THE OXFORD INTERN

THE OXFORD INTERNATIONAL LAW LIBRARY

General Editor: SIR FRANK BERMAN KCMG QC

This series features works on substantial topics in international law which provide authoritative statements of the chosen areas. Taken together they map out the whole of international law in a set of scholarly reference works and treatises intended to be of use to scholars, practitioners, and students.

Treaty Interpretation

Second Edition

RICHARD K GARDINER

OXFORD
UNIVERSITY PRESS

OXFORD
UNIVERSITY PRESS

Great Clarendon Street, Oxford, OX2 6DP,
United Kingdom

Oxford University Press is a department of the University of Oxford.
It furthers the University's objective of excellence in research, scholarship,
and education by publishing worldwide. Oxford is a registered trade mark of
Oxford University Press in the UK and in certain other countries

© Richard K Gardiner 2015

The moral rights of the author have been asserted

First Edition published in 2008
Second Edition published in 2015
First published in paperback 2017

Published in the United States of America by Oxford University Press
198 Madison Avenue, New York, NY 10016, United States of America

British Library Cataloguing in Publication Data
Data available

Library of Congress Cataloging in Publication Data
Data available

ISBN 978–0–19–966923–3 (Hbk.)
ISBN 978–0–19–880624–0 (Pbk.)

Contents

PART I. OVERVIEW, HISTORY, MATERIALS, AND *DRAMATIS PERSONAE*

The Vienna Rules

PART II. INTERPRETATION APPLYING THE VIENNA CONVENTION ON THE LAW OF TREATIES

A. The General Rule

Foreword to the First Edition

This is a book I should like to have written. The subject of treaty interpretation is one of great fascination and of great practical importance. I first heard of it in the pre-Vienna days when studying international law with Professor Clive Parry. My interest was further stimulated upon reading Yasseen's masterful (if brief, and now somewhat dated) introduction to articles 31–33 of the Vienna Convention on the Law of Treaties.

With the huge expansion of the volume and importance of treaties in recent times, an understanding of the rules for the interpretation of treaties becomes ever more important. Indeed, a proper understanding of the rules and processes of treaty interpretation is an essential tool for any international lawyer, whether in government, in private practice, or in the academic world. But it is not only public international lawyers who need to understand treaty interpretation, which is so different from interpretation of national laws and contracts. Questions of treaty interpretation arise more and more frequently in national courts, including in the UK.

On one level, it might be thought that there is not so much to be said on the subject. Interpretation is an art, not a science, and aside from the text of the rules set out in the Vienna Convention itself there is not much one needs beyond good sense and experience. Yet this is a mistaken approach. In the 40 years that have passed since the adoption of the Vienna Convention in 1969 a wealth of practice has developed, and it is chiefly through studying the practice that one learns the art.

There are different 'levels' of treaty interpretation. When a question of interpretation comes up in litigation, whether before an international court or a domestic one, it is usually examined in great depth, with full study by the parties—if not the court—of *travaux préparatoires* and context. When, on the other hand, a question of treaty interpretation has to be answered on the spot—often the case in the day-to-day work of a foreign ministry—it will, of necessity, be dealt with swiftly and even superficially. And there will be many situations between these two extremes.

The importance of treaty interpretation in modern international relations can be seen from the fact that almost all cases that have come before the International Court of Justice (and its predecessor the Permanent Court of International Justice), and most public international law arbitrations (including all investment treaty arbitrations) turn on the interpretation of treaties. All modern courts and tribunals take as their starting point (either expressly or implicitly) the rules set forth in articles 31–33 of the Vienna Convention on the Law of Treaties (the 'Vienna rules'), which are well established as rules of customary international law and are nowadays applied to treaties old and new.

Richard Gardiner was for a number of years a legal adviser in the UK's Foreign and Commonwealth Office and with the Attorney General's Office. He has been a private practitioner as well as an academic, and is the author of a recent text-book on international law. He has a particular interest in international aviation law, a field of international law dominated by bilateral and multilateral treaties and their interpretation. He is very well placed to write the present book analysing the Vienna rules, which is likely to become a classic in its field.

The merits of the book are manifold. Gardiner systematically analyses each element of the Vienna rules in detail, yet never loses sight of the overall approach to interpretation that is embodied in the Convention. It contains a meticulous, thorough, and sometimes critical study of the extensive case law that has developed on the Vienna rules. It contains enough theory to place the rules in context (explaining, for example, the heated debates in the International Law Commission and at the Vienna Conference), while remaining essentially a practical guide. And it contains a host of useful examples taken from real-life situations.

This book will be particularly useful for the practitioner, especially the practitioner involved in litigation or contemplating litigation. It will be consulted by judges and arbitrators, who may be moved to apply the Vienna rules more systematically as a result. And even (perhaps especially) the hurried interpreter, who needs to understand instinctively the process of treaty interpretation if he or she is to give good advice on the spot, will benefit greatly from Gardiner's exposition of the rules.

Sir Michael Wood, KCMG.
London, February 2008

Preface to the Second Edition

The need for a user's guide to the rules of treaty interpretation has not greatly diminished in the years since the first edition of this book. The book's message remains the same: the rules on treaty interpretation in the 1969 Vienna Convention on the Law of Treaties are a starting point and guide for treaty interpretation and to use them properly requires being aware of their entirety. In the most visible instances of reasoned interpretation – the decisions of courts and tribunals – increased reference to these rules has nevertheless shown some continuing and quite widespread misunderstanding and misuse of them. The two most prominent misconceptions are that the opening reference in the Vienna Convention to the ordinary meaning of terms in a treaty constitutes the whole of the general rule and that in all cases any consideration of a treaty's preparatory work is subject to the same restrictive preconditions. There is, however, also much more in the rules which needs explanation and illustration.

The focus of the changes in this second edition is expansion of examples and of the explanations of practicalities of treaty interpretation. The number of cases in which specific mention is made of the Vienna rules on treaty interpretation has grown greatly. Likewise, there has been growth in the number of cases in which treaties have been interpreted without specific reference to the rules but which nevertheless illuminate understanding of them. Those included here are cases which illustrate particular points, but there are now countless others. Since the first edition there has also been much investigation of treaty interpretation, both of a general nature and in relation to particular areas. On topics such as the law of international trade, human rights, investment agreements, and international tax issues, valuable studies have been published making far more extensive analysis of cases in those particular areas than is possible here, but providing great assistance in illustrating the rules by extensive examples.

Further, there is the work of the International Law Commission which has completed its Guide to Practice on Reservations to Treaties. This includes guidelines and commentaries on interpretative declarations, a topic inadequately addressed in the Vienna rules. Some notice has also been taken in this edition of the Commission's work on subsequent agreements and subsequent practice in relation to interpretation of treaties; but the Commission's conclusions remain in draft and those seeking more detail on these topics would do well to consult the extensive reports and draft commentaries already produced and, in due course, the completed work.

In response to the helpful suggestions of reviewers, concluding summaries have been added to each of the analytical chapters in Part II and a new chapter has been added to give some pointers to particular trends and issues in treaty interpretation, and to provide some conclusion to the whole work.

Thanks are due to those who have provided ideas, indications of material, and other aid and assistance for this and the previous edition. These include Rukhsana Ali,

Julian Arato, Anthony Aust, Danai Azaria, Craig Barker, Frank Berman, Eirik Bjorge, Eileen Denza, Christian Djeffal, Jörg Fedtke, Shireen Fisher, Malgosia Fitzmaurice, Douglas Guilfoyle, Duncan Hollis, David Hutchinson, Tomoko Ishikawa, John Avery Jones, Kenneth Keith, Rahim Moloo, Gemma Pountney, Anneliese Quast, Catherine Redgwell, Sam Ricketson, Philippe Sands, Dan Sarooshi, Antonios Tzanakopoulos, Ingo Venzke, Michael Waibel, John Walters, Colin Warbrick, Christopher Whomersley, Ralph Wilde, Elizabeth Wilmshurst, Michael Wood, all those involved in the Nottingham Treaty Project directed by Michael Bowman and Dino Kritsiotis, as well as many others who have offered comments and suggestions. Responsibility remains entirely with the author.

Richard Gardiner
28 February 2015

Acknowledgements

The case study of *Hitchcock v Outhwaite* in Chapter 1 is adapted from text by R K Gardiner, 'Interpreting Treaties in the United Kingdom' in M Freeman (ed), *Legislation and the Courts* (Aldershot: Dartmouth Publishing Company Limited, 1997), by permission of Michael Freeman.

Abbreviations

AJIL	*American Journal of International Law*
ATNIF	Australian Treaties not in Force
ATS	Australian Treaty Series
B C Int'l & Comp L	*Boston College International and Comparative Law Review*
BITs	Bilateral Investment Treaties
BYBIL	*British Year Book of International Law*
CJEU	Court of Justice of the European Union
DSB	Dispute Settlement Body of the WTO
ECHR	European Convention on Human Rights
ECtHR	European Court of Human Rights
ECJ	European Court of Justice
ECT	Energy Charter Treaty
EJIL	*European Journal of International Law*
EL Rev	*European Law Review*
EPC	European Patent Convention
GATS	General Agreement on Trade in Services 1994
GATT	General Agreement on Tariffs and Trade
ICC	International Criminal Court
ICJ	International Court of Justice
ICLQ	*International and Comparative Law Quarterly*
ICSID	International Centre for Settlement of Investment Disputes
ILC	International Law Commission
ILDC	International Law in Domestic Courts
IMCO	Inter-Governmental Maritime Consultative Organization
J Church & St	*Journal of Church and State*
LDA	London Debt Agreement
MFN	Most Favoured Nation
Mich J Int'l L	*Michigan Journal of International Law*
MOU	Memorandum of Understanding
NAFTA	North American Free Trade Association/Agreement
NILR	*Netherlands International Law Review*
OECD	Organization for Economic Co-Operation and Development
OED	*Oxford English Dictionary*
OSPAR Convention	Convention for the Protection of the Marine Environment of the North-East Atlantic
PCIJ	Permanent Court of International Justice
TRIPS	Trade-Related Aspects of Intellectual Property Right
UKTS	UK Treaty Series
UNHCR	UN High Commissioner for Refugees
UNTS	UN Treaty Series

Va J Int'l L	*Virginia Journal of International Law*
VCLT	Vienna Convention on the Law of Treaties, 1969
WHO	World Health Organization
WTO	World Trade Organization

Note on Citations

Citations follow OSCOLA (*Oxford Standard for Citation of Legal Authorities*) (4th Edn, 2012), with modifications, at: http://www.law.ox.ac.uk/publications/oscola.php.

Where the same work is cited in an uninterrupted succession of footnotes on the same page only the name of the author is repeated.

Where recent cases are cited, these may be available only (or most conveniently) via the Internet, but with the caution that web addresses (URLs) often change. The URLs for common websites are not repeated in the footnotes where sufficient particulars are given to enable location of reports at the appropriate URL. The following are URLs of websites providing reports of many of the cases cited:

International Court of Justice:
 www.icj-cij.org

European Court of Human Rights:
 http://www.echr.coe.int/ECHR/EN/Header/Case-Law/HUDOC/
 HUDOC+database/

World Trade Organisation Dispute Settlement Body:
 http://www.wto.org/english/tratop_e/dispu_e/dispu_e.htm

International Centre for Settlement of Investment Disputes:
 https://icsid.worldbank.org/

North American Free Trade Agreement:
 http://www.state.gov/s/l/c3439.htm

Treaties are accessible in the UN's electronic collection: https://treaties.un.org/. This is very cumbersome to search. Preference is therefore given here to citation in the Australian Treaty Series (ATS) or Australian Treaties not in Force (ATNIF):
 http://www.austlii.edu.au/au/other/dfat/

Table of Cases

Table of Treaties and Legislation

NATIONAL LEGISLATION

PART I

OVERVIEW, HISTORY, MATERIALS, AND *DRAMATIS PERSONAE*

'The Vienna Rules'[1]

Section 3. Interpretation of Treaties

Article 31
General rule of interpretation

1. A treaty shall be interpreted in good faith in accordance with the ordinary meaning to be given to the terms of the treaty in their context and in the light of its object and purpose.
2. The context for the purpose of the interpretation of a treaty shall comprise, in addition to the text, including its preamble and annexes:
    (*a*) any agreement relating to the treaty which was made between all the parties in connection with the conclusion of the treaty;
    (*b*) any instrument which was made by one or more parties in connection with the conclusion of the treaty and accepted by the other parties as an instrument related to the treaty.
3. There shall be taken into account, together with the context:
    (*a*) any subsequent agreement between the parties regarding the interpretation of the treaty or the application of its provisions;
    (*b*) any subsequent practice in the application of the treaty which establishes the agreement of the parties regarding its interpretation;
    (*c*) any relevant rules of international law applicable in the relations between the parties.
4. A special meaning shall be given to a term if it is established that the parties so intended.

Article 32
Supplementary means of interpretation

Recourse may be had to supplementary means of interpretation, including the preparatory work of the treaty atnd the circumstances of its conclusion, in order to confirm the meaning resulting from the application of article 31, or to determine the meaning when the interpretation according to article 31:

(*a*) leaves the meaning ambiguous or obscure; or
(*b*) leads to a result which is manifestly absurd or unreasonable.

---

[1] Rules for treaty interpretation from the Vienna Convention on the Law of Treaties, signed at Vienna, 23 May 1969: UN Doc A/Conf 39/28; UNTS 1155, p 331; UKTS 58 (1980), Cmnd 7964; ATS 1974 No 2; (1969) 8 ILM 679; text here as in UN print of 2005 at <http://legal.un.org/ilc/texts/instruments/english/conventions/1_1_1969.pdf>.

Article 33
Interpretation of treaties authenticated in two or more languages

1. When a treaty has been authenticated in two or more languages, the text is equally authoritative in each language, unless the treaty provides or the parties agree that, in case of divergence, a particular text shall prevail.

2. A version of the treaty in a language other than one of those in which the text was authenticated shall be considered an authentic text only if the treaty so provides or the parties so agree.

3. The terms of the treaty are presumed to have the same meaning in each authentic text.

4. Except where a particular text prevails in accordance with paragraph 1, when a comparison of the authentic texts discloses a difference of meaning which the application of articles 31 and 32 does not remove, the meaning which best reconciles the texts, having regard to the object and purpose of the treaty, shall be adopted.

1

A Single Set of Rules of Interpretation

Principles of general application—interpretation as single combined operation with supplementary means—rules endorsed and applicable internationally and nationally—key treaty concepts and nature of rules—illustrative cases

The reason why the United Nations had entrusted it [the International Law Commission] with the codification of international law, and in particular the law of treaties, was that the main objective was certainty of the law; and certainty of the law of treaties depended mainly on certainty of the rules of interpretation.[1]

1. Introduction

The increasing number and significance of treaties has given added importance to the art of their interpretation. The assertion that interpretation is an art has been criticized as having been made 'rather too glibly'. 'The question', as the author of that criticism noted, 'was whether there were any rules for practising that art'.[2] There is now no doubt that there are such rules. These are set out in a treaty: the Vienna Convention on the Law of Treaties, signed at Vienna, 23 May 1969.[3] The Convention entered into force on 27 January 1980; but its rules on interpretation

---

[1] R Ago, Chairman of International Law Commission, 726th Meeting, 19 May 1964, [1964] *Yearbook of the ILC*, vol I, p 23, para 34. The International Law Commission (ILC) is the body established by the General Assembly of the United Nations to fulfil its mandate 'to initiate studies and make recommendations for the purpose of... encouraging the progressive development of international law and its codification' (Charter of the United Nations, article 13). The prominent role of the ILC in drawing up the rules on treaty interpretation is considered throughout this book.

[2] Ago, vol I, p 23, para 34. This book is concerned with the practice of interpretation. Whether an art can usefully be the subject of rules is not investigated here but is assumed to be the case; cf M K Yasseen, indicating that the ILC had confined itself to 'stating a few rules which could be considered the scientific basis of the art of interpretation', ILC's 871st Meeting, 16 June 1966, [1966] *Yearbook of the ILC*, vol I, p 197, para 48.

[3] UN Doc A/Conf 39/28; UNTS 1155, 331; UKTS 58 (1980), Cmnd 7964; ATS 1974 No 2; 8 ILM 679. References in this work to the abbreviated form 'the Vienna Convention' are to this treaty, other conventions signed at Vienna being given their full titles. Similarly, references to 'articles' without attribution to a treaty are references to provisions of this Vienna Convention. The rules of treaty interpretation are in articles 31–33 of the Vienna Convention; these are referred to here as 'the Vienna rules', the term 'rules' in this context being the common usage; on the meaning of 'rule' and 'rules', see further section 4.3 below.

(throughout this book abbreviated as 'the Vienna rules') apply to treaties generally, including those made before 1980, as is explained below.[4] Those who would
practise the art need to understand the rules. This book explains the Vienna rules,
mainly using examples of interpretations reached by applying them. No claim is
made that the Vienna rules resolve all problems of interpretation or lead directly
to a necessarily 'correct' result in every case. Nor are the rules an exclusive compilation of guidance on treaty interpretation, other skills and principles that are
used to achieve a reasoned interpretation remaining admissible to the extent not
in conflict with the Vienna rules. What is suggested here is that the Vienna rules,
constituting a single framework for treaty interpretation, can now be identified
as generally applicable and that those rules should be understood and used by all
engaged in treaty interpretation. They are now an essential infrastructure, although
using them in particular circumstances requires skills and techniques which go well
beyond their brief prescriptions.

Probably the most common response to the question 'How are treaties to be
interpreted?' is along the lines that 'You must look for the intention of the parties.'
If the questioner presses for more detail, the further answer that is often given is
that one should look for the 'spirit' of the treaty. Neither element—the intention
of the parties or the spirit of the treaty—is remote from the objective of treaty
interpretation; but neither element is explicitly mentioned in the Vienna rules as
a guiding principle.[5] While a central idea is that interpretation has a focus on the
agreement of the parties expressed in the treaty, the general rule of interpretation
does refer in its opening propositions to the 'object and purpose' of the agreement,
which could be viewed as an objective repository of the collective intentions of
the parties, although this reference is in the context of a specific element of the
rules. Ascertainment of intention is one consequence of the exercise if the Vienna
rules are properly applied; but this is intention in the sense of the meaning of the
treaty as properly interpreted. This refers to the meaning within the *agreement* of
the parties rather than their intention distinct from their agreement (although
all too often a specific intention on a point in issue could never be ascertained as
the point was not considered by the negotiators or their principals). Nevertheless,
an 'intention' is commonly ascribed in the course of interpretation.[6] As stated
by the International Court of Justice (ICJ), which is the principal judicial organ of
the United Nations, a treaty provision must be interpreted 'in accordance with the
intentions of its authors as reflected by the text of the treaty and the other relevant
factors in terms of interpretation'.[7]

---

[4] Section 2 below.

[5] Intention is only mentioned in the Vienna rules in article 31(4); but that is in the context of a
very specific rule, indicating that a treaty term is to be given a 'special' meaning 'if it is established that
the parties so intended'.

[6] For an account of current work of the ILC relating 'presumed intent' to a meaning evolving over
time, see Chapter 10, section 3.3.

[7] *Dispute Regarding Navigational and Related Rights (Costa Rica v Nicaragua)* [2009] ICJ Reports
214, at 237, para 48.

The approach of the Vienna rules was explained in the International Law Commission's (ILC) Commentary which accompanied its draft articles for the 1968–69 Vienna Conference at which the text of the Convention was adopted:

... the text must be presumed to be an authentic expression of the intention of the parties; ... in consequence, the starting point of interpretation is the elucidation of the meaning of the text, not an investigation *ab initio* into the intention of the parties.[8]

At the Vienna conference one of the delegates, noting that many of the issues that arise in treaty interpretation are not ones which the treaty's originators had ever even contemplated, and that many parties which accede to a treaty have not participated in its preparation, stated:

... it was wiser and more equitable to assume that the text represented the common intentions of the original authors and that the primary goal of interpretation was to elucidate the meaning of that text in the light of certain defined and relevant factors.[9]

The ICJ has pronounced that the Vienna rules are in principle applicable to the interpretation of all treaties. This proposition now constitutes a statement of customary international law, with the effect that the rules apply to any treaty interpretation whether the states involved are parties to the Vienna Convention or not.[10] As the cases cited in this book show, this position has also been accepted by other international tribunals, by states pleading before such courts and tribunals, and by several courts considering treaties within national legal systems.[11]

In view of this general acceptance and application of the Vienna Convention's rules, why is it necessary to do more than invite lawyers, legislators, diplomats, arbitrators, and judges to read and apply them? The short answer is that the rules are not a set of simple precepts that can be applied to produce a scientifically verifiable result. More guidance is needed to set the ground for a 'correct' result, or at least one which has been correctly ascertained. Somewhat controversial when drawn up, the rules leave some important issues incompletely resolved. Much is left to nuance and the ILC itself saw the rules as quite general: '...the Commission confined itself to trying to isolate and codify the comparatively few general principles which appear to constitute general rules for the interpretation of treaties.'[12]

---

[8] UN Conference on the Law of Treaties, Official Records: Documents of the Conference, A/CONF.39/11/Add2, p 40, para 11, and [1966] *Yearbook of the ILC*, vol II, p 220, para 11. The Vienna Conference took place in two stages (1968–69) but for convenience is described below as 'the Vienna Conference, 1969' where the date is merely necessary to distinguish it from the many other Vienna conferences.

[9] I Sinclair, UN Conference on the Law of Treaties, First Session (26 March–24 May 1968), Official Records: Summary Records, p 177, para 6.

[10] Cases of the ICJ stating the general applicability of the rules are cited and considered in sections 2.1 and 2.2 below. On the rules in a treaty applying to agreements between states and international organizations and between international organizations, see Chapter 4, section 2.2. The preamble to the Vienna Convention affirms that the rules of customary international law continue to govern questions not regulated by the Convention's provisions.

[11] See section 2 below and Chapter 4, section 4.2.

[12] [1966] *Yearbook of the ILC*, vol II, pp 218–19, paras 4–5. As to 'canons' of interpretation or construction and 'maxims', see Chapter 2, section 3 for some of their history and Chapter 8, section 4.5.4 for the modern position.

Examination of the growing case law suggests that systematic use of the rules as a practical means of treaty interpretation still has scope for improvement. In some instances the case law shows that they are paid no more than lip service, even giving rise to the suspicion that some lawyers and judges perhaps lack familiarity with their actual content and manner of application. Likewise, selection of a particular rule to bolster an argument without application of the rules as a whole may indicate lack of awareness of their status as the applicable body of rules and of their manner of application, although in other instances the rules are correctly applied, specific mention of them being made only where there is some point of controversy about the interpretative process.

The core of this book is a set of chapters in Part II giving an account of the rules, with guidance for their practical application from examples of how they have actually been applied so as to provide precedent (in a loose sense) and analogy.[13] A full understanding of the rules also requires some awareness of the rest of the law of treaties, at least as regards the processes of their formation and implementation. Preparatory material, records of negotiations, ancillary instruments, interpretative declarations, reservations, amendments (and so on), can all be relevant to interpretation. Chapter 3 addresses these matters and gives a brief guide to relevant aspects of treaty-making. Necessary elements of general international law and general principles are introduced as and when appropriate.[14]

The obvious starting point is to consider articles 31–33 of the Vienna Convention. These are so short that to pick out key features risks doing harm to the holistic approach which the ILC intended to pervade their structure and use. They should therefore be read, or re-read, as a prelude to the detailed analysis in Part II. For present purposes it is only necessary to note that (reduced to broad terms) the 'general rule' (that is, the whole of article 31[15]) requires: good faith in giving the ordinary meaning to the words used in their context and in the light of the object and purpose of the treaty; consideration of related instruments of defined types; attention to agreement of the parties as to the meaning, whether specifically recorded or demonstrated through practice; giving special meaning to terms where this is intended; and application of relevant rules of international law. Further, the preparatory work and circumstances of conclusion of a treaty may be taken into consideration as usually the most significant of supplementary means of interpretation, to be used in the manner and circumstances directed by the rules (though in practice often more readily taken into account than that). Provision is also made in the rules for dealing with issues which may arise when treaty terms are in different languages. All these elements are grouped in the three articles set out on pp. 3–4 above and entitled: Article 31 'General rule of interpretation'; Article

---

[13] See Chapters 5–9 below.
[14] See further J Crawford, *Brownlie's Principles of Public International Law* (Oxford: OUP, 8th edn, 2012), R Gardiner, *International Law* (Harlow: Pearson/Longman, 2003), and A I Aust, *Modern Treaty Law and Practice* (Cambridge: CUP, 3rd edn, 2013).
[15] On the use of the singular in the term 'general rule', see section 4.2 below.

32 'Supplementary means of interpretation'; and Article 33 'Interpretation of treaties authenticated in two or more languages'.

This book is not about theory. It is about the practical use of the Vienna rules. Much theory can, however, be readily tracked down from the sources cited in Chapter 2 below, on the history and development of the rules, and also in the concluding chapter. In fact, a fairly simple theory or scheme underlies the Vienna rules (though not expressed by the ILC in the way that follows). Three general approaches were considered by the ILC. Their general nature is clear from the labels commonly given to them: (1) literal; (2) teleological; (3) intention. In a very general sense, the ILC adopted a combination of the literal and teleological approaches, viewing application of these as yielding up the intention—that is, (1) + (2) = (3).

Of course, the elaboration of the rules, of their dynamics and nuances, is much more complex than this may suggest; but the general significance of the approach is that by combining consideration of all relevant elements mandated by the Vienna rules, the resulting interpretation should achieve due respect for the intentions of the parties as recorded in the treaty text, taking account of the treaty's object and purpose, but without making a wide-ranging search for intentions from extraneous sources. The danger, however, in using the labels 'literal', 'teleological', and seeking 'intention' in treaty interpretation is that these become shorthand substitutes for understanding and applying the actual Vienna rules. Use of such substitutions continues to impair practical treaty interpretation, but the concepts do have an analytical value which is given some evaluation in the concluding chapter of this book.

The ILC's approach was much criticized at the Vienna Conference in 1969 by Professor McDougal, speaking for the American delegation. He saw the scheme of the articles on interpretation as relegating context (to which he gave a wider meaning than do the Vienna rules) too far into the background. He also saw the approach in the Vienna rules as evading a search for the true intentions of the parties, that is intentions which he considered could be derived from a greater range of sources than those specified in the rules.[16] His approach seeks what has been described by some as the 'subjective' intention, as contrasted with 'objective' intention (or its substitute when absent) inherent in the agreed text as properly interpreted. One theme of this book is that the Vienna rules as interpreted and applied in practice have generally not proved so restrictive as to preclude investigation of sufficient material to reveal the properly recorded intentions of the negotiators as carried through into the treaty. But that is not the whole story...

1.1 Guide to analytical approach

As the Vienna rules are set out in a treaty, they are themselves to be interpreted by application of the very rules that they state. The primary aim here is to show how

---

[16] See further Chapter 2, section 9.

the Vienna rules are, and are to be, interpreted and applied. Interpretation of rules by applying them to themselves may sound rather circular and formulaic: but the result need not be too artificial if the flexibility which the rules were intended to retain is respected.[17] However, as the rules are not here being applied to a specific issue (as would usually be the case in a particular dispute), some adjustments in approach are required.

A key to understanding how to use the Vienna rules is grasping that the rules are not a step-by-step formula for producing an irrebuttable interpretation in every case. They do indicate what is to be taken into account (in the sense of text, preamble, annexes, related agreements, preparatory work, etc) and, to some extent, how to approach this body of material (using ordinary meanings in context, in the light of the treaty's object and purpose, distinguishing a general rule from supplementary means, and so on). There is in the rules a certain inherent logical sequence. They are not, however, all of use every time or always sequentially applicable. The idea underlying a 'general rule' composed of several elements was expressed in the ILC's Commentary on the draft articles on interpretation:

All the various elements, as they were present in any given case, would be thrown into the crucible, and their interaction would give the legally relevant interpretation.[18]

This 'crucible' approach, in rejection of any hierarchy within the general rule, is designed to result in 'a single combined operation'.[19] It is, therefore, somewhat in opposition to this design to take the rules to bits and examine each component in isolation. In the absence of specific disputes over particular terms of an identified treaty, however, presentation of the Vienna rules is as much a descriptive and analytical exercise as one of treaty interpretation. For these reasons, in the 'core' chapters below (Chapters 5–9), where the elements of the rules are examined in detail, these elements are necessarily treated in a manner which is somewhat different from the approach that would be taken in resolving a dispute or advising on a specific problem over interpretation. The general approach in those chapters is to outline the main features and history, the issues that may arise in understanding

---

[17] It has been noted as a curious feature of the Vienna Convention's rules on interpretation that they have themselves to be interpreted, which requires application of pre-existing rules, and so on in infinite regression: J Klabbers, 'International Legal Histories: The Declining Importance of *Travaux Préparatoires* in Treaty Interpretation?' (2003) 50 NILR 267, at 270. Fortunately, however, rules of treaty interpretation are also part of customary law and the Vienna rules are now generally recognized as stating those customary rules.

[18] United Nations Conference on the Law of Treaties: Official Records: Documents of the Conference, A/CONF.39/11/Add.2, p 39, para 8 and [1966] *Yearbook of the ILC*, vol II, pp 219–20, para 8. The Commentary accompanied the draft articles considered by the Vienna Conference in 1969 as the starting point for its preparation and adoption of the Vienna Convention. The role of such a commentary is considered further in the context of preparatory work in Chapters 3 and 8.

[19] Commentary above, para 8, and in para 9: 'it was considerations of logic, not any obligatory legal hierarchy, which guided the Commission in arriving at the arrangement proposed in the article'; see further Chapter 5, section 3.1. Any suggestion that elements of the general rule beyond the ordinary meaning, or stated subsequent to the opening paragraph of the general rule, are subordinate is inconsistent with the proper interpretation of the rules and with the ILC's clear explanation of how they are to be used.

the rules, and to describe how such issues are handled in practice. However, just as one instance of a 'live' interpretation of a treaty provision does not precisely follow the form of another, so in the analysis of the rules, an identical sequence of treatment is not always the best one (nor is it required by the Vienna rules).

One way in which this approach differs from that mandated by the Vienna Convention is that in the Vienna rules the preparatory work is a supplementary means of interpretation of the treaty, to be used to confirm the meaning resulting from application of the general rule, or to determine the meaning when interpretation according to the general rule leaves the meaning ambiguous or obscure, or leads to a result which is manifestly absurd or unreasonable. In principle, therefore, preparatory work has a supporting role. Even if recounted at an earlier stage, preparatory work assumes its function after the application of the general rule, that is, after application of the whole of article 31, including examination of the practice in implementing the treaty. In an analytical consideration of the present kind, however, it would be impractical when presenting an account of a rule to postpone all the history of a provision until after showing the practice in application of the rule.

An attempt is also made here to demonstrate that practice in use of preparatory work has, in any event, already shown a marked divergence from a strict reading of the Vienna rules. In the practice of some tribunals, the history of a treaty provision is stated as part of the relevant law, after setting out the facts in a case. Thus, the preparatory work is clearly already present in the minds of those deciding on the interpretation, even if in their reasoning they formally draw on the preparatory work only after applying the general rule, as indicated by article 32 of the Vienna Convention. This is illustrated by the first of the five complete examples included at the end of this chapter to show the rules at work rather than taken to bits as they are later.[20] These examples show practice in both international and domestic courts and tribunals.

The Vienna rules provide for account to be taken of subsequent practice in the application of a treaty which establishes the agreement of the parties regarding its interpretation. A difference of approach adopted here is that the practice (in the, admittedly incomplete, sense of reported decisions) is set out to illustrate how a particular element of the rules has been or may be used, rather than to show that there is concordant practice establishing definitively the interpretation of the rule. Although there are now many reported decisions which allude to the Vienna rules, there has been insufficiently long practice in their application to show that points of detail have received uniform interpretation under the Vienna Convention. It is nevertheless useful to be aware of what reasoning and decisions there have been in relation to a particular point. Such practice may provide a useful starting point and give helpful guidance. If progressively and sufficiently supported, a clear enough trend may emerge in the practice to establish the approach as correct.

---

[20] See section 5 below.

Of course, treaty interpretation is not only undertaken in disputes before courts and tribunals. It takes place much more frequently in the day-to-day work of governments, legislatures, government departments (increasingly not just Ministries of Foreign Affairs), and of legal advisers and lawyers generally. Only a small amount of that surfaces into the public domain. When it does so it is likely to be because there is some controversy. Where such controversy is between states, most differences on points of treaty interpretation are settled between the parties by negotiation. This happens with most legal disputes within national systems of law, but with the important difference that those in dispute internationally over a treaty are commonly representatives of the actual originators of the treaty terms in issue, or are at least later parties to the treaty. Hence their interpretation has a special value (considered below, particularly in connection with the role of subsequent practice).[21]

All these instances of treaty interpretation form part of general practice in treaty interpretation, but those instances outside case reports are not readily accessed or assimilated into clear guidance. There is, however, at least a substantial body of material in case law to point to the approach that is to be taken. Such case law is not only that of international courts and tribunals. Some decisions of national courts contain useful indications of how treaty interpretation is to be approached.

Precedent does not have the same formal and binding character in international tribunals as in some national legal systems. There is no hierarchy of courts extending throughout the international legal system. However, it seems likely that the accounts of the practice of many international courts and tribunals may prove to be the most helpful guide to understanding the Vienna rules and to their use in connection with new issues of interpretation that arise. The best examples of their application are offered here from wherever they may be found. Attempting to avoid the invidious task of evaluating the merits of different judges and arbitrators, where possible majority views of the ICJ have been given pride of place, but some references to potentially useful or clarificatory opinions given by individual judges separately or in dissent have been included. Decisions of other bodies have been included without assessing them on the basis of the standing of the particular

---

[21] This was stated, perhaps somewhat starkly, by Mr J M Ruda in the ILC's work on the draft Vienna rules: 'Interpretation occurred at two different levels. First, as between States the only legally valid interpretation of a treaty was the authentic interpretation by the parties to the treaty. The other level was that of arbitration, for which there were fundamental principles...'. ILC's 765th Meeting, 14 July 1964, [1964] *Yearbook of the ILC*, vol I, p 277, para 34. However, the ILC's Special Rapporteur (Waldock) encountered the same problem noted in the text here, remarking in his introduction of the first draft of what became the Vienna rules that he 'had tried to take into account State practice, though evidence of it was difficult to obtain as not much was to be found in publications of State practice which for the most part were content to reproduce the decisions of international tribunals and were not concerned with the interpretation of treaties by States themselves'. *Yearbook of the ILC*, vol I, p 275, para 2. Cf S Rosenne, *An International Law Miscellany* (Dordrecht: Nijhoff, 1993), at 441: 'Most international interpretation is not the fruit of judicial action, but is performed through the diplomatic channel. Furthermore, probably the greater part of it is undertaken not as part of the settlement of a dispute, but as part of the negotiating and drafting processes and often with the object of trying to avoid future disputes.' See further Chapters 3 and 4.

court or tribunal but rather selecting them for the cogency of their argument or effective deployment of the Vienna rules. Similarly, in the case of decisions of national courts, generally only those of the highest courts have been included, but judgments of lower courts receive occasional mention. Chapter 4 gives a general outline of where treaty interpretation takes place and of the main factors to be taken into account where particular courts, tribunals, or other bodies may show individual characteristics.

Even taking this rather flexible approach to selection of cases, examples making specific reference to the Vienna rules have not been found illustrating all points to be addressed. Some cases from before the adoption of the Vienna rules are therefore used where they provide particularly good examples which, it is believed, would be likely to prove useful in reasoning out an interpretation under the Vienna rules. However, because the focus here is on the Vienna rules, no attempt is made to provide a comprehensive guide to all the previous case law. Even if remotely feasible, such an account would make for an extremely long work; and there are already many thorough studies of the earlier law. What is included here is an overview of the earlier material (Chapter 2) leading up to, and including an account of, the work of the ILC in preparing the draft treaty for consideration at the Vienna conference in 1969.

2. Applicability of the Vienna Rules Generally

It is now well established that the provisions on interpretation of treaties contained in Articles 31 and 32 of the Convention reflect pre-existing customary international law, and thus may be (unless there are particular indications to the contrary) applied to treaties concluded before the entering into force of the Vienna Convention in 1980. The International Court of Justice has applied customary rules of interpretation, now reflected in Articles 31 and 32 of the Vienna Convention, to a treaty concluded in 1955…and to a treaty concluded in 1890, bearing on rights of States that even on the day of Judgment were still not parties to the Vienna Convention… *There is no case after the adoption of the Vienna Convention in 1969 in which the International Court of Justice or any other leading tribunal has failed so to act.*[22]

---

[22] *Arbitration Regarding the Iron Rhine ("IJzeren Rijn") Railway (Belgium/Netherlands)*, Award of 24 May 2005, XXVII RIAA 35, p 62, para 45, (emphasis added). For the history of endorsement by the ICJ and other courts and tribunals, see below for a range of cases in which the Vienna rules have been used in international and domestic courts and tribunals, see L Crema, 'Subsequent Agreements and Subsequent Practice within and outside the Vienna Convention', chapter 2 in G Nolte (ed), *Treaties and Subsequent Practice* (Oxford: OUP, 2013), at 14–15 fns 6–8. For rejection of a suggestion that when being invoked as a matter of customary law the Vienna rules should not 'be applied with the same kind of minute and analytical rigour as would be the case if it were itself binding as between the Parties', see *Case Concerning the Auditing of Accounts (Netherlands/France)*, Award of 12 March 2004, para 77 (Permanent Court of Arbitration's unofficial translation at <http://pca-cpa.org/showpage.asp?pag_id=1156>), considered further in section 5.2 below.

This quotation from an arbitral award of a very distinguished tribunal recognizes the general applicability of the Vienna rules (with article 33 being added in where language issues arise) and that neither the ICJ nor other leading tribunals have ever denied that applicability (even if positive affirmation took a little while). The unreserved recognition and endorsement of the Vienna rules is now so well evidenced in judgments and opinions of the ICJ, and likewise widely in arbitral awards and decisions of national courts, that it is tempting to cite only the key cases supporting the proposition and leave it at that. For the sake of completeness, however, the ICJ's gradual progression to affirmation of the Vienna rules is traced here in some detail.

2.1 History of recognition by the ICJ of the Vienna rules

There are no specific indications that the ICJ had particular criticisms of the Vienna rules when the Vienna Convention was concluded. However, in its judgments (that is, the collective or majority judgments) the Court was quiet about their status for quite a long time thereafter. A good analysis of how the Court came to regard them as generally applicable customary law is that by a learned commentator, former Registrar, and ad hoc judge of the Court, S Torres Bernárdez. Writing in 1998, he noted that 'the process of recognition by the Court, in so many words, of the declaratory nature of these rules has been hesitant, uneven and lengthy, going on for much longer than in the case of other rules of the Vienna Convention—more than twenty years in fact!'.[23]

Torres Bernárdez divides the progression to the Court's explicit and complete endorsement of the Vienna rules into successive periods. The first he describes as 'the initial silence' from 1970 to 1980. In this period the only references to the rules were those by individual judges in separate or dissenting opinions. He identifies Judge Ammoun as the first to refer to article 31 in 1970, the year after the Vienna Convention was concluded.[24] He also notes that in 1980, at the other end of this first decade of the existence of the Vienna rules, again in a separate opinion, Judge Sette-Camara included an assertion that, though the Vienna rules did not apply to the matter in hand by virtue of treaty obligation, its provisions would apply 'inasmuch as they embody rules of international law to which the parties would be subject independently of the Convention (Art.3(b))'.[25] In relation to international agreements not within the scope of the Vienna Convention, its article 3(b)

---

[23] S Torres Bernárdez, 'Interpretation of Treaties by the International Court of Justice following the Adoption of the 1969 Vienna Convention on the Law of Treaties' in G Hafner et al. (eds), *Liber Amicorum: Professor Ignaz Seidl-Hohenveldern in Honour of His 80th Birthday* (Kluwer Law International: The Hague, 1998), 721 at 723.

[24] Torres Bernárdez, at 723, citing the judge's Separate Opinion in the *Barcelona Traction* case, [1970] ICJ Reports 304.

[25] Sette-Camara, Separate Opinion in *Interpretation of the Agreement of 25 March 1951 between the WHO and Egypt* (Advisory Opinion), [1980] ICJ Reports 178, at 184; and see Torres Bernárdez, at 724.

provides that the fact that the Convention does not apply is not to affect the application to such agreements of any of the rules set out in the Convention to which they would be subject under international law independently of the Convention. That clear proposition, coupled with the now established practice of regarding the Vienna rules as codified customary law, is the cornerstone of the (equally accepted) proposition that the Vienna rules apply generally, including application to treaties concluded before the Vienna Convention itself.

The second period in the development of the Court's endorsement of the Vienna rules (1980–90) is described by Torres Bernárdez as 'ensuing hesitations' of the Court with regard to the rules.[26] Nevertheless, even if it can be taken that 'hesitation' was the reason why the Court as a whole made no specific reference to the rules, Torres Bernárdez demonstrates that in the jurisdiction and admissibility phase of the *Nicaragua* case[27] the ICJ used implicitly the method and substance of the rules (although in some other cases in the same period no such close concurrence was apparent).[28] Nevertheless, individual judges made increasing reference to the rules and, in 1989, a Chamber (a panel of judges rather than the full court) of the ICJ recounted their invocation by one of the parties (Italy).[29]

Positive affirmations that the Vienna rules are of general application have become more frequent and have taken an increasingly assertive form over the years. In 1991 the ICJ referred, somewhat hesitantly, to principles of treaty interpretation which it had enunciated before the Vienna Convention was drawn up and stated:

These principles are reflected in Articles 31 and 32 of the Vienna Convention on the Law of Treaties, which may in many respects be considered as a codification of existing customary international law on the point.[30]

This judgment and that of a Chamber of the Court in the following year,[31] are classified by Torres Bernárdez as 'the first textually oriented recognitions of the rules of interpretation laid down by the Vienna Convention'.[32] Among the criticisms he makes of the first judgment recognizing the rules is that in its harking back to the Court's earlier approaches to treaty interpretation, despite its explicit acknowledgement of the Vienna rules, the Court failed to do full justice to the rules themselves

---

[26] Torres Bernárdez, 'Interpretation of Treaties by the International Court of Justice', at 727–29.

[27] [1984] ICJ Reports 392.

[28] Torres Bernárdez, at 727–29.

[29] *Elettronica Sicula* [1989] ICJ Reports 15, at 70, para 118; and see Torres Bernárdez, at 729–80, who saw this recognition as more formal than real, the Court providing in some judgments of the period a 'textually qualified recognition' and perhaps reflecting a remaining division of opinion among the judges between a 'textualist' approach and 'subjective', 'functional', or 'teleological' approaches: Torres Bernárdez, at 734.

[30] *Arbitral Award of 31 July 1989 (Guinea-Bissau v Senegal)* Judgment, [1991] ICJ Reports 53, at 70, para 48.

[31] *Land, Island and Maritime Frontier Dispute (El Salvador/Honduras: Nicaragua intervening)* [1992] ICJ Reports 351, at 582, para 373.

[32] Torres Bernárdez, 'Interpretation of Treaties by the International Court of Justice', at 730–35.

and the system of interpretation they embody.[33] Similarly, the majority judgment of the Chamber of the ICJ in the 1992 *El Salvador/Honduras* case was viewed in his Separate Opinion by Torres Bernárdez (who as judge ad hoc gave a detailed critique) as relying excessively on the first paragraph of article 31 rather than using the whole article as an integrated rule (a serious misunderstanding of how the rules apply, but one sometimes made by various courts and tribunals).[34]

Even where the Court did not make express reference to the Vienna rules, evidence of a more comprehensive use of their substance could be seen. In *Maritime Delimitation in the Area Between Greenland and Jan Mayen (Denmark v Norway)*, the Court stated:

The Court has to pronounce upon the interpretation to be given to the 1965 Agreement. The Preamble to the Agreement states…The 1965 Agreement has in any event to be read in its context, in the light of its object and purpose…It is also appropriate to take into account, for purposes of interpretation of the 1965 Agreement, the subsequent practice of the Parties.…[35]

2.2 Express endorsement of the Vienna rules by the ICJ

The Court has in more recent times presented application of the rules as virtually axiomatic:

The Court now addresses the question of the proper interpretation of the expression 'without delay' in the light of arguments put to it by the Parties. The Court begins by noting that the precise meaning of 'without delay', as it is to be understood in Article 36, paragraph 1 (b), is not defined in the Convention [on Consular Relations]. This phrase therefore requires interpretation according to the customary rules of treaty interpretation reflected in Articles 31 and 32 of the Vienna Convention on the Law of Treaties.[36]

That the Court views the Vienna rules as general, or customary international law, seems incontrovertible. Evidence additional to the Court's express statements to that effect can be found in the Court's application of these rules to treaties made long before entry into force of the Vienna Convention.[37] This is also shown by its

---

[33] Torres Bernárdez, 'Interpretation of Treaties by the International Court of Justice', at 732.

[34] *Land, Island and Maritime Frontier Dispute (El Salvador/Honduras: Nicaragua intervening)* [1992] ICJ Reports 351, Separate Opinion of Torres Bernárdez, 629 at 719–23.

[35] [1993] ICJ Reports 51–52, paras 26–28.

[36] *Avena and Other Mexican Nationals (Mexico v United States of America)* [2004] ICJ Reports 37–38, para 83. For criticism of *how* the ICJ has applied the rules, see J Klabbers, 'On Rationalism in Politics: Interpretation of Treaties and the World Trade Organization' (2005) 74 *Nordic JIL* 405, at 421–26.

[37] See, for example, *Kasikili/Sedudu Island (Botswana/Namibia)* [1999] ICJ Reports 1045, at 1060, para 20: 'The Court will now proceed to interpret the provisions of the 1890 Treaty by applying the rules of interpretation set forth in the 1969 Vienna Convention…'. Note that as a matter of treaty relations (as contrasted with general or customary international law), the Vienna Convention states: 'Without prejudice to the application of any rules set forth in the present Convention to which treaties would be subject under international law independently of the Convention, the

application of the rules in cases where one or more parties to the litigation are not parties to the Vienna Convention. An example of the latter is in the judgment in *Sovereignty over Pulau Litigan and Pulau Sipadan (Indonesia/Malaysia)*:

> The Court notes that Indonesia is not a party to the Vienna Convention of 23 May 1969 on the Law of Treaties; the Court would nevertheless recall that, in accordance with customary international law, reflected in Articles 31 and 32 of that Convention: a treaty must be interpreted in good faith ... Moreover, with respect to Article 31, paragraph 3, the Court has had occasion to state that this provision also reflects customary law ... Indonesia does not dispute that these are the applicable rules.[38]

In other judgments of the same era, and subsequently, the Court gave the widest endorsement to the applicability of the Vienna rules to treaties generally as customary international law along the following lines:

> The Court would recall that, according to customary international law as expressed in Article 31 of the Vienna Convention on the Law of Treaties of 23 May 1969, a treaty must be interpreted ... Article 32 provides....[39]

It is to be noted that in its general pronouncements on the applicability of the Vienna rules, the ICJ tends to refer to articles 31 and 32 without mentioning article 33 (on the role of versions of a treaty in different languages). It seems reasonable to understand this as a consequence of the rather particular circumstances in which the latter provisions come into play, as contrasted with the likelihood of the need to consider application of the two preceding articles in every case. Where a difference between languages has been part of the interpretative argument, the ICJ has stated that the Vienna Convention provision reflects customary international law.[40]

Convention applies only to treaties which are concluded by States after the entry into force of the present Convention with regard to such States' (article 4).

[38] [2002] ICJ Reports 23–24, para 37.

[39] *Legal Consequences of the Construction of a Wall in the Occupied Palestinian Territory (Advisory Opinion)* [2004] ICJ Reports 136, at 174, para 94. On article 32 of the Vienna rules, the court also recalled it earlier affirmations in *Oil Platforms (Islamic Republic of Iran v United States of America), Preliminary Objections* [1996-II] ICJ Reports 812, para 23; see, similarly, *Kasikili/Sedudu Island (Botswana/Namibia)* [1999-II] ICJ Reports 1059, para 18, and *Sovereignty over Pulau Ligitan and Pulau Sipadan (Indonesia/Malaysia), Judgment* [2002] ICJ Reports 645, para 37. See also the ICJ's endorsements of the Vienna rules in *Oil Platforms (Islamic Republic of Iran v United States of America) (Merits)* [2003] ICJ Reports 161, at 182, para 41; *Case Concerning Legality of Use of Force (Serbia and Montenegro v United Kingdom) (Preliminary Objections)* [2004] ICJ Reports 36–37, para 98 and other cases by the same applicant on *Legality of Use of Force (Serbia and Montenegro v Belgium, Canada, France, Germany, Italy, Netherlands, Portugal)*; *Avena and Other Mexican Nationals (Mexico v United States of America)* [2004] ICJ Reports 37–38, para 83; *Application of the Convention on the Prevention and Punishment of the Crime of Genocide (Bosnia and Herzegovina v Serbia and Montenegro)* [2007] ICJ Reports 43, at 110, para 160; *Maritime Dispute (Peru v Chile)*, Judgment of 27 January 2014, para 57; and for an example of citation a specific proposition such as their applicability to interpreting provisions of treaties and international agreements concluded before the entry into force of the Vienna Convention listing earlier cases, see *Case concerning Pulp Mills on the River Uruguay (Argentina v Uruguay)* [2010] ICJ Reports 18, para 65.

[40] See, for example, *Kasikili/Sedudu Island (Botswana/Namibia)* [1999] ICJ Reports 1045, at 1062, at para 25, referring to article 33(3), and *LaGrand (Germany v USA)* [2001] ICJ Reports 466, at 502, para 101, referring to article 33(4).

2.3 Endorsement of the Vienna rules
by other international courts and tribunals

The view of the ICJ has been shared by several other international courts and tribunals. The European Court of Human Rights, for example, espoused use of the Vienna rules well before the ICJ gave its full endorsement.[41] The International Tribunal for the Law of the Sea has followed the rather more sedate approach taken by the ICJ, at first by borrowing the terminology and approach of the Vienna Convention's articles on interpretation, then explicitly holding that the rules of the Vienna Convention on the interpretation of treaties apply to the interpretation of provisions of the Convention on the Law of the Sea and the 1994 implementing Agreement.[42] Similarly, arbitral practice supports the ICJ's view that the rules constitute customary international law and that this is evidenced in the practice of states which are not parties to the Vienna Convention. Thus, for example, the United States of America (which is not a party to the Vienna Convention and which sought at the Vienna conference to modify the rules) has relied on the Vienna rules in arbitral and other international proceedings.[43] For example, in proceedings before the settlement dispute bodies of the World Trade Organization:

The United States argued that, in accordance with customary rules of international law concerning treaty interpretation, as reflected in the Vienna Convention on the Law of Treaties, the United States had looked to the plain meaning of the terms in their context and object and purpose. The plain meaning of 'more favourable treatment' did not mean that re-imports must be excluded from safeguard action. If that were the intent, the agreement would have so stated.[44]

In the World Trade Organization dispute settlement system, the Appellate Body has frequently indicated that the rules in articles 31 and 32 of the Vienna Convention have attained the status of customary or general international law.[45] The Appellate Body has, in different cases, invoked the various constituent elements of article 31, although in an early case it laid a slightly misleading initial trail by indicating that paragraph (1) of article 31 (rather than the whole of that article) of the Vienna Convention constituted the 'general rule' for interpretation of treaties, which has led to rather heavy emphasis on the textual aspect of treaty interpretation in some cases.[46]

---

[41] See, for example, the European Court of Human Rights in *Golder v United Kingdom* ECtHR No 4451/70 (judgment of 21 February 1975), para 32 and numerous cases thereafter.

[42] *Responsibilities and Obligations of States Sponsoring Persons and Entities with Respect to Activities in the Area* (Advisory Opinion) (2011) ITLOS Case No 17, para 58.

[43] See, for example, award of *Arbitral Tribunal for the Agreement on German External Debt, (Belgium, France, Switzerland, UK and USA v Federal Republic of Germany)* ('*Young Loan*' case, 1980) 59 ILR 495, at 529, para 16, and see Chapter 9, sections 4.5 and 4.9; for the US proposals at the Vienna conference, see Chapter 2, sections 9 and 10.

[44] *United States—Restrictions on Imports of Cotton and Man-Made Fibre Underwear* (8 November 1996) WT/DS24/R, at para 5.185.

[45] See, for example, *Japan—Alcoholic Beverages* IIWT/DS8,10–11/AB/R (1996), Part D, 10–12 and *United States—Measures Affecting the Cross-Border Supply of Gambling and Betting Services* (2005) WT/DS285/AB/R, passim.

[46] See Report on *US—Gasoline* (1996) WT/DS2/AB/R, 17.

Other arbitral bodies which have made use of the Vienna rules include those established under the auspices of the International Centre for Settlement of Investment Disputes and the Permanent Court of Arbitration, and those set up under the North American Free Trade Agreement.[47]

2.4 Endorsement of the Vienna rules by national courts

Courts within national legal systems frequently interpret treaties or legislation giving effect to them:

…in the deliberations that led to the drafting of what eventually became Articles 31–3 of the Vienna Convention…there is little that suggests awareness that by far the greater part in the judicial interpretation of international agreements falls to municipal, not international, tribunals.…[48]

There are different ways in which treaties come to be interpreted, depending very largely on the constitutional arrangements of each state. In those states where international law is fully integrated with the national legal order, treaties can become fully part of that order. Thus, states whose constitutions provide for treaties to have direct effect in the internal legal order once the state has become a party to a treaty and has published it, and which regard international law as fully part of domestic law, would encounter little difficulty in accepting the applicability of the Vienna rules either as treaty provisions (if the particular state is a party to the Vienna Convention) or, now that it is generally recognized that the rules are rules of customary international law, simply as applicable law.[49]

The position is less clear in countries following the common law tradition, which tend to view treaties as having application in the internal legal order only if there has been a specific legislative act. However, once there has been legislation, this immediately presents an uncertainty whether it is the treaty itself which is to be interpreted or the legislation giving effect to it. In the case of the Vienna rules, these issues are overlaid with the further consideration of whether domestic law mandates their use, irrespective of whether the state is a party to the Vienna Convention, because the rules state customary international law. In several states which follow the common law tradition reference to the Vienna rules in the course of interpreting treaties has become much more frequent. This use sometimes appears to be based on the idea of the rules being in some sense grafted onto the established approaches to treaty interpretation. In other cases, the rules are applied more systematically.[50]

Courts in the United Kingdom have followed a trail of progressive acceptance of the applicability of the Vienna rules to issues over treaty interpretation. The first sign of this was mention of the rules by four of the five judges in the House of

---

[47] See Chapters 2 and 5–9 below.
[48] C H Schreuer, 'The Interpretation of Treaties by Domestic Courts' (1971) 45 BYBIL 255.
[49] See further Chapter 4, section 4.2.1 below.
[50] See further section 5.4, Chapter 4, section 4, and examples in Chapters 5–9, below.

Lords in *Fothergill v Monarch Airlines*.[51] However, only Lord Diplock referred to the rules at any length and it was the possible use of preparatory work which mainly excited the judges. This left a rather incomplete impression of the Vienna rules. Though later cases have referred to the rules much more extensively, sometimes looking at particular elements in some detail, the strong influence of precedent has meant that *Fothergill v Monarch* has acted as something of a counterweight to their systematic use.[52]

The position in the USA, which is not a party to the Vienna Convention, is rather different from that in the UK and other countries having a common law tradition. The US Supreme Court has referred to the Vienna Convention but not to the rules on treaty interpretation, preferring to rely on its own precedents on interpretation.[53] In contrast, the US Courts of Appeals have made explicit reference to the Vienna rules. However, the position of the USA internationally is different from that adopted by its Supreme Court. In international proceedings the USA has argued that the Vienna rules do govern treaty interpretation.[54]

Courts in several other states have referred to the Vienna rules.[55] While their use may have been somewhat spasmodic and infrequent hitherto, there does not appear to have been any notorious incident of outright rejection of their applicability.

3. Definitions and Key Concepts

Preliminary explanations are given here of the main terms and concepts which are used frequently in the book. Some of these raise issues of controversy which are considered in more detail later. These definitions and key concepts are not a guide to all the relevant law of treaties, let alone international law generally. However, because of the potential importance when interpreting a treaty of identifying and using its preparatory work (and associated material such as interpretative declarations, reservations, etc), a brief account of how treaties are made is included in Chapter 3.

3.1 Treaty

Article 2 of the Vienna Convention, defining terms for the purposes of the Convention, states:

'treaty' means an international agreement concluded between States in written form and governed by international law, whether embodied in a single instrument or in two or more related instruments and whatever its particular designation...[56]

---

[51] [1981] AC 251 and see further Chapter 4, section 4.2.2 below.
[52] See Chapter 4, section 4.2.2 below.
[53] See E Criddle, 'The Vienna Convention on the Law of Treaties in U.S. Treaty Interpretation' (2003–2004) 44 Va J Int'l L 431, and Chapter 4, section 4.2.3 below.
[54] See section 2.3 above and Chapter 4, section 4.2.3 below.
[55] See Chapter 4, section 4.2 below.
[56] See further Aust, *Modern Treaty Law and Practice*, Chapter 2 and Gardiner, *International Law*, at 58–65.

Key features of this definition are that: (a) 'treaty' is the generic term for international agreements however each one is designated or named in its title; (b) such an agreement is between states; and (c) the agreement is governed by international law.

The name given to an international agreement is not decisive of whether it is a treaty, though it may provide some evidence. Items (b) and (c) above are the real determinants (with the addition of international organizations to item (b)). In one study, nearly 40 names were listed as having been used in the titles of treaties.[57] These ranged from those which had been used many times (including Treaty, Convention, Agreement, Protocol, Exchange of Notes) to those which had been used infrequently (including Accord, Charter, Plan, Compact, Code). Some in the list are more controversial. A 'resolution' would be less likely nowadays to be the title of a treaty, though it might be the means for agreeing a text of one or might be the instrument opening one for signature. There may be also be doubts about whether 'understanding' is a term appropriate for inclusion in the title for a treaty. The term 'treaty', when used for an agreement between states, always sets out rights and obligations governed by law, while 'understandings' more aptly signifies non-binding arrangements. However, if understandings accompany a treaty and are followed in practice, they may have a significant effect upon interpretation even though in themselves not binding nor falling within the definition of a treaty.[58]

The Vienna Convention's definition specifies that for its purposes the agreements to be viewed as treaties are those between states. The Convention does, however, specifically apply to any treaty which is the constituent instrument of an international organization and to any treaty adopted within an international organization.[59] International organizations are entities whose existence and acts on the international plane are governed by international law. Hence they also have the capacity to participate in international agreements. Provisions on interpretation, exactly the same in substance as those in the Vienna Convention, are included in a parallel convention regulating treaties between states and international organizations and between such organizations themselves.[60]

That a key element of the definition of 'treaty' for the purposes of the Vienna Convention is that the agreement is governed by international law does not, of course, mean that treaties are excluded from interpretation within national legal systems. Quite the contrary, many treaties are of a kind that lead to the probability that they will only, or chiefly, be interpreted within national legal systems. Obvious examples are private law conventions, such as the many conventions produced by the Hague Conference on Private International Law, those on carriage by air or sea, or treaties engaging domestic procedures such as extradition treaties or double

---

[57] D P Myers, 'The Names and Scope of Treaties' (1957) 51 AJIL 575, at 576.
[58] See further Chapter 3 below. [59] Vienna Convention, article 5.
[60] The Vienna Convention on the Law of Treaties between States and International Organizations or between International Organizations, Vienna, 1986.

taxation agreements; but there is a huge range of treaties beyond these which also have their principal effect in domestic law.

An important issue is whether a treaty should be interpreted in accordance with the Vienna rules when it is being applied within a national system of law. That this is appropriate seems almost too obvious to require mention, since international law is clearly the 'proper law' of the instrument. However, because some national legal systems view international law and municipal law as entirely separate, there may be scope for argument on whether it is the treaty which is to be interpreted or the implementing legislation, the latter being open to interpretation in the same way as any other legislation of the relevant state. It seems probable that the Vienna rules will continue to receive increasingly widespread application in national courts, this being the approach most likely to achieve results that are correct and consistent with states' obligations.

In principle, the same rules of treaty interpretation apply to all types of treaty, that is to say whether they be bilateral or multilateral, whether they relate to matters that only affect relations between states or are designed to have an effect within the internal legal order of states, and whether they ultimately regulate relations between a person (human or corporate) and the state. There are, however, aspects of the rules of treaty interpretation which undergo some modification because of the type of treaty involved. For example, in human rights treaties (which come within the last category mentioned above), states assume obligations in relation to one another, but individuals are the beneficiaries. This means that when interpreting rights to formulate reservations or exercise powers such as those to suspend safeguards (for example, habeas corpus), the interests to be evaluated are those of the particular state and the protection of the rights and freedoms of individuals, rather than an effect on relations between the parties.[61]

The utility of the Vienna rules has proved such that they have been used, by analogy and with appropriate caution, in interpreting some unilateral acts, such as declarations by states accepting the jurisdiction of the ICJ and resolutions of organs of international organizations.[62] It is, of course, the substance of the transaction which is to be examined in determining whether a treaty obligation arises. For example, the 'Algiers Accords' provided the means for settlement of issues between the USA and Iran after the latter's involvement in unlawful acts against the US embassy, consular personnel, and property. The breach of relations between the USA and Iran set difficulties in the way for direct settlement. The Algerian government, therefore, acting as an honest broker, made declarations (including provisions for a claims settlement tribunal) to which the USA and Iran adhered.

---

[61] See further Chapter 5 below.

[62] For examples of interpretation of declarations see Chapter 5, sections 2.4.2 and 4.2.4 below. On resolutions, see M C Wood, 'The Interpretation of Security Council Resolutions' Max Planck 2 *Yearbook of United Nations Law* (1998), 73 and M C Wood, 'Security Council Working Methods and Procedures' (1996) 45 ICLQ 50.

Though not in form a typical treaty, the result was clearly within the Vienna defini-tion and the Iran–United States Claims Tribunal has contributed considerably to the case law applying the Vienna rules.[63]

3.2 Party, signatory, etc

In the Vienna Convention the term 'party' means 'a State which has consented to be bound by the treaty and for which the treaty is in force'.[64] It is best to note this well and to adhere strictly to using the term 'party' as defined. One of the most fre-quently occurring confusions, even among lawyers as well as more widely, is using 'signatory' when meaning 'party'. This is often a dangerous misuse. Although in some cases signature of a treaty may result in a state becoming bound by the treaty without more, in a great many cases (and very generally in the case of modern multilateral treaties) signature is subject to ratification. In all these latter cases, a state on whose behalf a treaty has been signed only becomes a party by depositing an instrument of ratification (and on the treaty entering into force, if it has not already done so). A 'signatory state' is *not* a party in those cases; it is not bound by the treaty or subject to its obligations.[65] Further, states may become parties to trea-ties by 'accession', 'acceptance', and other similar processes which do not involve signature at all. Such a state never has been a 'signatory' of the treaty to which it accedes and never will be: yet as a party, it is bound in exactly the same way as a state which has both signed and ratified the treaty.[66]

The difference between the position of a signatory state and a party takes on particular significance in the area of treaty interpretation. So do other relevant categories such as: a 'negotiating' state, meaning one which took part in the drawing up and adoption of the text of the treaty but which may not have signed the treaty—though the state may still be eligible to become a party, for example by later accession; a 'contracting state' meaning a state which has consented to be bound by the treaty, whether or not the treaty has entered into force; or more simply a state may be one to which the treaty's final clauses give an open invitation to become a party but which has not been involved with the treaty in any way hitherto (historically the situation in which a state would 'accede' to the treaty).

---

[63] See C N Brower and J D Brueschke, *The Iran–United States Claims Tribunal* (The Hague: Martinus Nijhoff, 1998), at 264, note 1240; see also G H Aldrich, *The Jurisprudence of the Iran–United States Claims Tribunal* (Oxford: Clarendon Press, 1996).

[64] Vienna Convention, article 2(g).

[65] For the limited obligations incurred by signature where this is subject to ratification (broadly, not to defeat the object and purpose of the treaty), see article 18 of the Vienna Convention and R K Gardiner, *International Law*, at 73. Provisional application of a treaty or part of it is a possibility if the treaty itself so provides or the negotiating states have agreed this in some other way: article 25 of the Vienna Convention.

[66] See further, Aust, *Modern Treaty Law and Practice*, Chapter 7 and Gardiner, *International Law*, Chapter 2.

These processes affect the treaty relations between states and, potentially, the substance of the text in the sense that reservations may have been formulated which may or may not have been the subject of objections. Two important issues affecting treaty interpretation that may turn on these distinct categories of participation by states in the treaty process are the effect of subsequent treaties related to the one in question and the effect of subsequent practice under the treaty. Most disputed matters of interpretation of a treaty are resolved by discussion or negotiation between the parties to the treaty. This is appropriate because a treaty applies in the relations of states with one another. Hence the Vienna rules (reflecting customary international law) treat subsequent agreements between parties about interpretation, and also concordant practice of the parties in application of the treaty, as fully part of the general rule of interpretation. In fact, the major role of subsequent practice as an element in treaty interpretation is one of the more prominent features distinguishing this from the approach to interpretation of formal legal instruments (such as legislation) in many national legal systems.

It will, however, be immediately apparent that signatory states, negotiating states, and others eligible to become parties, have an interest in how interpretation of a particular treaty develops, as this may affect their decision on whether to become a party. Further, states which have played no part in negotiating a treaty but which may subsequently become a party (or a party to an amended treaty) have an interest in the extent to which preparatory work and acts by other states parties to the treaty can affect interpretation of the treaty, raising questions of the effect of such elements and accessibility to information about them. These matters are considered below, mainly in Chapter 3. What is stressed here is the importance of correctly ascertaining the status of an actual or potential party vis-à-vis the treaty whose interpretation is in issue and vis-à-vis any other relevant treaty.

3.3 Treaty relations

The chief aim of treaty interpretation is to identify correctly the rights and obligations of the parties. The extent of these rights and obligations is a function of the treaty relations established between relevant parties. This concept may take the preliminaries to treaty interpretation beyond the text of the treaty instrument itself. While the treaty text has the prime role in determining rights and obligations, additional elements may need to be considered in identifying the precise extent of treaty relations between any two parties. These may include interpretative declarations made by one or more states, reservations formulated by a party and any response to any such reservation, and other limitations or conditions on the obligations that have been established in accordance with procedures within the treaty. The term 'treaty relations' also requires account to be taken of the more mundane or routine prerequisites for one party to be bound vis-à-vis another party, such as time factors for entry into force of the treaty. These matters are considered further in Chapter 3.

3.4 Preparatory work

One of the most controversial aspects of treaty interpretation is what use may be made of preparatory work of a treaty. Philip Allott's definition of a treaty as 'a disagreement reduced to writing' reveals the nub of the difficulty, containing the implicit warning that one should expect preparatory work to reveal a good deal of divergence, disagreement, and lack of conclusive outcome as to meaning.[67]

The classification of such material in the Vienna rules as 'supplementary means of interpretation' has not in practical terms diminished its importance. Yet neither article 32 of the Vienna Convention nor the article containing definitions identifies the extent of material covered by this term. In its French form, the term has long been in use both in international courts and tribunals, and in national courts. Despite the use of the term 'preparatory work' in the authentic English text of the Vienna Convention, even in cases where they refer to the Vienna rules, judges in the UK seem to have retained a preference for '*travaux préparatoires*'.[68] However, McNair (author of the classic, but now dated, work on the law of treaties) preferred 'preparatory work' in the title and text of his chapter on that subject.[69] His usage, and that of the Vienna Convention, is followed here.

The ILC did not think that anything would be gained by trying to define *travaux préparatoires*, taking the view that 'to do so might only lead to the possible exclusion of relevant evidence'.[70] McNair described the term 'preparatory work' as 'an omnibus expression which is used rather loosely to indicate all documents, such as memoranda, minutes of conferences, and drafts of the treaty under negotiation'.[71] In the House of Lords, Lord Scarman gave some indication of the wide range of this resource, albeit obliquely and somewhat dismissively:

Working papers of delegates to the conference, or memoranda submitted by the delegates for consideration by the conference, though relevant, will seldom be helpful; but an agreed conference minute of the understanding on the basis of which the draft of an article of the convention was accepted may well be of great value.[72]

Preparatory work and the circumstances of conclusion of a treaty are allied in being mentioned together in article 32 of the Vienna Convention as being included within supplementary means of interpretation. What is meant by the circumstances of conclusion of a treaty is not described in the Vienna Convention and emerges somewhat imprecisely in cases referring to the Vienna rules. The circumstances surrounding the preparation and conclusion of a treaty may be mentioned in the preparatory work, but are nevertheless distinct from it. The extent of preparatory work is considered further in Chapter 3 and its role in treaty interpretation in

---

[67] P Allott, 'The Concept of International Law' (1999) 10 EJIL 31, at 43.
[68] See, for example, *Fothergill v Monarch Airlines* [1981] AC 251, at 282 and *R v Immigration Officer at Prague Airport ex parte European Roma Rights Centre* [2004] UKHL 55, [2005] 2 AC 1, at para 17.
[69] McNair, *The Law of Treaties*, chapter XXIII.
[70] [1964] *Yearbook of the ILC*, vol II, p 205, para 17 (footnote omitted).
[71] McNair, *The Law of Treaties*, at 411.   [72] *Fothergill v Monarch*, at 294.

Chapter 8. The nature of the circumstances of conclusion of a treaty is illustrated by examples in Chapter 8.[73]

3.5 Intertemporal law

This term is one used in international law generally. The rule is commonly formulated (in relation to international law generally) as stating:

…a juridical fact must be appreciated in the light of the law contemporary with it, and not of the law in force at the time when a dispute in regard to it arises or fails to be settled.[74]

This proposition has a second limb stating:

…the existence of the right, in other words its continued manifestation, shall follow the conditions required by the evolution of law.[75]

These formulations (considered in detail in Chapter 7) are, however, of limited value in the context of treaty interpretation. There are at least four circumstances in which time may be a relevant element of treaty interpretation. First, and most obvious, is in identifying treaty relations, that is ascertaining what instruments were in force at any relevant time or critical date. Second, whether provisions of such instruments are to be interpreted as they would have been at the time of their conclusion or entry into force. Third, what effect passage of time may have on the interpretation of a treaty provision. This is manifestly a concern if the treaty contains indications that it speaks to a particular date or dates or, in the converse case, if it is clearly intended to evolve and keep in tune with the times. Fourth, in application of the provision in the Vienna Convention requiring account to be taken of any relevant rules of international law applicable in the relations between the parties (article 31(3)(c)), does this refer to international law at the time of conclusion of the treaty, at the moment of interpretation, or at some other time?[76] These matters are considered further in Chapter 7.[77]

3.6 'Interpretation', 'application', and 'construction'

Waldock as Special Rapporteur of the ILC on the law of treaties endorsed an earlier description of interpretation:

The process of interpretation, rightly conceived, cannot be regarded as a mere mechanical one of drawing inevitable meanings from the words in a text, or of searching for and discovering some preexisting specific intention of the parties with respect to every situation

---

[73] See Chapter 8, section 4.5 below.
[74] *Island of Palmas* case (Permanent Court of Arbitration) (1928) 2 RIAA 829, at 845.
[75] *Island of Palmas* case, at 845.
[76] See, generally, R Higgins, 'Time and the Law: International Perspectives on an Old Problem' (1997) 46 ICLQ 501.
[77] See Chapter 7, section 1.2 below; see also E Bjorge, *The Evolutionary Interpretation of Treaties* (Oxford: OUP, 2014), Chapter 4.

arising under a treaty…In most instances interpretation involves *giving* a meaning to a text.[78]

This homes in on the idea that the interpreter is 'giving' a meaning to the treaty rather than finding one buried within it. Thus, while considerations prevailing at the time at which a treaty was drawn up may be relevant to interpretation in the circumstances described in the preceding section, treaty interpretation is not just a quest for finding the original meaning of a statement or text, nor for simply taking words at their face value. True, the Vienna rules start with the idea of approaching the terms of a treaty in good faith and giving them their ordinary meaning. This allows scope for viewing a reasonable first impression as a starting point; but that is swiftly dispelled by the immediate link which the rules make with context and with the requirement of consideration of the object and purpose of the treaty, even before the further elements of the general rule (such as practice and general international law) are taken into account. Inclusion of context and these further elements of the general rule in the treaty interpretation process take it way beyond attempting merely to recapture the meaning of words at the time of conclusion of the treaty.

Professor Falk introduced the whole difficulty of the task of defining treaty interpretation rather nicely by showing how dictionary definitions may record multiple ordinary meanings. This immediately indicates that skills of selectivity are needed by the interpreter even at the first stage of the search for meaning:

A point of departure is suggested by the contrast between the first and the third definitions of interpretation found in the Oxford English Dictionary: '1. The action of interpreting; explanation, exposition'; '3. The way in which a thing ought to be interpreted; proper explanation.' Dictionary definitions used as a starting-point for investigation disclose, as is so often the case, an ambivalence deeply embedded in the subject-matter itself. In the instance of interpretation there is disclosed the wavering between the autonomy and objectivity of the interpretative process, on the one side, and its normative, instrumental function on the other. This wavering, and the obscurity of meaning that results from it, makes interpretation at once fascinating and mysterious as an object of inquiry. In an age of propaganda, advertising, and subliminal manipulation it is essential to disentangle, as well as we can, the manipulative mode from more descriptive alternatives in our effort to comprehend the interpretative act.[79]

The underlying dilemma is a double one. First, following Professor Falk's analysis, there is the contrast between performing straightforward exegesis and introducing

---

[78] [1964] *Yearbook of the ILC*, vol II, p 53, para 1, citing Part III of the Harvard draft codification of international law in (1935) 29 AJIL Supp 653, at 946 (original emphasis); see further Chapter 2, section 4 below and M Bos, 'Theory and Practice of Treaty Interpretation' (1980) 27 NILR 3, at 13–15; and cf A Barak, *Purposive Interpretation in Law* (Princeton: Princeton University Press, 2007), 3: 'Legal interpretation is a rational activity that gives meaning to a legal text', which prompts the suggestion that one role of the Vienna rules is to provide the framework for a 'rational' scheme for giving meaning to treaties.

[79] R A Falk, 'On Treaty Interpretation and the New Haven Approach: Achievements and Prospects' (1967–1968) 8 *Va J Int'l L* 323, at 324.

some external or normative approach, the latter importing the idea that a treaty has a life of its own which needs taming in its interaction with the international law scene. Second, as intimated above (and not wholly separate from Professor Falk's point), is whether the interpreter should seek the 'original meaning', trying to work out what the parties meant at the time of conclusion of the treaty, or whether an objective approach should be taken to the text giving it a meaning at the time when an issue of interpretation and application arises. Since issues of interpretation commonly arise in circumstances not foreseen by the negotiators, which they may have deliberately avoided resolving, or which are generally within the purview of the provisions but only treated in principle rather than detail, some element of objective approach may be the only solution available in the absence of indication of the joint subjective approach of the parties. The Vienna rules address this problem by combining a clear indication of *what* should be taken into account with some rather less prescriptive pointers as to *how* to use the indicated material, and in the final analysis leaving a margin of appreciation for the interpreter to produce an outcome.

The term 'application' is used in the Vienna rules without definition or explanation.[80] It has been described in the Permanent Court of International Justice (PCIJ) as 'determining the consequences which [a] rule attaches to the occurrence of a given fact' or, in another sense, as 'the action of bringing about the consequences which, according to a rule, should follow a fact'.[81] In many, if not most, instances an *interpretation* of a treaty will be sought in connection with *application* of a treaty to a given situation or prospective occurrence. The situation, circumstance or occurrence will play a part in defining the issues for interpretation and may thus have an effect on the process of interpretation. However, interpretation—the giving of meaning to a text—is separate from application of the provision and, logically, must come before it. This is *pace* McNair who wrote:

The words 'interpret', 'interpretation' are often used loosely as if they included 'apply, application'. Strictly speaking, when the meaning of the treaty is clear, it is 'applied', not 'interpreted'. Interpretation is a secondary process which only comes into play when it is impossible to make sense of the plain terms of the treaty, or when they are susceptible of different meanings. The *Concise Oxford Dictionary* says: 'Interpret: expound the meaning of (abstruse words, writings, &c.); make out the meaning of.'[82]

It is with hesitation that any suggestion be made that Homer nodded; but even allowing for McNair's self-limitation to the *Concise Oxford* definition, it is difficult

---

[80] See also Chapter 7, section 4.2.3(i) below, and A Gourgourinis, 'The Distinction Between Interpretation and Application of Norms in International Adjudication' (2011) 2 *J Int'l Dispute Settlement* 31.

[81] *Factory at Chorzów (Jurisdiction)* (1927) PCIJ Series A No 9, 39 (Dissenting Opinion of Judge Ehrlich); on this, and on the difference between interpretation and application, see further Bjorge, *The Evolutionary Interpretation of Treaties*, 15–17.

[82] McNair, *The Law of Treaties*, at 365, note 1; on the possible connection between McNair's proposition and the maxim of Vattel that 'it is not permissible to interpret what has no need of interpretation' see Chapter 2, section 3 below.

to see how this sustains the distinction which he suggests between the circumstances for interpretation and for application, and the relationship which he attributes to them. There may be scope for proper inquiry into statistics when trying to evaluate his assertion that 'interpretation' is in fact now often used as if it included application; but that seems of little importance when set against his view that when the meaning of the treaty is clear it is applied, not interpreted. This sets on its head the natural sequence that is inherent in the process of reading a treaty: first ascribing meaning to its terms and then applying the outcome to a particular situation. McNair's approach seems to follow the Red Queen's 'sentence first, verdict afterwards'. In fact, the *Concise Oxford* definition which he supplies perhaps gets nearest to the nub of it in 'make out the meaning of'. Even 'when the meaning of the treaty is clear', this is the result of 'making out' that meaning. It may have been a simple task, certainly easier than in the case of expounding the meaning of 'abstruse words, writings, &c.'; but in every case meaning must be given to the terms, this necessarily being before they can be applied.

This was helpfully explained in the commentary on the Harvard draft convention on the law of treaties:

Interpretation is closely connected with the carrying out of treaties, for before a treaty can be applied in a given set of circumstances it must be determined whether or not it was meant to apply to those circumstances...In any particular case there may be no expressed doubt or difference of opinion as to the meaning of the treaty concerned; its purpose and applicability may be regarded as perfectly evident. Yet, even in such a case, the person or persons deciding that the meaning of the treaty is 'clear', and that it is plainly intended to apply to the given circumstances, must do so, consciously or unconsciously, by some process of reasoning based upon evidence.

In short, the 'application' of treaties, it would seem, must almost inevitably involve some measure of 'interpretation'. There is, however, a recognized distinction between the two processes. Interpretation is the process of determining the meaning of a text; application is the process of determining the consequences which, according to the text, should follow in a given situation.[83]

This conclusion finds some more recent support in an opinion of Judge Shahabuddeen at the ICJ, although he does also make clear that the two concepts, interpretation and application, are often difficult to divorce. In the context of whether a dispute existed over 'the interpretation or application' of the Headquarters Agreement between the USA and the UN, Judge Shahabuddeen stated:

The phrase 'interpretation and application' has occurred in one version or another in a multitude of disputes settlement provisions extending over many decades in the past...The phrase in this case happens to be 'interpretation or application'. Satisfaction of either element will therefore suffice. But, further, since it is not possible to apply a treaty save with reference to some factual field (even if taken hypothetically) and since it is not possible to apply a treaty except on the basis of some interpretation of it, there is a detectable view

---

[83] 29 (1935) AJIL Supp 938; on the Harvard draft convention, see Chapter 2, section 4 below.

that there is little practical, or even theoretical, distinction between the two elements of the formula…It seems arguable that the two elements constitute a compendious term of art generally covering all disputes as to rights and duties having their source in the controlling treaty….[84]

In stating that it is not possible to apply a treaty except on the basis of some interpretation of it, Judge Shahabuddeen confirms that logically interpretation must precede application, even though his conclusion was that, for the purposes of a typical treaty provision establishing means of settlement of disputes over interpretation or application, the two concepts tended to run together.[85]

Rather less clear is whether there is any useful distinction to be drawn between 'interpretation' and 'construction'. In treaty drafting and usage by interpreters, the terms are used with seeming lack of differentiation. For example, in the Charter of the United Nations the terms are used without apparent difference in meaning where article 80(1) has 'nothing in this Chapter shall be *construed*…', while article 80(2) states 'Paragraph 1 of this Article shall not be *interpreted* as…', the French text using 'interprétée' and 'interprété' respectively.[86] It is difficult to find anything in interpretative practice that turns on a distinction between these terms in the law of treaties, but there may be a possible contrast in analysis of interpretation (particularly in comparison with that of national constitutions).[87]

4. The Process of Interpretation and the Nature of the Rules

4.1 The process of interpretation
and the principle of autonomous interpretation

> One starts from the proposition that the interpretation of legal texts is not simply an exercise in the use of language and its application to fact patterns.[88]

---

[84] Separate Opinion of Judge Shahabuddeen in *Applicability of the Obligation to Arbitrate under Section 21 of the United Nations Headquarters Agreement of 26 June 1947* (Advisory Opinion) [1988] ICJ Reports 57, at 59.

[85] See further M K Yasseen, 'L'Interpretation des Traités d'après la Convention de Vienne sur le Droit des Traités', 151 Hague Recueil (1976–III) 1, at 10: 'L'interprétation…est une étape vers l'application', and also at 9, quoting and citing Georges Scelle: 'il n'y a pas d'application sans interprétation'. In similar vein, the ILC's Special Rapporteur on the law of treaties (Waldock) is recorded as stating 'that "interpretation" is an essential element in the application of treaties', commentary on draft article 55, [1964] *Yearbook of the ILC*, vol II, p 8, para 3.

[86] Emphasis added; ICJ Judge de Castro, noting the contrasting terminology, took the French version as using the term interpret 'in the somewhat non-technical sense', *Legal Consequences for States of the Continued Presence of South Africa in Namibia (South West Africa) notwithstanding Security Council Resolution 276 (1970)* (Separate Opinion) [1971] ICJ Reports 16, at 192–93; the ILC quoted Judge Huber in the *Island of Palmas* case as stating '…whatever may be the right *construction* of a treaty, it cannot be *interpreted* as disposing of the rights of independent third Powers' [1966] *Yearbook of the ILC*, vol II, p 226, para 20 (emphasis added, footnote omitted).

[87] See Chapter 10 below.

[88] C McLachlan, 'The Principle of Systemic Integration and Article 31(3)(c) of the Vienna Convention' (2005) 54 ICLQ 279, at 286.

As suggested at the beginning of this chapter (and generally confirmed throughout the literature on treaty interpretation), application of any rules on treaty interpretation, and in particular the Vienna rules, is not a purely mechanical process; but their proper application is the correct procedure and the best assurance of reaching the correctly ascertained interpretation. It may, of course, be asked whether there is always a single correct interpretation. If using the description of a treaty as 'a disagreement reduced to writing',[89] or (less cynically) if two or more negotiators have selected words capable of reflecting differing meanings which they have elaborated in the course of preparing the treaty, may there not be different meanings in relation to different parties? While this suggestion may seem a realistic and (in some circumstances) an attractive one, it is at odds with (a) the function of a treaty as an international agreement; (b) the mechanics of treaty relations; (c) the nature and content of the Vienna rules; and (d) with the process of treaty interpretation envisaged in the Vienna Convention.

As regards (a), whatever the history of disagreement preceding its conclusion, a treaty is concluded as an international agreement. Good faith requires that no party has, as it were, its fingers crossed behind its back. Further, under item (b), the mechanics for establishing treaty relations allow states to make reservations and interpretative statements (in either case where permitted or accepted), processes clearly aimed at having individual variants or concerns out in the open. Consequently, any differences in interpretation based on one party's individual concerns could only flow from these established mechanisms for adjusting the agreement in the treaty. As to (c), the elements of the Vienna rules which look back to the negotiating history and surrounding circumstances are those in article 32. These elements are considered in detail below, but it is sufficient to note here that there is no glimmer of a suggestion in article 32's references to 'the meaning' that the outcome could be variable meanings according to utterances of different negotiators.

The reference to the interpretative process in item (d) is to the scheme of the Vienna rules which is predicated on combined application of all the elements relevant to interpretation in any particular case so that there is only a single route to the outcome. Thus, referring to one of the judgments of the ICJ delivered a few years before the Court gave its unequivocal endorsement of the Vienna rules, Torres Bernárdez wrote:

> ...the judgment's reasoning underlines...one of the most distinctive features of the Vienna Convention system, namely that interpretation of a treaty, or a provision of a treaty, is a legal operation which should combine the various permitted elements and means of interpretation as they may be present in the case, while keeping *open* the interpretation until the very conclusion of the interpretative process.[90]

---

[89] Allott, 'The Concept etc' (1999) 10 EJIL 31, at 43; see further Chapter 10 below.

[90] See Torres Bernárdez, 'Interpretation of Treaties by the International Court of Justice following the Adoption of the 1969 Vienna Convention on the Law of Treaties', in Hafner et al. (eds), *Liber Amicorum: Professor Ignaz Seidl-Hohenveldern* ..., at 726, para 11 (emphasis in original).

This description marries up well with the metaphor used by the ILC that all the various interpretative elements, as present in any given case, should be thrown into the crucible and their interaction would give the legally relevant interpretation.[91] As the various elements in the Vienna rules are not given different values, beyond the indication that those in article 32 are 'supplementary' means of interpretation, no firm conclusion based on particular elements should be reached before the process has been completed.[92] As the ILC's Special Rapporteur on the law of treaties put it: 'the process of interpretation was essentially a simultaneous one, though logic might dictate a certain order of thought'.[93] Elements can only be taken up one at a time, but they are to be evaluated together. Thus interpretation may require going round the circle more than once if a factor presents itself under an element of the rules later in the list and which appears to outweigh one already taken up. A helpful description of the ILC's approach indicates:

> The understanding that emerged was of interpretation as a recursive and inelegant process that would spiral in toward the meaning of a treaty rather than as a rigidly linear algorithm tied to a particular hierarchical sequence. [94]

The issue of whether there is a single autonomous interpretation is well illustrated and analysed in the rejection by the UK's House of Lords of the suggestion that a treaty could accommodate a range of possible interpretations (as distinct from expressly permitting parties to select from a range of permitted acts). Parties to the UN Convention on Status of Refugees have adopted different interpretations on whether its provisions protect a person from being required to return to a country of origin where they risk persecution by non-state agents. The UK interprets the Convention as requiring such protection. In *Ex parte Adan*[95] the House of Lords had to consider whether the Secretary of State could properly certify that sending a refugee to a country taking the opposite view (not being the individual's country of origin) would be sending the person to a country which would not send the asylum seeker to his country of origin 'otherwise than in accordance with the Convention'. Issuing a certificate in such circumstances could only be on the basis that the different interpretation was in some way legitimate and that sending a person to a country which might return them to their country of origin on the basis that any persecution there would be by non-state actors would not breach the Convention. Firmly opposing this, Lord Steyn stated:

---

[91] See section 1.1 above.

[92] See Torres Bernardez, 'Interpretation of Treaties by the International Court of Justice following the Adoption of the 1969 Vienna Convention on the Law of Treaties', above.

[93] Waldock [1966] *Yearbook of the ILC*, vol II, p 206, para 36; and see Yasseen, stating that 'the purpose of interpretation was to determine the meaning and effect of the rules embodied in treaties' and that the ILC had proposed 'a general method for achieving that purpose...The means enumerated were...arranged, not in any order of precedence, but in a practical order, which was self-evident in view of the circumstances', ILC's 871st Meeting, 16 June 1966, [1966] *Yearbook of the ILC*, vol I, p 197, para 48.

[94] J D Mortenson, 'Is the Vienna Convention Hostile to Drafting History?' (2013) 107 AJIL 780, at 781.

[95] *R v Secretary of State for the Home Department, ex parte Adan* [2001] 2 AC 477.

It is necessary to determine the autonomous meaning of the relevant treaty provision. This principle is part of the very alphabet of customary international law...It follows that, as in the case of other multilateral treaties, the Refugee Convention must be given an independent meaning derivable from the sources mentioned in articles 31 and 32 [of the Vienna Convention] and without taking colour from distinctive features of the legal system of any individual contracting state. In principle therefore there can only be one true interpretation of a treaty...In practice it is left to national courts, faced with a material disagreement on an issue of interpretation, to resolve it. But in doing so it must search, untrammelled by notions of its national legal culture, for the true autonomous and international meaning of the treaty. And there can only be one true meaning.[96]

Similarly, Lord Slynn stated:

Just as the courts must seek to give a 'Community' meaning to words in the Treaty of Rome (Cmd 5179-II) ('worker') so the Secretary of State and the courts must in the absence of a ruling by the International Court of Justice or uniform state practice arrive at their interpretation on the basis of the Convention as a whole read in the light of any relevant rules of international law, including the Vienna Convention on the Law of Treaties (1980) (Cmd 7674). The Secretary of State and the courts of the United Kingdom have to decide what this phrase in this Treaty means. They cannot simply adopt a list of permissible or legitimate or possible or reasonable meanings and accept that any one of those when applied would be in compliance with the Convention.[97]

It has been suggested that the idea that 'autonomous interpretation' requires stepping outside any particular national legal culture (noted by Lord Steyn above) has a particular application in private law treaties:

...interpretation of a private law convention must proceed on the basis of its 'international character'. This directive serves a separating and elevating function. That is, it suggests an 'autonomous' interpretation free from the influence of national legal concepts and terminology, and even from the domestic interpretive techniques themselves. In doing so, this mandate amounts to an express direction to interpreters to view a convention as occupying an entirely different, elevated international dimension.[98]

This description of autonomous interpretation is in the particular context of treaties seeking to lay down uniform rules of private law, such as the Convention on International Sales of Goods, the Warsaw (and now Montreal) Convention on Unification of Certain Rules on Carriage by Air, and many of the Hague private international law conventions. The treaties are applied within national legal systems; but though the terms used in them are often drawn from concepts in use in national legal systems, once included in treaties they no longer attract the possibly varying character that they have nationally but assume a single meaning under the treaty, unless it states otherwise.[99]

---

[96] [2001] 2 AC, at 515–17, per Lord Steyn.   [97] [2001] 2 AC, at 509.
[98] M P Van Alstine, 'Dynamic Treaty Interpretation' (1998) 146 *University of Pennsylvania Law Review* 687, at 730–31 (footnote omitted) and see M Heidemann and A Knebel, 'Double Taxation Treaties: The Autonomous Interpretation Method in German and English Law' (2010) 38 *Intertax* 136–52.
[99] See further Chapter 5, sections 3.3.6 and 3.3.8, and Chapter 10, section 6.1, below.

There are, however, further considerations allied to the idea of an autonomous meaning of treaties. It is necessary to consider the nature of the treaty which is being interpreted in conjunction with any position on interpretation adopted by the parties to it. The ILC's Commentary on its draft articles on interpretation noted that an agreement as to the interpretation of a provision reached after the conclusion of the treaty 'represents an *authentic* interpretation by the parties which must be read into the treaty for purposes of its interpretation'.[100] That the agreement of the parties on an interpretation would usually trump other possible meanings seems obvious enough, given the nature of a treaty as an international agreement between its parties which, as it is sometimes put, they 'own'.[101]

There are several points to note. First, the idea that an interpretative agreement of the parties provides an 'authentic' interpretation of a treaty is not inconsistent with the conclusion reached above that a treaty has a single meaning, although it does illustrate a circumstance in which an autonomous interpretation is not required. Second, the notion of authentic interpretation was assumed rather than explained by the ILC. In its Commentary on the drafts which became articles 31 and 32, the Commission characterized the distinction between these provisions as being one between 'authentic and supplementary means of interpretation'.[102] This was restated rather more emphatically by Waldock at the Vienna Conference in explaining the division between the general rule and supplementary means of interpretation: 'The Commission had therefore considered that those elements of interpretation which had an authentic and binding character in themselves must be set apart...'.[103] This difference between the general rule and supplementary rules is reflected by the use of the mandatory verb 'shall' in each of the paragraphs of the general rule, while the supplementary means of interpretation are ones to which 'recourse may be had'.

The use of 'authentic' with reference to any interpretative agreement of the parties also provides a further reason to stress the importance of article 31(3)(a) in treaty interpretation in response to any assumption that the general rule is a literal one and is essentially that set out in the first paragraph of that article. The same importance attaches to article 31(3)(b), subsequent practice of the parties being treated in the Vienna rules as authentic interpretation where it shows the agreement of the parties.[104]

---

[100] [1966] *Yearbook of the ILC*, vol II, p 221, para 14 (emphasis added), and see citation by the ICJ of this part of the Commentary in *Kasikili/Sedudu Island (Botswana v Namibia)* [1999] ICJ Reports 1045, at 1075, para 49 and in the NAFTA arbitration *Methanex v USA (Merits)*, Award of 3 August 2005, (2005) 44 ILM 1345, at 1354, para 19; see also Chapter 4, section 1 and Chapter 6, section 1.2, below; the term 'authoritative' has sometimes been used as a synonym for 'authentic': see, for example, the quotation at the start of Chapter 4 below.

[101] For possible exceptions and further analysis, see Chapter 6, section 1.1 below.

[102] [1966] *Yearbook of the ILC*, vol II, p 220, para 10.

[103] United Nations Conference on the Law of Treaties, First Session (26 March–24 May 1968), Official Records: Summary Records, p 184, para 68; see also Jimenez de Arechaga, UN Conference on the Law of Treaties, First Session (26 March–24 May 1968), Official Records: Summary Records, at p 170, para 66, and H W Briggs, 'The *Travaux Préparatoires* of the Vienna Convention on the Law of Treaties' (1971) 65 AJIL 705, at 710–11.

[104] See Chapter 6 below.

It must, however, be stressed that determining the autonomous meaning of a treaty is the product of interpreting that particular treaty and in some instances the practice of the parties under the treaty may not be so useful. For example, in the case of human rights treaties it is assessment of the practice of one or more of the parties which is likely to be the focus of attention. Practice under the treaty to discern a meaning attributed to it by the parties is therefore less likely to offer a contribution to the autonomous meaning in such cases.[105]

4.2 A general 'rule' and 'rules' of interpretation

Article 31 of the Vienna Convention bears the title 'General rule of interpretation' (*Règle générale d'interprétation*). Article 31(3)(c) directs an interpreter of a treaty to take account of any relevant 'rules' of international law. The plural 'rules' is also the description commonly applied to articles 31–33.[106] Two questions arise at this point. First, what is the significance of 'rule' being in the singular in the title of article 31? Second, does the use of the term 'rules' in referring to the provisions of articles 31–33 indicate anything about their nature and effect? There is, of course, also an issue of interpretation of the term 'rules' in article 31(3)(c), but that is considered in the analysis of the separate elements of the Vienna rules below.[107] The widespread use of 'rules of interpretation' in referring to the Vienna Convention provisions is considered in the next section. Here, the first question identified above is addressed.

Determining what 'rule' in the title to article 31 signifies by being in the singular provides an opportunity to examine and illustrate how treaty interpretation calls for skills in selecting and applying elements in the Vienna rules. This is quite laborious. If the *Oxford English Dictionary* (*OED*) is taken as the starting point in a search for the 'ordinary' meaning of 'rule', selecting from the 23 main definitions and usages would be the first hurdle. In parenthesis, this plethora of meanings illustrates that the criticism sometimes made of the reference to 'ordinary meaning' in the opening words of the Vienna rules, on the grounds that words have no plain or natural meaning, fails to take account of the immediate link made in the Vienna rules between ordinary meaning and the context, and object and purpose of the treaty, as essential and linked elements in the quest for a meaning.

Many of the *OED* definitions of 'rule' exclude themselves, being limited to particular subjects, activities, or phrases (maths, grammar, etc). Looking for the

---

[105] See G Letsas, *A Theory of Interpretation of the European Convention on Human Rights* (Oxford: OUP, 2007), Chapter 2.

[106] See, for example, *Sovereignty over Pulau Litigan and Pulau Sipadan (Indonesia/Malaysia)* [2002] ICJ Reports 645, paras 37 and 38, where the Court refers to the contents of articles 31–32 as 'rules'; and *Case concerning Avena and other Mexican Nationals (Mexico v USA)* [2004] ICJ Reports 12, at 48, para 83, referring to its task as 'interpretation according to the customary *rules* of treaty interpretation reflected in articles 31 and 32 of the Vienna Convention on the Law of Treaties' (emphasis added). Article 33 only presents itself for inclusion in the rules when there is an issue over texts in different languages.

[107] See Chapter 7, section 4.1.2 below.

ordinary meaning of the term in the context of a Convention on the law of treaties might point one in the direction of those entries connected with law. The first of these is not apt: '4. *Law.* **a.** An order made by a judge or court, the application of which is limited to the case in connexion with which it is granted.[108] The second entry for law has some potential resonance with provisions in a treaty: '**b**...; an enunciation or doctrine forming part of the common law, or having the force of law...' Likewise, the explanation of 'rule of law' as the concept that 'the day-to-day exercise of executive power must conform to general principles as administered by the ordinary courts' associates 'rule' with a collection of principles—the singular with a plurality. However, the general definitions seem an equally appropriate starting point: '**1.1. a.** A principle, regulation, or maxim governing individual conduct...**3.a.** A principle regulating practice or procedure; a fixed and dominating custom or habit...'.[109]

Given that the particular feature under investigation of the term 'rule' in the title to article 31 is that it is in the singular, it would be appropriate to identify definitions fitting that distinctive feature. Here the dictionary does reveal some helpful history of the word. One of the early definitions of 'rule' in the *OED* is: '**2.** The code of discipline or body of regulations observed by a religious order or congregation.' Here a singular use is made in the context of a 'code' or 'body of regulations'. Similarly, in relation to definition 3.a. quoted above, the *OED* gives as examples 'rule of the road' and 'rule(s) of the sea', where in both cases the plural might nowadays be viewed as the established usage.

The Vienna rules require that account be taken of context, meaning text, preamble, and annexes (see further Chapters 3 and 6). Here, the immediate context shows 'rule' as part of a title of a set of principles or regulations, apparently forming part of a code of treaty interpretation, thus fitting in with certain of the definitions considered above. Looking more specifically for other uses in the Vienna Convention, the only other use of the term in the Vienna rules themselves is plural, in article 31(3)(c): 'relevant rules of international law'. The Vienna rules do not exclude other principles of interpretation of legal instruments. An accepted principle posits the initial position that the same word has the same meaning in the same document unless otherwise indicated. If the meaning of 'rules' in article 31(3)(c) had been defined or were a precise term of art, that might assist in the present investigation. Since, however, that plural use of the word is in the context of a reference to a complete body of law (international law) as contrasted with the singular use of the term in a title of one article of a treaty, little helpful guidance can be found there.

Elsewhere in the Vienna Convention there are several references to 'rule' and 'rules'. Those closest to the present use are the titles of articles 34 and 39 ('General rule regarding third States' and 'General rule regarding the amendment of treaties'). The first of these articles contains just one proposition (that a treaty does not create obligations or rights for a third state without its consent). The second also

---

[108] *Oxford English Dictionary* (Oxford, 2nd edn, 1989).   [109] *OED.*

only states one substantive principle (that a treaty may be amended by agreement between the parties) but, in elaboration of this, provides that 'the rules laid down in Part II' (the provisions of the Vienna Convention on conclusion and entry into force of treaties) apply to an amending agreement unless the treaty being amended provides otherwise. The title of article 39 is therefore analogous to that of article 31, in that it uses the singular 'rule' to cover a set of regulations albeit that in article 39 they are applied by reference rather than being set out in that article.

More remotely, 'rule' and 'rules' are mainly used in the Vienna Convention in two situations: to refer to a particular requirement of law or to refer to regulations or provisions set out in the Convention itself or elsewhere. So, for example, pre-ambular paragraphs of the Vienna Convention recite that the parties have reached their agreement:

> **NOTING** that the principles of free consent and of good faith and the *pacta sunt servanda* rule are universally recognized; [and]
>
> **AFFIRMING** that the rules of customary international law will continue to govern questions not regulated by the provisions of the present Convention.

Other references to 'rules' set out in the Convention occur in articles 3, 4, 27, 30, 42, 69, and 79. These all refer to propositions or requirements forming the content of treaty provisions. Instances in which the word is used in more particular senses are: article 5 (the Vienna Convention applies to treaties constituting international organizations, etc. but 'without prejudice to any relevant rules of the organization'); article 9 (adoption of a treaty text at a diplomatic conference is to be by two-thirds vote unless the negotiating states agree a different 'rule', ie a rule of procedure); and article 46 (a state may not invoke violation of internal law on competence to conclude a treaty, unless the violation was manifest and 'concerned a rule of its internal law of fundamental importance').

It may seem tedious to rehearse all the uses made of a term in a treaty; but the Vienna rules, through their definition of 'context' in article 31(2), require the interpreter to study the whole text (including the preamble, annexes, and specified related instruments) as part of the quest for the appropriate ordinary meaning of a term whose meaning is in issue. In this instance, the use of 'rule' and 'rules' in the rest of the Convention seems largely uncontroversial, but does not fully resolve the question of why 'rule' in the heading to article 31 is in the singular when the content of the article is a plurality of propositions on treaty interpretation.

In these circumstances (and in any event, as explained in Chapter 8), article 32 directs attention to the preparatory work of the Convention, which is mostly found in the records of the ILC, the Vienna Conference having changed little in the draft articles served up to it by the ILC and having debated little of the content of these provisions (with the exception of that on preparatory work). Most helpful is an explanation in the Commentary which the ILC submitted to the Vienna Conference to accompany the ILC's draft articles:

The Commission, by heading the article 'General rule of interpretation' in the singular and by underlining the connexion between paragraphs 1 and 2 and again between paragraph 3 and the two previous paragraphs, intended to indicate that the application of the means of interpretation in the article would be a single combined operation. All the various elements, as they were present in any given case, would be thrown into the crucible, and their interaction would give the legally relevant interpretation. Thus, Article 27 is entitled 'General *rule* of interpretation' in the singular, not 'General *rules*' in the plural, because the Commission desired to emphasize that the process of interpretation is a unity and that the provisions of the article form a single, closely integrated rule.[110]

From the fact of adoption by the Conference of a text retaining the title with 'rule' in the singular, and from the preceding analysis of the word in its context, one can reach the conclusion that 'rule' in the heading to article 31 has substantially the same meaning as other uses of the term in the Vienna Convention, referring to the content of provisions, or to regulations or requirements governing a situation, practice, or procedure. However, a distinct significance does attach to the use here of the singular 'rule', which may seem slightly archaic, but which is to be read as having the role of indicating how article 31 is to be applied, emphasizing the unity of its several paragraphs and its intended application as a single operation.

The practical significance of this exercise in treaty interpretation is twofold. First, as all the elements of article 31 of the Vienna Convention constitute the general rule, the interpretative exercise demands quite an extensive investigation. Second, while the Vienna rules mandate this laborious process, in practice this may result in recourse to the preparatory work which may sometimes (as here) offer the clearest explanation.

4.3 Are the Vienna rules 'rules'?

In the next chapter is a history of the rules of treaty interpretation. That history has been full of attempts to formulate sets of rules and principles of interpretation. In relation to compilations of rules of interpretation, Professor Crawford states:

care must be taken to ensure that such 'rules' do not become rigid and unwieldy instruments that might force a preliminary choice of meaning rather than acting as a flexible guide.[111]

However, the ILC confined itself to a more limited task which it described in its Commentary on the draft articles:

…the question raised by jurists is rather as to the non-obligatory character of many of these principles and maxims. They are, for the most part, principles of logic and good sense valuable only as guides to assist in appreciating the meaning which the parties may have intended to attach to the expressions that they employed in a document…Even when a

---

[110] United Nations Conference on the Law of Treaties: Official Records: Documents of the Conference, A/CONF.39/11/Add.2, p 39, para 8 and [1966] *Yearbook of the ILC*, vol II, p 219, para 8 (emphasis in original). Following the usage of the ILC here, the terms 'heading' and 'title' are treated as equivalents in the rest of this book when referring to words occupying this role in relation to provisions of treaties; on the significance of titles or headings, see Chapter 5, section 4.2.2 below.

[111] J Crawford, *Brownlie's Principles of Public International Law* (Oxford: OUP, 8th edn, 2012), 380.

possible occasion for their application may appear to exist, their application is not automatic but depends on the conviction of the interpreter that it is appropriate in the particular circumstances of the case. In other words, recourse to many of these principles is discretionary rather than obligatory...

Accordingly the Commission confined itself to trying to isolate and codify the comparatively few general principles which appear to constitute general rules for the interpretation of treaties.[112]

Greater leeway can be assumed when exploring the use of 'rules' as the label commonly attached to the Vienna Convention provisions on treaty interpretation. Use of the term 'rules' in this case is a matter of convenience, not being a Vienna Convention term of art or a precise signifier of the character of the provisions or how they are to be used.[113] Hence this use of 'rules' is no indication of the force or rigidity or the provisions on treaty interpretation. In any event, the primary dictionary definitions given above show that 'rule' does not denote something absolutely rigid in its requirements. A 'principle', or even 'a fixed and dominating custom', leaves some margin of appreciation.

This chimes in with the titles and content of articles 31 and 32. The title of article 31, 'General rule of interpretation', can be read as allied to, but contrasted with, that for article 32, 'Supplementary means of interpretation'. 'Means' suggests something less prescriptive than 'rules'. This may reflect a contrast between the mandatory language of article 31 ('A treaty *shall* be interpreted...') and the permissive form of article 32 ('Recourse *may* be had to supplementary means...'). However, it is clear from the immediate context, that the latter are 'supplementary' to the content of article 31 (and probably to that of article 33, where applicable). Hence, the provisions forming the general 'rule' in article 31 are to be read as much as 'means' of interpretation as 'rules'. Further, when the latter term is in the plural it is a general description of the three Convention articles on interpretation, and hence less of an indication of function than a handy means of reference.

Practice in the application of articles 31–33 shows that courts and tribunals habitually refer to these provisions as 'rules' while often applying them more as 'principles'.[114] This is consistent with the 'crucible' approach advocated by the ILC, which requires weighing the elements and allowing them to work together.[115] Where a rule makes it mandatory to consider a particular element, that must be done; but this does not directly indicate how this is to be. Thus, as noted above, if seeking the ordinary meaning of 'rule' in a dictionary as a starting point (which is not a prescribed approach), the Vienna Convention requires an interpreter to take into consideration the context. However, as also illustrated above, the fact that the treaty is about law does not require that the definition ascribed to 'law' usage is

---

[112] [1966] *Yearbook of the ILC*, vol II, pp 218–19, paras 4–5.
[113] The term 'canons' has often been used to describe precepts applied to the art of interpretation and in phrases such as 'canons of construction'; see further in Chapter 2 and Chapter 8, section 4.5.4 below. Its use is generally avoided in this account of the rules of interpretation to avoid unnecessarily complicating terminology where there is no clear distinction.
[114] See Chapters 5–9 below. [115] See section 1.1 and 4.2 above.

necessarily the starting point. Nor does the fact that 'rules' appears in the phrase 'relevant rules of international law' in article 31(3)(c) dictate that the general 'rule' of interpretation, and still less the use by courts and tribunals of the phrase 'rules of interpretation', import any element of rigidity or prescriptive character beyond that proper to each element of the rules.

In the course of the ILC's preparatory work for the Vienna Convention, its Special Rapporteur (Waldock) stated:

> The Commission was fully conscious…of the undesirability—if not impossibility—of confining the process of interpretation within rigid rules, and the provisions of [the draft Articles]…do not appear to constitute a code of rules incompatible with the required degree of flexibility…any 'principles' found by the Commission to be 'rules' should, so far as seems advisable, be formulated as such. In a sense all 'rules' of interpretation have the character of 'guidelines' since their application in a particular case depends so much on the appreciation of the context and the circumstances of the point to be interpreted.[116]

In the light of this explanation, and the fact that the Vienna rules are not exclusive of other compatible principles and techniques for treaty interpretation, the use of 'rules' when referring to the provisions of articles 31–33 should not be taken as defining their character. The Vienna rules are of mandatory application when interpreting treaties, but their manner of application is to be in the enlightened sense described by Waldock, treating them as regulations, principles, or guidelines as appropriate.[117]

While application of the Vienna rules is mandatory in the sense described above, there is no explicit 'show your workings' requirement of the kind some may have encountered in mathematics at school. As the Vienna rules become better known, courts and tribunals may view their familiarity as making express citation of them redundant. Some others, however, take pains to explain their approach with more detailed reference to the rules.

The important aspect is substance rather than form, in the sense that what matters is whether the interpretative process has been properly pursued. Thus in the '*Lucchetti*' case an *Ad hoc* Committee, in rejecting a claim for annulment of an arbitral award, identified as missing from the award under consideration 'some elements regarding the interpretation of [the provision in issue] which the *Ad hoc* Committee would have expected to find in an award applying international rules of treaty interpretation based on the Vienna Convention'.[118] It noted that 'treaty

---

[116] Extract from Sixth Report of Special Rapporteur (Waldock), [1966] *Yearbook of the ILC*, vol II, p 94, para 1.

[117] In adopting this approach, Waldock was again endorsing an earlier warning against viewing treaty interpretation as a mechanical operation: 'This is obviously a task which calls for investigation, weighing of evidence, judgment, foresight, and a nice appreciation of a number of factors varying from case to case. No canons of interpretation can be of absolute and universal utility in performing such a task, and it seems desirable that any idea that they can be should be dispelled.' [1964] *Yearbook of the ILC*, vol II, p 53, para 1, citing Part III of the Harvard draft codification of international law in (1935) 29 AJIL Supp 653, at 946.

[118] *Industria Nacional de Alimentos, S.A. and Indalsa Perú, S.A. v Peru*, ICSID Case No. ARB/03/4, (Decision on Annulment, 2007), para 114.

interpretation is not an exact science, and it is frequently the case that there is more than one possible interpretation of a disputed provision, sometimes even several', but that it (the *Ad hoc* Committee) was 'concerned solely with the process by which the Tribunal moved from its premise to its conclusion'.[119] The Committee also noted, apparently censoriously, that 'the Award does not give a full picture of the various elements which should be taken into account for treaty interpretation under the Vienna Convention'.[120] It strongly implied that it would have taken a different view as to possible annulment had the tribunal making the award 'disregarded any significant element of the well-known and widely recognized international rules of treaty interpretation'.[121]

5. Five Examples

The following five examples of treaty interpretations are included to give a preliminary idea of how the Vienna rules should guide treaty interpretation. Their purpose is also to show how rules which may appear to be framed in separate elements, and which for the sake of detailed analysis are separated into their components, must work together so as to avoid distortion by undue emphasis on any one principle.

The first example is a judgment of the European Court of Human Rights. This shows how a simple word may be correctly interpreted in a way which does not accord with its obvious or literal meaning. It also shows an increasingly typical approach of an international court or tribunal, setting out the history and preparatory work of the provision in issue and then applying the Vienna rules quite systematically. The second example, an ad hoc arbitration under held the auspices of the Permanent Court of Arbitration, shows an arbitral tribunal faithfully applying the Vienna rules but (in one of the arbitrator's separate opinion) providing an illustration of how it may be necessary to distinguish between determining the relevant meaning of a treaty and the application of the law to a case.

The third example, from an arbitration at the International Centre for Settlement of Investment Disputes, is a more complex sequence of interpretations, showing particularly the link between interpretation and application discussed above. The fourth example illustrates the potential effect of context and the preparatory work in interpretation. It shows this in a case from the last decade of the twentieth century, within the national legal system of the UK, where the correct interpretation of a treaty provision was eventually achieved only by Parliament legislating after the higher courts used a rather different approach from that in the Vienna rules.

---

[119] ICSID Case No. ARB/03/4, para 112.   [120] ICSID Case No. ARB/03/4, para 129.
[121] ICSID Case No. ARB/03/4, para 116; the dissenting arbitrator, Sir Franklin Berman, considered that the only possible conclusion was that 'the actual evidence of their Award does not sustain the supposition that the Tribunal did diligently and systematically apply the Vienna Convention rules at all, let alone with the particular care the situation would seem to have dictated' and concluded that the award crossed the threshold for annulment, (*Industria Nacional de Alimentos*, Dissenting Opinion, paras 12 and 18).

The practical significance of the case is the light it (inadvertently) sheds on the importance of correct use of preparatory work. The final example illustrates how awareness of the Vienna rules has become more of an established feature in cases in the UK.

5.1 Interpretation by the European Court of Human Rights— a typical approach

In *Witold Litwa v Poland*,[122] the European Court of Human Rights had to consider the meaning of 'alcoholics' in article 5(1)(e) of the European Convention on Human Rights which permits 'the lawful detention...of persons of unsound mind, alcoholics or drug addicts or vagrants'. The applicant had been taken by the police from a post office, where it was alleged he had been behaving drunkenly and offensively, to a 'sobering-up centre' where he was detained for six and a half hours until a doctor signed him off as sober. Was it permissible to apply a law to detain someone at a sobering-up centre whom the police alleged smelt of alcohol, and whom a doctor assessed as 'moderately intoxicated', or did the term 'alcoholics' in the Convention necessarily import a notion of addiction?

After stating the facts and relevant domestic law, the Court set out the preparatory work that led to the text in article 5(1)(e). Its genesis was a draft provision based on the right to 'freedom from arbitrary arrest, detention, exile and other measures, in accordance with articles 9, 10 and 11 of the United Nations Declaration on Human Rights...'. The Swedish delegate at the Consultative Assembly of the Council of Europe which was considering the draft provision for inclusion in the European Convention, had proposed adding: 'This provision should not exclude the right to take necessary measures to fight vagrancy and alcoholism or to ensure respect of [*sic*] obligations to pay a family upkeep allowance.'[123] This proposal was withdrawn on the basis that the Committee of Experts of the Council of Europe would include 'the right of signatory [sic] States to take the necessary measures for combating vagrancy and drunkenness [*l'alcoolisme* in the French text]'.[124] That thought (preserving the right of action over 'drunkenness [*l'alcoolisme*]') was retained in further development of the provision; but each subparagraph of article 5 was eventually recast into a standard form relating to the lawful detention of a person, the next English version being the ungrammatical 'for the prevention of the spreading of infectious diseases, of persons of unsound mind, alcoholic or drug addicts'. This apparently was tidied up to follow the French version, so that in the case of paragraph (e) the description became that related to a person (rather than a

---

[122] ECtHR App no 26629/95, Judgment of 4 April 2000; another copybook example of use of the Vienna rules is in award of *Arbitral Tribunal for the Agreement on German External Debt* ('*Young Loan*' case, 1980) 59 ILR 495, where the most prominent issue was over the significance of different languages: see Chapter 9, sections 4.5 and 4.9.
[123] ECtHR App no 26629/95 (Judgment of 4 April 2000), at para 34.
[124] ECtHR App no 26629/95, at para 36.

condition such as vagrancy or alcoholism). By this route 'drunkenness' had become transformed into 'alcoholics'.[125]

Explicitly applying the Vienna rules, the Court noted that the word 'alcoholics' in its common usage denoted persons who are addicted to alcohol. However, the immediate context in which the term was found in the Convention included other categories of individuals who were linked by the possibility of deprivation of liberty in order to be given medical treatment, because of considerations dictated by social policy, or on both these grounds.[126] This suggested that the predominant reason why the Convention allowed deprivation of liberty was not only that such persons were a danger to public safety, but also that their own interests might necessitate detention. The Court, therefore, saw the object and purpose of article 5 as not directed specifically to detention of persons in a clinical state of alcoholism, but as giving authority so that those 'whose conduct and behaviour under the influence of alcohol pose a threat to public order or themselves, can be taken into custody for the protection of the public or their own interests, such as their health or personal safety'.[127] The risk of public disorder or harm to the intoxicated person themselves arose whether or not they were addicted to alcohol.

In reaching this interpretation the Court did not rely on the provision of article 31(4) of the Vienna Convention which the Respondent government had argued allowed a special meaning to be given to the word 'alcoholics'. The Court relied on context, object and purpose to displace an apparently unequivocal ordinary meaning. It confirmed this view by reference to the preparatory work of the European Convention, noting that the commentary on the preliminary draft of the provision acknowledged the right of states to take measures to combat vagrancy and drunkenness ('*l'alcoolisme*' in the French version of the developing text).

Although the Vienna rules were not specifically designed to be applied sequentially, the Court in this case found it useful to follow them through from ordinary meaning to context, object and purpose, with further guidance from the preparatory work. In common with the approach in many other cases before diverse tribunals, however, the Court must have had in mind the preparatory work which had been presented to it before it formulated its judgment (and which it recounted in detail before explicitly working through the Vienna rules), even though formally in applying the rules, the Court used the preparatory work only *to confirm* the meaning it had derived from application of the general rule in article 31 of the Vienna Convention.

Thus, the judgment is perhaps one of the best examples of a central problem of treaty interpretation—the relationship between the general rule and supplementary means of interpretation. Somewhat unusual is the clarity of the preparatory work, showing that a literal reading of the provision in issue is at odds with its

---

[125] ECtHR App no 26629/95, at paras 37–39.

[126] ECtHR App no 26629/95, at para 60.

[127] ECtHR App no 26629/95, at paras 61–62. Note that the Court here looks to the object and purpose of the provision rather than the treaty. Hence its argument is more in relation to what the Vienna rules would view as context rather than object and purpose (see Chapter 6 below).

context. Although formally there is only a role for the preparatory work in this case to confirm the meaning, it clearly has a more persuasive function than even a very wide reading of the term 'confirm' in article 32 of the Vienna Convention suggests. Effectively, use of preparatory work commonly seems based on something of a sliding scale reflecting the explanation of the ILC's Special Rapporteur that, although not authentic means of interpretation, the *travaux* can provide evidence of meaning, 'and their cogency depends on the extent to which they furnish proof of the *common* understanding of the parties as to the meaning attached to the terms of the treaty.'[128]

5.2 An arbitral award illustrating the difference between treaty interpretation and application of law

The obligation of good faith in applying the Vienna rules sets limits to the interpretative exercise. Interpretation of a treaty is distinct from application of law to a case, although obviously interpretation may be a necessary and major part of the process leading to a decision. However, unless given power to do so, the interpreter is not to revise the terms of the treaty simply because a meaning properly ascribed to it produces what seems an unpalatable result. This can be illustrated by the *Rhine Chlorides* case.[129]

Among the measures to reduce chloride concentrations in the river Rhine, treaty provisions in a Convention and Protocol required France to store chlorides temporarily on land when concentrations in the river exceeded a specified amount in the flowing water. The cost of this was shared between the Netherlands, Germany, France, and Switzerland. In addition to the control on the storage requirement set by the concentrations in the river, there was an annual limit to France's obligation to store chlorides which was set at a total monetary amount fixed by reference to a fixed sum per ton stored ('ton' being used in the report as the translation of *tonne* in the original). The other states were to pay their annual share to France in advance of an auditing of accounts which, if France had not been required to store chlorides up to the limits permitted, would result in reimbursements to the contributors.

Over the period in question the river flow was less than forecast, the amount stored was well below the annual limits, and therefore substantial amounts were to be repaid to the contributors, including the Netherlands. The Netherlands sought repayment on the basis of the stated fixed amount per ton. France argued that that fixed amount stated in the treaties provided the basis for setting annual limits and

---

[128] Waldock, 'Third Report on the Law of Treaties' [1964] *Yearbook of the ILC*, vol. II, p 58, para (21), emphasis in original; see further Chapter 8, section 2.2 below.

[129] *Case Concerning the Auditing of Accounts Between the Kingdom of the Netherlands and the French Republic pursuant to the Additional Protocol of 25 September 1991 to the Convention on the Protection of the Rhine against Pollution by Chlorides of 3 December 1976 (Netherlands v France)*, Arbitral Award of 12 March 2004, 144 ILR 259 <http://www.pca-cpa.org/> (unofficial English translation; official French text reported at (2005) 25 RIAA 267); references here are to the unofficial English translation.

advance payments, but that the final accounting should be based on the actual expense of storage. This actual expense was considerably higher than the fixed amount per ton because the fixed amount had been designed primarily to set the maximum expenditure and its calculation presupposed a far greater requirement for storage than in fact proved necessary. Hence the actual unit cost of storage was greater than forecast.

Both litigants referred to the Vienna rules but France, which was not a party to the Vienna Convention, argued for a nuanced approach. The fact that the Vienna rules are applicable as a matter of customary law did not mean that the Vienna Convention could be applied 'with the same kind of minute and analytical rigour as would be the case if it were itself binding as between the Parties'.[130] France further argued that:

> ...the interpretation of these rules should not be rigidly confined within the compass of those articles, and that, furthermore, the reference to the text of the treaty that the Netherlands attempts to present as the essential basis for their interpretation does not have, under international law, the exclusive character that the Netherlands seeks to give it....Good faith, in particular, is the guiding principle that governs the interpretation and application of treaties. France emphasises that this principle requires that there be a reasonable interpretation of the Protocol and its Annexes[131]

The Tribunal did not accept that there was a distinction between application of the Vienna rules as customary law and as a matter of treaty relations, concluding that the Vienna provisions 'must be taken as a faithful reflection of the current state of customary law'.[132] It carefully examined case law of the ICJ and of other courts and tribunals, emphasizing that article 31 provided a number of elements all of which had to be taken into account, although the importance of one element in relation to the others would vary depending on the case. The Tribunal also stressed the fundamental role of good faith in treaty interpretation but noted that this did not alter the fact that the text must always be taken as the starting point.[133]

Assiduously examining the relationship between articles 31 and 32 of the Vienna Convention and the content of the latter article, the Tribunal corrected a common misunderstanding over the use of supplementary means of interpretation. It noted that article 32 does not restrict the use of supplementary means of interpretation to cases in which the result of the application of the general rule would be ambiguous, obscure, or manifestly absurd or unreasonable. Material provided by supplementary means could have a confirmatory role. This, it pointed out, was in line with judgments of the ICJ and arbitral practice. The Tribunal also examined similar supporting material for use of supplementary means in a determinative roles when

---

[130] 144 ILR 282, at para 43.   [131] 144 ILR 282, at para 43.
[132] 144 ILR 282, at 300, para 77; the Tribunal also noted that, although it did not need to consider the status of article 33 of the Vienna Convention as customary law relating to interpretation of treaties authenticated in different languages, the ICJ had observed that that provision also reflected customary international law: 144 ILR 282, para 79.
[133] 144 ILR 282, at 290–95, esp 294, paras 64–5.

application of the general rule leaves the meaning ambiguous or obscure or leads to a result which is manifestly absurd or unreasonable.[134]

In reaching its conclusion on the customary law status of the Vienna rules, the Tribunal made a useful observation on the character of the rules, noting that France had not drawn attention to any specific factors in support of its contention that customary rules might differ from Articles 31 and 32 of the Vienna Convention: 'Moreover, these articles are not as rigid in nature as France appears to claim; on the contrary, they leave the adjudicator a sufficient degree of latitude in the interpretation process.'[135]

The Tribunal dealt with many issues calling for detailed application of the Vienna rules, providing a textbook lesson in their use. Among these issues, in analysing the text the Tribunal had to consider whether use of slightly different expressions in the treaties necessarily attracted different meanings. Was a distinction to be drawn between 'the expressions "*dépenses engagées*" ["expenditures incurred"] and "*dépenses effectuées*" ["actual expenditures"]'?[136]

It would be the usual approach to expect different meanings where different words are used in a treaty; but the Tribunal used the context and the interchangeable use of terms in the treaty in German, French, and Dutch, to conclude that these references to expenditure were to the fixed amount per ton stored. In its reasoning, the Tribunal carefully considered all the elements in the general rule according to whether there was pertinent material relating to each one. It considered the preparatory work of the treaties which the arbitrators found did not lead to a different conclusion from that which they had established through the application of the general rule.

The outcome favoured the Dutch interpretation. The interpretation placed on the treaty through the use of the Vienna rules was the unanimous view of the Tribunal. Thus the application of the elements in the general rule of interpretation produced a result which could not be said to be 'manifestly absurd or unreasonable', in the terms of article 32 of the Vienna Convention. One arbitrator, however, noted that the cost assumptions at the time of negotiation of the arrangements had proved grossly incorrect in basing the unit cost per ton of chlorides stored on estimates produced in the negotiation of the treaties.[137] He suggested that this mismatch between estimated amounts for storage and actual unit costs would have constituted a 'fundamental change of circumstances' by the time of the final audit.

---

[134] 144 ILR 282, at 296, para 70, and see 296–300.

[135] 144 ILR 282, at 300, para 77.

[136] As set out in 144 ILR 306, para 92; the translator refers there to p 277, fn 2, of that report where it is explained that the English translation in the UN Treaty Series uses the same expression 'actual expenditure' for both terms, but noting further that: 'The present Award was signed in French. This translation of the Award gives the original French expressions used in the Protocol where the context so requires. As an informal aid to understanding, "*dépenses engagées*" might be taken to mean "expenditure incurred" and "*dépenses effectuées*" as "actual expenditure"'. On different meanings of same term in a single instrument, see Chapter 5, section 4.2.7 below.

[137] Declaration of Judge Guillaume, 144 ILR 259, at 342–47.

The Vienna Convention envisages terminating a treaty, withdrawing from it, or suspending its operation (as a separate measure or as a prelude to termination or withdrawal) if there has been a fundamental change of circumstances with regard to those existing at the time of the conclusion of a treaty, and which was not foreseen by the parties (subject to certain conditions and limitations).[138] This, the arbitrator noted, implies that where there is a fundamental change of circumstances, the parties have a duty to negotiate before taking such serious steps as termination etc. The parties had not given the Tribunal a power to revise the terms of the treaty. The resultant situation was, in his view, thoroughly regrettable in that it had led the Tribunal to adopt 'an unreasonable solution that should have been reviewed in the light of the new circumstances by good faith negotiations between the Parties'.[139]

What this opinion helpfully demonstrates in the present context is the distinction between application of the Vienna rules to interpret a treaty and the potentially broader application of the Vienna Convention as the law of treaties governing the relations between the parties under the treaty. The latter is application of international law to the case generally, but goes outside the role of guiding the interpretative process. Interpretation is a distinct exercise in application of rules or principles solely to give meaning to a treaty.[140]

5.3 An interpretation by an arbitral tribunal of the International Centre for Settlement of Investment Disputes (ICSID)— interpretation and application of a treaty

A more complex example shows the interaction of 'interpretation' and 'application' in the decision of an arbitral tribunal of the International Centre for Settlement of Investment Disputes ('the Centre') in *Ceskoslovenska Obchodni Banka, AS v The Slovak Republic (Jurisdiction)*.[141] This decision refers expressly to the Vienna rules only at a single point;[142] but the tribunal there affirms their general applicability to the type of agreement in issue, and their application can be detected at the many stages of the decision.

The claimant, a commercial bank (CSOB) set up under Czech law and in which the Czech Republic had the largest shareholding, alleged that the respondent state, in breach of its agreement with the claimant, had failed to cover losses incurred by a Slovak collection company (SCC) set up to deal with non-performing loans assigned to it by CSOB as part of the arrangements for the aftermath of the separation of the Czech and Slovak Republics. SCC was funded by CSOB under a loan agreement, repayment of the loan being secured under a 'consolidation agreement' by an obligation of the Ministry of Finance of the Slovak Republic.

---

[138] Article 62.   [139] 144 ILR 259, at 346–47.
[140] See further Chapter 7, section 4.3 below.
[141] ICSID Case No ARB/97/4, Decision of the Tribunal on Objections to Jurisdiction, 24 May 1999.
[142] ICSID Case No ARB/97/4, at 271–72, § 57.

The jurisdiction of the arbitral tribunal depended principally on three issues: first, whether the claimant was a 'national of another Contracting State' (ie another party to the ICSID Convention[143]); second, on the respondent Slovak Republic having given consent; and third, on there being a legal dispute arising 'directly out of an investment' within the meaning of the ICSID Convention. Three legal instruments were in issue, two of which were treaties: the ICSID Convention, a bilateral investment treaty (BIT) between the Czech and Slovak Republics,[144] and the consolidation agreement.

The first issue (whether a bank largely owned by the Czech Republic was a 'national' rather than an emanation of the state itself) involved interpreting and applying a phrase from the ICSID Convention. The tribunal's starting point was that the words of the Convention made it clear that the Centre did not have jurisdiction over disputes between states. The dispute settlement mechanism was set up to deal with disputes between an ICSID state and the nationals of another ICSID state. 'National' was not usefully defined beyond indicating that the term included both natural and juridical persons. The tribunal found, however, that the legislative history of the Convention provided some answers, including an indication that the term 'juridical persons' (and hence 'nationals') was not limited to privately owned companies but included companies wholly or partly owned by governments. This interpretation, the tribunal stated, had found general acceptance. The issue turned not on whether the company was state-owned but on whether it was acting as an agent for the government or was discharging an essentially government function—a test which was generally accepted and accepted by the parties to the present dispute.[145] Analysis of the facts showed that CSOB was not acting as an agent of the state or discharging essentially government functions. This last (and quite extensive) aspect of the exercise was the 'application' of the interpretation.

It can be seen that the tribunal's approach to this first issue looked to the language of the Convention (ordinary meaning and context), sought any definitions (special meanings), examined the Convention's legislative history (the preparatory work), and checked the accepted interpretations and tests in use (practice). Thus, the tribunal used some of the main features of the Vienna rules, looking to the language in its context and in the light of the treaty's object and purpose, taking practice into account, considering any special meaning and looking at the preparatory work.

A similar interpretative approach is seen with regard to the second issue (whether there was Slovak consent to ICSID jurisdiction). This required interpretation and application of the requirement in article 25(1) of the ICSID Convention that there

---

[143] Convention on the Settlement of Investment Disputes between States and Nationals of other States, Washington, 1965.

[144] Agreement between the Government of the Slovak Republic and the Government of the Czech Republic Regarding the Promotion and Reciprocal Protection of Investments, 23 November 1992; citations of this treaty in the decision are of its title and date of signature, without the place of the latter; whether it had entered into force, or had legal effects, was one of the issues (recounted below).

[145] ICSID Case No ARB/97/4, Decision, at paras 17 ff.

be consent in writing. Whether there was such consent in this case depended on whether it had been given in, or in connection with, the BIT between the Czech and Slovak Republics, or in the consolidation agreement between CSOB and the Slovak Republic. From the words of article 25(1) of the ICSID Convention the tribunal derived only that consent had to be in writing. It then looked at how an earlier ICSID decision had indicated agreements to arbitrate (such as the BIT) were to be interpreted:

…a convention to arbitrate is not to be construed restrictively, nor, as a matter of fact, broadly or liberally. It is to be construed in a way which leads [the tribunal] to find out and to respect the common will of the parties…Moreover…any convention, including conventions to arbitrate, should be construed in good faith, that is to say by taking into account the consequences of the commitments the parties may be considered as having reasonably and legitimately envisaged.[146]

The tribunal noted that 'written consent' in the form of an ICSID arbitration clause in a BIT had been held valid at the first such ICSID arbitration and had found acceptance in subsequent practice.[147] The problem in the present case, however, was whether the BIT had entered into force pursuant to its own requirements. These were twofold: first, each party was to give notice to the other that their respective constitutional formalities had been completed; and, second, that the BIT would enter into force on the date of the division of the state into two republics.

Considering the first requirement, the tribunal examined the language of article 25(1) (in the sense of the words used); it applied the 'principle of effectiveness', that is that a provision in a treaty should be given an interpretation such as would allow it some role rather than one which deprives it of any effect. Taking into account the rules on entry into force in the Vienna Convention (article 24), it considered that the notification requirement was not a mere formality; and it noted that the specified exchange of notifications had not taken place. The second part of the entry into force provision had been fulfilled in that Czechoslovakia had divided into two republics; but, the tribunal concluded, the proper interpretation was that the two elements were cumulative and that to regard the BIT as in force because the second element was in place would offend the principle of effectiveness in relation to the first.

Despite the failure to complete reciprocal notifications, Slovakia had published in its official journal a notice (withdrawn after the start of the dispute that led to the arbitration proceedings) proclaiming entry into force of the BIT as from the date of separation into two republics. The tribunal examined this proclamation in the light of general international law on obligations arising from unilateral statements and concluded that this did not result in the consent required by article 25(1) of the ICSID Convention. Ultimately, however, the tribunal found that there was

---

[146] ICSID Case No ARB/97/4, Decision, para 34, quoting from *Amco Asia et al v Indonesia (Decision on Jurisdiction)* (1983), (1984) 23 ILM 359.
[147] ICSID Case No ARB/97/4, Decision, paras 37–38.

written consent. A provision in the consolidation agreement between the claimant and the Slovak Republic referring to the agreement being governed by the BIT did satisfy the requirement for consent (even though the BIT was not in force) as it made the arbitration provision in the BIT part of the contract in the consolidation agreement. As with the first issue, use of elements of the Vienna rules are clearly discernible, including here (in addition to those mentioned above) use of article 31(3)(c) (relevant rules of international law applicable in the relations between the parties).

Addressing the third issue (whether there was a legal dispute arising 'directly out of an investment'), the arbitral tribunal started by noting that in the preparation of the ICSID Convention no attempt had been made to define the term 'investment'. This was because jurisdiction of the Centre was dependent on consent by the parties, and the Convention included a provision for states to declare in advance the classes of disputes which they would or would not consider submitting to the Centre (article 25(4)). The tribunal linked this (not unusual) opening reference to the preparatory work to a contextual analysis, the absence of a limiting definition being taken as an indication that a liberal approach should be taken to the term 'investment'. This in turn was supported by a reference in the preamble to the ICSID Convention noting the need of states for 'international cooperation for economic development, and the role of private international investment therein'. This preambular statement opened the way to an inference that an international transaction which contributed to cooperation designed to promote the economic development of a state party had the potential to be an investment under the Convention. 'Investment' is a term often defined in BITs, and although loans were not specifically mentioned in the present BIT's definition, the tribunal found that terms such as 'assets' and 'monetary receivables or claims', which were in the definition, were sufficiently broad to encompass loans. Further, the fact that the contractual arrangement in the consolidation agreement referred to the BIT showed that the parties to the dispute had viewed the loan as an investment (though their view did not bind the tribunal in its interpretation).

The broader picture, however, was complicated by the fact that it was not the loan to cover the costs of the Slovak collection company that had itself given rise to the dispute. The core issue was whether the tribunal had jurisdiction over the claim arising from the refusal of the Slovak Republic to cover the losses of the collection company which, the claimant argued, was the Republic's obligation under the consolidation agreement. If the loan was an investment, did the dispute arise 'directly' from it? On this the tribunal followed an earlier ICSID arbitral decision in which the immediate context of 'directly' had been seen as relating to how the dispute arose, rather than how the investment had been made. This led to the conclusion that the term 'directly' in article 25 extended to cover a dispute in connection with a transaction that formed 'an integral part of an overall operation that qualifies as an investment'.[148] The tribunal in the present case once again found

---

[148] ICSID Case No ARB/97/4, Decision, paras 71–72, quoting from *Fedax NV v Republic of Venezuela (Objections to Jurisdiction)* (1998) 37 ILM 1378, at paras 24–26.

help in a preambular statement, this one reciting that in the ICSID Convention the 'Contracting States [were]…bearing in mind the possibility that from time to time disputes may arise in connection with such investment between Contracting States and nationals of other Contracting States'. Hence, taken in isolation, even if the Slovak Republic's undertaking to cover losses was not itself an investment, it was sufficiently closely linked to a transaction that was an investment.

In this case one sees how many matters for interpretation were approached using appropriate elements of the Vienna rules. There was not, however, a systematic application of each part of the general rule, followed by assessment of whether to refer to supplementary means of interpretation (circumstances of conclusion and preparatory work). The tribunal applied such of the rules as were appropriate, including reference to accounts of the preparatory work at an early stage of its interpretation on one point. This is consistent with the practice adopted in many courts and tribunals, even if not with a narrow reading of the Vienna Convention. So widespread is this more liberal use of preparatory work that the approach can be viewed as concordant practice in interpretation of the Vienna rules (such practice being a relevant factor under article 31(3)(b) of the Vienna Convention). A further point that can be seen is that interpretation and application were not strictly separated. The tribunal applied interpretative approaches in the context of the arguments raised by the parties and of the facts. The tribunal formed interpretations that led into application of provisions as the reasoning progressed systematically through the issues.

5.4 Interpretation within a national legal system— contrasting application of Vienna rules and domestic precedent

Within a national legal system, legislation implementing a treaty is more likely to receive an interpretation in line with the correct interpretation of the treaty if the relevant provisions are clearly identifiable as treaty terms rather than legislation, and if the Vienna rules are applied. This is not always the case. In the UK, for example, legislative enactments may transform the wording of the treaty; and the courts, though recognizing that the Vienna rules are in principle applicable when interpreting a treaty, have applied them rather haphazardly. The effect of the contrasting approaches can be shown quite vividly.

In *Hiscox v Outhwaite* a key issue was where an arbitral award is 'made'.[149] The Arbitration Act 1975 gave effect to the Convention on Recognition and Enforcement of Foreign Arbitral Awards, New York, 1958. The Act did not set out or schedule the exact provisions of the Convention. However, in establishing the extent of application of the Convention by reference to the treaty's provision defining a 'Convention award', the Act used the same test as that in the

---

[149] [1992] 1 AC 562; and for a fuller account (on which this assessment is based), see R K Gardiner, 'Interpreting Treaties in the United Kingdom' in M Freedman (ed), *Legislation and the Courts* (Aldershot: Dartmouth, 1997), 115–32.

treaty: whether the award was one 'made…in the territory of a State…party [to the New York Convention]'. In *Hiscox v Outhwaite* all possible linking factors connected the arbitration with England and English law, except for one. The arbitrator took the text of the award with him to Paris and signed it there. If this action made it a French award rather than an English one, it would transform the whole legal framework under the treaty's terms, particularly affecting issues such as which state's courts had jurisdiction in relation to supervisory measures (questions of law arising out of the award, directions that further reasons be given, etc).

At first instance the judge adopted an approach based on interpretation which, in effect, applied the Vienna rules. He quoted, with approval, from an article by Dr F A Mann: 'In so far as the Conventions…are concerned, we know that article 31 of the Vienna Convention governs their interpretation.'[150] Dr Mann had shown that, on the question of where an arbitral award is 'made', the proper interpretation of the treaty, placing due weight on the context as described in the Vienna rules, led one to the arbitral seat, or (summarizing) to the place that was the central point of the arbitral proceedings. This connotes the seat of the arbitration in a legal sense.[151] It was not simply a question of where the award happened to have been signed. The judge accepted this. He pointed out that the situation would have been different, and the meaning unambiguous, had the provision in the treaty read 'signed' rather than 'made'. 'One must' he said 'look at the arbitration as a whole, and not just the place of signature…'.[152] Hence he found that the award had been made in England.

On appeal, the judge's conclusion was reversed. In the practice of English courts the question of whether there is an ambiguity in the words in the statute has been important in influencing the court's approach to looking at the treaty and its preparatory work.[153] Article 32 of the Vienna rules envisages broader circumstances than just ambiguity as justifying examining the preparatory work and allows their use for confirmation of the meaning, or establishing it in the prescribed circumstances. This may lead to a difficult question. What is the position if the preparatory work does not confirm the meaning established by the general rule but reveals a different possibility or clearly different intention?[154] However, in *Hiscox v Outhwaite.* as the judge at first instance had noted, 'made' was a different word from 'signed'. Thus, in a literal sense, there was an ambiguity.

---

[150] See [1991] 2 Lloyd's Rep 1, 7–8; for F A Mann's subsequent comment on the decision of the House of Lords see (1992) 108 LQR 6; see also F P Davidson, 'Where is an Arbitral Award Made?—*Hiscox v Outhwaite*' (1992) 41 ICLQ 637 and C Reymond, 'Where is an Arbitral Award Made?' (1992) 108 LQR 1.

[151] See further Davidson, 'Where is an Arbitral Award Made?', at 638.

[152] [1991] 2 Lloyd's Rep, at 8.

[153] In *Salomon v Commissioners of Customs & Excise* [1967] 2 QB 116 the Court of Appeal accepted that even where an Act makes no mention of a treaty, cogent extrinsic evidence to connect the treaty with the Act would permit the Court to look at the treaty to elucidate the Act, but that was before the Vienna rules and before the House of Lords endorsed consulting the preparatory work when interpreting a treaty.

[154] See Chapter 8, section 4.2.2 below.

However, to the judges in the Court of Appeal and House of Lords, 'made' was a word which, perhaps because they were conditioned by their acquaintance with English law and practice, could only be equated with 'signed'. This was not unreasonable as a starting point. Probably to most English lawyers, 'made' in connection with any legal instrument would have the clear meaning of 'executed', 'perfected', or (as in the present context) 'signed'. This would be so despite the dictionary including, as a definition of 'make', 'to draw up (a legal document)',[155] a definition somewhat supportive of the approach of the judge at first instance, since where the arbitrator 'drew up' his award was not necessarily the same place as where he signed it. What was stranger was the attention given by the higher courts to *Brooke v Mitchell*.[156] This was a decision in 1840 relating to *when*, rather than *where*, an arbitral award had been made. Nevertheless, it seems to have been more influential in the thinking of the House of Lords than were the Vienna rules (though these had been mentioned in argument).

Equally puzzling is that the higher courts did look at the preparatory work but found them little help, perhaps because of the approach they took to them and their preference for the English precedent. Yet, rather unusually for preparatory work, in this case it seems very clear what the delegates at the conference thought was the meaning or effect of the words they used. The UK's delegate had supported the initial draft put to the conference for defining the Convention's scope ('arbitral award made in the territory of a state…') as providing 'an objective and easily applicable criterion'.[157] The US delegate supported this on the basis that in the USA 'it was *the place of arbitration* which determined whether an award was a foreign award' (emphasis added).[158] The UK's delegate (who had supported what he described as a 'geographical' test) did not demur from the US delegate's interpretation of the draft rule as equating the geographical test in the words 'made in the territory of a state' to the 'place of arbitration'. Nor did other states.

That 'made' referred to the place of arbitration seems also to have been the clear understanding of the conference's Working Party No 1 to which the matter was referred. The working party found that the views of governments fell into two categories:

(a) those favouring the principle of the place of arbitration; and
(b) those favouring the principle of nationality of the arbitral award.

In reconciling these views the working party recommended wording in all material particulars the same as that ultimately in the Convention.[159] Thus it seems clear that in article 1 of the New York Convention the wording 'arbitral awards made in the territory of a State …' was retained to reflect (a) above (place of arbitration), while a second sentence ('It shall also apply to arbitral awards not considered as

---

[155] *Shorter Oxford English Dictionary* (OUP, 3rd edn, revised, 1973).
[156] (1840) 6 M & W 473.
[157] E/CONF.26/SR.5 in Gaja, *International Commercial Arbitration*, Vol III, at III.C.29–30.
[158] E/CONF.26/SR.5 in Gaja, *International Commercial Arbitration*, Vol III, at III.C.29–30.
[159] See E/CONF.26/L.42 and Gaja, *International Commercial Arbitration*, at III.B.4.2.

domestic awards in the State where their recognition and enforcement are sought') was added to the article to respond to the concerns in (b). The UK delegate was a member of the working party and did not record any dissent from the working party's report.

The conclusion of the House of Lords, simply equating 'made' with 'signed', has been reversed by legislation for subsequent interpretations.[160] Perhaps the lesson to be drawn from this case is that not only should the Vienna rules be applied where interpretation of a treaty is in issue in a municipal court, but also that the approach to application of those rules should be more closely aligned to that which an international lawyer or tribunal would take, including their approach to preparatory work. There are indications in recent domestic cases that courts in the UK have become much more familiar with the Vienna rules and how to use them.

5.5 Interpretation within a national legal system— increasing awareness of the Vienna rules in courts in the UK

Hiscox v Outhwaite remains a useful example of how an 'internationalist' approach to treaty interpretation would produce a different result from using the interpretative approach of a national system familiar with applying established rules to homogeneous legislation. The latter is no longer the approach taken in the courts in the UK to treaty interpretation. More recent cases show a willingness not just to apply the Vienna rules, but to do so in the light of their origins in international law. An example, but not an isolated one, is *R (on the application of Hoxha) v Special Adjudicator*.[161] The opinions of the judges in the House of Lords used the Vienna rules without any question as to their applicability.

The applicants were ethnic Albanians from Kosovo. They had been persecuted there by the Serb army and police before coming to the UK. They had had a well-founded fear of persecution in the terms of the definition of 'refugee' under the 1951 Geneva Convention relating to the Status of Refugees as extended by a Protocol of 1967. By the time of the legal proceedings, however, the Serb forces had left Kosovo and the applicants' claim proceeded on the basis of a past rather than present fear of persecution. The Convention provided that its protection ceased to apply where (in paraphrase) the circumstances for recognition as a refugee have ceased to exist. However, a proviso excluded from this cessation of Convention protection refugees who came within the terms of some treaties entered into before the 1951 Convention ('statutory refugees') where such refugees had compelling reasons arising out of past persecution not to avail themselves of the protection of the country of their nationality. Some parties to the 1951 Convention had extended to refugees falling within the Convention's general definition the same treatment in respect of past persecution which it only accorded to statutory refugees. In other words, some states allowed all refugees, not just statutory ones, to

---

[160] See Arbitration Act 1996, ss 53 and 100.
[161] [2005] 4 All ER 580; and see further Chapters 4, section 4.2.2 and 6, section 4.4 below.

retain the protection of refugee status, even if the grounds to fear persecution no longer persisted.

Lord Hope referred to article 31(1) of the Vienna Convention to underpin a distinction between the meaning of the words used to define entitlement to refugee status and the practices which parties had 'chosen to adopt in their discretion' to give effect to the humanitarian principles identified in the preamble to the Convention.[162] He traced the history of the definition of the qualifications for refugee status and identified the reason for the proviso excluding statutory refugees from withdrawal of the now redundant protection. This proviso had been included in recognition of the fact that refugees from Germany and Austria would be unwilling to return to the scene of the atrocities which they and their families had undergone, and could not be expected to do so even if they would be safe there. The drafting history showed that although there had been expression of regret that the proviso was limited to statutory refugees, it had been deliberately retained in the Convention:

There is, then, no getting away from the plain words of the proviso. The only conclusion that can properly be drawn from its terms, having regard to their context and the drafting history, is that the contracting parties were not willing at the time the convention was entered into to extend the benefit of the proviso to non-statutory refugees.[163]

That the preamble to the 1967 Protocol recorded the motivation behind it as a desire to bring later categories of refugees within the scope of the Convention and to give all refugees equal status did not alter the terms of the definition, particularly as the substantive provisions of the Protocol did not alter the provision in issue.[164]

Lord Brown similarly made explicit reference to the Vienna Convention in his opinion. He too traced the history of the provision and he considered studies of commentators on the Convention, as well as case law. Particularly noteworthy are his use of the Handbook by the UN High Commissioner for Refugees as an aid to interpretation of the definition of 'Refugee', and his consideration of the role of the practice of parties to the Refugee Convention as a significant interpretative element under article 31(3)(b) of the Vienna Convention.[165]

Lord Brown saw the Handbook as a statement of guidance and recommendation on procedures and criteria for determining refugee status. He concluded from the Handbook that procedures relating to cessation of refugee protection were separate and distinct processes from those for determination of refugee status. He found continuing support for this view in revised versions of the Handbook and other publications.[166] As regards practice, Lord Brown set out extracts from article 31 of the Vienna Convention, including paragraph 3(b) on subsequent practice. He noted that commentators had observed that to indicate a meaning of a treaty provision, subsequent practice must be the concordant practice of the parties, that is without

---

[162] [2005] 4 All ER, at 585, paras 8–9.   [163] [2005] 4 All ER, at 587, para 16.
[164] [2005] 4 All ER, at 588, para 20.
[165] On the role of material such as the Handbook, see further Chapter 8, section 4.5.3 below.
[166] [2005] 4 All ER 580, at 599–601, paras 57–64.

there being evidence of a clear difference of opinion between them, though the precise degree of universality of the practice was not firmly identifiable.[167] He concluded that in the present case, where evidence from a study by the UN High Commissioner for Refugees showed 15 out of 20 states in a survey gave the more generous standard of treatment, there was not a sufficient extent of concordant practice to interpret the amended Convention as requiring the protection of the proviso to be given to all refugees.[168]

Viewed in the round, this case shows judges in the UK using the Vienna rules very much as envisaged by the ILC when drawing them up. The ordinary and clear meaning was given to the words in issue, in their context and in the light of the object and purpose of the treaty. Subsequent practice was evaluated. The circumstances of conclusion of the Convention and Protocol, together with their drafting history, were also taken into account, not applying the requirements of article 32 of the Vienna Convention in any too literal sense. The possibility of evolutionary interpretation was also considered.

There are two further important features. First, the national court used international materials (reports, resolutions, studies, etc), very much as would an international tribunal and approached the task of treaty interpretation very much in the same way as an international tribunal. Second, the role of the Vienna rules is well illustrated. They provide a loose framework from which elements relevant to the particular case need to be selected, while respecting the scheme; and the application of these elements requires evaluation and balancing in the particular circumstances, such evaluation and balancing being the element of judgement which no rules could capture.

---

[167] [2005] 4 All ER 580, at 603–604, paras 72–74; see also Chapter 6, section 4.1.3 below.
[168] [2005] 4 All ER 580, at 606, para 82.

2

Development of Rules of Interpretation

The Greco-Roman era—Grotius, others, and canons of interpretation—Harvard Draft Convention—PCIJ—restrictive interpretation and effectiveness—Institut de Droit International—practice of ICJ before the Vienna Convention—New Haven School—ILC and Vienna Conference

Other jurists, although they express reservations as to the obligatory character of certain of the so-called canons of interpretation, show less hesitation in recognizing the existence of some general rules for the interpretation of treaties.[1]

1. Introduction

In drawing up the draft articles which became the Vienna Convention's rules on treaty interpretation, the International Law Commission (ILC) 'confined itself to trying to isolate and codify the comparatively few general principles which appear to constitute *general* rules for the interpretation of treaties'[2] The Convention's rules do not exclude other principles compatible with these general rules, leaving open to the interpreter's discretion recourse to the wealth of material on treaty interpretation which preceded the Convention. As well as shedding light on why the Vienna rules are as they are, this material can prove a useful quarry from which to extract principles, arguments, and examples to buttress or supplement particular applications of the rules. This chapter gives an overview of that material and the accompanying literature.

Anyone who has limited time but wants to delve into the history of the Vienna rules in greater detail than is given in the analysis of them in Chapters 5–9 should start by gaining some acquaintance with the records of the two ILC sessions (1964 and 1966) at which the main work on the draft articles on treaty interpretation was undertaken.[3] It is likely, in any event, that in using modern case law,

---

[1] Commentary on draft articles [1966] *Yearbook of the ILC*, vol II, p 218, para 1.

[2] [1966] *Yearbook of the ILC*, vol II, pp 218–19, para 5 (emphasis added).

[3] The records of the work of the ILC on the law of treaties can be located through the guide at <http://legal.un.org/diplomaticconferences/lawoftreaties-1969/lawoftreaties-1969.html>; and see section 10 and Chapter 3, section 4.1.3 below for further discussion of this material, as well as the historical accounts in Chapters 5–9 below.

those interpreting treaties will come across instances where judgments or arbitral awards refer to the work of the ILC for guidance on application of the rules. Not intended as a complete history of treaty interpretation, the Reports of the Special Rapporteur (Waldock) and the ILC debates contain the clearest and most directly relevant background to the Vienna rules, a good deal of the underlying principles, and the key case references, as well as the main arguments which determined the content of the rules. Now that the complete record of the work of the ILC on treaties is available electronically, access is easy.[4] The Vienna Conference adopted the ILC's draft rules on treaty interpretation with no substantive change apart from one addition to the provision on treaties authenticated in different languages. Thus the records of the conference provide little additional background, except for a substantial debate on whether the rules should remain divided between a general rule and subsidiary means of interpretation, and an explanation of the addition to the article on languages.[5]

The ILC's reports refer mostly to material from the decades immediately before the Vienna Convention was concluded. However, the history of treaty interpretation goes much further back than that. The classical era (Greco-Roman) has some telling pre-echoes of current issues in treaty interpretation. Already in those times there was developed practice in making treaties and in their interpretation. The competing arguments for adhering to a strictly textual approach and those for following the intent or spirit of the treaty were already being advanced. It was with Grotius, Pufendorf, and Vattel in the seventeenth and eighteenth centuries that efforts were made to identify detailed rules for treaty interpretation and shape them into codes. Lacking institutions for independent international adjudication, these codes relied as much on transposition of rules and practice from national legal systems as on any developed rules of international law, though a classical tradition held in common by these writers was plainly influential.

Increasing resort to arbitration from the late nineteenth century onwards, and encouragement of this by the Hague conferences at the start of the twentieth, resulted in a growing repository of decisions interpreting treaties. These necessarily considered how to undertake interpretation, as did the case law of the Permanent Court of International Justice. While the League of Nations made little progress in codification of the law of treaties, this was one of the subjects of the programme of research into international law under the auspices of the Harvard Law School in the late 1920s and early 1930s.[6] The Harvard Draft Convention on the Law of Treaties included not only proposed provisions on interpretation but also detailed

---

[4] See <http://legal.un.org/diplomaticconferences/lawoftreaties-1969/lawoftreaties-1969.html>.

[5] See section 10 below and Chapter 9, section 2 *ad fin.*

[6] For an account of codification in this era and generally, see R P Dhokalia, *The Codification of International Law* (Manchester: Manchester University Press, 1970); the Harvard research into international law was published in the supplementary issues of the *American Journal of International Law*. The Law of Treaties is in Part III of the Harvard draft codification of international law in (1935) 29 AJIL Supp 653.

commentaries expounding and analysing the history, literature, and case law on the subject.

The main lines of development which followed this were the challenge to the 'restrictive' approach to treaty interpretation made by Hersch Lauterpacht and the advancement of a much broader scheme based on a policy-oriented approach to law put forward by Myres McDougal and his associates (collectively given the soubriquet the 'New Haven School').[7] The restrictive approach had seen treaty interpretation coloured by extreme deference to the sovereignty of states, the presumption being in favour of assuming that a state intends to be bound by the least of any obligation which could be read from a provision of doubtful content or ambiguous expression.[8] Lauterpacht saw the restrictive approach as inconsistent with the principle of effectiveness which emphasizes the integrity of a treaty and the need to give effective content to all its terms.[9] His work was a major precursor to an influential resolution of the Institut de Droit International in 1956, a resolution which, although it did not follow the substance of the approach favoured by Lauterpacht, provided something of a model for a short statement of interpretative rules. Meanwhile the ICJ was developing its techniques of treaty interpretation, building on cases of the Permanent Court of International Justice (PCIJ), and from which six principles were extracted by Fitzmaurice shortly before he became one of the Court's judges. In the USA, the 'McDougal' or 'New Haven' approach went much further than this and, in a monumental work, both analysing practice and breaking new ground in extending its policy-oriented jurisprudence, suggested principles of content and procedure for treaty interpretation. The major features of this approach (oversimplifying it) were that it favoured admitting anything which the interpreter found helpful in identifying the shared expectations of the parties, and it set the whole process of interpretation in the framework of world public order.[10] It was this approach which set in motion the unsuccessful US initiative to change the ILC draft at the Vienna Conference by running together what are now articles 31 and 32 of the Vienna Convention.

---

[7] On the New Haven School generally, see I Scobbie, 'A View of Delft: Some Thoughts about Thinking about International Law', in chapter 3 of M Evans (ed), *International Law* (Oxford: OUP, 4th edn, 2014), and see section 9 below.

[8] Vattel placed the origins of this principle in the more general idea of the intent behind a law; see *The Law of Nations* (1758 edition, translated by C G Fenwick), (Washington: Carnegie Institution, 1916), Book II, ch XVII § 292 '*Restrictive interpretation,* which is the contrary of *extensive interpretation,* is founded on the same principle. Just as a provision is extended to cases which, although not included within the meaning of the terms, are included within the intention of the provision and are embraced by the motive which gave rise to it; so also a law or a promise may be restricted by following out the motive of the law or promise, contrary to the literal meaning of the terms.' (emphasis in original)

[9] See H Lauterpacht, 'Restrictive Interpretation and the Principle of Effectiveness in the Interpretation of Treaties' (1949) XXVI BYBIL 48.

[10] M S McDougal, H D Lasswell, and J C Miller, *The Interpretation of Agreements and World Public Order: Principles of Content and Procedure* (New Haven: Yale University Press, 1967 re-issued as *The Interpretation of International Agreements . . .* with a new introduction and appendices, 1994); for brevity, 'McDougal' or the 'New Haven School' is used in later references to these three authors collectively in relation to the cited work.

Thus, when the Special Rapporteurs of the ILC came to the law of treaties, there was underway a developing debate about treaty interpretation along with a considerable history of publications (of which those mentioned above are only major landmarks), and quite a wealth of practical judicial pronouncements. More detailed references to the work of the ILC on particular aspects of the Vienna rules are included in Chapters 5–9. What follows here is an outline of those elements of the history of treaty interpretation that bear on modern treaty interpretation and an introduction to the work of the ILC and the Vienna Conference.

2. Treaty Interpretation in the Greco-Roman Era

A study of treaty interpretation in the classical era reports that nearly 400 treaties made by the Greek city states before 338 BC are extant which, with the treaties of the Romans and others of that time, demonstrate a considerable body of practice.[11] The same study reveals that certain features of treaty interpretation of that era were similar to those of today and were transmitted to modern times through the work of Grotius and others at the effective foundation of modern international law.[12] The same dichotomy was already marked out between emphasis on strict adherence to text and words on the one hand, and intent and spirit on the other.[13] The classical era also revealed the importance of *who* interprets treaties as something significantly affecting the approach taken, in particular drawing a contrast between practitioners and jurists.[14]

The introductory comment to the Harvard Draft Convention on the Law of Treaties notes that there were pre-classical treaties, citing one of the earliest as that of 1272 BC between Ramses II, King of Egypt, and Khetesar, King of the Hittites.[15] However, the significance of taking the Greco-Roman era as a starting point for considering treaty interpretation is that this is when clear links between formation of treaties and the requirement of good faith in their implementation led on to the elaboration of some principles of treaty interpretation.[16] There also emerged the tension between the textual approach of jurists and the search for the intention which characterized the arguments of orators.[17] Similar links and tensions were among the concerns addressed in the development of the Vienna rules.

---

[11] D J Bederman, *Classical Canons: Rhetoric, Classicism and Treaty Interpretation* (Aldershot: Ashgate, 2001), at 46 ff.

[12] Bederman (*Classical Canons*), provides not only a complete guide to treaty making and interpretation in classical antiquity (his chapter III), but also shows how the transmission of the classical tradition of legal interpretation influenced early modern writers and ultimately the modern rules of treaty interpretation.

[13] Bederman, especially chapters II and V.

[14] Bederman, chapter IV.

[15] (1935) 29 AJIL Supp 12, at 666, and see account of the Harvard Draft below.

[16] See Bederman, *Classical Canons*, chapter II.

[17] See Bederman, at 98–99.

3. Grotius, Pufendorf, Vattel, and Canons of Interpretation

Grotius, publishing his work on the law of war and peace in 1625, saw the interpretation of treaties as sufficiently important to warrant a complete chapter.[18] Although the ILC referred to Grotius in its work on some of the other draft provisions for the law of treaties, it did not explicitly refer to his chapter on interpretation of treaties. His work was, however, acknowledged by writers to whom the ILC did refer.[19] He saw the proper role of interpretation as being to gather the intention of the parties from the best indications available, that is to say the words they had used and legitimate conjectures from those words.[20] His detailed canons of interpretation were largely derived from analysis of Greco-Roman texts, but supplemented by a natural law approach which, with its classification of 'favourable' promises and treaties of an 'odious' kind, could not appropriately be taken over as a direct basis for a code in the twentieth century. Further attempts at elaboration of sets of rules followed those of Grotius and his first glossator Pufendorf, one of the most significant effects of these works being to lead the ILC to reject the idea of an elaborate code of canons.[21]

The work of Vattel received direct attention from the ILC, but on interpretation only briefly for his first general maxim that 'it is not permissible to interpret what has no need of interpretation'.[22] The underlying idea of this proposition is in line with that of McNair.[23] Vattel's maxim has been picked out of its context and has attracted criticism, though some of this may be the result of his further rather unwieldy and extensive set of maxims.[24] Nor is the criticism entirely fair when the maxim is taken away from the context in which sited it as part of a set of maxims specifically aimed at preventing fraud and duplicity in interpretation. His chapter on interpretation does, in fact, open with the acknowledgement that, even if words in a treaty are capable of being 'clear, precise and susceptible only of one sense', there would still be need for interpretation because it is impossible to foresee every case that may arise.[25] Further, the maxim is only one of

---

[18] H Grotius, *De Jure Belli ac Pacis* (F W Kelsey trans) (New York: Oceana, reprint 1964), Bk II, ch 16; for a study of the work of Grotius and his followers on this topic, see Bederman, *Classical Canons*, chapter VII.

[19] See, for example, A D McNair, *The Law of Treaties* (Oxford: OUP, 2nd edn, 1961), at 364, referring to Grotius at the start of his chapter on interpretation.

[20] Grotius, *De Jure Belli ac Pacis,* sections I, IV, XVI, and XX.

[21] See ILC commentary on draft articles 27 and 28, [1964] *Yearbook of the ILC*, vol II, p 218, para 1.

[22] Vattel, *The Law of Nations*, at § 263; the maxim was introduced into ILC discussion in its Latin form (*In claris non fit interpretatio*) by J M Ruda, [1964] *Yearbook of the ILC*, vol. I, p 277, para 33.

[23] See McNair, *The Law of Treaties*, at 365, note 1: 'Interpretation is a secondary process which only comes into play when it is impossible to make sense of the plain terms of the treaty'; and see Chapter 1, section 3.6 above for criticism of this description of interpretation.

[24] Criticisms range from the mild observation of McNair that he found the maxim 'somewhat irritating' (*The Law of Treaties*, at 372) to McDougal's finding of 'fatal flaws' in it, the most crucial defect being that it is 'profoundly misleading' (McDougal, at 80–81).

[25] Vattel, *The Law of Nations,* opening of chapter XVII.

60 paragraphs, some containing more than one interpretative proposition, and *all* to be taken into consideration to the extent appropriate in any given case.[26] Bederman characterizes Vattel's first maxim as a 'ringing call for textualism' which 'is then countermanded by a bewildering pastiche of maxims, without any structure or schematic of analysis'.[27] Bederman saw Vattel's work as having 'exercised inordinate influence on the subsequent consideration of treaty interpretation problems by international law publicists'.[28] However, the general effect of Vattel's work, and that of subsequent compilers of canons of construction, was to turn the ILC away from any attempt at drawing up its own list of canons of interpretation, an effect which may be thought beneficial.[29]

Modern tribunals are unlikely to consider the canons of treaty interpretation as complete collections, tending just to use the odd one as a buttress for a particular interpretation. However, an arbitral award at the International Centre for Settlement of Investment Disputes does offer some reflections on the contrast between the Vienna rules and canons of interpretation:

> ... the Vienna Convention represents a move away from the canons of interpretation previously common in treaty interpretation and which erroneously persist in various international decisions today. For example, the Vienna Convention does not mention the canon that treaties are to be construed narrowly, a canon that presumes States can not have intended to restrict their range of action. Rather than cataloging such canons (which at best may be said to reflect a *general pattern*), the Vienna Convention directs the interpreter to focus upon the *specific case* which may, or may not, be representative of such general pattern. To say a canon reflects a widespread practice does not mean it reflects a universal one.[30]

4. The Harvard Draft Convention on the Law of Treaties

A landmark in the progression towards codification of international law was the publication of the fruits of research at Harvard in the form of draft conventions and associated materials in 1929 and the following years. In 1935 this collection included a draft convention on the law of treaties with detailed commentaries on each provision.[31] The fourteen pages of bibliography preceding the commentary

---

[26] Vattel, *The Law of Nations,* at § 322.

[27] Bederman, *Classical Canons,* 140, footnote omitted.

[28] Bederman, 140.

[29] The Chairman of the ILC (Ago), speaking as a member, saw Vattel's first maxim as implicit in the proposed articles, although he preferred not to lay much stress on a rule which he saw as a trap: [1964] *Yearbook of the ILC,* vol I, p 280, para 79. Vattel was also invoked by Mr Amado as providing support for certain elements in the draft Vienna provisions; [1966] *Yearbook of the ILC,* vol I, p 191, para 75.

[30] *Aguas del Tunari v Bolivia* (ICSID ARB/02/03), Decision on Respondent's Objections to Jurisdiction, 21 October 2005, para 91 (original emphasis, footnotes omitted). As to 'restrictive interpretation' see section 6 below.

[31] (1935) 29 AJIL Supp 653; for a modern appraisal, see A Aust, 'Law of Treaties', chapter 11 in J P Grant and J C Barker (eds), *The Harvard Research in International Law: Contemporary Analysis and Appraisal* (New York: W S Hein, 2007).

show that even in 1935 the available literature on the law of treaties was immense.[32] The present value of this work is twofold. First, it provides an important and informative background to the Vienna rules, in the sense of a scholarly repository of learning and legal literature. Second, and of more immediate practical relevance to treaty interpretation, the commentaries are full of examples from judgments of the PCIJ, from international arbitral awards, and from some national practice.[33] Although there is now a growing body of practice in the interpretation and application of the Vienna rules themselves, examples are not always to be found for all the issues that they cover. Used with care to ensure that the material is apt under the Vienna rules, the examples in the commentaries on the Harvard draft articles enrich the database of treaty interpretations.

The Harvard draft convention had been preceded by work on the law of treaties in the League of Nations and by the Pan American Union. The League of Nations had a Committee of Experts on Codification of International Law, but its efforts on the law of treaties were directed mainly towards codifying procedures for drafting and concluding treaties, rather than their implementation and application. That venture was not conspicuously successful, the task being transferred in 1925 to the League's secretariat, which had not produced a report by the time of the Harvard draft. Slightly more productive was the Pan American Union, whose work resulted in the Convention on Treaties, Havana, 1928.[34] This did not attract many parties. Its provision on interpretation was limited in scope, stating in article 3 (which followed one requiring that treaties be in writing): 'The authentic interpretation of treaties, when considered necessary by the contracting parties, shall likewise be in writing.'

The Harvard draft provision was more ambitious. It placed emphasis in treaty interpretation on achieving the 'purpose' of the treaty, to which its more precise references to separate elements were specifically directed. Similarly, where the treaty was in more than one language, a common meaning was to be sought which achieved the purpose of the treaty. The text is worth brief consideration because it provides a comparison and contrast between a formulation based on an extreme teleological or purposive approach and that adopted in the Vienna rules:

Article 19
Interpretation of Treaties

(a) A treaty is to be interpreted in the light of the general purpose which it is intended to serve. The historical background of the treaty, travaux préparatoires, the circumstances of the parties at the time the treaty was entered into, the change in these circumstances

---

[32] (1935) 29 AJIL Supp 653, at 671–85.

[33] The commentaries bearing on treaty interpretation are those on article 19 of the draft, 937–77.

[34] Appendix 1 to the Harvard draft. On 1 April 1935, the convention was in force for Brazil, Dominican Republic, Haiti, Nicaragua, and Panama: see (1935) 29 AJIL Supp 670 and appendix. The team which prepared the Harvard draft convention saw the absence of an explanation of the term 'treaties' as a fatal flaw in the 1928 convention, and added the comment: 'Nor can it be said that the principles embodied in the convention constitute any significant contribution to the clarification of the law of treaties' (at 670).

sought to be effected, the subsequent conduct of the parties in applying the provisions of the treaty, and the conditions prevailing at the time interpretation is being made, are to be considered in connection with the general purpose which the treaty is intended to serve.

(b) When the text of a treaty is embodied in versions in different languages, and when it is not stipulated that the version in one of the languages shall prevail, the treaty is to be interpreted with a view to giving to corresponding provisions in the different versions a common meaning which will effect the general purpose which the treaty is intended to serve.[35]

A significant similarity with the Vienna rules is that this draft article did not seek to codify or supplement the 'canons of interpretation'.[36] Quite the contrary, although listing twelve from the many publicists who have drawn up sets of canons, rules, or maxims from Grotius (1625)[37] to Ehrlich (1928),[38] and noting the use made of these by arbitral tribunals and the PCIJ, despite all this volume of doctrine, the commentary to the Harvard draft saw the modern trend as being to reduce rather than expand the number of rules.[39] Although the reliance placed in the Harvard draft on a teleological imperative was not adopted by the ILC, the ILC did choose the same course of avoiding a long list of canons.

As regards the use to be made of the more detailed components in paragraph 19(a) of the Harvard draft (historical background, *travaux préparatoires*, subsequent conduct, etc), the commentary noted that:

… the function of interpretation is to discover and effectuate the purpose which a treaty is intended to serve, and that this is to be accomplished, not automatically by the mechanical and unvarying application of stereotyped formulae or 'canons' to any and every text, but instead by giving considered attention to a number of factors which may reasonably be regarded as likely to yield reliable evidence of what that purpose is and how it may best be effectuated under prevailing circumstances.

The weight to be attributed to each of the factors enumerated in paragraph (a) will naturally vary with the individual case; hence no importance is to be attached to the order in which they are named. All that can be said is that all of them are or may be significant in arriving at a sound interpretation in a particular case, and that none of them should be overlooked by the person charged with interpreting a treaty. Each of them may contribute in some measure to giving an accurate and complete 'picture' of the treaty in its setting, and it is only when so viewed that its general purpose can be fully comprehended and intelligently effectuated. Only then can one undertake to say what the treaty 'means'.[40]

This approach is virtually identical with that intended by the ILC for the manner in which the Vienna rules are to be used (the 'crucible' approach[41]), albeit that the aim of the ILC's rules is not so narrowly directed to finding the purpose of the treaty, that the elements are somewhat different in content and expression, and

---

[35] (1935) 29 AJIL Supp 661.   [36] (1935) 29 AJIL Supp 661, at 937.

[37] Grotius, *De Jure Belli ac Pacis*, Bk II, ch 16.

[38] L Ehrlich, 'L'Interprétation des Traités' (1928) 24 *Recueil des Cours* 5.

[39] (1935) 29 AJIL Supp 661, at 939–44.   [40] (1935) 29 AJIL Supp 661, at 938.

[41] See Chapter 1, section 1.1.

that in the Vienna rules some appreciation of the 'weight' to be attributed to the constituent elements of the rules is suggested by their separation into the general rule and supplementary means of interpretation.

5. The Permanent Court of International Justice

The predecessor to the ICJ built up a substantial body of case law and frequently pronounced on points of treaty interpretation. While reference is still made to propositions enunciated by the PCIJ, recognition that the Vienna rules have come to reflect customary international law has reduced the frequency of their invocation. In his study of the jurisprudence of the PCIJ, Judge Hudson identified many features of its approach to interpretation which foreshadowed issues relating to the Vienna rules and their elements.[42] Starting with the distinction between interpretation and application, and then the function of interpretation, Hudson put at the head of his list of elements of interpretation the concept of 'authentic interpretation'. The focus of this was that the PCIJ had accepted that it must follow an interpretation of a treaty on which all parties to it are agreed.[43] This can be seen to be reflected in several components of the Vienna Convention's general rule of treaty interpretation, including the parties' agreements, interpretative instruments of various kinds, and subsequent practice.

Hudson noted that the judgments and opinions of the PCIJ contained numerous references to the intentions of the parties as a guide for interpretation. While, however, he saw it as of first importance that 'the definitely entertained and expressed intentions of the parties should be effectuated', he warned against using the intention of the parties as cover for interpretation by methods other than real ascertainment of such intentions.[44] He fully recognized the problems of identifying the intention, particularly where it was necessary to apply provisions to facts which were covered by the wording used but had not been foreseen. His caution over reliance on finding intention as the key solution to problems of treaty interpretation was followed by a sequence of considerations which were to be largely mirrored in the Vienna Convention: natural meaning as reflecting ordinary usage; the context as extending beyond a particular part of the instrument to the whole instrument; versions in different languages, and interrelated and interdependent instruments; and the nature and purpose of an instrument, favouring an interpretation that takes account of its object or purpose—all these elements not coming within any rigid sequence but the natural meaning preceding consideration of the purpose.[45]

---

[42] M O Hudson, *The Permanent Court of International Justice 1920–1942* (New York: Macmillan, 1943), 640–61; on the work of the PCIJ more generally, see O Spiermann, *International Legal Argument in the Permanent Court of International Justice: The Rise of the International Judiciary* (Cambridge: CUP, 2005).
[43] Hudson, *The Permanent Court of International Justice 1920–1942*, at 643 and 649–50.
[44] Hudson, at 643–44.   [45] Hudson, at 645–52.

Hudson also extracted from the jurisprudence of the PCIJ several propositions which parallel what became the supplementary means of interpretation in the Vienna rules. He noted that the Court had frequently used preparatory work to confirm interpretations over which it had no doubt, but that when it did decide to resort to the preparatory work, the PCIJ had not been very definite about the extent of its reliance.[46] While this, together with his acceptance of a role for the 'legal' and 'political and social background', also finds resonance in the Vienna rules (explicitly mentioning preparatory work and circumstances of conclusion), those rules suggest a somewhat firmer scheme for use of these supplementary means of interpretation.[47]

It should not, of course, be surprising that much of what is in the Vienna rules can be seen in Judge Hudson's analysis, sourced as it was to the case law of the PCIJ. However, it must also be acknowledged that the Vienna rules are couched in such general terms, and the case law interpreting them being still relatively limited, that a study of the jurisprudence of the PCIJ can reveal issues which practice under the Vienna Convention has not yet addressed.

6. Restrictive Interpretation and Effectiveness

This heading is a truncation of the title of an article by Hersch Lauterpacht closely following part of his report to the Institut de Droit International (see below).[48] The article is revealing both for its general observations on the task of interpretation and for the assistance it gives to understanding the principles of restrictive interpretation and of effectiveness, both of which have played a role in treaty interpretation but are not explicitly included in the Vienna rules. The notion of effectiveness is twofold: first, a general sense of realizing the objectives of the treaty and, second, a narrower function of preferring an interpretation which gives meaning to every term rather than depriving one or more words of any role at all. The latter function is commonly denoted in Latin *ut res magis valeat quam pereat* but sometimes in the French *effet utile*, though is also sometimes applied to the more general concept of effectiveness. These ideas are now both subsumed in the requirement of good faith with which the Vienna rules open.[49]

Lauterpacht had doubts about the value of rules for treaty interpretation. Nevertheless, he devoted considerable attention to the subject. His work was followed by a resolution of the Institut, albeit that the approach was significantly reworked on different lines by Fitzmaurice, his successor as Rapporteur. Lauterpacht acknowledged that international courts and tribunals, in particular the PCIJ and ICJ, had constantly applied rules of interpretation; but he

---

[46] Hudson, at 653–54.   [47] See Chapter 8 below.

[48] 'Restrictive Interpretation and the Principle of Effectiveness in the Interpretation of Treaties' (1949) XXVI BYBIL 48.

[49] See Chapter 5, section 2.4.5 below.

assessed the trend in the literature of international law as being to deprecate such rules and to stress their essential unhelpfulness.[50] He noted, however, that some authors had succumbed to the temptation to elaborate codes of rules. Lauterpacht himself concluded that re-examination of the main principles of interpretation was justifiable, though he felt that even these main principles were 'no more than the elaboration of the fundamental theme that contracts must be interpreted in good faith'.[51] He drew support for this from the single article on this in the German Civil Code (and other civil codes), an economy of drafting which fed through into the Vienna rules, in contrast with the lengthy codes of Vattel and others.[52]

In working towards identification of the main principles of treaty interpretation, Lauterpacht saw it as necessary to assess the two apparently opposing principles mentioned above which still need to be understood in the present day. 'Restrictive interpretation' is a substitute for the latin tag *in dubio mitius,* the principle that if an obligation is not clearly expressed its less onerous extent is to be preferred. Applied to treaty relations of states, this principle pays deference to each state's sovereignty by directing selection of the lesser obligation where the terms of a treaty are open to doubt. Lauterpacht saw this principle as of little value and noted that the PCIJ and ICJ had refrained from using it, with one exception of doubtful significance because it had been stated with no reference to a particular treaty.[53] He saw it as incompatible with the principle of effective interpretation and only applicable if all other principles, including that of effectiveness, had failed to produce a result.[54]

In contrast to the idea of restrictive interpretation, which he saw as no more than a form of words, Lauterpacht saw the principle of effectiveness as being applied to treaty interpretation both in national and international jurisprudence. In the USA the Supreme Court had repeatedly spoken of 'liberal interpretation', while in the UK the idea of liberal interpretation 'seems to have been used in a somewhat wider sense as connoting generous rather than pedantic interpretation, in accordance with principles of good faith'.[55] Lauterpacht saw the consistent practice of the PCIJ and the ICJ as placing great emphasis on the principle of effectiveness, particularly in the case of treaties conferring jurisdiction on it, those establishing the competence of international tribunals, and treaties protecting minorities (the precursors of human rights treaties).[56] In contrast to the development of the principle of effectiveness, space for restrictive interpretation has diminished. In *Navigational and Related Rights (Costa Rica v Nicaragua)* (2009) the ICJ expressly

---

[50] Lauterpacht, 'Restrictive Interpretation ...', at 48–52.
[51] Lauterpacht, at 56.
[52] Lauterpacht, at 56.
[53] Lauterpacht, at 62.
[54] Lauterpacht, at 67.
[55] Lauterpacht, at 67–68, and see Lord Wilberforce in *James Buchanan & Co Ltd v Babco Forwarding & Shipping (UK) Ltd* [1978] AC 141, at 152, stating that a treaty should be interpreted 'unconstrained by technical rules of English law, or by English legal precedent, but on broad principles of general acceptation'.
[56] Lauterpacht, 'Restrictive Interpretation', at 68; for later development of this principle, see Chapter 5, section 2.4.5 below.

applied the Vienna rules but prefaced that exercise with a rejection of any general principle of restrictive interpretation at least in territorial disputes:

While it is certainly true that limitations of the sovereignty of a State over its territory are not to be presumed, this does not mean that treaty provisions establishing such limitations, such as those that are in issue in the present case, should for this reason be interpreted *a priori* in a restrictive way.[57]

7. Institut de Droit International

The Institut was established in 1873 as a body of jurists eminent in international law. Among its aims is promoting codification of international law, to which end its members prepare reports and adopt resolutions. These have proved influential in the codification and development of international law generally. Its work on the law of treaties included two studies by Hersch Lauterpacht, who later served as the ILC's second Special Rapporteur on the law of treaties.[58] The culmination of this work was a resolution setting out principles for use in treaty interpretation:

L'Institut de Droit international

Estime que lorsqu'il y a lieu d'interpréter un traité, les Etats, les organisations et les juridictions internationales pourraient s'inspirer des principes suivants:

Article premier

1. L'accord des parties s'étant réalisé sur le texte du traité, il y a lieu de prendre le sens naturel et ordinaire des termes de ce texte comme base d'interprétation. Les termes des dispositions du traité doivent être interprétés dans le contexte entier, selon la bonne foi et a la lumière des principes du droit international.
2. Toutefois, s'il est établi que les termes employés doivent se comprendre dans un autre sens, le sens naturel et ordinaire de ces termes est écarté.

Article 2

1. Dans le cas d'un différend porté devant une juridiction internationale il incombera au tribunal, en tenant compte des dispositions de l'article premier, d'apprécier si, et dans quelle mesure, il y a lieu d'utiliser d'autres moyens d'interprétation.
2. Parmi ces moyens légitimes d'interpréter se trouvent:
    (a) Le recours aux travaux préparatoires;

---

[57] *Dispute regarding Navigational and Related Rights (Costa Rica v Nicaragua)* [2009] ICJ Reports 214, at 237, para 48; for further extracts and analysis, see Chapter 8, section 4.5.4 below.

[58] (1950) 43 *Annuaire de l'Institut de Droit International,* vol I, p 366, and (1952) 44 *Annuaire,* vol I, p 197. Most of the substance of these reports were included in Lauterpacht, 'Restrictive Interpretation and the Principle of Effectiveness in the Interpretation of Treaties'. Two sections of the reports (on the doctrine of plain meaning and preparatory work) which were not included in that article appear in English in E Lauterpacht (ed), *International Law, the Collected Papers of Hersch Lauterpacht* (Cambridge: CUP, 1978), vol 4, chapters 19 and 22 (a work which also conveniently includes other writings of Hersch Lauterpacht on treaty interpretation). Hersch Lauterpacht's work on this topic for the Institut was seen through to its completion in 1956 by Sir Gerald Fitzmaurice, with a significant change of direction.

(b) La pratique suivie dans l'application effective du traité;

(c) La prise en considération des buts du traité.[59]

The ILC's Special Rapporteur (Waldock) identified this resolution as one of the two main sources from which he had drawn inspiration in framing his draft articles.[60] It is easy to see the debt to this resolution owed by the Vienna rules in scale and style, as well as much of their content.

8. The Practice of the International Court of Justice Before the Vienna Convention

The practice of the ICJ on treaty interpretation had a considerable influence on the drawing up of the Vienna rules. This was mainly indirect in that it took effect through the analysis of the ICJ's case law made by Fitzmaurice before he became a judge of the Court.[61] Acknowledging the prime importance of this work, in conjunction with the resolution of the Institut, the ILC's Special Rapporteur (Waldock) introduced his commentary on his first set of draft articles on interpretation by stating the principles which Fitzmaurice had deduced from the ICJ's practice and had refined in his second study:

I. *Principle of actuality (or textuality).* Treaties are to be interpreted primarily as they stand, and on the basis of their actual texts.

II. *Principle of the natural and ordinary meaning.* Subject to principle VI below, where applicable, particular words and phrases are to be given their normal, natural, and unstrained

---

[59] Resolution of 19 April 1956 which is translated in [1964] *Yearbook of the ILC,* vol II, p 55, para 11: 'When a treaty is to be interpreted, States and international organizations and tribunals might be guided by the following principles:

Article 1

1. The agreement of the parties having been reached on the text of the treaty, the natural and ordinary meaning of the terms of that text should be taken as the basis of interpretation. The terms of the provisions of the treaty should be interpreted in the context as a whole, in accordance with good faith and in the light of the principles of international law.
2. However, if it is established that the terms employed should be understood in another sense, the natural and ordinary meaning of those terms is set aside.

Article 2

1. In the case of a dispute brought before an international tribunal, it will be for the tribunal, taking into account the provisions of article 1 to determine whether and to what extent other means of interpretation should be employed.
2. The following are among the legitimate means of interpretation:
   (a) consultation of the *travaux préparatoires*;
   (b) the practice followed in the actual application of the treaty;
   (c) the consideration of the objects of the treaty.'

[60] [1964] *Yearbook of the ILC,* vol II, p 55, para 10; the other source of inspiration was the set of principles identified by Fitzmaurice considered in the next section.

[61] G G Fitzmaurice, 'The Law and Procedure of the International Court of Justice 1951–4: Treaty Interpretation and Certain Other Points' (1951) 28 BYBIL 1 and G G Fitzmaurice, 'The Law and

meaning in the context in which they occur. This meaning can only be displaced by direct evidence that the terms used are to be understood in another sense than the natural and ordinary one, or if such an interpretation would lead to an unreasonable or absurd result. Only if the language employed is fundamentally obscure or ambiguous may recourse be had to extraneous means of interpretation, such as consideration of the surrounding circumstances, or *travaux préparatoires*.

III. *Principle of integration.* Treaties are to be interpreted as a whole, and particular parts, chapters or sections also as a whole.

Subject to the foregoing principles

IV. *Principle of effectiveness* (ut res magis valeat quam pereat). Treaties are to be interpreted with reference to their declared or apparent objects and purposes; and particular provisions are to be interpreted so as to give them their fullest weight and effect consistent with the normal sense of the words and with other parts of the text, and in such a way that a reason and a meaning can be attributed to every part of the text.

V. *Principle of subsequent practice.* In interpreting a text, recourse to the subsequent conduct and practice of the parties in relation to the treaty is permissible, and may be desirable, as affording the best and most reliable evidence, derived from how the treaty has been interpreted in practice, as to what its correct interpretation is.

Footnote to this principle. Where the practice has brought about a change or development in the meaning of the treaty through a *revision* of its terms, by conduct, it is permissible to give effect to this change or development as an agreed revision but not as an interpretation of its original terms.

VI. *Principle of contemporaneity.* The terms of a treaty must be interpreted according to the meaning which they possessed, or which would have been attributed to them, and in the light of current linguistic usage, at the time when the treaty was originally concluded.[62]

The extent to which these principles were reflected in the eventual Vienna rules is largely self-evident.[63] Only the last one was effectively lost from expression in the rules. However, the principle of effectiveness was somewhat abridged in its reflection in the rules. Nevertheless, it must be reiterated that the Vienna rules do not exclude other compatible interpretative principles and techniques. Thus, although the ILC found temporal factors too complex to include in a codification of general principles, the principle of contemporaneity continues to be one to be taken into account in appropriate circumstances. Likewise, the principle of effectiveness continues to play a significant role, not only by application of those aspects which find clear reflection in the Vienna rules, but also in the well-established principle that an interpretation is to be preferred which accords a meaning to every element of a treaty's text.[64]

Procedure of the International Court of Justice 1951–4: Treaty Interpretation and Other Points' (1957) 33 BYBIL 203.

[62] [1964] *Yearbook of the ILC*, vol II, p 55, para 12.

[63] Waldock explains the specific links between each of Fitzmaurice's principles and the first draft articles in his Third Report [1964] *Yearbook of the ILC*, vol II, pp 56–57, paras 13–15.

[64] On the principles of contemporaneity and effectiveness, see C Warbrick, Introduction to *The Iron Rhine ("IJzeren Rijn") Railway (Belgium–Netherlands) Award of 2005* (ed B Macmahon) (The Hague: TMC Asser Press, 2007), at 15–23 and on effectiveness, see Chapter 5, section 2.1 below.

9. The New Haven School and World Public Order

The only substantial work which was somewhat at odds with the approach taken by the ILC was a book by Professor McDougal in 1967 (with collaborators): *The Interpretation of Agreements and World Public Order*.[65] This was too late to affect the work of the ILC on treaty interpretation but it did influence the attitude of the USA at the Vienna Conference and was thus the foundation of the only major debate on treaty interpretation at the Vienna Conference. This work arose from the policy-oriented approach to jurisprudence which characterized the work of the New Haven School which McDougal led. An initial hurdle to the study of this approach to treaty interpretation is its dependence on a specific conception of a treaty:

The most comprehensive and realistic conception of an international agreement ... is ... not that of a mere collocation of words or signs on a parchment, but rather that of a continuing process of communication and collaboration between the parties in the shaping and sharing of demanded values.[66]

The core idea in this concept, that a treaty is a 'continuing process of communication', suffers from the difficulty that this generalization does not fit all, or even most, international agreements. True, pious statements about the continuing collaboration of the parties in implementation of the treaty are a common feature of some treaties, particularly those that are expected to need development or further elaboration in their lifetime, but there are many treaties not of that kind or which include no such expectation. A treaty embodying a one-off transaction or one which is to be applied routinely in a technical field are just two examples of those which may well not involve any further 'communication' between the parties once brought into force, and which involve collaboration only in the sense of each party faithfully applying the treaty in parallel with the other.

It can also be seen that a false dichotomy is set up in the extract above. The choice offered between 'a mere collocation of words or signs on a parchment' and the 'continuing process of communication' suggests that the options are an extreme literal approach or a completely open-ended relationship.[67] A treaty identifies

---

[65] McDougal et al., cited in section 1 above. A shorter guide to the application of the approach is given in the reissue of the work. There were many critical appreciations of the New Haven approach. These included: R A Falk, 'On Treaty Interpretation and the New Haven Approach: Achievements and Prospects' (1967–1968) 8 *Va J Int'l L* 323 and G G Fitzmaurice, '*Vae Victis* or Woe to the Negotiators! Your Treaty or Our "Interpretation" or it?' (1971) 65 AJIL 359; and, taking a more philosophical approach, G Gottlieb, 'The Conceptual World of the Yale School of International Law' (1968) 21 *World Politics* 108 and D N Weisstub, 'Conceptual Foundations of the Interpretation of Agreements' (1970) 22 *World Politics* 255.

[66] McDougal et al. (1967 edn), at xxiii.

[67] McDougal et al. (1967 edn), at xxiv: 'The important point is that the shared expectations of commitment, commonly called "agreement," in whatever degree achieved and maintained, are a function not of some single variable, such as a text or historic utterance, but of the entire process of interaction that has shaped and affected the expectations of the parties.'

commitments and establishes obligations, obligations which may or may not specifically envisage further communication between the parties or which, by virtue of the requirements of international law which governs treaties, may or may not lead to a necessity to enter into such communication. The Vienna Convention itself contains many requirements that necessarily involve communication between parties to treaties.[68] Specific treaty provisions commonly require that states negotiate before taking a dispute over the interpretation or application of a treaty to arbitration or other judicial settlement. Yet these requirements do not show that all treaties, or even most treaties, are inherently 'continuing processes of communication and collaboration between the parties in the shaping and sharing of demanded values'. The central issue of treaty interpretation is how to decide what an agreement requires. If communication between the parties helps to demonstrate what an agreement requires, this may form part of the process of interpretation; but a continuing process of communication is not part of the definition of a treaty.

Similar considerations affect the last part of the conception of an international agreement quoted above. The idea that there is a continuing process of 'shaping and sharing of demanded values' may fit some agreements. If treaties reflect values of a 'community' of states, whether on a universal or regional scale, that may well be subsumed in the object and purposes of each of the treaties. An obvious example is the substantial collection that has built up of human rights treaties. These embody rights of a kind whose interpretation may well need to take account of community values. That is part of the understanding of human rights and the way the treaties are framed. In contrast, a treaty may simply contain a deal done between two states. If the New Haven School is referring to values accepted by the parties as relevant, then they are explicitly or implicitly agreed rather than demanded. If derived from international sources independent of the participants, the values which may be imported into interpretation of the set of agreed obligations are those incorporated by international law as it applies in the relations between the parties, not demanded by nebulous community values. The Vienna Convention includes shared values in the process of treaty interpretation but in the more controlled and concrete form of rules of international law applicable in relations between the parties.

The approach of the New Haven School divided its guidance on treaty interpretation into 'principles of content' and 'principles of procedure'. The content of both of these categories was identified, analysed, and criticized. Then, on the basis of past practice and writings, recommended principles were elaborated. Principles of content included 'the contextuality principle', 'principles relating to the process of agreement', and 'principles relating to the decision process', the latter two sets of principles being further divided into several categories such as 'participants' or 'officials', 'objectives', 'base values', 'strategies', and 'outcomes'.

---

[68] See, for example, article 23(4) (withdrawal of a reservation to be formulated in writing), article 25(2) (notification of intention not to become a party), article 40(2) (notification of proposal to amend a treaty), etc.

It is impossible to do justice to such elaborate conceptions by attempting a summary. For example, in the category of 'strategies' in the principles of content, four
recommended principles are offered: (1) 'The Principle of Including All Strategic
Acts': this suggests adopting an interpretation which gives meaning to every element of the text of the agreement.[69] This is a principle underlying the Vienna
rules;[70] (2) 'The Principle of the Preferred Mode of Expression': this is essentially a
reiteration of the principle of contextuality, that is the idea of taking context into
account in the very broad sense of anything that could be construed as relevant.[71]
The Vienna rules rather more helpfully identify the primary elements to be taken
into account as part of the general rule and allow a rather broader sweep of supplementary means to be used in a controlled manner; (3) 'The Principle of Logical
Relationships': this really proposes no more than that decision-makers should take
account of 'the relevance or importance of examining syntax in the search for genu-
ine shared expectations of agreement', something which is axiomatic in the Vienna
rules;[72] (4) 'The Principle of Adapting the Level of Generality or Particularity to
the Other Features of the Context': this requires that assessment be made of the
weight to be given to general and particular propositions in treaties and how to
relate them to each other, a requirement which is inherent in the Vienna rules.

The New Haven approach tries to separate the substantive principles from procedural ones. In the chapter 'Trends in the Management of Principles of Procedure',
the New Haven approach puts the contextuality principle to work in marshalling
the various elements of interpretation to ensure that orderly and appropriate application is made of the principles of interpretation.[73] There is much to commend
Professor McDougal's call for a more overt revelation by a treaty interpreter of the
approach or principle being adopted at each stage of interpretation. While, however, courts and tribunals do disclose their reasons for selecting an interpretation,
with increasing reference to the Vienna rules, they cannot be expected to provide
a running commentary on how the rules are being applied.

If the above brief glimpse of some of the recommended principles gives a
taste of the New Haven approach, its real flavour can only be gained by working
through what has been described as an 'arresting and original' book but a 'very

---

[69] McDougal et al. (1967 edn), at 195–97; the example given there is the PCIJ case *Legal Status of
Eastern Greenland* PCIJ, Series A/B, no 53 (1933), which is of questionable value as guidance on treaty
interpretation. Among the questions under consideration in that case were whether a unilateral declaration could give rise to obligations (it could, but that does not necessarily mean such a declaration
always fully equates to a treaty), and whether there had been displays of sovereignty, such as by raising
a flag (which could certainly be relevant to sovereignty, but as a matter of identifying a substantive
right under international law rather than of interpretation of a treaty).

[70] See Fitzmaurice's principle III, 'the principle of integration', and Waldock's recognition of this
principle as underlying the first draft of the articles on interpretation, being reflected in the references
to good faith and context: Third Report on the Law of Treaties [1964] *Yearbook of the ILC*, vol II,
p 56, paras 13–14.

[71] [1964] *Yearbook of the ILC*, vol II, at 197–99.

[72] [1964] *Yearbook of the ILC*, vol II, at 199–200; the principle is considered more extensively in
the New Haven approach as part of the principles of procedure, [1964] *Yearbook of the ILC*, vol II,
at 330–43.

[73] [1964] *Yearbook of the ILC*, vol II, at 273–302.

difficult work to assimilate and, partly for that reason, to be fair to'.[74] It is difficult to extract practical interpretative guidance from the principles enumerated by the New Haven School or the broad prescription to take account of community values.

Where the Vienna rules do differ from the New Haven approach is that they give a firmer indication of the bounds on the scope of an interpretative inquiry and differentiate (though not in a watertight fashion) between the primary and supplementary means of interpretation. The New Haven principles were developed from theory and extrapolation from past practice. They set out in more detailed form 'principles of procedure' which the Vienna rules leave largely to emerge from the structure of the Vienna Convention's provisions (the loose division between general rules and supplementary means) and from indications worked into the substantive rules ('in the light of' the object and purpose, 'there shall be taken into account …' etc). The approach of the Vienna rules leaves with the interpreter the responsibility for assessing which elements to apply in any particular instance and, subject to specific indications (such as when to use preparatory work to 'confirm' and when to 'determine' the meaning), how the elements are to be weighed in relation to one another. The result, however, of applying the Vienna rules as they have been interpreted and applied in practice is, it is suggested, nowhere nearly as restrictive as Professor McDougal's criticisms expected them to be. At all events, it could reasonably be suggested that what is now clear is that the shared expectation of the parties to a treaty must be that it will be interpreted according to the Vienna rules.

10. The Work of the International Law Commission and the Vienna Conference

Chapter 1 of this book began with an extract from the records of the ILC and references to its work are prominent in the chapters that follow which analyse the Vienna rules separately. The status of the ILC records as preparatory work of the Vienna Convention is considered in the next chapter.[75] What follows here is a brief account of the working methods of the ILC and of its work on the law of treaties. This is to assist in understanding the many references to the work of the ILC and in finding and using its records if more detailed research into it is needed.

The ILC is a body of legal experts selected to reflect the range of legal systems throughout the world. It was established by the General Assembly of the United Nations in 1947 with a Statute providing that the 'Commission shall have for its object the promotion of the *progressive development* of international law and its *codification*.[76]

---

[74] Fitzmaurice, *'Vae Victis* or Woe to the Negotiators! Your Treaty or Our "Interpretation" of it?' (1971) 65 AJIL 359.

[75] See Chapter 3, section 4.1.3.

[76] Article 1(1) of the ILC Statute (emphasis added); Article 15 of the Statute describes 'progressive development' as meaning 'the preparation of draft conventions on subjects which have not yet been

Codification and progressive development are not necessarily entirely separate exercises. When a subject is being codified, gaps in the existing customary international law may be filled by complementing proposals in line with any discernible trends in that customary law or as otherwise thought desirable. A set of draft articles produced by the ILC may therefore contain a mixture of codification and progressive development. Thus it is not to be seen as surprising or unusual that the Vienna rules were not recognized as a statement of customary law immediately upon the Vienna Convention's signature or entry into force.

The Commission's usual procedure is to appoint an individual member as Special Rapporteur to work up each topic which it studies. A change in Special Rapporteur may take place during the course of study of a particular topic, hence the need to name the particular one concerned if their work is being cited. The ILC had four successive Special Rapporteurs for its work on the law of treaties: Brierly, Lauterpacht, Fitzmaurice, and Waldock. Only Waldock took up the subject of interpretation in the work of the Commission, although his two immediate predecessors had made detailed studies of the topic elsewhere.

The Special Rapporteur prepares reports for discussion at the Commission's annual session. The reports may include draft articles for inclusion in a convention or code and often provide the basis of the commentary which typically accompanies such draft articles when the Commission completes its work on a topic. In appropriate cases, governments and international organizations may be asked to provide information, such as texts of relevant laws, decrees, judicial decisions, treaties, and diplomatic correspondence. The Commission goes through a quasi-legislative process, with successive readings of draft articles and debates leading to approval of texts and commentaries. Each year the Commission submits a report to the General Assembly, setting out any draft provisions. These are also submitted to governments for their written observations. The Special Rapporteur studies the reactions, including any comments made in the debates of the Sixth Committee of the General Assembly and the views of governments. Eventually the Commission submits its final conclusions for the Assembly's consideration, which may lead to the Assembly deciding to take action itself to negotiate a treaty through to adoption or call a diplomatic conference to do this; or it could take a different approach such as endorsing a set of articles as a code or guide for states in their international legal relations.[77]

Fitzmaurice, the third Special Rapporteur on the law of treaties, produced his reports on the basis that the appropriate vehicle for a statement of the law of

---

regulated by international law or in regard to which the law has not yet been sufficiently developed in the practice of States'; it describes 'codification' as 'the more precise formulation and systematization of rules of international law in fields where there already has been extensive State practice, precedent and doctrine'.

[77] On codification and progressive development of international law, see A E Boyle and C Chinkin, *The Making of International Law* (Oxford: OUP, 2007), Chapter 4, and R P Dhokalia, *The Codification of International Law* (Manchester: Manchester University Press, 1970), 147–332; on the ILC, see I Sinclair, *The International Law Commission* (Cambridge: Grotius, 1987), and A Watts, *The International Law Commission, 1949–1998* (New York: OUP, 1999).

treaties was a code rather than a treaty.[78] His scheme envisaged considering validity of treaties, then their effects. Interpretation, which he viewed as closely allied to application, would fall within the latter part of the Commission's work.[79] He saw it as inappropriate that a code on the law of treaties should itself take the form of a treaty.[80] This objection probably reflected the thought that any rules should be ones which were already, or would become, customary international law. In the event, the rules on treaty interpretation have taken a while to become recognized as customary rules and thus be acknowledged as being of general application. But this does not seem to have followed from their being in a treaty. States which are not parties to the Vienna Convention have relied on its rules of treaty interpretation.[81]

The second ground given by Fitzmaurice for preferring a code does, however, have relevance to treaty interpretation. He saw much of the law of treaties as ill adaptable to inclusion in a treaty as it would at best include 'a certain amount of declaratory and explanatory material'.[82] Such material should be excluded from a treaty as treaties should state only rights and obligations, whereas in the code which he envisaged, inclusion of subsidiary matter would have the considerable advantage of making clear, 'on the face of the code itself', the legal concepts or reasoning on which its contents were based.[83] Fitzmaurice's doubts may have been one of the reasons why the Vienna rules were ultimately so laconic. Fitzmaurice also saw the multiplicity of forms of treaties as presenting one of the many difficulties of a code of general application to treaties, noting that:

The reader who, for instance, has mainly general multilateral conventions in mind, should remember that there are also such things as bilateral agreements and exchanges of notes, *and, moreover, that the latter outnumber the former by a very large margin.*[84]

In the event, the rules on treaty interpretation came to be embraced in treaty form, without distinction between application to multilateral and bilateral treaties. However, Fitzmaurice's doubts may have proved well-founded in some measure in that the interpreter has to look to the preparatory work and other interpretative means for explanation or clarification of concepts in the rules and how they were expected to work. The difference between the approach of the ILC and that of the New Haven School discussed above might, in part at least, arise from different appreciations as to the function of treaties, as shown by Fitzmaurice. Viewed through the distorting lens of generality, multilateral treaties dealing with group concerns may often be more amenable to consideration

---

[78] See Report of G G Fitzmaurice, [1956] *Yearbook of the ILC*, vol II, 106–7, para 9.

[79] [1956] *Yearbook of the ILC*, vol II, at 105, para 1.

[80] [1956] *Yearbook of the ILC*, vol II, at 107, para 9.

[81] For examples, see Chapter 1, sections 2.2 and 2.3 above.

[82] Report of G G Fitzmaurice, [1956] *Yearbook of the ILC*, vol II, 106–7.

[83] [1956] *Yearbook of the ILC*, vol II, 106–7.

[84] [1956] *Yearbook of the ILC*, vol II, at 107, para 10, emphasis in the original.

within a regime of 'community expectations', while bilateral agreements (especially those in exchanges of notes) tend to cover particular issues or activities of concern to only the two parties, or best managed by agreements tailored to their dual concerns.

As Special Rapporteur, Fitzmaurice never reached treaty interpretation in the five reports which he submitted to the ILC. Although he reached effects of treaties in his Fourth Report, he had by then decided that interpretation was sufficiently separate from application to warrant treatment of its own in a separate part of that chapter after the effects of treaties for third states (which was to be the subject of his Fifth Report).[85] Nevertheless, his approach to the topic was well-evidenced by his study of ICJ cases, which provided an analytical basis which was used by the next Special Rapporteur, Sir Humphrey Waldock.[86]

The first draft of the ILC's articles on treaty interpretation was in Waldock's 'Third Report on the Law of Treaties' (1964).[87] Debate on those drafts took place at the ILC's sessions in July 1964 and the drafts were reported to the General Assembly of the UN.[88] Waldock's Sixth Report (1966) notes the comments of governments on the draft articles and sets out his observations and proposals in response.[89] The Commission debated the further drafts in June 1966 and again in July on the report from the drafting committee.[90] The drafts were then adopted with little further debate.[91] Commentaries on the draft articles were agreed and the result was reported to the General Assembly.[92]

Details of the work of the ILC on particular elements of the Vienna rules are given in Chapter 5–9 below. As a preliminary to the history of those elements there are certain points from the general debate which indicate what the ILC was trying to achieve. The diffidence felt by the Special Rapporteur (Waldock) over including articles on interpretation comes through in his introduction to the articles which he had drafted in his Third Report, as well as in the Report itself. The emphasis on the attempt being to produce a 'few possible fundamental provisions', reflected the whole approach as one which tried to lay down only an infrastructure for treaty interpretation, not to elaborate codes or sets of canons as had been attempted in

---

[85] See [1959] *Yearbook of the ILC*, vol II, p 40, para 3.

[86] G G Fitzmaurice, 'The Law and Procedure of the International Court of Justice 1951–4: Treaty Interpretation and Other Points' (1957) 33 BYBIL 203, and see section 8 above.

[87] Doc A/CN.4/167 and Add.1–3 [1964] *Yearbook of the ILC*, vol II, p 4; the drafts on interpretation, as articles 70–75, were set out with commentary at 52–65. For detailed guides to the preparatory work of the Vienna rules, see S Rosenne, *The Law of Treaties: a Guide to the Legislative History of the Vienna Convention* (Leyden: A W Sijthoff, 1970) and D Rauschning and R Wetzel, *The Vienna Convention on the Law of Treaties: Travaux Préparatoires* (Frankfurt am Main: Metzner, 1978); see also J Klabbers, 'On Rationalism in Politics: Interpretation of Treaties and the World Trade Organization' (2005) 74 *Nordic JIL* 405, at 418–21.

[88] [1964] *Yearbook of the ILC*, vol I, pp 275–91, 296–99, 308–19, and 340–41.

[89] Doc A/CN.4/186 and Add.1–7 [1966] *Yearbook of the ILC*, vol II, p 51; for the comments, observations and proposals on the drafts on interpretation, as articles 69–73, see pp 91–103.

[90] [1966] *Yearbook of the ILC*, vol I, part II, pp 183–211 and 267–71.

[91] [1966] *Yearbook of the ILC*, vol I, part II, at pp 328–29.

[92] [1966] *Yearbook of the ILC*, vol I, part II, at pp 341 and 346–47; the final drafts, as articles, were set out in the ILC's Report as articles 27–29, [1966] *Yearbook of the ILC*, vol II, p 169, at 217–26.

the past.[93] Waldock was also realistic about the difficulties of taking account of state practice, a really huge body of the most important evidence which is very difficult to unearth, and which is as problematic to expose today as it was then:

> He [the Special Rapporteur] had tried to take into account State practice, though evidence of it was difficult to obtain as not much was to be found in publications of State practice which for the most part were content to reproduce the decisions of international tribunals and were not concerned with the interpretation of treaties by States themselves.[94]

Waldock's modest approach seems to have won over those of the ILC who might previously have opposed or been sceptical about inclusion of any provisions on interpretation. They now saw that the task was not going to be one of immense scale but rather working out a very basic scheme. If relief at this was the main cause of acceptance of the idea of inclusion of provisions of this kind in principle, it seems also to have led to a rather diffuse initial debate. Since there was to be no general attack on the principle of inclusion of provisions on interpretation, there was little to do but to keep powder dry for the more detailed debates on the content of the provisions.

It seems sensible to follow the same approach here, leaving detail for later. However, one point in the initial debate is worth a mention because of its subsequent omission. One member of the Commission pointed out that the group of articles under consideration indicated *how* treaties should be interpreted but did not specify *who* was to interpret them.[95] He considered that this should be taken up in the further work of the Commission on this topic either in draft provisions or in the commentary. While other members of the Commission raised a loosely related problem, that of interpretation in international organizations, the matter was not taken up in the further work of the Commission.[96] It can be seen that it would hardly have been appropriate to try to establish rules on who should interpret treaties, particularly given the approach adopted of framing general provisions on treaty interpretation; and it would in any event have proved difficult, if not impossible, to come up with useful provisions. However, there are some factors which are particular to different interpreters of treaties, and a brief indication of some of these considerations is therefore given in Chapter 4 below.

As regards the work of the Vienna Conference, what little this produced is taken up when the history and analysis of particular provisions on treaty interpretation are considered below. The conference adopted the ILC's proposals with only minor changes of drafting and one of substance. There was, however, a considerable debate in the Committee of the Whole.[97] This was on proposals to amend the scheme of the rules by amalgamating the separate general rule and supplementary

---

[93] [1964] *Yearbook of the ILC*, vol I, p 275, para 2.

[94] [1964] *Yearbook of the ILC*, vol I, p 275, para 2.

[95] Tsuruoka [1964] *Yearbook of the ILC*, vol I, p 280, para 72.

[96] The UN Secretariat did produce for the ILC a report on preparation of multilingual treaties in international organizations but this did not lead to detailed attention by the Commission to issues concerning interpretation of treaties in international organizations: see Chapter 9, section 2 below.

[97] UN Conference on the Law of Treaties, Summary Records of First Session (26 March–24 May 1968), pp 166–85; and for the texts proposed by the drafting committee and discussion of these,

means, intended by the USA to go some way towards the New Haven approach; but the proposals gained little support.[98] The substantive change was the inclusion of a reference to the object and purpose of a treaty as an element to be used in reconciling divergences between texts of a treaty in different languages which could not be otherwise reconciled.[99]

see pp 441–43. For the adoption of the rules in plenary, see UN Conference on the Law of Treaties, Summary Records of Second Session (9 April–22 May 1969), pp 57–59.

[98] The proposal was rejected by 66 votes to 8, with 10 abstentions; see Reports of Committee of the Whole, United Nations Conference on the Law of Treaties: Official Records: Documents of the Conference, A/CONF.39/14, p 150; for the summary record of disposition of the US proposal and other proposals considered in the same debate, see further Chapter 8, section 2.1 below.

[99] See Chapter 9, section 2 *ad fin,* below.

3

Interpretative Material Generated in Making Treaties

Treaty-making and documentation—varieties of instruments drawn up at conclusion of treaties—reservations and interpretative declarations—admissible preparatory work

International law itself prescribes neither form nor procedure for the making of international engagements....[1]

1. Introduction

This chapter describes elements of the treaty-making process that are of potential relevance to treaty interpretation. As 'preparatory work' and the 'circumstances of conclusion' of a treaty are the specific (but not exclusive) content of the supplementary means of interpretation set out in article 32 of the Vienna Convention, some knowledge of treaty-making is necessary to know where to look and what one may be looking for in seeking to use these elements. The scope of the concept 'preparatory work' is ill-defined, despite its regular invocation. Its identification in the interpretative process therefore needs attention.

It is also necessary to know the rudiments of treaty-making in applying the general rule in article 31. For included in the applicable context are 'any agreement relating to the treaty which was made between all the parties in connection with the conclusion of the treaty' and 'any instrument which was made by one or more parties in connection with the conclusion of the treaty and accepted by the other parties as an instrument related to the treaty' (article 31(2)). The treaty interpreter also needs to be able to differentiate between an interpretative statement and a reservation made on signature or ratification, accession, etc. The one concerns interpretation through the application of the Vienna rules, the other adjusts treaty relations and is tantamount to a permitted modification of the terms of the agreement to the extent identified in the reservation.

The next section of this chapter gives a brief outline of the steps in making a treaty. Subsequent sections pick up the major components of that process and their

---

[1] A D McNair, *The Law of Treaties* (Oxford: OUP, 1961), 6.

products, and point out links between those steps and relevant elements of the Vienna rules. This chapter is concerned with *identification* of the materials; their *use* in treaty interpretation is explained and analysed in the chapters that follow, principally in Chapters 6 and 8.

2. Making Treaties

2.1 Who initiates and negotiates treaties?

There is no single type of spark that provides the initial impulse for the negotiation of a treaty. It may be the policy of a single state, some development or irritant in relations between two states, a regional concern, the fulfilment of part of a programme of work of an international organization, the response to some significant event or catastrophe, or, doubtless, many other causes.[2] While it is clear that one cannot say of that initial impulse, whatever it may have been, that this is invariably the starting point for invocable preparatory work to be generated, investigation of why someone thought of having a treaty may assist in identifying the object and purpose of the eventual treaty if these are not clear from the text. Consideration of why a treaty was drawn up may also form part of the circumstances of conclusion of a treaty, these being a set of factors which the Vienna rules expressly admit as supplementary means of interpretation.

2.2 Negotiating and drawing up a treaty

The principal division in the next stage of treaty-making is between bilateral and multilateral negotiations. In both cases, some form of study group or working party may be set up, but in the case of bilateral negotiations, the more common procedure is for one side to produce a draft, once diplomatic contacts have established that there is the necessary willingness to negotiate. In the bilateral process, delivery of a draft may lead to a counter-draft and thence to agreement to negotiate on the basis of one or other version, or to agreement to attempt an amalgamation of the drafts topic by topic.

In the case of multilateral negotiations, probably the most common situation nowadays is for an international organization either to provide the expertise leading to a first draft or to act as the amanuensis for a group of representatives of

---

[2] International organizations have long been involved in the preparation of treaties. Their role in providing specialist input, negotiating facilities, secretarial functions, acting as depositary, publishing records of diplomatic conferences, etc has proved increasingly valuable. These roles are different from those of being a negotiating body, in which capacity international organizations can also act whenever, as entities governed by international law, they have capacity to enter into treaties. The Vienna Convention 1969 does not apply to treaties in which international organizations participate as parent rather than midwife. However, the Vienna Convention on the Law of Treaties between States and International Organizations or between International Organizations, Vienna, 1986 (not yet in force), sets out the same rules for treaty interpretation in its articles 31–33 as those in the Vienna rules.

Member States to achieve this. As a prelude to a draft treaty, studies may well be prepared on particular issues by the organization's officials, by interested states or, increasingly, by non-governmental organizations. In the case of a very structured process, such as that of the ILC, there may be something akin to a legislative process. The ILC, a body of experts (supported by the UN's permanent staff) works through successive readings of draft provisions. To assist the Commission in achieving a text likely to have reasonably widespread acceptability, there are opportunities to submit the work in progress to a political body (the Sixth Committee of the UN's General Assembly) for responsive assessment as preparation of a treaty text continues. Usually any commission or conference drawing up a treaty will at some point make use of a drafting committee to carry out what is colloquially known as the 'toilette', or tidying up (sometimes amounting to considerably more than just ensuring order, coherence, and textual alignment).[3]

If a sufficient measure of agreement emerges, the various preliminary phases can be expected to lead to terms of agreement expressed in a text for conclusion through a final negotiation. In the case of bilateral work, this may be simply a culminating round of a series of meetings of the negotiators. In the case of a multilateral treaty, a decision will usually be made to hold a diplomatic conference to produce the definitive text of the agreement, unless some broadly comparable procedure is available within an international organization.[4]

2.2.1 *Negotiation and full powers*

As multilateral treaties may attract widespread participation, which sometimes gathers over decades after their conclusion, and will often be difficult to change once signed, who participates in the negotiations and in any diplomatic conference can significantly affect the content of the treaty and in some cases may affect who has access to the preparatory work. The Vienna Convention identifies a negotiating state as one 'which took part in the drawing up and adoption of the text of the treaty' (article 2(1)(e)). The state's representative or representatives, for the purpose of adopting or authenticating the text of a treaty, or for the purpose of expressing the consent of the state to be bound by a treaty, include anyone furnished with 'full powers' unless, from the practice of the states concerned or from other circumstances, it is clear that their intention was to consider that person as representing the state for such purposes, dispensing with full powers.[5] The term 'full powers'

---

[3] See, eg, Report of the Drafting Committee of the ILC on parts two and three of draft articles on State responsibility, Chairman Mr Calero Rodrigues: 'The Drafting Committee had ... had two tasks to accomplish: first, to examine the draft articles dealing with international crimes which had been referred to it; and, secondly, to undertake the fine-tuning, or *toilette finale*, of all the articles in parts two and three.' [1996] *Yearbook of the ILC*, vol I, p 133, para 2.

[4] An example of the latter is adoption of a treaty by a resolution of the General Assembly of the UN, as, eg, in General Assembly resolution 59/38, Official Records of the General Assembly, Fifty-ninth Session, Supplement No 49 (A/59/49) adopting the 'United Nations Convention on Jurisdictional Immunities of States and Their Property, 2004'.

[5] Vienna Convention, article 7. Article 7(2) lists the representatives for whom full powers will be unnecessary: '(a) Heads of State, Heads of Government and Ministers for Foreign Affairs, for the

means 'a document emanating from the competent authority of a state designating a person or persons to represent the state for negotiating, adopting or authenticating the text of a treaty' (article 2(1)(c)).

These definitions use slightly different terminology. The Convention equates being a 'negotiating' state with participation in 'drawing up' a treaty, and associates full powers with 'negotiating' rather than 'drawing up'. But nothing seems to follow from any distinction which could be drawn between 'drawing up' and 'negotiating' a treaty. The only aspect of this which may be significant for treaty interpretation is whether or not a state has participated in the stages leading up to adoption of a treaty. In the case of multilateral treaties, there are often many more states attending the diplomatic conference, at which key obstacles to agreement must ultimately be resolved, than there are participants in working groups or preparatory commissions drawing up the early drafts. As well as the obvious possibility of influencing the content of a treaty through participation in its negotiation, participation in the final stage of its adoption will also enable a state to have an input into the interpretative material which surrounds adoption of a treaty, such as resolutions in the Final Act of the conference.

The significance of these matters lies in the part they may play in helping to assess whether a document produced by a particular individual or group, or statements by representatives at a conference, can be viewed as part of the preparatory work or as representing a generally accepted interpretation.[6] This is considered in greater detail below.

2.3 Adoption and authentication of a treaty text

The Vienna Convention uses the term 'adoption' without definition in the context of the process by which negotiators signify conclusion of the negotiation and acceptance of a text as final.[7] In the case of a multilateral treaty, adoption will commonly take place at a plenary meeting where a complete text of the treaty in the most recent of the conference documents is approved by consensus or by a vote. 'Authentication' (likewise undefined) is the means by which the text is established as definitive.[8] The latter term means, from its context and from practice, some formal indication of finality, such as signature, signature ad referendum, or

purpose of performing all acts relating to the conclusion of a treaty; (b) heads of diplomatic missions, for the purpose of adopting the text of a treaty between the accrediting State and the State to which they are accredited; (c) representatives accredited by States to an international conference or to an international organization or one of its organs, for the purpose of adopting the text of a treaty in that conference, organization or organ.'

  [6] In the case of a conference negotiating a multilateral treaty, the rules of procedure will play a key role in determining how drafts are introduced to the conference, how the committees are to proceed, and how the treaty is to be adopted; these are all matters which can be relevant to treaty interpretation when assessing the significance of particular elements of preparatory work.

  [7] See Vienna Convention, article 9, indicating that adoption is by consent, which if signified at an international conference is consent of two-thirds of those present and voting unless, by the same majority, they have decided to apply a different rule.

  [8] See Vienna Convention, article 10.

initialling by the representatives of the negotiating states of the text of the treaty or of the Final Act of a conference incorporating the text.[9] Thus, authentication is the stage at which a particular printed text of a treaty is identified as the definitive content of the treaty which will be the binding commitments for states which become parties to the treaty. In addition to the obvious importance of being able to identify a particular text as setting out the terms of a treaty in a form that will be binding, the process of authentication has a particular significance for treaty interpretation. In the formal words of conclusion or 'testimonium' (typically, 'Done at…' followed by spaces for signatures) there will be stated which languages are 'authoritative' (if more than one language has been agreed and their status has not been indicated in the final clauses). In some cases there will also be an indication that a particular language is to prevail if there is a divergence in meaning among the various languages. The significance of 'authoritative' languages and 'versions' in other languages, is considered in Chapter 9.

2.4 Concluded and other instruments

The characteristics of a treaty as an agreement between states governed by international law, and the role of signature, ratification (accession, approval, etc) in the process of a state becoming a party to a treaty, have been outlined in Chapter 1.[10] Although there is no set form, a modern treaty commonly consists of a single text that includes title, recital listing negotiating states (nowadays collectively as, eg, 'the States parties to the present Convention', rather than listing negotiating states as in older treaties), preamble, words of agreement, substantive provisions, final clauses, and the testimonium. There is, however, so much use of other elements, such as annexes and appendices, as well as variations or other supplementations of these typical features, that a measure of interpretative acumen may be required to identify what constitutes the totality of the text of the treaty. There are also other quite different forms of agreement, particularly in the case of bilateral treaties, such as an Exchange of Notes (usually identifiable as a treaty by a specific statement in the notes that together they are to constitute an agreement), which may provide a simpler vehicle for a formal record of treaty commitments.

---

[9] Vienna Convention, article 10, where these procedures are indicated as the default ones if no other is agreed; they are in fact the most common.

[10] See Chapter 1, section 3.2 above. The trend towards recognition of a wider range of instruments as treaties, and the difficulties which this raises, are illustrated by the contrasting conclusions in *Land and Maritime Boundary between Cameroon and Nigeria (Cameroon v Nigeria: Equatorial Guinea intervening)* [2002] ICJ Reports 303, at 429, para 263 (holding that the 'Maroua Declaration' constituted a treaty); *Maritime Delimitation and Territorial Questions between Qatar and Bahrain (Qatar v Bahrain) (Jurisdiction and Admissibility)* [1994] ICJ Reports 112 (exchanges of letters and minutes of discussions amounted to treaties); and *Dispute Concerning Delimitation of the Maritime Boundary between Bangladesh and Myanmar in the Bay of Bengal*, ITLOS case no 16, Judgment of 14 March 2012, paras 96–99 (agreed minutes signed by official without full powers did *not* constitute a treaty); and see D B Hollis, 'Defining Treaties' and A Aust, 'Alternatives to Treaty-Making: MOUs as Political Commitments', Chapters 1 and 2 in D B Hollis (ed), *The Oxford Guide to Treaties* (Oxford: OUP, 2012).

The description given above of the stages of treaty-making should suffice to give
a general idea of how and when material potentially relevant to treaty interpretation is generated. Surprisingly, however, there is continuing uncertainty as to when
a treaty is 'concluded'. This is because of the several stages that follow on from
completion of the negotiations. These include signature, ratification (if required),
other possibilities for participation (accession and the like), and entry into force.
While there has been a body of practice treating a single act, such as signature,
as the mark of conclusion, the concept has come increasingly to be recognized as
referring to a process stretching at its widest from the conclusion of negotiations
to ratification, or even entry into force. The term 'conclusion' has a particular
significance for treaty interpretation because it is used in both subparagraphs of
article 31(2) of the Vienna Convention in identifying the extended meaning of the
context in which terms are to be given their meaning. It is therefore considered in
detail in Chapter 6.[11] For present purposes it is sufficient to identify the processes
that produce a treaty and to distinguish a treaty from other documents relevant to
interpretation.

2.4.1 Final acts and protocols

Whatever the form or designation of a treaty (convention, agreement, pact, etc),
it may be accompanied by a range of other documents. At a multilateral conference, it is a common practice to draw up a 'Final Act'. This is a document which
records the transactions of the conference, the fact of conclusion of the treaty, and
may contain resolutions, declarations, or other statements relevant to the treaty
and its interpretation.[12] In earlier times the Final Act might include the text of
the agreement itself.[13] Nowadays a treaty is usually an instrument separate from
the related Final Act, but the latter can clearly fall within article 31(2)(a) of the
Vienna Convention, thus being regarded as part of the context for the purpose of
interpreting the treaty. Likewise, a resolution of an international organization may
have a broadly equivalent role to a Final Act. For example, the General Assembly
resolution adopting the United Nations Convention on Jurisdictional Immunities
of States and Their Property, 2004, included significant interpretative elements.[14]

---

[11] See Chapter 6, section 2.1.1 below.
[12] See, eg, Final Act of the United Nations Conference on the Law of Treaties A/CONF.39/26,
Official Records, Documents, 381.
[13] This was sometimes even the form for a bilateral treaty: see, eg, UK–US Final Act of the Civil
Aviation Conference, Bermuda, 1946, UKTS No 3 (1946) Cmd 6747, where some provisions were
in the body of the Final Act (such as those on capacity of air services) while others (such as those on
tariffs) were in a separate, appended agreement; cf the Air Transport Agreement between the USA
and the Member States of the European Community and the Community, Brussels 25 April and
Washington 30 April 2007, OJ L 134/4, 25.5.2007 where a 'Memorandum of Consultations' (at OJ
L 134/33–40) performs a similar function to a final act and has an interpretative role, affirming (for
example) that 'air transportation' covers charter flights even though not specifically mentioned in the
definition article, OJ L 134/33, para 4.
[14] Resolution 59/38, Official Records of the General Assembly, Fifty-ninth Session, Supplement
No. 49 (A/59/49); see further section 2.4.2 below.

In addition to schedules and annexes forming part of the treaty itself, there may be one or more 'protocols'. The term 'protocol' is used for a variety of instruments. Some are akin to schedules or annexes. Some are instruments setting out agreements related to a main treaty but kept conveniently separate to allow for a multiple range of choices by prospective state participants. 'Protocol' is also used to describe an independent treaty or one which amends an earlier treaty. A rather different creature, masquerading under the same banner, is the 'Protocol of Signature'. This description may be misleading. It commonly describes an instrument which is not a Protocol constituting a treaty itself or forming an adjunct instrument setting out additional terms. Nor, though signed or inserted at the point of signature, is it a means by which states sign the treaty itself. The Protocol of Signature functions more in the manner of a final act and might more appropriately be described as a protocol upon the occasion of signature. As an instrument drawn up at the time of conclusion of a treaty and accepted by the signatories as relating to it, a protocol of signature may have significant interpretative consequences, most clearly when it records understandings as to interpretation of particular provisions of the treaties.[15]

2.4.2 Distinguishing treaties from other instruments

A key element in identifying an instrument as a treaty is evidence of the intention of the parties to make commitments binding under international law.[16] That does not mean that instruments which are not in themselves binding have no legal effect on treaty interpretation. Just as a Protocol of Signature may record understandings as to interpretation of particular provisions, so likewise may other instruments, including a Memorandum of Understanding (MOU). The description 'Memorandum of Understanding' is unfortunately even more confusing than 'Protocol of Signature'. An 'understanding' can mean something different from an 'agreement', principally in that an understanding may be the description of how one party unilaterally views or interprets something; but when two or more reach the same understanding, is the result an agreement? Does it equate to a treaty? Not necessarily, and the absence of a clear-cut answer to this question can lead to confusing situations.

First, there are examples of understandings whose effects are explicitly interpretative. This is the case of the understandings annexed to the UN General Assembly resolution mentioned above adopting the Convention on Jurisdictional

---

[15] See, eg, the Protocol of Signature relating to the Convention on the Contract for International Carriage of Goods by Road considered in *Chloride Industrial Batteries v F & W Freight* [1989] 1 WLR 823. The Protocol of Signature included an understanding that the Convention would not be applicable to contracts for carriage by road between Northern Ireland and the Republic of Ireland. As a state which became party to the Convention by accession, the UK did not sign the Convention but was nevertheless bound by the interpretative effect of the Protocol, it being part of the context for the purposes of article 31(2) of the Vienna Convention; see further Chapter 6, section 2.2.

[16] For the definition of 'treaty' for the purposes of the Vienna Convention, see Chapter 1, section 3.1.

Immunities of States and Their Property, 2004. The annex to the Convention contains a set of understandings. It is explicitly stated to form an integral part of the Convention, but this is only for the purpose of providing interpretative understandings.[17]

More complex is the position over the outcome of the work of an ad hoc working group of the General Assembly's Sixth Committee (Legal Committee), a working group which the General Assembly subsequently converted into an Ad Hoc Committee.[18] A clear interpretative position is established by operative paragraph (2) of the General Assembly's resolution, which states that the General Assembly:

Agrees with the general understanding reached in the Ad Hoc Committee that the United Nations Convention on Jurisdictional Immunities of States and Their Property does not cover criminal proceedings.[19]

As the resolution was adopted by consensus, it seems clear that it is to be taken as part of the context of the treaty for the purposes of interpretation, the resolution being an instrument which was made in connection with the conclusion of the Convention. The statement is framed as an endorsement of a 'general understanding' reached in the preparation of the Convention, rather than as an agreement on the content of the understanding and thus on the meaning of the Convention's provisions. This is not, therefore, overtly an agreement relating to the treaty in the sense of an agreement falling within article 31(2)(a) of the Vienna Convention.[20] The resolution probably comes more appropriately within the class of instruments described in article 31(2)(b), being made by one or more of the parties in connection with the conclusion of the treaty and accepted by the other parties as an instrument related to the treaty.[21]

While the interpretative role of the understandings in the annex and in the operative paragraph quoted above is clear, less prominent (but no less important) is the interpretative role of the statement by Mr Gerhard Hafner (who had chaired both the working group and Ad Hoc Committee). This was made when introducing the report of the Ad Hoc Committee in the General Assembly's Sixth Committee.

---

[17] See Resolution 59/38 cited in n 14 above, article 25 and the annex to the resolution; see G Hafner and U Köhler, 'The United Nations Convention on Jurisdictional Immunities of States and Their Property' (2004) XXXV NYIL 3, at 42 stating that article 25 is 'counterbalanced by the chapeau for the Understandings, which defines the purpose of the annex as "setting out understandings relating to the provisions concerned". Consequently the annex is to be considered part of the Convention, but serves interpretation purposes only. It qualifies therefore as part of the context of a treaty in accordance with Article 31 [of the Vienna Convention], so that the [UN] Convention is to be read in conjunction with the Understandings. These Understandings, however, are not able to alter the text of the agreement.'

[18] See Hafner and Köhler, at 8–9.

[19] Resolution 59/38 (footnote omitted).   [20] See further Chapter 6, section 2.

[21] See Hafner and Köhler, 'The United Nations Convention on Jurisdictional Immunities', at 46, invoking article 31(2)(b) of the Vienna Convention in this context, and noting also that, as the exclusion of application to criminal proceedings was included in the ILC's commentary and had never been contested in the negotiation process, article 32 of the Vienna Convention could also bring preparatory work into the interpretative process (were there any doubt about the resolution qualifying under article 31(2)(b)).

A preambular reference to this statement is included in the General Assembly's resolution.[22] This statement may have considerable interpretative significance. For example, a matter of some controversy was whether there should be an explicit exclusion of all military matters from the Convention's coverage. It has been noted that the ILC's Commentary was not clear on this and that only where there are specific treaties, such as status of forces agreements, is it clear that the Convention does not affect the rights and obligations of states parties to those agreements.[23] However, the statement by the Chairman reflected his impression that there was a general understanding in the negotiation process that military activities were not covered by the Convention. As this was not controverted but was mentioned in the preamble to the General Assembly's resolution, it has greater interpretative weight by being noted in an instrument which is part of the treaty's context rather than merely being recorded in the preparatory work.

More difficult to place is an MOU. This is because an MOU may contain terms of agreement or, even if both or all sides are agreed on the understandings, it may be designedly an instrument not binding in itself but having potential legal consequences for interpretation of a treaty. Part of the problem is lack of clarity and absence of uniform practice in the terms used to describe various instruments that are not treaties in established form, but also, and even more of an obstacle in assessing whether the instrument is binding, is the absence of systematic differentiation in use of language in the content of the instrument. Thus, for example, the term 'understanding' has an established meaning when the US Senate attaches a rider to its approval of a treaty as something which is not a reservation:

Understandings, by contrast [with reservations], are interpretive statements that clarify or elaborate, rather than change, the provisions of an agreement and that are deemed to be consistent with the obligations imposed by the agreement.[24]

Clearly, in that context an 'understanding' is not of the same status as a reservation modifying treaty relations. Yet the USA views an MOU as a vehicle for treaty provisions.[25] The UK has in recent decades tried to develop a practice of distinguishing between 'understandings' and 'agreements'. In trying to maintain this distinction, the UK has sought to avoid using in MOUs mandatory language of the kind typically found in treaties ('agree', 'shall', 'undertake', etc) and instead keep to words which do not indicate an intention to be bound ('intend', 'will',

---

[22] The preamble to the resolution includes the recital: '*Taking into account* the statement of the Chairman of the Ad Hoc Committee introducing the Report of the Ad Hoc Committee', Resolution 59/38, (footnote omitted); and see Hafner and Köhler, 'The United Nations Convention on Jurisdictional Immunities', at 9–10.

[23] See Hafner and Köhler, at 46–47.

[24] *Treaties and other International Agreements: The Role of the United States Senate,* Senate Committee on Foreign Relations, 106th Congress, *2d Session,* S. PRT, 106–71 (2001), at 125; see also extracts from other sources in Commentary on the draft guidelines on reservations to treaties provisionally adopted by the Commission on first reading, [1999] *Yearbook of the ILC,* vol II, p 99, para 8, fn 318.

[25] See, eg, J H McNeill, 'International Agreements: Recent US–UK Practice Concerning the Memorandum of Understanding' (1994) 88 AJIL 821.

'expect', etc).[26] However, there is no uniform practice on this, nor has the UK itself been entirely consistent in its own practice.

Writing of the title 'Memorandum of Understanding' nearly 50 years ago, McNair described the term as 'comparatively new' and wrote: 'To an increasing extent it is being used to denote an informal but nevertheless legal agreement between two or more states…'[27] He noted, presumably as evidence of their legal character, that many such memoranda of understanding had appeared in the UK Treaty Series and in the UN Treaty Series.[28] Appearance in the latter series follows upon registration of an instrument with the UN as a treaty, the requirement of article 102 of the UN Charter being that every treaty and every international agreement be so registered. It is, however, the content of the instrument and evidence of the intent of the makers of the instrument which are the real determinants. Failure to register a treaty with the UN carries the sanction that the instrument may not be invoked before UN organs rather than changing its status. There are countless memoranda of understanding and confidential memoranda of understanding which are not registered. If, as often is the case, they have been worded in a form to avoid any indication of an intention to be binding (and assuming there is no such intention), they are not treaties and are not eligible for registration as treaties.[29] Nevertheless, their significance for treaty interpretation may be considerable.

The status of an inter-governmental MOU was in issue in the *US–UK Heathrow Airport User Charges Arbitration*.[30] One matter in the arbitration concerned a provision in the Air Services Agreement between the USA and the UK allowing that user charges at airports 'may provide for a reasonable rate of return on assets'. Following differences over the user charges levied at London Heathrow Airport, a 1983 US–UK MOU included understandings as to how returns on assets were to be assessed and on appropriate procedures for setting the structure of user charges. The arbitral tribunal rejected arguments that the MOU was a treaty within the meaning of article 2(1)(a) of the Vienna Convention, but held that the MOU constituted 'consensual subsequent practice of the Parties' and 'certainly as such, is available to the Tribunal as an aid to the interpretation of [the Air Services Agreement] and, in particular, to clarify the meaning to be attributed to expressions used in the Treaty and to resolve any ambiguities'.[31] The Tribunal noted that if, contrary to its impression, 'the MOU were intended…to create independent legally enforceable obligations as opposed to merely recording the understandings

---

[26] For an analysis of practice and theory relating to MOUs, see A I Aust, *Modern Treaty Law and Practice* (Cambridge: CUP, 3rd edn, 2012), Chapter 3. For the interpretation of 'shall', see *Churchill Mining PLC and Planet Mining Pty Ltd v Republic of Indonesia* ICSID Case No. ARB/12/14 and 12/40 (Decision on Jurisdiction, 24 February 2014), at paras 162–231, and see Chapter 5, section 3.3.7 and Chapter 9, section 4.4 below.

[27] McNair, *The Law of Treaties*, 15; cf McNeill, 'International Agreements: Recent US–UK Practice Concerning the Memorandum of Understanding', at 821.

[28] McNair, at 15, fn 1.

[29] See Aust, *Modern Treaty Law and Practice*, chapter 3.

[30] 102 ILR 215, Award of 30 November 1992.

[31] 102 ILR 215, Arbitral Award, chapter 6, p 353, para 6.7; see also note on the arbitration in Contemporary Practice of the US relating to International Law, M Nash (Leich) (1994) 88 AJIL 738.

of the Parties', it would have lacked jurisdiction to rule on those obligations as its jurisdiction was solely in relation to disputes arising under the Air Services Agreement. The Tribunal concluded that the MOU was available to it as a 'potentially important aid to interpretation but [it] is not a source of independent legal rights and duties capable of enforcement in the present Arbitration'.[32]

While that conclusion relates solely to the particular MOU, it strongly supports the view that where an instrument which is not intended to be binding as a treaty is relevant to an issue of interpretation of a treaty to which it is related, it may provide evidence of consent to the establishment of subsequent practice which will be admissible as an element of treaty interpretation under article 31(3)(b) of the Vienna Convention.

3. Reservations and Statements or Declarations Affecting Interpretation of Treaties

During the negotiation of treaties, and at or after their conclusion, states often seek to put on record their own interpretation of provisions in the treaty or its draft text. Loosely classed as falling within the description 'interpretative declarations', such a statement is something distinct from formulating a reservation to a provision of the treaty, a reservation being a unilateral act by a state in effect adjusting (where permitted) the terms of the treaty to accord with those acceptable to the particular state. Reservations are not in themselves interpretative acts. They affect the formation of treaty relations. However, the occasion for making a reservation may also be one of those used for making an interpretative declaration. Sometimes reservations are disguised as interpretative declarations. Reservations and interpretative declarations therefore need to be considered together, although it is only the latter which are pertinent to treaty interpretation once the scope and formal content of treaty relations has been identified.

3.1 Reservations

A state may be permitted to indicate adjustments to a treaty regime by formulating reservations upon signature, ratification, or when using a process akin to ratification (accession, approval, etc). The permissibility of formulating a reservation may be indicated in the particular treaty but otherwise depends on how the rules in the law of treaties determine the position for the particular treaty and reservation.

Any such reservation is essentially unilateral in nature even if formulated jointly by several states or international organizations. Article 2(1)(d) of the Vienna Convention provides:

'reservation' means a unilateral statement, however phrased or named, made by a State, when signing, ratifying, accepting, approving or acceding to a treaty, whereby it purports to

---

[32] ILR 215, Arbitral Award, chapter 6, p 353, para. 6.8.

exclude or to modify the legal effect of certain provisions of the treaty in their application to that State...

The Vienna Convention sets out rules on formulating, accepting, and challenging reservations.[33] However, these rules do not provide a complete set of provisions covering all aspects of reservations. The ILC has therefore drawn up a Guide to Practice on Reservations to Treaties ('the Guide') which is a set of guidelines with commentaries based on law and practice relating to reservations.[34] The Guide and commentary were developed through the ILC's work based on 17 reports by its Special Rapporteur (Pellet) and endorsed by the General Assembly of the United Nations. Bearing in mind that the task of the ILC is progressive development of international law as well as codification, the guidelines are not solely statements of clear existing law, but, with the commentaries and the Special Rapporteur's Reports, they provide an invaluable study of relevant law and practice, extending over nearly 650 pages, as well as providing clarification and guidance which may help shape practice in the future.

Details of the law relating to reservations, such as the right to formulate a reservation, the procedures for accepting and rejecting reservations, the consequences of such responses to reservations, and the many other aspects of the regime for reservations are beyond the scope of the present work.[35] In summary, however, possible consequences of a reservation, and of any responses to it, for treaty relations are that: (a) the treaty applies in the relations of the reserving state with one or more other parties but with effects as excluded or modified by the reservation; (b) the treaty applies in those relations but without the provisions affected by the reservation; or (c) the treaty does not give rise to treaty relations between a state so specifying and the reserving state.

The significance of reservations for treaty interpretation is their contribution to identification of what is to be interpreted. Although they do not alter the actual text of a treaty, they produce a similar result to a 'modification'. Their words combine with those of the treaty provisions (with the exclusions or modifications) to change the legal effect from that which the treaty in its unaffected form would have in relation to the state making the reservation and others affected by it.

---

[33] Articles 19–23. Parallel provisions are included in the 1986 Vienna Convention on the Law of Treaties between States and International Organizations or between International Organizations. In the work of the ILC that is considered below, acts of states and international organizations in relation to reservations and interpretative declarations are treated together unless specific differences are indicated for the latter; in the present text reference to a state includes reference to an international organization wherever appropriate.

[34] Addendum to Report of the International Law Commission, Sixty-third session (2011), UN General Assembly Official Records, Sixty-sixth Session, Supplement No. 10, A/66/10/Add.1, <http://legal.un.org/ilc/reports/2011/english/addendum.pdf>. The Guide received endorsement by the General Assembly in resolution A/RES/68/111 (2013); references in the following text and notes to 'the Guide' and to any numbered 'guideline' are references to the text in this document and to text with commentary in the Addendum cited above.

[35] See further J Crawford, *Brownlie's Principles of Public International Law* (Oxford: OUP, 8th edn, 2012), at 374–77, Aust, *Modern Treaty Law and Practice,* Chapter 8, A Clapham, *Brierly's Law of Nations* (Oxford: OUP, 2012), 320–36, and Gardiner, *International Law,* at 75–78.

'Modification' is the term used by the Vienna Convention where two or more parties to a multilateral treaty conclude an agreement to adjust the treaty as between themselves alone (see Part IV and article 41 of the Convention). It is convenient to use the same concept in an analogous sense in the present context. The difficulties which this might present if one or more contracting states accept an interpretation in a declaration which others regard as a reservation are considered below.

Reservations are typically formulated in a statement or declaration made in connection with processes for becoming a party to a treaty. There is no set form. In their many variants, some instruments do not clearly indicate whether they purport to exclude or modify particular effects of a treaty, whether they purport to affect its interpretation, or whether they have only some political or practical significance. Where a reservation is formulated, its nature as a reservation is confirmed by the content of the statement. Although reservations affect treaty relations rather than interpretation, in its recent work developing the Guide the ILC found it appropriate to address statements or declarations constituting 'interpretative declarations' at the same time as considering draft guidelines relating to reservations. [36]

The framework adopted in the Guide is the same for reservations and interpretative declarations although the substance differs considerably. After setting out definitions, the Guide provides guidelines on 'procedure' which are essentially an account of how states and organizations make and communicate reservations and interpretative declarations and their responses to them. By this means the respective positions of the parties are clarified, to the extent that they participate in the process. The Guide then deals with 'permissibility', a term used to denote the considerations affecting substantive validity of reservations and interpretative declarations, competence to assess the permissibility of reservations, consequences of impermissibility, and permissibility of reactions to reservations and interpretative declarations. The next part of the Guide deals with the legal effects of reservations and interpretative declarations, which requires a combined assessment of the positions of the parties and the permissibility of the reservations and interpretative declarations.

3.2 Interpretative declarations

A state or international organization may announce its understanding of a term of a treaty, or indicate the meaning which it sees that provision as bearing, at almost any stage in the preparation of the text, or in the lifetime of a treaty (that is, at or after its conclusion). Thus, interpretative statements may be recorded in the preparatory work, in a document at the time of signature, or appended to the

---

[36] Although an essential feature of interpretative declarations is that they are unilateral acts (even if made as joint or coordinated statements), the ILC has completed its work on another topic under the title 'unilateral acts', which is primarily concerned with acts that are not within treaty relationships: see explanations in the Fifth Report on Unilateral Acts of States by V Rodríguez Cedeo, Special Rapporteur, UN Doc A/CN.4/525, and the earlier and later Reports of the Special Rapporteur on the same topic.

actual signature itself, may be made at the occasion of depositing an instrument of ratification (accession, etc), or at any convenient time or occasion thereafter.[37]

The Vienna Convention does not offer a definition of an interpretative declaration, but the Guide has one:

'Interpretative declaration' means a unilateral statement, however phrased or named, made by a State or an international organization, whereby that State or that organization purports to specify or clarify the meaning or scope of a treaty or of certain of its provisions.[38]

The law and practice on making interpretative declarations is rather less developed than that on reservations, though the ILC's Guide shows that both need extensive clarification and the Guide seeks to provide it.

3.2.1 Interpretative declarations in preparatory work and at, or after, conclusion

In his Third Report on the law of treaties, the Special Rapporteur (Waldock) noted that a particularly important question was whether an agreed statement or understanding as to the meaning of a provision before the conclusion of the treaty was to be considered as part of the context or merely as part of the preparatory work.[39] He recorded that the Court had adopted the latter view in the *Conditions of Admission to Membership* case, but he advised the ILC to prefer the line taken by the ICJ in the *Ambatielos* case where it had said: 'The provisions of the declaration are in the nature of an interpretation clause, and, as such, should be regarded as an integral part of the Treaty.'[40] This observation of the Special Rapporteur was, however, made before the elements of the context of a treaty had been clearly identified and incorporated into the general rule of interpretation in article 31 of the Vienna Convention.

The Advisory Opinion in the *Admissions* case excluded from consideration statements or interpretative understandings forming part of the negotiations preceding the treaty, not because of any principle relating to interpretative declarations but because the majority of the Court considered that the terms of the treaty in that particular case were clear and did not require resort to the preparatory work. In the *Ambatielos* case, the interpretative declaration was an instrument agreed by

---

[37] See Fourth Report on the Law of Treaties, by the Special Rapporteur (Waldock), [1965] *Yearbook of the ILC,* vol II, p 49, para 2.

[38] Guideline 1.2. On interpretative declarations see generally F Horn, *Reservations and Interpretative Declarations to Multilateral Treaties* (Amsterdam: North-Holland, 1988); D M McRae, 'The Legal Effect of Interpretative Declarations', (1978) 49 BYBIL 155; R Sapienza, 'Les Déclarations Interprétatives Unilatérales et l'Interprétation des Traités' (1999) 103 *Revue Generale de Droit International Public* 601; L D M Nelson, 'Declarations, Statements and "Disguised Reservations" with respect to the Convention on the Law of the Sea' (2001) 50 ICLQ 767; and M Benatar, 'From Probative Value to Authentic Interpretation: The Legal Effect of Interpretative Declarations' (2011) 44 *Revue Belge de Droit International* 170.

[39] [1964] *Yearbook of the ILC,* vol II, p 58, para 19.

[40] *Conditions of Admission to Membership* (Advisory Opinion) [1948] ICJ Reports 63; *Ambatielos (UK v Greece)* (Preliminary Objection) [1952] ICJ Reports 43, at 75.

the parties to a bilateral treaty as a clarification of its entry into force provision and its effect on any matters governed by a previous treaty which this bilateral treaty replaced. Such an agreed declaration relating to a bilateral treaty is more akin to an interpretative agreement than an interpretative declaration of the kind considered here.

Two years later, in response to an observation by a government that it should be made clear whether the 'context' of a treaty could include a unilateral document and a document on which several but not all parties to a multilateral instrument have agreed, the Special Rapporteur (Waldock) referred to the *Anglo–Iranian Oil Company* case, noting that the ICJ had 'upheld the relevance of a purely unilateral declaration for the interpretation of an unilateral instrument'.[41] The Special Rapporteur thought it clear that a unilateral document could not be regarded as part of the 'context' for the purpose of interpreting a treaty unless the other parties acquiesced in its relevance to interpretation.[42] It should be noted, however, that in the *Anglo–Iranian Oil Company* case, the ICJ was considering a declaration accepting the jurisdiction of the Court, a type of instrument which is quite distinct from interpretative declarations supplying an understanding as to the meaning of a provision in a treaty.

This background to interpretative declarations needs to be supplemented by recalling that the work of the ILC resulted in an element of the Vienna Convention's general rule of interpretation which includes an instrument made by one or more parties 'in connection with the conclusion of the treaty' (article 31(2)), quite distinct from the preparatory work.[43]

It is this element of the general rule which in a general sense, without expressly referring to them, identifies the main occasions for making interpretative declarations of the kind considered here. Statements recorded in the preparatory work are a separate matter, to be considered according to how they may become admissible as supplementary means of interpretation.[44] The Guide makes it clear that it addresses only 'interpretative declarations' made after the text of the provision of the treaty concerned has been finally adopted.[45]

3.3 Differentiating between reservations and interpretative declarations

3.3.1 The nature of the difference

Efforts to assimilate interpretative declarations with reservations were rejected by the ILC when preparing draft articles on the law of treaties.[46] The Special

---

[41] [1966] *Yearbook of the ILC,* vol II, p 98, para 16 referring to ICJ Reports (1952) 105.
[42] [1966] *Yearbook of the ILC,* vol II, p 98, para 16.   [43] See Chapter 6 below.
[44] See Chapter 8 below.
[45] Guideline 2.4.4, commentary para (6); for the effect of interpretations recorded in preparatory work see Chapter 8, section 4.4.8 below.
[46] For a thorough account of the work of the ILC and the Vienna Conference on this topic, see Horn, *Reservations and Interpretative Declarations to Multilateral Treaties,* 231–4.

Rapporteur (Waldock) observed that 'statements of interpretation' had not been dealt with by the ILC in the section on reservations for the simple reason that they were not reservations and concerned interpretation rather than the conclusion of treaties.[47]

It can be seen from the definition of 'reservation' in the Vienna Convention and the definition of 'interpretative declaration' in the Guide that the most significant contrast for present purposes is between the purport of a reservation ('to exclude or to modify the legal effect of certain provisions of the treaty') and that of an interpretative declaration ('to specify or clarify the meaning or scope attributed by the declarant to a treaty or to certain of its provisions'). Thus, a reservation adjusts a treaty's effects by specifying that certain of its terms are to be excluded or modified with effect from the moment when the reserving state becomes bound. An interpretative declaration provides evidence of the meaning attributed by the declarant to the terms of the treaty and to be considered whenever these come to be interpreted.

It is to be noted that article 21 of the Vienna Convention indicates that a reservation 'modifies…the provisions of the treaty'. This phraseology is consistent with article 41 on 'modification' of treaties (described above). Since the effect to be brought about by a reservation is expressed in words, and results in a different set of words apt to describe the rights and obligations of those affected by the reservation, thinking of the result in textual terms may not be such a bad approach, provided one remembers that the adjusted terms apply only in relations between those states or organizations specifically affected. Such an approach helps one to see the reservation as akin to a modifier of what the treaty is, in contrast to the interpretative declaration which affects how the treaty is to be understood. Put in a nutshell, a reservation affects *what* is to be interpreted; an interpretative declaration seeks to affect *how* something is to be interpreted, that is what meaning is to be attributed to it.

3.3.2 Wrinkles in the distinction
and 'conditional interpretative declarations'

Although the practice of making interpretative declarations is well established, and the contrast with reservations just drawn seems clear and simple, distinguishing between the two is not quite so easy as it may appear. The ILC notes that the practice of making declarations to accompany treaties dates back to the appearance of multilateral treaties, instancing the British declarations on exchange of instruments of ratification of treaties agreed at the Congress of Vienna in 1815.[48] The example is significant because the British declaration (stating that the British understood the treaty as a commitment to complete the defeat of Napoleon but not to impose a particular government on France) was clearly an interpretative

---

[47] Horn, 231–4.   [48] Guideline 1.2, commentary para (1), fn 128.

declaration, a characterization which distinguishes this type of statement from a reservation (of which there was an example in another treaty in the same set).[49]

Any distinction, however, between an interpretative declaration and a reservation that had its roots in 1815 was blurred by subsequent use of interpretative declarations as opportunities to attempt to formulate reservations in disguise. This may be done sometimes because an interpretation simply has a 'nicer', or less contentious, appearance than a reservation; but there is a particular incentive to attempt a reservation disguised as an interpretative declaration in instances where reservations to a treaty are specifically excluded or are otherwise impermissible.[50] Additional difficulties in making the distinction are: confusing terminology, uncertain weight to be attached to the characterization given to a statement or declaration by its maker, and the dual use declaration which is formulated as an interpretation upon which the maker purports to make its consent to be bound by the treaty conditional.

This last category is described by the ILC as a 'conditional interpretative declaration', which is defined in the Guide:

A conditional interpretative declaration is a unilateral statement formulated by a State or an international organization when signing, ratifying, formally confirming, accepting, approving or acceding to a treaty, or by a State when making a notification of succession to a treaty, whereby the State or international organization subjects its consent to be bound by the treaty to a specific interpretation of the treaty or of certain provisions thereof.[51]

The Guide seeks to clarify the status of conditional interpretative declarations by stating: 'Conditional interpretative declarations are subject to the rules applicable to reservations.'[52] This makes the resultant status of a conditional interpretative declaration clear, but leaves the modalities of characterizing a declaration as a conditional interpretation to be resolved by the means indicated elsewhere in the Guide through the processes considered below (principally 'recharacterization').

3.3.3 *Confusing terminology: statements and declarations*

The ILC has noted that while in French one encounters few terms other than *réserves* and *declarations*, in English the equivalent usages extend beyond 'reservation' and '(interpretative) declaration' to include 'statement', 'understanding',

---

[49] Guideline 1.2, commentary para (1), fn 128.
[50] Guideline 1.2, commentary para (1), fn 131 citing the Danish response to the ILC's questionnaire on reservations.
[51] Guideline 1.4, para (1); this clarifies the difficulty in terminology noted in the first major analysis of the issues presented by such declarations see D M McRae, 'The Legal Effect of Interpretative Declarations' (1978) 49 BYBIL 155, where he distinguished between a 'mere interpretative declaration' and a 'qualified interpretative declaration', at (160–61); the Swiss government also used the description 'qualified interpretative declaration' in its submissions to the European Court of Human Rights in *Belilos v Switzerland*, ECtHR case no 20–1986/118/167, judgment of 23 March 1988, paras 42 and 46.
[52] Guideline 1.4, para 2.

'proviso', 'interpretation', 'explanation', and others.[53] While the ILC attributes to the English usage the advantage that the variety of terms correctly shows that unilateral declarations do not necessarily contain just reservations or interpretative declarations (see below on political, practical, and other possible content of declarations), the absence of defined and systematic usage may make identification of the legal outcome difficult.

The root of the difficulty is confusing the vehicle with its passengers. A declaration may be the vehicle for conveying a reservation or an interpretation (or an understanding, explanation, etc). The operative distinction is in what is conveyed and in the purported effects; but the form lends scope for disguise. This is because the term 'declaration' has the potential to include the formulation of a reservation as well as a purely interpretative statement. However, the practice of describing the dichotomy as being between 'declarations' and 'reservations' is too well established to displace.[54] The Guide provides some clarification. Taking the lead from the Vienna Convention's definition of 'reservation' as a 'statement', the ILC's definition of 'interpretative declaration' also casts this in terms of a statement. Thus the 'statement' becomes the vehicle, allowing the 'declaration' to be the passenger.

3.3.4. *Differentiating in practice*

Earlier practice and case law reflects some uncertainties in the distinction between reservations and interpretative declarations. This is in part because of lack of clarity as to what significance is to be attached to the way in which the maker of a statement characterizes its intended legal effect.

As an example of practice, a number of declarations were made on signature and ratification of the Treaty for the Renunciation of War, 1928 ('the Pact of Paris' or 'Kellogg–Briand Pact'). Some declarations concerned the possibility of sanctions being imposed by the League of Nations, while others stated rights of self-defence.[55] In disagreeing with these when it acceded to the treaty, the Soviet Union described the declarations as 'reservations'.[56] The true effect of the declarations was not resolved, although it appears that most other states and writers regarded them as interpretative declarations rather than reservations.[57]

Practice in distinguishing reservations and declarations was taken little further forward when India made a statement with its ratification of the Convention on the Inter-Governmental Maritime Consultative Organization (IMCO) in 1948. The thrust of the statement was that Indian measures of support for its shipping industries and national measures were consistent with the purposes of the IMCO.[58] Circulation of the statement by the Secretary-General of the UN as depositary

---

[53] Guideline 1.2, commentary para 7.

[54] As the foremost depositary of treaties, the Secretary General of the UN appends to treaty status lists 'Declarations and Reservations', followed by objections: See *Multilateral Treaties deposited with the Secretary General*, ST/LEG/SER.E/24 (2005), now available electronically on the UN treaty database.

[55] See Horn, *Reservations and Interpretative Declarations to Multilateral Treaties*, 274 ff.

[56] Horn, at 275.   [57] Horn, at 275.

[58] Horn, 268 ff.

led to negative responses by individual states and to discussion in the General Assembly.[59] The Indian representative eventually announced in the Assembly that the statement on ratification did not contain reservations but was a statement of policy.[60] On this basis the Council of the IMCO accepted India as a member but recorded that the Indian statement had no legal effect.[61] This resulted in a variety of approaches by other states in later declarations, some explicitly stating that they were only policy statements, others purporting to be interpretative declarations.[62]

The case law of other courts and tribunals offers some further examples but little in the way of comprehensive guidance. In the *UK–French Continental Shelf* case the Court of Arbitration considered three French reservations to the 1958 Geneva Convention on the continental shelf.[63] The UK argued that one of these was a mere 'interpretative declaration'. The Court rejected this and found the three reservations to be permissible as reservations. It therefore considered the consequences of reservations and the responses which had been made to them, but it did not shed any light on the role of interpretative declarations in the interpretation of treaties.

In *Belilos v Switzerland* the European Court of Human Rights (ECtHR) considered declarations on the interpretation of article 6 of the European Convention on Human Rights (ECHR).[64] The Swiss instrument of ratification declared that the Convention was ratified with appended reservations and interpretative declarations.[65] The European Convention explicitly permits reservations relating to a particular provision of the Convention to the extent of any domestic law not in conformity with the provision. However, it excludes reservations 'of a general character' and requires any reservation relating to non-conforming domestic law to contain a brief statement of the law concerned (article 64). The relevant Swiss declaration on interpretation of article 6 stated that the Swiss Federal Council considered that the provisions of the Convention guaranteeing a fair trial were 'intended solely to ensure ultimate control by the judiciary' over acts, decisions, or determinations of public authorities relating to rights and obligations or criminal charges.[66]

After reviewing the domestic processes which led the Swiss authorities to make an interpretative declaration rather than a reservation, the ECtHR found that the reference to 'ultimate control by the judiciary' was ambiguous and imprecise, leading to uncertainty over the application of protection of article 6, particularly as regards decisions in criminal matters made by administrative authorities. The Court found, therefore, that 'the objective reality of the actual wording of the declaration' led to the conclusion that the declaration was a reservation of the impermissible general character.[67]

---

[59] See Horn, *Reservations*, chapter 28 on the functions of depositaries.
[60] Horn, at 269.   [61] Horn, at 269.
[62] Horn, at 269.   [63] 54 ILR 6.
[64] Case number 20–1986/118/167, judgment of 23 March 1988.
[65] Case number 20–1986/118/167, at para 28.
[66] Case number 20–1986/118/167, at para 28.
[67] Case number 20–1986/118/167, para 55.

These cases and the examples discussed by Horn[68] show how statements and declarations, in combination with any responses, have been interpreted and characterized in practice, but that uniformity and consistency is lacking.

3.3.5 *The scheme for differentiation envisaged in the ILC's Guide*

The ILC's guidelines differentiate reservations and interpretative declarations by combining definitions with procedures for identifying any positions taken by the parties to a treaty and with principles of permissibility of reservations and declarations. A particular feature of the procedures identified in the Guide is 'recharacterization' of an interpretative declaration as a reservation.

Hence, after the definitions, the Guide combines a statement of principle with guidelines for its implementation. The statement of principle is that:

The character of a unilateral statement as a reservation or as an interpretative declaration is determined by the legal effect that its author purports to produce.[69]

However, this principle is *not* to be read in the sense that it is entirely for the maker of a statement to decide whether his creature is a reservation or an interpretative declaration. What the maker of a statement intended to achieve is clearly part of the picture, and it lies within the maker's hands to determine what is purported to be done by the statement. That, however, is not the whole story. The same content may be given a different description by different makers of the same statement.[70] What the maker intends or claims to be doing does not give sufficient certainty if the substance and effect lead to a result different from that intended.

The Guide therefore includes its own principles of interpretation of statements which could be reservations or interpretative declarations. The statement is to be interpreted 'in good faith in accordance with the ordinary meaning to be given to its terms, with a view to identifying therefrom the intention of its author, in light of the treaty to which it refers', and that 'the phrasing or name of a unilateral statement provides an indication of the purported legal effect'.[71] There is a presumption that if the treaty prohibits reservations to all or certain of its provisions, a unilateral statement in respect of those provisions is to be presumed not to constitute a reservation unless the statement purports to exclude or modify for the author of the statement the legal effect of the treaty or certain provisions of it, in which case it is treated as a reservation.[72]

It can be seen that this interpretative approach is analogous to the first part of the general rule of the Vienna rules, but it allows for some account to be taken of the proponents' view of what they were trying to do, though implying that priority must be given to the actual text of the declaration over the intention of

---

[68] Horn, *Reservations and Interpretative Declarations*.....   [69] Guideline 1.3
[70] See Guideline 1.2, commentary para (6).   [71] Guidelines 1.3.1 and 1.3.2.
[72] Guideline 1.3.3.

its maker.[73] Where a state itself distinguishes in a statement between reservations and declarations, that act is a persuasive indicator of intent and effect, but it is not conclusive.[74]

3.4 Other declarations

In its work on draft guidelines on reservations, the ILC has noted that unilateral statements which states and international organizations make in relation to treaties, and which are not reservations or interpretative declarations, are too numerous and diverse be listed individually.[75] Nevertheless, although such statements are not within the scope of its draft guidelines, the Commission has listed the main categories of such statements since these might be confused with reservations or interpretative declarations. The ILC has provided a commentary on each category, but they require no analysis here:

1. Statements purporting to undertake unilateral commitments;
2. Unilateral statements purporting to add further elements to a treaty;
3. Statements of non-recognition (made by a state or international organization to indicate that its participation in a treaty does not imply recognition of an entity which it does not recognize);
4. Statements concerning the territorial application of a treaty;
5. General statements of policy (expressing a state's or international organization's views on a treaty or its subject matter without purporting to produce a legal effect on the treaty);
6. Statements concerning the manner of implementation of a treaty domestically (not purporting to affect rights and obligations between parties but giving relevant information); and
7. Unilateral statements made under an optional clause (made in accordance with a treaty provision expressly authorizing the parties to accept an obligation not otherwise imposed by the treaty or where a treaty allows or requires parties to choose between two or more of its provisions).[76]

3.5 Procedure relating to interpretative declarations

There is little to note in the guidelines on procedures for formulating interpretative declarations. Except where the treaty itself specifies conditions on these matters, the form, timing, modification, and withdrawal of interpretative declarations is left open to the choice of the declarant.[77] The procedures for communication of interpretative declarations is as for reservations.[78] There are two main points of general difference in

---

[73] Guideline 1.3.1, commentary paras (9)–(13) and guideline 1.3.2, commentary paras (7)–(11).
[74] Guideline 1.3.1, commentary para (14) and guideline 1.3.2.
[75] See draft guideline 1.4 and commentary, [1999] *Yearbook of the ILC*, vol II, p 113.
[76] Summary of list in Guideline 1.5 and the commentary thereto.
[77] Guidelines 2.9.5 ff.   [78] Guideline 2.9.7.

procedures for formulating reservations and those for interpretative declarations. First, the former (reservations), if made on signature subject to ratification, require confirmation by repetition upon subsequent consent to be bound. Second, there are time elements specified by the Vienna Convention relating to reservations and objections to them which are not applicable to interpretative declarations.

In relation to reactions to interpretative declarations the Guide has rather more to offer. In addition to silence (the most common response), three possible reactions to purported interpretative declarations can be described in general terms, but the Guide adds definition and precision. The first possibility is to express agreement (in the Guide 'approval'). The second is to deny that the declaration gives a correct interpretation (in the Guide 'opposition'). The third is to deny that the statement is an interpretative declaration and to treat it as a reservation (in the Guide 'recharacterization'). The first two of these may be combined with a declaration stating an alternative interpretation, asserting this to be the correct one.

There are three general points. First, approval or opposition is not to be presumed, though one or other may be inferred, in exceptional cases, from the conduct of the states or international organizations concerned, taking into account all relevant circumstances.[79] Second, in somewhat similar vein, approval of an interpretative declaration is not to be inferred from mere silence.[80] A comment in the Guide seems an equally apt conclusion on both the first and second general points:

It therefore seems impossible to provide, in the abstract, clear guidelines for determining when a silent State has, by its inaction, created an effect of acquiescence or estoppel. This can only be determined on a case-by-case basis in the light of the circumstances in question.[81]

The third general point is that the Guide indicates that any approval, opposition, or recharacterization 'should, to the extent possible, indicate the reasons why it is being made'.[82] Underlying this point is the aim of encouraging for interpretative declarations something equivalent to the ILC's proposed 'reservations dialogue', the idea being that any difficulties over interpretative declarations should be resolved consensually wherever possible.[83]

3.5.1 Approval of an interpretative declaration

The Guide describes practice with respect to positive reactions to interpretative declarations as 'virtually non-existent', but it identifies a positive reaction, where this does occur, as 'approval'.[84] The commentary remarks that it is as if states

---

[79] Guideline 2.9.8; the commentary to this guideline gives an extract from an arbitral decision considering conduct which might constitute acquiescence or implied or tacit agreement, but without specific reference to interpretative declarations, (para (8) of commentary).

[80] Guideline 2.9.9.   [81] Guideline 2.9.9, commentary para (9).   [82] Guideline 2.9.6.

[83] For the Conclusions on the Reservations Dialogue, see Annex to Addendum to Report of the International Law Commission, Sixty-third session (2011), UN General Assembly Official Records, Sixty-sixth Session, Supplement No. 10, A/66/10/Add.1.

[84] Guideline 2.9.1. gives the definition: '"Approval" of an interpretative declaration means a unilateral statement made by a State or an international organization in reaction to an interpretative declaration in respect of a treaty formulated by another State or another international organization,

'considered it prudent not to expressly approve an interpretation given by another party'.[85] While this applies to the marked absence of examples of approving statements in response to declarations, a real assessment would require identifying practice of states actually conforming to an interpretation in another state's declaration, which is much more difficult to discover. Parenthetically it may be noted that the same problem bedevils any overall assessment of interpretative declarations, indeterminate influence being one of their main characteristics.

As noted above, interpretative statements may be made at various stages in treaty-making, including in the course of negotiations, at conclusion of treaties, and subsequently. Express approval may occur when an interpretation is advanced in the course of negotiation of a multilateral treaty, but such forms of interpretative declarations are not covered in the Guide.[86] Informal expressions of interpretation may occur if one state circulates an interpretation on a point in a treaty already in force and other states agree with that interpretation. The primary concern here, however, is responses to declarations made at signature or upon ratification, accession, etc, or subsequently.

The only two examples of approval given in the Guide were both positive statements by a single state in response to an interpretative declaration relating to a multilateral treaty.[87] Both are nuanced rather than outright approval, in one the response being taken as an opportunity to interpret the declaration in a particular way, in the other to emphasize that the declaration was only interpretative and not to be taken as a reservation.[88]

The key point to note here is that an affirmative response is described in the Guide as 'approval' to distinguish such response from 'acceptance' of a reservation. Acceptance of a reservation has the effect of the treaty taking effect between the reserving and accepting states with the reservation having a governing role. The Guide explains that 'approval' of an interpretative declaration 'expresses the idea of agreement or acquiescence without prejudging the legal effect actually produced'.[89]

3.5.2 Opposition to an interpretative declaration

The commentary in the Guide[90] notes that examples of negative reactions to an interpretative declaration, 'while not quite as exceptional as positive reactions, are

---

whereby the former State or organization expresses agreement with the interpretation formulated in that declaration.'

[85] Guideline 2.9.1, commentary para (1).

[86] See, for example, the account of the part of the 1951 Geneva Conference where, in negotiating the Convention Relating to Status of Refugees, the Conference President ruled that a delegate's statement on the meaning of 'return (refoulement)' was to be placed on record: *Sale v Haitian Centers Council* 509 US 155 (1993), at 184–87, considered further in Chapter 8, section 4.4.8.

[87] *Sale v Haitian Centers Council* 509 US 155 (1993), at paras (3)–(4).

[88] Guideline 2.9.1, commentary paras (3)–(4).   [89] Guideline 2.9.1, commentary para (6),

[90] Guideline 2.9.2. gives the definition: '"Opposition" to an interpretative declaration means a unilateral statement made by a State or an international organization in reaction to an interpretative declaration in respect of a treaty formulated by another State or another international organization, whereby the former State or organization disagrees with the interpretation formulated in the interpretative declaration, including by formulating an alternative interpretation.'

nonetheless sporadic'.[91] To give just one example here of a declaration and response, in the list of declarations and reservations accompanying the instrument of accession to the Vienna Convention deposited by Syria, the fourth item ('D') stated:

The Government of the Syrian Arab Republic interprets the provisions in article 52 as follows:

The expression 'the threat or use of force' used in this article extends also to the employment of economic, political, military and psychological coercion and to all types of coercion constraining a State to conclude a treaty against its wishes or its interests.[92]

The United Kingdom rejected the interpretation and drew attention to what it saw as the more authoritative treatment of the point:

The United Kingdom does not accept that the interpretation of Article 52 put forward by the Government of Syria correctly reflects the conclusions reached at the Conference of Vienna on the subject of coercion; the Conference dealt with this matter by adopting a Declaration on this subject which forms part of the Final Act....[93]

A response to an interpretative declaration may be thought necessary to protect the position on interpretation in relation to contracting states and potential parties as well as, or other than, the declarant. Such was evidently the case with this declared refusal by the UK to accept the interpretation placed on article 52 by Syria as the UK made a further statement which precluded treaty relations under this Convention between it and Syria:

The United Kingdom objects to the reservation entered by the Government of Syria in respect of the Annex to the Convention and does not accept the entry into force of the Convention as between the United Kingdom and Syria....[94]

3.5.3 Recharacterization of an interpretative declaration

The ILC reports that there are 'countless examples' of states objecting to purported interpretative declarations by asserting them to be reservations.[95] Horn gives examples of this type of response (as well as responses of the other kinds indicated above).[96] The same list of declarations and reservations accompanying the instrument of accession to the Vienna Convention deposited by Syria (considered above), provides an example in the USA's response. This expressed concern at the

---

[91] Guideline 2.9.2, commentary para (1).
[92] *Status of Multilateral Treaties Deposited with the Secretary-General of the United Nations,* UN document ST/LEG/SER.E/24 (2005), at p 380, now on the UN treaty database (electronic), Syrian Declaration D; and see the commentary to Guideline 2.9.2, listing this and other examples, including those relating to the UN Convention on the Law of the Sea 1982 which has provisions that prohibit reservations but authorize interpretative declarations.
[93] UN document ST/LEG/SER.E/24 (2005), at p 380.
[94] UN document ST/LEG/SER.E/24 (2005), at p 380.
[95] See Guideline 1.2, commentary para (14), fn 149, where a selection of examples is given.
[96] Horn, *Reservations and Interpretative Declarations to Multilateral Treaties,* Chapter 26.

Syrian interpretation but, characterizing it as a reservation, stated that in view of the USA's 'intention to reject treaty relations with the Syrian Arab Republic under all provisions in Part V to which reservations C and D relate, we do not consider it necessary at this time to object formally to those reservations'.[97]

A response to a purported interpretative declaration in the form of an assertion that the declaration is in fact a reservation is now described in the Guide as 'recharacterization', which is defined:

'Recharacterization' of an interpretative declaration means a unilateral statement made by a State or an international organization in reaction to an interpretative declaration in respect of a treaty formulated by another State or another international organization, whereby the former State or organization purports to treat the declaration as a reservation.'[98]

Recharacterization is somewhat different in nature from approval of, or opposition to, an interpretative declaration in that it does not directly engage the content of the message in the declaration so much as challenge its essential nature and consequent legal effects. The state making this challenge thus establishes its own position with regard to the status of the declaration and may need to follow this up by whatever action is appropriate in response to a reservation.

3.6 Effects of interpretative declarations

The effects of interpretative declarations are not stated in the Vienna rules. When the ILC was considering reservations in its work before the Vienna Conference, the Special Rapporteur (Waldock) observed: 'Statements of interpretation were not dealt with by the Commission in the present action for the simple reason that they are not reservations and appear to concern the interpretation rather than the conclusion of treaties.'[99] In the provisions on interpretation, however, no specific mention was made of such statements or declarations. It was left to be assumed that if made in connection with the conclusion of a treaty, and accepted as such by other parties, a declaration in a unilateral instrument will be admitted into consideration under article 31(2)(b). Likewise, statements or declarations made before the conclusion of a treaty may be contained in the preparatory work and therefore admissible in the circumstances set out in article 32 of the Vienna Convention.

In considering the significance of interpretative declarations in the interpretation of treaties, McRae considered that where a state is silent in the face of another state's interpretative declaration, such inaction could not be treated as acquiescence.[100] He

---

[97] *Status of Multilateral Treaties Deposited with the Secretary-General of the United Nations,* UN document ST/LEG/SER.E/24 (2005), at p 384, now on the UN treaty database (electronic).

[98] Guideline 2.9.3; the commentary to this guideline gives several examples of responses to interpretative declarations amounting to recharacterization.

[99] Fourth Report [1965] *Yearbook of the ILC,* vol II, p 49, para 2; the word 'action' in the ILC record appears to mean the 'section' of the draft.

[100] D M McRae, 'The Legal Effect of Interpretative Declarations' (1978) 49 BYBIL 155, at 169; and see M Benatar, 'From Probative Value to Authentic Interpretation: The Legal Effect of Interpretative Declarations' (2011) 44 *Revue Belge de Droit International* 170.

considered that the legal significance of interpretative declarations lay in the provision of evidence of intention in the light of which the treaty is to be interpreted.[101] It seems clear that this does not refer just to the unilateral intention of the declarant, as McRae notes that the response of other states becomes significant in determining what weight is to be attached to the interpretative declaration as evidence of meaning:

A State making an interpretative declaration, therefore, is taking the opportunity in advance to influence any subsequent interpretations of the treaty, the extent of that influence in part being affected by the reaction of other States to the declaration.[102]

Interpretative declarations have the nature of understandings as to meaning. A study of aspects of treaty-making prepared for the US Senate concluded that understandings are a means of clarification and reassurance.[103] This conclusion could be transposed to apply helpfully to interpretative declarations *mutatis mutandis:*

The actual effect of any particular proposed understanding may, of course, be debatable. What may seem to the Senate to be a reasonable interpretation, and therefore an understanding, might appear to the other country or countries involved to be an important modification, and therefore a reservation, particularly if it concerns an aspect of the agreement that is considered fundamental. If that is the conclusion of another party to a treaty, the mere characterization of a condition as an understanding rather than a reservation will do little to change that conclusion. True understandings are commonly used in the ratification of both multilateral and bilateral treaties as a means of clarification and reassurance rather than revision.[104]

The present Guide takes the same approach, stating:

An interpretative declaration does not modify treaty obligations. It may only specify or clarify the meaning or scope which its author attributes to a treaty or to certain provisions thereof and may, as appropriate, constitute an element to be taken into account in interpreting the treaty in accordance with the general rule of interpretation of treaties.[105]

It is, however, understandable that the Guide can offer little in the way of help on the effects of such declarations. The content of the Guide is firmly anchored in the Vienna Conventions on the Law of Treaties. The absence from those Conventions of 'parent' provisions on interpretative declarations, coupled with limited reference to them in court and arbitral practice, provides scant basis for guidelines.

3.6.1 *Effects of general agreement to an interpretative declaration*

Only where there is general agreement to a stated position on interpretation is the outcome reasonably clear. The Guide, somewhat cautiously, indicates that an interpretative declaration approved by all the contracting states 'may' constitute an

---

[101] McRae, 'The Legal Effect of Interpretative Declarations', at 169.
[102] McRae, at 169–70, citation and footnotes omitted.
[103] *Treaties and other International Agreements: The Role of the United States Senate*, Senate Committee on Foreign Relations, 106th Congress, *2d Session*, S PRT (2001), 106–71.
[104] *Treaties and other International Agreements: The Role of the United States Senate*, at 125–6.
[105] Guideline 4.7.1.

agreement regarding the interpretation of the treaty.[106] Hesitancy seems to derive from uncertainty as to which element of the general rule of interpretation in article 31 of the Vienna Convention is the appropriate link; that is, whether the product is an agreement between all the parties in connection with the conclusion of the treaty, a subsequent agreement, agreement through subsequent practice etc. This seems largely dependent on the way in which agreement of all relevant states has been established, but there seems little doubt that unanimous agreement by these states as to the meaning of a treaty provision must be taken into account in its interpretation.

3.6.2 *Effects of approval by only one state or fewer than all*

Much more difficult is assessing what account, if any, is to be taken of an interpretative declaration which has only limited approval, whether by stated response or in practice. The Guide stresses that 'an interpretative declaration may in no way modify "the legal effect of certain provisions of a treaty or of the treaty as a whole with respect to certain specific aspects".'[107] However, it also indicates that, as well as taking into account the declaration in the general sense of the conclusion noted above: '… account shall also be taken, as appropriate, of the approval of, or opposition to, the interpretative declaration, by other contracting States or contracting organizations.'[108]

Thus, for example, in the case of one state approving a declaration by another in relation to a multilateral treaty, the obvious question is whether, in such a situation, account is to be taken of this? The role of subsequent agreement in treaty interpretation is based on the principle that the parties to a treaty, being the ones entitled to change or terminate it, must axiomatically have the power to agree authoritatively what their treaty means.[109] Does this entail an underlying assumption that *all* parties to a multilateral treaty would need to assent to any subsequent agreement reached through a response to an interpretative declaration, or that what is envisaged is an interpretative trail being opened up by bilateral action, or that the result is merely a joint interpretative position?

An early formulation by the Permanent Court of International Justice referred to the interpretative power lying with the person or body who could 'modify' the treaty.[110] 'Modify' may have been terminology intended loosely to suggest 'amend' or simply 'change'. It was a use of wording long before the 1969 Vienna Convention established the clear distinction between 'amendment' (broadly, a change to a treaty open to all parties and prospective parties to it) and 'modification' (a change to a treaty made by two or more parties as between themselves alone).[111]

---

[106] Guideline 4.7.3.
[107] Guideline 4.7.1, commentary para (70), quoting from the definition of 'reservation' in Guideline 1.1.
[108] Guideline 4.7.1, para 2.
[109] See Chapter 6, section 3.1.2 below where Sinclair's analysis is set out of the proposition of the Permanent Court in the *Jaworzina* case that 'the right of giving an authoritative interpretation of a legal rule belongs solely to the person or body who has power to modify or suppress it', PCIJ Advisory Opinion of 6 December 1923, Series B no 8, at p 37.
[110] See preceding note.   [111] Articles 40 and 41.

Were a positive reaction to an interpretative declaration to be viewed as establishing a bilateral interpretation of a multilateral provision, there would be implications for other parties. What if a third state made an interpretative declaration indicating a different meaning in relation to the same treaty provision? If the third state's declaration were to be approved by a fourth state, would this suggest that one or other of the interpretations so established is wrong or that it amounts to a reservation?

It seems unlikely for it to be possible simply to treat an interpretation bilaterally established through declaration and response as being effectively a 'modification' of a multilateral treaty. This is because, within the scheme envisaged by the Vienna Convention and the Guide, modification is in the same realm as reservations—that is, *altering* or *adjusting* the legal effect of a treaty provision. In contrast, as indicated in the Guide, the role of an interpretative declaration is to *specify* or *clarify* meaning. Nevertheless, it is difficult to see a court or tribunal refusing to give some consideration to what is effectively an agreement between two parties on the meaning which they attach to a treaty unless the court or tribunal finds that they have gone beyond interpretation or there is insufficient evidence that the meaning is one which all parties accept.

In the case of approval of an interpretative declaration, the two or more states concerned understand the declaration not to amount to a reservation. The possibility of 'recharacterization' is a reflection of practice which accompanies a negative reaction to a declaration, rather than approval. Hence any court or tribunal faced with differing responses to an interpretative declaration will need to decide whether the purported interpretative declaration is just that or whether it must be treated as a reservation.

Where does this leave a court or tribunal faced with a typical 'mere' interpretative declaration, which is unquestionably not a reservation, is in an instrument clearly accepted by all other relevant states as connected with conclusion of a treaty, and which has not excited any opposition? The Guide gives accounts of differing views from the theoretical point of view on the extent to which attention may be paid to such a declaration.[112] The main difference of views is on whether the general rule of the Vienna Convention requires account to be taken of unilateral statements made in connection with the conclusion of a treaty only if the other relevant states accept the content of the statement or merely accept that the instrument containing the declaration is an instrument related to the treaty, a matter considered in relation to the appropriate element of the general rule below.[113]

As a unilateral statement, the content of such an interpretation is not binding without the assent of the other relevant states. As a statement of the position taken by the declarant state, there is a very strong case that it should be held to the interpretation if the other elements of treaty interpretation point in the same direction. Otherwise, such a declaration may be one among the elements to be considered in an interpretative exercise, its admissibility depending on whether it is classed

---

[112] Guideline 4.7.1, commentary paras (7)–(24).　　　[113] See Chapter 6, section 2.3.

as one of the elements in the general rule of interpretation or as supplementary means, and its weight to be assessed according to the extent to which it plays a part in showing the common understanding of the parties (and potential parties) to the treaty.

3.6.3 Decisions of courts and tribunals on interpretative declarations

The decisions of courts and tribunals on interpretative declarations shed more light on the interpretation of such declarations themselves than on how such declarations affect interpretation of treaties. The older decisions turn out to be addressing atypical declarations rather than 'plain' interpretative declarations relating to multilateral treaties, while more recent ones focus again on distinguishing interpretative declarations from reservations and whether the former are disguised formulations of the latter.

That a declaration establishing the position of the declarant state itself has interpretative relevance finds support in the Advisory Opinion of the ICJ on the *International Status of South West Africa* (1950):

Interpretations placed upon legal instruments by the parties to them, though not conclusive as to their meaning, have considerable probative value when they contain recognition by a party of its own obligations under an instrument. In this case the declarations of the Union of South Africa support the conclusions already reached by the Court.[114]

The point addressed in this part of the Opinion concerned statements made by the government of South Africa to the effect that it would continue to administer South-West Africa in the spirit of the mandate it had been given pursuant to the defunct Covenant of the League of Nations. The Court concluded that the declarations supported the interpretation it had established on other grounds. Not, therefore, an interpretative declaration associated with the conclusion of a treaty, the principle nevertheless transposes well to the present regime, as is accepted by the Guide.[115]

If the principle that a declarant should be held to their interpretation seems reasonably clear, little else has been revealed by case law about the interpretative role of declarations. Thus the outcome, in a more recent ICJ case, of argument over an interpretative declaration seems negative or at best inconclusive as to the general role of interpretative declarations. This arose in the case concerning *Maritime Delimitation in the Black Sea (Romania v Ukraine)* before the ICJ.[116] A central issue was the significance of an island off the coast of the two disputants ('Serpents' Island') for claims to the continental shelf and exclusive economic zone in those waters. In its interpretative declaration made on signature of the UN Convention

---

[114] *International Status of South West Africa*, Advisory Opinion of 11 July 1950, [1950] ICJ Reports 128, at 135–36.

[115] Guideline 4.7.1, commentary paras (25)–(26).

[116] ILC, Sixty-first session, Fourteenth Report on Reservations to Treaties by Alain Pellet, A/CN. 4/614, 2 April 2009, at paras 47–51, referring to the judgment of the ICJ of 3 February 2009.

on the Law of the Sea, and confirmed on ratification, Romania had declared in relation to article 121 of that Convention (the regime of islands), that:

...according to the requirements of equity—as it results from Articles 74 and 83 of the Convention on the Law of the Sea—the uninhabited islands without economic life can in no way affect the delimitation of the maritime spaces belonging to the mainland coasts of the coastal States.[117]

In an Additional Agreement to the Treaty on the Relations of Good Neighbourliness and Co-operation between Romania and Ukraine, both of 1997 and containing provisions on delimitation of maritime areas, it was agreed that among the principles for resolving the dispute would be 'the principle stated in article 121 of the United Nations Convention on the Law of the Sea of December 10, 1982, as applied in the practice of states and in international case jurisprudence'.[118] Romania argued that Ukraine's acceptance of this reference to Article 121 clearly indicated that the two States had agreed in 1997 that Serpents' Island could receive no other effect additional to those effects already produced by it on the delimitation of the territorial seas of the two parties. Ukraine invoked the ILC's work on interpretative declarations to support its contention that its silence in the face of Romania's declaration on article 121 could not amount to consent, there being no obligation to respond to such a declaration.[119] The ILC's Special Rapporteur subsequently noted that the ICJ 'seems to have admitted that point of view', but he left consideration of the implications of this to the promised study of the effects of interpretative declarations.[120] The Court had stated:

Finally, regarding Romania's declaration, quoted in paragraph 35 above, the Court observes that under Article 310 of UNCLOS, a State is not precluded from making declarations and statements when signing, ratifying or acceding to the Convention, provided these do not purport to exclude or modify the legal effect of the provisions of UNCLOS in their application to the State which has made a declaration or statement. The Court will therefore apply the relevant provisions of UNCLOS as interpreted in its jurisprudence, in accordance with Article 31 of the Vienna Convention on the Law of Treaties of 23 May 1969. Romania's declaration as such has no bearing on the Court's interpretation.[121]

It is difficult to see that much can be deduced from the Court's statement. It effectively confirms that silence does not automatically signify acquiescence to an interpretative declaration. It may also be seen as going a little further than that in as much as Ukraine's specific agreement to application of article 121 of UNCLOS was not seen as encompassing any approval of Romania's declared interpretation of that provision. Hence it is not obvious what role the declaration may have had other than perhaps as an open invitation to any other state to agree specifically with it.

---

[117] [2009] ICJ Reports 61, at 76, para 35.
[118] [2009] ICJ Reports 61, at 75, para 33(a).
[119] ICJ, Verbatim Record, 12 September 2008 CR 2008/29, paras 63–68.
[120] Fourteenth Report on Reservations to Treaties (see above), paras 50–51.
[121] [2009] ICJ Reports 61, at 78, para 42.

Noting the Court's observation as 'rather peremptory' and as casting 'serious doubt on the utility of interpretative declarations', the commentary in the Guide sees the inclusion in the judgment of the words that the declaration 'as such' has no bearing on the Court's interpretation as allowing the possibility that, while not binding, Romania's unilateral interpretation is not precluded from having an effect 'as a means of proof or an element that might corroborate the Court's interpretation "in accordance with Article 31 of the Vienna Convention on the Law of Treaties".'[122] The Guide finds further traces of such an approach in a case at the European Court of Human Rights and in pleadings by states at the ICJ putting forward interpretative declarations as supportive in a 'subdued manner'.[123]

One British case in which an interpretative declaration played an assisting role concerned the issue whether international law established universal jurisdiction over internationally defined acts of torture and required a state to afford civil remedies where torture was alleged to have been committed in another state's territory.[124] The claimants had relied on arguments based on US cases, but the House of Lords noted that the USA when ratifying the Torture Convention in 1984 had communicated its understanding that the Convention required a party 'to provide a private right of action for damages only for acts of torture committed in territory under the jurisdiction of that State Party'.[125] The court noted that that understanding was not a reservation, had provoked no dissent, and was expressly recognized by Germany as not touching upon the obligations of the USA as a party to the Convention.[126] Hence the court concluded that it was unlikely that the USA would now subscribe to a rule of international law requiring exercise of universal jurisdiction for civil claims in respect of torture committed outside the forum state. However, even this use of an interpretative declaration was in support of an argument regarding the formation of a customary rule of international law, rather than on a specific issue of treaty interpretation.

3.7 Conclusion on interpretative declarations

It is difficult to go much further in summarizing the effects of interpretative declarations than did Waldock as Special Rapporteur on the law of treaties in 1965. He referred to the draft provisions amplifying the context of a treaty so as to include instruments related to the treaty and drawn up in connection with its conclusion, provisions on subsequent agreements and subsequent practice, special meanings, and further means of interpretation, including preparatory work and the circumstances of the treaty's conclusion, noting that:

Any of these provisions may come into play in appreciating the legal effect of an interpretative declaration in a given case...the legal significance of an interpretative

---

[122] Guideline 4.7.1, commentary paras (28).
[123] Guideline 4.7.1, commentary paras (29)–(30).
[124] *Jones v Ministry of Interior Al-Mamlaka Al-Arabiya AS Saudiya (the Kingdom of Saudi Arabia)* [2006] UKHL 26.
[125] [2006] UKHL 26, at para 20.   [126] [2006] UKHL 26, at para 20.

statement must always depend on the particular circumstances in which it is made.[127]

The present Guide slightly improves on the situation by clarifying the nature of declarations and suggesting practices which might lead to more activity by way of response to interpretative declarations, and particularly identifying conditional interpretative declarations as apt for recharacterization as reservations.

4. Preparatory Materials

Definitions of 'preparatory work' as a key concept in treaty interpretation have been given in section 3.4 of Chapter 1. However, McNair's characterization there of this term as 'an omnibus expression which is used rather loosely' is sufficient evidence of its uncertain content.[128] The present section gives indications of *what* may be admissible in treaty interpretation as preparatory work. *When* and *how* preparatory work is to be used are matters considered in Chapter 8.

Issues as to what is admissible as preparatory work include: how far back an interpreter may go in the history of a treaty; whether documents relating to another treaty can be included; whether preparatory work can be differentially admissible, that is (for example) opposable to other parties which participated in the negotiations but not to states which have only been involved in the treaty processes occurring after conclusion; whether the particular negotiating procedure can suggest that some documents are admissible while others are to be excluded; and whether documents from a unilateral source can ever be admitted.

4.1 How far does preparatory work trace history?

There is no single prescription for how far back in the history of a treaty or its provisions the interpreter is to delve for guidance. Courts and tribunals tend to seize on anything that looks helpful and they assess admissibility by applying the principle that clarificatory information must attest to a meaning which can be said to have been accepted (at least implicitly) by prospective parties. Individual recollections and memoirs do not qualify. In the latter category, Proust is reported to have been interested in the process of negotiation of the 1919 treaties in Paris. When Harold Nicholson told him that the conference's committees usually started their work at 10 a.m., Proust interrupted him to press for more detailed information about what preceded the start of the meetings.[129] Preparatory work does not extend to considering the effect of what the negotiators had for breakfast (although

---

[127] [1965] *Yearbook of the ILC,* vol II, p 49, para 2.

[128] Dictionary definitions do not capture the rather open-ended character of the term: see, for example the use made by an arbitral tribunal of *Black's Law Dictionary* (7th edn) defining *travaux préparatoires* as '(French "preparatory works") Materials used in preparing the ultimate form of an agreement or statute, and esp. of an international treaty, materials constituting a legislative history', *Pope & Talbot v Canada (Award in respect of Damages)* (NAFTA) (2002) 41 ILM 1347, at 1353, para 28, fn 13.

[129] M Macmillan, *Peacemakers* (London: John Murray, 2001), 160.

an airline's breakfast menu was invoked as a contextual analogy in interpreting the 'Warsaw Convention' on carriage by air[130]). The point was put rather more formally by the US Supreme Court, but in a manner reflecting well the position in international practice (albeit this is only by analogy with international law as the agreement in issue was between states of the USA):

It has often been said that, when the meaning of a treaty is not clear, recourse may be had to the negotiations, preparatory works, and diplomatic correspondence of the contracting parties to establish its meaning...But that rule has no application to oral statements made by those engaged in negotiating the treaty which were not embodied in any writing and were not communicated to the government of the negotiator or to its ratifying body.[131]

4.1.1 What illuminates a common understanding?

The principle that preparatory work extends to material which can be characterized as 'illuminating a common understanding' is often applied only implicitly, but it was spelt out in the *Iron Rhine* arbitration (2005).[132] One issue in that case was the nature of the bargain underlying the 1839 Treaty of Separation between Belgium and the Netherlands. Was the right of transit granted by that treaty to Belgium an exchange for Limburg becoming part of the Netherlands, or had Limburg in fact been swapped for part of Luxembourg? The tribunal found that extracts from the extended negotiations before the 1839 treaty did not have the character of *travaux préparatoires* on which the tribunal could 'safely rely as a supplementary means of interpretation under Article 32 of the Vienna Convention'.[133] This was because although the extracts may have shown the desire or understanding of one or other of the negotiators at particular moments, they did not 'serve the purpose of illuminating a common understanding as to the meaning' of the various provisions in issue.[134] The Tribunal was of the view that there were very many elements in play and no single one was determinative. Nevertheless, the Tribunal stated that it would 'remain mindful of the circumstances of the conclusion of each of the applicable treaties, as required in Article 32 of the Vienna Convention'.[135]

4.1.2 Tracing a historical line

In the *LaGrand* case, the ICJ had to decide whether its order indicating provisional measures was binding so that by failing to take all measures at its disposal to ensure that Walter LaGrand was not executed pending the final decision of the Court, the USA was in breach of such obligations.[136] The Court concluded it was

---

[130] *Corocraft v Pan American Airways* [1969] 1 QB 616, at 633; see further Chapter 9, section 4.8.
[131] *State of Arizona v State of California* 292 US 341, at 359–60 (1934).
[132] *Arbitration regarding the Iron Rhine ("IJzeren Rijn") Railway (Belgium/Netherlands),* (2005) XXVII RIAA 35, p 63 para 48.
[133] (2005) XXVII RIAA 35, p 63 para 48.   [134] (2005) XXVII RIAA 35, p 63 para 48.
[135] (2005) XXVII RIAA 35, p 63 para 48.
[136] *LaGrand (Germany v USA)* [2001] ICJ Reports 466, Judgment of 27 June 2001, and see further Chapter 9, sections 4.4, 4.5, and 4.9.

not necessary to resort to the preparatory work in order to determine the meaning of the relevant provision of the Statute as this could be achieved by applying the general rule. A particularly significant element in this process was that the object and purpose of the Statute was to enable the Court to settle international disputes by binding and effective judgments. Nevertheless, the Court did examine relevant preparatory work of the Statute and attached significance to finding that it did not preclude the conclusion that such orders had binding force.[137] The ICJ's Statute is identical to that of its predecessor, the PCIJ (except for references to organs of the UN rather than the League of Nations). The Court therefore looked back to the stage at which a proposal had been made for inclusion in the draft Statute of the PCIJ of an article on provisional measures, the text being based on an earlier bilateral treaty between the USA and Sweden.[138] The Court then followed the drafting history, particularly in the aspects relevant to the apparent differences between the French and English texts. Thus the Court treated preparatory work as extending to indications of the origin of the text not only in the predecessor treaty to that under consideration, but also to the more remote bilateral source of the wording. Such historical tracing of a provision is a common occurrence in treaty interpretation.

4.1.3 *Looking at the main source*

It may not always be feasible to implement the principle that preparatory work can extend to the actual origin of particular wording, nor will it always be particularly helpful. What may prove a significant factor in assessing whether something is admissible preparatory work is whether an interpreter can identify in it a main source of a text. In the case of one-off multilateral treaties, where a sequence of work by ad hoc preparatory bodies has been followed by a diplomatic conference, there is a risk that the records may be diffuse. The later stages, such as a preparatory commission and diplomatic conference have increasingly had their records collected; but the contribution of earlier work, particularly that of nongovernmental organizations (sometimes only having an input at national level), is unlikely to be fully recorded in the treaty depositary's archives.[139]

In contrast, many a modern treaty text has been worked up under the aegis of an international organization where the records are likely to be well maintained and disseminated. However, even at the time of the conference which produced the Vienna Convention, there was some uncertainty whether the work of the ILC itself would be regarded as admissible preparatory work. Rosenne, a greatly respected authority in his work outside the Commission as well as within it, doubted whether

---

[137] *LaGrand,* [2001] ICJ Reports 466, at para 104.

[138] *LaGrand,* at para 105.

[139] Some records which were originally published by the depositary, but not very widely circulated, have become more available thanks to the availability of materials electronically . For example, the records of the 1944 Chicago conference on international civil aviation were originally published by the US State Department, but have become much more widely available after transfer by the International Civil Aviation Organization to its website.

the ILC's records of its work on a treaty constituted preparatory work.[140] He saw the Commission's drafts as 'rather remote from diplomatic conferences', another significant factor in his view being that members of the Commission acted in a personal capacity rather than as state representatives.[141] On the substantive work of the Commission, he saw its records as contributing to an understanding of the development of the Commission's collective thoughts, but noted the possibility that states might have a different understanding upon adoption of a treaty provision.[142] Rosenne did, however, end his statement of doubts by indicating he would not wish to prejudice the status of the ILC's records in any concrete situation.

In the same ILC debate, Yasseen (the Chairman, but speaking as a member of the Commission) expressed a very different view. Although members of the Commission were obviously not acting as representatives of parties to a treaty, all the material which the parties had had before them when drafting the final text was relevant preparatory work when it came to interpretation. He noted that at a diplomatic conference working on a draft prepared by the ILC the representatives of states quite often adopted articles as they stood, taking account of the Commission's commentaries. He considered that the Commission's work formed part of the preparatory work for conventions concluded on the basis of its drafts.[143] Subsequent history and practice has overwhelmingly tended to follow Yasseen. Particularly in the field of treaty interpretation, liberal use is made of the guidance to be derived from the records of the ILC, which was the main source of the learning on treaty interpretation at the Vienna Conference and fed into the Convention's provisions.[144]

Given the nature of treaty interpretation, if the dialectic of negotiation is helpful in analysis of possible meanings, one can expect arguments and stated understandings to be attributed to their sources. That certainly is the approach taken in this book and, it is suggested, it illuminates a characteristic of the task of treaty interpretation, that is the need to deploy a capacity for evaluation of a range of materials and for balancing of arguments and approaches. Of course, if one admits records of ILC debates into the canon of preparatory work for the purpose

---

[140] [1966] *Yearbook of the ILC*, vol I, part II, p 201, para 35.
[141] [1966] *Yearbook of the ILC*, vol I, part II, p 201, para 35.
[142] [1966] *Yearbook of the ILC*, vol I, part II, p 201, para 35.
[143] [1966] *Yearbook of the ILC,* vol I, part II, p 205, para 25. It should also be recalled that the Final Act of the Vienna Conference notes that the Conference had before it the relevant records of the International Law Commission (Final Act, para 11(a), Documents of the Conference, p 283, at 284). Further, the Official Records of the two sessions of the Conference each has a note immediately before the start of the summary records stating: 'For the reports of the successive Special Rapporteurs on the law of treaties and the discussion of the topic in the International Law Commission, see the *Yearbooks of the International Law Commission* for the years 1949 to 1966' (Official Records, First Session p xxxi, Second Session p xxiii). Hence adoption of the text of the Vienna rules by the conference with very little change proceeded on the basis of work of the ILC drawn to the attention of the participants in the Vienna conference.
[144] See, eg, *Kasikili/Sedudu Island (Botswana/Namibia)* [1999] ICJ Reports 1045, at 1076, para 49 (quoted in Chapter 6, section 4 below) and the European Court of Human Rights in *Bankovic & others v Belgium & others*, App no 52207/99, Decision on Admissibility (2001), para 18.

of interpreting the Vienna rules, one is likely to be led to admit the documents on which those debates were centred. But the Special Rapporteur (Waldock) in his reports also gave his sources. One could hardly describe all the case law and practice to which he refers as preparatory work for particular provisions of the Vienna Convention; but the work of earlier Special Rapporteurs (in particular Fitzmaurice), or the learning contained in the commentaries on the earlier Harvard draft articles on the law of treaties, can in appropriate circumstances be invoked to assist in clarifying the meaning or application or a particular element in the Vienna rules if no more contemporary wisdom has been found. However, it is suggested here that this would be as supplementary means in article 32 of the Vienna Convention (which are not confined to preparatory work and circumstances of conclusion), rather than by a lengthening thread of connective tissue within the preparatory work.

4.1.4 *Using all material available to negotiators*

It may seem a contradiction of the last observation above to take up Yasseen's guide to what is admissible as preparatory work as being all material that was available to the treaty negotiators. But this should be taken as meaning all of the documents gathered into the negotiating process, and thus available to the negotiators collectively, rather than the wealth of outside material that they may have individually been able to use.

In a recent example of identification of such material, the *Chilean Price Band System* case, a World Trade Organization (WTO) Panel found admissible the reports of various agriculture committees established over the years by participants in the 1947 General Agreement on Tariffs and Trade (GATT).[145] The Panel accepted these documents as an aid to interpretation of the terms 'variable import levy' and 'minimum import price' in the 1994 GATT, finding that the treaty's text and context alone did not enable them to determine the meaning of those terms without ambiguity.[146] The Panel found that the documents were 'strictly speaking not part of the preparatory work' but were admissible under article 32 of the Vienna Convention.[147] This was partly on the basis that they formed part of the 'circumstances of conclusion of the treaty' (article 32 of the Vienna Convention), but also in reliance on Yasseen's statement above.[148] The Appellate Body considered that the Panel had not properly applied article 32 of the Vienna Convention, though from the Appellate Body's subsequent focus on the general

---

[145] *Chile—Price Band System and Safeguard Measures Relating to Certain Agricultural Products* WT/DS207/R, 3 May 2002, paras 7.35–7.36.

[146] *Chile—Price Band System*, at para 7.36.

[147] *Chile—Price Band System*, at para 7.35.

[148] See [1966] *Yearbook of the ILC,* vol. I, Part II, p 205, para 25: 'But the very nature of a convention as an act of will made it essential to take into account all the work which had led to the formation of that will—all the material which the parties had had before them when drafting the final text.'

rule of interpretation, this criticism may have related more to the use of supplementary means than admission of material which was not acknowledged not to be preparatory work.[149]

In fact, however, Yasseen was supporting the view that the work of the ILC was preparatory work of the various conventions to which their labours led. Thus the material in issue was rather different from that considered by the Panel in the *Chilean Price Band System* case. Given that international courts and tribunals tend to recount the content of documents which can be seen to be relevant to the development of a particular treaty provision, admissibility may well be a matter of whether something can be seen as generally within the scope of article 32 of the Vienna Convention without further precision. For documents which are less closely connected with the eventual wording of a provision of a treaty, their consideration as part of the circumstances of conclusion of the treaty depends very much on the assessment by the interpreter of the evidence that they had some significant contribution to make in relation to inclusion of the terms in the treaty.

4.2 Whether preparatory work can be differentially admissible

The principle that there is only one 'correct' interpretation of a treaty points firmly to the conclusion that there can only be one set of preparatory work which is admissible whoever is interpreting the treaty. Although this does not appear to have been an issue recently, it was not always thought so obvious. In considering the citation of preparatory work against what he described as 'third parties', McNair referred to the situation where states which had not participated in the negotiation of a treaty had become parties by accession.[150] Accession, though more widely used now, was commonly the means by which states which had not participated in the negotiation of a treaty became party to it. He pointed to a case at the Permanent Court where material was excluded because three of the states before the Court had not participated in the relevant work of the Versailles conference.[151] This did not, however, deal with the question of whether confidential documents could have been opposable as preparatory work to other parties which *had* participated in the negotiations and *did* have access to them. To allow differential admissibility in modern times would be inconsistent with the principle stated above of there being one correct interpretation, and also somewhat out of line with the ethos of avoiding secret treaties. While there may be good reasons to

---

[149] *Chile—Price Band System and Safeguard Measures Relating to Certain Agricultural Products* WT/DS207/AB/R, 23 September 2002, para 230, and see fn 206, which leaves it unclear whether the Appellate Body disagreed on admissibility of the material or simply ignored it because it felt able to reach an interpretation without it.

[150] McNair, *The Law of Treaties*, at 420–1.

[151] McNair, at 420–1, referring to the *Case concerning the Jurisdiction of the International Commission of the River Oder*, PCIJ Rep, Series A, No 26 (1929); and see S Rosenne, 'Travaux Préparatoires' (1963) 12 ICLQ 1378.

respect the confidentiality of position statements and of the bargaining strengths of each party in the process of negotiation of a treaty, those factors would not provide any justification for later differential admissibility of material as preparatory work according to whether parties to a dispute had or had not been involved in the negotiation of a treaty in issue.

With the greater availability of preparatory work, it has been suggested that any rule that preparatory work may not be invoked if one or more of the litigating parties was not involved in the negotiations has been 'quietly rescinded'.[152]

4.3 Documents associated with treaty negotiations

Some documents that are prepared during treaty negotiations are not specifically intended to contribute to particular provisions in the eventual text of the treaty, even though related to its subject. An example is provided in the WTO *Gambling* case.[153] During the negotiation of the General Agreement on Trade in Services 1994 (GATS), one of the issues that arose was how states would define their commitments in relation to particular services. Since each state would draw up its own schedule of commitments in terms appropriate to its specific wishes, this was not a matter that would be elaborated in the treaty. Nevertheless, in an attempt to encourage some degree of standardization, the GATT secretariat prepared two documents during the negotiations. One was numbered W/120 and was entitled 'Services Sectoral Classification List' (1991), containing elements comparable to those in a United Nations compilation (the 'Provisional Central Product Classification'). The other was described as an 'Explanatory Note'. It became known as the '1993 Scheduling Guidelines', covering what items should be put in a state's schedule of commitments and how they should be entered.[154]

The WTO Appellate Body found that these documents were not part of the context of the GATS as they had not been accepted by all the parties at the time of conclusion of the treaty as related to it. The Explanatory Note had stated that it was only intended to be of assistance and not an authoritative interpretation of the GATS.[155] Nor could it be shown that use of the documents revealed an interpretative agreement. However, the Appellate Body did accept that both documents were admissible under article 32 of the Vienna Convention, finding supporting arguments to show that they were preparatory work and circumstances relevant to the conclusion of the GATS.

The documents in this example were different from Explanatory Reports of the kind that accompany Council of Europe Conventions or the article-by-article

---

[152] Rosenne, 'Travaux Préparatoires' at 1380.
[153] *United States—Measures affecting the cross-border supply of gambling and betting services,* WT/DS285/AB/R, Report of Appellate Body, 7 April 2005, and see Chapter 8, sections 4.3.1, 4.4.1, and 4.4.6 for fuller consideration of this case.
[154] WT/DS285/AB/R, Report of Appellate Body, 7 April 2005, at paras 172–73.
[155] WT/DS285/AB/R, Report of Appellate Body, 7 April 2005, at para 176.

commentary provided by the ILC for its draft articles. Those clearly relate to interpretation of the treaties with which they are associated. The Reports look to be 'context' by virtue of their endorsement at the time of conclusion of the treaties, while the ILC commentaries remain part of the preparatory work. Given that article 32 of the Vienna Convention instances preparatory work and circumstances of conclusion as prominent examples of a wider (but not particularized) range of supplementary means of interpretation, it seems likely that courts and tribunals will tend to use a broad-brush approach. If they do not find documents related to the treaty to be context, they will admit them as preparatory work or part of the circumstances of conclusion, or otherwise as supplementary means if sufficiently closely connected to the preparation of a treaty and having a direct bearing on the interpretation and application of the treaty.

4.4 Admissibility of documents from a unilateral source

The admission of material generated by one party needs to be carefully approached in the light of the principle that preparatory work should illuminate a common understanding of the agreement, not unilateral hopes and inclinations. Obviously where unilateral material has been specifically endorsed, such as a document proposing an amendment to a draft treaty provision which is then adopted, it becomes part of the preparatory work.

In some instances, international courts and tribunals have looked to truly unilateral material, such as explanations given to a legislative body when a state is preparing to ratify a treaty.[156] Explanation of this in clear terms of the material being preparatory work is hard to find. It may be possible to introduce the material on some other basis, skirting round the question of whether it forms preparatory work. For example, in *Mondev v USA* an International Centre for Settlement of Investment Disputes (ICSID) arbitral tribunal had to decide whether the minimum standard of treatment of an alien corporation and the requirement of according 'fair and equitable treatment', which were guaranteed in the relevant treaty, were a reflection of numerous bilateral investment treaties containing concordant terminology.[157] The USA had repeatedly informed its Senate that numerous bilateral investment treaties, as well as the NAFTA treaty in issue in the particular case, were intended to incorporate principles of customary international law.[158] The tribunal held that whether or not statements by a party to its own legislature could

---

[156] See, eg, *Belilos v Switzerland*, ECtHR case no 20–1986/118/167, judgment of 23 March 1988, paras 31–32 and 48, where the European Court of Human Rights took account of Swiss preparatory work regarding its declaration: '...the Court recognises that it is necessary to ascertain the original intention of those who drafted the declaration. In its view, the documents show that Switzerland originally contemplated making a formal reservation but subsequently opted for the term "declaration". Although the documents do not make the reasons for the change of nomenclature entirely clear, they do show that the Federal Council has always been concerned to avoid the consequences which a broad view of the right of access to the courts...would have...' (para 48).

[157] Case No. ARB(AF)/99/2, Award of 11 October 2002.

[158] Case No. ARB(AF)/99/2, at para 111.

constitute preparatory work 'they can certainly shed light on the purposes and approaches taken to the treaty, and thus can evidence *opinio juris*'.[159]

In approaching this conclusion, the tribunal mentioned two cases as ones where the potential of unilateral material to constitute preparatory work had been considered.[160] In the first of these, the ICJ had taken the Iranian legislative records as confirmation that Iran's declaration accepting the jurisdiction of the ICJ was to exclude disputes relating to treaties accepted by it before ratification of the declaration.[161] Where, as in such a situation, a domestic document is part of the preparatory work of what is essentially a unilateral act related to a treaty, there is a more obvious justification for its admission.[162]

The ICJ did admit and consider material of unilateral origin in the *Oil Platforms* case.[163] In issue was a treaty provision that 'there shall be firm and enduring peace and sincere friendship between the United States...and Iran'. In determining that this amounted to an objective rather than a specific obligation, the Court found confirmation of this in a memorandum sent by the US State Department to the US embassy in China explaining the same wording in a treaty negotiated in the same series as that with Iran. It found further confirmation in the message of the Secretary of State transmitting several treaties of the same kind to the Senate for advice and consent to ratification.[164] The Court had expressly referred to articles 31 and 32 of the Vienna Convention. Although it did not pin this material to article 32, its admission under article 32 seems the reasonable conclusion from the Court's position in the judgment on this point and from the sequence of interpretative argument. It is to be noted, however, that the US documents were introduced by both parties in the case. Their admissibility consequently raised less of an issue.

More questionable as preparatory work, but nevertheless sometimes admitted as interpretative material, are reports or records of negotiations drawn up during or after the process of conclusion of a treaty. These may include commentaries on the treaty prepared during or after that process. For example, in the *US–UK Heathrow Airport User Charges Arbitration,* a commentary prepared by a British government lawyer for restricted circulation immediately after a bilateral negotiation was disclosed in the course of discovery of documents.[165] The USA referred to it and the Tribunal quoted it in its award.[166] Admission of such material is not always on the basis that it is preparatory work, or not solely on that basis. A commentary prepared during negotiations but connected with the conclusion of a treaty (for example, by being approved by representatives of signatory states) may form part

---

[159] Case No. ARB(AF)/99/2, at para 111. This conclusion might suggest that the material would more appropriately be admitted to consideration under article 31(3)(c) of the Vienna Convention (relevant rules of international law).

[160] Case No. ARB(AF)/99/2, at para 111.

[161] *Anglo–Iranian Oil Company Case (Preliminary Objections)* [1952] ICJ Reports 93 at 106–7.

[162] See, eg, *Belilos v Switzerland* and *Anglo-Iranian Oil Company* case, fn 121 above.

[163] *Case concerning Oil Platforms (Islamic Republic of Iran v United States of America) (Preliminary Objection)* [1996] ICJ Reports 803.

[164] [1996] ICJ Reports 803, at 814, para 29.

[165] 102 ILR 215, at 292–93, Award of 30 November 1992.   [166] 102 ILR 215, at 292.

of the preparatory work or may come within the context of the treaty as set out in article 31(2) of the Vienna Convention.[167] Somewhat different is a set of explanations prepared unilaterally within one state as part of the parliamentary process for approval of a treaty before ratification. Such material will not commonly be expressly approved by other parties to the treaty, but where presented to an arbitral by one such other party it may be viewed by the tribunal as admissible.[168]

[167] See, for example, the confirmatory use made of the Explanatory Report on the Convention on the Transfer of Sentenced Persons that had been submitted to the Committee of Ministers of the Council of Europe in *R v Secretary of State for the Home Department, ex parte Read* [1989] AC 1014, at 1052, where the House of Lords regarded the Report as admissible both as part of the preparatory work and under article 31 of the Vienna Convention.

[168] See *HICEE B.V. v Slovak Republic*, PCA Case No. 2009-11, Partial Award, 23 May 2011 where Dutch Explanatory Notes were admitted on presentation to the tribunal by Slovakia, principally on the basis that preparatory work and circumstances of conclusion were not the exclusive supplementary means of interpretation envisaged in article 32 of the Vienna Convention: see Chapter 8, section 4.5.4 below; cf consideration of detailed accounts of negotiation of a bilateral agreement retained in the archives of one of the parties: *Churchill Mining PLC and Planet Mining Pty Ltd v Republic of Indonesia* ICSID Case No. ARB/12/14 and 12/40 (Decision on Jurisdiction, 24 February 2014), at paras 208–30.

4

Who Uses the Vienna Convention
to Interpret Treaties?

...it is an established principle that the right of giving an authoritative interpretation of a legal rule belongs solely to the person or body who has power
to modify or suppress it.[1]

1. Introduction

In the present context, the principle underlying the above proposition of the
PCIJ is that the parties to a treaty ultimately control its interpretation. One
significant effect which this has in treaty interpretation is to underline the
importance of two elements in article 31(3) of the Vienna Convention. The
heavy emphasis which some courts and tribunals place on the ordinary meaning, context, and object and purpose in paragraph (1) of article 31 might lead to
the belief that subsequent agreement of the parties on interpretation of a treaty
provision, and subsequent practice establishing such an agreement, are subsidiary elements in the general rule of interpretation or only come into play if the
ordinary meaning is unclear. That is not the case. The importance attached to
subsequent practice, in particular, is a distinctive feature of treaty interpretation,
and subsequent practice and subsequent agreements have their full place in the
general rule of interpretation.

The principle in the quotation was mentioned in one of the debates at the ILC
on the draft Vienna rules.[2] But it should not be taken as indicating that agreement
between the parties is the *only* means of achieving an authoritative interpretation.

---

[1] *Delimitation of the Polish–Czechoslovakian Frontier (Question of Jaworzina)* PCIJ Advisory
Opinion, Series B, No 8, p 37; for uses of the terms 'authoritative' and 'authentic', and possible limitations on the interpretative role of the parties' understandings, see Chapter 6, section 1.1; but for the
different uses of 'authentic' and 'authoritative' contrasting finalization of a treaty text and the status
of a particular language or languages where the treaty is in more than one language, see Chapter 9,
section 2 below.

[2] See, eg, Mr Ruda 765th meeting, 14 July 1964, [1964] *Yearbook of the ILC*, p 277, para 34:
'Interpretation occurred at two different levels. First, as between States, the only legally valid interpretation of a treaty was the authentic interpretation by the parties to the treaty. The other level was that
of interpretation by arbitration, for which there were fundamental principles...'.

For they have often agreed that differences that may arise between them over interpretation and application of a treaty are to be resolved by a third party. True, an interpretation by the parties can trump all other interpretations, as happens occasionally when an interpretation in an arbitral award or judicial judgment is displaced by subsequent agreement;[3] but this could as readily be viewed as an amendment to the treaty as an interpretation displacing a judicial one. This distinction may be significant for treaties implemented in national legal systems, as some would require constitutional procedures to be followed for an amendment but could apply an interpretation without such measures.

Leaving principle to one side, however, the answer to the question 'who most frequently interprets treaties' is that it is the parties to the treaty themselves. In reality this means in the case of each state party to a treaty, the government, its legal advisers and officials, the state's legislature or courts, lawyers, and nongovernmental bodies.[4] There is no universally applicable system, each state's processes being governed by its constitution and legal system. Such unilateral interpretation must, however, reflect faithfully obligations in the agreement between the parties, defects in a state's domestic law being no defence if a party breaches these obligations.[5]

It is, of course, almost too obvious to mention that most treaty provisions that are in daily use are applied with little need to undertake any formal exercise of interpretation. If, however, the parties differ over interpretation, they most commonly discuss their difference and negotiate its resolution. The outcome may be an explicit agreement adopting an interpretation in, for example, an exchange of notes, an amendment to the treaty, or some less formal record of their interpretation, such as an agreed minute, or memorandum of understanding in language not constituting a treaty but forming the basis for actual practice which will then constitute an effective interpretation under article 31(3)(b) of the Vienna Convention.[6]

Thus internationally, issues over treaty interpretation will commonly be a matter for discussion, negotiation, and agreement between states or for resolution within an international organization, with judicial or arbitral determination covering only

---

[3] See, eg, *Beagle Channel Arbitration and subsequent agreement between Chile and Argentina following Papal mediation*, Arbitral Awards at (1978) 17 ILM 738 and *Argentina–Chile Negotiation and Conclusion of Border Dispute Agreement* (1985) 24 ILM 1, and L Lindsley, 'The Beagle Channel Settlement: Vatican Mediation Resolves a Century-Old Dispute' (1987) 29 *J Church & St* 435, and see *Pope & Talbot v Canada*, cited at the end of section 2.1 below.

[4] Those regularly involved in interpretation of treaties on a particular subject, including officials in international organizations, may develop something of a collective approach: see I Johnstone, 'Treaty Interpretation: the Authority of Interpretive Communities' (1990–91) 12 *Michigan JIL* 371; for example, see the extensive study, literature, and case law on tax treaties considered in F Engelen, *Interpretation of Tax Treaties under International Law* (Amsterdam: IBFD Publications BV, 2004); on 'Diverse Treaty Interpreters and Interpretive Communities' generally, see M Waibel, 'Uniformity versus specialization (2): A uniform regime of treaty interpretation?' Chapter 13 in C J Tams, A Tzanakopoulos, and others (eds), *Research Handbook On The Law Of Treaties* (Cheltenham: Edward Elgar, 2014), 397–405.

[5] See Vienna Convention, articles 26 and 27.

[6] See *US–UK Heathrow Airport User Charges* Arbitration 102 ILR 215, Award of 30 November 1992 and Chapter 3, section 2.4.2 above.

a small minority of cases. However, the test which many lawyers use in giving advice on matters of international law is what an independent tribunal would find the law to be.[7] This test may be particularly appropriate where no specific international court, tribunal, or other body is identifiable as having competence to give an authoritative ruling in relation to a particular treaty. Thus the idea is to predict what a putative arbitral tribunal composed of persons competent to apply the Vienna rules would decide.

The purpose of this chapter is not to identify particular authoritative adjudicators on questions of interpretation of treaties, or to suggest the relative value of the determinations provided by different tribunals and courts. It is rather to give an indication of which courts, tribunals, or other bodies may yield up materials containing arguments and examples which could assist in understanding the Vienna rules and may provide models, ideas, or analogies for use in differing circumstances. It must be clearly recognized that these are not producers of binding precedents, and their arguments and solutions are to be regarded as the best on offer if they assist or, in diplomatic parlance, à *toutes fins utiles*.

This chapter therefore examines factors to be taken into account when using materials from these varied sources. International courts and tribunals are often part of international institutions. Even international arbitral tribunals are commonly associated with some organization (however loosely), unless set up by agreement as free-standing. However, since the emphasis in the present work is, when considering international interpretation, on examples provided by international courts and tribunals rather than international organizations, they are considered separately, after some considerations affecting international organizations. Factors which generally affect the approaches taken by courts in national legal systems and their use of the Vienna rules are also considered here; but it is a major premise of treaty interpretation that there is no reason for different application of the rules within a national legal system from their application in an international setting.

2. International Organizations

2.1 General interpretative competence in international organizations

International organizations are entities having structures and powers defined in their constitutive instruments, the latter almost invariably being treaties.

In international organisations, it is generally accepted that each organ, within its function, is called upon to interpret the treaties which concern it although the interpretations

---

[7] Cf *The Restatement of the Law (Third), The Foreign Relations Law of the United States* (St Paul, Minn: American Law Institute, 1987), 3: '… this Restatement represents the opinion of The American Law Institute as to the rules that an impartial tribunal would apply if charged with deciding a controversy in accordance with international law'.

of some, especially judicial, organs may in some cases be binding on the other organs as well.[8]

There is no need to labour over the situation where a treaty provides for a judicial or quasi-judicial determination to resolve questions of interpretation. From the standpoint of examples provided of application of the rules of treaty interpretation, if the treaty makes this the authoritative means of interpretation, the consistent jurisprudence of the authorized tribunal can be viewed as subsequent practice or as providing examples of issues of interpretation in case law. More complex is the situation where competence is distributed within an organization, where an appeal system may shed potential doubt on consistent practice of the lower court or tribunal, or where a political organ has ultimate competence to determine the application of a treaty but will normally defer to a judicial organ on questions of interpretation.[9]

2.2 The two Vienna Conventions on the Law of Treaties

In addition to the convention of 1969 which provides the Vienna rules that are the main subject of this book, there is the Vienna Convention on the Law of Treaties between States and International Organizations or between International Organizations, 1986 (not yet in force).[10] The provisions on treaty interpretation in the latter are identical to those of the 1969 Convention.[11] It seems reasonable to predict that the rules on interpretation as replicated in the 1986 Convention will be subject to gravitational pull and will come to be regarded as stating customary international law in the same way as those of the 1969 Convention; but there is insufficient practice to assert this definitely.[12]

---

[8] P Reuter, *Introduction to the Law of Treaties* (London: Kegan Paul, 2nd edn, 1995), 95–6.

[9] See, for example, article 1131 of the North American Free Trade Association Agreement, which provides that an interpretation by the NAFTA Commission shall be binding on tribunals established under that provision; and for difficulties in the application of this provision, see *Arbitration under Chapter Eleven of NAFTA, Pope & Talbot v Canada (Award in respect of Damages)* (2002) 41 ILM 1347.

[10] UN Doc.A/CONF.129/15, Australian Select Documents on International Affairs No 44 (1996). At 21 March 2015, 31 states and 12 international organizations had ratified or completed the necessary procedures to become bound by the treaty. However, the treaty had not entered into force, requiring 35 states to ratify or otherwise bind themselves to become parties to it (article 85); international organizations, although they can be parties to the Convention, are not counted for purposes of entry into force.

[11] The 1986 provisions were carried over from the 1969 Convention without debate in the ILC: see [1982] *Yearbook of the ILC*, vol I, pp 22 and 260; likewise at the 1986 Conference which adopted the treaty; the1986 provisions have occasionally been cited in legal proceedings: see, eg, *Prosecutor v Kallon and Others* [2004] 3 Law Report of the Commonwealth 658, Special Court for Sierra Leone (Appeals Chamber), at 671–72, para 43, referring to article 31(1).

[12] The observer of the ILO (Jenks) at the 1968–69 Vienna Conference, speaking with reference to article 3 excluding treaties to which international organizations are parties, noted that ILO practice on interpretation had involved greater recourse to preparatory work than was envisaged in the eventual article 32 of the Vienna Convention; Official Record of UN Conference on the Law of Treaties, Summary Records, First Session, at 37, para 12. The ILO nevertheless has agreed to be bound by the 1986 Convention (formal confirmation deposited on 31 July 2000).

The 1969 Vienna Convention applies to any treaty which is the constituent instrument of an international organization and to any treaty adopted within an international organization without prejudice to any relevant rules of the organization.[13] As noted above, in most instances it is the organs themselves which interpret the constitutive treaties which grant them powers and competencies. Most international organizations will have their own legal advisers as part of the secretariat who can give advice on interpretation of such treaties. Some organizations have courts or other legal tribunals which can give advisory opinions in some cases and make determinations on points of law in others. This section considers interpretation within international organizations, except for interpretation by courts and tribunals, which are considered separately below.

One general issue is whether treaties setting out the constitutions of international organizations form a distinct class of treaties and thus may attract different rules of interpretation from other treaties. This is not explored in detail here because there is insufficient evidence to show that the Vienna rules are displaced. The provision of the 1969 Vienna Convention mentioned above (applying the Convention to constituent instruments of an international organizations) shows that the normal rules of interpretation should apply but, by including the proviso that this is without prejudice to any relevant rules of the organization, something of a special class is also indicated.

The most helpful approach may be that of Brölmann who, in examining specialized rules of treaty interpretation in connection with international organizations, notes that:

the [Vienna Convention] framework itself is famously broad, subsidiary and not very hierarchically structured. As a result, it may be best to approach treaty interpretation in this context, not as a separate regime, but rather as a version of the [Vienna Convention] framework to which additional or supplementary approaches have emerged in light of the 'special' characteristics that these constitutive instruments possess.'[14]

2.3 The United Nations and other organizations

The organs of the United Nations have built up extensive practice in interpretation of the UN Charter and associated instruments. A comprehensive record of this is being compiled and published.[15] Other international organizations similarly

---

[13] Vienna Convention 1969, article 5. It does not, however, apply to treaties between states and international organizations or between international organizations themselves: article 3. Such treaties are covered by customary international law and the rules set out in the Vienna Convention of 1986 (see above).

[14] C M Brölmann, 'Specialized Rules of Treaty Interpretation: International Organizations', Chapter 20 in D B Hollis (ed), *The Oxford Guide to Treaties* (Oxford: OUP, 2012), 508–9 (footnote omitted). One particularly prominent topic is that of subsequent practice as an element of the general rule and whether practice within an organization can constitute such practice: see Chapter 6, section 4.8 below.

[15] See, eg, *Repertory of Practice of United Nations Organs* and the *Repertoire of the Practice of the Security Council* accessible at <http://www.un.org/law/repertory> and <http://www.un.org/depts/dpa/

have a wealth of experience in interpreting their constituent instruments and other treaties, but this is not always so accessible; nor does this material readily yield up insights into application of rules of treaty interpretation.

Resolutions of the UN Security Council raise particular issues of interpretation, primarily over interpretation of mandatory resolutions addressed to UN members. These are often resolutions requiring implementation of sanctions against miscreants. Such resolutions are interpreted both by Member States and by 'sanctions committees' established by the Council. With regard to resolutions and decisions of the Security Council, it has been suggested that because there is little authority on the interpretation of non-treaty texts, it is convenient to approach the interpretation of Security Council resolutions with the Vienna rules in mind but also having regard to the fact that such resolutions may be more akin to a unilateral act than a treaty[16]

The ICJ took a somewhat guarded approach in the *Kosovo Unilateral Declaration of Independence* case:

While the rules on treaty interpretation embodied in Articles 31 and 32…may provide guidance, differences between Security Council resolutions and treaties mean that the interpretation of Security Council resolutions also require that other factors be taken into account. Security Council resolutions are issued by a single, collective body and are drafted through a very different process than that used for the conclusion of a treaty.…Security Council resolutions can be binding on all Member States…irrespective of whether they played any part in their formulation. The interpretation of Security Council resolutions may require the Court to analyse statements by representatives of members of the Security Council made at the time of their adoption, other resolutions of the Security Council on the same issue, as well as the subsequent practice of relevant United Nations organs and of States affected by those given resolutions.[17]

The Seabed Disputes Chamber of the International Tribunal for the Law of the Sea has adopted the approach taken by the ICJ in using the Vienna rules, by analogy, to provide guidance for interpretation of instruments that are not treaties, such as Regulations adopted by the International Seabed Authority relating to Polymetallic Nodules and Polymetallic Sulphides, these being instruments setting

---

repertoire>, and, on progress made in updating these, Report of the Secretary-General to UN General Assembly, Sixty-second session, Doc A/62/124, 12 July 2007.

[16] See M C Wood, 'The Interpretation of Security Council resolutions' (1998) 2 *Max Planck Yearbook of United Nations Law* 73, 85–86; see also *Prosecutor v Dusko Tadić* [1999] ICTY 2, 124 ILR, at 183–84, paras 303–4, where the Court, having concluded that it did not need to consult the preparatory work relating to its statute, stated that this did not mean that it did not view statements made in the Security Council as having interpretative weight if there were ambiguity, paras 52–62; 'Report and Recommendations made to by the Panel of Commissioners concerning the First Instalment of "E2" Claims', adopted in Decision 53 (S/AC.26/Dec.53 (1998)) by the Governing Council of the UN Compensation Commission, paras 52–62; and D Caron, 'The United Nations Compensation Commission for Claims arising out of the 1991 Gulf War: the "Arising Prior To" Decision' (2004–2005) 14 *Journal of Transnational Law & Policy* 309, 326–33.

[17] *Accordance with International Law of the Unilateral Declaration of Independence in Respect of Kosovo* (Advisory Opinion) [2010] ICJ Reports 404, at 442, para 94.

out binding texts negotiated by states and adopted through procedures similar those of multilateral conferences.[18]

2.4 The European Community and European Union

The establishment of the European Community and Union by a succession of treaties between the growing number of Member States locates those instruments within the ambit of international law. From its early days, however, the members, with guidance of the European Court of Justice (ECJ), saw the Community as a new legal order rather than just another international organization operating under international law.[19] In its internal aspect, that is viewing relations between the Member States themselves, the Community is an organism for collective exercise of sovereignty in matters over which competence is transferred to the Community by treaty. In its external aspect, the Community functions as an international organization, entering into treaties in matters within its competence. Thus, the treaties setting up the European Community have produced a legal system with its own institutions, including a Court, functioning with some of the characteristics of a state (such as a legislative power). This arrangement differentiates the task of interpreting those treaties, and the legal acts and instruments created pursuant to them, from those in the general range of treaties. Within the legal order of the European Community, the institutions interpret for themselves, at least initially, their areas of competence which are defined by the treaties. The ECJ exercises ultimate judicial control over the interpretation of the treaties as they affect the legal order of the European Community and, through its advisory role, in relation to the competence of organs and the procedures to be followed in entering into external relations through treaties.[20]

3. International Courts and Tribunals

3.1 International Court of Justice

The way in which the ICJ has come to embrace the Vienna rules has been described in Chapter 1.[21] There are four considerations to be borne in mind when considering

---

[18] *Responsibilities and Obligations of States Sponsoring Persons and Entities with respect to Activities in the Area* (Advisory Opinion) (2011) ITLOS Case No 17, para 60.

[19] *Van Gend en Loos*, Case 16/62 (1963) ECR 1, judgment, section II B; and see D R Verwey, *The European Community, the European Union and the International Law of Treaties* (The Hague: TMC Asser Press, 2004) 209 ff. More recent usage refers to the Court of Justice of the European Union (CJEU), but as it is the work of the European Court of Justice which is mainly considered in this chapter, the abbreviation 'ECJ' has been retained. Differences between the legal regimes of the European Community and European Union are not considered here, save to note that within the European Union competence with regards to the EU treaty establishing the Common Foreign and Security Policy remains with the Member States.

[20] On the role of the ECJ, see section 3.6 below.

[21] See Chapter 1, sections 2.1 and 2.2 above.

the output of the ICJ. First, only the parties are bound by judgments of the ICJ in a contentious case and only in respect of the particular case.[22] However, this does not detract from the value of pronouncements of the Court on aspects of the Vienna rules in such cases. The Court seeks to act consistently and often recounts its own jurisprudence on an issue when it recurs. Similarly, advisory opinions of the ICJ are given to any organization or body authorized to request an opinion for the guidance of that body in relation to the particular matter which it has raised, but this does not diminish the authority of pronouncements by the Court indicating how the Vienna rules are to be used.

Second, judgments and opinions of the ICJ are collegiate products but are commonly accompanied by separate and dissenting opinions of individual judges or groups of judges. Such separate and dissenting opinions may cover points of particular interest or value in relation to the Vienna rules. They are considered here where an opinion seems particularly apt or helpful, but obviously such opinions will usually be regarded as carrying less weight than the collective pronouncements of the Court. Third, many of the judgments of the Court concern matters of jurisdiction, admissibility, and issues of a procedural character. In particular, they may concern consent to the jurisdiction of the ICJ given in a treaty, as it often is. There is no reason to suppose that the application of the Vienna rules is changed in these circumstances.

Fourth, where, however, consent to the jurisdiction of the Court is not contained in a treaty or ad hoc agreement, the jurisdiction of the Court is typically founded on declarations of the parties under the 'optional clause'.[23] States make such declarations unilaterally and, in construing them, the Court is not interpreting a treaty:

The régime relating to the interpretation of declarations made under Article 36 of the Statute is not identical with that established for the interpretation of treaties by the Vienna Convention on the Law of Treaties…Spain has suggested in its pleadings that '[t]his does not mean that the legal rules and the art of interpreting declarations (and reservations) do not coincide with those governing the interpretation of treaties'. The Court observes that the provisions of that Convention may only apply analogously to the extent compatible with the *sui generis* character of the unilateral acceptance of the Court's jurisdiction.[24]

With this caveat, the Court has applied the principles of the Vienna rules in such circumstances, and special considerations which apply are noted where appropriate.

3.2 Arbitration

International arbitrations which consider questions of treaty interpretation are usually determined by arbitral tribunals appointed pursuant to procedures set out in

---

[22] Article 59 of the ICJ Statute.
[23] Article 36(2) of the Statute of the International Court of Justice.
[24] *Fisheries Jurisdiction Case (Spain v Canada) (Jurisdiction and Preliminary Objections)* [1998] ICJ Reports 432, at 455, para 46.

a treaty. The reliability of the views expressed in awards of such tribunals on issues of interpretation is therefore dependent on the competence and experience of the arbitrators in matters of international law. The composition of these tribunals may range from those which include judges of the ICJ to those which are composed of arbitrators selected more for some particular expertise, such as their knowledge of economics or international trade. Arbitrators nominated from those on the list kept by the Permanent Court of Arbitration are persons 'of known competency in questions of international law'.[25]

3.3 The World Trade Organization Dispute Settlement Understanding

Disputes between members of the WTO arising from the WTO Agreement and the various associated treaties and instruments are resolved by a procedure established by the Dispute Settlement Understanding of 1994.[26] The procedure includes submission of complaints to a panel of three experts, the panel being established by the WTO Dispute Settlement Body (DSB). If there is an appeal from a panel's report it is heard by the Appellate Body, which is a standing tribunal established by the DSB. The Appellate Body may only deal with questions of law and its reports are automatically adopted by the DSB unless that body decides by consensus not to adopt a report.

Questions of treaty interpretation arise at the panel stage, but the members of the panels are not chosen just for their competence in international law generally but rather their possession of the requisite skills for considering complex trade disputes. Because the Appellate Body has a stable composition and concentrates on questions of law, the use it has made of the Vienna rules in many cases helpfully reveals their appropriate application and discloses issues that may arise in this process.[27]

---

[25] Article 44 of the Convention for the Pacific Settlement of International Disputes, The Hague, 1907 (English translation of the authoritative French published by the Permanent Court at <http://www.pca-cpa.org>).

[26] See J G Merrills, *International Dispute Settlement* (Cambridge: CUP, 2005), at 213–31, J Collier and V Lowe, *The Settlement of Disputes in International Law* (Oxford: OUP, 1999), 99–104, and for the case law resulting from this dispute settlement procedure see I Van Damme, *Treaty Interpretation by the WTO Appellate Body* (Oxford: OUP, 2009).

[27] Because the Appellate Body has sought to apply the Vienna rules systematically, the panels also make frequent reference to them. The case law of these WTO bodies is extensive and has been the subject of a growing body of literature examining interpretation, including: G White, 'Treaty interpretation: the Vienna Convention "Code" as applied by the World Trade Organization Judiciary' (1999) 20 *Australian Yearbook of International Law* 319; J Cameron and K R Gray, 'Principles of International Law in the WTO Dispute Settlement Body' (2001) 50 ICLQ 248; J Pauwelyn, 'The Role of Public International Law in the WTO: How Far Can We Go?' (2001) 95 AJIL 535; J Meltzer, 'Interpreting the WTO Agreements—A Commentary on Professor Pauwelyn's Approach' (2003–2004) 25 *Mich J Int'l L* 917; J Pauwelyn, 'Reply to Joshua Meltzer' (2003–2004) 25 *Mich J Int'l L* 924; Malgosia Fitzmaurice, 'Canons of Treaty Interpretation: Selected Case Studies from the World Trade Organization and the North American Free Trade Agreement' (2007) 10 *Austrian Review of International and European Law* 41.

There are two particular considerations to be taken into account when using decisions of the panels or Appellate Body. First, it is to be noted that the Appellate Body is bound to give effect to interpretations of the WTO treaties and associated instruments where such interpretations have been adopted by the WTO ministerial conference and general council of the WTO. This requirement, however, to conform to such interpretations does not detract from the value to be extracted from the use made by the Appellate Body of the Vienna rules. Interpretations by the Ministerial Conference or General Council are in line with what is envisaged in Article 31(3)(b) of the Vienna Convention (subsequent agreement of the parties as to interpretation). Their deployment in the interpretative process is simply an example of what is envisaged by the Vienna rules.

The second point is a little more complex, though linked with the first. The dispute settlement mechanism of the WTO provides for the reports of panels (and also of the Appellate Body) to become final rulings unless the DSB (which consists of all WTO members) rejects them by consensus. However, while these decisions of panels and of the Appellate Body on disputes between Member States of the WTO provide interpretations of treaty provisions which may become effective in relation to a particular dispute, the Appellate Body has indicated that panel reports do not constitute subsequent practice for the purposes of article 31(3)(b) of the Vienna Convention. In *Japan—Alcoholic Beverages,* the Panel had found that panel reports adopted by the Contracting Parties constituted subsequent practice in a specific case.[28] In reversing the Panel's findings on this issue, the Appellate Body stated that it did not believe that the parties to the General Agreement on Tariffs and Trade (GATT), in deciding to adopt a panel report, intended that their decision would constitute a definitive interpretation of the relevant provisions of GATT 1947. Nor did it believe that this was contemplated under GATT 1994:

There is specific cause for this conclusion in the WTO Agreement. Article IX:2 of the WTO Agreement provides: 'The Ministerial Conference and the General Council shall have the exclusive authority to adopt interpretations of this Agreement and of the Multilateral Trade Agreements'. Article IX:2 provides further that such decisions 'shall be taken by a three-fourths majority of the Members'. The fact that such an 'exclusive authority' in interpreting the treaty has been established so specifically in the WTO Agreement is reason enough to conclude that such authority does not exist by implication or by inadvertence elsewhere.

For these reasons, we do not agree with the Panel's conclusion...that 'panel reports adopted by the GATT Contracting Parties and the WTO Dispute Settlement Body constitute subsequent practice in a specific case' as the phrase 'subsequent practice' is used in Article 31 of the Vienna Convention.[29]

---

[28] *Japan—Taxes on Alcoholic Beverages*, AB-1996–2, Report of 4 October 1996, WT/DS8/AB/R, WT/DS10/AB/R, WT/DS11/AB/R.
[29] *Japan—Taxes on Alcoholic Beverages*, at 14.

Nevertheless, the decisions of the WTO panels are treated in successive cases as if they were case law, and in *Japan—Alcoholic Beverages* the Appellate Body acknowledged their role, noting in relation to earlier versions of the GATT:

Adopted panel reports are an important part of the GATT acquis. They are often considered by subsequent panels. They create legitimate expectations among WTO Members, and, therefore, should be taken into account where they are relevant to any dispute. However, they are not binding, except with respect to resolving the particular dispute between the parties to that disputed.[30]

For present purposes these two points are not a detriment to finding guidance on use of the Vienna rules, decisions being cited for the issues raised and solutions offered. As with judgments and decisions quoted or cited here from all sources, the absence of a formal system of precedent in treaty interpretation means that the reports cannot be presumed to be authoritative. They depend for their strength on the quality of their argument, their coherence, and their consistency with other applications of the rules of interpretation to the same or analogous issues. Thus, for example, the Appellate Body stated in explanation of the first paragraph of article 31 of the Vienna Convention:

A treaty interpreter must begin with, and focus upon, the text of the particular provision to be interpreted. It is in the words constituting that provision, read in their context, that the object and purpose of the states parties to the treaty must first be sought. Where the meaning imparted by the text itself is equivocal or inconclusive, or where confirmation of the correctness of the reading of the text itself is desired, light from the object and purpose of the treaty as a whole may usefully be sought.[31]

This description of how article 31(1) is to apply suffers from two self-evident drawbacks. There is little elsewhere to suggest that the second and third of these sentences correctly reflect the proper approach to the first part of the general rule of treaty interpretation, even if they may follow a typical or logical process of thought. First, article 31(1) does not refer to the object and purpose of the particular treaty provision being found in the particular provision in issue; it refers to the object and purpose of the treaty as part of the process of finding the ordinary meaning of the terms of that provision. True, construing a provision and giving meaning to its terms may necessarily involve understanding their object and purpose. Further, the object and purpose of the treaty in combination with

---

[30] *Japan—Taxes on Alcoholic Beverages*, AB-1996–2, Report of 4 October 1996, at 14 (footnote omitted).

[31] *United States—Import Prohibition of Certain Shrimp and Shrimp Products*, WTIDS58/AB/R, 12 October 1998, para 114, citing I Sinclair, *The Vienna Convention on the Law of Treaties* (Manchester: Manchester University Press, 2nd edn, 1984), 130–1. Sinclair, in a much fuller explanation reflecting the nuances of the Vienna rules, indicated that: 'The initial search is for the "ordinary meaning" to be given to the terms of the treaty in their "context" '; he continued that 'it is *in the light* of the object and purpose of the treaty that the initial and preliminary conclusion must be tested and either confirmed or modified' (emphasis in the original); but his approach acknowledges that the (possibly multifarious) objects and purposes are those of the treaty; and, though the object and purpose may be more or less valuable in helping identify the ordinary meaning, identifying that meaning is its role.

the context (as defined in the Vienna Convention), by denoting more extensive concepts must also embrace the narrower notions of immediate context and the object and purpose of a particular provision as part of the interpretative process; but the quoted passage does not properly capture the requirement that the whole of the first part of the general rule must be applied, not merely some elements sequentially and incrementally. Second, as regards the role of the object and purpose of the treaty, article 31 of the Vienna Convention does not subject their use to the qualifying criteria of the ordinary meaning of terms being equivocal or inconclusive (in contrast with article 32 which does include tests of that kind).[32]

This is not to say that the Appellate Body in fact applied article 31 incorrectly in the particular case. It actually appears to have done a thorough job in correcting the approach taken by the panel and it applied the Vienna rules appropriately. However, if the Appellate Body's description of what it thought should be done were taken from the passage quoted above, without looking to see what it actually did, the wrong impression of the general rule in the Vienna Convention might be gained.

More generally, case law produced by the WTO Dispute Settlement procedures, and particularly from the Appellate Body, provides a substantial quarry for finding examples of how the Vienna rules are applied in the most varied situations and how the framework which they provide can be used as the base for an interpretative superstructure. This case law has been the subject of a comprehensive study by Van Damme with a specific focus on treaty interpretation.[33]

3.4 The International Centre for Settlement of Investment Disputes (ICSID)

The ICSID is a centre for mediation, conciliation, and arbitration of disputes arising between a foreign individual or company on the one hand and a state party to the Washington Convention of 1965, on the other.[34] The agreement to arbitrate is frequently contained in one of the over 2,500 bilateral investment treaties designed to overcome the problems faced by foreign investors who may find themselves subjected to expropriation or other detrimental measures taken by a host state.[35] These treaties have led to a great number of arbitrations, many of which concern interpretation of the bilateral treaties. Although an early arbitration under the aegis

---

[32] See D Shanker, 'The Vienna Convention on the Law of Treaties, the Dispute Settlement System of the WTO and the Doha Declaration on the TRIPs Agreement' (2002) 36 *Journal of World Trade* 721, at 741–2.

[33] I Van Damme, *Treaty Interpretation by the WTO Appellate Body* (Oxford: OUP, 2009).

[34] See C H Schreuer, *The ICSID Convention: A Commentary* (Cambridge: CUP, 2001) and Collier and Lowe, *The Settlement of Disputes in International Law*, 59–73.

[35] The International Institute for Sustainable Development reports that there are some '3,000 investment treaties, including bilateral investment treaties between two states, regional agreements, and investment protection provisions in free trade agreements between two or more countries': <http://www.iisd.org/investment/law/treaties.aspx> (2013).

of the Centre applied customary rules of interpretation formulated in the tribunal's own way, more recent ones have used the Vienna rules as a statement of the applicable interpretative regime.[36] However, despite frequent reference to the Vienna rules, accurate and full application of them by ICSID tribunals (and by other tribunals concerning investment disputes) does not always follow.[37]

3.5 The European Court of Human Rights

The present court replaced the previous combination of court and commission set up within the framework of the Council of Europe.[38] Cases before the court and its predecessors have mostly been initiated by individuals but there has been a small number of cases between states. The court was one of the earliest to apply the Vienna rules and it has built up a considerable body of jurisprudence around their use. There are three points to note here about the European Court of Human Rights (ECtHR). First, the court is almost exclusively concerned with the interpretation of one treaty. The rights stated in that treaty are not particularized in great detail, yet have to be applied to a very wide range of facts. This sets the work of the court in rather a particular framework, but does not appear to colour its interpretation of the Vienna rules in a manner which makes its approach to the rules different from their normal application by other courts and tribunals.

Second, the court is part of a regional institution and its work is grafted onto a substructure of national legal systems which, though very different in their nature and development, nevertheless share common principles of justice and fairness. This again does not appear to colour the application of the Vienna rules, even if it does affect application of the treaty to particular facts. Third, the court has developed a structure for its judgments which set out the facts and the law before the arguments and reasoned conclusions. This results in the preparatory work of the relevant provisions of the European Convention on Human Rights being set out before the Vienna Convention's rules are applied. This appears to reverse the natural sequence of general rule and supplementary means of interpretation in the Vienna rules;, but the Court's approach is to make its interpretative analysis after setting out the facts and legislative history of the relevant Convention provisions. When it reaches the stage of this analysis, the Court follows the Vienna rules carefully, respecting their structure and content in their natural sequence, and using supplementary means in the manner specified in article 33 of the Vienna Convention.[39]

---

[36] For an example of a tribunal elaborating its own version of customary rules of interpretation, see *Asian Agricultural Products Ltd (AAPL) v Sri Lanka* (1991) 30 ILM 580; examples of ICSID tribunals using the Vienna rules are given in Part II below.

[37] See Chapter 10, section 6.2 below.

[38] Protocol 11 to the European Convention on Human Rights entered into force in 1998.

[39] See *Litwa v Poland*, discussed in Chapter 1, section 5.1 and on the ECtHR's case law more generally, see Chapter 10, sections 4.2, and 5.1 below.

3.6 The European Court of Justice
(Court of Justice of the European Union)

The European Court of Justice (ECJ) has developed a distinct approach to interpretation of treaties and other instruments within the European Community.[40] This does not correspond exactly with the scheme of the Vienna rules. In contrast, customary international law as reflected in the Vienna rules clearly applies in the external relations of the Community; that is to any treaties which the Community has made, alone or with its members, with non-Member States. As an intergovernmental organization, the European Community is not a party to the Vienna Convention of 1969 but could become a party to the Vienna Convention of 1986.[41] As the sets of rules on interpretation in the 1969 and 1986 treaties are the same, and the latter are likely to be taken as representing customary international law in the same way as the former, separate consideration of them here is unnecessary.

Any relevant and effective distinction, however, is not between the different treaties on the law of treaties. It is between the approach taken by the ECJ to treaties and instruments in the European Community's legal order on the one hand, and to the treaties in its external relations on the other. There are three types of instruments which may involve treaty interpretation: (1) the treaties founding the Community; (2) treaties to which the Community is a party with non-Member States; and (3) instruments of a legislative character within the Community which give effect to obligations established by such treaties with non-members.

3.6.1 The treaties founding the Community

The ECJ has viewed the founding instruments of the European Community more as a constitution of a new legal order than as treaties applying in relations between states parties to them.[42] Distinguishing the legal order of the Community in this way from public international law has generally resulted in the ECJ not applying the Vienna rules to these treaties.[43] Explanation of the Court's abstention from use of the rules in this context has been rather oblique. In *France v Commission*, a

---

[40] More recent usage refers to the Court of Justice of the European Union (CJEU), but as it is the work of the European Court of Justice which is mainly considered in this chapter, the abbreviation 'ECJ' has been retained.

[41] See section 2.2 above and P Manin, 'The European Communities and the Vienna Convention on the Law of Treaties Between States and International Organizations or Between International Organizations' (1987) 24 CMLRev 457.

[42] See *Van Gend en Loos*, Case 16/62 (1963) ECR 1, judgment, section II B, and see section 2.4 above; see also F Hoffmeister, 'The Contribution of EU Practice to International Law', chapter 3 in M Cremona (ed), *Developments in EU External Relations Law* (Oxford: OUP, 2008).

[43] A distinction needs to be made in the case of the EU treaty which is amenable to interpretation in the relations of states parties to it, and therefore likely to attract the application of the Vienna rules, in particular in the case of the Common Foreign and Security Policy which is not subject to judicial supervision by the ECJ: see M G Ketvel, 'The Jurisdiction of the European Court of Justice in Respect of Common Foreign and Security Policy' (2006) 55 ICLQ 77 and Hoffmeister, 'The Contribution of EU Practice to International Law'.

case concerning an agreement between the Commission and the USA, it had been argued that practice of the organs of the European Community was relevant.[44] The Advocate General rejected the notion of interpretation revealed by practice of the institution[45] Although it accepted that the agreement in issue fell squarely within the definition of 'treaty' in the 1986 Vienna Convention, the Court did not refer to the interpretation provisions of that Convention but simply said that 'a mere practice cannot override the provisions of the [EEC] Treaty'.[46] As regards preparatory work, in the early years some antipathy to their use was detectable in the practice of the Court.[47] This was put down to the paucity or inaccessibility of records of the founding instruments.[48]

A more general explanation of the Court's attitude to interpretation points to the approach of the Court to instruments within the Community's legal order, the difference from the approach of other international courts and tribunals being one of emphasis and objective:

> In EU law...there is a greater tendency to stress the objectives pursued by the act or provision in question, in particular (but not exclusively) as regards essential provisions of the founding treaties. This is the so-called teleological method of interpretation, and even if its importance is sometimes exaggerated, it is indisputable that it plays a significant role in the case law of the EU Courts.[49]

3.6.2 Treaties to which the Community is a party with non-Member States

The purposive or teleological approach adopted by the ECJ to legal instruments is seen by Arnull as just one of a range of methods used by the Court.[50] Arnull suggests that the approach taken by the ECJ is 'not out of keeping with Article 31(1) of the Vienna Convention'.[51] However, it appears that the Court has found some

---

[44] [1994] ECR I-3641, at 3674, para 25 of the Advocate General's opinion.

[45] [1994] ECR I-3641, at 3657–658, paras 28–29. See criticism of this by P J Kuijper, 'The Court and Tribunal of the EC and the Vienna Convention Law of Treaties 1969' [1998] *Legal Issues in European Integration*, part 1, at p 10, and the view of Advocate General Jacobs that subsequent practice should be taken into account in interpreting the Euratom treaty: *Commission of the European Communities v Council of the European Union* C-29/99, [2002] ECR I-11221, at 11246, paras 147–49.

[46] [1994] ECR I-3641, 3656, at 3661, paras 25 and 36 of the judgment.

[47] See, eg, A Arnull, *The European Union and its Court of Justice* (Oxford: OUP, 2nd edn, 2006), Chapter 16, 'Interpretation and the limits of literalism', 614.

[48] Arnull, at fn 46; there is no longer any general reluctance to use preparatory work of legal instruments generated within the Community's own legal order: S Schonberg and K Fric, 'Finishing, refining, polishing: on the Use of Travaux Préparatoires as an Aid to the Interpretation of Community Legislation' (2003) 28(2) EL Rev 149, at 170.

[49] P Eeckhout, *External Relations of The European Union* (Oxford: OUP, 2004), 257; see also D Shelton, 'Reconcilable Differences? The Interpretation of Multilingual Treaties' (1997) 20 *Hastings International and Comparative Law Review* 611, at 631: 'The European Court of Justice also takes a teleological approach, much more than sanctioned by the Vienna Convention. It frequently looks to the underlying object and purpose of the provision in question, rather than taking a strictly textual approach.'

[50] Arnull, *The European Union and its Court of Justice*, Chapter 16, 'Interpretation and the limits of literalism', 607.

[51] Arnull, at 614.

difficulty in shaking off the approach to interpretation described above, even when it has turned to interpretation of treaties with non-members. As has been noted in the case of other courts (most prominently the ICJ), acceptance of the applicability of the Vienna rules has been rather slow and incremental. In the case of the ECJ this has not overtly progressed beyond the first paragraph of article 31 of the Vienna Convention, though the Court has accepted that treaties between the Community and non-members are of a different order from the constitutional instruments of the Community. Sometimes the terms of a treaty in the external relations of the EU are the same as those in instruments in the internal EU legal order. For the reason just given, the ECJ has recognized that identity of wording does not result necessarily in identical interpretation.[52]

Until relatively recently, the Court's approach to treaty interpretation put the emphasis on a teleological approach. In *Polydor v Harlequin Records,* a case concerning an agreement between the EEC and Portugal, the Court stated that it was necessary to interpret the provisions of the treaty in issue 'in the light of both the object and purpose of the agreement and of its wording', a statement which does not quite reflect the dynamics of article 31(1).[53] It has been suggested that the Court 'succeeds fairly well' in basing 'the *exceptional* character of the Community legal order on *normal* rules of treaty interpretation'.[54] Yet in *Polydor* the Court's approach was much closer to the purposive approach of the Harvard draft than to the Vienna rules.[55] Article 31(1) of the Vienna Convention carefully links the object and purpose of a treaty to the ordinary meaning of the terms used. As stated by Sinclair: 'The initial search is for the "ordinary meaning"…; it *is in the light of* the object and purpose of the treaty that the initial preliminary conclusion must be tested and either confirmed or modified.'[56] In *Polydor,* the object and purpose of the treaty are viewed as if they were separate elements, having their own independent role.

In *Opinion 1/91*, the ECJ stated that: 'An international treaty is to be interpreted not only on the basis of its wording but also in the light of its objectives.'[57] This is closer to the Vienna Convention's provisions than the Court's approach in *Polydor,* and the Court did continue by quoting article 31(1) of the Convention. The Court has also endorsed application of article 31 in more recent cases concerning treaties with non-members, though it generally limits its attention to paragraph (1) of

---

[52] See *Hauptzollamt Mainz v CA Kupferberg* C-104/81, [1982] ECR 3641 and *Polydor v Harlequin Records,* below.

[53] [1982] ECR 329, para 8.

[54] Kuijper, 'The Court and Tribunal of the EC and the Vienna Convention Law of Treaties 1969' [1998] *Legal Issues in European Integration,* part 1, at 3.

[55] See Chapter 2, section 4 above.

[56] Sinclair, *The Vienna Convention on the Law of Treaties,* at 130; puzzlingly, Sinclair describes reference to the object and purpose of a treaty as 'as it were, a secondary or ancillary process in the application of the general rule' (at 130), but this is out of line with the crucible approach of the ILC and, use of the introductory phrase 'as it were' may suggest that this is really a description of sequence of thought rather than an observation on hierarchy.

[57] [1991] ECR I-6079, at 6101, para 14.

that article.[58] In *Anastasiou*, however, the Court did refer to practice in application of an Association Agreement, though in this instance it found practice to be insufficient to establish unequivocally the existence of an interpretative agreement between the parties within the meaning of article 31 of the Vienna Convention.[59] In the same case, the Court rejected invocation of propositions of international law which might have been regarded as relevant rules of international law applicable in relations between parties to interpret an agreement relating to Cyprus.[60]

Community practice takes into account article 33 of the Vienna Convention.[61] There was some evidence of this in *Simutenkov v Ministerio de Educación* in the Commission's argument based on that provision.[62] The case arose from rules in Spain which limited the number of foreign football players who could play in professional games at national level. A Russian player had both a residence permit and a work permit in Spain. A 'Partnership and Cooperation Agreement' between the Russian Federation and the European Community and its members included a provision that, subject to their own laws, the Community and its members were to 'ensure that the treatment accorded to Russian nationals, legally employed in the territory of a Member State shall be free from any discrimination based on nationality, as regards working conditions, remuneration or dismissal, as compared to its own nationals'. An issue arose over the nature of this obligation.

The Agreement had been authenticated in ten languages. Seven, including the Russian text, used the equivalent of the English 'ensure', thus pointing to an obligation to achieve the result; three used phrases indicating endeavours (translated into English as 'shall use every endeavour', 'shall watch that', and 'shall take care that'), suggesting that only best efforts were required.[63] The Advocate General considered that: 'In view of the linguistic divergences it appears, however, to be necessary to consider the intention of the parties and the object of the provision to be interpreted.[64] In a broad sense this can be viewed as an approximation for article 33(4) of the Vienna Convention. The Court itself simply stated that it follows from the wording of Article 23(1) of the Communities–Russia Partnership Agreement that a prohibition on discrimination was laid down by the provision 'in clear, precise and unconditional terms', without indicating the path to that conclusion.[65]

---

[58] See *Metalsa* [1993] ECR I-3751, at 3772–3, para 10, *El-Yassini v Secretary of State* C-416/96. [1999] ECR I-01209, at 1242, para 47, and *Jany v Staatssecretaris van Justitie* [2001] ECR I-8615, at 8675–6, para 35; and see Hoffmeister, 'The Contribution of EU Practice to International Law'.

[59] [1994] ECR I-3087, at 3134, para 50.   [60] [1994] ECR I-3087, at 3132, para 43.

[61] See Hoffmeister, 'The Contribution of EU Practice to International Law'.

[62] *Simutenkov* C-265/03, [2005] ECR I-2579, and Hoffmeister, 'The Contribution of EU Practice to International Law'.

[63] See Opinion of Advocate General Stix-Hackl [2005] ECR I-2579, para 15.

[64] [2005] ECR I-2579, at para 20.

[65] Judgment, *Simutenkov* [2005] C-265/03, ECR I-2579, at para 22; see also *Christina Kik v OHIM (Trade Marks and Designs)* T-120/99 [2001] All ER (D) 161 (Jul), at para 43, where the Court of First Instance rehearsed a reference by the Greek government to article 33 of the Vienna Convention, without specifically basing its reasoning on this provision.

It is disappointing that the ECJ has not explicitly endorsed the application of the complete set of Vienna rules. That it has made reference to paragraph (1) of article 31 and has not repudiated the rules when the full set has occasionally been mentioned by the Advocates General, may suggest that the Court would not in principle be averse to applying the complete rules in due course.[66]

3.6.3 Community instruments giving effect to treaties with non-members

The implementation within the European Community of treaties to which the Community is a party leads to constitutional issues and questions of direct effect of a complexity which it is not necessary to investigate here. There are, however, two propositions which bear on the Court's approach to treaty interpretation. First, in relation to treaties, the ECJ has stated that 'it is for the Court, within the framework of its jurisdiction in interpreting the provisions of agreements to ensure their uniform application throughout the Community'.[67] Second, as regards legislation implementing treaties, the Court has stated:

When the wording of secondary Community legislation is open to more than one interpretation, preference should be given as far as possible to the interpretation which renders the provision consistent with the Treaty...Similarly, the primacy of international agreements concluded by the Community over provisions of secondary Community legislation means that such provisions must, so far as is possible, be interpreted in a manner that is consistent with those agreements.[68]

The effect of these two principles is that the ECJ could be expected to have to interpret treaties in order to ensure uniform application and when there are issues before the Court requiring interpretation of Community legislation implementing treaties. The ECJ could be expected to apply the full Vienna rules to interpretation of treaties, although the second of the principles suggests that it may be difficult for the Court to reach issues of treaty interpretation if the secondary Community legislation is wholly unambiguous.[69] Hitherto, the manner of interpretation of these treaties has not been directly in issue, other than to the extent described in the preceding section. There is, however, potential for this to become important if the ECJ has to interpret treaties which are primarily within the orbit of the

---

[66] See, eg, references to article 31–33 by Advocates General Van Gerven in *Fédération de l'industrie de l'huilerie de la CEE (Fediol) v Commission* C-70/87 [1989] ECR 1781, at 1808–9, para 14, Saggio in *Portuguese Republic v Council of the European Union* Case C-149/96 [1999] I-8410–11, para 20, and Jacobs in *Commission v Council* C-29/99 [2002] I-11221, at 11246, para 83; cf the General Court of the CJEU which shows signs of incomplete awareness of the Vienna rules in extracting from article 31 of the Vienna Convention only the substance of the first paragraph: *Stichting Natuur en Milieu and Pesticide Action Network Europe v European Commission* (Case T-338/08), Judgment of 14 June 2012, para 72.

[67] *Hauptzollamt Mainz v CA Kupferberg* C-104/81 [1982] ECR 3641, at 1342–3, para 2.

[68] *Commission v Germany (International Dairy Arrangement)* C-61/94 [1996] ECR I-3989, at 4020–21, para 52.

[69] This is the same problem that can arise in the approach of courts in the UK: see section 4.2.2 below.

WTO. This has been a matter that has so far been somewhat mired in questions of whether the relevant treaties have direct effect or can be otherwise examined by the Court, without reaching a conclusion on whether the ECJ will take the same detailed approach to application of the Vienna rules that has characterized the approach to dispute settlement within the WTO.[70]

None of the above is to suggest that the ECJ is acting illegitimately in largely neglecting the Vienna rules. As regards both the EC internal legal order and also the Community's conduct of external relations, the ECJ acts more in the manner of a national court interpreting a constitution. Further, viewed as an international organization, the ECJ's observance of its own code is in line with what is acknowledged by the Vienna Convention as admissible.[71]

3.7 Other international courts and tribunals

There are many other international courts and tribunals, mostly having competence to deal with cases concerning specialist subject areas such as human rights, international trade, the law of the sea, etc, or dealing with particular matters such as the Iran–US Tribunal, the International Criminal Tribunal for the former Yugoslavia, etc. The judgments and decisions of some of these courts and tribunals feature in the chapters below analysing the Vienna rules.[72]

4. National Legal Systems

4.1 Implementation of treaties

Wherever a treaty is being applied, the Vienna rules are the appropriate framework for its interpretation. Treaties, being agreements between states governed by public international law, are authoritatively interpreted in the relations of the parties themselves on the international plane through direct state-to-state communication or by agreed third party adjudication. However, there have long been treaties requiring application within national legal systems. Their number has grown greatly in recent years. International law prescribes no general means for implementation of treaties save the obligation in the Vienna Convention that every treaty which is in force must be performed by the parties in good faith (article 26) and that a party may not invoke the provisions of its internal law as justification for its failure to perform a treaty (article 27). Apart from those treaties which do

---

[70] See C J Kuijper and M Bronckers, 'WTO Law in the European Court of Justice' (2005) 42 CMLRev, 1313 and Hoffmeister, 'The Contribution of EU Practice to International Law'.

[71] Article 5 states: 'The present Convention applies to any treaty which is the constituent instrument of an international organization and to any treaty adopted within an international organization without prejudice to any relevant rules of the organization.'

[72] For the range of courts and tribunals, past and present, see the synoptic chart drawn up in the Project on International Courts and Tribunals at <http://www.pict-pcti.org>.

prescribe particular modes of implementation, states are free to use whatever methods their constitutions afford provided they comply with these two provisions of
customary law as stated in the Vienna Convention.[73]

The bodies within a state which are most likely to be involved in treaty
interpretation are the executive, the legislature, and the judiciary. Most commonly it is the executive, that is to say the government, which has responsibility for international relations, though this may be subject to some form
of parliamentary approval, direction, or scrutiny. As the leading body in the
negotiation of treaties, their conclusion and implementation, the government
and its officials necessarily have to interpret treaties. Different states have very
different methods for establishing internal consent to be bound by a particular treaty and then, according to their differing constitutional arrangements,
there are variations in methods for implementation of treaties. Even where
such methods involve wholesale textual incorporation, the nature of the obligations in a treaty may be such as to require further action by legislation or
other process. In some states there are councils having a constitutional role
which may include involvement in treaty acceptance and implementation.[74]
Any such components of the executive or legislative organs of the state may
need to determine the interpretation of a treaty in the course of performing
their functions.

It is, however, likely that the most common venue for airing issues of treaty
interpretation in public will be the courts. Judgments interpreting treaties increasingly reveal use of the Vienna rules. While these are not sufficiently numerous or
systematic to show a structured approach to application of the rules, they can be
helpful in revealing the issues that arise and providing examples of application of
particular elements in the rules. In interpretation of treaties, the Vienna rules are
the 'proper law', to borrow a term from private international law.[75] Where national
courts and other bodies apply the Vienna rules they do so not only because they
have selected the proper law, but also because this makes the outcome most likely
to accord with the obligations in the treaty in issue. Thus, domestic case law is
treated in this book as providing useful examples of problems and suggested solutions, even though there may not yet be sufficient practice to make this jurisprudence authoritative.

The main division over how treaties are implemented is between those states
whose constitutions make the text of the treaty automatically part of the internal
legal order of the state once it has become a party to the treaty, and those states
which transform the treaty into domestic law by legislative process to give effect
to the commitments in the treaty whether in the words of the treaty itself or by

---

[73] See R K Gardiner, *International Law* (Harlow: Pearson/Longman, 2003), 138–62.

[74] An example of this is the role of the *Conseil d'État* in France: see P M Eisemann and R Rivier,
on 'France' in D B Hollis, M R Blakeslee, and L B Ederington (eds), *National Treaty Law and Practice*
(Leiden, Boston: Martinus Nijhoff, 2005), 253 at 261–3 on legislative approval and 270–3 on
interpretation.

[75] See Chapter 1, section 3.1.

converting them into legislative provisions. This division does not provide a precise demarcation of groups of states; but these loose categories do have implications for treaty interpretation. In the first place, in the case of those states whose legal systems automatically take the whole of the treaty text into their internal legal order upon becoming a party to the treaty, it will be readily apparent when a treaty provision is being interpreted. It would also seem inherently more probable that such interpretation would attract application of the Vienna rules in those states parties to the Convention. In contrast, a particular problem in those states which transform treaties into domestic law by legislation is that it has not always been clear whether the courts will apply their own principles of interpretation, that is those used for any other domestic law, or whether they will import the rules of international law as the appropriate rules for an instrument governed by international law.[76]

In some states the process which leads to approval for the state to become a party to a treaty includes submission of the treaty to a legislative or other body, often accompanied by an explanatory memorandum or other guide to the obligations in the treaty. While such guides include interpretations of treaty provisions, they are essentially unilateral understandings of the meaning to be attributed to the terms. Nonetheless, reference has occasionally been made to such guides in the course of treaty interpretation arising from a difference over the meaning of the treaty.[77]

In the case of states which transform the treaty provisions into domestic legislative language, any difference in wording from that of the treaty's text may be taken as indicating an understanding attributed by the legislature to the terms of the treaty. There are also instances of legislation being passed at a later date indicating understandings of the legislature as to how a treaty is to be interpreted.[78]

4.2 Judicial interpretation within national legal systems

4.2.1 Parties to the Vienna Convention generally

For those states whose constitutions provide for incorporation of treaties into domestic law on becoming a party to them, formal promulgation of the text in an official journal or equivalent publication is commonly required. This has the advantage that courts and tribunals more readily accept that they are interpreting the treaty itself rather than implementing legislation. Until there is a comprehensive comparative study of case law it will remain difficult to assess how thorough is the use made of the Vienna rules by national courts. There are certainly many examples of explicit reference to the Vienna rules, though it is not always easy to tell exactly how this has informed judgments. In many instances courts mention

---

[76] See, eg, the *Hiscox v Outhwaite* case, considered in Chapter 1, section 5.4.
[77] See Chapter 3, section 4.4 above.
[78] See, eg, in the UK, the Arbitration Act 1996, ss 53 and 100 (considered in Chapter 1, section 5.4) and the Carriage by Air and Road Act 1979, s 2(1), cited in *Fothergill v Monarch Airlines* [1981] AC 251, at 271 (see section 4.2.2 below).

the Vienna rules but do not set out in their judgments detailed analysis of how the rules affect their reasoning.

Thus, for example, the German Federal Supreme Court (*Bundesgerichtshof*) cited articles 31–33 of the Vienna Convention when interpreting The Hague Convention on International Child Abduction, 1980.[79] The Court used appropriate elements of the Vienna rules in deciding whether courts of a state could make a custody order notwithstanding a decision that a child was to be returned to another jurisdiction. The Court examined the text and the purpose of the Convention, the practice of several other states, and the Explanatory Report on the Convention, deciding that a decision on the merits of a custody application was not permitted by the Convention in the particular circumstances. The Court further decided that in the light of the specific commitment to take appropriate measures to achieve the objects of the Convention, it was obliged to suspend pending custody proceedings.[80]

There are numerous further examples showing widespread willingness of national courts to refer to, and apply, the Vienna rules.[81]

4.2.2 The common law tradition

Legal systems which follow the common law tradition have tended to view international law as a separate system of law, its invocation in a court calling for explanation. The tendency has been to try to domesticate international law, whether by transforming treaties into statutes or seeking to harmonize rules of international law with domestic concepts familiar to practitioners and judges. In interpreting

---

[79] XII ZB 210/99, BGHZ 145, 97, 16 August 2000, at 145,100, and see full text, and summary by the Permanent Bureau of the Hague Conference on Private International Law, at <http://www.incadat.com>.

[80] See also *Proceedings on The Constitutional Complaint* BVerfG, 2 BvR 1290/99 of 12/12/2000 at <http://www.bverfg.de/entscheidungen/rk20001212_2bvr129099en.html> where the German Federal Constitutional Court (*Bundesverfassungsgericht*), in a case concerning the interpretation of Article II and VI of the Convention on the Prevention and Punishment of the Crime of Genocide 1948, affirmed the applicability of articles 31 and 32 of the Vienna Convention to treaties generally.

[81] See, eg, *Norddeutscher Rundfunk State Treaty* 90 ILR 366 (German Federal Administrative Court), where the Vienna rules were used in the case of treaty between the constituent states (*Länder*); *BS and KG v AR and AR*, Labour Court of Appeals, Brussels (5th Chamber), *International Law in Domestic Courts* (ILDC, electronic, OUP) ILDC 50 (BE 2002); *CIGNA Insurance Company of Europe NVEA v Transport NIJS BVBA*, Cour de Cassation (Belgium), C.97.0176.N, 30.03.2000, stating that violation of the rules of interpretation (expressly mentioning article 31 of the Vienna Convention) could only lead to a decision being overturned (cassation) if the result was that the treaty being interpreted was itself violated; and *AG v Germany* 88 ILR 679, at 682–83 where the Spanish Supreme Court confirms the applicability of the Vienna Convention and its relevance to interpretation of a treaty as part of the internal order; *A Holding ApS v Federal Tax Administration* 8 ITLR 536, decision of Swiss Federal Court (2005), at 556, para 3.4.1 (recognizing applicability of the Vienna Convention's rules to a treaty made before its entry into force); *Belgium v GW and VR-M* 7 ITLR 442, Belgian Cour de Cassation (recognizing applicability of the general rule in article 31 of the Vienna Convention); and for references to the Vienna rules by courts in Japan, see written statement submitted by the Japan Fellowship of Reconciliation to the UN Sub-Commission on the Promotion and Protection of Human Rights, Fifty-fourth session, Doc E/CN.4/Sub.2/2002/NG0/22 of 24 July 2002.

law having its origins in obligations in treaties, these tendencies may have delayed full recognition and use of the Vienna rules.

A brief outline of the progression of the courts in the UK to acceptance of the applicability of the Vienna rules is given below, followed by reference to their acceptance in other jurisdictions within the Commonwealth.[82] Cases in courts in the UK show that the Vienna rules have often been regarded merely as an aid to interpretation, a fashion accessory adorning a particular point, rather than a framework for the interpretative exercise. This may be because they have been found useful in offering an approach to a particular problem or justifying inclusion in the reasoning of particular element. It may, however, be that the system of implementing treaties in the UK has made it difficult for courts to perceive treaty interpretation as something distinct from statutory interpretation.

The first stage in the acknowledgement in courts in the UK of the applicability of the Vienna rules was in 1980 in *Fothergill v Monarch Airlines*.[83] Parenthetically, it is to be noted that this was the same year as Judge Sette Câmara's Separate Opinion in the ICJ tentatively linking the Vienna rules with customary international law.[84] In *Fothergill v Monarch Airlines* one judge (Lord Diplock) in the UK's highest court effectively endorsed the view that what the Vienna Convention said in articles 31 and 32 (of which he quoted the whole of article 32 but only paragraph (1) of article 31) amounted to customary international law. This was in the context of making use of preparatory work:

...international courts and tribunals do refer to travaux préparatoires as an aid to interpretation and this practice as regards national courts has now been confirmed by the Vienna Convention on the Law of Treaties (Cmnd. 4140), to which Her Majesty's Government is a party and which entered into force a few months ago. It applies only to treaties concluded after it came into force...; but what it says in Articles 31 and 32 about interpretation of treaties, in my view, does no more than codify already-existing public international law.[85]

Confusingly, however, Lord Diplock failed to draw the full consequences from his assertion that this was a codification of existing law. For it would follow that the rules applied to treaties pre-dating the Vienna Convention, though it would have been difficult to pinpoint the moment at which the rules had crystallized, their status remaining a matter of some uncertainty even after the Vienna Convention's entry into force.[86] This general applicability is something which has been accepted

---

[82] See also Chapter 1, section 2.4 above; an account of the practice of English courts up to 1986 is in F A Mann, *Foreign Affairs in English Courts* (Oxford: OUP, 1986), at 102–14; and for a list of some early cases in the English courts, see T-C Yü, *The Interpretation of Treaties* (New York: Columbia University, 1927) 81–2, note 1.

[83] [1981] AC 251.   [84] See Chapter 1, section 2.1 above.

[85] [1981] AC 251, at 282; and see Lord Scarman, at 290: 'Faced with an international treaty which has been incorporated into our law, British courts should now follow broadly the guidelines declared by the Vienna Convention on the Law of Treaties.'

[86] Lord Diplock, however, saw the rules as applying essentially to treaties given effect after entry into force of the Vienna Convention: 'By ratifying that Convention, Her Majesty's Government has undertaken an international obligation on behalf of the United Kingdom to interpret future treaties in this manner...', [1981] AC 251, at 283; some uncertainty may have remained: see, eg, R Higgins, 'United Kingdom', chapter 7 in F Jacobs and S Roberts (eds), *The Effect of Treaties in Domestic Law*

or assumed later by courts in the UK. The clear markers in *Fothergill v Monarch Airlines* that the Vienna rules warranted attention was overshadowed by the emphasis in that case on the preparatory work of a treaty. It was probably because of this that for some years thereafter, use of the Vienna rules in English courts was rather uneven and incomplete.[87] However, isolated indication of awareness of the Vienna rules was the start of intermittent attention being paid by individual judges in the UK to the rules.[88] This was followed by gradual progress towards their more general endorsement.[89] In this way, the English judiciary has followed a path broadly parallel to that of the ICJ. Endorsement of the Vienna rules for interpreting treaties (including those pre-dating entry into force of the Vienna Convention) is now unqualified, though their use is not always overt and systematic.[90] In *Sepet v Secretary of State for the Home Department* Lord Bingham set out the whole of articles 31 and 32 of the Vienna Convention, introducing them by stating:

The task of the House [of Lords] is to interpret the 1951 [Status of Refugees] Convention and, having done so, apply it to the facts of the applicants' cases…In interpreting the Convention the House must respect articles 31 and 32 of the Vienna Convention on the Law of Treaties 1969….[91]

(London: Sweet & Maxwell, 1987), 139: 'It would be unsafe to assume that Articles 31 to 33 are fully reflective of customary international law—in any event, this is not an aspect the courts seem much inclined to discuss.'

[87] It was noted in comment on *Fothergill v Monarch* that there were difficulties at the time with the different approaches of the judges, the consequence flowing from the majority conclusion that interpretation was to be 'an exercise in divining not Parliament's will but that of the treaty makers': V Lowe and D Williams, 'A Shirt, a Pair of Sandals, a Cardigan' (1981) 44 MLR 452, at 453; at that time it remained uncertain whether the Vienna rules represented not codification but progressive development, leaving the position in the English courts under a shadow (at 454). See also R K Gardiner, 'Treaty Interpretation in the English Courts since *Fothergill v. Monarch Airlines* (1980)' (1995) 44 ICLQ, 620, and Gardiner, 'Interpreting Treaties in the United Kingdom' in M Freeman (ed), *Legislation and the Courts* (Aldershot: Dartmouth, 1997), 115–32.

[88] See Gardiner, 'Treaty Interpretation in the English Courts since *Fothergill v. Monarch Airlines* (1980)' above.

[89] For a detailed account of the English case law on interpretation of treaties, see F Shaheed, *Using International Law in Domestic Courts* (Oxford: Hart Publishing, 2005), Chapters 4 and 5.

[90] Application to treaties made before the Vienna Convention entered into force is shown by recognition of the rules as a stating customary international law and by applying them to such earlier treaties: see, eg, *R (European Roma Rights Centre and others) v Immigration Officer at Prague Airport* [2005] 2 AC 1, at 31, paras 17–18 (applying the Vienna rules to a treaty of 1951).

[91] [2003] 1 WLR 856, at 861, para 6. It is still possible, however, to detect some lingering suggestions of the idea that the general rule is contained in paragraph (1) of article 31, downplaying its other elements and blurring the differentiation from the supplementary means in article 32. For example Lord Steyn's opinion in *Deep Vein Thrombosis and Air Travel Group Litigation* quotes article 31(1) and states that: 'This is the starting para of treaty interpretation to which other rules are supplementary: see articles 31.2; 31.3; 31.4; and 32. The primacy of the treaty language, read in context and purposively, is therefore of critical importance' [2006] 1 Lloyd's Rep 231, at 238.

Were it not for the express reference to the rest of the rules, and the instruction that the language is to be read in context and purposively, the description of the other rules as 'supplementary' would give an emphasis to article 31(1) which is not within the text of the rules (which reserve 'supplementary' for article 32); nor is this consistent with the approach of the ILC, which clearly indicated that *all* relevant elements identified in the general rule are to be thrown into the crucible, and even the notion of 'supplementary' in the article 32 means of interpretation is given a rather liberal meaning in practice (see Chapter 8 below).

While the principle that the Vienna rules apply for treaty interpretation in the United Kingdom, their use continues to be uneven and piecemeal at times. The UK Supreme Court in *Assange v The Swedish Prosecution Authority* placed considerable weight on part of the rules, though undervaluing their force in its first reference to them. This stated that article 31(3)(b) '*permits* recourse, as an *aid* to interpretation, to "any subsequent practice in the application of the treaty which establishes the agreement of the parties regarding its interpretation".'[92] This formulation suggests an *à la carte* approach and is out of line with the mandatory and unitary character of general rule which does not simply 'permit recourse' as an 'aid' to interpretation. Subsequent practice has a much stronger role than that, for it potentially equates to agreement of the parties as to meaning and thus is authentic evidence of interpretation. Later references in the *Assange* judgment to article 31(3)(b) did, however, give a more faithful account of the provision.[93]

The general influence of *Fothergill v Monarch* still tends to hamper full deployment of the rules. In *Laroche v Spirit of Adventure (UK) Ltd* the Court of Appeal in England quoted, and apparently accepted, a set of propositions which had been applied by the judge at first instance. These were *not* the Vienna rules, though some propositions had some resemblance to parts of them.[94] There are, however, hopeful, if somewhat ambivalent, signs that there may be movement away from complex lists of principles compounded from case law mixed with gobbets of the Vienna rules and towards more direct application of the latter. In *Ben Nevis v HMRC*, the Court of Appeal acknowledged a set of principles by Mummery J in *IRC v Commerzbank* (which it had itself approved), but stated:

The rules of interpretation set out in arts 31 and 32 of the Vienna Convention are rules of customary international law and therefore binding on all states regardless of whether or not they are parties to that Convention. (See *Fothergill* [1981] AC 251 per Lord Diplock at p. 82.) Furthermore, the principles stated by Mummery J are largely derived from the Vienna Convention to which he refers in the passage cited above. Accordingly, it is appropriate to have regard to arts 31 and 32 of the Vienna Convention in this appeal. There is no conflict between these principles and the formulation by Mummery J. However, that formulation was in the nature of a summary and the corresponding articles of the Convention deal with

---

[92] [2012] UKSC 22, at para 67 (emphasis added).

[93] [2012] UKSC 22, at para 67, and see similarly para 130 where article 31(3) is quoted; but cf *Ministry of Justice, Lithuania v Bucnys* [2013] UKSC 71, at paras 38–39, where the UK Supreme Court noted that in *Assange* it had been procedural reasons which ruled out a late challenge to the applicability of the Vienna Convention and to consideration of state practice as potentially relevant to construction of a Framework Decision of the Council of the European Union; in *Lithuania v Bucnys* the Court now doubted the applicability of the Vienna Convention to the Decision as a matter of European Law and questioned the reliability of the available state practice as a guide, even if otherwise admissible; see also *William Frederick Ian Beggs v Her Majesty's Advocate* [2010] SCCR 681, at 757, where the Scottish High Court of Justiciary, citing academic comments in the latter part of the last century, referred to 'the tendency of English courts to "cherry pick" from the principles of interpretation set out in art 31 of the Vienna Convention...making occasional reference to isolated aspects of them in order to support particular interpretations rather than treating them as the framework for interpretation...It is a tendency which remains perceptible'.

[94] [2009] 2 All ER 175, at 180.

certain matters which are not included in the *Commerzbank* formulation. It is convenient to set out at this point arts 31 and 32 of the Vienna Convention on Treaties.[95]

A direct invocation of the Vienna rules, coming nearer to their systematic application, was made by the Court of Appeal in *Kairos Shipping Limited, The Standard Club Limited v Enka & Co LLC* endorsing the proposition that: 'It is important not to compartmentalise the approach to the Convention; it must be interpreted as a whole but one inevitably has to start at the beginning.'[96]

One difficulty which has dogged the courts in the UK is that the legal system does not have a single means of implementing treaties. Treaties are not normally brought into domestic law wholesale. Even where the text is set out in a schedule to an Act of Parliament, this is usually only in the most economical terms, that is setting out the substantive provisions of the treaty (or just those seen as creating obligations) without its final clauses. In cases where the text of the treaty has been transformed into statutory provisions reflecting the substance of the obligations but without using the exact provisions of a treaty, the courts will look to the treaty itself only if the Act itself refers to it or if, where the Act does not refer to the treaty, there is leeway in the wording of the statute and there is compelling evidence that the provisions of the statute were included to give effect to the treaty.[97]

In either approach, however, lies the difficulty that the courts have in the past viewed themselves as interpreting a statute, with the treaty in the background as a possible aid if the meaning of the statute is open to more than one interpretation. If a court determines that it is appropriate to look at the treaty, is the next stage further statutory interpretation or treaty interpretation? This is not a purely theoretical matter. The courts have long recognized that treaties are different in character from statutes. The judges have acknowledged that they are undertaking a different task from one of purely statutory interpretation. Yet they must make their interpretation of a treaty in the context of the statutory provisions, and any other relevant domestic law, so that the process has not been seen as one purely of treaty interpretation.[98]

---

[95] *Ben Nevis (Holdings) Ltd v Revenue and Customs Commissioners* [2013] EWCA Civ 578, 15 ITLR1003, at 1016, paras 17–18; the court quoted two of the three Vienna articles on interpretation, but the effect was somewhat outweighed by its much longer list of what it described as a 'summary of principles applicable to the interpretation of treaties' from *IRC v Commerzbank AG* [1990] STC 285 which it had approved in *Memec v IRC* [1998] STC 754.

[96] [2014] EWCA Civ 217, para 26, citing *CMA CGM SA v Classica Shipping Co Ltd (The "CMA Djakarta")* [2004] EWCA Civ 114, para 12; it is not clear whether the reference to 'the Convention' is to the Vienna Convention or to the Convention being interpreted (the International Convention on Limitation of Liability for Maritime Claims 1976), though the latter is systematically abbreviated as 'the 1976 Convention' elsewhere in both judgments; in any event, the stated principle applies to both Conventions.

[97] See *Salomon v Commissioners of Customs & Excise* [1967] 2 QB 116.

[98] For an illustration of problems of this kind, see the analysis of *Hiscox v Outhwaite* [1992] 1 AC 562 in Chapter 1, section 5.4 above; and for residual ambivalence over the role of the Vienna rules, see Lord Bingham in *R (European Roma Rights Centre and others) v Immigration Officer at Prague Airport* [2005] 2 AC 1, at 31: 'This...approach to interpretation of a Convention...*gains support, if support be needed,* from article 31(1) of the Vienna Convention...' (emphasis added); however, Lord Bingham then invoked further elements of the Vienna rules, without qualifying their status; see also Lord Bingham in *K v Secretary of State for the Home Department* [2007] 1 All ER 671, at 679: '*in case*

This ambivalence seems unfortunate. There are two separate issues. Is the wording of the statute (including any text of the treaty included in the statute) so clear that the court must apply it without recourse to interpretation of the treaty as a treaty? Second, if it is appropriate to consider the treaty itself, how are its terms to be interpreted? There is no obvious reason why, at the second stage, the Vienna rules should not be used as the foundation of interpretation, rather than in the auxiliary role which has characterized much of the case law in the UK since *Fothergill v Monarch Airlines*. However, considerable progress has been achieved since 1986 when F A Mann said, in the considering treaty interpretation: 'In England, unfortunately, the courts have displayed a remarkable disrespect for treaty law.'[99] There has, however, been movement towards interpreting treaties as treaties, not as if in statutory guise. Thus, Lord Bingham, referring to the 1951 United Nations Convention relating to the Status of Refugees, as amended by a Protocol of 1967, stated:

The Convention must be interpreted as an international instrument, not a domestic statute, in accordance with the rules prescribed in the Vienna Convention on the Law of Treaties.[100]

One may conclude that use of the Vienna rules by courts in the UK has been more pragmatic than systematic. Nevertheless, a combination of increasing frequency of their invocation and more detailed attention to their application suggests that some progress is being made towards using the Vienna rules as the foundation for treaty interpretation in place of the previous mixture of domestic precedents and intermittent selection from the rules.[101]

Courts in other Commonwealth jurisdictions have used the Vienna rules in a similar fashion or sometimes more comprehensively. For example, courts in Australia have referred to the Vienna rules on several occasions, and in principle apply them to issues of treaty interpretation, though with some glosses. In 1983, in *Commonwealth v Tasmania (The Tasmanian Dam)*, judges in the High Court of Australia accepted that the Vienna rules applied to treaty interpretation, though distinguishing their application from that in *Fothergill v Monarch Airlines* on the ground that the Australian case concerned interpretation of the Convention for the Protection of the World Cultural and Natural Heritage, Paris, 1972, as an international agreement, not as Australian law.[102] Later, the Full Court of the Federal Court of Australia set out articles 31 and 32 of the Vienna Convention in *QAAH*

---

of doubt arts 31–33 of the Vienna Convention ... may be invoked *to aid* the process of interpretation' (emphasis added); cf Lord Phillips in the Court of Appeal in *The Republic of Ecuador v Occidental Exploration* [2007] All ER (D) 51 (Jul), at paras 25–26, where the court set out the whole of articles 31 and 32 of the Vienna Convention in response to the judge at first instance having quoted part only of article 31(1).

[99] Mann, *Foreign Affairs in English Courts*, 110.

[100] *Januzi v Secretary of State for the Home Department* [2006] 2 AC 426, at 439, para 4.

[101] See, for example, *Adams v Secretary of State for Justice* [2011] UKSC 18, where the UK Supreme Court considered the Vienna rules more comprehensively, including references to articles 31(3)(b), 32, and 33; see also *R (ST) v Secretary of State for the Home Department* [2012] UKSC 12.

[102] (1983) 158 CLR 1, see judgment of Gibbs CJ, at para 77.

v Minister for Immigration & Multicultural & Indigenous Affairs with some further explanations of the approach taken by the Australian courts to treaty interpretation, characterized there as an 'ordered, yet holistic' one.[103]

Other courts in states whose legal systems follow the common law tradition have similarly used the Vienna Convention's rules on treaty interpretation.[104]

4.2.3 States which are not parties to the Vienna Convention

One hundred and fourteen states, out of some 190, are parties to the 1969 Vienna Convention.[105] Among those that are not parties, it is difficult to detect any which have developed a particularly distinctive and comprehensive approach to treaty interpretation that differs radically from that of the Vienna Convention. This is hardly surprising as application of the Vienna rules as a statement of customary international law would not compromise any position taken in opposition to other provisions of the Vienna Convention.[106] Thus, in *Re Société Schneider Electric*, the French Conseil d'État cited the conclusions of the Commissaire du Gouvernement in which he recounted how since 1980 the Conseil has developed an approach to interpreting treaties guided by the general principles of public international law set out in articles 31–33 of the Vienna Convention.[107]

One state whose courts have developed extensive practice on treaty interpretation is the USA.[108] The Vienna Convention has been signed but not ratified by the USA. Consideration of US case law must take account of the fact that the

---

[103] [2005] FCAFC 136, and see *Qenos Pty Ltd v Ship 'APL Sydney'* [2009] FCA 1090, paras 11–17; *Secretary, Department of Families, Housing, Community and Indigenous Affairs v Mahrous* [2013] FCAFC 75, para 55: 'The principles set out in the Vienna Convention apply to both multilateral and bilateral treaties'; and for systematic application of the general rule, see *Li v Zhou* (Court of Appeal, New South Wales) [2014] NSWCA 176.

[104] See, eg, *Attorney-General v Zaoui* [2006] 1 NZLR 289 where the New Zealand Supreme Court accepted articles 31 and 32 of the Vienna Convention as stating customary international law, acknowledged the rules to be part of the law of New Zealand, and followed their scheme systematically; see also *Crown Forest Industries Ltd v Canada* [1995] 2 SCR 802, where the Canadian Supreme Court referred to articles 31 and 32 of the Vienna Convention, and many later cases where the higher courts in Canada have referred to elements of the Vienna rules, eg *Gulfmark Offshore N.S. Limited v Canada* [2007] FCA 302, *Takeda Canada Inc. v Canada (Health)* [2011] FC 1444, *Ezokola v Canada* [2013] SCC 40, and *Peracomo Inc. v TELUS Communications Co.* [2014] SCC 29; *Trinidad Cement Ltd v Co-operative Republic of Guyana* (Caribbean Court of Justice) (2009) 74 WIR 302.

[105] Multilateral Treaties Deposited with the Secretary-General of the UN, UN treaty database at <http://untreaty.un.org> as at 30 September 2014.

[106] See, for example, *Jethmalani and others v Union of India* (Supreme Court of India 14 ITLR 1, at 26, para 60 (referring to article 31(1) of the Vienna Convention, although India was not a party) and *Sølvik v Staten v/Skatt Øst* (Supreme Court of Norway) 11 ITLR 15, at 34, para 47 (applying article 31(1) of the Vienna Convention as being 'generally accepted as the international norm', although Norway was not a party).

[107] 4 ITLR 1077, at 1106 and 1115–16, judgment of 28 June 2002; and see *State v Mhlungu and Others* [1995] 2 LRC 503, at 551, where the South African Constitutional Court referred to the significance of context in article 31(1) of the Vienna Convention as support for an interpretative approach to the South African constitution.

[108] For a long list of early American cases, see T-C Yü, *The Interpretation of Treaties* (New York: Columbia University Press, 1927), 81–2, note 1.

approach of the courts was well developed before the Vienna rules were drawn up, though the executive, to which the courts pay considerable respect, acknowledges the rules as customary international law. The fact that the USA has not ratified the Vienna Convention has not prevented the deployment of the Vienna rules by the USA in international proceedings.[109] More generally, the US State Department has stated that it accepts the Vienna Convention as in large part 'the authoritative guide to current treaty law and practice'.[110] Further, the courts have long paid heed to international law; and if the Vienna rules do reflect customary law, the approach of the US courts could be expected to be broadly in line with them. It is suggested here that any divergence from the approach taken in the Vienna rules probably consists mainly of a slightly greater willingness to admit a broader range of evidence of the intention of the parties.

The reason why the USA has not ratified the Convention was not the rejection by the Vienna Conference of the US proposal to modify the draft Vienna rules by combining the content of the eventual articles 31 and 32 into a single provision with all the elements on the same footing. Rather, it was because the Senate required that the President deposit an instrument of ratification with a special understanding or interpretative statement regarding article 46 of the Convention.[111] That article provides that a state may not invoke any domestic irregularity which has led to its consent to a treaty being given in breach of its internal law. Such a violation of internal law does not invalidate a state's consent unless 'that violation was manifest and concerned a rule of its internal law of fundamental importance' (article 46). The understanding proposed by the Senate was to the effect that it is a rule of the internal law of the USA of fundamental importance that no treaty is valid for the USA, nor is the giving of consent for the USA to be bound by a treaty permissible, unless the Senate has given its advice and consent to that treaty, or the treaty's terms have been approved by law.[112] Such an interpretative statement could have prejudiced the position in the case of 'executive agreements', that is treaties (in the sense of the Vienna Convention rather than that of the US Constitution) which, by established practice in the USA, have long been concluded by the executive, alone or with legislative support but without advice and consent of the Senate. Failure by the executive and Senate to agree on this issue precluded ratification.

Some courts in the USA below the level of the Supreme Court have accepted that the Vienna rules apply to treaty interpretation. This is evident, first, from general acceptance by the courts of the Vienna Convention ('We therefore treat the Vienna Convention as an authoritative guide to the customary international law of treaties'[113]); and, second, from specific acknowledgement of applicability of

---

[109] See Chapter 1, section 2.3 above.

[110] S Exec Doc L, 92d Cong, 1st Sess 1 (1971); see *Chubb & Son, Inc v Asiana Airlines* 214 F3d 301 (2d Cir 2000), at 308, and material cited there.

[111] See E Criddle, 'The Vienna Convention on the Law of Treaties in U.S. Treaty Interpretation' (2003–2004) 44 *Va J Int'l L* 435, at 442.

[112] Criddle, 'The Vienna Convention on the Law of Treaties', at 442.

[113] *Chubb & Son, Inc v Asiana Airlines* at 309, citing several US cases referring to the Vienna Convention and the practice of the State Department.

the rules ('…both federal and state courts have acknowledged and employed the principles of interpretation codified in the Vienna Convention'[114]). The amount of attention given to the Vienna Convention by the lower courts in the USA has been considerably surpassed by study and analysis of treaty interpretation in American academic literature. While much of this is devoted to constitutional, domestic, and theoretical issues, there are some studies which examine US practice in the light of international law.[115]

The US Supreme Court has referred to the definition of 'treaty' in the Vienna Convention in order to make the contrast between that international definition and the more limited meaning in the US Constitution's provision referring to instruments to which the USA has become a party after following the specific procedure in the Constitution relating to treaties.[116] It has not referred to the Vienna rules. The Supreme Court was, of course, interpreting treaties long before the Vienna Convention was signed and came into force. The Court adopted what might be described as a largely 'internationalist' approach, recognizing treaties as creatures of international law. Hence it has been observed that: 'Most notably the canon of "good faith" and its corollary, "liberal interpretation", dominated US treaty interpretation from the late nineteenth until the middle of the twentieth century, reflecting an internationalist attitude reminiscent of the writings of Grotius and Vattel'.[117] It has continued to apply this approach in the era of the Vienna Convention but with, some suggest, increasingly 'nationalist' overtones and deference to executive discretion.[118] A number of factors have been suggested as distinguishing the modern Supreme Court's approach from that of the Vienna Convention.[119] These are summarized here, taking first a general criticism, then

---

[114] *Busby v State of Alaska* 40 P3d 807 (Alaska Ct App, 2002), at 814 and at fn 13 citing further cases; see also Criddle, 'The Vienna Convention on the Law of Treaties', at 447, fns 72–73; for consideration of further issues in *Busby v State of Alaska*, see Chapter 9, section 4.7 below.

[115] For major studies which do consider the Vienna Convention, see Criddle, 'The Vienna Convention on the Law of Treaties', and M Frankowska, 'The Vienna Convention on the Law of Treaties before United States Courts' (1987–1988) 28 *Va J Int'l L* 281, and D J Bederman, *Classical Canons* (Aldershot: Ashgate, 2001), Chapters IX–X.

[116] See *Weinberger v Rossi* 456 US 25 (1982), at 29, fn 5 and US Constitution [Article II, para 2]. Justice Blackmun mentions the Vienna Convention in a dissenting opinion in *Sale v Haitian Centers Council* 509 US 155, at 191 (1993), using the Convention in support of the treaty interpretation element relying on 'ordinary meaning'.

[117] H P Aust, A Rodiles, and P Staubach, 'Unity or Uniformity?: Domestic Courts and Treaty Interpretation' (2014) 27 *Leiden Journal of International Law* 75, at 85; and for an early example of the Supreme Court taking into account practice evidenced by the law of other states, see *Tucker v Alexandroff* 22 S.Ct. 195 ('crew' included a member of a small advance party sent to take over a warship on which he had not set foot and which had ben launched but not commissioned) in respect of which Yü saw the approach of the majority judgment as based on good faith in achieving "the high purpose" of the treaty: Yü, *The Interpretation of Treaties*, at 207.

[118] See Criddle, 'The Vienna Convention on the Law of Treaties', at 467 ff; Aust and others, 'Unity or Uniformity?: Domestic Courts and Treaty Interpretation' at 86–8; but see also M K Madden, '*Abbott v. Abbott*: Reviving Good Faith and Rejecting Ambiguity in Treaty Jurisprudence' (2012) 71 *Maryland LR* 575.

[119] Madden, at 435–36 and 463, and see Bederman, *Classical Canons*, Chapter XII for a thorough and critical account of 13 'significant' US Supreme Court treaty interpretation cases since 1986.

three specific points on which the Supreme Court's practice is said to diverge from the Vienna rules.

A general criticism is made by Bederman: 'One consistent pathology of treaty interpretation by U.S. courts has been an avid willingness to depart from the actual terms of the treaty instrument and to seek confirmation of meaning in outside sources…In short, the threshold of tolerable textual ambiguity in treaties has been set quite low…'.[120] Bederman helpfully distinguishes two types of ambiguity which have led the Supreme Court to step away from the text of a treaty: first, 'slip of the pen' cases, where bad drafting has omitted wording usually included in such a treaty or present in a related instrument; and second, 'situational obscurity' where apparently clear language does not meet the situation that has actually arisen.[121] These do not seem to be extreme extensions of the notion of ambiguity.

The first real divergence from the Vienna rules is the Supreme Court's acceptance of a wider notion of context, potentially allowing reference to a broader range of evidence of a state's intent, including material revealing a party's own documentation not forming part of the preparatory work. This (unsurprisingly) is in line with the proposal made by the US delegation at the Vienna Conference to put the content of article 32 of the Vienna Convention (supplementary means, including circumstances of conclusion and preparatory work) on the same footing as the other elements in the Vienna rules; but it goes rather further than that by extending the notion of preparatory work and surrounding circumstances to include, as indicated above, material of unilateral origin. Second, the Supreme Court's approach may also pay less regard to relevant rules of international law applying in the relations between the parties to the treaty under interpretation. Third, it has further been suggested that the Supreme Court pays excessive deference to the views of the Executive on the meaning of a treaty, rather than forming its own view by reference to the international rules codified in the Vienna Convention.[122]

Referring to the first of these ways in which the practice of the US Supreme Court is said to diverge from the Vienna rules, it should be acknowledged that international courts and tribunals have not given a very clear indication of what constitutes preparatory work. However, it is fair to say that documents showing unilateral positions of states in negotiations would not usually be given weight by international tribunals unless clearly brought into public view and endorsed by the other treaty-making states. There are some examples of the Supreme Court having used extrinsic material which has not been so endorsed by other parties.[123] While this does not necessarily mean that the Supreme Court reached the wrong conclusion in those cases, it does mean that these instances are not good examples of what constitutes a proper approach to interpretation of treaties were the Vienna rules being used.

---

[120] Bederman, *Classical Canons*, at 246.   [121] Bederman, at 251.
[122] See Criddle, 'The Vienna Convention on the Law of Treaties', at 459–60.
[123] Criddle, at 452–3.

There are two aspects to the second criticism, that the Supreme Court does not pay sufficient regard to international law. The first, which is clearly well founded, is that if the Court does not use the Vienna rules when interpreting a treaty, it is less likely to reach a conclusion on a question of interpretation which accords with the USA's treaty obligations. The second aspect is whether the Supreme Court departs from the principle in article 31(3)(c) of the Vienna Convention and fails to apply to the interpretation of treaties any relevant rules of international law applicable in the relations between the parties. It is only recently that much attention has been focused on this provision in international courts and tribunals. Its scope has not been precisely defined. Criticism of the approach taken by the Supreme Court may be more aptly directed to whether it has paid sufficient regard to the rules of international law applying to the situation before it as distinct from relevant rules of international law as an element in treaty interpretation. Thus, for example, in *Sale v Haitian Centers Council*, the Supreme Court majority found that the USA had not acted inconsistently with the UN Refugee Convention in turning back boatloads of escaping Haitians on the high seas.[124] The Court's conclusion that 'return (*refouler*)', a term used with its parenthetical French equivalent in the Convention, referred to treatment of refugees who had succeeded in entering a state party to the Convention was supported by reference to the preparatory work.[125] This use of the preparatory work was criticized by a dissenting Justice who came closer to the Vienna rules in preferring the ordinary meaning of the words used in their context. Had the Court used the Vienna Convention's general rule, it would also have had regard to subsequent practice and the other obligations incumbent on the USA which have considerably extended the prohibition on sending people to states where they will be likely to be tortured or persecuted.[126]

In contrast, in the *Alvarez-Machain* case, the Supreme Court considered whether the abduction of a Mexican national in Mexico and his conveyance to the USA for trial there was in breach of the US–Mexico Extradition treaty.[127] There might well be grounds for holding that there had been a clear violation of Mexican sovereignty, and there may have been an arguable case that an appropriate response would be that in order to prevent injustice to an accused, or to discourage further illegalities by the authorities, jurisdiction in such circumstances should not be maintained; but it is less clear what issue of treaty interpretation would have been assisted by application of relevant rules of international law applicable in relations between the USA and Mexico.

The third criticism, that the Supreme Court pays excessive heed to the views of the executive, suggests that the result is an excessively nationalist interpretation,

---

[124] 509 US 155 (1993), at 184–87, considered further in Chapter 8, section 4.4.8; see also H H Koh, 'The "Haiti Paradigm" in United States Human Rights Policy' (1993–1994) 103 *Yale LJ* 2391.

[125] See Chapter 8, section 4.4.8 below.

[126] See UNHCR, 'Advisory Opinion on the Extraterritorial Application of Non-refoulement' Obligations under the 1951 Convention relating to the Status of Refugees and its 1967 Protocol [2007] *European Human Rights LR* 484 and G S Goodwin-Gill and J McAdam, *The Refugee in International Law* (Oxford: OUP, 3rd edn, 2007), Chapter 5.

[127] *US v Alvarez-Machain* 504 US 655 (1992).

rather than an internationalist one. However, in view of the assertions by the executive of the applicability of the Vienna rules to treaty interpretation, this seems a factor which would be likely to draw the Supreme Court indirectly *towards* application of the Vienna rules. It is also to be noted that the position in the USA is, in general terms, little different from that likely to be encountered in most national legal systems. The executive, alone or in combination with the legislature, is likely to be in an influential, if not commanding, position as regards treaty interpretations in the internal legal order. Courts in national legal systems are applying treaties which have been domesticated and legislation can usually be introduced to establish an interpretation if this is thought necessary. For this reason, and because it is desirable that a state should speak with one voice in matters of foreign relations, it is no more than prudent for courts to keep themselves aware of the executive's interpretations of a treaty.

In facing some contemporary issues of treaty interpretation, the Supreme Court has shown signs of resuming a somewhat more international approach. In *Abbott v Abbott* some attention was paid to the significance of subsequent practice in the decisions of courts in other jurisdictions.[128] A brief for the United States as amicus curiae had noted that: '[a]lthough the United States has not ratified the Vienna Convention on the Law of Treaties, the United States generally recognizes the Convention as an authoritative guide to treaty interpretation'.[129] Similarly, the brief for the Petitioner before the Supreme Court noted that: 'the Department of State has indicated both that 'the [Vienna] Convention is already generally recognized as the authoritative guide to current treaty law and practice', and that: '[m]ost provisions of the Vienna Convention, including Articles 31 and 32 ... are declaratory of customary international law'.[130] Thus, although, in the event, the Supreme Court did not itself refer to the Vienna rules, these briefs helped to shape the argument along the lines of the approach in the Vienna Convention.

In *Abbott v Abbott*, various orders were made in the family courts in Chile in respect of a child whose parents separated there. The mother was to have custody and the father had access or visitation rights, there being a statutory prohibition under Chilean law, as well as a court order (*ne exeat*), forbidding either parent from removing the child from the country without the other parent's consent. The central issue was whether the *ne exeat* prohibition gave the father a 'right of custody' within the meaning of the Hague Convention on the Civil Aspects of International Child Abduction. If it did, the Convention provided a right for the father to apply to the Courts in the USA to have the child returned to Chile as the child's country of habitual residence after being taken to the USA in violation

---

[128] *Abbott v Abbott*, 130 S.Ct. 1983 (2010); see M K Madden, '*Abbott v. Abbott*: Reviving Good Faith and Rejecting Ambiguity in Treaty Jurisprudence' (2012) 71 *Maryland LR* 575.

[129] *Abbott v Abbott*, 2009 WL 3043970 (U.S.), FN 6, citing *Fujitsu Ltd. v Federal Express Corp.*, 247 F.3d 423,433 (2d Cir.), cert. denied, 534 U.S. 891 (2001).

[130] Attributed to Dep't of State, Letter of Submittal to the President, S. Exec. Doc. L., 92d Cong., 1st Sess. 1 (1971), and Letter from Roberts B. Owen, Legal Advisor of the Dep't of State, to Sen. Adlai Stevenson III (Sept. 12, 1980) respectively: 2009 WL 2978245 (U.S.), FN 6.

of the *ne exeat* order.[131] The Convention defines 'rights of custody' as including 'rights relating to the care of the person of the child and, in particular, the right to determine the child's place of residence'. They are distinguished from 'rights of access', which are to include 'the right to take a child for a limited period of time to a place other than the child's habitual residence'.[132] The particular mention of the right to determine a child's place of residence as a custody right raises the issue whether a *ne exeat* order comes within this category of rights.

The analysis in the opinion of the Supreme Court looked to the inclusion in the Convention's definition of 'rights of custody' of a reference to the right to 'determine the child's place of residence'. The Court considered that: '"place of residence" encompasses the child's country of residence, especially in light of the Convention's explicit purpose to prevent wrongful removal across international borders'.[133] Noting that one of the dictionary definitions of 'determine' is 'to set bounds or limits to', the Court found that a right entitling a parent to set limits to the child's place of residence was a custodial right.[134]

This initial investigation of the ordinary meaning in the light of the object and purpose of the Convention was set in the context of the scheme of the Convention, among other things distinguishing rights of custody from rights of access. After a brief acknowledgement of the support of the State Department, the Court made a thorough examination of the practice in the decisions of courts of other parties to the treaty. It considered that international case law confirmed 'broad acceptance of the rule that *ne exeat* rights are rights of custody'.[135] In conjunction with this subsequent practice evidenced by decisions of courts, the Supreme Court considered the history of the Convention, particularly through examination of an Explanatory Report published soon after conclusion of the Convention, as well as giving more detailed attention to the purposes of the Convention. The Court adopted what might now be viewed as an 'evolutionary' interpretation:

Scholars agree that there is an emerging international consensus that *ne exeat* rights are rights of custody, even if that view was not generally formulated when the Convention was drafted in 1980. At that time, joint custodial arrangements were unknown in many of the contracting states, and the status of *ne exeat* rights was not yet well understood.[136]

Is this judgment of the US Supreme Court in line with the Vienna rules even though it does not refer to them? It certainly seems to reflect not only key elements of the rules but also their intended manner of application. Contrary to the

---

[131] Convention on the Civil Aspects of International Child Abduction, The Hague, 1980, articles 3 and 8.

[132] Convention on the Civil Aspects of International Child Abduction, The Hague, 1980, article 5.

[133] *Abbott v Abbott* 130 S.Ct. 1983, at 1990–91.   [134] 130 S.Ct. 1983, at 1991–93.

[135] 130 S.Ct. 1983, at 1993; see also *Lozano v Montoya Alvarez* (US Supreme Court, Slip Opinion 12-820, 5 March 2014) where the Court declined to apply the principle of 'equitable tolling' (waiving the limitation period) to the time limit specified in the Hague Abduction Convention, taking account (among other things) of the decisions of courts in other treaty parties; cf the treatment of subsequent practice by the House of Lords in *R (on the application of Hoxha) v Special Adjudicator*, Chapter 1, section 5.5 above.

[136] 130 S.Ct. 1983, at 1994.

criticism that the rules are based on an excessively literal approach, the judgment shows well how the reference to ordinary meaning in the rules demands consideration of context and of the object and purpose of a treaty if it is to have realistic application. The practice in application of the treaty, where it shows subsequent agreement of the parties as to meaning—an element of the Vienna rules having peculiar significance given the nature and role of treaties in legal relations between states—is given suitable prominence and, likewise, appropriate use is made of supplementary means of interpretation. The Court's approach is also in line with the loose manner which the ILC envisaged for use of the rules, there being no hierarchy or mandated sequence for deployment of elements in the general rule. Thus even without express reference to the Vienna rules, the interpretative process would have been within their flexible framework.[137]

As in the United Kingdom, although with significant constitutional differences, how treaties are given effect in domestic law has played a part in shaping the approach taken by courts in the USA to treaty interpretation, and the practice of those courts is still developing.[138] It may reasonably be concluded that the approach taken by the US Supreme Court does differ from that in the Vienna rules, most significantly in its willingness to take into account a broader range of materials in an attempt to ascertain the intention of the parties or achieve a purposive result. However, this does not necessarily lead to a very different result because the Court weighs relevant factors in a broadly similar manner to that required by the Vienna rules, although its general approach to treaty interpretation varies with changes in the Court's composition.[139]

---

[137] The three dissenting judges characterized a *ne exeat* order as a 'travel restriction' which they saw as associated with rights of access rather than custody.

[138] See, eg, J Coyle, 'Incorporative Statutes and the Borrowed Treaty Rule' (2010) 50 *Virginia JIL* 655; and see Madden, '*Abbott v. Abbott*: Reviving Good Faith and Rejecting Ambiguity in Treaty Jurisprudence' at 615–8, suggesting that '*Abbott v Abbott* represents a missed opportunity by the supreme court to distinguish treaty from statutory interpretation'; see also F E Marouf, 'The Role of Foreign Authorities in U.S. Asylum Adjudication' (2013) 45 *NYU J Int'l L & Pol* 391.

[139] See, eg, *Sumitomo v Avalgiano* 457 US 176 (1982), where the Court considered that a provision in a bilateral treaty between the USA and Japan required a subsidiary of a Japanese company to be treated as a company of the USA because it was, in the words of the treaty, 'constituted under the applicable laws and regulations' of New York. The Court gave priority to the clear meaning of the terms used, given added weight by both states parties to the treaty agreeing to this interpretation; but cf *BG Group plc v Argentina* Slip Opinion No. 12–138 of 5 March 2014 (US Supreme Court) upholding the arbitrators' powers to interpret and apply provisions in a bilateral investment treaty when deciding the extent of their own jurisdiction, the US Supreme Court approached the matter as if the treaty were a contract, but between nations, and considered that, where a court is asked to interpret a treaty pursuant to a motion to vacate or confirm an arbitral award made in the USA under the Federal Arbitration Act, 'it should normally apply the presumptions supplied by American law' (at pp 10–11); and see C J Mahoney, 'Treaties as Contracts: Textualism, Contract Theory, and the Interpretation of Treaties' (2006–2007) 116 *Yale L J* 824.

PART II

INTERPRETATION APPLYING THE VIENNA CONVENTION ON THE LAW OF TREATIES

A. The General Rule

5

The General Rule: (1) The Treaty, its Terms, and their Ordinary Meaning

Treaty—good faith—ordinary meaning—terms—context—object and purpose

Interpretation under Article 31 of the Vienna Convention is a process of progressive encirclement where the interpreter starts under the general rule with (1) the ordinary meaning of the terms of the treaty, (2) in their context and (3) in light of the treaty's object and purpose, and by cycling through this three step inquiry iteratively closes in upon the proper interpretation. In approaching this task, it is critical to observe two things about the general rule... First, the Vienna Convention does not privilege any one of these three aspects of the interpretation method. The meaning of a word or phrase is not solely a matter of dictionaries and linguistics....[1]

Article 31

General rule of interpretation

1. A treaty shall be interpreted in good faith in accordance with the ordinary meaning to be given to the terms of the treaty in their context and in the light of its object and purpose.
2. The context for the purpose of the interpretation of a treaty shall comprise, in addition to the text, including its preamble and annexes:
   (a) any agreement relating to the treaty which was made between all the parties in connection with the conclusion of the treaty;
   (b) any instrument which was made by one or more parties in connection with the conclusion of the treaty and accepted by the other parties as an instrument related to the treaty.

...

This chapter is the first of those making an analytical study of the Vienna rules. This means taking them to bits and applying the rules to each term. It is necessary, therefore, to preface these chapters with the warning that in an exercise of treaty interpretation where application of the rules is to an actual dispute or issue, the Vienna rules are to be applied together, not in bits. Necessary here to make the exercise manageable in the circumstances of a detailed exposition of the rules, the risk of application of individual rules of treaty interpretation in isolation from one another was the main reason why the whole of article 31 is described as the

---

[1] *Aguas del Tunari v Bolivia* (ICSID ARB/02/03), Award of 21 October 2005, para 91.

(singular) 'general rule'.[2] Similarly, too often 'ordinary meaning' in the opening paragraph of that article is taken as a separate, or even the sole, interpretative element without its immediately associated reference to context and to object and purpose, while the latter (object and purpose) is sometimes taken as merely a mandate for a general teleological approach.

Concern for the need to safeguard against 'excessive molecularization' of the Vienna rules led to the formulation of the first paragraph of the rules placing in combination several elements rather than itemizing them separately.[3] A strong note of caution must be sounded over the extract from the arbitral award at the head of this chapter. Helpfully describing interpretation under article 31 as a process of 'progressive encirclement', and rightly pointing out that all three components of article 31(1) which the extract identifies must be used to close in on the proper meaning of terms, the extract should not be taken as putting the elements of the rest of the general rule in article 31 out of view. Quite the contrary, the 'progressive encirclement' description holds good for the whole of article 31, the 'crucible' analogy described in Chapter 1 requiring that *all* relevant elements identifiable by the Vienna rules, and presenting themselves in any given instance, are ultimately taken together in each exercise of treaty interpretation.

The second paragraph of article 31 is a definition of 'context' for the purposes of interpretation. What comes within paragraphs 2(a) and (b) of that definition (agreements and instruments in connection with conclusion of a treaty) has been considered in Chapter 3; the role which those agreements and instruments play in treaty interpretation is considered in Chapter 6. The principal elements of article 31(1) which are considered here are: (1) 'a treaty'; (2) 'good faith'; (3) 'ordinary meaning of terms'; (4) 'context'; and (5) 'object and purpose'.

1. A 'Treaty'

The opening reference to 'a treaty' is to be interpreted by giving the term 'treaty' its particular or 'special' meaning established by the Vienna Convention in its definition provision (article 2).[4] This is required by article 31(4) of the Convention (a special meaning is to be given to a term if it is established that the parties so intended). In relation to this definition of 'treaty' a distinction is to be noted between application of the Vienna rules as provisions of a treaty and as a statement of customary international law. While it is now beyond question that the Vienna rules (ie articles 31–33) are rules of customary international law, the rest of the Vienna Convention has not all been confirmed as stating customary

---

[2] See further Chapter 1, section 4.2 above.
[3] See Observations of the Government of Israel [1966] *Yearbook of the ILC*, vol II, p 92.
[4] For definition and comment on it, see Chapter 1, section 3.1 above.

law. Hence the Vienna Convention's definition of 'treaty' cannot necessarily be taken to be part of customary international law. Definitions perform an adjectival role, their content being contextually constricted, so that considering whether they are 'rules' of customary international law is actually a rather stilted exercise. The definitions are adjuncts to rules and the real question is therefore how far the definition of 'treaty' controls the extent of applicability of the Vienna rules.

Article 2 of the Vienna Convention introduces its definition with the limitation: 'For the purposes of the present Convention'. This negates any initial presumption that by reason of its link with use of the term in article 31(1) (acknowledged to be customary international law), the definition of 'treaty' could be taken to identify the content of that term for customary international law generally. This does not exclude a more general utility of this (and the other definitions in article 2) based on their good sense; nor does it rule out the possibility that the definitions may assume a defining role in usage of the terms in propositions of customary international law. In its commentary on the draft of article 2 the ILC records:

This article, as its title and the introductory words of paragraph 1 indicate, is intended only to state the meanings with which terms are used in the draft articles.[5]

This extract from the preparatory work is in line with the ordinary and clear meaning of the opening words of article 2. The correct interpretation, therefore, appears to be that application of the Vienna rules as a matter of treaty relations is limited to instruments falling within the definition in article 2. The ICJ has indicated that where rules are codified in a treaty, customary law continues to occupy a parallel field on the same subject matter.[6] While all treaties covered by the definition in the Vienna Convention are within any customary law meaning of a treaty, the definition adopted for the purposes of the Convention is more limited than the meaning ascribed by customary law. For example, the latter would not be limited to agreements between states but would include agreements governed by international law involving international organizations.[7] Oral agreements and some multilateral instruments involving states and other entities have also been assimilated to treaties.[8] There is no reason why tribunals should not apply customary rules of treaty interpretation (as stated in the Vienna rules) if they regard such instruments as of the character of treaties.

---

[5] United Nations Conference on the Law of Treaties: Official Records: Documents of the Conference, A/CONF.39/11/Add.2., p 39, para 8 and [1966] *Yearbook of the ILC*, vol II, p 188, para 1.

[6] *Military and Paramilitary Activities in and against Nicaragua (Nicaragua v United States of America) (Merits)* [1986] ICJ Reports 14, at paras 174–79.

[7] Such treaties are governed by the same rules as the Vienna rules: see the Vienna Convention on the Law of Treaties between States and International Organizations or between International Organizations, Vienna, 1986: see Chapter 4, section 2.2 above.

[8] See A Aust, *Modern Treaty Law and Practice* (Cambridge: CUP, 3rd edn, 2013), at 7–8, 16, and 55 ff, and Agreements between Belgium (Brussels-Capital, Flanders, Wallonia Regional Governments),

1.1 The 'treaty' and its 'terms'

> ...the meaning of a sentence may be more than that of the separate words, as a melody is more than the notes, and no degree of particularity can ever obviate recourse to the setting in which all appear, and which all collectively create.[9]

The first paragraph of the general rule, which provides the immediate context in which the word 'treaty' is used, can be seen as formulated to differentiate between a treaty and its 'terms'. It is the *treaty* which is to be interpreted; it is the *terms* whose ordinary meaning is to be the starting point, their context moderating selection of that meaning, and the process being further illuminated by the treaty's object and purpose.

There is, however, an obvious ambiguity in the reference to 'the terms of the treaty'. 'Terms' could refer simply to the words or provisions of the treaty or it could mean the bargain struck by the parties. The context clearly suggests the former, but this is considered further in section 3.2 on 'ordinary meaning' below. However, a more controversial point is that the formulation of the complete first paragraph of the general rule seems to have been mainly the product of a difference in approach founded on a supposed contrast between text and intention. An underlying question in the ILC's initial debates on rules of interpretation was 'whether interpretation should be by reference to the text itself or to the intention of the parties'.[10] The ILC's approach favoured the text as the starting point on the basis that this was the best evidence of the finally agreed intent of the parties.

The first draft put to the ILC by its fourth Special Rapporteur on the law of treaties (Waldock) had opened by stating that the 'terms of a treaty' were to be interpreted in good faith, etc. The opening appears to have been changed in the course of the ILC's work to reflect more closely the 1956 Resolution of the Institute of International Law and the formulation of principles by Sir Gerald Fitzmaurice which together inspired the wording of the ILC draft.[11] The former had opened its proposed rules of interpretation by reciting the 'agreement of the parties having been reached on the text of the treaty...'. Fitzmaurice had described a principle of 'actuality (or textuality)', stating: 'Treaties are to be interpreted primarily...on the basis of their actual texts.' This he coupled with other principles including that

France, and Netherlands on the Protection of the Rivers Meuse and Scheldt, Charleville Mezieres, 1994, (1995) 34 ILM 851.

[9] Judge Learned Hand in *Helvering v Gregory Revenue* 69 F 2d 809, at 810–11 (US Court of Appeals, 2nd Circuit) (1934).

[10] Mr de Luna [1964] *Yearbook of the ILC*, vol I, p 276, para 16; see also Mr Bartos, at p 279, para 64: 'The draft articles were based on the general concept, so dear to the English school of legal thought, that interpretation meant interpretation of the text rather than of the spirit of a treaty.'

[11] See Third Report of Special Rapporteur (Waldock) [1964] *Yearbook of the ILC*, vol II, pp 55–6 and Chapter 2, section 8 above; see also the observation of Mr Amado that 'in fact, a treaty consisted of a number of texts, contexts and terms; what had to be interpreted was the treaty itself, not its terms...', [1964] *Yearbook of the ILC*, vol I, p 277, para 28.

of 'integration': 'Treaties are to be interpreted as a whole...'[12] The formulation ultimately adopted by the ILC thus reflects the idea that, while it is the text of the treaty that must be taken as the authentic expression of the agreement of the parties, the treaty is to be read as a whole and respect paid to its object and purpose, rather than simply taking words that are the subject of controversy and digging out their meaning solely from dictionary, grammar, and syntax.

The principle of textuality has been helpfully summarized:

This aspect of the primacy of the text has been recognized by international tribunals in a number of recurring situations. First, it seems to be generally recognized that an interpretation that does not emerge from the text cannot be accepted, however plausible it may be in view of the circumstances, unless failure to do so would lead to an obviously unreasonable result. Accordingly, tribunals have usually rejected otherwise reasonable interpretations because to accept them would have been tantamount to rephrasing or otherwise altering the actual text. Second, interpretations suggested by means of interpretation not derived from the text cannot be justified by referring to general custom, usage, or even recognized rules of international law unless sufficiently supported by the text. Last, when two or more reasonable interpretations exist, all of which are consistent with the text, the one that appears to be the most compatible with the text should prevail in the absence of persuasive evidence in support of another interpretation.[13]

1.2. The sound of silence—absent and implied terms

Sometimes the absence of something means simply that it is not there.[14]

One of the most difficult areas of treaty interpretation is how to cope with silence, or absent terms. If the treaty does not expressly make provision for the matter in issue, must it be assumed that it is not covered? This depends on what 'it' is, on the nature of the treaty and the interaction of the various elements of the Vienna rules. If there is a list of items which the treaty covers, something which is not capable of coming within any meaning within the list is excluded, but even this can be infused with an element of flexibility by the *eiusdem generis* rule. The more complicated issue is where a treaty authorizes one thing but leaves it unclear whether the interpreter is to deduce that other similar matters are to be the subject of later negotiation or are not regulated by the treaty (therefore leaving the parties free to act as they will). The nature of the treaty may be a key factor here. For example, a constitution of an international organization may require a greater degree of

---

[12] See Chapter 2, section 8.

[13] R H Berglin, 'Treaty Interpretation and the Impact of Contractual Choice of Forum Clauses on the Jurisdiction of International Tribunals: the Iranian Forum Clause Decisions of the Iran–United States Claims Tribunal' (1986) 21 *Texas International Law Journal* 39, at 44 (footnotes omitted).

[14] *Canada—Term of Patent Protection* Report of WTO Appellate Body, WT/DS170/AB/R (2000), para 78; and see J Klabbers, 'On Rationalism in Politics: Interpretation of Treaties and the World Trade Organization' (2005) 74 *Nordic JIL* 405, at 418, criticizing rule-governed interpretation, but commending this statement.

readiness to accept implied powers to exercise its functions, in contrast to a treaty in which precision is the key, such as one fixing a boundary.[15]

As to the nature of the treaty, this may have an effect on interpretation in different, and not always predictable, ways. The arbitral award in *Air Services Agreement (USA v France)* (1978)[16] shows this. Bilateral air services agreements in the second half of the twentieth century were treaties providing very detailed regulation of air services, at least until the concept of 'open skies' came to the fore. In this case an American airline proposed to operate large aircraft from the USA to London and then decant the passengers into smaller aircraft which the airline proposed to operate for onward travel to European destinations, including Paris. Such a switch from larger to smaller aircraft in operating an air service was known in the trade as 'change of gauge'. The French government asserted that the proposed change of gauge was not permitted. The bilateral agreement between France and the USA governing air services between the USA and Paris (with other possible points on the route, such as London), prohibited change of gauge *within the territory of the two parties*. Did the agreement allow change of gauge elsewhere? The majority held that the proposed change of gauge was permitted by the treaty. They found that there were many details of aviation practice which were not spelt out in the treaty and developments in aviation (such as the introduction of jet aircraft) and which had been accommodated without negotiation of amendments.[17] A contrary view was that the nature of the agreement as a whole suggested that what is not expressly granted is not permitted, at least in matters which the treaty regulated, though even this would need to be assessed in the light of practice.[18] Even though the dissenting opinion showed that a very different conclusion was possible, the significance of the award on this point is that the treaty's silence on the precise point required the whole treaty to be construed and not just the one provision that did touch on the subject.

In contrast, a different interpretative approach could be expected towards treaties which do not regulate fine detail but set out broad principles intended to apply in a wide range of circumstances and over a period long enough to expect social changes. Human rights treaties are an obvious example of this. Nevertheless, the general principle remains that the approach is a textual one:

In interpreting the [European Convention on Human Rights], as any other treaty, it is generally to be assumed that the parties have included the terms which they wished to include and on which they were able to agree, omitting other terms which they did not

---

[15] See *Certain Expenses of the United Nations* [1962] ICJ Reports 151.

[16] *Case concerning the Air Services Agreement of 27 March 1946 (United States v France)* 54 ILR 304.

[17] The majority did, however, acknowledge that because of the limited time available they had not been able to make a detailed examination of comparable agreements and relevant practice of the parties, although to the extent that they had seen these, they did not appear inconsistent with the tribunal's conclusion: *Case concerning the Air Services Agreement of 27 March 1946 (United States v France)* at 335, para 71.

[18] See Reuter (dissenting), 54 ILR 304, at 343; see also L F Damrosch, 'Retaliation or Arbitration—Or Both? The 1978 United States–France Aviation Dispute' (1980) 74 AJIL 785, and R K Gardiner, 'UK Air Services Agreements 1970–80' (1982) 8 *Air Law* 2, at 9–10.

wish to include or on which they were not able to agree. Thus particular regard must be had and reliance placed on the express terms of the Convention, which define the rights and freedoms which the contracting parties have undertaken to secure. This does not mean that nothing can be implied into the Convention. The language of the Convention is for the most part so general that some implication of terms is necessary, and the case law of the European court shows that the court has been willing to imply terms into the Convention when it was judged necessary or plainly right to do so. But the process of implication is one to be carried out with caution, if the risk is to be averted that the contracting parties may, by judicial interpretation, become bound by obligations which they did not expressly accept and might not have been willing to accept. As an important constitutional instrument the Convention is to be seen as a 'living tree capable of growth and expansion within its natural limits' (Edwards v Attorney General for Canada [1930] AC 124, 136 per Lord Sankey LC), but those limits will often call for very careful consideration.[19]

The significance of absent terms is a matter which comes up at many points in treaty interpretation. In establishing the ordinary meaning of a term, the absence of defining or qualifying words can be significant.[20] At a more conceptual level, the choice of one word rather than another could amount to a telling omission of that other.[21] Good faith has been considered as a constraining factor on the scope for implying terms into a treaty.[22]

2. 'Good Faith'

When courts and tribunals refer to good faith in treaty interpretation, they tend to stress its fundamental importance.[23] In this vein Hersch Lauterpacht wrote: 'Most of the current rules of interpretation, whether in relation to contracts or treaties...

---

[19] *Brown v Stott* [2003] 1 AC 681, at 703 (UK, Privy Council); see also *In re B (FC) (2002), R v Special Adjudicator ex parte Hoxha* [2005] UKHL 19, at para 9, opinion of Lord Hope linking the approach in *Brown v Stott* to article 31(1) of the Vienna Convention and stating: 'There is no warrant in this provision for reading into a treaty words that are not there. It is not open to a court, when it is performing its function, to expand the limits which the language of the treaty itself has set for it'; and *R v Immigration Officer at Prague Airport and another ex parte European Roma Rights Centre and others* [2004] UKHL 55, at para 18 per Lord Bingham: 'It is in principle possible for a court to imply terms even into an international convention. But this calls for great circumspection...'; and see further Chapter 6, section 4.6 below.

[20] See, eg, *Sovereignty over Pulau Litigan and Pulau Sipadan (Indonesia/Malaysia)* [2002] ICJ Reports 625, at 648, para 42, where an issue was whether a line in a treaty establishing the line of a boundary across an island could be interpreted as extending beyond the coast: 'The Court observes that any ambiguity could have been avoided had the Convention expressly stipulated that the 4° 10' N parallel constituted, beyond the east coast of Sebatik, the line separating the islands under British sovereignty from those under Dutch sovereignty. In these circumstances, the silence in the text cannot be ignored. It supports the position of Malaysia.'

[21] See, eg, *Hiscox v Outhwaite* in Chapter 1, section 5.4 above, where the use of 'made' rather than 'signed' in the New York Convention on Recognition etc of Arbitral Awards, would have led the courts to acknowledge that the former did not necessarily mean the latter.

[22] See, eg, *R v Immigration Officer at Prague Airport ex parte European Roma Rights Centre*, above; and see further section 2.4.1 below.

[23] On good faith in international law generally, see J F O'Connor, *Good Faith in International Law* (Dartmouth: Aldershot, 1991).

are no more than the elaboration of the fundamental theme that contracts must be interpreted in good faith.'[24] Yet in most instances it is difficult to see any precise application of it or independent role for it. This may be because good faith is subjective in the sense that it attaches to a person, rather than objectively forming an attribute of an interpretation. That good faith is an accompaniment to an activity may partly explain why it is difficult to extract from judgments a clear dividing line between interpretation and application. When judgments refer to good faith as an element in treaty interpretation they sometimes link this with the notion of abuse of rights, the latter relating to how a right is exercised rather than how its content is determined. The borderline between interpretation and application becomes blurred.

It is usually difficult to detect any evidence that an interpretation has been proffered in bad faith, still less that an interpretation in a judgment or arbitral award has been reached in bad faith. Where good faith is specifically included in the justification for an interpretation, this is usually to buttress some other line of reasoning without providing any obviously additional criterion. Sometimes it seems little more than a synonym for 'reasonable'; but good faith is also invoked to justify express references to finding the intention of the parties, an objective to which the Vienna rules are directed but which they do not explicitly state. The concept is also used in the Vienna rules as an umbrella for the specific principle that an interpretation of a term should be preferred which gives it some meaning and role rather than one which does not. In international practice this principle is often given its Latin form *ut res magis valeat quam pereat* (abbreviated here as '*ut res*').

Good faith differs from most of the other elements of the Vienna rules in that, at least in the way it is expressed in the opening words of the rules, it applies to the whole process of interpreting a treaty rather than solely to the meaning of particular words or phrases within it. Although it is difficult to give precise content to the concept generally, it does include one principle that applies to interpretation of specific terms used in a treaty. This is commonly described as the principle of 'effectiveness', of which one meaning is the *ut res* rule (considered further in section 2.4.5 below). The other aspect of the principle of effectiveness—preferring an interpretation which fulfils the aims of the treaty—is considered in section 5.3.6, on 'object and purpose'. These two aspects of effectiveness are not always clearly distinguished.

2.1 History and preparatory work relating to 'good faith'

In the work of the ILC, when the Commission was still undecided on whether to include draft rules on treaty interpretation, the Special Rapporteur included a reference to existing rules in the description of the general principle of the law of treaties that a treaty is binding on the parties who must perform its obligations in

---

[24] H Lauterpacht, 'Restrictive Interpretation and the Principle of Effectiveness in the Interpretation of Treaties' (1949) XXVI BYBIL 48, at 56.

good faith (*pacta sunt servanda*). The link between this proposition and the open-ing words of the Vienna rules ('A treaty shall be interpreted in good faith') was both conceptual and textual. It was conceptual in that interpretation is a stage compre-hended in the proper and honest performance of a treaty. It was textual because the ILC's first elaboration of *pacta sunt servanda* linked interpretation with it:

A treaty is binding upon the parties and must be applied by them in good faith in accord-ance with its terms and in the light of the general rules of international law governing interpretation of treaties.[25]

However, the inclusion of good faith in the Vienna rules seems to have been as much because of the difficulty of dealing with maxims and canons of interpreta-tion, and because of the desire to respect the principle of effectiveness,[26] as the recognition of what seemed an obvious consequence of the role of good faith as underpinning the law of treaties.

The wording referring to good faith in the first draft of what was to become article 31 of the Vienna rules was derived from proposals in the 1954 Resolution of the Institute of International Law mentioned above. This was used by the Special Rapporteur (Waldock) in combination with six principles formulated by Sir Gerald Fitzmaurice, which in turn were derived from the jurisprudence of the 'World Court' (a term used by several writers to refer jointly to the ICJ and its predecessor, the PCIJ).[27] These principles did not explicitly refer to good faith, but the Special Rapporteur linked good faith with two of them. Principle III was headed 'Principle of integration' and provided: 'Treaties are to be interpreted as a whole, and particu-lar parts, chapters or sections also as a whole.' The Special Rapporteur character-ized this principle as 'one both of common sense and good faith'.[28] Principle IV was headed 'Principle of effectiveness (*ut res magis valeat quam pereat*)' and stated:

Treaties are to be interpreted with reference to their declared or apparent objects and purposes; and particular provisions are to be interpreted so as to give them their fullest weight and effect consistent with the normal sense of the words and with other parts of the text, and in such a way that a reason and a meaning can be attributed to every part of the text.[29]

This principle of effectiveness provided the basis for a separate draft article 72 in the first set of draft articles on interpretation proposed by the Special Rapporteur.[30] However, he set out reasons for hesitating to include the principle of 'effective' interpretation among the general rules. One was that effective interpretation, cor-rectly understood, could be said to be included in interpretation made in good

---

[25] Waldock, Third Report, [1964] *Yearbook of the ILC*, vol II, p 7, draft article 55(1). That draft included elements of the content of good faith, a paragraph which did not survive into the Vienna Convention: 'Good faith, *inter alia*, requires that a party to a treaty shall refrain from any acts calcu-lated to prevent the due execution of the treaty or otherwise to frustrate its objects.'

[26] Waldock, Third Report, [1964] *Yearbook of the ILC*, vol II, p 7, at 55.

[27] Waldock, Third Report, at 55 and see Chapter 2, section 8 above.

[28] Waldock, Third Report, at 56.   [29] Waldock, Third Report, at 55.

[30] Waldock, Third Report, at 53, article 72 and commentary at 60–61.

faith, or to be implicit in that notion.[31] In ILC debate about draft article 72, speakers supported the inclusion of the principle of effective interpretation, but not as a separate provision. The consensus that emerged was that it should be included in the opening paragraph of the rules, the preponderant view being that: 'An interpretation given in good faith and taking account of the object and purpose of a treaty would always necessarily seek to give a meaning to the text.'[32]

Thus, not only was the scene set for a broad view of good faith but that concept was also linked from the start with other elements of the general rule, such as the role of object and purpose.

2.2 Ordinary meaning of 'good faith'

'Good faith' is an excellent example of a term whose 'ordinary meaning' is elusive. The dictionary reference to the phrase 'good faith' takes one to a separate entry for 'bona fides', via the definition (unhelpful in the present context) as 'fidelity, loyalty'.[33] 'Bona fides' is itself a relatively recent usage, the very much older one being the adverbial or adjectival 'bona fide'.[34] That notion of acting honestly, without fraud or intent to deceive, is too general and ill-fitting to help in the context of treaty interpretation. To find the proper interpretation of the term 'good faith', a fuller application of the Vienna rules to the term is necessary. The difficulty of finding an ordinary meaning does, however, lend confirmation to the view to which Professor Cheng drew attention:

> It is said that we cannot define 'impossibility' of discharging duties. Certainly not; any definition would be either so wide as to be nugatory, or too narrow to fit the ever-varying events of human life. Neither can we define other terms applicable to human conduct, such as 'honesty,' for instance, or 'good faith,' or 'malice';... Such rudimentary terms elude *a priori* definition; they can be illustrated, but not defined; they must be applied to the circumstances of each case...[35]

The few cases illustrative of good faith in connection with treaty interpretation are considered below. More generally, the term has received varying amounts of attention in national legal systems,[36] but while looking for any approximation to an 'ordinary' meaning for the term 'good faith', the Latin origins suggest a further line of conceptual approach. Professor Schwarzenberger explained good faith, in this context, as a product of treaty rights to be contrasted with rights in international

---

[31] Waldock, Third Report, at 60, para 27, and 61 para 29.

[32] Chairman of ILC (Yasseen, speaking as a member of the Commission), [1964] *Yearbook of the ILC*, vol I, p 290, para 106.

[33] *Shorter Oxford English Dictionary* (1973 revised edn).

[34] *Shorter Oxford English Dictionary*.

[35] *Russell v Russell* [1897] AC 395, at 436 per Lord Hobhouse; and see Bin Cheng, *General Principles of Law as applied by International Courts and Tribunals* (London: Stevens and Sons, 1953), Part Two, 'The Principle of Good Faith' at 105 ff.

[36] For a general account of good faith both in different national laws and international law, see that of Lord Hope in *R v Immigration Officer at Prague Airport ex parte European Roma Rights Centre* [2004] UKHL 55, at paras 57–63.

customary law. Characterizing the latter as *jus strictum*, he described the rights in customary law as absolute in the sense that 'their exercise, however harsh, does not amount to an abuse of rights'.[37] Thus (in his example), the right of the diplomatic representative to immunity is absolute but is balanced by the absolute right of the host state's government to declare such a representative *persona non grata* without the requirement of any justification. In contrast, Schwarzenberger describes treaty rights as rules of *jus aequum*, signifying the typical intention of the parties, in creating treaty relations, that such rights should be equitably interpreted, that is 'in a spirit of good faith, common sense and reasonableness'.[38] Good faith, therefore, means more than simply *bona fides* in the sense of absence of *mala fides*, or rejection of an interpretation resulting in abuse of rights (though, of course, it includes such absence and rejection).[39] It signifies an element of reasonableness qualifying the dogmatism that can result from purely verbal analysis. As discussed above, the term is also capable of a sufficiently broad meaning to include the principle of effective interpretation.

Translating the requirement of good faith into a practical outcome is only easy in the extreme case. Vattel instances the account of how Tamerlane, having agreed with those in the city of Sebastia that if they capitulated he would shed no blood, then, when they had fulfilled their part of the deal, caused all the soldiers of the garrison to be buried alive.[40] This extreme case illustrates the principle well but it does not throw much light on how a principle which is so dependent on particular circumstances can be reduced to a definition.

Good faith colours a key part of the general rule of treaty interpretation, giving the more generous approach to texts of treaties that characterizes many a decision of international tribunals, probably to the consternation of those lawyers who have a literalist disposition, but perhaps going some way to meet the vehement criticism of the New Haven school.[41]

2.3 'Good faith' in context and in the light of the Convention's object and purpose

The immediate context of the term 'good faith' is in the interpretation of a treaty as contrasted with the immediately following elements of article 31(1) which refer to how the treaty's terms—that is its words—are to be approached. Thus, the term 'in good faith' indicates *how* the task of interpretation is to be undertaken. This needs to be considered in conjunction with the position of the term, which is: (a) in the opening phrase of an article headed 'General rule of interpretation'; (b) in a paragraph which leads on to a broad definition of the context for the purposes of interpretation; and (c) in this paragraph, which ends with a reference to the object and

---

[37] G Schwarzenberger, 'Myths and Realities of Treaty Interpretation' (1968) 9 *Va J Int'l L* 1, at 9.
[38] Schwarzenberger at 9–10.   [39] Schwarzenberger at 10.
[40] *The Law of Nations* (1758 edn, trans C G Fenwick) (Washington: Carnegie Institution, 1916), Book II, ch XVII, § 273.
[41] See Chapter 2, section 9 above.

purpose of the treaty, not just to particular terms in it. The significance of (a) is that the process of interpretation is seen as an accumulation of elements rather than a succession, all the items in article 31 constituting the general rule. Thus, good faith does not have an entirely independent function. The significance of (b) is that the opening and closing parts of article 31(1) are aligned with one another in looking to the whole treaty, balancing the central part of the paragraph which addresses the component terms of the treaty. The significance of (c) is that the combination of good faith and taking account of object and purpose results in an outcome that is more likely to reflect effectively the true intentions recorded in the text than would a purely literal approach.

As has been noted above, good faith has both general application in the law of treaties and one specific interpretation. In its general role, good faith is included in the Vienna Convention's fundamental proposition on the law of treaties, in its article 26, that treaties establish binding obligations for the parties 'and must be performed by them in good faith'.[42] In its specific application to the interpretation of treaties, in article 31, *Oppenheim's International Law* notes that the concept of good faith strongly implies an element of reasonableness and that the requirement that a treaty is to be interpreted in good faith, as well as being necessary 'as a matter of general principle…follows from article 26…'.[43]

2.4 Issues and practice

2.4.1 'Good faith' generally

The ICJ has had little to say about good faith as such in treaty interpretation beyond referring to it as part of its frequent reiteration of article 31(1) of the Vienna rules as customary law applicable to treaty interpretation. Thirlway accounts for this by observing that 'what may be in question is the good faith of the parties; an interpretation by the Court in which the Court itself was animated by something other than good faith is not to be thought of'.[44] Since that observation was written, however, Judge Schwebel has invoked good faith in a dissenting opinion to question whether an ICJ majority judgment had applied the Vienna rules properly when deciding whether Qatar and Bahrain had agreed that either state might refer their dispute to the ICJ. The majority had asserted that whatever may have been the motives of the parties, the Court would view the words used in certain Minutes (which formed an agreement) as expressing their

---

[42] Article 26 uses as its heading the Latin maxim in relation to treaties '*Pacta sunt servanda*'. This is fleshed out in the text of the article as: 'Every treaty in force is binding upon the parties to it and must be performed by them in good faith.'

[43] Jennings and Watts (eds), *Oppenheim's International Law* (London: Longman, 9th edn, 1992), 1272, § 632 and note 7.

[44] H Thirlway, 'The Law and Procedure of the International Court of Justice 1960–1989 Part Three' (1991) LXII BYBIL 1, at 17. He further considered it 'difficult to conceive circumstances in which the Court would find it necessary to reject an interpretation advanced by a party on the sole ground that it was not made in good faith'.

common intent, rather than looking to the preparatory work to elucidate their intent. Judge Schwebel wrote:

The Court's choice of the word 'motives' is revealing of its devaluation of the intention of the Parties. But the fundamental flaw in its reasoning, as I see it, is the contention that it adheres to the actual terms of the Minutes 'as the expression of their common intention' when I believe that it is demonstrable—and has been demonstrated—that their common intention could not have been to authorize unilateral application to the Court.

Thus in my view the Court's construction of the Doha Minutes is at odds with the rules of interpretation prescribed by the Vienna Convention. It does not comport with a good faith interpretation of the treaty's terms...Moreover, the Court's failure to determine the meaning of the treaty in the light of its preparatory work results, if not in an unreasonable interpretation of the treaty itself, in an interpretation of the preparatory work which is 'manifestly...unreasonable'....

The Court provides no more explanation of why the travaux préparatoires do not provide it with conclusive supplementary elements for the interpretation of the text adopted than described above. But it also implies...that it discounts the travaux préparatoires on the ground that they do not confirm the meaning to which its analysis has led. In my view, *such a position, if it be the position, would be hard to reconcile with the interpretation of a treaty 'in good faith' which is the cardinal injunction of the Vienna Convention's rule of interpretation.* The travaux préparatoires are no less evidence of the intention of the parties when they contradict as when they confirm the allegedly clear meaning of the text or context of treaty provisions.[45]

The suggestion that an approach which does not give sufficient or proper weight to the preparatory work (or which gives that work an unreasonable interpretation) does not 'comport' with a good faith interpretation raises a diplomatically oblique challenge to the good faith of the majority's view, the essence of the charge seeming to be that it would be improper to disregard evidence merely because that evidence does not accord with an interpretation achieved by textual analysis.[46]

---

[45] *Maritime Delimitation and Territorial Questions between Qatar and Bahrain (Qatar v Bahrain) (Jurisdiction and Admissibility)* [1995] ICJ Reports 6, at 35–37 and 39 (emphasis added); for further consideration of this case, see Chapter 8, section 4.2.2 below.

[46] Other dissenting judges have referred to the requirement of good faith. In *Kasikili/Sedudu Island (Botswana/Namibia)* [1999] ICJ Reports 1045, a core issue was which of two branches of a river was 'the main channel' for the purposes of a treaty of 1890 which had specified the centre of that channel as the boundary between two states. Judge Fleischhauer, in his dissenting opinion, considered that where the expectation in 1890 of large-scale navigability of the river had proved mistaken over the subsequent century, it would not be an interpretation in good faith for that mistaken belief to be held against a party so as to deprive it of an equitable share of the channel which has in recent years been of some use for tourism (Dissenting Opinion of Judge Fleishhauer, 1196, at 1203–204, para 9). It is difficult to see how this appeal to good faith substantially buttresses a conclusion which is dependent on contested issues as to the navigability of the channels and whether navigability was, in any event, the correct test in a treaty addressing the respective spheres of influence of Britain and Germany in Africa. Good faith has also been invoked by a dissenting judge in interpreting a state's declaration accepting the jurisdiction of the ICJ: see Judge Torres Bernárdez in *Land and Maritime Boundary between Cameroon and Nigeria (Cameroon v Nigeria: Equatorial Guinea intervening), (Preliminary Objections)* [1998] ICJ Reports 275, at 670–71, paras 237–39.

Bin Cheng points to a much earlier reference to good faith directly illustrating its role in an interpretative context. Venezuela had proposed to certain states ('the allied Powers'), and agreed with them, that 'all claims against Venezuela' should be the subject of special guarantees. The question then arose whether 'all claims' in the eventual Protocol meant that those of every creditor state should be given exactly the same guaranteed funding (including 'neutral Powers') or whether the allied Powers which had negotiated the treaty should be paid off first. Finding in favour of the latter interpretation, an arbitral tribunal stated:

... The good faith which ought to govern international relations imposes the duty of stating that the words '*all claims*' used by the representative of the Government of Venezuela in his conferences with the representatives of the allied Powers ... could only mean the claims of these latter and could only refer to them. ... [47]

In the more recent arbitration *Rhine Chlorides (Netherlands/France)* (2004), the tribunal paid considerable attention to the role of good faith in the interpretation of treaties. In the course of this the tribunal had to consider a French argument that although the Vienna rules reflected customary international law, where neither of the states involved in the arbitration was a party to the Vienna Convention, it was the actual rules of customary international law which applied rather than those of the Vienna Convention applied in an analytical and taxonomical fashion (*façon analytiqe et cédulaire*) as under the Convention's obligations. [48] In a careful analysis leading to the conclusion that the Vienna rules faithfully reflected customary international law and were applicable to the case, the Tribunal referred to an earlier award in which certain general rules for treaty interpretation had been formulated, including the proposition:

In so far as the text is not sufficiently clear, it is allowable to have recourse to the intentions of the parties concerned. If, in this case, the intentions are clear and unanimous, they must prevail over every other possible interpretation. If, on the contrary, they diverge or are not clear, that meaning must be sought which, within the context [*dans le cadre du texte*], best gives either a reasonable solution of the controversy, or the impression which the offer of the party which took the initiative must reasonably and in good faith have made on the mind of the other party. ... [49]

Here the approach is similar to the Venezuelan case, requiring the interpreter, in the case of uncertainty or divergent texts, to look to the proposal that led to the

---

[47] *Venezuelan Preferential Claims Case* (1904) 1 HCR 55, at 60–61; and see Bin Cheng, *General Principles*, at 107–8. Note also, however, that in preferring the claims of the allied Powers, the tribunal appears to have placed great weight on the negotiating history and surrounding circumstances, which provided evidence not revealed on the face of the treaty.

[48] *Case Concerning the Auditing of Accounts Between the Kingdom of the Netherlands and the French Republic pursuant to the Additional Protocol of 25 September 1991 to the Convention on the Protection of the Rhine against Pollution by Chlorides of 3 December 1976 (Netherlands v France)*, Arbitral Award of 12 March 2004, 144 ILR 259, at 290–300, paras 54–79 (unofficial translation from authentic French): <http://www.pca-cpa.org>; see further Chapter 1, section 5.2.

[49] *Rhine Chlorides* 144 ILR 259, at 298, para 74, quoting the award in the *Georges Pinson Case France v Mexico* (Mixed Claims Commission) 19 October 1928, § 50 as translated in Annual Digest of Public International Law Cases (now ILR) 1927–28, p 426.

text and the good faith of the parties in negotiating on that basis. The tribunal in the *Netherlands/France* case considered that this application of good faith was reflected in article 32 of the Vienna rules, with its reference to the preparatory work and surrounding circumstances.

It seems clear that the approach indicated above and in the Vienna rules aims to elucidate what is unclear in the text of a treaty, not to invoke good faith in order to fill gaps in a manner which would impose additional obligations. This was the theme in a decision in the UK by the House of Lords where good faith played a prominent role. In *R v Immigration Officer at Prague Airport ex parte European Roma Rights Centre*[50] a central issue was whether a provision in the Convention on the Status of Refugees required a person to be afforded an assessment of their status as a possible refugee in the country of intended asylum, the broader allegation being that by stationing immigration officers in the claimants' country of origin, the UK authorities had improperly circumvented the Convention to prevent potential refugees reaching the UK at all. Specific issues of interpretation, such as the meaning of the term 'return' ('*refoulement*') of individuals, were tackled with the help of the Vienna rules. However, though the judges did invoke the reference to good faith in Vienna article 31, rather than using it to find the meaning of terms such as 'return', they really used it in a more general way in assessing whether circumventing the Convention by preventing an individual entering the UK conflicted with implementation of the treaty in good faith. Thus, Lord Bingham, after quoting from some of the ICJ's observations on good faith, referred to articles 26 and 31 of the Vienna Convention and stated:

Taken together, these rules call for good faith in the interpretation and performance of a treaty, and neither rule is open to question. But there is no want of good faith if a state interprets a treaty as meaning what it says and declines to do anything significantly greater than or different from what it agreed to do. The principle that pacta sunt servanda cannot require departure from what has been agreed. This is the more obviously true where a state or states very deliberately decided what they were and were not willing to undertake to do.[51]

Lord Steyn also referred to the role of good faith in interpretation, indicating important limitations:

...It is true, of course, that the Refugee Convention is a living instrument and must be interpreted as such. It must also be interpreted in accordance with good faith: article 31 of the Vienna Convention on the Law of Treaties. These are very important principles of interpretation. But they are not capable of filling gaps which were designedly left in the protective scope of the Refugee Convention....[52]

---

[50] [2004] UKHL 55, [2005] 2 AC 1.

[51] *R v Immigration Officer at Prague Airport ex parte European Roma Rights Centre* [2004] UKHL 55, at para 19; and cf *Cox v Canada* (1994) UN Human Rights Committee, 114 ILR 347, at 372–73.

[52] [2004] UKHL 55, at para 43.

Lord Hope also conflated good faith in treaty interpretation with its broader role:

…in practice, this general principle of law has only marginal value as an autonomous source of rights and duties…good faith is always related to specific behaviour or declarations. What it does is invest them with legal significance and legal effects…

The question then is whether the appellants are seeking to do no more by appealing to this principle than insist that the rights and obligations which the 1951 Convention creates are exercised within the law…or whether they are seeking to enlarge what it provides so as to impose new obligations on the contracting states. In my opinion the answer to this question must be found in the language of the Convention, interpreted in good faith in accordance with the ordinary meaning to be given to the terms of the treaty in their context and in the light of its object and purpose, as article 31 of the Vienna Convention requires. The argument that good faith requires the state to refrain from actions which are incompatible with the object and purpose of the treaty can only be pressed so far. Everything depends on what the treaty itself provides.[53]

Thus, Lord Hope returned to the provisions of the treaty and saw good faith, context, and object and purpose as interpretative tools to be applied within the confines of the text rather than in an external and tangential setting.

2.4.2 'Good faith' meaning reasonableness

The ICJ has had to consider the role of good faith in other contexts in the law of treaties. In *Nicaragua v USA* the Court considered modification or withdrawal without notice of a declaration accepting the Court's jurisdiction, and said of such declarations:

It appears from the requirements of good faith that they should be treated, by analogy, according to the law of treaties, which requires a reasonable time for withdrawal from or termination of treaties that contain no provision regarding the duration of their validity.[54]

Read in the same spirit of analogy, this bears out the suggestion that one component of good faith in interpretation is reasonableness.[55] The Court has also stated that although the principle of good faith is 'one of the basic principles governing the creation and performance of legal obligations…it is not in itself a source of obligation where none would otherwise exist'.[56] Again this is not direct guidance on good faith in interpretation; but in its references to performance and to good faith not being a source of obligation, this extract illustrates the aspect of good faith that goes to the manner of performance of obligations and in relation to their

---

[53] [2004] UKHL 55, at paras 62–63, attributions and citations omitted.

[54] *Military and Paramilitary Activities in and against Nicaragua (Nicaragua v United States of America) (Jurisdiction and Admissibility)* [1984] ICJ Reports 420, para 63.

[55] See R Jennings and A Watts (eds), *Oppenheim's International Law*, vol I (London: Longman, 9th edn, 1992), 1272.

[56] *Border and Transborder Armed Actions (Nicaragua v Honduras) (Jurisdiction and Admissibility)* [1988] ICJ Reports 69, at 105, para 94. This proposition was reaffirmed in *In re Land and Maritime Boundary between Cameroon and Nigeria (Cameroon v Nigeria)* [1998] ICJ Reports 275, at 297, para 39.

extent leaves scope for application of the test of good faith to the reasonableness of an interpretation that is being advanced and the approach to be adopted in evaluating such an interpretation.

A more specific suggestion that good faith may demand a form of balancing of rights and obligations, and hence reasonableness, is in relation to article 7 of the Agreement on Trade-Related Aspects of Intellectual Property Right (TRIPS Agreement) which sets objectives for the promotion and protections of intellectual property rights calling for them to be conducive to (inter alia) 'a balance of rights and obligations'.[57] Slade shows by examination of case law within the WTO dispute settlement system how this provision could act as 'a form of good faith principle', particularly in precluding arbitrary action and abusive use of rights.[58]

2.4.3 'Good faith' limiting interpretation of a power

In a separate opinion in the ICJ case *Territorial Dispute (Libyan Arab Jamahiriya/ Chad)* Judge Ajibola reviewed the role of good faith in treaty interpretation.[59] He referred to the situation where a treaty affects the exercise of a power by a state. In one example which he gave, an arbitral tribunal limited the state's power to make regulations on fishing off Canada by reference to good faith:

But from the Treaty results an obligatory relation whereby the right of Great Britain to exercise its right of sovereignty by making regulations is limited to such regulations as are made in good faith, and are not in violation of the Treaty.[60]

Clearly, it would be contrary to good faith to interpret the grant of powers as permitting their use to deny rights under the treaty.[61] However, the position appears to be somewhat different where interpretation of a power of derogation from a human rights treaty is in issue. By such treaties states 'submit themselves to a legal order within which they, for the common good, assume obligations not in relation to other States, but towards all individuals'.[62] Hence, rather than looking to the effect of relations between the parties, the application of the test of good faith is more directed to securing the object and purpose for individuals when,

---

[57] A Slade, 'Good Faith and the Trips Agreement: Putting Flesh on the Bones of the Trips "Objectives"' (2014) 63 ICLQ 353.

[58] Slade, 'Good Faith and the Trips Agreement'.

[59] [1994] ICJ Reports 6, at 51, paras 79–87.

[60] *North Atlantic Coast Fisheries (USA v Great Britain)* (1910) 4 AJIL 948, at 967; see also *Rights of Nationals of the USA in Morocco* [1952] ICJ Reports 212.

[61] Cf article 5 of the Convention on International Civil Aviation, Chicago, 1944, where the power of a state party to impose 'such regulations, conditions or limitations as it may consider desirable' on non-scheduled commercial flights was interpreted by the Council of the International Civil Aviation Organization as allowing parties to impose what restrictions they chose, but that it was understood that this right to restrict non-scheduled flights 'would not be exercised in such a way as to render the operation of this important form of air transport impossible or non-effective' (ICAO Doc 7278/2).

[62] *Effect of Reservations on the Entry into Force of the American Convention* (OC-2/82) Inter-American Court of Human Rights, Advisory Opinion of 24 September 1982, 67 ILR 559, at 568, para 29.

for example, interpreting rights to formulate reservations to human rights treaties or assessing exercise of powers such as those to suspend safeguards such as *habeas corpus*.[63]

2.4.4 'Good faith' requiring balancing of treaty elements

In the context of trade treaties, the WTO Appellate Body has referred to the principle of good faith in interpreting and applying a provision (article XX of GATT 1994), allowing members of the WTO to impose measures which would otherwise conflict with obligations of the GATT. This issue arose when the USA adopted a scheme to restrict imports of shrimps from states which did not ensure adequate protection against incidental taking of sea turtles in the course of commercial shrimp trawl-harvesting. Permitted exceptions listed in GATT, article XX included measures necessary to protect human, animal, or plant life or health, and those relating to the conservation of exhaustible natural resources. However, both these exceptions (as well as several others) were listed after an opening clause, or '*chapeau*', subjecting any excepted measure to the requirement that they were not to be applied 'in a manner which would constitute a means of arbitrary or unjustifiable discrimination between countries where the same conditions prevail, or a disguised restriction on international trade'. In interpreting and applying these provisions, the Appellate Body said:

The chapeau of Article XX is, in fact, but one expression of the principle of good faith. This principle, at once a general principle of law and a general principle of international law, controls the exercise of rights by states. One application of this general principle, the application widely known as the doctrine of *abus de droit*, prohibits the abusive exercise of a state's rights and enjoins that whenever the assertion of a right 'impinges on the field covered by [a] treaty obligation, it must be exercised bona fide, that is to say, reasonably.'[156] An abusive exercise by a Member of its own treaty right thus results in a breach of the treaty rights of the other Members and, as well, a violation of the treaty obligation of the Member so acting. Having said this, our task here is to interpret the language of the chapeau, seeking additional interpretative guidance, as appropriate, from the general principles of international law.[157]

The task of interpreting and applying the chapeau is, hence, essentially the delicate one of locating and marking out a line of equilibrium between the right of a Member to invoke an exception under Article XX and the rights of the other Members under varying substantive provisions (eg Article XI) of the GATT 1994...

[156] B. Cheng, *General Principles of Law as applied by International Courts and Tribunals* (London: Stevens and Sons, Ltd., 1953), Chapter 4, in particular, p. 125 elaborates:

...A reasonable and bona fide exercise of a right in such a case is one which is appropriate and necessary for the purpose of the right *(i.e.,* in furtherance of the interests which the right is intended to protect). It should at the same time be *fair and equitable as between the parties* and not one which is calculated to

[63] See *Habeas Corpus in Emergency Situations* (OC-8/87) Inter-American Court of Human Rights, Advisory Opinion of 30 January 1987, 96 ILR 392, at 397, para 16, applying *Effect of Reservations* Opinion in preceding note.

procure for one of them an unfair advantage in the light of the obligation assumed. A reasonable exercise of the right is regarded as compatible with the obligation. But the exercise of the right in such a manner as to prejudice the interests of the other contracting party arising out of the treaty is unreasonable and is considered as inconsistent with the bona fide execution of the treaty obligation, and a breach of the treaty.... (emphasis added)

Also see, for example, Jennings and Watts (eds.), *Oppenheim's International Law*, 9th ed, Vol. I (Longman's, 1992), pp. 407–410, *Border and Transborder Armed Actions Case*, (1988) I.C.J. Rep. 105; *Rights of Nationals of the United States in Morocco Case*, (1952) I.C.J. Rep. 176; *Anglo-Norwegian Fisheries Case*, (1951) I.C.J. Rep. 142.

[157] Vienna Convention, Article 31(3)(c).[64]

The opening words of this extract give further evidence that the boundary between relying on good faith as part of the process of interpretation and as part of performance of treaty provisions is not always readily drawn. Here the Appellate Body sees itself as carrying out a combined task of interpreting and applying the requirements of the chapeau with good faith as a guiding principle ensuring that the operation of the exceptions was reasonable.

2.4.5 'Good faith' and the principle of effectiveness
(ut res magis valeat quam pereat)

The Latin maxim, requiring preference for an interpretation which gives a term some meaning rather than none, is the more specific limb of the principle of effectiveness. The other limb guides the interpreter towards an interpretation which realizes the aims of the treaty. The ILC took the view that insofar as the maxim amounts to a true general rule of interpretation, it is 'embodied' in article 31(1):

When a treaty is open to two interpretations one of which does and the other does not enable the treaty to have appropriate effects, good faith and the objects and purposes of the treaty demand that the former interpretation should be adopted.[65]

The ILC subsumed both elements of the principle of effectiveness under two elements in article 31(1) jointly, that is 'good faith' and 'object and purpose'. It seems appropriate, however, for analytical purposes to consider the maxim in the context of good faith and realization of the aims of the treaty as an aspect of the object and purpose of a treaty. The dual aspect of the principle of effectiveness can be seen in the Court's judgment in *Territorial Dispute (Libyan Arab Jamahiriya/Chad)*.[66] Libya argued that only certain boundaries were definitive among those identified in instruments listed in an Annex to a 1955 treaty between Libya and France (the latter being one of the colonial powers which had been responsible for territory adjacent to Libya). The ICJ applied the principle of effectiveness to confirm that

---

[64] *United States—Import Prohibition of Certain Shrimp and Shrimp Products* WTO Report of Appellate Board AB-1998–4, WT/DS58/AB/R, 12 October 1998, paras 158–59.

[65] Commentary on draft articles, [1966] *Yearbook of the ILC*, vol II, p 219, para 6.

[66] *Territorial Dispute (Libyan Arab Jamahiriya/Chad) (Merits)* [1994] ICJ Reports 6.

the reference in article 3 of the treaty to 'the frontiers' meant all the frontiers resulting from those instruments to which reference was made in the legal instruments: 'Any other construction would be contrary to the actual terms of article 3 and would render completely ineffective the reference to one or other of those instruments in Annex I.'[67] This application of the principle of effectiveness (in the maxim *ut res*) was supplemented by the Court's application of the more general principle of effectiveness in the context of the aim of the treaty.[68]

The principle *ut res* has been expressly recognized as part of the general rule for treaty interpretation in the decisions of the Appellate Body of the WTO: 'A fundamental tenet of treaty interpretation flowing from the general rule of interpretation set out in Article 31 [of the Vienna Convention] is the principle of effectiveness *(ut res magis valeat quam pereat)*.'[69] This has received continuing and expanding application in the WTO:

…We have also recognized, on several occasions, the principle of effectiveness in the interpretation of treaties *(ut res magis valeat quam pereat)* which requires that a treaty interpreter:

> '…must give meaning and effect to all the terms of the treaty. An interpreter is not free to adopt a reading that would result in reducing whole clauses or paragraphs of a treaty to redundancy or inutility.'

In light of the interpretive principle of effectiveness, it is the *duty* of any treaty interpreter to 'read all applicable provisions of a treaty in a way that gives meaning to *all* of them, harmoniously.' An important corollary of this principle is that a treaty should be interpreted as a whole, and, in particular, its sections and parts should be read as a whole. Article II:2 of the *WTO Agreement* expressly manifests the intention of the Uruguay Round negotiators that the provisions of the *WTO Agreement* and the Multilateral Trade Agreements included in its Annexes 1, 2 and 3 must be read as a whole.[70]

The principle extends to interpretation of related treaties. Where the 'Agreement on Safeguards' and a provision of GATT 1994 were both in issue, the Appellate Body held:

…a treaty interpreter must read *all* applicable provisions of a treaty in a way that gives meaning to all of them, harmoniously. And, an appropriate reading of this 'inseparable

---

[67] [1994] ICJ Reports 6, at 23, para 47. See also a straightforward application of the principle in *Application of the International Convention on the Elimination of All Forms of Racial Discrimination (Georgia v Russian Federation), (Preliminary Objections),* [2011] ICJ Reports, at paras 133–34, where the ICJ considered that in a provision granting a right to submit 'a dispute' qualified by the words 'which is not settled' by certain specified peaceful means of resolution, reliance on the mere fact there was a subsisting dispute did not afford the latter phrase any useful effect and hence it was necessary to show there to have been some resort to the specified means; cf *Application of the Interim Accord of 13 September 1995 (The Former Yugoslav Republic of Macedonia v Greece)* [2011] ICJ Reports 644, at 673, para 92 where the ICJ rejected the contention that a phrase lacked legal effect unless interpreted in the manner proposed because there was an alternative possible meaning having 'legal significance'.

[68] See further consideration of this case in the practice under 'object and purpose' below.

[69] *Japan—Taxes on Alcoholic Beverages,* AB-1996-2, WT/DS8, 10 &11/AB/R (1996).

[70] *Korea—Definitive Safeguard Measure on Imports of Certain Dairy Products,* AB-1999-8, WT/DS98/AB/R, p 24, paras 80–81(1999) (emphasis in original, footnotes omitted).

package of rights and disciplines' must, accordingly, be one that gives meaning to *all* the relevant provisions of these two equally binding agreements.[71]

3. 'Ordinary Meaning'

> In accordance with the general rule on interpretation...the object of treaty interpretation is to give their 'ordinary' meaning to the terms of the treaty...The difficulty about this approach to the issue is that almost any word has more than one meaning. The word 'meaning' itself, has at least sixteen different meanings.[72]

> ...the ordinary meaning of a term is not to be determined in the abstract but in the context of the treaty and in the light of its object and purpose.[73]

First and foremost, in considering the role of the 'the ordinary meaning to be given to the terms of the treaty', it is necessary to stress that the ordinary meaning is not an element in treaty interpretation to be taken separately when the general rule is being applied to a particular issue involving treaty interpretation. Nor is the first impression as to what is the ordinary meaning of a term anything other than a very fleeting starting point. For the ordinary meaning of treaty terms is immediately and intimately linked with context, and then to be taken in conjunction with all other relevant elements of the Vienna rules.

For present purposes, however, the notion of an ordinary meaning is taken separately for ease of analysis and exposition. Further, identifying the starting point in no way detracts from the importance of the other elements of the general rule. One has to start somewhere. Given that the starting point is reading the words in the treaty, the act of reading almost axiomatically involves giving them the meaning which the reader takes to be usual (at least initially) or as one of a range of meanings. This section is therefore concerned with identifying what the Vienna rules direct is to be taken as the starting point, always with the caveat in mind that this is not the complete or independent interpretative process.

---

[71] *Argentina—Safeguard Measures on Imports of Footwear*, AB-1999-7, WT/DS121/AB/R, p 27, para 81 (1999) (emphasis in original, footnote omitted). The Board also in that decision held that the principle *ut res* does not apply to require meaning to be given to an omission: 'We believe that, with this conclusion, the Panel failed to give meaning and legal effect to *all* the relevant terms of the *WTO Agreement*, contrary to the principle of effectiveness (*ut res magis valeat quam pereat*) in the interpretation of treaties. The Panel states that the "*express omission* of the criterion of unforeseen developments" in Article XIX:1(a) from the *Agreement on Safeguards* "must, in our view, have meaning." On the contrary, in our view, if they had intended to *expressly omit* this clause, the Uruguay Round negotiators would and could have said so in the *Agreement on Safeguards*. They did not' (at para 88 (emphasis in original, footnotes omitted)).

[72] G Schwarzenberger, 'Myths and Realities of Treaty Interpretation: Articles 27–29 of the Vienna Draft Convention on the Law of Treaties' (1968) 9 *Va J Int'l L* 1, at 13, where he cites dictionaries and recalls: 'In the Note Verbale of October 10, 1967, from the Permanent Representative of the United States of America at the United Nations, it is justly pointed out that the "basic problem is that words can have many meanings, and what may be an ordinary meaning in one set of circumstances may be an extraordinary one in another." U.N. Doc. A/CONP 3915, vol 1 at 205'.

[73] ILC Commentary on draft articles, [1966] *Yearbook of the ILC*, vol II, p 221, para 12.

3.1 History and preparatory work

A distinctly literal approach may have found its place in some past approaches to treaty interpretation, particularly at the hands of lawyers whose national legal systems placed great sanctity on the text of legal instruments. This was buttressed by earlier writers, probably the most quoted being Vattel in the exposition following his heavily criticized statement in 1758 that 'it is not allowable to interpret what has no need of interpretation'.[74] He characterized this as the first maxim of interpretation and explained it thus:

When a deed is worded in clear and precise terms,—when its meaning is evident, and leads to no absurd conclusion,—there can be no reason for refusing to admit the meaning which such deed naturally presents. To go elsewhere in search of conjectures, in order to restrict or extend it, is but an attempt to elude it. If this dangerous method be once admitted, there will be no deed which it will not render useless. However luminous each clause may be,—however clear and precise the terms in which the deed is couched,—all this will be of no avail, if it be allowed to go in quest of extraneous arguments, to prove that it is not to be understood in the sense which it naturally presents.[75]

Earlier, however, Grotius had stated: '*If there is no implication which suggests a different conclusion*, words are to be understood in their natural sense, not according to the grammatical sense which comes from derivation, but according to current usage' (emphasis added).[76] Thus Grotius's opening words effectively support the approach taken in the Vienna rules in that they start with the ordinary meaning but allow for different implications. Further, Vattel linked primacy of the text to the intention of the parties and allowed for the ordinary meaning to be modified.[77] The dictum in his first maxim included the immediate qualifier 'when the meaning is evident *and leads to no absurd conclusion*' (emphasis added). This must also be read in the context of his sixty paragraphs on treaty interpretation, many of which are in line with the Vienna rules and which end with the statement: 'All the rules contained in this chapter ought to be combined together, and the interpretation be made in such manner as to accord with them all, so far as they are applicable to the case.'[78]

The ILC in its preparation of the draft Vienna Convention adopted the same principle of an accumulation rather than a prescribed sequence of rules but saw

---

[74] Vattel placed the origins of this principle in the more general idea of the intent behind a law; see *The Law of Nations* (1758 edn, trans C G Fenwick) (Washington: Carnegie Institution, 1916), Book II, ch XVII § 263.

[75] Vattel, § 263.

[76] H Grotius, *De Jure Belli ac Pacis* (F W Kelsey trans) (New York: Oceana, reprint 1964), Bk II, Ch XVI at 409 (footnote omitted), and see Chapter 2, section 3 above.

[77] This was in his antidote to 'quibbles on words': 'All these pitiful subtleties are overthrown by this unerring rule: When we evidently see what is the sense that agrees with the intention of the contracting parties, it is not allowable to wrest their words to a contrary meaning. The intention, sufficiently known, furnishes the true matter of the convention,—what is promised and accepted, demanded and granted. A violation of the treaty is rather a deviation from the intention which it sufficiently manifests, than from the terms in which it is worded: for the terms are nothing without the intention by which they must be dictated.' Vattel, *The Law of Nations* at § 274.

[78] Vattel, at § 320.

the starting point as a combination of the ordinary meaning, context, and object and purpose:

The elements of interpretation in the article have in the nature of things to be arranged in some order. But it was considerations of logic, not any obligatory legal hierarchy, which guided the Commission in arriving at the arrangement proposed in the article. Once it is established—and on this point the Commission was unanimous—that the starting point is the meaning of the text, logic indicates that 'the ordinary meaning to be given to the terms of the treaty in their context and in the light of its object and purpose' should be the first element to be mentioned.[79]

3.2 Ordinary meaning of 'ordinary meaning to be given to the terms of the treaty'

Since it is the 'terms' in this phrase that attract an ordinary meaning, it is necessary to consider what the word 'terms' encompasses. Are 'terms' simply synonymous with 'words', or is 'terms' a collective expression for the bargain reflected in the treaty? Whichever is the case, 'terms' is apt to point to the recorded matter, which under the Vienna Convention's definition of 'treaty' in article 2(1) is what has been written down. In giving meaning to what has been written down, defining words, construing and parsing them must be prerequisites to identifying the content of the stipulations.

In the Vienna Convention, the context (in the form of the complete text of the Convention), gives good guidance on the meaning of 'terms'. In the immediate context of article 31, paragraph (4) provides for a special meaning to be ascribed to a term if the parties so intended. The most obvious evidence of such an intention is inclusion of a definition article. In the same section of the Vienna Convention dealing with interpretation, article 33(3) provides for 'terms' to be presumed to have the same meaning in each authentic text. That article deals with treaties in different languages. Both these provisions are clearly addressed to the meaning of words used, or perhaps their particular significance as terms of art. Further afield, the definitions in article 2 come under the heading 'Use of Terms' and are couched in the form of single words or pairs within quotation marks, followed by a definition. The same article provides in its paragraph (2) that the provisions of paragraph (1) on use of terms in the Convention are 'without prejudice to the use of those terms or to the meanings which may be given to them in the internal law of any State'. The cumulative effect of the references to 'terms' in their context in the Vienna Convention is that the word is concerned with meanings of words and phrases rather than bargains or packages of stipulations.

It is precisely because 'ordinary' includes the meaning 'regular, normal or customary'[80] that such importance must attach to context. For 'regular', 'normal',

---

[79] [1966] *Yearbook of the ILC*, vol II, p 220, para 9.
[80] *Oxford English Dictionary* (1989).

and 'customary' do not in any way indicate that there is necessarily a *single* meaning that is the ordinary meaning of a word (as that triple definition of ordinary—itself only one of several definitions—shows). Nevertheless, courts and tribunals often make an attempt at finding a meaning for a term by use of a dictionary or, particularly in technical areas, specialist books that define the term in issue.

That the rule is formulated as indicating the ordinary meaning 'to be given' to the terms of the treaty suggests an approach in line with the second definition of interpretation noted by Professor Falk (see Chapter 1, section 3.6), that is 'the way in which a thing ought to be interpreted; proper explanation', suggesting a normative approach to selecting ordinary meanings. This, however, is a point of marked difficulty, the plain, normal, or ordinary meaning being a thing of potential variety rather than objectively ascertainable in most cases. Further, the word 'given' in the phrase 'to be given' is apt to emphasize that the meaning is not inherent in the text but something to be attributed by the interpreter, albeit using the text in the manner required by the rules. Whether the reader is an expert in the terminology and whether the meaning is what is ordinary at the time of interpretation or at the time of conclusion of the treaty are among the obvious issues that these words raise.

Waldock, invited to the Vienna Conference as the former Special Rapporteur most familiar with the work of the ILC on the law of treaties, emphasized that the reference to 'ordinary meaning' did not mandate a narrow dictionary approach:

> With regard to the expression 'ordinary meaning', nothing could have been further from the Commission's intention than to suggest that words had a 'dictionary' or intrinsic meaning in themselves. The provisions of article 27, paragraph 1, [now article 31(1) VCLT] clearly indicated that a treaty must be interpreted 'in good faith' in accordance with the ordinary meaning of the words 'in their context'. The Commission had been very insistent that the ordinary meaning of terms emerged in the context in which they were used, in the context of the treaty as a whole, and in the light of the object and purpose of the treaty. So much so that, quite late in the Commission's deliberations, it had even been suggested that paragraph 4 of article 27 [now article 31(4)] could safely be omitted. It was said with some justice during those discussions that the so-called 'special' meaning would be the natural meaning in the particular context.[81]

3.3 Issues and practice

3.3.1 Role of ordinary meaning

Even before the conclusion of the Vienna Convention, the role of the ordinary meaning of the terms of a treaty was not understood as producing an interpretation

---

[81] Waldock, United Nations Conference on the Law of Treaties, First Session (26 March–24 May 1968), Official Records: Summary Records, p.184, para 70.

divorced from context. The ordinary meaning might have a determinative role but only if the context confirmed this and if there were no other factors leading away from that conclusion. This was confirmed in 1991 by the ICJ at a time when the Vienna rules were advancing to their present governing role. In *Arbitral Award of 31 July 1989 (Guinea-Bissau v Senegal)*[82] the ICJ considered whether an arbitral tribunal had acted in manifest breach of the competence conferred on it by an arbitration agreement. The Court endorsed observations on the role of 'ordinary meaning' in judgments it had given before the Vienna Convention was concluded. The Court indicated that those observations represent the position under the Vienna rules:

An arbitration agreement (*compromis d'arbitrage*) is an agreement between States which must be interpreted in accordance with the general rules of international law governing the interpretation of treaties. In that respect

'the first duty of a tribunal which is called upon to interpret and apply the provisions of a treaty, is to endeavour to give effect to them in their natural and ordinary meaning in the context in which they occur. If the relevant words in their natural and ordinary meaning make sense in their context, that is an end of the matter. If, on the other hand, the words in their natural and ordinary meaning are ambiguous or lead to an unreasonable result, then, and then only, must the Court, by resort to other methods of interpretation, seek to ascertain what the parties really did mean when they used these words.' (*Competence of the General Assembly for the Admission of a State to the United Nations, Advisory Opinion*, I.C.J. Reports 1950, p. 8.)

The rule of interpretation according to the natural and ordinary meaning of the words employed

'is not an absolute one. Where such a method of interpretation results in a meaning incompatible with the spirit, purpose and context of the clause or instrument in which the words are contained, no reliance can be validly placed on it.' (*South West Africa, Preliminary Objections, Judgment*, I.C.J. Reports 1962, p. 336.)

These principles are reflected in Articles 31 and 32 of the Vienna Convention on the Law of Treaties, which may in many respects be considered as a codification of existing customary international law on the point.[83]

It must immediately be parenthetically noted that the ICJ has in other cases firmed up its view in the last part of this extract so that the Vienna rules are now accepted as the generally applicable law on treaty interpretation, even if it was controversial at the time of conclusion of the Vienna Convention whether the Vienna rules were actually a codification. However, the main thrust of the extract is that the ordinary meaning is the starting point of an interpretation, but only if it is confirmed by investigating the context and object and purpose, and if on examining all other relevant matters (such as whether an absurd result follows from applying a literal interpretation) no contra-indication is found, is the ordinary meaning determinative.

---

[82] [1991] ICJ Reports 53.   [83] [1991] ICJ Reports 53, at 69–70, para 48.

3.3.2 *Dictionaries and other sources of definitions*

Dictionaries and other sources of definitions play their part in three ways:

(i) the basic discovery of ordinary meanings of a term;

(ii) the identification of a 'functional' meaning, in the sense of a meaning appropriate to the subject matter be it international law, hydrology, or whatever; and

(iii) ascertaining different language meanings, either to seek concepts peculiar to a language or as a prelude to comparing texts (in substance, the province of article 33 of the Vienna Convention).

An example of dictionary function (i) is in the WTO Appellate Body's start of its interpretation of 'a benefit' as part of the definition of a subsidy:

In addressing this issue, we start with the ordinary meaning of 'benefit'. The dictionary meaning of 'benefit' is 'advantage', 'good', 'gift', 'profit', or, more generally, 'a favourable or helpful factor or circumstance'.[85] Each of these alternative words or phrases gives flavour to the term 'benefit' and helps to convey some of the essence of that term. These definitions also confirm that the Panel correctly stated that 'the ordinary meaning of "benefit" clearly encompasses some form of advantage.'[86] Clearly, however, dictionary meanings leave many interpretive questions open.

[85] *The New Shorter Oxford English Dictionary*, (Clarendon Press, 1993), Vol. I, p. 214; *The Concise Oxford Dictionary*, (Clarendon Press, 1995), p. 120; *Webster's Third New International Dictionary* (unabridged), (William Benton, 1966), Vol. I, p. 204.

[86] Panel Report, para. 9.112.[84]

The note of caution at the end of this extract was amplified in the WTO's *US—Measures Affecting Gambling* case, where the core issue was whether 'sporting' includes gambling:

...But dictionaries, alone, are not necessarily capable of resolving complex questions of interpretation,[192] as they typically aim to catalogue *all* meanings of words—be those meanings common or rare, universal or specialized...In this case, in examining definitions of 'sporting', the Panel surveyed a variety of dictionaries and found a variety of definitions of the word....[193]

[192] Appellate Body Report, *US—Softwood Lumber IV*, para. 59; Appellate Body Report, *Canada—Aircraft*, para. 153; and Appellate Body Report, *EC—Asbestos*, para. 92.

[84] *Canada—Measures Affecting the Export of Civilian Aircraft*, WTO Appellate Body Report AB-1999–2 of 2 August 1999, WT/DS70/AB/R, p 39, para 154. See also *Marvin Feldman v Mexico* ICSID Case No. ARB(AF)/99/133–34, para 96. See also: Chang-Fa Lo, 'Good Faith Use of Dictionary in the Search of Ordinary Meaning under the WTO Dispute Settlement Understanding' (2010) 1 *J Int'l Dispute Settlement* 431; I Van Damme, 'On 'Good Faith Use of Dictionary in the Search of Ordinary Meaning under the WTO Dispute Settlement Understanding'—A Reply to Professor Chang-Fa Lo' (2011) 2 *J Int'l Dispute Settlement* 231; Chang-Fa Lo, 'A Clearer Rule for Dictionary Use Will Not Affect Holistic Approach and Flexibility of Treaty Interpretation—A Rejoinder to Dr Isabelle Van Damme' (2012) 3 *J Int'l Dispute Settlement* 89; D Pavot, 'The Use of Dictionary by the WTO Appellate Body: Beyond the Search of Ordinary Meaning' (2014) 4 *J Int'l Dispute Settlement* 29.

193 The 13 different dictionary definitions consulted by the Panel are set out in paragraphs. 6.55–6.59 of the Panel Report. Some of the definitions appear to contradict one another. For instance, the *Shorter Oxford English Dictionary* definition quoted by the Panel defines 'sporting' as both 'characterized by sportsmanlike conduct'; and '[d]esignating an inferior sportsman or a person interested in sport from purely mercenary motives'. (Panel Report, para. 6.55).[85]

Function (ii) is more complicated. It presupposes that it is appropriate to find something more than an 'ordinary' dictionary definition as a starting point; yet the degree of specialism in the term being interpreted is not such as to warrant an argument that the parties intended it to have a special meaning of the kind to which article 31(4) of the Vienna Convention refers. An example of this is the ICJ's use of specialist works in its attempt to find an ordinary meaning of the 'main channel' of a river (the Chobe):

The Court finds that it cannot rely on one single criterion in order to identify the main channel of the Chobe around Kasikili/Sedudu Island, because the natural features of a river may vary markedly along its course and from one case to another. The scientific works which define the concept of 'main channel' frequently refer to various criteria: thus, in the Dictionnaire français d'hydrologie de surface avec équivalents en anglais, espagnol, allemand (Masson, 1986), the 'main channel' is 'the widest, deepest channel, in particular the one which carries the greatest flow of water' (p. 66); according to the Water and Wastewater Control Engineering Glossary (Joint Editorial Board Representing the American Public Health Association, American Society of Civil Engineers, American Water Works Association and Water Pollution Control Federation, 1969), the 'main channel' is 'the middle, deepest or most navigable channel' (p. 197)....[86]

The difficulty of using such works to produce an interpretation is illustrated further below. Yet courts and tribunals show some willingness to make use of specialist dictionaries, with or without 'ordinary' dictionaries, if they feel this to be useful in the circumstances.[87]

Function (iii) above is a twofold one: where the authoritative text of a treaty is in a different language from that of the court or tribunal, a dictionary or specialist work may show the meaning of the term or the concept it signifies; otherwise, or additionally, investigation of meanings in another language may be a prelude to application of article 33 of the Vienna Convention to resolve differences between authentic texts in different languages.

In the *Golder* case, the European Court of Human Rights had to consider whether the provision ensuring a fair and public hearing (under article 6 of the European Convention on Human Rights) 'in the determination of his civil rights and obligations' entitled a prisoner to consult a lawyer so as to institute

---

85 *United States—Measures Affecting the Cross-Border Supply of Gambling and Betting Services* WTO Appellate Body Report of 7 April 2005, WT/DS285/AB/R, p 54, paras 164–65.

86 *Kasikili/Sedudu Island (Botswana/Namibia)* [1999] ICJ Reports 1045, at 1064, para 30.

87 [1999] ICJ Reports 1045 and cf dissenting opinion of Arbitrator Pharand in *Dispute concerning Filleting within the Gulf of St Lawrence ("La Bretagne")(Canada/France)* (1986) 82 ILR 591, at 660, using a French dictionary of international law terms and the *Oxford English Dictionary* to assist in giving a meaning to 'equal footing'.

civil proceedings or only gave the right to a hearing in proceedings that were already in train. After stating that the Vienna rules applied, the Court accepted a dictionary definition of a French term advanced by the British government, but expanded this with a further 'ordinary' sense of the word from another dictionary:

> The clearest indications are to be found in the French text, first sentence. In the field of 'contestations civiles' (civil claims) everyone has a right to proceedings instituted by or against him being conducted in a certain way—'équitablement' (fairly), 'publiquement' (publicly), 'dans un délai raisonnable' (within a reasonable time), etc.—but also and primarily 'à ce que sa cause soit entendue' (that his case be heard) not by any authority whatever but 'par un tribunal' (by a court or tribunal) within the meaning of Article 6 para. 1 ... (Ringeisen judgment of 16 July 1971, Series A no. 13, p. 39, para. 95). The Government have emphasised rightly that in French 'cause' may mean 'procès qui se plaide' (Littré, Dictionnaire de la langue française, tome I, p. 509, 5°). This, however, is not the sole ordinary sense of this noun; it serves also to indicate by extension 'l'ensemble des intérêts à soutenir, à faire prévaloir' (Paul Robert, Dictionnaire alphabétique et analogique de la langue française, tome I, p. 666, II-2°)....[88]

Courts in the USA have made use of dictionaries in seeking the 'plain' meaning of terms expressed in treaties in a foreign language, one such court optimistically stating that:

> One of the simplest methods 'of determining the meaning of a phrase appearing in a foreign legal text' is 'to consult a bilingual dictionary'.[89]

However, while accepting the use of dictionaries as a primary method for defining terms, the US Supreme Court has recognized that 'dictionary definitions may be too general for purposes of treaty interpretation'.[90]

The ICJ has also had occasion to conclude, by reference to dictionary meanings of different language texts, that the search for the meaning of 'without delay', in the context of consular contact with a prisoner under a consular convention, would not be assisted by dictionaries:

> Article 1 of the Vienna Convention on Consular Relations, which defines certain of the terms used in the Convention, offers no definition of the phrase 'without delay'. Moreover, in the different language versions of the Convention various terms are employed to render the phrases 'without delay' in Article 36 and 'immediately' in Article 14. The Court observes that dictionary definitions, in the various languages of the Vienna Convention, offer diverse meanings of the term 'without delay' (and also

---

[88] *Golder v United Kingdom* ECHR App no 4451/70 (Judgment of 21 February 1975), para 32.

[89] *Ehrlich v American Airlines* 360 F 3d 366, at 377 (US Court of Appeals, 2nd Circuit, 2004), and using dictionaries to explore the meaning of words in the phrase '*dommage survenu en cas*' in the 'Warsaw Convention' system treaties on carriage by air: see at 376–78. In referring to the Vienna Convention in a context which did not expressly include the Vienna rules, the court noted: 'Although the United States has never ratified the Vienna Convention, we "treat the Vienna Convention as an authoritative guide to the customary international law of treaties"' (at 373, fn 5).

[90] *Eastern Airlines v Floyd* 499 US 530, at 537 (1991).

of 'immediately'). It is therefore necessary to look elsewhere for an understanding of this term.[91]

At risk of seeming over-repetitive, it must be stressed that the multiplicity of meanings offered by dictionaries for most words serves to answer criticisms levelled against the Vienna rules for their alleged over-reliance on the 'ordinary meaning'. That there are so many dictionary meanings makes almost inevitable immediate recourse to context and the other aids prescribed by the rules for selection of the appropriate ordinary meaning. This was graphically illustrated by Judge Anderson at the International Tribunal for the Law of the Sea when considering the word 'bond'. He found twelve different meanings in Webster's Dictionary and fourteen in the *Oxford English Dictionary* (including, he noted, the name of the type of special paper used for the originals of the judgment in the case which the Court was deciding). These he could narrow down to the two meanings having a financial and a legal connotation as these were the ones directly pertaining to the issues in the case, with a specific focus on the latter because the use of a bond to enable release of an arrested vessel was clearly part of a legal process rather than a purely financial transaction.[92]

3.3.3 Literal meanings of single terms

The description 'single terms' refers here to a word or words which constitute a single concept as the starting point for an issue of interpretation. That the meaning of a single term is clear does not lead to the conclusion that the task of interpretation is complete. If, for example, a dictionary (used in the manner of dictionary function (i) above), or a common understanding of a term, produces an apparently incontrovertible meaning, it is still necessary to locate this in its context to see if the result could be different from what the ordinary meaning produces. Examples which have already been examined, where a clear meaning seemed to exist, are 'alcoholics' and 'make (an arbitral award)'.[93] In both these cases the apparently clear meaning was ultimately displaced. It may, of course, be that the clear meaning remains clear, as in *Luedicke, Belkacem and Koç v Germany* at the European Court of Human Rights.[94] The applicants had been tried in criminal proceedings conducted in a language foreign to them so that they had needed interpretation. This had been provided at no cost to them before conviction. Afterwards, they were sent the bill, the cost of interpretation being added to their penalties and court costs (or *other* court costs). The Court had to interpret article 6(3)(e) of the European Convention on Human Rights, which provides that one of the minimum rights of everyone charged with a

---

[91] *Case concerning Avena and other Mexican Nationals (Mexico v USA)* Judgment of 31 March 2004 [2004] ICJ Reports 12, at 48, para 84. Consideration of the object and purpose of the treaty (see below), and the preparatory work, assisted the Court towards a meaning in this case.

[92] Judge Anderson (dissenting) in *The 'Volga' case (Russian Federation v Australia) (2002)*, (2003) 42 ILM 159, at 188–90 and 192.

[93] See Chapter 1, sections 5.1 and 5.4 above, describing *Witold Litwa v Poland* ECtHR App no 26629/95 (Judgment of 4 April 2000) and *Hiscox v Outhwaite* [1992] 1 AC 562. (In the latter case an interpretation in line with the Vienna rules was achieved by legislatively reversing the judicial decision.)

[94] Application nos 6210/73, 6877/75, 7132/75 (1978) 2 EHRR 149 (Judgment of 28 November 1978).

criminal offence is 'to have the free assistance of an interpreter if he cannot understand or speak the language used in court'. The Court found the meaning of 'free' to be unambiguous, but nevertheless (in application of the Vienna rules) went on to investigate whether there were any circumstances that might displace the clear meaning of 'free' (but concluded there were not):

The Court finds, as did the Commission, that the terms 'gratuitement'/'free' in Article 6 para. 3 (e)...have in themselves a clear and determinate meaning. In French, 'gratuitement' signifies 'd'une manière gratuite, qu'on donne pour rien, sans rétribution' (Littré, Dictionnaire de la langue française), 'dont on jouit sans payer' (Hatzfeld et Darmesteter, Dictionnaire général de la langue française), 'à titre gratuit, sans avoir rien à payer', the opposite of 'à titre onéreux' (Larousse, Dictionnaire de la langue française), 'd'une manière gratuite; sans rétribution, sans contrepartie' (Robert, Dictionnaire alphabétique et analogique de la langue française). Similarly, in English, 'free' means 'without payment, gratuitous' (Shorter Oxford Dictionary), 'not costing or charging anything, given or furnished without cost or payment' (Webster's Third New International Dictionary).

Consequently, the Court cannot but attribute to the terms 'gratuitement' and 'free' the unqualified meaning they ordinarily have in both of the Court's official languages: these terms denote neither a conditional remission, nor a temporary exemption, nor a suspension, but a once and for all exemption or exoneration. It nevertheless remains to be determined whether, as the Government contend, the context as well as the object and purpose of the provision in issue negative the literal interpretation.[95]

The Court found that there were no such negative indications.

3.3.4 No ordinary meaning or no single one?

In *Kasikili/Sedudu Island (Botswana/Namibia)*,[96] the ICJ interpreted a treaty of 1890 between Great Britain and Germany which stated:

In Southwest Africa the sphere in which the exercise of influence is reserved to Germany is bounded:...To the east by a line...[which] runs eastward...till it reaches the river Chobe, and descends the centre of the main channel [Thalweg des Hauptlaufes] of that river to its junction with the Zambesi....[97]

The Court considered that

the real dispute between the Parties concerns the location of the main channel where the boundary lies...the Court will therefore proceed first to determine the main channel. In so doing, it will seek to determine the ordinary meaning of the words "main channel" by reference to the most commonly used criteria in international law and practice, to which the Parties have referred.[98]

---

[95] Application nos 6210/73, 6877/75, 7132/75 [1978] 2 EHRR 149 (Judgment of 28 November 1978), at 160–161, para 40.

[96] *Kasikili/Sedudu Island (Botswana/Namibia)* [1999] ICJ Reports 1045.

[97] 1999] ICJ Reports 1045, at 1060, extracted from para 21, with German text added from that paragraph.

[98] [1999] ICJ Reports 1045, at 1062–63, para 27.

The problem was choosing between two channels around an island. Both changed substantially in different seasons and the river generally did not allow for through navigation. One channel was narrower and shallower, though with the recent growth in tourism is now used by flat-bottomed boats. The other was not always identifiable because at times of flood it merged with a great spread of water; but it was larger and deeper.

The Court found differing dictionary definitions of 'main channel', including 'the widest, deepest channel, in particular the one which carries the greatest flow of water' and 'the middle, deepest or most navigable channel', as well as other potentially relevant factors.[99] It therefore purported to apply all the criteria proffered by the parties. In her declaration concurring in the result, Judge Higgins cast doubt on the approach in the judgment:

In my view, although there are commonly used international law criteria for understanding, e.g., the term 'thalweg', the same is not true for the term 'main channel'. And it seems that no 'ordinary meaning' of this term exists, either in international law or in hydrology, which allows the Court to suppose that it is engaging in such an exercise. The analysis on which the Court has embarked is in reality far from an interpretation of words by reference to their 'ordinary meaning'. The Court is really doing something rather different. It is applying a somewhat general term, decided upon by the Parties in 1890, to a geographic and hydrographic situation much better understood today.[100]

Agreeing that the Court was entitled to look at all the suggested criteria, Judge Higgins indicated that this was not 'to discover a mythical "ordinary meaning" within the Treaty, but rather because the general terminology chosen long ago falls to be decided today'.[101] While the narrower channel was edged by a ridge which would provide a very visible frontier, Judge Higgins agreed that the other channel met the proper interpretation of the treaty, being the broader and more important channel and thus the main one 'in the generalized sense intended by the Parties'.[102]

It is difficult to tell in the circumstances of this case whether the criticism to be made of the approach of the majority was that it was trying to find a mythical 'ordinary meaning' or that it was in fact trying to find a single or unified ordinary meaning, being a single set of obvious or accepted criteria fulfilling the sense of the term. For this reason Judge Higgins' characterization of the majority's quest for a 'mythical' ordinary meaning seems apt, and thus raised to greater significance the object and purpose (to choose a channel which would mark clearly the limits of the parties' interests), also making the case an appropriate one for taking into account supplementary means (the circumstances of conclusion indicating the parties' interests).

---

[99] [1999] ICJ Reports 1045, at 1064–65, para 30; and see section 3.3.2 above.
[100] Declaration of Judge Higgins [1999] ICJ Reports 1113, para 1.
[101] [1999] ICJ Reports 1113, at 1114, para 3.
[102] [1999] ICJ Reports 1113, at 1115, para 10.

3.3.5 *Generic terms*

In *Aegean Sea Continental Shelf (Greece v Turkey)*[103] at issue was a Greek reservation in its accession to the 1928 General Act for Pacific Settlement of International Disputes. Part of this reservation excluded from Greece's acceptance of jurisdiction of the Permanent Court and its successor the ICJ 'disputes relating to the territorial status of Greece'. Greece had a dispute with Turkey over the extent of its continental shelf in the Aegean where Turkey was exploring for oil in areas claimed by Greece. Was a dispute over the extent of continental shelf excluded from the jurisdiction of the Court by the term 'territorial status' as used in a treaty before the concept of the continental shelf had become known? The ICJ characterized 'territorial status' as a 'generic term denoting any matters properly to be considered as comprised within the concept of territorial status under general international law'.[104] The Court viewed such a term as being of continuing application and keeping pace with the development of the law. This was supported by the nature of the commitment in the treaty as one which was designed to last for a long period. Hence the Court took the view:

Once it is established that the expression 'the territorial status of Greece' was used in Greece's instrument of accession as a generic term denoting any matters comprised within the concept of territorial status under general international law, the presumption necessarily arises that its meaning was intended to follow the evolution of the law and to correspond with the meaning attached to the expression by the law in force at any given time.[105]

The case concerning the river Chobe provides a contrast. Judge Higgins pointed out:

The term 'the main channel' is not a 'generic term' (cf. *Aegean Sea Continental Shelf* case, *I.C.J. Reports 1978*, para. 77)—that is to say, a known legal term, whose content the Parties expected would change through time. Rather, we find ourselves closer to the situation of the Arbitral Tribunal in the *Laguna del Desierto* case of 1994 (see para. 20 of the Court's Judgment). The Tribunal there stated that it could not accept Chile's argument:

'that to apply the 1902 Award in light of geographical knowledge acquired subsequently would be equivalent to its revision through the retrospective consideration of new facts. The 1902 Award defined, in the sector with which this Arbitration is concerned, a frontier which follows a natural feature that, as such, does not depend on accurate knowledge of the area but on its true configuration. The ground remains as it has always been... [t]his Judgment is... faithfully applying the provisions of the Award of 1902.' *(International Law Reports*, Vol. 113, p. 76, para. 157.)

This dictum retains a certain relevance, notwithstanding that the fact situation in the *Laguna* case is somewhat different from ours.[106]

---

[103] [1978] ICJ Reports 3; for consideration of generic terms in the context of evolutionary interpretation, see Chapter 10, section 4 below.

[104] [1978] ICJ Reports 3, at 31–32, para 76.

[105] [1978] ICJ Reports 3, at 32, para 77.

[106] *Kasikili/Sedudu Island (Botswana/Namibia)*, Declaration of Judge Higgins [1999] ICJ Reports 1113–14, para 2. Cf *Dispute concerning Filleting within the Gulf of St Lawrence ("La Bretagne") (Canada/France) (1986)* 82 ILR 591, at 619 where, using slightly different wording, the arbitrators found that 'the authors of the 1972 Agreement used the term "fisheries regulations" as a generic formula covering

The point of broader significance which this extract offers is that the concept of a 'generic term' includes 'a known legal term, whose content the Parties expected would change through time'.

3.3.6 'Ordinary' to whom?

In some cases the ordinary meaning of a term may only be apparent to someone who has some knowledge of the field. For example, not everyone would immediately understand (though they might guess) that 'iontophoretically' sampling a substance from a living human or animal body for diagnostic purposes has to be considered a 'diagnostic method' within the ordinary meaning of that term in article 52(4) of the European Patent Convention.[107] More equivocally, in a case requiring interpretation of an extradition treaty, the court had to decide whether the German definition of a crime amounting to fraud and the English crime of obtaining by false pretences (the latter being limited to misrepresentations as to existing facts) were sufficiently close to satisfy the treaty's double criminality rule where the alleged misrepresentation was as to a future fact. Finding that the core element of dishonesty was present in both types of crime, and that the general nature of the defined crimes in the two national legal systems was sufficiently close, Lord Chief Justice Widgery said:

The words used in a treaty of this kind are to be given their general meaning, general to lawyer and layman alike. They are to be given, as it were, the meaning of the diplomat rather than the lawyer, and they are to be given their ordinary international meaning and not a particular meaning which they may have attracted in England, or in certain branches of activity in England.[108]

While the exclusion of any meaning peculiar to England or English law clearly follows from the international character of treaty relations, this extract seems internally inconsistent, describing the test as the meaning which would be ascribed to a term by a lawyer, diplomat, and layman alike but giving pre-eminence to the meaning a diplomat would find ordinary. There may be some wisdom to this approach in the case of many treaties which show greater signs of diplomatic than legal drafting, but in the case of extradition treaties it could be expected that lawyers would be more likely to have a key input than in many treaties not so focused on legal matters. In any event, the observation is directed to 'a treaty of this kind'. Whether or not the test of what a diplomat would understand to be the ordinary

---

all the rules applicable to fishing activities...' (emphasis added). See also Chapter 7, sections 1.2 and 4.2, where 'generic terms' were considered in the context of the Vienna Convention's article 31(3)(c) and the application of the 'inter-temporal law' in an arbitral award (the *Iron Rhine* case).

[107] European Patent Office, Technical Board of Appeal, 29 June 2001, Case no T 0964/99–3.4.1.

[108] *R v Governor of Pentonville Prison ex parte Ecke* (1981) 73 Cr App R 223, at 227 (the judgment was given in 1973 but included in these reports belatedly). This case does not refer to the Vienna rules but the quoted proposition was an extrapolation from *Re Arton (No 2)* [1896] 1 QB 509. A tenuous link is made via reference to the latter judgment in an Australian case in a context which did refer to the Vienna rules: Deane J in *Riley and Butler v The Commonwealth* 87 ILR 144, at 153. On interpretation of extradition treaties in the UK, see *Government of Belgium v Postlethwaite* [1988] AC 924 (HL).

meaning is most apt for an extradition treaty, at least it purports to take into account the kind of treaty involved thus, in effect, reflecting the formula in the Vienna rules that the ordinary meaning is directly linked to context and the object and purpose of the treaty. Thus the test is not necessarily what the ordinary person would understand a term to mean but could take account of the subject matter of the treaty so as to seek what a person reasonably informed in that subject, or having access to evidence of what a reasonably informed person would make of the terms as a starting point.

This was the approach taken by the European Court of Human Rights in *Bankovic and Others v Belgium and Others:*

(b) The meaning of the words 'within their jurisdiction'

As to the 'ordinary meaning' of the relevant term in Article 1 of the Convention, the Court is satisfied that, from the standpoint of public international law, the jurisdictional competence of a State is primarily territorial. While international law does not exclude a State's exercise of jurisdiction extra-territorially, the suggested bases of such jurisdiction (including nationality, flag, diplomatic and consular relations, effect, protection, passive personality and universality) are, as a general rule, defined and limited by the sovereign territorial rights of the other relevant States....[109]

3.3.7 Treaty language and terms

International law does not prescribe a linguistic style for treaties, but there are usages that are too well-established to be changed. Some seem pointless, while others have a real and useful significance. Examples of the former are 'High Contracting Party' for 'party' (the latter being used in the Vienna Convention), or 'State' for 'state'.[110] These have little bearing on the essentially practical character of treaties and are to be contrasted with established terminology which serves to distinguish the provisions of a treaty as characteristically mandatory.

As instruments of obligation rather than vehicles for propaganda, treaties use the distinctive mandatory language which mirrors or adopts the approach of some domestic legislative acts. Thus in *OSPAR Arbitration (Ireland v UK)* an arbitration concerning access to information on effects of nuclear reprocessing on the marine environment, the tribunal stated:

For the achievement of these aims the framers of the OSPAR Convention have carefully applied differential language to provide for stipulated levels of engagement of treaty obligation to achieve these objectives. There is a cascading standard of expression providing for the particular obligations imposed on a Contracting Party. For example, there are mandatory provisions that provide for Contracting Parties:

— to take some act ('shall apply', 'shall include', 'shall undertake', 'shall co-operate' or 'shall keep');

---

[109] Application no 52207/99, Decision on Admissibility, 12 December 2001, para 59.
[110] See further, Gardiner, *International Law*, at 19–20.

— actively to work towards an objective ('take all possible steps', 'implement programs', 'carry out programs');

— to deal with issues of planning for the objective ('establish programs', 'adopt', 'define', 'draw up', 'develop', 'take account of'); and

— to take measures ('take', 'adopt', 'plan', 'apply', 'introduce', 'prescribe', 'take into account').

At a lesser level of engagement, other provisions provide for information to be dealt with ('collect', 'access information') or that systems be set up ('provide for', 'establish').

When read as a whole (including the Annexes), it is plain to the Tribunal that the entire text discloses a carefully crafted hierarchy of obligations or engagement to achieve the disparate objectives of the OSPAR Convention. Those who framed the OSPAR Convention expressed themselves in carefully chosen, rather than in loose and general, terms. They plainly identified matters for mandatory obligation for action by Contracting Parties....[111]

While this extract shows the variety of levels of mandatory requirements in the particular case, further study of the OSPAR Convention text which the Award was considering reveals the more general point that the mandatory term 'shall' is used in conjunction with each verb to indicate an obligation to perform, the term 'may' being the auxiliary used for acts that are permitted but optional.

There are numerous instances in which courts and tribunals have referred to the use of a term in other treaties as indicative of possible meanings. Whether this is in pursuit of the 'ordinary' meaning of a term, is a practice adopted in implementation of the Vienna rules, is an application of rules of international law applicable in relations between the parties (article 31(3)(c)), is part of the circumstances of the adoption of the treaty (article 32), or is some other supplementary means of interpretation, often may not be explained.[112] At least two things are clear. First, it happens. Second, in a number of instances the word or words in issue do have an identifiable meaning in several treaties on the same subject, and if on the same or a similar subject may help in selecting an ordinary meaning.[113]

3.3.8 Terms and concepts

While the ordinary meaning of a term in a treaty may seem clear, interpretation may lead into investigation of the concept which the term embraces. Thus, for example, where individual applicants had been deprived of their property by

---

[111] *Dispute Concerning Access to Information under Article 9 of the OSPAR Convention (Ireland v United Kingdom)* (PCA) (2003) 42 ILM 1118, at 1142, paras 129–30, concerning the Convention for the Protection of the Marine Environment of the North-East Atlantic, 1992. For the interpretation of 'shall', see *Churchill Mining PLC and Planet Mining Pty Ltd v Republic of Indonesia*, ICSID Case No. ARB/12/14 and 12/40 (Decision on Jurisdiction, 24 February 2014), at paras 162–231, and see Chapter 9, section 4.4 below.

[112] See F D Berman, 'Treaty "Interpretation" in a Judicial Context' (2004) 29 *Yale Journal of International Law* 315, at 317.

[113] This is particularly common in the case of treaties following a model or having closely comparable objectives: see, eg, treaties on tax, F Engelen, *Interpretation of Tax Treaties under International Law* (Amsterdam: IBDF Publications BV, 2004).

operation of law (a statute allowing occupants of property for a term (lease) to buy the property against the owner's wishes) the European Court of Human Rights had to consider a provision in a Protocol stating:

Every natural or legal person is entitled to the peaceful enjoyment of his possessions. No-one shall be deprived of his possessions except in the public interest and subject to the conditions provided for by law and by the general principles of international law.[114]

The applicant property owners argued that 'no-one' was a term with only one meaning and that therefore they could not deprived of their property except under conditions including those provided for by the 'general principles of international law'. The general principles of international law do indeed set down minimum standards for state-directed deprivation of property, but only in protection of the rights of aliens; nationals have not traditionally been protected by general international law against expropriation by their own state. Thus, while the body of rules that was indicated by the term 'general principles of international law' was clear enough, only by entering into the content of that law and its internal limiting factors, could the correct interpretation be achieved (viz, that the protection of the minimum standard of treatment under international law is only applied by the Protocol to protect aliens). The Court found that to interpret the phrase in question as extending the general principles of international law beyond their normal sphere of applicability was less consistent with the ordinary meaning of the terms used in the Convention.[115]

In another European human rights case, whether the applicant was entitled to the protection of a provision of the Convention depended on whether the 'regulatory offence' of which the applicant had been convicted was a 'criminal offence'. German law had been amended to remove petty offences, such as certain motoring offences, from the sphere of the criminal law. Nonetheless, the European Court of Human Rights noted that, while the changes in German law represented more than a simple change of terminology, in interpreting the Convention:

... according to the ordinary meaning of the terms, there generally come within the ambit of the criminal law offences that make their perpetrator liable to penalties intended, inter alia, to be deterrent and usually consisting of fines and of measures depriving the person of his liberty.[116]

Hence the Court found the concept of criminal law clear enough to cover an offence punishable by a fine even if it was categorized in domestic law as 'regulatory' rather than 'criminal'.[117]

---

[114] Article 1 of the First Protocol to the European Convention on Human Rights.

[115] Judgment of 22 January in *James and Others v UK*, ECtHR case no 3/1984/75/119, at para 61 and judgment of 22 January 1986 in *Lithgow and Others v UK,* ECtHR case no 2/1984/74/112–118, para 114.

[116] Judgment of 25 January 1984 in *Öztürk v Germany,* ECtHR case no 8544/79, para 53.

[117] ECtHR case no 8544/79, para 53.

4. 'Context'

No one has ever made an 'acontextual' statement. There is always some context to any utterance, however meagre.[118]

There are two main roles for the references to 'context' in the Vienna rules and two principal aspects of use of context in treaty interpretation under the rules. The first role of the reference to context is as an immediate qualifier of the ordinary meaning of terms used in the treaty, and hence context is an aid to selection of the ordinary meaning and a modifier of any over-literal approach to interpretation. The second role is the identification in the Vienna rules of the material which is to be taken into account as forming context. Context is defined by spelling out this second role, directing attention to the whole text of the treaty, its preamble, and any annexes.

The fact that context is spelt out broadly in this latter role does not exclude the common meaning of reading something in context as meaning reading words in their immediate surroundings. If a word forms part of a phrase, that is the obvious initial contextual assessment that must be made. The second aspect of use of context is in application of the wider definition. This directs the interpreter to look to many factors ranging from those that are fairly immediate, such as the wording of surrounding provisions, headings of articles and punctuation, to more remote elements such as comparisons with other provisions on similar matters or using similar wording, extending to the function of the context as a bridge to the further element in the first paragraph of the general rule, that is 'the object and purpose'.

An important preliminary point is that in article 31 the Vienna Convention is using the term 'context' in the role and extent described in the provision. The looser usage sometimes made of 'context' to indicate surrounding circumstances is not what this article concerns. The Vienna rules use a separate term for the more general investigation of pertinent matters relating to a treaty by permitting recourse, as a supplementary means of interpretation, to 'the circumstances of its conclusion' (article 32).

The distinction needs to be emphasized or the terminology can be confused. In *Czech Republic v European Media Ventures SA* a statement of the Vienna rules was followed by careful consideration of the interpretative elements in the general rule.[119] However, the focus on context slipped from assessing the treaty's terms in

---

[118] Lord Hoffmann in *Kirin-Amgen Inc v Hoechst Marion Roussel Ltd* [2004] UKHL 46, at para 64; in the context of the Protocol on the Interpretation of article 69 of the European Patent Convention, Lord Hoffmann continued: '"Acontextual meaning" can refer only to the conventional rules for the use of language, such as one finds in a dictionary or grammar. But then, to compare acontextual meaning in that sense with contextual meaning is to compare apples with pears. The one refers to a general rule about how words or syntax should be used and the other to the fact of what on a specific occasion the language was used to mean. So, to make any sense of the terms "primary, literal or acontextual meaning" in the Protocol questions, it must be taken to mean a construction which assumes that the author used words strictly in accordance with their conventional meanings.'

[119] [2007] EWHC 2851 (Comm), para 14 ff.

their context to rather vaguer reference to 'evaluating a treaty's context' and the heading 'Contextual Material'.[120] Under the latter heading were included references to 'material relating to the politico-economic background' and other items which, in terms of the Vienna rules, were clearly within the realm of 'circumstances of conclusion', not context. That the Court implicitly recognized this is shown by the judge's statement (dismissing this material) in his 'Conclusion on Contextual Material' that: 'It seems to me that the court or tribunal's task is to interpret the treaty rather than to interpret the *supplementary means of interpretation*'.[121] To avoid confusion in following the scheme of the Vienna rules, it seems preferable to confine the terms 'context' and 'circumstances of conclusion' to their allocated content and functions.

4.1 Background and context

The immediate context in which reference to 'context' is made in the Vienna rules is that of closest connection with the 'ordinary meaning'.[122] This indicates that the primary reason for looking to the context is to confirm an ordinary meaning if a single contender emerges or to assist in identifying the ordinary meaning if two or more possibilities come forward. In performing these roles the context, once linked with one or more ordinary meanings, is to be considered under the guidance provided by the object and purpose of the treaty. This exercise may be somewhat short-circuited if a provision in the treaty, that is the wider context, provides in a definition the meaning of a term which is not displaced by any other of the Vienna rules. Special meanings, such as those provided by definition provisions, are considered in the last part of Chapter 7 below.

Little time was spent in the deliberations of the ILC on the general role of context in interpretation. This was probably because, as the Special Rapporteur (Waldock) noted: 'the natural and ordinary meaning of terms is not to be determined in the abstract but by reference to the context in which they occur'.[123] This was one of the principles which he found to have 'repeatedly been affirmed by the World Court'.[124]

Comprised within the meaning of context are the agreements and instruments identified in article 31(2) of the Vienna Convention. What constitutes the agreements and instruments to which the paragraph refers, is considered in Chapter 3 above. The role of article 31(2) is to define 'context' for the purpose of the Vienna rules, thus furnishing a special meaning of the kind envisaged in article 31(4).

---

[120] [2007] EWHC 2851, at paras 20 and 24.

[121] [2007] EWHC 2851, at para 31 (emphasis added); on circumstances of conclusion, see Chapter 8, section 4.5.

[122] Cf Judge Learned Hand in *Commissioner of Internal Revenue v National Carbide Corp* 167 F 2d 304, at 306 (US Court of Appeals, 2nd Circuit) (1948): '...but words are chameleons, which reflect the color of their environment...'.

[123] [1964] *Yearbook of the ILC*, vol II, p 56. This was affirmed in the ILC's Commentary on the draft articles which formed the Vienna rules: [1966] *Yearbook of the ILC*, vol. II, p. 221, para (12).

[124] [1964] *Yearbook of the ILC*, vol II, p 56.

4.2 Issues and practice

4.2.1 Immediate context—grammar and syntax

The immediate context includes the grammatical construction of the provision or phrase within which a word in issue is located. An ICJ judgment illustrating this, and the more extensive role of the context, is *Land, Island and Maritime Frontier Dispute (El Salvador/Honduras: Nicaragua intervening)*, where an issue was whether a Chamber of the ICJ had authority to delimit disputed maritime boundaries.[125] For this the Chamber had to have been given a mandate to do so, either in express words, or according to the true interpretation of the Special Agreement made by the parties to confer jurisdiction on the Court. The question on the wording was whether the phrase in the Agreement 'determination of a legal situation...' (*'Que determine la situación jurídica...'*) could be equated with 'delimitation', the latter being the usual term for a tribunal drawing boundaries. The ICJ Chamber stated:

...If account be taken of the basic rule of Article 31 of the Vienna Convention on the Law of Treaties...No doubt the word 'determine' in English (and, as the Chamber is informed, the verb *'determinar'* in Spanish) can be used to convey the idea of setting limits, so that, if applied directly to the 'maritime spaces' its 'ordinary meaning' might be taken to include delimitation of those spaces. But the word must be read in its context; the object of the verb 'determine' is not the maritime spaces themselves but the legal situation of these spaces. No indication of a common intention to obtain a delimitation by the Chamber can therefore be derived from this text as it stands.

This conclusion is also confirmed if the phrase is considered in the wider context, first of the Special Agreement as a whole, and then of the 1980 General Treaty of Peace, to which the Special Agreement refers. The question must be why, if delimitation of the maritime spaces was intended, the Special Agreement used the wording 'to delimit the boundary line...' (*'Que delimite la línea fronteriza...'*) regarding the land frontier, while confining the task of the Chamber as it relates to the islands and maritime spaces to 'determine [their] legal situation...' (*'Que determine la situación jurídica...'*). The same contrast of wording can be observed in Article 18 of the General Treaty of Peace, which, in paragraph 2, asks the Joint Frontier Commission to 'delimit the frontier line in the areas not described in Article 16 of this Treaty', while providing in paragraph 4, that 'it shall determine the legal situation of the islands and maritime spaces'. Honduras itself recognizes that the islands dispute is not a conflict of delimitation but of attribution of sovereignty over a detached territory. It is difficult to accept that the same wording 'to determine the legal situation', used for both the islands and the maritime spaces, would have a completely different meaning regarding the islands and regarding maritime spaces.[126]

This extract shows how a possible meaning of a word, if taken in isolation, is excluded by the immediate grammatical context, a conclusion reinforced by contrasting the wording with the term's use elsewhere (the wider context as defined by the Vienna rules). This is carried yet further to include a comparison with the

---

[125] [1992] ICJ Reports 351.　　[126] [1992] ICJ Reports 351, pp 582–4, paras 373–74.

analogous wording of a related treaty, linked by a reference to it in the Special Agreement. This further treaty does not form part of the context within the opening words (chapeau) of article 31(2) of the Vienna Convention. Nor does it fit well within article 31(2)(a) since that is worded to cover the case of an agreement made at the time of, or after, the one that is being interpreted. In contrast, the Special Agreement appears to have been contemplated by the Treaty of Peace, and could itself therefore be viewed as within article 31(2)(a) if sufficiently proximate to have been made 'in connection with the conclusion' of that treaty. Nevertheless, if the wording of a treaty links it to another one, it is clear that consideration must be given to the express linkage and consequently to concordant interpretation, as appropriate, between the two instruments. Reliance for this on a specific provision of the Vienna Convention is made unnecessary by the express reference.

In the same case there was still further reference to context in the assertion by Honduras that the ordinary meaning of the term 'maritime spaces' in the context of the modern law of the sea must have extended to delimitation of maritime areas, including, for example, the territorial sea and the exclusive economic zone. In the light of this, the rights of coastal states over areas off their coasts, and the asserted object and purpose of the Special Agreement being to dispose completely of long-standing disputes, Honduras argued that the principle of effectiveness, or of effective interpretation, required delimitation if any judgment was to attain its objective of the final solution for the dispute between the parties. It seems that an attempt to bring in the modern law of the sea as part of the context was inappropriate, relevant rules of international law being the subject of article 31(3)(c) of the Vienna Convention. In the event, the Chamber considered that what Honduras was arguing amounted to recourse to the 'circumstances of the conclusion' of the Special Agreement, a supplementary means of interpretation under article 32 of the Vienna rules which was only accessible on the specified conditions being met.[127]

The potential and varied consequences of syntax forming part of the context are too obvious to warrant copious examples, syntax being very much allied to construing phrases and thus fixing the ordinary meaning of terms in their context.[128]

4.2.2 Title, headings, and chapeaux

Contextually, the title may be the obvious starting point for identifying the ambit of a treaty, or a section or provision in it. However, titles are often too general to provide precise guidance, though they may occasionally contribute to a specific interpretation. For example, in the jurisdictional phase of the *Oil Platforms* case[129] one issue before the ICJ was whether 'commerce' in the relevant 1955 treaty meant

---

[127] [1992] ICJ Reports 351, at paras 375–76.

[128] See, eg, the analysis by the WTO Appellate Body of contrasting tenses as context in its Report in *Chile—Price Band System and Safeguard Measures Relating to Certain Agricultural Products* WT/DS207/R (3 May 2002), at paras 205–11.

[129] *Oil Platforms (Islamic Republic of Iran v United States of America), (Preliminary Objections)* [1996–II] ICJ Reports 803.

only acts of purchase and sale or could include associated activities. After looking at dictionary definitions, the Court noted that

in the original English version, the actual title of the Treaty of 1955 (contrary to that of most similar treaties concluded by the United States at the time, such as the treaty of 1956 between the United States and Nicaragua) refers, besides 'Amity' and 'Consular Rights', not to 'Commerce' but, more broadly to 'Economic Relations'.[130]

This supported a wider reading.

Articles of treaties frequently have titles or descriptive headings. These are clearly part of the context for the purposes of interpretation, unless otherwise indicated.[131] The term 'chapeau' is not defined or used in the Vienna Convention. It is, however, in vogue, mainly to describe the opening words of a provision which consists of a subset of terms.[132] The importance of titles as part of the context is well illustrated in the Vienna rules themselves. The use of the singular in the title of article 31 of the Vienna Convention 'General rule of interpretation' was carefully adopted to make it clear that the whole of the article was to be applicable to the extent that as many of its components as are relevant in any particular case, they must be applied together. This title also links to that of article 32 'Supplementary means of interpretation' in that the latter not only indicates that the means of interpretation described in that provision were additional to those in article 31, but that the general rule had primary sway in determining the meaning of terms in issue.

A title or heading may, of course, be relevant because it is used as a reference point in a treaty's text; but the content of the heading may also help with interpretation. Both aspects were apparent in *Plama v Bulgaria*, an ICSID arbitration.[133] In making a decision on its jurisdiction the tribunal had to consider the Energy Charter Treaty (ECT), a multilateral convention for cooperation in the energy sector. Part III of the ECT gives protection to investors engaged in energy-related activities in the territory of states parties of a different nationality than their own. Part V of the ECT contains provisions for dispute settlement in article 26. Article 17 (in Part III) is entitled 'Non-Application of Part III in Certain Circumstances'. Under this provision parties reserve 'the right to deny the advantages of this Part' (ie the substantive protection for investors under Part III) to any legal entity owned or controlled by nationals of a state not party to the ECT if that entity has no substantial business activities in a party in which it is set up. Objecting to the tribunal's jurisdiction, Bulgaria argued that because it was entitled to deny the claimant

---

[130] *Oil Platforms (Islamic Republic of Iran v United States of America), (Preliminary Objections)* [1996–II] ICJ Reports 803, at 819, para 47.

[131] The role of titles to articles may be specifically limited as in the United Nations Framework Convention on Climate Change, New York, 1992. In that treaty, a note to the title of Article 1 (Definitions) states: 'Titles of articles are included solely to assist the reader.' See also consideration of specific instructions in a treaty as to use of headings in it in *Turbon International GmbH v Oberfinanzdirektion Koblenz* (Case C-250/05) [2006] All ER (D) 384.

[132] See the example in section 2.4.4 above; and see *Dispute concerning Access to Information under Article 9 of the OSPAR Convention (Ireland v UK)* (2003) 42 ILM 1118, at para 163, where the Tribunal took into account the title in considering the scope of article 9.

[133] ICSID Case No ARB/03/24, Decision on Jurisdiction, 8 February 2005.

the advantages of Part III in application of article 17, there could be no relevant 'advantages' under Part III capable of giving rise to any claim and hence no ground for jurisdiction under Part V.

The tribunal relied on the heading to Part III to confirm its interpretation that denial of protection under article 17 would only exclude the advantages of Part III and would not preclude it exercising jurisdiction under Part V to determine whether on the facts article 17 had been properly invoked:

In the Tribunal's view, the Respondent's jurisdictional case here turns on the effect of Articles 17(1) and 26 ECT, interpreted under Article 31(1) of the Vienna Convention. The express terms of Article 17 refer to a denial of the advantages 'of this Part', thereby referring to the substantive advantages conferred upon an investor by Part III of the ECT. The language is unambiguous; but it is confirmed by the title to Article 17: 'Non-Application of *Part III* in Certain Circumstances' (emphasis supplied). All authentic texts in the other five languages are to the same effect. From these terms, interpreted in good faith in accordance with their ordinary contextual meaning, the denial applies only to advantages under Part III. It would therefore require a gross manipulation of the language to make it refer to Article 26 in Part V of the ECT. Nonetheless, the Tribunal has considered whether any such manipulation is permissible in the light of the ECT's object and purpose.[134]

4.2.3 Context showing structure or scheme

As well as referring to the context in the sense of immediate surroundings and the more extensive meaning as defined in article 31(2), context may be taken as including any structure or scheme underlying a provision or the treaty as a whole.[135] The exploration of context leading to such a structure is shown in the WTO Appellate Body's decision in *Canada—Measures Affecting the Export of Civilian Aircraft*.[136] This tribunal had to consider the argument of Canada (the appellant) that evaluation of a 'benefit', which was part of the definition of 'subsidy' in the Agreement on Subsidies and Countervailing Measures (the SCM Agreement), should include the cost to a government. Canada agreed with the finding of the Panel (the tribunal whose decision was under appeal) that the ordinary meaning of the term 'benefit' is 'advantage'; but Canada argued that the Panel had not applied the Vienna rules properly when assessing whether there had been a benefit in that it used commercial benchmarks to the exclusion of the cost to the government.

After considering dictionary definitions, the Appellate Body looked to the immediate context in the definition of 'benefit' in article 1 of the SCM Agreement, then expanding this inquiry into investigation of other relevant elements of the Agreement and the structure of the provision. In its analysis, the Appellate Body stated:

A 'benefit' does not exist in the abstract, but must be received and enjoyed by a beneficiary or a recipient. Logically, a 'benefit' can be said to arise only if a person, natural or legal, or a

---

[134] ICSID Case No ARB/03/24, Decision on Jurisdiction, 8 February 2005, at para 147.

[135] For an example of an arbitral award which carefully distinguishes the immediate context and the context in the sense of the entire text of the treaty, see *Dispute concerning Filleting within the Gulf of St Lawrence ("La Bretagne")(Canada/France)* (1986) 82 ILR 591, at 620–21, paras 38–39.

[136] Decision AB-1999–2 of 2 August 1999, WT/DS70/AB/R.

group of persons, has in fact received something. The term 'benefit', therefore, implies that there must be a recipient. This provides textual support for the view that the focus of the inquiry under Article 1.1(b) of the *SCM Agreement* should be on the recipient and not on the granting authority. The ordinary meaning of the word 'confer', as used in Article 1.1(b), bears this out. 'Confer' means, *inter alia*, 'give', 'grant' or 'bestow'. The use of the past participle 'conferred' in the passive form, in conjunction with the word 'thereby', naturally calls for an inquiry into *what was conferred on the recipient.* Accordingly, we believe that Canada's argument that 'cost to government' is one way of conceiving of 'benefit' is at odds with the ordinary meaning of Article 1.1(b), which focuses on the *recipient* and not on the *government* providing the 'financial contribution'.[137]

The Appellate body then considered the context in the sense of a related provision in the same treaty:

We find support for this reading of 'benefit' in the context of Article 1.1(b) of the *SCM Agreement.* Article 14 sets forth guidelines for calculating the amount of a subsidy in terms of 'the benefit to the recipient'. Although the opening words of Article 14 state that the guidelines it establishes apply '[f]or the purposes of Part V' of the *SCM Agreement*, which relates to 'countervailing measures', our view is that Article 14, nonetheless, constitutes relevant context for the interpretation of 'benefit' in Article 1.1(b). The guidelines set forth in Article 14 apply to the calculation of the 'benefit *to the recipient* conferred *pursuant to paragraph 1 of Article 1*'. (emphasis added) This explicit textual reference to Article 1.1 in Article 14 indicates to us that 'benefit' is used in the same sense in Article 14 as it is in Article 1.1. Therefore, the reference to 'benefit *to the recipient'* in Article 14 also implies that the word 'benefit', *as used in Article 1.1*, is concerned with the 'benefit *to the recipient'* and not with the 'cost to government', as Canada contends.[138]

The clinching contextual reasoning of the Appellate Board took up the structure of article 1 of the SCM Agreement which defined 'subsidy' as existing if: '(a) there is a financial contribution by a government or any public body within the territory of a Member…and (b) a benefit is thereby conferred'. The Board reasoned:

The structure of Article 1.1 as a whole confirms our view that Article 1.1(b) is concerned with the 'benefit' to the recipient, and not with the 'cost to government'. The definition of 'subsidy' in Article 1.1 has two discrete elements: 'a financial contribution by a government or any public body' and 'a benefit is thereby conferred'. The first element of this definition is concerned with whether the *government* made a 'financial contribution', as that term is defined in Article 1.1(a). The focus of the first element is on the action of the government in making the 'financial contribution'. That being so, it seems to us logical that the second element in Article 1.1 is concerned with the 'benefit…conferred' on the *recipient* by that governmental action. Thus, subparagraphs (a) and (b) of Article 1.1 define a 'subsidy' by reference, first, to the action of the granting authority and, second, to what was conferred on the recipient. Therefore, Canada's argument that 'cost to *government'* is relevant to the question of whether there is a 'benefit' to the *recipient* under Article 1.1(b) disregards the overall structure of Article 1.1.[139]

---

[137] Decision AB-1999–2 of 2 August 1999, at pp 39–40, para 155 (emphasis in original).
[138] Decision AB-1999–2 of 2 August 1999, at p 40, para 156 (emphasis in original).
[139] Decision AB-1999–2 of 2 August 1999, at p 40, para 157 (emphasis in original).

Another good example of the significance of the context as defined in the Vienna rules is in the judgment of the House of Lords in *R v Secretary of State for the Home Department, Ex parte Read*.[140] This case shows how use of context leads to clarification of particular terms by comparison with those in other provisions of the treaty, and how the underlying scheme of the treaty can buttress an emerging interpretation. A man was convicted in Spain of an offence of introducing there counterfeit currency to an approximate value of £4,000. He was sentenced to imprisonment of 12 years and one day, the minimum term for that offence under Spanish law. He was transferred to the UK to serve his sentence under arrangements governed by a Convention.[141] Pursuant to the Convention, the UK Secretary of State fixed the period of sentence to be served by adapting the Spanish sentence to one of 10 years' imprisonment which was the maximum term prescribed for a similar offence committed in the UK. The prisoner argued that in applying the Convention's provisions the Secretary of State should have adapted the sentence to the much lesser period of imprisonment that a court would have given had the same offence been committed in Britain.

The House of Lords looked at the scheme in the Convention which was that the authorities in the state to which the prisoner was being transferred would either 'continue the enforcement of the sentence' of the convicting state's court or 'convert the sentence' to its own equivalent sentence. The UK had exercised its right under the Convention to opt in all cases for 'continuation' of sentence rather than 'conversion'. The Convention spelt out the modalities of continuation as including the requirements that the administering state was to be bound 'by the legal nature and duration of the sentence as determined by the sentencing state'; but if the sentence was 'by its nature or duration incompatible with the law of the administering state' that state could 'adapt the sanction to the punishment or measure prescribed by its own law for a similar offence'. However, the punishment had, as far as possible, to 'correspond with that imposed by the sentence to be enforced', though it was not to 'exceed the maximum prescribed by the law of the administering state '.[142]

Further, an administering state using the 'continuation' approach was bound by 'the duration of the sentence as determined by the sentencing state' with the equivalent prescription in the case of 'conversion' that the administering state was to be 'bound by the findings as to the facts in so far as they appear explicitly or implicitly from the judgment imposed in the sentencing state'. The latter envisaged the particular characteristics of the acts of the prisoner to be in the frame, the former did not. If circumstances particular to the prisoner's acts had been taken into account, that would have eliminated any significant distinction between the continuation and the conversion schemes. Hence the power to adapt the punishment to one prescribed by law in the UK for a 'similar offence' did not mean looking to the circumstances of the particular prisoner's acts but rather to an offence having

---

[140] [1989] AC 1014.
[141] Convention on the Transfer of Sentenced Persons, Strasbourg, 1983.
[142] Convention on the Transfer of Sentenced Persons, Strasbourg, 1983, article 10.

similar legal characteristics. It can be seen that the contrasting wording and the very framework of having two distinct schemes played their part in the interpretation of the provision, an interpretation which was confirmed by the 'Explanatory Report' adopted at the time of conclusion of the Convention.[143]

4.2.4 Related and contrasting provisions

Even where the provisions in issue do not form a distinct scheme in themselves, their relationship, or a comparison of their roles, may assist in their interpretation. In relation to a dispute between Nicaragua and Honduras, the ICJ had to consider two provisions of a treaty which made provision for the Court to have jurisdiction.[144] Article XXXI of the Pact of Bogotà was in a form which seemed to amount to a declaration by states parties to the Pact that they accepted the jurisdiction of the ICJ under the provision in the ICJ's Statute for such declarations ('the Optional Clause'). Article XXXII provided that if the conciliation procedure of the Pact had not led to resolution of a dispute and if the disputants did not agree to submit the matter to arbitration, either of the parties could have recourse to the ICJ, whose jurisdiction was in those circumstances to be compulsory under the Statute's provision for accepting jurisdiction in a treaty. An issue was whether these provisions were to be read together, the former establishing the jurisdiction of the Court and the latter setting out the prerequisites for reference of the particular dispute, or whether they provided two separate bases for jurisdiction. The Court was able to contrast the two provisions, noting (among other points) that the provisions fitted in with separate ways of accepting its jurisdiction in accordance with its Statute.[145]

4.2.5 Preamble

The preamble (where there is one) usually consists of a set of recitals.[146] These recitals commonly include motivation, aims, and considerations which are stated as having played a part in drawing up the treaty. Specifically mentioned as an element of the context as defined in the Vienna rules, preambles are of both textual and teleological significance. Their textual significance is as part of the apparatus for selecting and modifying the ordinary meaning of terms used.[147] By stating the

---

[143] On the status of the Explanatory Report, see Chapter 6, section 2.1.1 below.

[144] *Border and Transborder Armed Actions (Nicaragua v Honduras) (Jurisdiction and Admissibility)* [1988] ICJ Reports 69.

[145] *Border and Transborder Armed Actions (Nicaragua v Honduras) (Jurisdiction and Admissibility)* at 88–89, paras 42–45; see also *Certain Questions of Mutual Assistance in Criminal Matters (Djibouti v France)*, [2008] ICJ Reports 177, at 232–3, paras 154–56.

[146] See generally E Suy, 'Le Préambule', in E Yakpo and T Boumedra (eds), *Liber Amicorum Judge Mohammed Bedjaoui* (The Hague: Kluwer, 1999), at 253–69.

[147] See, eg, *Border and Transborder Armed Actions (Nicaragua v Honduras), (Jurisdiction and Admissibility)* [1988] ICJ Reports at 106, para 97, where the ICJ relied on a draft of the preamble and its similar wording in the Final Act of a conference adopting a treaty to show that dispute settlement

aims and objectives of a treaty, as preambles often do in general terms, they can help in identifying the object and purpose of the treaty.[148] It should not, however, be assumed that all preambles are of equal value. Some are very carefully negotiated, others cobbled together more or less as an afterthought. In the case of major modern multilateral treaties, where there are usually good records of the negotiating history, the preparatory work will reveal whether there has been thorough attention to the content of the preamble.[149]

The recitals in the preamble are not the appropriate place for stating obligations, which are usually in operative articles of the treaty or in annexes. However, they may impose interpretative commitments, such as in a Protocol 'EMPHASIZING that this Protocol shall not be interpreted as implying a change in the rights and obligations of a Party under any existing international agreements'.[150] Hence if the terms of a substantive provision offered a choice of meanings, those which ran counter to rights and obligations under other instruments would be excluded. Put more generally, the substantive provisions will usually have greater clarity and precision than the preamble; but where there is doubt over the meaning of a substantive provision, the preamble may justify a wider interpretation, or at least rejection of a restrictive one.[151]

4.2.6 Punctuation and syntax

A reader that pointeth ill, a good sentence may often spill.[152]

The essential link between the meaning of a single word and its immediate context also requires considering punctuation and syntax. Probably one of the best known instances where punctuation was crucial to the interpretation of a treaty concerned article 6 of the Nuremberg Charter, 1945.[153] The provision listed the crimes over which the International Military Tribunal was to have jurisdiction. Paragraphs (a) and (b) listed crimes against peace and war crimes. Paragraph (c) covered two groups of crimes against humanity:

Crimes against humanity: namely, murder, extermination, enslavement, deportation, and other inhumane acts committed against any civilian population, before or during the war;*

---

procedures in the treaty were not intended to exclude the right of recourse to other competent international forums; see also WTO Appellate Body in *Canada—Term of Patent Protection* WT/DS170/AB/R (2000), para 59; and see Suy, 'Le Préambule', at 258–63.

[148] See section 5.3.2 above.   [149] See Suy, 'Le Préambule', at 256.

[150] Cartagena Protocol on Biosafety to the Convention on Biological Diversity of 5 June 1992, Montreal, 2000 [2000] *Australian Treaties Not In Force* 4.

[151] This loosely paraphrases Suy, 'Le Préambule', at 262: '*De façon générale, le dispositive offrira, en raison de sa plus grande précision, plus de clarté, de sorte qu'un recours à l'interprétation au moyen du préambule s'avérera sans effet réel. Mais en cas de doute quant à la portée du dispositif, le préambule peut en justifier une interprétation extensive—ou au moins justifier le rejet d'une interprétation restrictive.*'

[152] *Oxford English Dictionary*, sub nom 'point', attribution there to G Chaucer, *The Romaunt of the Rose* ('A reder that poyntith ille, A good sentence may ofte spille').

[153] Agreement for the Prosecution and Punishment of the Major War Criminals of the European Axis, and Charter of the International Military Tribunal, London, 8 August 1945, in *Trial of Major War Criminals before the International Military Tribunal*, Vol 1, Documents (London: HMSO, 1947). See further E Schwelb, 'Crimes Against Humanity' (1946) 23 BYBIL, 178 at 188 and 193–95.

or persecutions on political, racial or religious grounds in execution of or in connection with any crime within the jurisdiction of the Tribunal, whether or not in violation of the domestic law of the country where perpetrated.

The semi-colon (marked here with an asterisk) appeared in the English and French texts, but in the equally authentic Russian text there was a comma at this point. A semi-colon would have marked a firm separation between the defined group of 'persecutions' in the second half and the group of 'inhumane acts' listed in the first half. Yet the requirement of a connection with one of the specified crimes, and the clarification that domestic law was irrelevant, appears only in the second half of the paragraph. A semi-colon would have strongly suggested (if not dictated) that this requirement and clarification related solely to persecutions rather than both groups of crimes against humanity. One decidedly odd consequence would have been that the specific exclusion of domestic defences (such as superior orders) would have been linked only to persecutions and not the inhumane acts (such as murder, extermination, enslavement, etc). Equally, the Tribunal would have had jurisdiction over the specified inhumane acts at large, rather than only when committed in conjunction with crimes against peace and war crimes. Accordingly, an amending Protocol was concluded by which a comma was substituted for the semi-colon in the English text to bring this in line with the Russian version.[154]

Punctuation and syntax are (it goes without saying) only part of the picture. They may be of assistance but, as is the case with the other elements of treaty interpretation, are only one part of the whole. This is illustrated by the approach taken by the ICJ in *Aegean Sea Continental Shelf (Greece v Turkey)*.[155] At issue was a Greek reservation in its accession to a 1928 treaty for pacific settlement of disputes. This reservation, which was lodged in French, excluded from Greece's acceptance of the jurisdiction of the Court 'disputes concerning questions which by international law are solely within the domestic jurisdiction of States, and in particular [Fr: *et, notamment,*] disputes relating to the territorial status of Greece...'. Greece had a dispute with Turkey over the extent of its continental shelf in the Aegean where Turkey was exploring for oil in areas claimed by Greece. Greece argued that the dispute over delimitation of its continental shelf was not excluded by the quoted reservation because territorial disputes were only excluded if they raised questions which by international law were solely within the domestic jurisdiction of Greece. Since its dispute with Turkey was international in character it could not (Greece argued) fall within the exclusion.

---

[154] Protocol Rectifying Discrepancy in Text of Charter, Berlin, 6 October 1945, in *Trial of Major War Criminals...* (see preceding note). The Protocol made the same change in the French text, but also altered that text in a way which made it clear that inhumane acts and persecutions were both conditioned by the two elements noted in the text above.

[155] [1978] ICJ Reports 3; cf *Sovereignty over Pulau Litigan and Pulau Sipadan (Indonesia/Malaysia)* [2002] ICJ Reports 625, at 646–47, paras 39–40, where the equally authentic texts in English and Dutch differed in punctuation as to a colon or semi-colon; but the Court found that the difference in punctuation did not assist in elucidating the meaning with regard to the point in issue.

In reaction to Greece's citation of French dictionaries to show that 'et, notamment,' were words 'most often used to draw attention to one or more particular objects forming part of a previously designated or understood whole',[156] the ICJ noted that what it described as the 'grammatical argument' advanced by Greece had the peculiar legal consequence of integrating into one category 'territorial disputes' and 'domestic jurisdiction', which were two separate legal concepts (and reflected as separate in the 1928 treaty), with the consequence that the former concept was deprived of any significance. The Court found that the 'grammatical argument' was not compelling:

In the first place, the grammatical argument overlooks the commas placed both before and after '*notamment*'. To put the matter at its lowest, one possible purpose of these commas might have been to make it clear that in the phrase 'et, *notamment, les différends*' etc., the word '*et*' is intended to be a true conjunctive introducing a category of '*différends*' additional to those already specified.

Another point overlooked by the argument is that the meaning attributed to 'et, *notamment*,' by Greece is grammatically not the only, although it may be the most frequent, use of that expression. Robert's *Dictionnaire* itself goes no further than to say of the word *notamment* that it is 'most often' used to draw attention to one of several particular objects forming part of a collectivity previously indicated or implied. The question whether in the present instance the expression 'et, *notamment*,' has the meaning attributed to it by Greece thus depends on the context in which those words were used in Greece's instrument of accession and is not a matter simply of their preponderant linguistic usage. Even a purely grammatical interpretation of reservation (*b*), therefore, leaves open the possibility that the words '*et, notamment, les différends ayant trait au statut territorial de la Grèce*' were intended to specify an autonomous category of disputes additional to those concerning matters of domestic jurisdiction, which were also specifically 'excluded from the procedures described in the General Act'.

In any event, 'the Court cannot base itself on a purely grammatical interpretation of the text' *(Anglo–Iranian Oil Co., I.C.J. Reports 1952,* p. 104).[157]

Where purely grammatical analysis produces an untenable result, the narrowly grammatical interpretation may have to be ignored. For example, in the *US–UK Heathrow Airport User Charges Arbitration* a provision in an Air Services Agreement required that '[user charges imposed or permitted to be imposed by a Party on the designated airlines of the other Party] are equitably apportioned among categories of users'.[158] The tribunal rejected a construction of this which required apportionment by the UK authorities to be equitable merely as among US airlines rather than equitably among different types of users of all nationalities. The tribunal also noted that although grammatically the apportionment was to take place after the charges had been imposed, this was clearly not what was meant. 'For both these reasons, a narrowly grammatical interpretation of the "equitable apportionment" condition must be discarded as untenable.'[159]

---

[156] [1978] ICJ Reports 3, at 21, para 51 (stating the ICJ's translation of an entry in Robert's *Dictionnaire*).

[157] [1978] ICJ Reports 3, at 22, para 53; see also problems of punctuation in different languages considered in Chapter 9, section 4.8.

[158] 102 ILR 215, Award of 30 November 1992, at 307.   [159] 102 ILR 215, at 307.

4.2.7 Different meanings of same term in a single instrument

It is a general principle in interpretation of a well-drafted document to expect the same term to have the same meaning throughout a single instrument. A related, or perhaps obverse, principle is that different terms can be expected to have different meanings. Neither of these is an absolute rule and departures may be more likely in the case of treaties, particularly where there have been many negotiators, sometimes with different groups working on different parts of the text, and sometimes using several languages, some of which may have a greater and more nuanced range of words on a particular topic than do other languages. In the Award in the *Rhine Chlorides* case, the Tribunal noted that:

> ...the mere fact that a treaty uses two different terms (but which are very close in meaning) does not mean that it must immediately conclude, without further analysis, that the parties intended to create a significant distinction. Naturally, each treaty is presumed to be consistent in the way it uses its terms, but this presumption cannot be regarded as an absolute rule.[160]

Context, as an element of the general rule of interpretation in the Vienna Convention, is defined to include the whole of the treaty although the primary use of context is as an aid to identifying the ordinary meaning of terms. This is a wider use of context that a common usage in relation to a word or phrase, where it refers to the most immediate surroundings. However, the greater definition of context includes the lesser. In the absence of any specific indication in a treaty that a term has a particular meaning in a specific part of the treaty (such as a definition provision for a particular part), it is both the immediate context and the wider context which will be significant determinants of the meaning.

A good example of context suggesting different meanings of the same term is in the references in the general rule of interpretation to 'in connection with conclusion' of a treaty, which at one point suggests a single moment and at another seems more apt to refer to a process.[161] An example of different terms in one language being found to have been used interchangeably, or at least haphazardly in other languages, is in the Award in the *Rhine Chlorides* case (above). In that case it was in large measure the context which led the Tribunal to reject an argument that references to expenses (with various qualifiers) meant the sums specified in the treaty in relation to each ton of chlorides stored, rather than the actual cost of storage.[162]

---

[160] *Case Concerning the Auditing of Accounts (Netherlands v France)*, Arbitral Award of 12 March 2004, 144 ILR 259, at 305, para 91.

[161] See Chapter 6, section 2.1 below; see also the example of 'responsibility' meaning to have an obligation ('responsibility to ensure') and 'responsibility' meaning liability ('responsibility and liability for damage') in *Responsibilities and Obligations of States Sponsoring Persons and Entities with respect to Activities in the Area* (Advisory Opinion) (2011) ITLOS Case No 17, paras 64–71, and see Chapter 9, section 4.7 below.

[162] See Chapter 1, section 5.2 above.

4.2.8 Link with object and purpose

The linking factor in the first paragraph of the general rule of treaty interpretation between the context and the object and purpose of the treaty is that these are elements pertinent to finding the ordinary meaning of terms used in the treaty. Context in the Vienna rules denotes the idea of the focus of the interpreter's attention expanding out from the provision under consideration to the broader vision provided by the context as described by article 31, and then using this wider view to help home back in on the meaning of the term or terms in issue. While the object and purpose of the treaty, as analysed below, is a distinct element assisting the interpreter towards giving meaning to the relevant term in a similar way to the assistance provided by the context, a role for the object and purpose of a particular treaty provision (as distinct from the object and purpose of the treaty as a whole) is not singled out in the general rule.

The expansive role for context includes consideration of matters identified above, such as titles or headings, structure or scheme, contrasting provisions etc. These all offer pointers to what a provision is trying to convey. It is therefore no surprise that, in this process of examination of context, interpreters sometimes look to the object of a particular provision. Thus, in a case where it identified articles 31 and 32 of the Vienna Convention as governing the matter as customary international law, the ICJ looked to such an object:

> it would be contrary to the object of the provision [article VI of the Genocide Convention] to interpret the notion of "international penal tribunal" restrictively in order to exclude from it a court which, as in the case of the ICTY, was created pursuant to a United Nations Security Council resolution adopted under Chapter VII of the Charter.[163]

Although the Court did not link this approach to a particular provision in the general rule of interpretation, it is consistent with reading a provision in its context to take account of the provision's object and purpose.[164] It is difficult to see any reason why this should not apply in treaty interpretation generally.

---

[163] *Application of the Convention on the Prevention and Punishment of the Crime of Genocide (Bosnia and Herzegovina v Serbia and Montenegro)* [2007] ICJ Reports 43, at 227, para 445 and stating, at 110, para 160, that the Court was applying articles 31 and 32 of the Vienna Convention; see also: *Case concerning Legality of Use of Force (Serbia and Montenegro v Belgium)* (Preliminary Objections) [2004] ICJ Reports 279, at 312, para 109; *Nuclear Tests (Australia v France)*, [1974] ICJ 253, at 332, para 41, and *Case Concerning the Barcelona Traction, Light and Power Company, Limited (New Application: 1962) (Belgium v Spain)* [1964] ICJ. 6, at 136: 'The ratio legis, the object, of these two provisions of the Statute is the same...'; the Court has also made numerous references to the object and purpose of particular rules in its Rules of Court.

[164] Cf the commentary in the Guide to Practice on Reservations to Treaties (considered in Chapter 3, section 3.1 above) where there are examples of objections to reservations on the basis of inconsistency with the object and purpose of particular provisions: Addendum to Report of the International Law Commission, Sixty-third session (2011), UN General Assembly Official Records, Sixty-sixth Session, Supplement No. 10, A/66/10/Add.1, p 486, fn 2270 and p 514, fn 2400.

5. 'Object and Purpose'

It is by no means easy to put together in a single formula all the elements to be taken into account, in each specific case, in determining the object and purpose of the treaty. Such a process undoubtedly requires more 'esprit de finesse' than 'esprit de géométrie', like any act of interpretation, for that matter—and this process is certainly one of interpretation.[165]

The final words of article 31(1) of the Vienna Convention bring the teleological element into the general rule. These words can also be seen as allowing for consideration of the principle of 'effectiveness' in its more general sense. In English case law since *Fothergill v Monarch*,[166] the label 'purposive approach' has often been given to this element of treaty interpretation and that label has sometimes been used to describe the whole approach to be taken by courts in the UK to treaty interpretation.[167] However, in the Vienna rules, object and purpose function as a means of shedding light on the ordinary meaning rather than merely as an indicator of a general approach to be taken to treaty interpretation. The main issues relating to 'object and purpose' are what these terms signify, how they are to be identified, and what use is to be made of them. Also within the ambit of this concept is the second meaning of the 'principle of effectiveness'. This is the notion that an objective of treaty interpretation is to produce an outcome that advances the aims of the treaty, a notion which is obviously dependent on identifying the object and purpose of the treaty. It is to be noted, however, that this element of the rule is not one allowing the general purpose of a treaty to override its text. Rather, object and purpose are modifiers of the ordinary meaning of a term which is being interpreted, in the sense that the ordinary meaning is to be identified in their light. However, the precise nature, role, and application of the concept of 'object and purpose' in the law of treaties present some uncertainty and it has been described in the title of the leading study of the topic (to which reference should be made for a full account of its history and the concepts involved) as an 'enigma'.[168]

---

[165] Addendum to Report of the International Law Commission, Sixty-third session (2011), UN General Assembly Official Records, Sixty-sixth Session, Supplement No. 10, A/66/10/Add.1, pp 359–60, guideline 3.1.5.1, commentary para (1), footnote omitted; see also the full commentary on this guideline for a useful analysis of the practice of the ICJ and other courts and tribunals on this matter <http://legal.un.org/ilc/reports/2011/english/addendum.pdf>.

[166] [1981] AC 251.

[167] More recently, however, these courts have adopted a somewhat closer focus on the Vienna rules, at least to the extent of invoking article 31(1); see, eg, in the opinion of Lord Hope *In re B (FC) (2002), R v Special Adjudicator ex parte Hoxha* [2005] UKHL 19, at paras 8–9, before referring to article 31(1): 'A large and liberal spirit is called for when a court is asked to say what the Convention means. But there are limits to this approach. The court must recognise the fundamental fact that the Convention is an agreement between states. The extent of the agreement to which the states committed themselves is to be found in the language which gives formal expression to their agreement. The language itself is the starting point…'.

[168] I Buffard and K Zemanek, 'The "Object and Purpose" of a Treaty: An Enigma?' (1998) 3 *Austrian Review of International and European Law* 311.

5.1 History and preparatory work relating to 'object and purpose'

The use of this phrase in the Vienna rules had its origins in the link made with treaty interpretation in the original version of the provision reflecting the obligation of states to implement treaties in good faith (*pacta sunt servanda*), now article 26 of the Vienna Convention. That first draft included a requirement that 'a party to a treaty shall refrain from any acts calculated to prevent the due execution of the treaty or otherwise to frustrate its objects'.[169] Use of the term 'objects' was in turn drawn from another draft provision concerning the obligation of a state which had signed but not yet ratified a treaty. Such a state was to be under an obligation 'to refrain from any action calculated to frustrate the objects of the treaty or to impair its eventual performance'.[170] The combining of 'object' and 'purpose' appears to have been the result of the observation made by a member of the ILC in relation to the draft article on the obligation to comply with treaties ('*pacta sunt servanda*'):

Mr Reuter... thought that in paragraph 2 of the article, the English word 'objects' might be better rendered in French by the expression '*l'objet et la fin;* that was the wording used by the International Court of Justice in connexion with the reservations to the Convention on the Prevention and Punishment of Genocide; in other cases it had used the French word '*but*' alone as the equivalent of the English word 'object'. If it adopted that suggestion, the Commission would be introducing a teleological nuance... But that question of form also affected the substance, for the object of an obligation was one thing and its purpose was another.[171]

Rather tantalizingly, the distinction thus observed was not further exposed in the work of the ILC but may have reflected the distinction in French public law (considered below).

5.2 Ordinary meaning of 'object and purpose' in context

It is difficult in English to distinguish the terms 'object' and 'purpose', which may explain why these words are commonly treated as a composite item when referring

---

[169] Waldock, Third Report on the Law of Treaties [1964] *Yearbook of the ILC*, vol II, p 7, draft article 55(2).

[170] Waldock, Special Rapporteur, First Report on the Law of Treaties [1962] *Yearbook of the ILC*, vol II, p 46, draft article 9(2)(c). The original reference to 'objects' may have been derived from the Special Rapporteur's acknowledged inspiration for the draft articles in the 1956 Resolution of the Institute of International law and in the work of Sir Gerald Fitzmaurice formulating major principles of treaty interpretation. The 1956 Resolution included among the 'legitimate means of interpretation' in the case of a dispute brought before an international tribunal: 'the consideration of the objects of the treaty'. Sir Gerald Fitzmaurice's Principle IV '*Principle of Effectiveness*' included the proposition: 'Treaties are to be interpreted with reference to their declared or apparent objects and purposes...' (Waldock, Third Report on the Law of Treaties [1964] *Yearbook of the ILC*, vol II, p 55).

[171] [1964] *Yearbook of the ILC*, vol I, p 26, footnotes omitted; the usage by the Court in the *Reservations to the Genocide Convention* case appears in fact to have been slightly different: it did refer to '*les fins poursuivies*', translated as 'objects pursued', [1951] ICJ Reports 15, at 23; but in conjunction with '*l'objet*' the Court used '*et le but*', translated as 'the object and purpose', at 24. Thus the French text came to use '*but*' rather than '*fin*' in each place where 'object and purpose' occurs in the English version, the term '*fin*' being used in the Vienna Convention mainly in phrases signifying 'termination' of a treaty (see, eg, articles 45, 60, etc), the exception being article 8 (representation for a particular '*fin*' or 'purpose').

to their use in the Vienna rules. Dictionary definitions include for 'object' 'goal, purpose, or aim', and for 'purpose' 'the object which one has in view'.[172] Given, however, the apparent French source for the language ultimately used for this phrase in the Convention, not to mention the equal authenticity of the French text, it is particularly appropriate to consider the terminology in French and any equivalence which should be provided in English.

Buffard and Zemanek explain that French public law has developed a distinction between '*l'objet*' of a legal act or instrument, that is what it does in the sense of creating a particular set of rights and obligations, and '*le but*' as the reason for establishing '*l'objet*':

> According to this French doctrine the term 'object' indicates thus the substantial content of the norm, the provisions, rights and obligations created by the norm. The object of a treaty is the instrument for the achievement of the treaty's purpose, and this purpose is, in turn, the general result which the parties want to achieve by the treaty. While the object can be found in the provisions of the treaty, the purpose may not always be explicit and be prone to a more subjective understanding.[173]

One of the commonly mentioned sources of guidance on the object and purpose of a treaty is its preamble. However, in keeping with the approach of the Vienna rules generally, and their definition and use of context in particular, it is the whole text (and associated matter as indicated in article 31(2)) which is to be taken into account. Courts and tribunals sometimes simply state the object and purpose without explaining precisely how they have deduced these, but presumably it is simply from their reading of the text. Some treaties have provisions in their substantive articles specifically listing the treaty's object and purpose. Article 1 of the United Nations Charter, stating the purposes of the UN in conjunction with provisions for their fulfilment in article 2, is a good example of this.[174] Sometimes the treaty may be of a type which itself attracts an assumption of a particular object and purpose. For example, treaties resolving boundary disputes may be taken by courts and tribunals as intended to produce a final fixing of frontiers; and agreements establishing jurisdiction over a particular dispute may be taken as having final determination of the dispute as their end. However, the examples given below show that this does not mean that such object and purpose are to be taken as affording the court or tribunal a very general interpretative mandate. The inclusion in the Vienna rules of this reference to object and purpose is so as to shed light on the terms actually used in their context, rather than introduce an alternative option for finding the meaning. A further form in which much the same idea is sometimes clothed in treaty interpretation is that guidance on interpretation and

---

[172] *Oxford English Dictionary* (1989).
[173] Buffard and Zemanek, 'The "Object and Purpose" of a Treaty: An Enigma?', at 326, and see 325–28 for a fuller explanation.
[174] For an example in a bilateral treaty, see article I of the US–Iran Treaty of Amity, Economic Relations and Consular Rights, Tehran, 1955, and extracts from ICJ judgments in *Oil Platforms (Iran v USA)* below in section 5.3.1.

application is to be gained from the 'spirit' of the treaty. Caution, however, is advisable on this as the 'spirit' may suggest a nebulous formulation of what animates the treaty. 'Object and purpose' is a more specific point of reference.

The term 'object and purpose' is used in several other provisions of the Vienna Convention. In the immediate context of interpretation, article 33(4) uses regard for the object and purpose of the treaty as the means for reconciling texts where a treaty has been authenticated in two or more languages, no text has been agreed to prevail in the case of divergence, and comparison of authentic texts discloses a difference of meaning which is not resolved by application of the rest of the Vienna rules. More remotely the term is used in:

- Article 18—obligation 'not to defeat the object and purpose of a treaty prior to its entry into force' in the case of a state which has signed but not yet ratified a treaty, or which has given consent but the treaty has not yet come into force.

- Article 19—entitlement to make a reservation if doing this is not 'incompatible with the object and purpose of the treaty', where the reservation is not prohibited by the treaty and the treaty does not limit entitlement to only specified reservations.

- Article 20 (2)—a reservation requires acceptance by all the parties when it appears from the limited number of the negotiating States and 'the object and purpose of a treaty that the application of the treaty in its entirety between all the parties is an essential condition of consent of each one to be bound by the treaty'.

- Article 41—modification of multilateral treaties between certain of the parties only in specified circumstances and if the modification 'does not relate to a provision, derogation from which is incompatible with the effective execution of the object and purpose of the treaty as a whole'.

- Article 58—suspension of the operation of a multilateral treaty by agreement between certain of the parties only in specified circumstances and if the modification 'is not incompatible with the object and purpose of the treaty'.

Examination of the practice in the application of these other provisions could extend the range of examples of how the object and purpose of a treaty is to be ascertained; but there are sufficient examples for present purposes arising in the specific context of interpretation.

Practice shows that courts and tribunals have tended to treat the term 'object and purpose' as a single but broad remit, in the sense that it is difficult to find any reasoned distinction being drawn between the object and purpose of a treaty, and sometimes there seems no particularity in distinguishing between the object and purpose of the treaty and the purpose of particular provisions. These may, of course, be justifiably elided; but the purpose of a particular provision, in the sense of its role in the structure of the treaty and its delineating function in the scheme of the treaty is as much (or more) part of the context as an aid to identifying the ordinary meaning. The 'object and purpose' of a treaty is a phrase which is also to be distinguished from the 'circumstances of its conclusion' in article 32 of the Vienna Convention, the latter being a supplementary means of interpretation. Such supplementary material may, however, shed light on the object and purpose if these are difficult to ascertain from the text.[175]

5.3 Issues and practice

5.3.1 Singular object and purpose

In the judgments of the ICJ there has been a hint that object and purpose will not always be regarded as a combined concept. At the preliminary objection phase of the *Oil Platforms* case the ICJ at several points referred to objects and purposes together (having made specific reference to the Vienna Convention); but it also refers to 'object' separately, 'objective', 'spirit', and what the 'whole of these provisions is aimed at'.[176] In that case the ICJ was concerned with an argument over the meaning of provisions of the Treaty of Amity, Economic Relations and Consular Rights between the United States of America and Iran, Tehran, 1955. Iran argued that 'in adopting a patently hostile and threatening attitude towards the Islamic Republic that culminated in the attack and destruction of the Iranian oil platforms, the United States breached the object and purpose of the Treaty of Amity, including articles I and X (1)…'. The Court examined article I which provided that '[t]here shall be firm and enduring peace and sincere friendship' between the two states. The Court considered that 'such a general formulation cannot be interpreted in isolation from the object and purpose of the Treaty in which it is inserted''.[177] It contrasted treaties of friendship generally with the present Treaty of Amity. The former tended to follow such a provision as the article I in issue with clauses aimed at clarifying the conditions of application of such a general formulation. The Court noted that the 1955 treaty was not the same type, its fuller title of the present treaty was a treaty of 'Amity, Economic Relations and Consular Rights' whose object was, according to the terms of the Preamble, the 'encouraging [of] mutually beneficial trade and investments and closer economic intercourse generally' as well as 'regulating consular relations' between the two states.[178] After identifying the scope of particular provisions the Court found:

It follows that the object and purpose of the Treaty of 1955 was not to regulate peaceful and friendly relations between the two States in a general sense… Rather, by incorporating into the body of the Treaty the form of words used in Article I, the two States intended to stress that peace and friendship constituted the precondition for a harmonious development of

---

[175] The ILC seems to have assumed that the main guidance on identifying the object and purpose of a treaty would be its preamble: 'Again the Court has more than once had recourse to the statement of the object and purpose of the treaty in its preamble in order to interpret a particular provision' (Commentary on draft articles [1968] *Yearbook of the ILC*, vol II, p 41 (footnotes omitted). It must, however, be emphasized that the ILC was there stressing the importance of considering the treaty as a whole.

[176] [1996–II] ICJ Reports 803, at paras 27, 28, 31; 52; and 36, respectively.

[177] [1996–II] ICJ Reports 803, at para 27.   [178] [1996–II] ICJ Reports 803.

their commercial, financial and consular relations and that such a development would in turn reinforce that peace and that friendship. It follows that Article I must be regarded as fixing an objective, in the light of which the other Treaty provisions are to be interpreted and applied.

This conclusion is in conformity with that reached by the Court in 1986, when, on the occasion of its interpretation of the Treaty of Friendship of 1956 between the United States and Nicaragua, it stated in general terms that:

> 'There must be a distinction... in the case of a treaty of friendship, between the broad category of unfriendly acts, and the narrower category of acts tending to defeat the object and purpose of the Treaty. That object and purpose is the effective implementation of friendship in the specific fields provided for in the Treaty, not friendship in a vague general sense.' (I.C.J. Reports 1986, p. 137, para. 273.)[179]

It can be seen that in this case the object and purpose was viewed as a singular feature, helping to classify the treaty as different from more general treaties of friendship and peace and assisting the Court to the conclusion that the general pronouncement in article I of the 1955 treaty stated a treaty objective but not the basis for the Court's jurisdiction:

In the light of the foregoing, the Court considers that the objective of peace and friendship proclaimed in Article I of the Treaty of 1955 is such as to throw light on the interpretation of the other Treaty provisions, and in particular of Articles IV and X. Article I is thus not without legal significance for such an interpretation, but cannot, taken in isolation, be a basis for the jurisdiction of the Court.[180]

It would be unrealistic, however, to assume that because article 31(1) directs the interpreter to a singular object and purpose, such an object and purpose will be identifiable (or useful) in every case. The view of the Appellate Body at the WTO is a realistic generalization:

... most treaties have no single, undiluted object and purpose but rather a variety of different, and possibly conflicting, objects and purposes. This is certainly true of the *WTO Agreement*. Thus, while the first clause of the preamble to the *WTO Agreement* calls for the expansion of trade in goods and services, this same clause also recognizes that international trade and economic relations under the *WTO Agreement* should allow for 'optimal use of the world's resources in accordance with the objective of sustainable development', and should seek 'to protect and preserve the environment'. The Panel in effect took a one-sided view of the object and purpose of the *WTO Agreement* when it fashioned a new test not found in the text of the Agreement.[181]

5.3.2 Finding object and purpose from preamble and substantive provisions

The phase of the *Oil Platforms* case described above provides an example of how the object and purpose of the 1955 treaty was taken from the treaty's preamble, at least as a starting point. This was confirmed by reference to the full text where a further

---

[179] [1996–II] ICJ Reports 803, at para 28.　　　[180] [1996–II] ICJ Reports 803, at para 31.
[181] *US—Import Prohibition of Certain Shrimp and Shrimp Products* WT/DS58/AB/R (1998), para 17.

formulation of the 'objective' was found with significance for interpretation. While the preamble may seem an obvious starting point for ascertaining the object and purpose of the treaty, caution is necessary because preambles are not always drafted with care and a preamble itself may need interpreting. Thus, for example, in a dispute over the boundaries between territories previously affected by colonial activities, an issue was whether a particular treaty provision related only to land boundaries covered maritime boundaries too. The relevant preamble stated that the parties were 'desirous of defining the boundaries between the Netherlands possessions in the island of Borneo and the States in that island which are under British protection'. The ICJ rejected the contention that this indicated an objective of defining all boundaries in the area:

The Court considers that the object and purpose of the 1891 Convention was the delimitation of boundaries between the parties' possessions within the island of Borneo itself, as shown by the preamble to the Convention, which provides that the parties were 'desirous of defining the boundaries between the Netherland possessions *in* the Island of Borneo and the States *in that island* which are under British protection' (emphasis added by the Court). This interpretation is, in the Court's view, supported by the very scheme of the 1891 Convention.[182]

Judge Weeramantry has described earlier practice of the ICJ and of arbitral tribunals:

An obvious internal source of reference is the preamble to the treaty. The preamble is a principal and natural source from which indications can be gathered of a treaty's objects and purposes even though the preamble does not contain substantive provisions. Article 31(2) of the Vienna Convention sets this out specifically when it states that context, for the purpose of the interpretation of a treaty, shall comprise in addition to the text, the preamble and certain other materials. The jurisprudence of this Court also indicates, as in the case concerning *Rights of Nationals of the United States of America in Morocco*[3] and the *Asylum (Colombia/Peru)* case,[4] that the Court has made substantial use of it for interpretational purposes. In the former case, a possible interpretation of the Madrid Convention was rejected for its lack of conformity with the preamble's specific formulation of the purposes of the Convention. In the latter case the Court used the objects of the Havana Convention, as indicated in its preamble, to interpret Article 2 of the Convention. Important international arbitrations have likewise resorted to the preamble to a treaty as guides to its interpretation.[5]

[3] *I.C.J. Reports 1952*, p. 176, at p. 196.
[4] *I.C.J. Reports 1950*, p. 266, at p. 282.
[5] See paras. 19 and 20, *the Beagle Channel Arbitration*, 1977, Wetter, *The International Arbitral Process*, 1979, Vol. 1, p. 276, at pp. 318–319.[183]

---

[182] *Sovereignty over Pulau Litigan and Pulau Sipadan (Indonesia/Malaysia)* [2002] ICJ Reports 625, para 51; for further judgments and opinions of the PCIJ and ICJ referring to the preamble in treaty interpretation, see Suy, 'Le Préambule' at 255, note 6.
[183] *Case concerning the Arbitral Award of 31 July 1989 (Guinea-Bissau v Senegal)*, Dissenting Opinion [1991] ICJ Reports 53, at 142.

While, however, the preamble may be used as the source of a convenient summary of the object and purpose of a treaty, both the Vienna Convention (article 31(2)) and practice make it clear that an interpreter needs to read the whole treaty. Thus, the substantive provisions will provide the fuller indication of the object and purpose. The Appellate Body at the WTO has referred to preambles on a number of occasions, but it does so in the course of very detailed consideration of the relevant treaty's substantive provisions.[184]

5.3.3 Can the object and purpose be used to counter clear substantive provisions?

The *Oil Platforms* case considered above is but one of several ICJ cases which have been concerned with the extent of the jurisdiction conferred upon it, or another tribunal, by the parties to a dispute. The Court has in this context considered the object and purpose of the parties as requiring great care not to stretch jurisdiction beyond that specifically conferred by those parties. In doing so, and for the purposes of treaty interpretation more generally, it has answered in the negative the question that heads this section. Thus, in *Arbitral Award of 31 July 1989 (Guinea Bissau v Senegal)*, where the dispute was whether an arbitral tribunal's award was invalid because of failure to resolve all the issues as put before the tribunal, the ICJ stated:

... when states sign an arbitration agreement they are concluding an agreement with a very specific object and purpose: to entrust an arbitral tribunal with the task of settling a dispute in accordance with the terms agreed by the parties, who define in the agreement the jurisdiction of the tribunal and determine its limits.[185]

However, the arbitral tribunal had been asked two specific questions: the first on the validity of an agreement determining the boundary, and the second as to where the boundary should be drawn if the agreement were found invalid. Thus, the second function of the tribunal, drawing the line itself, only arose if it found the line had not been determined by the previous agreement. Finding that the previous agreement was valid and binding on the parties, the tribunal had nevertheless found that the agreement only dealt with sea areas as known at the time of the earlier agreement. Hence the line was incomplete, but the tribunal did not proceed to draw the rest of it. The ICJ found that this was not a failure of the tribunal to act as required by the reference to arbitration:

... although the two States had expressed in general terms in the Preamble of the Arbitration Agreement their desire to reach a settlement of their dispute, their consent thereto had only been given in the terms laid down by Article 2.[186]

---

[184] See, eg, *US—Import Prohibition of Certain Shrimp and Shrimp Products* (1998) WT/DS58/AB/R, paras 12 and 17; *EC—Measures Concerning Meat and Meat Products (Hormones)* (1998) WT/DS26/AB/R and WT/DS48/AB/R, para 70; *Chile—Price Band System* (2002) WT/DS207/AB/R, paras 196–97; see also Reports of the Panel in *European Communities—Measures Affecting the Approval and Marketing of Biotech Products* (2006) WT/DS291/R, WT/DS292/R, WT/DS293/R, para 4.162.
[185] [1991] ICJ Reports 53, at 70, para 49.   [186] [1991] ICJ Reports 53, at 72, para 56.

Similarly in *Land, Island and Maritime Frontier Dispute (El Salvador/Honduras: Nicaragua intervening)* a chamber of the ICJ did not accept the argument by Honduras that jurisdiction was sufficiently established by a general reference in a preamble to the special agreement on jurisdiction to the object and purpose as being to dispose completely of very long-standing disputes; regard must be had to the common intention of the parties actually expressed in the words of the agreement. The Court saw Honduras as really invoking the 'circumstances of conclusion' of the special agreement, such circumstances being a supplementary means of interpretation in article 32 of the Vienna rules and therefore an inappropriate basis on which to enlarge the meaning of the express terms.[187]

That the object and purpose of a treaty cannot be used to alter the clear meaning of a term of treaty is also well illustrated by an award of the US–Iran Claims Tribunal over a requirement that Iran maintain funds in a 'Security Account' with a third party bank at a certain level:

Even when one is dealing with the object and purpose of a treaty, which is the most important part of the treaty's context, the object and purpose does not constitute an element independent of that context. The object and purpose is not to be considered in isolation from the terms of the treaty; it is intrinsic to its text. It follows that, under Article 31 of the Vienna Convention, a treaty's object and purpose is to be used only to clarify the text, not to provide independent sources of meaning that contradict the clear text.[188]

5.3.4 *Object and purpose identifying general scope of treaty*

While the general rule in article 31 of the Vienna Convention sees the treaty's object and purpose as shedding light on the ordinary meaning of terms used in their context, interpretation of a treaty may raise issues of more general applicability. This is interpretation of terms in a somewhat broader sense than that apparent in the general rule.

Thus, in *Maritime Delimitation in the Area Between Greenland and Jan Mayen (Denmark v Norway)* a principal issue was whether a bilateral treaty between Denmark and Norway which identified principles for delimitation of continental shelf boundaries between them (such as use of the 'median line') was applicable to *all* such boundaries, including those between their remoter territories viz Danish Greenland and the Norwegian Jan Mayen island to the north of Iceland. The ICJ considered that despite the generality of the provision referring to the areas of the continental shelf over which Denmark and Norway had sovereign rights to explore and exploit, the fact that their agreement specifically identified points on the boundary in the North Sea, coupled with the manner in which both states had implemented the Geneva Convention on the Continental Shelf, 1958,

---

[187] [1992] ICJ Reports 351, at 584, paras 375–76.
[188] *USA, Federal Reserve Bank v Iran, Bank Markazi* Case A28, (2000–02) 36 Iran–US Claims Tribunal Reports 5, at 22, para 58 (footnotes omitted).

showed that the object and purpose of the bilateral agreement had been to achieve a delimitation in the North Sea in terms of the continental shelf, as then defined, and that the parties could not have had in mind the possibility of a shelf delimitation between Greenland and Jan Mayen island.[189]

A further example of such a case is *Islam v Home Secretary*, in which Lord Hoffmann used the object and purpose to identify the general scope of the treaty so as to identify groups of people who might come within the 1951 Geneva Convention relating to the Status of Refugees as amended by the 1967 Protocol:

The travaux préparatoires for the Geneva Convention shed little light on the meaning of 'particular social group.' It appears to have been added to the draft at the suggestion of the Swedish delegate, who said that 'experience had shown that certain refugees had been persecuted because they belonged to particular social groups.' It seems to me, however, that the general intention is clear enough. The preamble to the Convention begins with the words:

'*Considering* that the Charter of the United Nations and the Universal Declaration of Human Rights approved on 10 December 1948 by the General Assembly have affirmed the principle that human beings shall enjoy fundamental rights and freedoms without discrimination...'

In my opinion, the concept of discrimination in matters affecting fundamental rights and freedoms is central to an understanding of the Convention. It is concerned not with all cases of persecution, even if they involve denials of human rights, but with persecution which is based on discrimination. And in the context of a human rights instrument, discrimination means making distinctions which principles of fundamental human rights regard as inconsistent with the right of every human being to equal treatment and respect...

In choosing to use the general term 'particular social group' rather than an enumeration of specific social groups, the framers of the Convention were in my opinion intending to include whatever groups might be regarded as coming within the anti-discriminatory objectives of the Convention.[190]

5.3.5 Object and purpose in a particular provision

Sometimes courts give the appearance of taking the object and purpose of the treaty as something that is so obvious as to be brought into consideration directly in the context of a particular provision. Thus in a case concerning consular access to prisoners:

As for the object and purpose of the Convention, the Court observes that Article 36 provides for consular officers to be free to communicate with nationals of the sending State, to have access to them, to visit and speak with them and to arrange for their legal representation. It is not envisaged, either in Article 36, paragraph 1, or elsewhere in the Convention, that consular functions entail a consular officer himself or herself acting as the legal representative or more directly engaging in the criminal justice process. Indeed, this is confirmed by the wording of Article 36, paragraph 2, of the Convention. Thus, neither the terms of

---

[189] [1993] ICJ Reports 38, at 50–51, paras 26–28.
[190] [1999] 2 AC 629, at 650–51.

the Convention as normally understood, nor its object and purpose, suggest that 'without delay' is to be understood as 'immediately upon arrest and before interrogation'.[191]

A somewhat similar approach has been taken by the Appellate Board of the WTO:

A treaty interpreter must begin with, and focus upon, the text of the particular provision to be interpreted. It is in the words constituting that provision, read in their context, that the object and purpose of the states parties to the treaty must first be sought. Where the meaning imparted by the text itself is equivocal or inconclusive, or where confirmation of the correctness of the reading of the text itself is desired, light from the object and purpose of the treaty as a whole may usefully be sought.[192]

5.3.6 Principle of effectiveness (general)

Realization of the object and purpose of a treaty, or securing the effectiveness of the general objectives of the treaty, appears to fulfil a larger aim than interpreting terms in the light of the object and purpose of the treaty. Nevertheless, the ICJ has harnessed the idea underlying the principle of effectiveness to the task of interpretation of treaties. The dual aspect of this can be seen in the Court's judgment in *Territorial Dispute (Libyan Arab Jamahiriya/Chad)*.[193] The Court's application of the principle in the maxim *ut res* has been described in the section on good faith above. This led to the conclusion that the reference in article 3 of a 1955 treaty to frontiers recognized as being 'those that result from the international instruments' defined in the Annex to the treaty, meant all the frontiers resulting from those instruments. This application of the principle of effectiveness in its narrow (or 'technical') form was supplemented by the Court's application of the more general principle of effectiveness. The Court saw the aim of the treaty as being to resolve all the issues over the frontiers:

... The text of Article 3 clearly conveys the intention of the parties to reach a definitive settlement of the question of their common frontiers. Article 3 and Annex I are intended to define frontiers by reference to legal instruments which would yield the course of such frontiers. Any other construction would be contrary to one of the fundamental principles of interpretation of treaties, consistently upheld by international jurisprudence, namely that of effectiveness (see, for example, the *Lighthouses Case between France and Greece, Judgment, 1934, P.C.I.J. Series A/B. No. 62, p. 27; Legal Consequences for States of the Continued Presence of South Africa in Namibia (South West Africa) notwithstanding Security Council Resolution 276(1970), I.CJ. Reports 1971*, p. 35, para. 66; and *Aegean Sea Continental Shelf I.C.J. Reports 1978*, p. 22, para. 52).

Reading the 1955 Treaty in the light of its object and purpose one observes that it is a treaty of friendship and good neighbourliness concluded, according to its preamble, 'in a spirit of mutual understanding and on the basis of complete equality, independence and

---

[191] *Case concerning Avena and other Mexican Nationals (Mexico v USA)* Judgment of 31 March 2004, para 85, and see section 3.3.2 above.
[192] *United States—Import Prohibition of Certain Shrimp and Shrimp Products* WTO Report of Appellate Board AB-1998–4, WT/DS58/AB/R, 12 October 1998, para 114 (footnote omitted).
[193] *Territorial Dispute (Libyan Arab Jamahiriya/Chad) (Merits)* [1994] ICJ Reports 6.

liberty'. The parties stated in that Preamble their conviction that the signature of the treaty would 'serve to facilitate the settlement of all such questions as arise for the two countries from their geographical location and interests in Africa and the Mediterranean', and that they were 'Prompted by a will to strengthen economic, cultural and good-neighbourly relations between the two countries'. The object and purpose of the Treaty thus recalled confirm the interpretation of the Treaty given above, inasmuch as that object and purpose led naturally to the definition of the territory of Libya, and thus the definition of its boundaries. . . . [194]

Thus the Court applied this principle of effectiveness in the framework of the object and purpose of a treaty establishing frontiers, relying on earlier case law showing that the aim of any treaty of that kind should be interpreted to establish a precise, complete, and definitive frontier. Referring to the preamble of the particular treaty, the Court found that the same object and purpose led naturally to the definition of the territory of Libya, and thus the definition of its frontiers: 'To "define" a territory is to define its frontiers.'[195]

6. Conclusions

Article 31(1) has probably been cited more than any other of the Vienna rules. This may be because cursory attention to the Vienna Convention's provisions might lead some to think this paragraph is the general rule, whereas use of it is only a starting point for interpretation. Underlying its architecture is the relationship between the treaty's terms and the treaty as a whole. An issue may centre on one or more provisions. Any such provision is to be read selecting the ordinary meaning for the words used. But finding the ordinary meaning typically requires making a choice from a range of possible meanings. The immediate and more remote context is the next textual guide to making this choice, with the treaty's object and purpose as a further aid to this phase of an exercise in interpretation. The rest of the general rule, set out in the later paragraphs of the same article, must be taken into account. They are not subordinate or subsidiary provisions, but are equally elements of the general rule. Good faith is required throughout the exercise.

---

[194] [1994] ICJ Reports 6, at pp 25–6, paras 51–52.
[195] [1994] ICJ Reports 6, at pp 25–6, paras 51–52; and see also at p 23, para 47.

6

The General Rule: (2) Agreements as Context, Subsequent Agreements, and Subsequent Practice

Agreements at conclusion and subsequently—concordant practice showing agreement

The Commission considered that subsequent practice establishing the understanding of the parties regarding the interpretation of a treaty should be included...as an authentic means of interpretation alongside interpretative agreements.[1]

Article 31
General rule of interpretation

...

2. The context for the purpose of the interpretation of a treaty shall comprise, in addition to the text, including its preamble and annexes:
   (a) any agreement relating to the treaty which was made between all the parties in connection with the conclusion of the treaty;
   (b) any instrument which was made by one or more parties in connection with the conclusion of the treaty and accepted by the other parties as an instrument related to the treaty.
3. There shall be taken into account, together with the context:
   a) any subsequent agreement between the parties regarding the interpretation of the treaty or the application of its provisions;
   b) any subsequent practice in the application of the treaty which establishes the agreement of the parties regarding its interpretation;

...

1. Introduction

1.1 The linking notion of agreement

The core of this chapter is the notion of agreement between the parties on interpretation of a treaty. This is considered in two forms: first, a recorded agreement,

---

[1] [1966] *Yearbook of the ILC*, vol II, p 222, para 15.

and second, concordant practice of parties where this reveals their agreement on a point of interpretation. The first part overlaps with the subject of the preceding chapter in that 'context' is a feature of both chapters. Agreements on interpretation adopted in connection with the conclusion of a treaty, as well as interpretative initiatives in connection with conclusion of a treaty that are of a unilateral character but are accepted by the other parties as related to the treaty, are defined in the Vienna rules as part of the context. These are, however, listed as categories of relevant matter separate from the treaty text itself (the preamble and any annexes being part of the text).

While agreement is the theme linking the present treatment of article 31(2)(a) and (b) and 31(3)(a) and (b) of the Vienna Convention, article 31(2)(b) is to a somewhat different effect from the other three subparagraphs. Those three address the possibility of a complete interpretative agreement. This is *potential* in the case of article 31(2)(a), being dependent on whether the agreement made in connection with the conclusion of the treaty addresses the particular issue of interpretation under investigation. It is *explicit* in the case of paragraph (3)(a), the stipulation there defining an agreement as being one regarding the interpretation of the treaty or the application of its provisions. A complete interpretative agreement is *resultant* in the case of paragraph (3)(b), the requirement there being sufficient practice to establish such an agreement. In contrast, in article 31(2)(b), the agreement of the parties lies only in their acceptance of an instrument of unilateral or group origin as being related to the treaty. Whether such acceptance of an instrument provides an authoritative interpretation or merely records an interpretative understanding which may contribute evidence pointing towards an interpretation, is a further stage in the process, not spelt out in the Vienna rules but considered below.

It is to be noted, however, that the ILC saw the agreements and instruments in paragraph (2) of article 31 as so closely related to the text as to be equivalent to context, while the elements in paragraph (3) are extrinsic to the text. However, the ILC Commentary on its draft articles stated of paragraph (3): 'But these three elements are all of an obligatory character and by their very nature could not be considered to be norms of interpretation in any way inferior to those which precede them.'[2]

If taking account of subsequent agreement between the parties constitutes a norm of interpretation not in any way *inferior* to the preceding elements of the general rule of treaty interpretation, to what extent may the converse be true? Does a particular or superior value attach to the interpretation which the parties place on their agreement? The short answer is that a clear agreement of the parties as to what their treaty means will *usually* be the strongest element in the crucible of interpretation.[3]

---

[2] [1966] *Yearbook of the ILC*, vol II, p 220, para 9; the third element to which the comment refers is the provision on relevant rules of international law, the main subject of Chapter 7 below.

[3] Cf *Azpetrol v Azerbaijan*, ICSID Case No. ARB/06/15, Award of 8 September 2009, at para 64: 'English law does not normally admit reference to the subsequent conduct of the parties as an aid to

As Professor Crawford has put it: 'it is too often forgotten that the parties to a treaty, that is, the states which are bound by it at the relevant time, own the treaty. It is their treaty. ... International law says that the parties to a treaty own the treaty and can interpret it. ...'[4] However, he also asks in relation to subsequent agreements: 'But if "agreement" means "agreement", why then do you only "have regard" to it? Why is the agreement not dispositive?'[5] The two reasons which he gives are to the effect that agreements may range from formal to almost ephemeral, and may themselves be open to difficulties of interpretation: 'Not every coming together of states is equal to every other coming together of states. Not every press release is equal to every other press release.'[6]

This is very much in line with the approach taken by Waldock as the ILC's Special Rapporteur that the cogency of indications of meaning in preparatory works 'depends on the extent to which they furnish proof of the *common* understanding of the parties as to the meaning attached to the terms of the treaty'.[7] Further, the ILC in its Guide to Practice on Reservations to Treaties has commented that 'when an interpretative declaration made in respect of a bilateral treaty is accepted by the other party, it constitutes *the authentic interpretation thereof*'.[8] Noting the PCIJ's statement that: 'the right of giving an authoritative interpretation of a legal rule belongs solely to the person or body who has power to modify or suppress it', the ILC commentary continues with the observation that:

in the case of a bilateral treaty this power belongs to both parties. Accordingly, if they agree on an interpretation, that interpretation prevails and itself takes on the nature of a treaty, regardless of its form. ...[9]

Thus in the particular circumstances of bilateral interpretative agreements, the ILC equates an 'authentic' interpretation by the parties with an 'authoritative' one and asserts its supremacy over other meanings. Obviously such an interpretation only holds good in relation to the particular treaty. A state which has made a 'shared' interpretative declaration of a bilateral provision will not necessarily be

---

the interpretation of a contract. Again, this is in marked contrast to the approach taken by international law, in which the subsequent practice of the parties can be of the utmost importance in the interpretation of a treaty' (footnotes omitted).

[4] J Crawford, 'Subsequent Agreements and Practice from a Consensualist Perspective', Chapter 3 in G Nolte (ed), *Treaties and Subsequent Practice* (Oxford: OUP, 2013), at 31.

[5] Crawford, at 31.

[6] Crawford, at 31–32.

[7] Waldock, 'Third Report on the Law of Treaties' [1964] *Yearbook of the ILC*, vol II, p 58, para 21 (footnotes omitted, emphasis in original) and see Chapter 8, section 2.2 below.

[8] Guideline 1.6.3, commentary para (2) (footnote omitted, emphasis added) in Addendum to Report of the International Law Commission, Sixty-third session (2011), UN General Assembly Official Records, Sixty-sixth Session, Supplement No. 10, A/66/10/Add.1, <http://legal.un.org/ilc/reports/2011/english/addendum.pdf>.

[9] Guideline 1.6.3, commentary para (2); the statement of the PCIJ is reproduced at the head of Chapter 4 above and cited there.

held to have given an identical interpretation to the same words in another of treaty of the same kind.[10]

However, the principle of the supremacy of the parties' interpretation may not apply across the board, as the ILC has noted in its later and continuing work on subsequent agreements and subsequent practice that:

The character of subsequent agreements and subsequent practice of the parties...as 'authentic means of interpretation' does not, however, imply that these means necessarily possess a conclusive, or legally binding, effect. According to the chapeau of article 31(3), subsequent agreements and subsequent practice shall, after all, only 'be taken into account' in the interpretation of a treaty, which consists of a 'single combined operation' with no hierarchy among the means of interpretation which are referred to in article 31.[11]

It is difficult, however, to find any practical examples where a clear indication of the parties' agreement on interpretation has been outweighed by other interpretative considerations. As the Commission has noted, its comment quoted above 'does not exclude that the parties to a treaty, if they wish, may reach a binding agreement regarding the interpretation of a treaty'.[12] The problematic case is therefore likely to be at the opposite end of the scale and involve a questionable interpretative agreement or incomplete evidence of one, particularly in the latter case where this evidence is sought from practice.[13] The need for caution is demonstrated by the emerging difficulties where interpretative competence is allocated both to future agreement of the parties and to third party adjudication, particularly where the treaty is one which has direct implications for the acquired rights of individuals and corporations.[14] Caution is also particularly warranted if reaching an interpretation which places weight on a subsequent agreement or on subsequent practice but appears to change the meaning of a treaty without following any amendment procedure which the treaty lays down.[15]

---

[10] Cf, however, *Daimler v Argentina*, ICSID Case No. ARB/05/1, Award of 22 August 2012, at para 272, where an arbitral tribunal guardedly considered an exchange of diplomatic notes between Argentina and Panama with an 'interpretive declaration' of a most favoured nation clause in their investment treaty noting that, although an interpretive declaration issued by a state after a dispute had already arisen could not be considered as a definitive guide to the state's original intentions—particularly when the declaration related to a different treaty—nevertheless the fact that Argentina and Panama had distanced themselves from the understanding endorsed by an earlier tribunal was indicative of their mutual disapproval of that holding. This appears to have been among the many factors which the tribunal found helped its decision.

[11] ILC Report on the work of its Sixty-fifth session (2013) General Assembly Official Records Sixty-eighth Session, Supplement No. 10 (A/68/10), Chapter 4, p 21 para (4).

[12] ILC Report on the work of its Sixty-fifth session para (5).

[13] Cf the difficult position where a different interpretation was agreed by the parties after an arbitral tribunal had delivered its decision but not yet awarded damages in the *Pope & Talbot v Canada* case considered in section 4.7 below.

[14] See, for example, A Roberts, 'Power and Persuasion in Investment Treaty Interpretation: The Dual Role of States' (2010) 104 AJIL 179.

[15] See the detailed consideration of this in the development of Draft Conclusion 11 in Nolte (ILC Special Rapporteur), 'Second Report on Subsequent agreements and subsequent practice

In as much as the agreements on interpretation considered here can arise at different stages in the life of a treaty—principally at the time of conclusion of the treaty or subsequently, these interpretative elements may have a particularly prominent role when time factors are an issue. Time factors are present in various guises, notably in the questions whether a treaty is to be interpreted as it would have been at the moment of its conclusion or at the time when it is actually being interpreted; more narrowly, whether interpretation takes account of the law as at the former or latter of these instances; and, usually with a focus on a particular term or provision of a treaty, whether the interpretation is to be 'evolutionary' (or 'evolutive'), that is taking account of other changes than just those of law, such as changes in meaning of words, changes in the relevant practices, technology, social and political changes, and so on.

This chapter only considers evolutive or evolutionary interpretation to the extent relevant to interpretative agreements. Time factors relevant to changes in rules of international law are considered in the next chapter.[16] Evolutive or evolutionary interpretation is considered more generally in the concluding chapter.[17]

Study of the role of subsequent agreement and subsequent practice has benefitted greatly from recent work in the ILC, initially under the description of 'Treaties over Time', then 'Subsequent Agreements and Subsequent Practice in Relation to Interpretation of Treaties'.[18] The formulation by the ILC of draft 'Conclusions', with commentaries, represents development toward a clarificatory code on this aspect of treaty interpretation.[19] Further, the ILC work highlights the importance of this set of elements of treaty interpretation, a necessary antidote to the occasional misunderstanding which suggests that the first part of the general rule is the main rule to which the rest is somehow subsidiary. Another misunderstanding which is sometimes met is that the general rule is only concerned with the treaty's text. Although the text is the obvious starting point, the provisions considered in this chapter, particularly those on agreements evidenced by practice, show that the interpretative exercise is not exclusively textual.[20]

---

in relation to interpretation of treaties', A/CN.4/671 (26 March 2014), pp 50–71 and see section 4.7 below.

[16] See Chapter 7, section 1 below.　　[17] See Chapter 10, section 4 below.

[18] See First and Second Reports of the Special Rapporteur (Nolte), A/CN.4/660 (2013) and A/CN.4/671 (2014), and Report of the International Law Commission (2013), (Sixty-eighth Session, Supplement No. 10 A/68/1), Chapter 4, and the extensive and invaluable research and analysis in Nolte, *Treaties and Subsequent Practice*.

[19] ILC 2013 Report above; see also Report of the International Law Commission (2014), (Sixty-eighth Session, Supplement No. 10 A/69/1), Chapter VII which includes draft conclusions (inter alia) on what constitutes subsequent agreements and subsequent practice, on their possible effects, and on the weight to be attached to them.

[20] See helpful analysis and examples in R Moloo, 'When Actions Speak Louder Than Words: The Relevance of Subsequent Party Conduct to Treaty Interpretation' (2013) 31 *Berkeley JIL* 39, at 43–4.

1.2 Substantial identity of effect of subsequent agreements on interpretation as of those at time of conclusion

Although their link to the conclusion of a treaty firmly separates in time agreements within article 31(2)(a) from subsequent agreements within article 31(3)(a), it would be difficult to distinguish their legal effects. In principle, agreements and instruments accepted at the time of the conclusion of the treaty are part of the context to be used in ascertaining the ordinary meaning of the terms used. In contrast, subsequent agreements are 'to be taken into account, together with the context'. Since all relevant parts of the general rule, that is the whole of article 31 of the Vienna Convention, are to be applied in any interpretation (as well, of course, as articles 32 and 33, if appropriate), it is difficult to discern any difference in practical consequence between an agreement on interpretation which is to be treated as part of the context and one which is made later. If their content is clear, both types of agreements, being specifically directed to interpretation, will have an equally decisive effect on meaning.

In the commentary on the draft articles in its Report that formed the basis for the text adopted at the Vienna Conference in 1968–69, the ILC explained that the fact that the two classes of document now defined in article 31(2) were to be regarded as part of the context did not mean that they were necessarily to be regarded as integral parts of the treaty (which depended on the intention of the parties in the particular case). However, they were not to be treated as mere evidence to be used only to resolve any ambiguity or obscurity but rather 'as part of the context for the purpose of arriving at the ordinary meaning of the terms of the treaty'.[21] Referring to paragraph 3(a) of the same draft article (subsequent agreements), the ILC pointed out that questions of fact might arise as to whether an understanding reached during the negotiations on the meaning of a provision constituted an agreed basis for its interpretation:

> But it is well settled that when an agreement as to the interpretation of a provision is established as having been reached before or at the time of the conclusion of the treaty it is to be regarded as forming part of the treaty...Similarly, an agreement as to the interpretation of a provision reached after the conclusion of the treaty represents an authentic interpretation by the parties which must be read into the treaty for purposes of its interpretation.[22]

The idea that subsequent agreements on interpretation must be 'read into' the treaty places such agreements pretty much on a par with those reached at the time the treaty is made.

In one national case an attempt was made to draw a distinction between agreements on interpretation coming under article 31(2)(a) and those under article 31(3)(a). In *Coblentz v Canada*[23] the Canadian Court of Appeal considered whether a lump

---

[21] [1966] *Yearbook of the ILC*, vol II, p 221, para 13.
[22] [1966] *Yearbook of the ILC*, vol II, para 14.
[23] [1997] 1 FC 368, (1996) Can LII 4091 (Federal Court of Appeal).

sum pension payment was exempt from taxation in Canada under a 1980 treaty between the USA and Canada of the type colloquially described as a 'double taxa-tion' treaty (meaning for avoidance of double taxation).[24] A few months after the treaty was signed the US Treasury Department published a 'Technical Explanation' explaining the treaty's provisions and giving examples of its application. The treaty did not enter into force until protocols were concluded in 1983 and 1984 to deal with certain 'technical problems' in the original text and taking account of US legislation on pensions. In transmitting the Convention and first Protocol to the US Senate for advice and consent to ratification, the US President asserted that 'the Protocol resolves these technical problems by clarifying the language of the Convention to assure that its original intent is fulfilled'.[25] Four months after the Convention entered into force in 1984, the Canadian Department of Finance confirmed that a revised Technical Explanation of 1984, superseding one issued in 1981, accurately reflected understandings reached in the course of negotiations with respect to the interpretation and application of the various provisions in the 1980 Tax Convention as amended.[26] The Technical Explanation, in one of its examples, effectively resolved the question whether the lump sum was taxable in Canada. The Court, in deciding that the Technical Explanation was admissible to provide an interpretation, considered which provision of the Vienna Convention made it so, and explored possible consequences of deciding one way or the other:

... it may be asked whether the Technical Explanation falls within Article 31(2) or 31(3) ... Correlatively, it may be asked whether the words 'shall be taken into account' found in Article 31(3) lessen the interpretative weight to be given to documents which fall within its boundaries, at least when compared to those documents that come within the ambit of Article 31(2)... As I understand the taxpayer's argument here, the Technical Explanation falls within Article 31(3) and, therefore, the Explanation cannot be used to contradict the ordinary meaning of Article XVIII of the Convention. The argument, of course, is premised on the understanding that the Explanation is not a document made 'in connection with the conclusion of the treaty' as required under Article 31(2). It is also premised on the understanding that there is a substantive difference between Article 31(2) which speaks of the interpretative 'context' and Article 31(3) which speaks in terms of taking into 'account'. In short, it is argued that a document which falls within the latter article must be given less weight than one which comes within the former. Above all, the taxpayer maintains that the Explanation cannot be used to contradict an article of the Convention. Counsel for the Minister sidesteps this line of attack by insisting that his argument rests on the ordinary meaning of the terms found within paragraph 1 of Article XVIII... I am of the view that the Technical Explanation facilitates our understanding of paragraph 1 of Article XVIII and does not contradict it.[27]

---

[24] Convention Between the United States of America and Canada with Respect to Taxes on Income and on Capital, Washington, September 26, 1980, as amended: at <http://www.irs.gov/pub/irs-trty/canada.pdf>.
[25] Convention Between the United States of America and Canada as amended, at p 40.
[26] *Coblentz v Canada* [1997] 1 FC 368, (1996) CanLII 4091 (Federal Court of Appeal), paras 10–18.
[27] *Coblentz v Canada* paras 12–16.

This example is of more help for the issues which it raises than any conclusion it may imply. Whether an elucidation of treaty provisions is provided at the time of conclusion of a treaty or later seems of little importance if the parties concerned have clearly indicated that they view the elucidation as a correct interpretation. Their agreement on this is the essence of the matter. The suggestion that there should be a difference between something that is part of the context, to be used in establishing the ordinary meaning of a term, and something which is drawn up later and therefore only to be 'taken into account', seems at first reading to fit the wording and scheme of the Vienna Convention. Similarly, the idea that the former circumstance allows an instrument accompanying the text to 'contradict' a provision of the treaty, while the latter would not be admissible for this purpose, seems a plausible distinction. On closer examination, however, there are cogent reasons for concluding that this is not a distinction which the Vienna rules mandate or permit.

First, a separate instrument adopted at the same time as the treaty, such as a Protocol of Signature (see below), giving an apparently different meaning to a term of the treaty than its 'obvious' one, is not inherently more cogent by reason of the circumstances of its adoption than a later agreement doing exactly the same thing. In fact the latter may be said to be more cogent if it is an agreement on interpretation drawn up to meet a point that has actually arisen in practice: it represents the agreement of the parties on a point which has crystallized.

Second, while it is correct that the difference in wording governing the role of the agreement or instrument made in connection with conclusion and a subsequent one could initially suggest different roles, the whole of article 31 of the Vienna Convention is the 'general rule'. Using the consequence attached by the ILC to this characterization, if all relevant matter is to go into the crucible of interpretation, once an element has gone in, any difference in weight must result from its inherent characteristics, not its position in the crucible.

Third, although the ILC was responsible for the formulation of the provisions which make the apparent distinction, the ILC commentary treats both classes of interpretative agreement as on a par.[28] This is explained by the history of the provisions. In his first draft, the Special Rapporteur (Waldock) had included subsequent practice as 'other evidence or indications of the intentions of the parties' which was treated as on a par with the preparatory work of the treaty and only to be used in the circumstances, and to the same ends, as such work.[29] However, the Commission developed the division between the general rule and supplementary means. In response to an observation by the USA, that in the draft text of what became the general rule there might be a certain appearance of conflict between the primacy given to the ordinary meaning and the rule concerning a subsequent agreement between the parties regarding the interpretation of the treaty, the Special Rapporteur (Waldock) noted:

This observation does not perhaps give full weight to the opening phrase of paragraph 3: 'There shall also be taken into account, together with the context: *(a)* any agreement

---

[28] See section 1.1 *ad fin* above.
[29] [1964] *Yearbook of the ILC*, vol II, p 52, draft article 71(2).

between the parties etc.' These words were intended by the Commission to put such inter-pretative agreements on the same level as the 'context' and to indicate that an interpretative agreement is to be taken into account as if it were part of the treaty.[30]

It is to be noted that this is reinforced by the whole of article 31 constituting the general rule. Realistically, if an accompanying document does appear to contradict the ordinary meaning of the terms of a treaty, the problem is no different whether that document was adopted at the same time as the treaty or is a later one directly addressed to it. The key issue is whether the interpretative instrument is one to which the parties have given their concordant blessing.

Thus agreements and instruments of the kind described that are made in con-nection with the conclusion of the treaty and which bear on its interpretation are likely to deal with some point of doubt, difficulty, or specific application which it was not thought appropriate to cover in the treaty itself but which could be foreseen or which might possibly arise. Subsequent agreements on interpretation are likely to be concluded to cover specific issues which have actually arisen between the parties. Agreement resolving such difficulties may be recorded in a formal instrument of the same legal standing as the original treaty or in a less formal record of agreement or understanding on interpretation. Hence it can be seen that all these agreements and instruments have a similar function of clarifying the meaning of provisions of treaties, albeit in slightly different circumstances.[31]

1.3 Interpretative agreement in subsequent practice

Subsequent practice in relation to a matter covered by a treaty which establishes the agreement of the parties on its interpretation is clearly a category distinct from the matters covered in article 31(2) and (3)(a). However, for the purpose of treaty interpretation, such practice is examined for evidence of agreement and it can therefore be viewed as fulfilling a similar function to formally recorded agreements. The difference is essentially evidentiary: the coincidence of subsequent practice may show agreement as to meaning without the expressed meeting of minds which

---

[30] [1966] *Yearbook of the ILC*, vol II, p 95, para 6.
[31] An example of how an agreement at the time of conclusion and a subsequent one may have the same effect on interpretation is in connection with the Air Transport Agreement between the USA and Peru, Lima, 27 December 1946 (UNTS No 390). In the first Exchange of Notes accompanying this Agreement, the parties recorded understandings that as Peru was not able to designate under the agreement an airline that met the then normal requirements that it be 'substantially owned and effectively controlled' by Peru or its nationals, Peru could (for the first ten years of the Agreement's operation) designate an airline with at least 30 per cent Peruvian capital and the remainder would be American or Canadian, with a difference of no more than 20 per cent between the latter interests. Six months later it was realized that this formula did not achieve the intended aim of not permitting either US or Canadian interests to exceed 42 per cent. Hence a further Exchange of Notes took place recording this and other interpretative corrections. Both these (and other) Exchanges of Notes were registered (together with the treaty itself) with the UN at the same time. The interpretative effect of the Notes six months after conclusion appears to be no different from that of the Notes at conclusion of the treaty.

the term 'subsequent agreement' indicates. However, the potential difficulties in establishing whether there has been clear and sufficient practice to show agreement of the parties are obviously much greater than in the case of a specifically recorded agreement. There is one point at which the categories intersect. This is where there is a recorded agreement on interpretation which is informal but which has been put into practice. In this situation an informal record of understanding as to interpretation may, through the confirming practice, acquire a force of the same standing as a formal agreement.

In consequence of the roles described above for agreements and practice in interpretation of treaties, this chapter examines first agreements and instruments made in connection with conclusion of a treaty, second, subsequent agreements, and, third, subsequent practice.

2. Agreements and Instruments Made in Connection with Conclusion of a Treaty

A general description of the procedures which may produce the range of instruments within article 31(2)(a) and (b) has been given in Chapter 3 above. The general role of context in the Vienna rules has been considered above and in Chapter 5. This section considers in more detail the elements of paragraphs (2) (a) and (b), the function in treaty interpretation of such agreements and instruments, and how they fulfil that function.

2.1 Meaning of 'Conclusion' of a treaty

To identify what is connected with conclusion of a treaty it is necessary first to pinpoint what is 'conclusion' of a treaty and when it occurs. Unfortunately, this is not a term having a clear meaning.[32] It is the common practice for purposes of identification to regard a treaty as concluded when it is signed. Hence the accepted manner of reference is to couple the treaty's name with the place and date of signature. This may suggest that 'conclusion' matches the words often put in capital letters in the testimonium, as in the Vienna Convention: 'DONE at Vienna, this twenty-third day of May, One thousand nine hundred and sixty-nine.'[33]

It seems clear, however, that in some provisions of the Vienna Convention, 'conclusion' has a broader meaning. Most prominently, in Part II ('Conclusion and Entry into Force of Treaties'), Section 1 ('Conclusion of Treaties') contains provisions relating not only to drawing up a treaty, its authentication, and signature, but also on how states consent to be bound by signature (in those cases where signature conveys such consent), ratification, accession, etc.

---

[32] A thorough study of the issues is in E W Vierdag, 'The Time of the "Conclusion" of a Multilateral Treaty: Article 30 of the Vienna Convention and Related Provisions' (1988) LIX BYBIL 75.

[33] United Nations Conference on the Law of Treaties, Official Records, Documents, p 301.

The titles (above) read together imply that conclusion is a distinct step in a process. However, it is clear from the text, context (that is the whole treaty), and the history of the provisions that the titles do not provide any indicator of the precise moment or stage in the process that can be viewed as conclusion, since the section's title and content are open to being read as covering the processes leading to conclusion as much as some point at completion of the process. The first three articles of this Section identify the capacity of states to conclude treaties and the means by which representatives of a state can be identified as authorized for the purpose of adopting or authenticating the text of a treaty or for the purpose of expressing the consent of the State to be bound. Articles 9 and 10 concern 'adoption' and 'authentication' of the text of a treaty. The later provisions of the Section (articles 11–17) refer to different means of 'consent to be bound by a treaty', thus presupposing existence of a treaty.

'Treaty' is defined as an 'international agreement concluded etc.' (article 2(1)). This suggests that by the time of the procedures in articles 11–17 conclusion has already taken place, assuming a concluded agreement is a synonym for a concluded treaty. The switch from reference to 'text of a treaty', the phrase used in articles covering development of the treaty text, to reference to 'treaty' *(tout court)* comes between article 10 (authentication of the text) and article 11 (means of expressing consent), but this is hardly sufficient to pinpoint a moment of conclusion.

Among the many provisions referring to conclusion, article 4 of the Vienna Convention provides for the Convention's application to treaties 'concluded' by states after its entry into force. This suggests that conclusion of a treaty occurs on an identifiable date, different from entry into force (the context within the article being use of two distinct terms), and necessarily preceding the treaty's entry into force (that being the very last moment of the 'process' possibility considered below), but without indicating at what point in the Part II procedures the date of conclusion falls. Paragraphs (2) and (3) of article 40 seem based on a distinction between entitlement to negotiate and conclude a treaty and entitlement to become a party; but, again, while these provisions make quite clear that negotiation and conclusion are distinct, no clear pointer is given as to the moment of conclusion, the use here appearing to indicate participation in the drawing up of a treaty as distinct from becoming a participant in the result of that effort.[34]

In these circumstances it is appropriate to look at the preparatory work. The draft articles presented by the Special Rapporteur (Brierly) after the ILC's first discussion of the law of treaties started with a provision on conclusion of treaties.[35] This identified conclusion as occurring when the agreed text had been established in final written form and, in the typical case of a treaty produced by an international

---

[34] For an analysis and comparison of the Vienna Convention's articles mentioning conclusion, see Vierdag, 'The Time of the "Conclusion" of a Multilateral Treaty: Article 30 of the Vienna Convention and Related Provisions' above.

[35] In the draft article in his First Report on the Law of Treaties, Brierly had referred simply to states 'making' treaties: see [1950] *Yearbook of the ILC*, vol II, p 223, draft article 3 and at 233 ff, draft chapter III headed 'The Making of Treaties'.

conference, 'either such text or the Final Act of the conference has been duly signed or initialled *ne varietur* on behalf of two or more States represented at the conference'.[36] Brierly supported this approach by referring to examples of words frequently used in the formal parts of treaties, identifying 'agreed' and 'concluded' as most commonly used.[37]

When Fitzmaurice took over from Hersch Lauterpacht as Special Rapporteur on the law of treaties, he made a more detailed analysis of the framing and conclusion of treaties as part of proposed provisions on the validity of treaties. He saw conclusion as the second of four stages: authentication, conclusion, participation, and entry into force.[38] He acknowledged, however, that 'conclusion' was an ambiguous term and had always given rise to difficulties, but stated that 'there is no doubt that a treaty is always given the date of its signature (i.e., conclusion), never that of its entry into force unless that coincides with signature'.[39] His solution was to treat conclusion as the stage beyond acknowledging the text as finally established and as the point at which states indicate that that text is also the one by which they are willing to be bound if they become bound at all.[40]

When Waldock took over as fourth Special Rapporteur on the law of treaties, the nature of the exercise had changed. He was preparing draft provisions on conclusion, entry into force, and registration of treaties either as a stand-alone convention or as part of a larger one. He noted that Fitzmaurice had pointed out that conclusion of treaties could be regarded either as a *process* or as a *substantive matter* relating to the validity of treaties.[41] Homing in on the former (the process approach), now that validity of treaties was no longer included in the part of the exercise which addressed conclusion of treaties, efforts at finding a definition of 'conclusion' were discarded. Conclusion became the description of the process preceding entry into force. As indicated above, however, some provisions in the Vienna Convention point to an act or moment rather than a process. Most obvious are those involving time factors, such as the ones on successive treaties.

In the light of these difficulties both in the text of the Convention and the preparatory work, the most appropriate meaning of 'conclusion' for present purposes seems the contextual and pragmatic one. In article 31(2)(a) an 'agreement...in connection with the conclusion' is to be contrasted with 'subsequent agreement' in article 31(3)(a). Hence, 'conclusion' in this context would generally be the date of adoption and opening for signature (the first Fitzmaurice sense). This is the moment of collective action (though signature can be a moveable feast, with a treaty open for signature over an extended period rather than on a single occasion). However, this would not exclude from consideration as part of the context a later agreement (such as an amendment required to bring the treaty into force)

---

[36] Second Report on the Law of Treaties [1951] *Yearbook of the ILC*, vol II, p 70.
[37] [1951] *Yearbook of the ILC*, vol II, at p 71.
[38] Fitzmaurice, First Report [1956] *Yearbook of the ILC*, vol II, p 121, paras 48 and 52.
[39] [1956] *Yearbook of the ILC*, vol II, at para 50.
[40] [1956] *Yearbook of the ILC*, vol II, at para 51.
[41] Waldock, First Report [1962] *Yearbook of the ILC*, vol II, p 30, para 9.

which does not specifically provide an interpretation, provided it is one to which all those who participated in the treaty's conclusion agree.[42] Practice on this is considered below.

The immediate context is slightly different in the case of instruments made by one or more parties unilaterally (article 31(2)(b)). There is no contrasting provision in article 31(3). Nor is there the same sense of collective action involving all parties reaching agreement as to an interpretation (as distinct from agreement that an instrument is related to the treaty concerned). Yet on occasion such as deposit of an instrument of ratification may be just the moment for making a unilateral interpretative declaration. Hence 'conclusion' in article 31(2)(b) may more appropriately attract the 'process' meaning since such instruments may accompany ratification, accession, etc as much as signature.

2.1.1 Issues arising as to 'in connection with conclusion' of a treaty

The uncertainty over the moment of conclusion of a treaty, or of the completion of the process of conclusion, has resulted in doubts as to whether a document associated with a treaty but prepared before the treaty was adopted or opened for signature forms part of the preparatory work or is connected with conclusion of the treaty. This was illustrated in *R v Secretary of State for the Home Department, Ex parte Read*.[43] There the House of Lords found confirmation of its interpretation of a treaty in an Explanatory Report, but hedged its bets as to the basis of the Report's admissibility for interpretative purposes:

Although it does not purport to be an authoritative interpretation of the Convention, it is available as an aid to construction as part of the 'travaux preparatoires' and under article 31 of the Vienna Convention on the Law of Treaties 1969 (Cmnd. 4818).[44]

As an instrument published at the behest of the Committee of Ministers of the Council of Europe when opening the Convention for signature, the Explanatory Report can be viewed as an 'agreement relating to the treaty which was made between all the parties in connexion with the conclusion of the treaty' (article 31(2)(a)), and hence part of the context;[45] but as a document drawn up by the Committee of Experts preparing the text for conclusion by the Committee of Ministers, it also appears to form part of the preparatory work. That such a report can be characterized as within the meaning of context is significant in that it is to be taken into account as part of the general rule of interpretation, rather than admitted as a supplementary means of interpretation admitted on the conditions prescribed for use of preparatory work.

---

[42] Cf Vierdag, 'The Time of the "Conclusion" of a Multilateral Treaty: Article 30 of the Vienna Convention and Related Provisions', at 83–4.

[43] [1989] AC 1014; the facts and other issues are considered in Chapter 5, section 4.2.3 above.

[44] [1989] AC 1014, at 1052; see further Chapter 8, section 4.5.3 below.

[45] See I Sinclair, *The Vienna Convention on the Law of Treaties* (Manchester: Manchester University Press, 2nd edn, 1984), 129–30.

From the discussion above about the meaning of 'conclusion' of a treaty, it can be seen that there may also be uncertainty whether a particular agreement falls within the category of those made 'in connection with the conclusion of the treaty' or constitutes a 'subsequent agreement' regarding interpretation or application of the treaty (which is a category considered later in this chapter). It is likely to be most commonly correct that the existence of agreement on interpretation or application of a treaty is more important than the form or timing of the agreement. If all the parties to a treaty agree on its meaning, this will usually be the correct meaning. There may be difficulties if the parties make an interpretative agreement while an interpretative process that affects third parties is underway (such as where investors are relying on bilateral investment treaties) or if, for example, there is a body within an organization endowed with competence to determine the interpretation.

Examples of such situations are hard to find.[46] However, the potential for uncertainty as to whether an agreement is in connection with conclusion or is a subsequent one can be illustrated by the sequence of the UN Convention on the Law of the Sea 1982 and the Agreement relating to the Implementation of Part XI of the Convention adopted in July 1994 before the Convention itself entered into force later that year. Although problems of categorization of the kind considered here in relation to interpretation do not appear to have arisen, (probably because of skilful construction of provisions establishing the relationship between the Agreement and the Convention), it can be seen that an implementing agreement making adjustments necessary to enable further states to participate in a convention could affect the potential for the convention to enter into force. If such an implementation agreement adjusted the terms on which states which had already signed the convention become parties to it, could it be viewed as made in connection with the convention's conclusion? It seems more probable that in such a case the convention would be regarded as having been concluded when the text was adopted or signed. An implementing agreement would thus be viewed as having been made subsequent to the conclusion of the convention and therefore one potentially relating to its interpretation or application within paragraph (3)(a) rather than (2)(a) of article 31 of the Vienna Convention.[47]

In the case of both subparagraphs (a) and (b) of article 31(2) there is a problem in the use of the term 'parties', at least of a theoretical kind. 'Party' is a term defined in article 2(1)(g) of the Vienna Convention as 'a State which has consented to be bound by the treaty and for which the treaty is in force'. This combination of consent and entry into force means that there will not be parties to a treaty until after conclusion of a treaty, except in the case where conclusion and entry into force are simultaneous (such as those treaties which enter into force upon signature). The

---

[46] Cf *Arbitration under Chapter Eleven of NAFTA, Pope & Talbot v Canada (Award in respect of Damages)* (2002) 41 ILM 1347 considered in section 4.7 below.

[47] For an example of factors which may bear on determining in which category interpretative understandings may need to be considered, see K Heller, 'The Uncertain Legal Status of the Aggression Understandings' (2012) 10 *Journal of International Criminal Justice* 229 and section 2.3 below.

use of 'parties' in these two subparagraphs is therefore either proleptic or, more probably, intended to be read as looking at the position when the treaty is being interpreted after entry into force and is being applied in treaty relations between the parties. The point does not appear to have raised problems in connection with these two subparagraphs, in contrast with the use of 'parties' in article 31(3)(c) of the Vienna Convention but further possible issues in relation to article 31(2)(b) are considered below.[48]

It would obviously be more convenient if 'conclusion' could be fixed in a way which would simplify the interpretation of article 31(2) of the Convention. This may be possible for some purposes. In its current work on subsequent agreements and subsequent practice in relation to the interpretation of treaties the ILC has identified, in its commentary on the proposed definition of such agreements and practice, a specific stage in the treaty making process. Noting that various provisions of the Vienna Convention show that a treaty may be 'concluded' before its actual entry into force, for the purposes of the Commission's present work, '"conclusion" is whenever the text of the treaty has been established as definite'.[49]

2.2 Interpretative role of agreements connected with conclusion of a treaty

Some formal agreements concluded in connection with a treaty specifically indicate that they address interpretation. For example, the 'Protocol on the Interpretation of Article 69 of the European Patent Convention'[50] gives guidance on how to interpret and apply the Convention's direction that the extent of the protection conferred by a European patent (in the sense of what is the area monopolized by the invention) is to be determined by the terms of the claims, using also the description and any drawings in the specification. The Protocol sought to establish a balance between an unduly narrow and literal construction of the claims on the one hand and, on the other, an excessively general approach resulting from viewing the claims as merely an aid to finding the essence of the invention and protecting that.[51]

---

[48] See section 2.3.1 below, and Chapter 7, section 3.3 where the various subparagraphs are compared, together with the use of 'parties' in article 31(3)(a) on subsequent agreements on interpretation.

[49] ILC Report on the work of its Sixty-fifth session (2013) General Assembly Official Records Sixty-eighth Session, Supplement No. 10 (A/68/10), Chapter 4, p 31 commentary para (2).

[50] See Convention on the Grant of European Patents (European Patent Convention), Munich 1973 and Protocol on the Interpretation of article 69 of the Convention, adopted at the Munich Diplomatic Conference for the setting up of a European System for the Grant of Patents on 5 October 1973 at <http://www.european-patent-office.org/legal/epc/e/ar69.html>; a revised text of the Protocol has been adopted: Act Revising the Convention on the Grant of European Patents, Munich, 29 November 2000; cf the First Protocol on the Interpretation by the Court of Justice of the European Communities of the Convention on the Law Applicable to Contractual Obligations (UKTS 33 (2004)), which concerns acceptance of jurisdiction of the Court of Justice to interpret the treaty, rather than specific matters of interpretation.

[51] For a more detailed history and analysis of the Protocol, see *Kirin-Amgen Inc v Hoechst Marion Roussel Limited* [2005] RPC 9, judgment of Lord Hoffmann at paras 23–30.

While this Protocol shows well the role of a fairly typical interpretative instrument, setting out guidance on how to exercise interpretative discretion in relation to the plain rule in the text of the treaty, the Protocol is not a typical example of the way in which such an interpretative Protocol is related to the treaty. This is because the Protocol is specifically mentioned in a list of associated instruments in article 164 of the European Patent Convention, which are to be regarded as integral parts of the Convention; it could therefore probably be viewed as admissible within article 31(1) of the Vienna rules rather than article 31(2)(a).

The substance, however, is clearly more important than the form or classification; and this example provides an opportunity to recall that the whole of article 31 of the Vienna Convention is to be applied as the 'general rule'. Hence, pedantic distinctions need not be drawn between interpretative elements that form part of the context and those derived from other relevant matter.

A similar role to a protocol on interpretation, though not so explicit in the title, is performed by a Protocol of Signature. This refers to an instrument concluded at the time of signature of a treaty; but as a description it is somewhat misleading as it is not directly concerned with the process of signature of a treaty.[52] Such a Protocol is described in a UN guide:

> A Protocol of Signature is an instrument subsidiary to a treaty, and drawn up by the same parties. Such a Protocol deals with ancillary matters such as the interpretation of particular clauses of the treaty, those formal clauses not inserted in the treaty, or the regulation of technical matters....[53]

Other such protocols concern matters at the blurred line between interpretation and application. For example, article 3 of the Customs Convention on Containers, Geneva, 1972,[54] requires parties to grant temporary admission to containers, subject to conditions prescribed in the treaty, whether loaded with goods or not. The second declaration in the Protocol of Signature attached to the treaty states: 'The terms of the present Convention shall not preclude the application of national provisions or of international agreements, not of a Customs nature, regulating the use of containers.' This can be read as interpreting the extent of the general obligation in article 3 or simply as an understanding for avoidance of doubt as to the reach of the treaty. The latter seems a better analysis as the same treaty provides in its article 13 for a compilation of interpretations to be made. This is in the set of 'Explanatory Notes' in Annex 6 to the treaty. These notes provide an interpretation

---

[52] The unfamiliar and perhaps confusing description of such an instrument may have been the reason why the Court of Appeal in one case described a protocol of signature as 'a protocol of the United Kingdom signature of the Convention' (when in fact the UK had acceded to the treaty, a process that does not involve signature) and to assume that there must have been 'a further protocol of the United Kingdom's accession to the Convention' allowing for territorial extension (when in fact article 46 of the relevant treaty provided for such extension by notification to the Secretary General of the UN): *Chloride Industrial Batteries Ltd. v F & W Freight Ltd* [1989] 1 WLR 823, at 827–28; see also Chapter 3, section 2.4.1.

[53] UN Treaty Collection, Treaty Reference Guide, Definition of key terms, at <https://treaties.un.org/Pages/Overview.aspx?path=overview/definition/page1_en.xml>.

[54] [1967] ATS 3 where a Protocol of Signature is also reproduced.

of some of the provisions of the Convention, not modifying them but making their contents, meaning, and scope more precise. Those 'notes' include details such as: 'The term "insulated container" is to be taken to include refrigerated and iso-thermic containers' (para 4.2.1.(c)), the type of definition or specification which clearly falls within the notion of interpretation showing an intention of the parties to give the term a special meaning (Vienna Convention, article 31(4)).

2.3 Interpretative role of instruments made by one or more parties

That the context for the purposes of interpretation of a treaty is to include any instrument made by one or more parties in connection with conclusion of the treaty and accepted by the other parties as an instrument related to it, raises two main issues. The first is what these instruments are. The second is how they can assist interpretation.

2.3.1 *Instruments covered by article 31(2)(b) of the Vienna Convention*

As to what the 'instruments' are, it seems clear that this term is not specifically linked to unilateral statements or interpretative declarations. It is the instrument that is identified in article 31(2)(b), not the content. The term is apt to cover a document.[55] The Vienna Convention uses 'instrument' in this sense in the defini-tion of a treaty ('an international agreement concluded between States in written form and governed by international law, whether embodied in a single instrument or in two or more related instruments': article 2(1)(a). It also uses the term in many other articles, but none appears to refer to a particular item in the content of a document rather than the document itself. Self-evidently, however, instruments containing statements relevant to interpretation and, in particular, those claiming to state interpretative understandings are the prime candidates for consideration. In contrast, when unilateral statements or interpretative declarations are recorded in preparatory work these are admissible in the interpretative process to the extent stated in article 32.

Among the most obvious instruments produced by a state unilaterally in con-nection with a treaty are 'instruments of ratification, acceptance, approval or acces-sion' (a phrase used in article 16 and elsewhere in the Convention). Are these instruments 'in connection with conclusion of a treaty'? As has been indicated above, the moment of 'conclusion' of a treaty is not clearly identified in the Vienna Convention and the term may signify a process rather than a single act.[56] If sig-nature is taken as the moment of conclusion, and the treaty is the instrument

---

[55] The *Oxford English Dictionary* (1989) offers as its fifth definition of 'instrument', in usage relat-ing to law: 'A formal legal document whereby a right is created or confirmed, or a fact recorded; a for-mal writing of any kind, as an agreement, deed, charter, or record, drawn up and executed in technical form, so as to be of legal validity.'

[56] See section 2.1 above.

being signed, there could be scope for doubting whether an appended interpretative statement is properly described as 'an instrument...made...in connection with the conclusion of the treaty'. The instrument is the document being signed. A statement could be written under the signature or may be in a separate document, the latter being more probable and clearly being capable of description as an instrument. Yet the interpretative value can hardly be dependent on the precise process used to record it if the circumstances of its making are essentially of the same kind. There seems little doubt that an interpretative statement made at the moment of signature will be admissible in the interpretative process, the niceties of the wording of article 31(2)(b) notwithstanding.

Likewise, such a statement made (or repeated) on ratification, accession, etc ought clearly to be admissible under this provision. It is to be noted, however, that this was not so certain in the work of the ILC. There was some doubt initially whether instruments of ratification should be taken into account in interpretation and, logically anterior to that issue, whether 'instrument' was an appropriate term since (it was suggested) it could be read as excluding declarations.[57] Nevertheless, it was pointed out that not only ratifications accompanied by reservations but other instruments containing declarations might affect interpretation.[58] A suggestion by Rosenne included the words 'instrument related to the treaty and accepted by the parties in connection with its conclusion';[59] and this thought seems later to have shaped the eventual wording, without there being significant discussion of precisely what instruments might be covered.

In its Guide to Practice on Reservations to Treaties, the ILC has noted doubts about the admissibility of interpretative declarations under articles 31 and 32, although it has indicated their interpretative relevance, particularly where confirmatory of meaning.[60] Any doubt seems based on earlier work of the ILC preceding the adoption of its draft provisions for the Vienna rules, and on the lack of authority as to the common understanding of the parties that the unilateral character of an interpretative declaration can sustain. It seems clear, however, that the ILC ultimately opted for identifying the conditions on which an instrument could have interpretative potential rather than offering criteria on which the interpretative weight of the instrument's contents should be assessed.

Thus there can be little doubt that the ordinary meaning of the phrase in article 31(2)(b) can include documentation associated with an instrument of ratification so that an interpretative declaration lodged with such an instrument is to be taken into account. Indeed, this is the material most likely to emerge within the ambit of this subparagraph. If it were excluded, this would leave little effect for the Vienna

---

[57] [1964] *Yearbook of the ILC*, vol. I, pp 310–13.

[58] [1964] *Yearbook of the ILC*, vol. I, pp 311 and 313.

[59] [1964] *Yearbook of the ILC*, vol. I, p 313, para 54.

[60] Addendum to Report of the International Law Commission, Sixty-third session (2011), UN General Assembly Official Records, Sixty-sixth Session, Supplement No. 10, A/66/10/Add.1, <http://legal.un.org/ilc/reports/2011/english/addendum.pdf>, Guideline 4.7.1, commentary para (24) ff; and see Chapter 3, section 3 above.

provision; and if acceptance of the substance of a declaration by all other relevant states were a precondition for consideration of the interpretative declaration, the resultant agreement on meaning would make the Vienna provision unnecessary as the agreement would be included either under article 31(2)(a) or 31(3)(a).

One particular treaty-related instrument which warrants attention is the 'Final Act' of a diplomatic conference. Closer in time to conclusion of a treaty, if conclusion is taken as the adoption of the text or its signature, a final act comes well within the description of an instrument made in connection with the treaty's conclusion and is likely to be readily seen as one accepted by the parties as an instrument related to the treaty. However, this again casts some doubt over which parties are meant and how their agreement is signified.[61]

The term 'party' in the Vienna Convention refers to a state which has become bound by a treaty and for whom it is in force. In as much as such states have accepted that the treaty's adoption or opening for signature has been properly agreed as recorded in the final act or equivalent instrument, so too it seems likely that their acceptance of that instrument as being related to the treaty has been agreed by them. If specific acceptance that the instrument is related to the treaty had to be shown for each state participating in a conference, as well as those which eventually become parties but did not participate in the negotiations, many final acts would lose interpretative significance, there being in several cases no formal record of which states were actually present and participating in the session of the conference which approved or adopted the final act by consensus.[62] It should be emphasized that acceptance that an instrument is related to a treaty is quite different from agreement to propositions within the instrument. A final act may record matters of differing kinds and states may need to take a position on these and, if appropriate, give effect to their position by, for example, reservation or interpretative declaration when they become a party.

2.3.2 *Role of unilateral instruments covered by article 31(2)(b)*

The role of such instruments was equally little discussed in the ILC debates. The assumption seems to have been that the opportunities for unilateral declarations were sufficiently varied to leave them as a flexible element whose possible role in shaping an interpretation was dependent on the circumstances of each particular case.[63] In its work preparing the draft articles on the law of treaties, the ILC

---

[61] See section 2.1 above.

[62] Cf a different view in K Heller, 'The Uncertain Legal Status of the Aggression Understandings' (2012) 10 *Journal of International Criminal Justice* 229 concerning amendments to the Rome Statute of the International Criminal Court adopted at a review conference where understandings were recorded relating to the definition of 'aggression'; analysis of that situation is made more difficult by the nature of the amending instrument, the differing procedures by which states become parties to the amended Statute, and the possibility of a further review conference before the amendments come into force.

[63] See F Horn, *Reservations and Interpretative Declarations to Multilateral Treaties* (Amsterdam: North-Holland, 1988), at 231–3, and Chapter 3, section 3 above.

therefore focused on the source (the instrument) rather than the substance of the interpretative material. That omission has thus far only been partly remedied in the recent work of the ILC on guidelines on reservations.[64]

There has been little published practice on the effect of interpretative declarations. There is no express reference to them in the Vienna rules. The most substantial consideration of the processes surrounding them (formulation, approval, disapproval, recharacterization, etc) is in the Guide to Practice on Reservations to Treaties which is the product of the ILC's work on reservations. Because the ILC linked interpretative declarations with reservations and integrated the procedural aspects of the two types of statement with their effects, the whole topic of interpretative declarations has been covered in the consideration of interpretative material in Chapter 3 above.[65] Article 31(2)(b) also covers instruments made by two or more parties, if accepted by the other parties to the treaty. For example, in the *East German expropriation* case the German Federal Constitutional Court had to consider whether the Treaty on the Final Settlement of 12 September 1990, which finally ended the occupation of Germany, dealt with the issue of expropriations made by the occupying power of the German Democratic Republic.[66] Although that treaty contained no provision on the question of restitution of expropriated properties, there had been a joint letter of the Federal Foreign Minister and the Minister President of the German Democratic Republic to the foreign ministers of the victorious powers in the talks which preceded the treaty. The Court concluded:

This correspondence, therefore, under Article 31.2 letter b of the Vienna Convention on the Law of Treaties of 23 May 1969 (Federal Law Gazette 1985 II p. 926), was to be consulted in interpreting the Treaty on the Final Settlement and to be understood to the effect that the Federal Republic of Germany had committed itself vis-à-vis the victorious powers to leave the expropriations on the basis of sovereign acts by occupying powers untouched.[67]

3. Subsequent Agreements

Two aspects of article 31(3)(a) are quite clear: the provision refers to interpretative agreements made after conclusion of a treaty (that is, not made 'in connection' with its conclusion), and it clearly covers treaties which embody agreements on interpretation or application of a treaty. In place of 'made in connection with the conclusion of the treaty' (the linkage envisaged for agreements and instruments in article 31(2)), subsequent agreements (not being ones with that link) are specified in article 31(3)(a) as agreements 'regarding the interpretation of the treaty or the application of its provisions'. Whether an agreement falls within this description will be uncontroversial if it is explicitly directed to interpretation or application

---

[64] See Chapter 3, section 3.1 above.   [65] See Chapter 3, section 3 above.
[66] BVerfG, 2 BvR 955/00 of 10/26/2004, at <http://www.bverfg.de/entscheidungen/rs20041026_2bvr095500en.html>.
[67] BVerfG, 2 BvR 955/00 of 10/26/2004, at para 63 (translation by the Court).

of the treaty whose interpretation is in question, but may be less clear where, for example, there is a later treaty between the same parties which can be viewed as on the same subject, or related ones, but which reveals no specific reference to, or relationship with, the earlier treaty.

In the *Jan Mayen* case *(Denmark v Norway)*, the ICJ touched on this latter issue, although it confusingly opened its consideration of the matter by referring to taking account of subsequent practice rather than agreement (perhaps indirectly reinforcing the point that it is agreement of the parties as to interpretation that is significant rather than the form that agreement takes).[68] The Court had to decide whether reference to use of a median line in a 1965 agreement between Denmark and Norway on delimitation of their continental shelves could be shown to be of general application between them because, among other factors, their 1979 Agreement on delimitation of the continental shelf in the area between the Faroe Islands and Norway used the median line. The Court considered that if the 1965 Agreement had been designed to commit the parties to the median line in all ensuing shelf delimitations, a reference would have been made to it in the 1979 Agreement (which there was not). The absence of a relationship between the two agreements was explicitly confirmed by a communication by the Norwegian government to the Norwegian parliament ruling out application of the 1965 agreement to the area between the Faroe Islands and Norway.[69] Clearly, there must be a relationship between the putative subsequent agreement and the treaty which is being interpreted sufficient to warrant the subsequent agreement being seen as providing evidence of meaning by way of interpretation or application.[70]

Further issues that arise are: (1) whether there is any difference in legal effect between subsequent agreements and those reached at the time of conclusion; (2) whether subsequent agreements or understandings recorded by a less formal means than a treaty are envisaged; and (3) (linked to the previous issue) whether in the case of less formal understandings over interpretation, additional support needs to be found for any understanding by showing that it has been implemented in practice, thus making an overlap with the topic of article 31(3)(b). The lack of significant difference in effect between subsequent agreements and those made at the time of conclusion of a treaty has been considered above.[71]

3.1 Fact of agreement, not form, is the key factor

In considering whether the Vienna rules envisage a subsequent agreement as having any particular form, the starting point is the meaning of 'agreement' in article 31(3)(a). In the title of an international instrument 'agreement' usually denotes

---

[68] *Case concerning Maritime Delimitation in the Area between Greenland and Jan Mayen (Denmark v Norway)*, [1993] ICJ Reports 38, at 51 para 28; see further Chapter 5, section 5.3.4 above.

[69] [1993] ICJ Reports 38, at 51, paras 28–9.

[70] See further L Crema, 'Subsequent Agreements and Subsequent Practice within and outside the Vienna Convention', Chapter 2 in Nolte, *Treaties and Subsequent Practice*, section 3.

[71] See section 1.2.

binding commitment and is synonymous with a treaty. Similarly, in the most common form of a treaty, the opening recital of the states involved and any pre-ambular paragraphs are followed by words of 'agreement', viz '…have agreed as follows:…'. So too in the substantive provisions of a treaty, the word 'agree' in any form provides strong evidence that the intention was to create binding legal relations. However, while all these indicators (particularly when present together) will usually show conclusively that the intention is to set out the terms of a treaty, that is not the issue over article 31(3)(a). It is not a question of whether that provision adds to the assessment that any given instrument was intended to be a binding treaty, but whether the parties to a treaty have, subsequent to its conclu-sion, reached a firm agreement on what one of its provisions means. Thus it does not necessarily follow that such an agreement will be recorded in one of the forms commonly used for a treaty. Conversely, however, if a firm agreement has been reached between two states with the intention of creating a legal relationship, this will amount to a treaty (subject to the further requirements, if one is following the definition in article 2(1)(a) of the Vienna Convention, that the agreement must be in writing, etc).

3.1.1 History and analysis

The ILC linked subsequent agreements to understandings reached during negotia-tion of a treaty:

> A question of fact may sometimes arise as to whether an understanding reached during the negotiations concerning the meaning of a provision was or was not intended to constitute an agreed basis for its interpretation. But it is well settled that when an agreement as to the interpretation of a provision is established as having been reached before or at the time of the conclusion of the treaty, it is to be regarded as forming part of the treaty…Similarly, an agreement as to the interpretation of a provision reached after the conclusion of the treaty represents an authentic interpretation by the parties which must be read into the treaty for purposes of its interpretation.[72]

The first of these quoted sentences suggests that the underlying issue is what con-stitutes 'an agreed basis' for a treaty's interpretation. The implication is that 'an understanding' could constitute such a basis where reached during the negotia-tions, albeit that this would depend on whether a clear intention was manifested. The commentary then notes that if an agreement on interpretation is established as having been reached before or at conclusion of a treaty, this is clearly to be read as forming part of the treaty. Hence it seems that the test for use of a subsequent agreement in treaty interpretation ought to be whether there was a manifest inten-tion that the understanding would constitute an agreed basis for interpretation. Regrettably, however, the ILC's recorded comment is not framed in such a way as to make this entirely clear because the explanation, in the case of an agreement

---

[72] [1966] *Yearbook of the ILC*, vol II, p 221, para 14.

before or at the time of conclusion of a treaty, switches from the term 'understanding' to the term 'agreement' without clearly indicating whether a distinction is intended. However, it seems reasonable to conclude from all the circumstances that 'agreement' does not have to be in treaty form but must be such as to show that the parties intended their understanding to be the basis for an agreed interpretation.

These rather obvious points in analysis of article 31(3)(a) of the Vienna Convention assume greater significance when seen in the context of the all too common situation where some issue of everyday interpretation of a practical treaty is the subject of discussion between officials of two or more parties. They reach an understanding or compromise over some minor interpretative controversy but record this in a 'minute', 'memorandum of understanding', or simply a letter, perhaps not considering that the matter warrants the hassle of domestic legislative procedures and of international requirements such as registration of a treaty with the UN. Can such a process, or rather its outcome, be regarded as a subsequent agreement on interpretation? The answer (which is still only lightly evidenced, but is considered further below) seems twofold. First, there is the issue of whether the official is sufficiently senior to have the authority to make an agreement binding the state. Second, if an understanding is actually put into effect in applying a treaty, that less formal agreement (whether recorded in a letter, agreed record of discussions or whatever), merges with the next element of treaty interpretation in the Vienna rules (subsequent practice).

That practical resolution of difficulties of interpretation is often achieved in the course of implementation of a treaty may be one reason why article 31(3)(a) refers to subsequent agreements regarding the interpretation of the treaty 'or the application of its provisions'. The addition of the words 'or the application of its provisions' was one of the few changes made at the Vienna conference to the ILC draft articles on interpretation. The conference took up the addition proposed by Pakistan to cover cases 'where the parties entered into subsequent agreements concerning the implementation of the treaty, which might shed light on their intentions'.[73] There is no explanation why the drafting committee preferred 'application' to 'implementation', but the former is in the heading of the part of the Vienna Convention in which the Vienna rules appear and is the term used several times elsewhere in the Convention. It also sensibly reflects an ordinary usage by which parties are as likely to agree that the treaty 'applies', 'is to apply', or 'that they will apply it', to some new situation or object, as they are to specify that they interpret it in that way. Whether such formulations of application point to interpretation or extension is a matter for assessment in each particular case but is considered further below.[74]

---

[73] United Nations Conference on the Law of Treaties, First Session (26 March–24 May 1968), Official Records: Summary Records of Committee of the Whole, p 168, para 53.

[74] Cf Nolte (ILC Special Rapporteur), Second Report on Subsequent Agreements etc, A/CN.4/671 (26 March 2014) pp 4–5, paras 4–6 suggesting a slightly different analysis of the relationship between interpretation and application in the Vienna rules, and at pp 49–69 bearing on the relationship between interpretation and change in meaning of a treaty.

3.1.2 ICJ looks for fact of agreement, not form

In its judgment in the *Botswana/Namibia* case in 1999 (concerning the location of part of the river boundary between those states), the ICJ affirmed the role of subsequent agreements in treaty interpretation, quoting the last sentence of the extract from the ILC's commentary in the section above.[75] The ICJ noted that both parties in the case accepted that interpretative agreements and subsequent practice constitute elements of treaty interpretation, though disagreeing over the consequences to be drawn from the facts for purposes of interpretation of the treaty in issue.[76] The Court examined relevant events and dealings between the predecessors to the disputing states and concluded that these events demonstrated the absence of agreement. Hence, the Court found, those events could not constitute subsequent practice in the application of the treaty which established the agreement of the parties regarding its interpretation (quoting article 31(3)(b)):[77] 'A fortiori, they cannot have given rise to an "agreement between the parties regarding the interpretation of the treaty or the application of its provisions" (ibid., Art 31, para 3 (a)).'[78]

In looking at the history of dealings between the relevant authorities to see whether they had reached any agreement subsequent to the historic treaties establishing where the river boundary lay, the ICJ rather worked backwards to the conclusion that there can have been no subsequent agreement from the starting point of an assessment that the various moves to resolve the difficulties between the states' predecessors did not amount to subsequent practice showing agreement on an interpretation. This approach seems to suggest that the concepts of a subsequent agreement and subsequent practice establishing agreement over interpretation have some potential overlap at the point of less formal agreements or understandings. More significant in the present context, the ICJ seems to have reached its conclusion on the premise that 'any subsequent agreement' refers to the fact of agreement, rather than presupposing a formal instrument.

In relation to subsequent agreements, Sinclair writes:

It follows naturally from the proposition that the parties to a treaty are legally entitled to modify the treaty or indeed to terminate it that they are empowered to interpret it... This having been said, it is rarely that one comes across subsequent agreements between the parties bearing upon the interpretation of a treaty which they have concluded.[79]

---

[75] *Kasikili/Sedudu Island (Botswana/Namibia)* [1999] ICJ Reports 1045, at 1076, para 49.
[76] [1999] ICJ Reports 1045, at para 51.   [77] [1999] ICJ Reports 1045, at para 63.
[78] [1999] ICJ Reports 1045, at para 63.
[79] Sinclair, *The Vienna Convention on the Law of Treaties* at 136. Sinclair cites an advisory opinion of the PCIJ showing this proposition to be uncontroversial. He also reports there Yasseen's explanation for the paucity of examples of interpretative agreements, namely that there has to be a high level of desire to reach an understanding (ambiguity is often in the interest of one of the parties) and that it requires a delicate touch to reach agreement on interpretation, which becomes even more difficult where a multilateral treaty is in issue. For an example of a formal agreement on interpretation, see Exchange of Notes constituting an Agreement between Governments of Australia and others and the Government of Italy, concerning the Interpretation of Article 7 of the Agreement respecting Graves of British Soldiers in Italy of 11 May 1922 (Rome, 6 August 1936) [1936] ATS 5 (electronic); cf so-called agreements on interpretation which are actually agreements on application: Agreement on

It is difficult to determine why agreements on interpretation or application are not too commonly encountered.[80] It could be that in instances where differences are resolved by agreement in the course of practical application of a treaty the matter is not reported at all, or not with the prominence of a dispute that goes to international adjudication. Another possibility is that, particularly where there is more than one difficulty in the application of treaty, the parties to the treaty may be more likely to enter a further agreement which does not specifically identify itself as directed to interpretation. This perhaps carries the implication that in addition to considering the role of subsequent agreements (such as there are) specifically on interpretation or application of a treaty, one should also consider whether an amending agreement may have implications for interpretation. For the latter may in fact be designed to clarify the meaning and, in the case of a multilateral treaty which is being amended among some parties only, may have implications for the interpretation of the unamended treaty. It is also appropriate to consider whether an informal subsequent agreement on the meaning of a treaty provision takes effect as an instrument within the Vienna Convention's article 31(3)(a) (subsequent agreement) or whether, if implemented in practice, it lays the groundwork for applying article 31(3)(b) (subsequent practice).

The judgment of the ICJ in the *Botswana/Namibia* case (considered above) was cited by the Arbitral Tribunal in *Methanex v USA*, in conjunction with other material, as showing that article 31(3)(a) does not envisage that a subsequent agreement need be concluded with the same formal requirements as a treaty for such an agreement to play a role in treaty interpretation.[81]

3.2 Less formal or informal agreement

In its reference to 'any subsequent agreement' in article 31(3)(a), the Vienna Convention does not specify that such an agreement must constitute a treaty or have the same formal status as the instrument which is interpreted. Hence any good evidence that parties to a treaty have reached agreement on its interpretation seems admissible. The approach of the ICJ in the *Botswana/Namibia* case has been noted above. That case was decided in the light of the Vienna rules. Before those rules received widespread application, whether agreement had been achieved on

---

Interpretation and Application of Articles VI, XVI, and XXIII of the General Agreement on Tariff s and Trade of 30 October 1947 (Subsidies and Countervailing Duties Code) (Geneva, 12 April 1979) [1981] ATS 28; see also understandings on the interpretation of the various GATT articles annexed to the Marrakesh Agreement establishing the World Trade Organization (WTO Agreement), Marrakesh, 1994 [1995] ATS 8.

[80] For consideration of the paucity of interpretative agreements in the case of investment treaties, see A Roberts, 'Power and Persuasion in Investment Treaty Interpretation: The Dual Role of States' (2010) 104 AJIL 179, at 215–17.

[81] *International Arbitration under Chapter 11 of the North American Free Trade Agreement and the UNCITRAL Arbitration Rules, Methanex v USA (Merits)*, Award of 3 August 2005 (2005) 44 ILM 1345, at 1354, paras 18–21; and see Contemporary Practice of the United States, 'Statements by Parties as "Subsequent Agreement" in Treaty Interpretation' (2001) 95 AJIL 887.

interpretation was sometimes viewed in terms of estoppel: had one of the treaty partners adopted a position which precluded it from arguing any further for a different interpretation from that propounded by another party? Informal records and evidence of statements might make the case.

By their nature, however, informal agreements and records are less likely to surface than formal ones. They tend to be buried in the files of government departments. Sometimes, however, such instruments emerge and have a clear role in interpretation. Even those that appear to have a less formal character than a commonly identifiable treaty have been held to constitute a binding agreement. For example, in the *European Molecular Biology Laboratory Arbitration*[82] the laboratory (EMBL) was an international organization with a permanent staff under a Director-General and having its headquarters in the Federal Republic of Germany pursuant to a treaty ('Headquarters Agreement'). Differences arose between EMBL and Germany over the extent of exemptions from tax and duties accorded by the Headquarters Agreement to both EMBL and the Director-General. Did the exemptions in relation to official activities cover income generated from the operation of a canteen and guest house used by staff and scientists visiting EMBL, and was the Director-General exempt from import duties and value added tax on goods purchased and imported for his or her personal benefit? In the case of the Director-General, article 10 of the Headquarters Agreement stated that the exemptions were inapplicable to goods purchased or imported for the personal benefit of the Director-General and staff of EMBL, but article 19 accorded the Director-General the immunities and privileges of a diplomatic agent as in the multilateral convention on diplomatic relations, which generally exempts diplomatic agents from tax and duties.[83]

In 1977 the Federal Ministry for Research and Technology (BMFT) sent a letter to EMBL confirming that the Director-General's status under article 19 was not restricted by article 10, thus apparently recognizing the broad entitlement to tax exemption of a diplomatic agent. Nevertheless, the Federal Foreign Ministry stated in 1982, in a communication purporting to revoke the BMFT's 1977 letter, that goods purchased or imported for the Director-General's benefit were not exempt. In 1987 negotiations led to a 'Settlement'; but in relevant respects this only set out guidelines for interpreting the Headquarters Agreement and, in relation to the official activities of the organization, merely repeated the statement of purposes and responsibilities in the EMBL's constitutive instrument. Thus the differences over interpretation continued.

In the ensuing international arbitration the tribunal considered that both the Ministry's letter of 1977 and the Settlement of 1987 constituted subsequent agreements within the meaning of article 31(3)(a) of the Vienna Convention(s).[84] As

---

[82] *European Molecular Biology Laboratory Arbitration (EMBL v Germany)*, Award of 29 June 1990, 105 ILR 1.

[83] Vienna Convention on Diplomatic Relations, Vienna, 1961 [1968] ATS 3, article 34 (with listed exceptions).

[84] The Arbitral Tribunal noted that both the 1969 Vienna Convention and the 1986 Vienna Convention on the Law of Treaties between States and International Organizations or between

regards the BMFT's letter of 1977, the Federal Government had disputed its binding effect, but not on the basis that it did not follow 'the usual and well tested form of communication in public international law'.[85] Rather it had relied on an assessment of the contents of the letter, asserting that it was just an intermediate link in the controversy. The Tribunal, however, saw the letter as more than a unilateral statement, being a reply to a question put by the other side in a dispute, a reply which constituted an agreement on interpretation.[86] It is evident from this Award that, in assessing whether there was a subsequent agreement for the purposes of the Vienna rules, the Tribunal attached value to identifying a binding agreement on interpretation, binding through being conclusive of a dispute rather than through compliance with forms for international agreements.

A further example of an informal record of agreement on interpretation is in the UK case *Seaboard World Airlines Inc v Department of Trade*.[87] There the judgment recorded that difficulties had arisen between the UK and the USA as to the meaning of the route descriptions in a bilateral agreement on air services, and that representatives of the two governments had discussed the matter. The problem had been over the interpretation of the route schedule which set out possible points in four columns, listing successively departure points, intermediate points, destination points, and 'points beyond'. Each of these columns had a note under the heading 'Any one or more of the following if desired'. One of the issues was whether this note permitted omission of all destination points and if so whether 'points beyond' could still be served. The result of the discussions between representatives of the two governments was recorded in an attachment to a 'Memorandum Summarising a Portion of the Discussions':

The two delegations discussed the meanings to be attributed to the headings of the columns...

The delegations were in agreement (a) that these headings should remain unchanged and (b) that the headings as they stand permit the designated carriers of either party to serve as desired any, several or no points listed in any of those columns. Even if no point listed in the 'Destination' column is served, such designated carriers may serve any point or points listed as 'Intermediate points' or 'Points beyond', including terminating flights at any of these points, unless there is a precise provision in the route description to the contrary.[88]

In the light of this record of discussions, which the judge described as 'the interpretation agreements reached between the two governments', it would be difficult to maintain that a destination point had to be served on an outward journey, even

---

International Organizations contain the same provision on this point which applied in the present case as a matter of general customary international law: *European Molecular Biology Laboratory Arbitration (EMBL v Germany)*, Award of 29 June 1990, 105 ILR 1, at 25 and 53.

[85] *European Molecular Biology Laboratory Arbitration (EMBL v Germany)*, Award of 29 June 1990, 105 ILR 1, at 54; presumably the Tribunal was making the contrast with communications such as a diplomatic note, aide-memoire or formal Exchange of Notes constituting an agreement.

[86] *European Molecular Biology Laboratory Arbitration (EMBL v Germany)*, Award of 29 June 1990, 105 ILR 1, at 54–56, where the Tribunal cited the well-known conclusion of the PCIJ on the binding effect of a declaration in the *Legal Status of Eastern Greenland (Denmark v Norway)* PCIJ Series A/B53.

[87] [1976] 1 Lloyd's Rep 42.   [88] [1976] 1 Lloyd's Rep 42, at 45.

though absence of such a point made nonsense of the notion of a 'beyond' point (there being nothing appropriate for it to be beyond) and meant that an outward journey included no point in the state granting the right to operate the route and thus established no connection between the air service and that route outbound.[89]

Although these two cases do not provide a great weight of authority, they do support the suggestion that the *fact* of subsequent agreement is likely to be taken as what is required rather than agreement evidenced by conclusion through the usual treaty formalities. There is, however, more than a hint of a relationship between subsequent agreements and subsequent practice. The less formal the agreement, the greater the significance of subsequent practice confirming the less formal agreement or understanding.

3.3 Formal amendment and changed wording

3.3.1 *Effect of amending agreements*

If a treaty amends an earlier one, the function of 'amending' is not always carefully distinguished in its title from the function of clarifying, amplifying, or supplementing an earlier treaty. A protocol may, for example, state in its title that it is 'amending' or 'supplementing' a particular treaty; but this does not exhaust the possibilities or indicate the effect of every provision. For present purposes the question is whether a later agreement, including any described as an 'amending' one, has an amending or an interpretative effect on an earlier one.[90] In some situations the answer may not matter. In others it does.

An example of the former was in *Territorial Dispute (Libyan Arab Jamahiriya/ Chad)*.[91] In investigating the boundary between Libya and Chad, the ICJ had to consider a Convention of 8 September 1919 signed at Paris between Great Britain and France. The Convention itself stated that it was 'Supplementary to the Declaration signed at London on March 21, 1899, as an addition to the Convention of June 14, 1898, which regulated the Boundaries between the British and French Colonial Possessions'. The Court was dismissive of whether the 1919 Convention was an interpretation or modification of the earlier treaty:

There is thus little point in considering what was the pre-1919 situation, in view of the fact that the Anglo-French Convention of 8 September 1919 determined the precise endpoint

---

[89] The judgment in this case at first instance was followed a few days later by a decision in another case in the Court of Appeal relating to the same treaty on air services in which that Court said that because such agreements were not incorporated into English law, the courts had no business to be interpreting them: see *Pan-American World Airways Inc v Department of Trade* [1976] 1 Lloyd's Rep 257. Thus, as a formal precedent the judgment was trumped. Nevertheless, the example given in the text here remains a good factual one to show the potential effects of an informal agreement on interpretation of a treaty.

[90] Cf issues over whether subsequent practice which appears to diverge from the meaning of a treaty provision constitutes an interpretation or tacit amendment which are considered in section 4.7 below.

[91] [1994] ICJ Reports 6.

of the line in question ... The text of the 1919 Convention presents this line as an interpretation of the Declaration of 1899; in the view of the Court, for the purposes of the present Judgment, there is no reason to categorize it either as a confirmation or as a modification of the Declaration. Inasmuch as the two States parties to the Convention are those that concluded the Declaration of 1899, there can be no doubt that the 'interpretation' in question constituted, from 1919 onwards, and as between them, the correct and binding interpretation of the Declaration of 1899.[92]

Thus the last of the instruments was dispositive, whatever its true characterization. This does not, however, mean that there is never a significance in whether a later treaty is truly an amendment to an earlier one. Treaties which amend earlier ones sometimes contain provisions aimed at resolving problems that have arisen over interpretation of the original treaty. These amending treaties are not necessarily designated or described as agreements on interpretation. Their construction may present difficulties where a different wording in relation to the same matter may be viewed as a clearer wording to reflect a meaning which is thereby confirmed, as a change to cope with a situation which the earlier wording did not cover or for which it produced unexpected results, or with no very clear indication either way. This may be an important matter not just for states which do not become party to the amending treaty. It can also be significant for those that do become bound by the 'amendments' if they continue to be parties to the original treaty; for this will continue to apply in their relations with states parties only to that original instrument. If provisions in the later treaty are truly amendments, and produce obligations incompatible with those of the earlier instrument, states may not be able to reconcile these and be party to both.[93]

An example of a circumstance in which an amending instrument was considered as interpreting the unamended version was in *El Al v Tseng* (US Supreme Court).[94] An intrusive body search at an airport led to a claim based on assault and false imprisonment (among other claims), but alleging no bodily injury. Article 17 of the Warsaw Convention provides that a carrier by air 'is liable for damage sustained in the event of the death or *wounding* of a passenger or any other *bodily injury* suffered by a passenger, if the *accident* which caused the damage so sustained

---

[92] [1994] ICJ Reports 6, at 29, para 60; see also paras 31, 30–33, and 59.

[93] This raises complex issues over successive treaties on the same subject matter and amendment and modification of treaties. See, for example, the Convention for the Unification of Certain Rules relating to International Carriage by Air, Warsaw, 1929 (see fn 95 below), which through its uniform regime, definition of 'international carriage', prescription of jurisdictions, and prohibition of substantive reservations made it quite clear that a group of parties could not modify the treaty *inter se*, but left it less clear whether and how the parties collectively could implement amending protocols if only some of them became bound by these later instruments; see *R v Secretary of State for the Environment, Transport and the Regions, ex parte IATA* [1999] 2 CMLR 1385, R K Gardiner, 'Revising the Law of Carriage by Air: Mechanisms in Treaties and Contract' (1998) 47 ICLQ 278, Gardiner, 'Treaty Relations in the Law of Carriage by Air: Article 55(1) of the Montreal Convention' [2000] *The Aviation Quarterly* 24–61, and see generally A Aust, *Modern Treaty Law and Practice* (Cambridge: CUP, 3rd edn, 2012), Chapters 12 and 15.

[94] 525 US 155, 119 S Ct 662.

took place on board the aircraft or in the course of any of the operations of embarking or disembarking'.[95] Although the claimant's cause of action could be loosely described as being for 'personal injury', there had been no accident and the claim did not come within the ordinary meaning of 'wounding' or 'other bodily injury' (unless the latter could cover purely mental or psychological harm, a controversial matter in application of the Convention). The claimant therefore sought to claim outside the Convention (ie under local law) but encountered difficulty because of article 24 of the Convention:

(1) In the cases covered by Articles 18 and 19 any action for damages, however founded, can only be brought subject to the conditions and limits set out in this Convention.
(2) In the cases covered by Article 17 the provisions of the preceding paragraph also apply....

In issue was whether the words 'In the cases covered by Article 17' meant that where circumstances matched all the conditions in article 17 a claim could only be brought on the basis of that provision, or whether article 24 meant that article 17 provided the sole and exclusive source or remedy for all personal injury claims relating to the carriage by air. The Supreme Court held that the Convention remedy was exclusive so that claims based on local laws were not available if a claim could not succeed under the Convention. In reaching this conclusion, one element which the Court considered was a provision in a 1975 Protocol 'to amend' the Warsaw Convention, even though it had not been in force for the USA at the relevant time. This replaced article 24 so that it would read:

(1) In the carriage of passengers and baggage, any action for damages, however founded, can only be brought subject to the conditions and limits set out in this Convention. ...[96]

The Court considered that this made the Convention's 'pre-emptive' effect quite clear. It can be seen, however, that, framed as an amendment, in a collection of amendments, in an amending Protocol, there could be a question whether this amounted to a clarificatory interpretation or was an amendment changing the meaning. The Supreme Court held that the revised article 24 merely clarified the meaning and did not alter the unamended Convention's rule of exclusivity. It reached this conclusion on the basis of the text, drafting history, and underlying purpose of the Convention, together with the concordant views of courts in other countries applying the original Convention.[97]

---

[95] Convention for the Unification of Certain Rules relating to International Carriage by Air, Warsaw, 1929 [1963] ATS 18 (emphasis added).

[96] Article 24 as amended by Montreal Protocol No 4 to amend the Convention for the Unification of Certain Rules relating to International Carriage by Air, signed at Warsaw on 12 October 1929, as amended by the Protocol done at The Hague on 28 September 1955 (Montreal, 25 September 1975) [1998] ATS 10.

[97] *El Al v Tseng* 525 US 155, at 174–79.

3.3.2 *Changed wording in related or comparable agreements*

An illustration of an issue to which such a changed wording can give rise is provided by the attempt to address the persistent uncertainty whether most favoured nation (MFN) provisions in bilateral investment treaties apply only to provisions protecting investors within a state party's legal system or also allow claimants to invoke from other such treaties provisions that establish procedures for dispute settlement, such as arbitral jurisdiction.

Thus, for example, some bilateral agreements in the last couple of decades have included of a provision on the lines: 'For the avoidance of doubt it is confirmed that the treatment provided above' (viz MFN treatment) shall apply to listed provisions which include those on dispute settlement.[98] However, this wording is really recognition that there could be doubt as to the proper interpretation of the earlier agreements that did not include it. Hence such a statement could only become something of an interpretative indicator for treaties which did not include it if both parties had adopted the changed wording systematically and if there were indications that this was to apply to their existing agreements.[99]

4. Subsequent Practice

The prominent role accorded to the practice of parties to a treaty in its interpretation is one of the features of the Vienna rules which marks out a difference from the approach taken in some legal systems to interpretation of legal texts of purely domestic origin. Words are given meaning by action. This is, at least in part, because treaties differ in character from national legal instruments, bearing an exact analogy neither to contract nor to legislation. Closer to the former than the latter, being compacts or recorded agreements, treaties embody the common understanding of the parties to them. Hence concordant practice of the parties is best evidence of their correct interpretation. In a judgment in 1999, the ICJ affirmed the role of subsequent practice in treaty interpretation, endorsing the ILC:

As regards the 'subsequent practice'... the Commission... indicated its particular importance in the following terms:

'The importance of such subsequent practice in the application of the treaty, as an element of interpretation, is obvious; for it constitutes objective evidence of the understanding of the parties as to the meaning of the treaty. Recourse to it as a means of interpretation is well-established in the jurisprudence of international tribunals.'[100]

---

[98] See examples in *National Grid plc v The Argentine Republic*, UNCITRAL arbitration, Decision on Jurisdiction, 20 June 2006, paras 66 ff and 85; for later cases on MFN clauses, see Chapter 10, section 6.2.3 below.

[99] Cf the different interpretative technique adopted by Argentina and Panama which exchanged diplomatic notes containing an 'interpretative declaration' of the MFN clause in their bilateral investment treaty to the effect that the MFN clause did not extend to dispute resolution clauses, and that this had always been their intention: as described in *National Grid* at para 85.

[100] *Kasikili/Sedudu Island (Botswana/Namibia)* [1999] ICJ Reports 1045, at 1076, para 49, quoting from [1966] *Yearbook of the ILC*, vol II, p 221, para 15. In that case the Court also noted that it

4.1 Elements of subsequent practice

4.1.1 History and development of the provision

In his original proposals to the ILC on treaty interpretation, the Special Rapporteur (Waldock) included subsequent practice in a draft article permitting reference to 'other evidence or indications of the intentions of the parties' in specified circumstances similar to those in the present article 32 of the Vienna Convention for affording recourse to supplementary means of interpretation.[101] However, the Commission decided to make subsequent practice a distinct element in the general rule which had the effect, in the Commission's view, of making subsequent practice an authentic interpretation comparable to an interpretative agreement.[102] The Special Rapporteur noted that: 'Clearly, to amount to an "authentic interpretation", the practice must be such as to indicate that the interpretation has received the tacit assent of the parties generally.[103]

The text of article 31(3)(b) of the Vienna Convention offers four elements for consideration or notice: (1) the meaning of 'subsequent practice'; (2) that it be in the application of the treaty; (3) which parties need to participate in the practice; (4) what it is that establishes interpretative agreement.

4.1.2 Meaning of 'subsequent practice'

The dictionary definition of 'practice' emphasizes 'action' or 'doing something', meanings which it develops to include the 'habitual doing or carrying on of something' and 'customary or constant action'.[104] In relation to interpretation of treaties the two important qualifying characteristics of practice are that the practice is 'in the application of the treaty' and is practice 'which establishes the agreement of the parties regarding its interpretation'. These characteristics do not, however, give an indication of what factually comprises such practice or what evidence is admissible to demonstrate that it has occurred.

What subsequent practice comprises will vary according to the subject matter of the treaty in issue. The essence of it is what can be shown to have been done systematically or repeatedly in implementation and application of a treaty, whether

---

had itself frequently examined the subsequent practice of the parties in the application of that treaty, giving as examples: *Corfu Channel, Merits, Judgment* [1949] ICJ Reports 25; *Arbitral Award Made by the King of Spain on 23 December 1906, Judgment* [1960] ICJ Reports 206–7; *Temple of Preah Vihear, Merits, Judgment* [1962] ICJ Reports 33–35; *Certain Expenses of the United Nations (Article 17, paragraph 2, of the Charter), Advisory Opinion* [1962] ICJ Reports 157, 160–61, and 172–75; *Military and Paramilitary Activities in and against Nicaragua (Nicaragua v United States of America), Jurisdiction and Admissibility, Judgment* [1984] ICJ Reports 408–13, paras 36–47; *Territorial Dispute (Libyan Arab Jamahiriya/Chad), Judgment* [1994] ICJ Reports 34–37, paras 66–71; *Legality of the Use by a State of Nuclear Weapons in Armed Conflict, Advisory Opinion* [1996–I] ICJ Reports 75, para 19.

[101] Third Report, draft article 71(2) [1964] *Yearbook of the ILC*, vol II, p 52.

[102] See Waldock, Sixth Report [1966] *Yearbook of the ILC*, vol II, pp 98–9, para 18 and Commentary on draft article 27(3)(b), at 221–22, para 15.

[103] Waldock, [1966] *Yearbook of the ILC*, vol II, at p 99, para 18.

[104] *Shorter Oxford English Dictionary* (Oxford: Clarendon Press, 1973).

it be the levying of tax in a matter governed by a double taxation convention or, in the classic case of the 'veto' in the United Nations Security, regularly treating the absence of any negative vote as satisfying the requirement for 'concurring' votes even if there is an abstention or absence of a permanent member.[105]

It would be difficult to offer a list of what may constitute 'practice'. The notion is well known in general international law in the widespread use of the description of a source of international law as 'international custom, as evidence of a *general practice* accepted as law'.[106] Obviously, with a focus on treaty interpretation any such description transforms 'general' into 'specific' practice revealing what the parties accept as the meaning of a particular provision. However, this cognate description of practice in general international law suggests something of the range of evidence that can be used to show practice. Crawford lists as material sources of international custom:

…diplomatic correspondence, policy statements, press releases, the opinions of government legal advisers, official manuals on legal questions (e.g. manuals of military law), executive decisions and practices, orders to military forces (e.g. rules of engagement), comments by governments on drafts and accompanying commentary, state legislation, international and national judicial decisions, recitals in treaties and other international instruments (especially when in 'all states' form), a pattern of treaties in the same terms, the practice of international organs, and resolutions relating to legal questions in UN organs, notably the General Assembly.[107]

This list requires some qualifying in application to treaty interpretation. Statements and records of a position taken with regard to a treaty provision need to be linked to something actually done unless they are in a form which itself amounts to an official act or committed policy that is being, or will be, implemented. However, while recalling that the essence of the definition of practice is repeated action, the typical evidence as demonstrated by the general list set out above is the written record or account of any practice. It can be seen that, in the context of customary international law, several of the items in the list relating to general practice may record unilateral approaches to a legal matter which need replication more widely to show practice sufficient to found a customary rule (in conjunction there with evidence that the practice is carried out under a sense of obligation). When searching for practice relating to interpretation of a particular treaty provision, the defining test is that the practice must establish the agreement of the parties. This dictates that relevant evidence is that which shows the 'concordant' conduct of the parties, that is that they have done essentially the same thing expressly in pursuance of the treaty or, if the conduct is unilateral, that it reveals the agreement of the other party or parties.

---

[105] See below for elaboration of both these examples.
[106] Statute of the International Court of Justice, article 38 (emphasis added).
[107] J Crawford, *Brownlie's Principles of Public International Law* (Oxford: OUP, 8th edn, 2012), 24 (footnotes omitted).

4.1.3 *Frequency and uniformity of practice*

It is inherent in the combination of the term 'practice' and establishment thereby of agreement of the parties as to meaning that the relevant conduct of parties to the treaty be concordant. However, although the term 'concordant' was used in ILC debate and in its draft commentary to characterize practice which could amount to authentic interpretation of a given agreement or treaty, in its final version of the commentaries on the draft articles as taken up at the Vienna conference, the ILC stated: 'The value of subsequent practice varies according as it shows the common understanding of the parties as to the meaning of the terms.'[108] Thus, rather than suggesting a threshold of concordant practice must be crossed before this element of interpretation is engaged, the ILC looked to the result, that is whether practice is sufficiently extensive to demonstrate 'a common understanding'. Somewhat in contrast, the Appellate Body of the World Trade Organization in *Japan—Alcoholic Beverages* tried to identify features of practice with specific reference to article 31(3)(b):

Generally, in international law, the essence of subsequent practice in interpreting a treaty has been recognized as a 'concordant, common and consistent' sequence of acts or pronouncements which is sufficient to establish a discernable pattern implying the agreement of the parties regarding its interpretation. [109]

It is to be noted that Sinclair, as the source cited by the WTO Appellate Body, considered that the '*value and significance* of subsequent practice will naturally depend on the extent to which it is concordant, common and consistent'.[110] It thus seems best to consider the criteria 'concordant, common and consistent' as indicators of the cogency with which practice evidences agreement of the parties as to the proper meaning of a term or treaty which is being interpreted. These criteria are not aids to interpretation independent of such agreement. In its current work on subsequent agreements and subsequent practice Nolte, the ILC's Special Rapporteur, has noted that the ICJ, and most other international courts and tribunals, have not taken up the formula 'concordant, common and consistent', while tribunals established through the Centre for the Settlement of Investment Disputes have adopted divergent positions on it.[111]

---

[108] [1966] *Yearbook of the ILC*, vol II, p 222, para 15; and for earlier consideration see [1964] *Yearbook of the ILC*, vol I, p 282, paras 3 and 5, p 296, para 39, p 298, paras 56–7, p 299, para 64, etc; and [1964] *Yearbook of the ILC*, vol II, Report of the Commission to the General Assembly, p 204, para 13.

[109] *Japan—Taxes on Alcoholic Beverages*, AB-1996-2, Report of 4 October 1996, WT/DS8/ AB/R, WT/DS10/AB/R, WT/DS11/AB/R, pp 12–13; and see *Chile—Price Band System and Safeguard Measures Relating to Certain Agricultural Products*, AB-2002-2, (2002) WT/DS207/AB/R, at paras 213–14, where the Appellate Body took the view that the assertion that no country that had had a price band system in place before the Uruguay Round had actually converted it into ordinary customs duties did not reveal a discernible pattern of acts or pronouncements, since this only showed the alleged practice of some members of the WTO.

[110] Sinclair, *The Vienna Convention on the Law of Treaties* (2nd edn, 1984), 137 (emphasis added); see also Yasseen, 'L'interprétation des traités d'après la Convention de Vienne sur le Droit des Traités' (1976-III) 151 *Recueil des Cours* 1 at 48.

[111] 'Second Report on Subsequent agreements and subsequent practice in relation to interpretation of treaties', A/CN.4/671 (26 March 2014), pp 21–4 where extensive supporting material is cited.

In its draft conclusions, the ILC has therefore avoided use of the formula 'concordant, common and consistent' and has suggested:

1. The weight of a subsequent agreement or subsequent practice as a means of interpretation under article 31, paragraph 3, depends, inter alia, on its clarity and specificity.
2. The weight of subsequent practice under article 31, paragraph 3(b), depends, in addition, on whether and how it is repeated....[112]

If this is necessary to avoid the impression that the formula 'concordant, common and consistent' is to be taken as a statement of established entry criteria for practice to be assessed, it does the job. However, if it can be recognized that there is something of a sliding scale, the extent to which the practice can be shown to be concordant, common, and consistent may strike more of a chord with interpreters making the assessment as to whether agreement on meaning can be shown.

4.1.4 Practice may consist of executive, legislative, and judicial acts

A simpler classification of conduct that may amount to practice of states is in terms of executive, legislative, and judicial acts. Of these, 'executive' is not limited to the conduct of a central government nor, where it is acts of a central government that are being considered, only those acts that have an obvious international connection. Any body charged with the authority of the state may carry out relevant acts if these demonstrate a position in relation to the state's treaty commitments or entitlements.

Legislative acts may take a position on interpretation at a time when effect is given to a treaty's provisions in the course of meeting constitutional requirements to enable the state to become party to a treaty. Legislation may also, however, specifically address points of interpretation that arise at a later stage. Examples of the latter in the UK are: section 2(1) of the Carriage by Air and Road Act 1979, which provided in relation to the 1929 Warsaw Convention on carriage by air as amended at The Hague in 1955 that references to 'damage' were to be construed as including loss of contents of a passenger's baggage,[113] and section 100 of the Arbitration Act 1996, which provides that for the purposes of the 1958 New York Convention on recognition and enforcement of foreign arbitral awards an award

---

[112] Report of the International Law Commission (2014), (Sixty-eighth Session, Supplement No. 10 A/69/1), Chapter VII, draft conclusion 8, and see commentary on that draft conclusion, paras (7)–(11); for an example of assessing the practice by reference to the number of parties adopting it, see *Yugraneft Corporation v Rexx Management Corporation* [2010] 1 SCR 649, para [21] (Canadian Supreme Court).

[113] See *Fothergill v Monarch Airlines* [1981] AC 251 where, after reporting damage to a suitcase at the airport, the passenger discovered loss of some of its contents after arrival home. The House of Lords applied the same interpretation as the legislation (not then in force) and found that such loss was included in the term 'damage' (which had to be reported within a specified number of days). For an example of French legislation being specifically identified as subsequent practice for the purposes of the Vienna rules, see *R v Secretary of State for the Home Department ex parte Mullen* [2004] UKHL 18, at para 47.

is to be treated as made at the seat of the arbitration, regardless of where it was signed, despatched, or delivered to any of the parties.[114]

Judicial decisions, as conduct which may contribute towards subsequent practice, can be separated into national and international ones. Decisions of a state's courts are commonly taken as capable of constituting practice, though it is really necessary to see where ultimate authority to interpret treaties lies within the state to be sure that a court's judgment does truly represent the interpretative position of the state. In the UK, the principle, put very generally, is that where a matter concerning the foreign relations of the UK is before the courts, the courts try to speak 'with the same voice' as that of the government or Parliament if the matter is also within the foreign affairs competence of these bodies.[115] This principle applies implicitly whenever legislation in the UK implements a treaty and the courts follow and apply that legislation. It has also been explicitly stated to apply to treaty interpretation. Where Parliament legislated in 1999 to give effect to a ruling by the European Court of Human Rights (ECtHR) that admission in evidence of answers given by defendants under compulsion was contrary to the European Convention right to fair trial,[116] Lord Hoffmann observed:

> Given that Parliament had accepted the ECtHR interpretation when it passed the 1999 Act, it seems to me very likely that the courts would also have done so. If Parliament considered that the law should be changed to comply with an international obligation, it would be strange for the courts to say that it had been unnecessary. Parliament and the courts should speak with one voice on such issues.[117]

Thus in identifying the practice of the UK in interpreting treaties, one can generally expect the pronouncements of the courts, the government, and Parliament to be in alignment but in exceptional cases care may need to be taken to consider later legislation designed to adjust an interpretation made by a court.[118]

A note of caution also needs to be sounded over the characterization of some decisions of international courts and tribunals as subsequent practice for the purposes of article 31(3)(b) of the Vienna Convention. International judicial proceedings take place by consent of the parties. Commonly the parties agree that the decisions of international courts and tribunals shall be final and binding (though some arbitral agreements provide for an 'advisory' award or qualify in some other

---

[114] This effectively reversed the interpretation adopted by the House of Lords in *Hiscox v Outhwaite* [1992] 1 AC 562, on which see Chapter 1, section 5.4 above; see also section 53 of the same Act.

[115] *Rio Tinto Zinc Corporation v Westinghouse* [1978] AC 547, at 617.

[116] See Youth Justice and Criminal Evidence Act 1999, Sch 3, para 5, and *Saunders v UK* (1996) 23 EHRR 313 and *IJL, GMR and AKP v U K* 19 September 2000, ECtHR, Series A no 285-C.

[117] *R v Lyons* [2003] 1 AC 976, at 997, para 46.

[118] In one instance the British government disavowed an interpretation by the House of Lords of a treaty. In *Philippson v Imperial Airways* [1939] AC 332, the House interpreted a contractual reference to 'High Contracting Parties to the Warsaw Convention' as applying to Belgium. Belgium had signed the Convention but had not deposited an instrument of ratification. The British government told the US government that in its view the interpretation by the House of Lords was a misinterpretation; see Cheng, 'The Law of "International" and "Non-International Carriage"' (1963) 60 *Law Society Gazette* 444, at 445–46; and see *Hiscox v Outhwaite* (fn 114 above).

way the obligation to implement an award). Although each judgment or award is only binding on the parties to it, successive judgments or awards in the same sense but between different parties can show a consistent practice effective to establish the interpretation as that agreed by the parties in the case. The reason for care, however, is that in some instances the decision of a court or tribunal established within an international organization is linked with some other body within the organization which has power to make a further decision.[119]

4.1.5 'Subsequent practice' and 'subsequent conduct' distinguished

The most obvious distinction is that practice requires an element of constancy, a feature which is reinforced by the context in that subsequent practice must be sufficient to reveal the agreement of the parties on interpretation. Conduct merely denotes the behaviour of the parties, which may constitute an instance of relevant practice or may not. Thus Sinclair emphasizes the requirement for a plurality of acts: 'A practice is a sequence of facts or acts and cannot in general be established by one isolated fact or act, or even by several individual applications.'[120] Nevertheless, in the context of 'subsequent practice' courts and tribunals do refer to 'conduct' and to the 'attitude' of a party.

In *Kasikili/Sedudu Island (Botswana/Namibia)*,[121] the ICJ considered the history of dealings between relevant states concerning a disputed island, assessed facts and incidents relating to it, including the use made of the island by people from the neighbouring territories since a treaty of 1890, the principal one in issue. The Court noted that for any such conduct to constitute relevant practice, the various elements in the history traced by the Court would need to meet at least two criteria: first, that they were linked to a belief on the part of those responsible for the conduct that it reflected a position taken on the interpretation of the treaty; and, second, that the other state concerned was fully aware of and accepted the conduct as a confirmation of the Treaty boundary.[122] The Court concluded that, in the particular case, none of the facts or incidents in the history presented to it amounted to the necessary elements to constitute subsequent practice in the application of the 1890 treaty within the meaning of article 31(3)(b) of the Vienna Convention.[123] The Court's approach was criticized by Judge Oda in his separate opinion:

The Judgment refers to various acts or conduct…I accept that these facts and the survey reports are extremely important for the Court's consideration of the matter. However, I am unable to accept the Court's position that such facts and reports could be considered only as possible evidence of…[a subsequent agreement or subsequent practice] within the

---

[119] See, eg, the WTO Dispute Settlement Understanding, under which the Member States acting as the DSB have powers to reject by consensus Reports of the Panels and Appellate Body.
[120] Sinclair, *The Vienna Convention on the Law of Treaties*, at 137.
[121] *Kasikili/Sedudu Island (Botswana/Namibia)* [1999] ICJ Reports 1045; see Chapter 5, section 3.3.4 above.
[122] [1999] ICJ Reports 1045, at para 74.
[123] [1999] ICJ Reports 1045, at paras 63, 75, and 78–79.

meaning of Article 31, paragraph 3, of the Vienna Convention on the Law of Treaties, to be taken into account when interpreting the 1890 Anglo-German Treaty. The Court, after a lengthy analysis (paras. 47 to 70), comes to the conclusion that the facts and documents in question cannot be regarded as constituting 'any subsequent agreement' or 'any subsequent practice' to be used for the interpretation of the 1890 Treaty, although the Court ultimately found that these facts 'nevertheless support the conclusions which it has reached by interpreting Article III, paragraph 2, of the 1890 Treaty in accordance with the ordinary meaning to be given to its terms' (para. 80). I would rather suggest that these facts and documents should be considered at their face value, as historical background to the present case but without having any bearing on the provisions of the Vienna Convention, in order to assist the Court in determining the boundary.[124]

It is respectfully suggested that Judge Oda was here swimming against the tide. With the increasing acceptance that the Vienna rules are the rules generally applicable to treaty interpretation, approaches which link analysis to components of those rules are appropriate. To do this it is necessary to examine conduct to see whether it does meet the tests in article 31(3)(b). It would be strange if such conduct were *inconsistent* with the ordinary meaning of a term for no remark to be made by a court or tribunal. Hence it seems reasonable for the Court to have noted its consistency in this case.

The analysis of 'conduct' of one party as 'practice' is not actually inconsistent with the requirement of the Vienna rule if the conduct is sufficiently constant and repeated as to amount to practice, always recalling that the rest of the rule must also be observed so as to show that the 'practice' establishes the agreement of the parties. This is illustrated by a case before the Iran–US Claims Tribunal in which it was argued that a judgment in a domestic court created a debt or obligation distinct from the claim that had led to the judgment. In deciding that a judgment in a domestic US court did *not* amount to a claim within the meaning of the Algiers Accords (the treaties setting up and applied by the Tribunal), the Tribunal noted that in suspending execution of judgments against Iran as well as suspending claims in US courts unresolved at the time the Accords took effect, the US had recognized that a judgment had no distinct status under the Accords independent of the claim on which it was based.[125] This was in a case brought by US nationals against Iran. Hence the conduct of the US courts in implementation of a treaty of the USA could be seen as practice of the USA under the treaty when it accorded with the interpretation of the treaty advanced by Iran.

Somewhat similar was the view taken in a case before the same Tribunal but where the claimant was Iran. In holding that where export of Iranian property had been banned under US export control laws before the Algiers Accords, such a ban could be continued after their entry into force, the Tribunal found that:

... this interpretation is consistent with the subsequent practice of the Parties in the application of the Algiers Accords and, particularly, with the conduct of the United States ... a

---

[124] Separate Opinion at para 7.
[125] *Burton Marks and Harry Umann v Iran* 8 Iran–US Claims Trib Rep 290, at 295–96.

practice, according to Article 31(3)(b) of the Vienna Convention...to be taken into account in the interpretation of a treaty.[126]

In relying on this conduct, the Tribunal appears also to have taken into account that in its communication informing Iran of its refusal of export approval, the USA acknowledged Iran's right to compensation for the value of the property. This may have encouraged the Tribunal to place unilateral conduct under a somewhat more generous characterization of the idea of practice than would usually be the case.

4.1.6 Practice 'in the application of the treaty'

That relevant practice is that 'in application *of the treaty* plainly indicates that this is not limited to conduct specifically referable to a particular provision or provisions in issue. A good illustration of this is the ICJ's Advisory Opinion in the *IMCO Maritime Safety Committee* case.[127] This concerned the composition of a committee of an international organization whose constitutive treaty provided that in the membership of the committee 'not less than eight shall be the largest ship-owning nations'. Did 'largest ship-owning nations' mean those having the greatest registered tonnage flying their flag (which would have led to inclusion of 'flags of convenience' states) or did this mean states having the greatest tonnage of ships beneficially owned by their nationals? The Court noted that the practice of the Assembly of the organization (and thus implicitly of states party to the treaty setting up the organization) in implementing other provisions of the treaty used registered tonnage of a flag state, and therefore considered it unlikely that any criterion other than registered tonnage was contemplated.[128]

A further issue which could arise over the phrase 'in the application of the treaty' is when relevant practice begins. At first sight it would seem probable that the practice must be that after the treaty has entered into force and be the practice of parties to the treaty. Only such practice seems strictly in application of the treaty.[129] However, the position may not be quite so clear cut. Signatory states and other potential parties may also have an interest in development of practice in relation to matters to be governed by the treaty when it enters into force and may

---

[126] *The Islamic Republic of Iran v The USA* 19 Iran–US Claims Trib Rep 273, at 294–95, para 68. See also C N Brower and J D Brueschke, *The Iran–United States Claims Tribunal* (The Hague: Martinus Nijhoff, 1998), at 283–85 and G H Aldrich, *The Jurisprudence of the Iran–United States Claims Tribunal* (Oxford: Clarendon Press, 1996), at 372.

[127] Advisory Opinion on *Constitution of the Maritime Safety Committee of the Inter-Governmental Maritime Consultative Organization* [1960] ICJ Reports 150; see also H Thirlway, 'The Law and Procedure of the International Court of Justice 1960–1989' (1991) LXII BYBIL, Part Three, at 49–50.

[128] Advisory Opinion on *Constitution of the Maritime Safety Committee of the Inter-Governmental Maritime Consultative Organization* [1960] ICJ Reports 150, at 168–69 (practice under the IMCO Convention) and 169–70 (international practice under various other conventions).

[129] See G Hafner, 'Subsequent Agreements and Practice: Between Interpretation, Informal Modification, and Formal Amendment' in Nolte *Treaties and Subsequent Practice*, Chapter 10, 118.

establish their practice through implementing legislation given effect before entry into force.[130]

Taking conclusion as the moment when the text of a treaty 'has been established as definite', the ILC has stated in its commentary on one of its draft conclusions on subsequent agreements and subsequent practice that:

> It is after conclusion, not just after entry into force, of a treaty when…subsequent practice can occur. Indeed, it is difficult to identify a reason why an agreement or practice which take[s] place between the moment when the text of a treaty has been established as definite and the entry into force of that treaty should not be relevant for the purpose of interpretation.[131]

4.2 Deduction from absence of subsequent practice

4.2.1 Absence of action

The flip side of the requirement of subsequent practice being open to characterization as 'in the application of the treaty' is consideration of practice where a treaty provision might be thought to be applicable but in practice has not been applied. Taking subsequent practice as an element of treaty interpretation involves drawing conclusions from what has been constantly done. Examining what interpretation has been demonstrated through conduct makes an association with, or adaptation of, what has been stated in writing. Hence, although it does not apply literally, the maxim *expressio unius exclusio alterius* may be applied in a somewhat analogous manner. This seems to be the effect of the ICJ's approach in its advisory opinion to the UN General Assembly on *Legality of the Threat or Use of Nuclear Weapons*.[132] On the question whether treaty provisions prohibiting use of poisonous and asphyxiating weapons (the Second Hague Declaration 1899, the Hague Regulations 1907, and the Geneva Protocol 1925) should be interpreted as barring nuclear weapons, the ICJ stated:

> The Court will observe that the Regulations annexed to the Hague Convention IV do not define what is to be understood by 'poison or poisoned weapons' and that different interpretations exist on the issue. Nor does the 1925 Protocol specify the meaning to be given to the term 'analogous materials or devices'. The terms have been understood, in the practice of States, in their ordinary sense as covering weapons whose prime, or even exclusive, effect

---

[130] See, for example, D H Anderson, 'British Accession to the UN Convention on the Law of the Sea' (1997) 46 ICLQ 761, at 762, indicating that British practice, through modernisation of maritime legislation in the period after completion of the UN Convention on the Law of the Sea in 1982, came to be based in many respects on the content of the Convention, apart from its Part XI, even though the United Kingdom only became a party following its accession to the Convention and ratification of the Implementing Agreement in July 1997, some years after the Convention's entry into force in November 1994.

[131] International Law Commission Report 2013 (Sixty-eighth Session Supplement No. 10 A/68/1), p31, Commentary on draft Conclusion 4, para (2) (footnote omitted).

[132] [1996–I] ICJ Reports 226.

is to poison or asphyxiate. This practice is clear, and the parties to those instruments have not treated them as referring to nuclear weapons.

In view of this, it does not seem to the Court that the use of nuclear weapons can be regarded as specifically prohibited on the basis of the above-mentioned provisions of the Second Hague Declaration of 1899, the Regulations annexed to the Hague Convention IV of 1907 or the 1925 Protocol (see paragraph 54 above).[133]

In terms of acts and conduct, the proscription of 'asphyxiating, poisonous or other gases, and of all analogous liquids, materials or devices' affirmed by the 1925 Geneva Protocol has been recognized as having secured the non-repetition of the use made in the First World War of gas (with some notorious exceptions), but there was no evidence that a self-denying ordinance had been understood to apply to nuclear weapons. However, it would have been more difficult to pin the absence of a bar on nuclear weapons on practice in this sense had the ban on poisoned weapons, etc not been accompanied by practice in the sense of further treaty practice. The latter included the negotiation, conclusion, and ratification of the 1977 Additional Protocol I to the 1949 Geneva Conventions, in the course of which it was made clear that the new rules did not regulate or prohibit nuclear weapons. Express statements to this effect were not challenged or contradicted.[134]

The ECtHR has viewed consistent absence of action, where measures might have been expected, as practice indicative of interpretative agreement. In *Bankovic & Others v Belgium & Others*, a central issue was whether NATO action in Serbia provided a basis for claims against NATO participating states of violation of the European Convention on the basis that military action in Serbia came within their jurisdiction.[135] The Court found state practice in the application of the Human Rights Convention to be indicative of a lack of any apprehension on the part of the parties that they might attract responsibility under the Convention in respect of military operations in which they had participated outside of their territories.[136]

---

[133] [1996–I] ICJ Reports 226, at 248, paras 55–56.

[134] It is difficult to pinpoint the evidence leading to the Court's conclusion on practice in relation to these particular treaty provisions. Written submissions of the USA and the Russian Federation provide supporting assertions, references, and citations of relevant material, while the USA addressed arguments raised on the meaning of poison and gas weapons at the oral proceedings (ICJ, *Compte Rendu* 15 November 1995, *CR 95/34*). There was, of course, much broader evidence of treaty practice acknowledging the possession of nuclear weapons in, for example, the Treaty on the Non-Proliferation of Nuclear Weapons, Washington, London, and Moscow, 1968; but it is difficult to describe that as practice in relation to the three treaty provisions discussed here. See also: *Legal Consequences for States of the Continued Presence of South Africa in Namibia (South West Africa) notwithstanding Security Council Resolution 276* (1970) [1971] ICJ Reports 16, at 36, para 69, where the ICJ concluded that the fact that the General Assembly decided not to set up a temporary subsidiary body to assist it in the exercise of its supervisory functions over the former League of Nations mandates could not be interpreted as implying that the General Assembly lacked competence or could not itself exercise its functions in that field; and *Oil Platforms (Iran v USA) (Preliminary Objections)* [1996] ICJ Reports 803, at 815, para 30, where the ICJ viewed as relevant practice the fact that neither party had, in previous cases between them before the ICJ, referred to the treaty provision under consideration.

[135] Application no 52207/99, Decision on Admissibility, 12 December 2001.

[136] Application no 52207/99, Decision on Admissibility, 12 December 2001, at para 62. See also Lord Bingham in *R (on the application of Al-Jedda) v Secretary of State for Defence* [2007] UKHL 58, at para 38, referring to absence of a practice of making derogations under article 15 of the European

Practice evidencing their agreement on this was found in the lack of derogations under article 15 of the Convention.

While subsequent practice in the form of another treaty or treaties may confirm a possible reading of the text, subsequent practice evidenced by conduct in relation to a different agreement is not admissible to establish an interpretation which does not lie in the words used in the text being interpreted. This is shown by the analysis by a Chamber of the ICJ in *Land, Island and Maritime Frontier Dispute (El Salvador/Honduras: Nicaragua intervening).*[137] One aspect of the dispute was whether the special agreement which referred the dispute to a Chamber of the ICJ empowered the court to 'delimit' the maritime boundary. The special agreement asked the court to 'determine the legal situation of the island and the maritime spaces', in contrast with conferring jurisdiction on the court 'to delimit the boundary line' regarding the land frontier. The significance of this distinction lay in the position of the disputing parties as to the legal status of the waters in question. El Salvador claimed that they were subject to a condominium in favour of the three coastal states and that delimitation would therefore be inappropriate, whereas Honduras argued that there was a community of interests among the coastal states which necessitated a judicial delimitation of the maritime space.

Having considered the ordinary meaning of the terms of the special agreement and the context, and finding that these excluded its jurisdiction to delimit, the Chamber considered the argument of Honduras that pursuant to identical wording in a General Treaty of Peace between the same parties in 1980, a Joint Frontier Commission acting under that treaty had entertained proposals in relation to maritime delimitation. The Chamber held, with specific reference to article 31(3)(b) of the Vienna Convention, that practice under a different treaty could not prevail over the absence of a specific reference to delimitation in the text on which Honduras sought to base jurisdiction. Further, the practice in other special agreements conferring jurisdiction on the Court to make a delimitation had been to spell out very clearly what was asked of the court.[138] Evidently, practice under agreements of the same type as that in issue could be taken into account to support the ordinary meaning of terms used in their context, particularly where the established practice had not been followed.

4.2.2 Combining action with absence of reaction

To find agreement on meaning from practice may require examining a combination of action by one or more states with subsequent responsive action or inaction by others. The principle that there may be circumstances in which an act by one state calls for a reaction by another has been recognized by the ICJ. In the *Temple* case, a dispute between Cambodia and Thailand as to sovereignty over

---

Convention on Human Rights when conducting peacekeeping operations under UN auspices as an element of interpretation admissible under article 31(3)(b) of the Vienna Convention.

[137] [1992] ICJ Reports 351.   [138] [1992] ICJ Reports 351, at 585–86, paras 379–80.

the region of the Temple of Preah Vihear, relevant maps had been handed over. Even if there had had been no acknowledgement by conduct that these maps had been delivered, the Court found that 'it is clear that the circumstances were such as called for some reaction, within a reasonable period, on the part of the Siamese authorities'.[139]

Fifteen years later, a Court of Arbitration, in the *Beagle Channel* case between Argentina and Chile, noted that the Vienna Convention provision on subsequent practice did not specify the ways in which agreement could be manifested. In the context of acts of jurisdiction by Chile, which were public and well-known to Argentina and which could only derive from the treaty in issue, the Court held that 'the silence of Argentina permits the inference that the acts tended to confirm an interpretation of the meaning of the Treaty independent of the acts of jurisdiction themselves'.[140]

The significance of absence of responsive conduct can also be illustrated by the *Assange* case before the UK Supreme Court (although the application of the Vienna Convention to the Council of the European Union's Framework Decision on the European Arrest Warrant was not expected by the parties).[141] A European Arrest Warrant issued by the Swedish Prosecuting Authority requested the arrest and surrender of Julian Assange then in England. The issue was whether a state prosecutor constituted a 'judicial authority', the entity competent to issue such a warrant under the Framework Decision.

That several states had public prosecutors issuing warrants at the time at which the Framework Decision was drawn up is more a pertinent circumstance of conclusion than a matter of interpretative practice. However, that prosecutors in several different states functioned as judicial authorities in implementing the Decision without a murmur of dissent from states which had appointed judges for this function, and as the reports to the bodies reviewing operation of the system did not voice any objection, in the view of the majority of the judges there was sufficient practice to amount to agreement on the meaning of the term. Hence the practice consisted of action on the part of those states which appointed prosecutors as judicial authorities, while there was absence of action by those who might have objected. The judges approved the helpful account by Villiger of what the Vienna provision requires:

… it requires active practice of some parties to the treaty. The active practice should be consistent rather than haphazard and it should have occurred with a certain frequency.

---

[139] *Case Concerning the Temple of Preah Vihear (Cambodia v Thailand)* [1962] ICJ Reports 6, at 23; and on silence as a possible element of an agreement under article 31 (3), see further Nolte, (ILC Special Rapporteur), 'Second Report on subsequent agreements and subsequent practice in relation to interpretation of treaties', A/CN.4/671 (26 March 2014), pp 29–33, paras 58–70, and Nolte, *Treaties and Subsequent Practice*, 192–5.

[140] *Dispute between Argentina and Chile concerning the Beagle Channel* XXI (Pt II) UNRIAA 53, Award of 18 February 1977, at 187, para 169(a).

[141] *Assange v The Swedish Prosecution Authority* [2012] UKSC 22; on the approach of the UK Supreme Court to the Vienna rules in this case, see Chapter 4, section 4.2.2 above.

However, the subsequent practice must *establish the agreement of the parties regarding its interpretation.* Thus, it will have been acquiesced in by the other parties; and no other party will have raised an objection.[142]

4.3 Parties participating in the practice

4.3.1 Practice must be attributable to parties

The Vienna rule refers to 'any subsequent practice' which establishes 'the agreement of *the parties*'. To be relevant, practice must be attributable to the parties to the treaty.[143] Hence the first issue is what acts or pronouncements are attributable to parties (generally states, but also potentially international organizations). The principle is that practice must be under the authority of the state, meaning here any manifestation of its executive, legislative, or judicial branches. Thus, in considering its jurisdiction over claims involving standby letters of credit in a dispute between the USA and Iran, an arbitral tribunal rejected an assertion that settlements between American and Iranian banks could be viewed as subsequent practice in interpretation of a treaty because, although the Iranian Bank Markazi, as the central bank of Iran, was an entity of the Iranian state, the US banks were not entities of the USA.[144] The fact that the respective banks had alluded to standby letters of credit in their own settlement negotiations did not amount to practice showing that such letters of credit were included within the deposits and assets covered by the agreement between the two states so as to bring the matter within the tribunal's jurisdiction.

4.3.2 Agreement, not practice, of all parties is required

A second issue is the relationship and effect of the words 'any' subsequent practice and agreement of 'the parties'. The wording of article 31(3)(b) does not require that the practice be performed by all the parties; but does the agreement have to be that of *all* parties? Ordinarily, the definite article before parties would suggest 'all' rather than 'some' parties. That this was meant to be the case is confirmed by the development of the provision as recorded in the work of the ILC:

The text provisionally adopted in 1964 spoke of a practice which 'establishes the understanding of all the parties.' By omitting the word 'all' the Commission did not intend to

---

[142] *Assange v The Swedish Prosecution Authority* [2012] UKSC 22, at para 130, quoting M E Villger *Commentary on the 1969 Vienna Convention on the Law of Treaties* (Leiden: Nijhoff, 2009), 431, at para 22 (footnotes omitted; original emphasis); but cf *Ministry of Justice, Lithuania v Bucnys* [2013] UKSC 71, at paras 38–9, considered in Chapter 4, section 4.2.2 above.

[143] In its work on subsequent agreements and subsequent practice in relation to interpretation of treaties, the ILC has proposed in draft conclusion 5 that subsequent practice 'may consist of any conduct in the application of a treaty which is attributable to a party to the treaty under international law', borrowing phraseology from it articles on the responsibility of States for internationally wrongful acts: Report on the work of its sixty-fifth session (2013) General Assembly Official Records Sixty-eighth Session, Supplement No. 10 (A/68/10), Chapter 4, p 41 and commentary at pp 42–7.

[144] Case A16 *USA v Iran*, 5 Iran–US Claims Trib Rep 57, at 62–64 and 70–71.

change the rule. It considered that the phrase 'the understanding of the parties' necessarily means 'the parties as a whole.' It omitted the word 'all' merely to avoid any possible misconception that every party must individually have engaged in the practice where it suffices that it should have accepted the practice.[145]

Noting that the wording ultimately adopted in the Convention up-rated the concept of 'understanding' to 'agreement', it nevertheless seems clear that participation of all the parties in the practice is not required. What is required is their manifested or imputable agreement. Participation in the practice is obviously the clearest evidence of this. Thus the principle appears to be that there must be a sufficient nexus between the parties to the treaty and the practice, as distinct from actual participation of all parties in the practice concerned.

An oblique illustration of this was the dispute between Indonesia and Malaysia over certain islands.[146] This involved historical investigation of conduct of predecessor states. Dealings between the Dutch government and the local Sultan may well have taken account of a 1891 Convention between the Dutch government and Great Britain; and amendments in 1893 to the earlier Dutch 'Contracts of Vassalage' with the Sultan of Bulungan may have provided a further indication of the interpretation given by the Netherlands government to the 1891 Convention (as was asserted by Indonesia). Nevertheless, Great Britain (one of the links in the chain of Malaysia's asserted title) had had no part in this and the ICJ concluded that these transactions were *res inter alios acta* for Great Britain.[147] Great Britain had therefore not concurred in the practice.

4.3.3 Practice of some parties only does not interpret a treaty 'inter se' unless so agreed

Quite a different question is whether some states parties to a multilateral treaty can through their practice establish an interpretation which becomes binding on them alone even though it differs from that of the majority of the parties. There are two clear grounds for rejecting this possibility, but one argument appears, at least initially, to go in its favour. First, the principle underlying the rule on use of subsequent practice in treaty interpretation is that a correct interpretation can only emerge from concordant practice coupled with unalloyed agreement—that latter being at a very minimum evidenced by the absence of any disagreement. This requirement for the agreement of all parties is underlined in the ILC Report quoted above. Second, the principle of autonomous interpretation precludes the possibility of legitimate differences of interpretation among states (always bearing

---

[145] [1966] *Yearbook of the ILC*, vol II, 222, para 15.
[146] *Sovereignty over Pulau Litigan and Pulau Sipadan (Indonesia/Malaysia)* [2002] ICJ Reports 625; see further section 4.4 below.
[147] *Sovereignty over Pulau Litigan and Pulau Sipadan (Indonesia/Malaysia)* at para 64.

in mind the distinction between this proposition and the case of the treaty provision whose single, correct interpretation allows for a range of possible acts or applications).[148]

The only wrinkle in this clear position might be thought to lie in the provisions of the Vienna Convention which allow 'modification' of treaties in certain circumstances, 'modification' meaning in this context a change effective for some parties only (article 41). If this can be achieved by explicit agreement, why not by convergent practice of just some parties? First, it is to be noted that article 41 includes procedural requirements as well as specific conditions for modification. Article 41(2) requires that the states making the modification notify the other parties of their intention to conclude an agreement doing this, and of the modification to the treaty which the agreement is to make. Such notifications do not fit within the notion of convergent practice. If there is a preliminary agreement sufficient to enable states to announce an intention to modify, then the next step envisaged by the Vienna Convention is the agreement doing that, not convergent practice. More generally, in the absence of clear guidance in case law (or elsewhere), modification by practice of some parties only would be inconsistent with the two principles stated immediately above. The interpretative value of subsequent practice, which by definition is not a formal, textual agreement, is wholly dependent on the practice being concordant, the agreement being that of all parties and the resultant interpretation being a single autonomous one.

4.3.4 Practice of some parties in absence of that of others

More difficult is the position in the case of a multilateral treaty where some parties have established a practice which other parties have not had occasion to emulate or on which to act differently. This may be a matter of how to view the evidence of agreement (considered in the next section) or it may be the result of the way a particular provision is framed and is intended to work. Where the language in issue is of a kind that the meaning can really only be elucidated by practice, such practice as there is may indicate considerations to be taken into account and factors which are to be balanced in applying the treaty without revealing an all-purpose meaning.

An example of this is the provisions of the Vienna Convention on Diplomatic Relations which requires parties to take all appropriate steps to protect the premises of another state's diplomatic mission 'against any intrusion or damage and to prevent any disturbance of the peace of the mission or impairment of its dignity' (article 22) and in relation to a diplomatic agent to 'take all appropriate steps to prevent any attack on his person, freedom or dignity' (article 29). The term 'dignity', and what constitutes its impairment or an attack on it, leaves open quite a range of possibilities.

---

[148] See Chapter 1, section 4.1 above and *R v Secretary of State for the Home Department, ex parte Adan* [2001] 2 AC 477.

In *Minister for Foreign Affairs and Trade v Magno*[149] the Australian High Court considered these treaty provisions in the context of a protest against the conduct of the Indonesian authorities in East Timor. The protestors placed a number of white crosses on public land within 50 metres of the Indonesian embassy in Australia. The Australian Minister certified that the presence of these objects on that land could lead to the impairment of the dignity, or to disturbance of the peace, of the mission or the head, or other diplomatic agent, of the mission. In interpreting the term 'dignity', the court found little help in dictionary definitions, identified the purposes of the treaty regime, and (in the leading judgment) examined state practice. The judgment found that in the context of the defined functions of a diplomatic mission (article 3 of the Vienna Convention on Diplomatic Relations), the purpose of articles 22 and 29 was to permit diplomatic representatives to operate with maximum efficiency, quality, and freedom of action and that the extent of any interference with the functions of a diplomatic mission must be highly relevant in considering the obligation to protect impairment of dignity. However, the judgment noted that international application of the Convention by democratic countries showed that another consideration, particularly significant when dealing with political demonstrations outside embassies, was taking account of the legal principle of freedom of speech. Giving close attention to the position in the USA and the UK, where there was substantial evidence of practice, the judgment found:

… both of these major countries have taken a restrictive view of 'impairment of dignity', linking it to breaches of the peace, and the disruption of the mission's essential functions. In both countries only actual interferences are proscribed. Both nations have interpreted the Convention obligations in a way which takes into account and gives considerable weight to freedom of expression. The United States, in particular, has narrowly interpreted its obligation with respect to preventing the impairment of dignity.…

The importance of this State practice is that it suggests that a narrow interpretation is consistent with compliance with the Convention obligations. If the practices of the United States and the United Kingdom are insufficient to make a conclusive finding as to what ought to be the Australian interpretation of the Convention, they certainly provide influential examples of how two important democratic countries with experience in the field have interpreted it.[150]

It should be noted, however, that this was a case where application and interpretation ran very closely together. The notion of 'dignity' is somewhat elastic when it has to be fitted to novel facts.[151]

4.4 'Establishing' agreement

To be admissible under the rule, the practice must be such as to establish the agreement of the parties. This is widely taken as requiring that the practice be 'concordant', that is identical or sufficiently close to identical as to show that the parties

---

[149] 112 ALR 529, 37 FCR 298.   [150] 37 FCR 298, at 337–38.
[151] See *Aziz v Aziz and Others* [2007] EWCA Civ 712.

have demonstrated their agreement.[152] It does not, however, necessarily mean that there has been abundant practice by all parties to the treaty. It is sufficient if there is practice of one or more parties and good evidence that the other parties have endorsed the practice. Hence the matter may be largely one of how a court or other interpreter views the evidence. The example given above in the Australian decision in *Magno* indicates how practice may help in showing the boundaries of a range of acceptable meanings.

The difficulty of locating, collating, and assessing evidence of practice of states makes short-cuts particularly attractive. This is, of course, quite admissible where reputable studies have been carried out by international organizations, research institutes, and others. For example, in the case of the UN Refugee Convention:

The Preamble to the Convention notes that the United Nations High Commissioner for Refugees is charged with the task of supervising international conventions providing for the protection of Refugees...The UNHCR Handbook [on Procedures and Criteria for Determining Refugee Status] was published in 1979 upon the request (as its Preface shows) of the Executive Committee of the High Commissioners Programme to consider the possibility of issuing—for the guidance of Governments—a handbook relating to procedures and criteria for determining refugee status...

...the issue we must decide is whether or not, as a matter of law, the scope of Art.1A(2) extends to persons who fear persecution by non-State agents in circumstances where the State is not complicit in the persecution, whether because it is unwilling or unable (including instances where no effective State authority exists) to afford protection. We entertain no doubt but that such persons, whose case is established on the facts, are entitled to the Conventions protection... This interpretation is supported by the approach taken in paragraph 65 of the UNHCR Handbook. We have described the Handbook's genesis, to which we attach some importance. While the Handbook is not by any means itself a source of law, many signatory States have accepted the guidance which on their behalf the UNHCR was asked to provide, and in those circumstances it constitutes, in our judgment, good evidence of what has come to be international practice within Art.31(3)(b) of the Vienna Convention.[153]

Obviously the extent and evidence of state practice required to establish an interpretation may be affected by the context of the treaty provision in issue and the scheme of the particular Convention. For example, the Vienna Convention on Diplomatic Relations, 1961 provides in its article 47 that parties are not to discriminate between states in application of the convention, but that it will not be regarded as discrimination where the receiving state applies any of the provisions restrictively because of a restrictive application of that provision to its mission in the sending state, or where by custom or agreement states extend to each other more favourable treatment than is required by the Convention. This implicitly acknowledges scope for establishing the precise level of treatment by practice, with

---

[152] See, eg, *Japan—Alcoholic Beverages*, section 4.1.3 above; and Sinclair, *The Vienna Convention*, at 137.

[153] *R v Secretary of State for the Home Department, ex parte Adan* [2001] 2 AC 477, at 490 and 500.

an assurance of bilateral reciprocity. Thus practice may establish an interpretation where generally accepted by the diplomatic corps in a particular capital.

An instance illustrating this in the UK is *Jimenez v Inland Revenue Commissioners*[154] where one issue was whether the appellant, although a member of the service staff of a diplomatic mission, was disqualified from exemption from taxation by reason of being permanently resident in the UK within the meaning of article 37(3) of the Vienna Convention on Diplomatic Relations. In holding that she was permanently resident in this sense, the judge considered a longstanding circular that had been issued by the Foreign and Commonwealth Office to the Heads of Diplomatic Missions in London giving guidance on the determination of whether or not particular persons employed in diplomatic missions should be regarded as persons permanently resident in the UK. Although the context of the circular was the administration of diplomatic relations between the government and foreign missions, and included a consultation procedure to resolve any 'difference of opinion' which might arise between a Mission and Her Majesty's Government as to whether an individual was permanently resident in the UK, the judge held that it constituted practice for the purposes of interpretation:

In accordance with article 31(3) of the Vienna Convention on the Law of Treaties... I ought to take into account 'any subsequent practice...'.... [T]he provisions of the 1969 FCO Circular...have never been challenged by the Heads of Mission in the United Kingdom...Therefore I consider I should have regard to it in accordance with article 31(3) of the Vienna Convention on the Law of Treaties, and I further consider that it is reflective of customary international law which, by the fifth indent of the Preamble to the 1961 Convention 'should continue to govern questions not expressly regulated by the provisions of the [1961] Convention'.[155]

Most commonly, it will be a question of assessing each instance of practice to take account of all the evidence. In the Indonesia/Malaysia islands dispute, the ICJ examined a number of elements that were put forward as subsequent practice.[156] The central issue was whether what was essentially a land frontier, which had been developed through a series of transactions involving treaties made by predecessors of the disputing states from the nineteenth century onwards, extended out to sea to identify sovereignty over two islands. Indonesia sought to characterize as subsequent practice a map in an Explanatory Memorandum drawn up by the Dutch government to accompany its draft law ratifying a Convention of 1891 with the Great Britain. Although this Memorandum and map had been reported to the British government by their diplomatic agent at The Hague, it was not in any way a document recording any dealings between the parties to the Convention or endorsed by the British government and thus the Court found that this particular item was not subsequent practice for the purposes of the Vienna rule.[157]

---

[154] [2004] STC (SCD) 371; [2004] STI 1939.
[155] [2004] STC (SCD) 371, at para 69.
[156] *Sovereignty over Pulau Litigan and Pulau Sipadan (Indonesia/Malaysia)* [2002] ICJ Reports 625, at 656–65, paras 59–80.
[157] [2002] ICJ Reports 625, at 656, paras 59–61.

The Court also excluded from consideration as subsequent practice transactions between the Netherlands and the local Sultan following the 1981 Convention. These transactions could not reveal any agreement of Great Britain as it was not a party to them. The Court did, however, find that the work of a mixed Commission and Agreements of 1915 and 1928 were relevant to the interpretation of the 1891 Convention (showing that there had been scope for a more exact delimitation of the boundary, not its extension out to sea). The Court's attention was also directed to internal consideration by the Dutch authorities over where maritime boundaries should be drawn, one possibility being an extension of the land boundary. This was not taken up with the British government but was seen by the Court as further evidence that the Dutch had not understood the 1891 Convention to extend boundaries seawards generally. Later limitations in grants of oil concessions by Indonesia and Malaysia themselves could not be seen as referable to an interpretation of the 1891 Convention. 'In view of all the foregoing', the Court stated that it 'considers that an examination of the subsequent practice of the parties to the 1891 Convention confirms the conclusions at which the Court has arrived...'.[158] One can see, therefore, that the Court viewed the various acts and transactions put to it as potentially within the ambit of 'subsequent practice', though in relation to particular elements it applied the requirements underlying the Vienna rule to ensure that they reflected agreement.

What is clear is that a mere headcount does not satisfy the requirement to show sufficient practice to evidence agreement (unless the result clearly shows unanimity). How to evaluate the number of participants in a practice can be illustrated by the contrasting situations in the UK cases of *Hoxha* and *Assange*.[159] In *Hoxha* the evidence that a substantial number of states gave refugee status to a range of people extending beyond that required by the text did not indicate an agreed interpretation that such treatment was a requirement of the treaty. In *Assange* a number of states had designated a prosecutor as a judicial authority for the purposes of issue of European Arrest Warrants. That this was not a uniform practice of all Member States did not prevent this type of designation being viewed as showing a subsequent practice having interpretative effect when such designations had been the subject of reports to the European Parliament and the Council of Ministers in several rounds of mutual evaluations and no objection had been raised to the practice.[160]

However, any assessment is dependent on evaluating all the circumstances as is shown by the ICJ's view in the *Whaling* case that the claimant and intervening states had overstated the legal significance of the recommendatory resolutions and the Guidelines of the International Whaling Commission in as much as:

many IWC resolutions were adopted without the support of all States parties to the Convention and, in particular, without the concurrence of Japan [the Respondent state].

---

[158] [2002] ICJ Reports 625, at 665, para 80.

[159] *R (on the application of Hoxha) v Special Adjudicator* [2005] 4 All ER 580 and *Assange v The Swedish Prosecution Authority* [2012] UKSC 22; for a fuller account of *Hoxha* see Chapter 1, section 5.5 above; and cf *Yugraneft Corporation v Rexx Management Corporation* [2010] 1 SCR 649, para [21] (Canadian Supreme Court).

[160] *Assange*, at paras 68–71; but cf *Ministry of Justice, Lithuania v Bucnys* [2013] UKSC 71.

Thus, such instruments cannot be regarded as subsequent agreement to an interpretation of Article VIII [of the Whaling Convention], nor as subsequent practice establishing an agreement of the parties regarding the interpretation of the treaty within the meaning of subparagraphs (a) and (b), respectively, of paragraph (3) of Article 31 of the Vienna Convention on the Law of Treaties.[161]

4.5 Subsequent practice linked with informal agreement, understandings, or other instruments

Subsequent practice is sometimes confirmatory of an interpretation recorded or intimated in an instrument related to a treaty but not falling precisely within one or other of the categories in the Vienna rules. If the practice yields a clear interpretation, it does not matter too much what the precise status is of the instrument that fostered it. Thus, for example, the Explanatory Reports that accompany Council of Europe conventions have been viewed as preparatory work (ie within article 32, since they are prepared before the treaties are concluded) or as falling within article 31 (as agreements or instruments within paragraph (2)).[162] As preparatory work, these reports would strictly be only supplementary means of interpretation for use in the circumstances indicated in article 32 of the Vienna Convention. If within article 31(2), they form part of the context. However, once implemented in practice, their interpretative effect is confirmed, whatever their correct designation.[163]

Subsequent practice may also have a significant role in interpretation of instruments to which the Vienna rules are applied by analogy, or which are derived from a treaty or made under powers in one. For example, the rules may apply to the UN Security Council's resolutions where later resolutions may constitute subsequent interpretative practice, as might the work of Sanctions Committees overseeing implementation of mandatory resolutions of the Security Council.[164]

---

[161] *Whaling in the Antarctic (Australia v Japan: New Zealand intervening)*, Judgment of 31 March 2014, para 83.

[162] See *R v Secretary of State for the Home Department, Ex parte Read* [1989] AC 1014, at 1052.

[163] Cf *Pulp Mills on the River Uruguay (Argentina v Uruguay)* [2010] ICJ Reports 14, at 63, para 131, where the ICJ concluded that an understanding recorded in minutes of a meeting of foreign ministers of Argentina and Uruguay would have had the effect of relieving Uruguay of its obligations under a treaty establishing procedures relating to the river Uruguay only if Uruguay had complied with the terms of the understanding; see also *R v Secretary of State for the Home Department, ex parte Mullen* [2004] UKHL 18, at para 48, where prospective state practice, which would be based on an Explanatory Report, was expressly recognized as directly relevant to interpretation of a treaty provision by virtue of article 31(3)(b) of the Vienna Convention.

[164] See M Wood, 'The Interpretation of Security Council resolutions' (1998) 2 *Max Planck Yearbook of United Nations Law* 73, at 92, where the possibility of application of the Vienna rules is advanced with caution; see also at 94–95, suggesting that subsequent practice of states, in implementing such resolutions, or for example in their legislation to comply with orders of the International Criminal Tribunal for the Former Yugoslavia, even if not sufficient to establish agreement might nevertheless have an interpretative role as supplementary means.

4.6 Subsequent practice and 'evolutive' interpretation distinguished

Where a provision in a treaty is open to different possible interpretations, practice of the parties may coalesce to provide a clear common approach. However, such a firming-up process does not occur in every case. Obviously the establishment of practice is dependent on states having occasion to take some action in application of the treaty. The process also depends to some extent on how the provisions come to be open to different possible interpretations. Practice may resolve deliberate or unrealized ambiguity, or may be part of the development of the application of a treaty; but some treaties in their nature are designed to allow for a more progressive development or elaboration of the treaty.

The latter has given rise to the idea of 'evolutive' interpretation. In a joint dissenting opinion, seven judges of the European Court indicated the difference between subsequent practice and evolutive interpretation.[165] The issue was whether entitlement to health benefits under statutory social security schemes gave rise to 'civil rights and obligations' and thus required the 'fair and public hearing within a reasonable time by an independent and impartial tribunal established by law' guaranteed in article 6(1) of the European Convention on Human Rights. After finding that state practice had not developed to the point where the parties could be said to be agreed on the 'civil' or other character of an entitlement to such health benefits, the dissenting judges found that an evolutive interpretation of article 6(1) led to no different conclusion. The judges explained:

An evolutive interpretation allows variable and changing concepts already contained in the Convention to be construed in the light of modern-day conditions . . . but it does not allow entirely new concepts or spheres of application to be introduced into the Convention: that is a legislative function that belongs to the Member States of the Council of Europe. The desirability of affording proper safeguards for the adjudication of claims in the ever-increasing field of social security is evident. There are, however, limits to evolutive interpretation and the facts of the present case go beyond those limits as far as Article 6 (1) para. 1 (art. 6–1) is concerned.[166]

---

[165] *Feldbrugge v Netherlands*, ECtHR case no 8/1984/80/127 (Judgment of 23 April 1986); for further consideration of evolutionary (evolutive) interpretation, see Chapter 10, section 4 below.

[166] Joint dissenting opinion at paras 23–24; cf the position where practice allows a margin of appreciation to parties as in *Ireland v United Kingdom* (1978) 2 EHRR 25 at 96, para 220 where, in relation to derogations from the European Convention on Human Rights in circumstances of a public emergency threatening the life of the nation, the ECtHR concluded that 'the interpretation of article 15 must leave a place for progressive adaptations'. Somewhat similar is the view taken in the UN Human Rights Committee as explained by G Nolte (ILC Special Rapporteur) in his First Report on Subsequent Agreements etc, A/CN.4/660 (13 March 2013), at para 21: 'One important aspect of the Human Rights Committee's interpretative approach is its evolutive understanding of the rights of the Covenant. For example, in the case of *Yoon and Choi v The Republic of Korea*, the Committee stressed that any right contained in the Covenant evolved over time, and by this reasoning justified a certain departure from its own prior jurisprudence. However, in the case of *Atasoy and Sarkut v Turkey*, the Committee has emphasised that evolutive interpretation "cannot go beyond the letter and spirit of the treaty or what the States parties initially and explicitly so intended".' (footnotes giving case citations omitted)

The indication that evolutive interpretation must be based on concepts already in the treaty suggests that this has more limited potential for extending meanings than does concordant practice of the parties. Since the parties are, acting collectively through their concordant practice, sovereign to make further treaty provisions, they can take interpretation further than can a person or body charged with the role of independent interpretation. Saying this, however, takes the matter into investigation of whether the parties really are interpreting the treaty or reach a point at which they amend it through their practice, which is the topic of the next section.[167]

4.7 Subsequent practice and amendment differentiated

Whether subsequent practice in the application of the treaty which establishes the agreement of the parties regarding its interpretation is in fact interpretation or amendment is not always easy to discern. Does this distinction matter? Even if the outcome is properly construed as an amendment, for the purposes of application of a provision, the effect should be no different whether what is being applied is an interpretation reflecting the agreement of the parties or an amendment reflecting the agreement of the parties. Further, if one accepts that every application of a treaty is preceded, no matter for how fleeting a moment, by an act of interpretation, any subsequent practice or subsequent agreement to an amendment constituted by practice would each form a valid component of an interpretation.

To accept this, however, would be to ignore the importance of treaty relations, procedural difficulties, and the fact that decisions of courts and tribunals, though in principle only binding on the parties to the proceedings, do have an effect comparable to precedent (albeit their authority will depend more on the cogency of the reasoning than the status of the adjudicator). Thus treaty relations may suppose that a procedure has been followed for amendment giving not only parties but potential parties an opportunity to participate (for example, in a revision conference for a multilateral treaty). Procedural difficulties may occur where one body is empowered to interpret a treaty while another has authority to determine disputes. In such circumstances a tribunal determining a dispute may have to decide whether an act described as an interpretation really is one.[168]

The potential importance of practice constituting agreement of the parties on interpretation, and the relatively lesser importance of whether the meaning constitutes an interpretation of the terms of the treaty or an agreed departure from them,

---

[167] On evolutionary interpretation, see further Chapter 10, section 4 below.

[168] See, eg, *Arbitration under Chapter Eleven of NAFTA, Pope & Talbot v Canada (Award in respect of Damages)* (2002) 41 ILM 1347, where the Free Trade Commission, a body empowered to give interpretations of the North American Free Trade Agreement issued an 'interpretation' relating to a point on which an arbitral tribunal had made a decision but had not yet awarded damages. The Tribunal found that had it been required to adjudicate on the nature of the Commission's act, it would have found it not to be an interpretation but an amendment: Award of 31 May 2002, *Arbitration under Chapter Eleven of NAFTA, Pope & Talbot v Canada (Award in respect of Damages)* (2002) 41 ILM 1347, at para 47.

was presciently described by Waldock in his introduction of proposed articles on interpretation:

Subsequent practice when it is consistent and embraces all the parties would appear to be decisive of the meaning to be attached to the treaty, at any rate when it indicates that the parties consider the interpretation to be binding upon them. In these cases, subsequent practice as an element of treaty interpretation and as an element in the formation of a tacit agreement overlap and the meaning derived from the practice becomes an authentic interpretation established by agreement. Furthermore, if the interpretation adopted by the parties diverges, as sometimes happens, from the natural and ordinary meaning of the terms, there may be a blurring of the line between the *interpretation* and the *amendment* of a treaty by subsequent practice.[169]

There are, however, only some isolated suggestions that practice may be taken into account in the course of interpreting and applying a treaty in such a way that a result can be found which acknowledges the practice without the distinction between interpretation and amendment proving an obstacle.[170] This can be illustrated by two judgments of the ECtHR. In its judgment in *Soering v the United Kingdom*[171] the Court accepted that an established practice among parties to the European Convention on Human Rights could give rise to an amendment of the Convention, and held that a general abolition of capital punishment in states' penal policy could amount to subsequent practice establishing the agreement of the parties to abrogate the exception in article 2(1) of the Convention (right to life except in execution of a sentence of a court in accordance with the law).[172] The Court found, however, that by adopting a specific protocol (no 6) committing parties to the protocol to abolish capital punishment in time of peace, the parties to the Convention showed an intention to use the normal method for its

---

[169] Waldock, Third Report, [1964] *Yearbook of the ILC*, vol II, p 60, para 25, footnote omitted, emphasis in original; but care is needed in considering the question of amendment through practice because of the history of rejection of explicit provision for this at the Vienna Conference: see Nolte (ILC Special Rapporteur), 'Second Report on subsequent agreements and subsequent practice in relation to interpretation of treaties', A/CN.4/671 (26 March 2014), pp 51–53, paras 117–123. Note, however, the issue here is one of whether there is a distinction to be drawn between 'interpretation' and 'amendment', not between 'interpretation' and 'modification'. In the Vienna Convention 'modification' is carefully distinguished from 'amendment' (though this had not been finally established when the ILC drafts were first considered at the Vienna Conference). This distinction is significant in the case of interpretation of a treaty in that 'modification' in the Convention's sense could never be achieved purely by practice as envisaged in article 31(3)(b) because that provision is predication on agreement of *all* the parties, while modification is by the Vienna Convention's usage (article 41 in particular) operative for only *some* of the parties. 'Modification' is, however, commonly used in discussion of the present issue to refer to change effective for all parties, even though this blurs the Convention's clear usage.

[170] See, eg, *Air Transport Arbitration (USA v France)*, Award of 22 December 1963, 38 ILR 182, where an arbitral tribunal found that a schedule to a bilateral treaty specifying points which could be served on an air route had been extended by repeated permission to serve a point not listed and consequent operation of services including that point, but this case was before the conclusion of the Vienna Convention and the tribunal seems to have been describing something more akin to estoppel than interpretation or amendment; see also Nolte (ILC Special Rapporteur), 'Second Report' (26 March 2014), p 56, paras 130–31.

[171] Judgment of 7 July 1989, Series A no 161, p 40.

[172] Judgment of 7 July 1989, at para 103.

amendment. Accordingly, the practice of the parties did not at that time lead to article 3 of the same Convention (prohibition of inhuman or degrading treatment) being interpreted to encompass prohibition of the death penalty.[173]

In contrast, when the same Court came to consider the same point more recently in *Öcalan v Turkey* its view was that it could not now exclude the possibility that the parties to the European Convention on Human Rights had agreed through their practice to change the effect of article 2 as regards capital punishment in peacetime, so that the implementation of the death penalty could now be regarded as inhuman and degrading treatment contrary to article 3.[174] This took account of the fact that 43 of 44 parties had abolished the death penalty in peacetime and the forty-fourth had imposed a moratorium on executions. That practice was to be assessed along with the fact that all parties had signed the Protocol requiring abolition of the death penalty in peacetime and all but three had ratified it. This was combined with the policy of the Council of Europe requiring all new members to abolish the death penalty, also taking account of the adoption of a further Protocol proscribing the death penalty even in time of war (which supported the assessment of the policy).[175] The Court did not have to reach a firm decision on this point as it found that to implement a death sentence following what in the particular case had been an unfair trial would run counter to the Convention in any event. Nevertheless, the reasoning illustrates how interpretation of a treaty provision could be affected by practice of the parties revealing, in combination with other elements, an agreement which substantially changes the original meaning of a text albeit there was the rather particular circumstance in the situation posited by the ECtHR that the practice was in proleptic application of a properly adopted amendment.[176]

An example of interpretation by reference to practice which is often cited is in an advisory opinion of the ICJ. This concerned the well-known matter of the voting practice in the UN Security Council under article 27(3) of the UN Charter and that treaty's prescription relating to votes of the five permanent members in relation to the rest of the total of 15 members. The provision requires that decisions of the Security Council in all matters other than procedural ones are made 'by an *affirmative* vote of nine members including the *concurring* votes of the permanent members' (emphasis added). The combination of 'affirmative' and 'concurring' very strongly suggests that on these matters all the permanent members must vote in favour of a resolution for a decision to be duly made. Yet from virtually its earliest days, the requirement of 'concurring' in relation to the votes of permanent members was interpreted as fulfilled by abstention or absence as much as by a vote

---

[173] Judgment of 7 July 1989, at paras 103–4.
[174] Application no 46221/99 (Judgment of 12 March 2003).
[175] Application no 46221/99 (Judgment of 12 March 2003), paras 192–98.
[176] See also *Al-Saadoon and Mufdhi* v *UK*, Application no 61498/08 (Judgment of 2 March 2010) which follows the reasoning in *Öcalan v Turkey*; but on the particular circumstances, see further Nolte (ILC Special Rapporteur), 'Second Report on Subsequent agreements and subsequent practice in relation to interpretation of treaties', A/CN.4/671 (26 March 2014), pp 56–7, paras 133–35.

in favour. This converted the apparently ordinary meaning of 'concurring votes' in the case of permanent members to (in effect) not casting a negative vote (leading to such a negative vote being generally labelled a 'veto'). The ICJ has acknowledged this interpretation.[177]

While there may be scope for questioning whether practice by an organ of limited membership within an organization may itself constitute practice which establishes the agreement of the parties to the constitution of the organization (on which see next section), assuming that the absence of objection over a long period amounts to practice complying with the Vienna rule's requirements, this seems an example of an interpretation close to accepting amendment by practice, particularly given that the preparatory work of the Charter suggests an intent contrary to the adopted practice on the part of the eventual permanent members of the Security Council.[178]

The ICJ has given further apparent support to the possibility that subsequent practice may produce a departure from what might have been the interpretation contemporaneous with conclusion of the treaty, a departure based on tacit agreement between the parties. In its judgment in the *Dispute regarding Navigational and Related Rights (Costa Rica v Nicaragua)*, the ICJ prefaced its analysis of the case with some general propositions on taking account of a change in the meaning of a treaty provision where a term's meaning is no longer the same as it was at the date of conclusion. [179]

The case concerned the extent of Costa Rica's rights on the section of the San Juan river where the right bank, ie the Costa Rican side, marks the border between Costa Rica and Nicaragua pursuant to an 1858 'Treaty of Limits'. In considering whether the right of vessels of Costa Rica to navigate the river included the right to conduct activities such as tourism and navigation of government vessels, the Court first determined that the Spanish phrase *con objetos de comercio* meant 'for the purposes of commerce' rather than 'with articles of trade'. Thus a key question which the Court had to determine was whether 'commerce' was limited to what that term embraced at the time of the 1858 treaty or whether it should take account of subsequent changes in the term's meaning.

The Court accepted that a treaty was be interpreted in the light of the determination of the parties' common intention as reflected in the treaty, that is necessarily contemporaneous with the treaty's conclusion but as identified through the text.[180] The Court followed this by stating: 'This does not however signify that,

---

[177] See *Legal Consequence for States of the Continued Presence of South Africa in Namibia (South West Africa)* [1971] ICJ Reports 16, at 22, para 22; and see Aust, *Modern Treaty Law and Practice* (Cambridge: CUP, 3rd edn, 2012), 215–16.

[178] Aust, *Modern Treaty Law and Practice*, at 216.

[179] [2009] ICJ Reports 214, at 237, para 47.

[180] [2009] ICJ Reports 214, at 242, para 63; it should be noted parenthetically that the Court was avowedly applying the Vienna rules, was not embarking on a search for the 'intention' of the parties by any means other than the rules, but indicated that the relevant provision was to be interpreted 'like any other provision of a treaty, i.e. in accordance with the intentions of its authors as reflected by the text of the treaty and the other relevant factors in terms of interpretation' (Judgment, para 48).

where a term's meaning is no longer the same as it was at the date of conclusion, no account should ever be taken of its meaning at the time when the treaty is to be interpreted for purposes of applying it.'[181] The Court noted the latter occurrence includes situations where 'the subsequent practice of the parties, within the meaning of Article 31 (3) (b) of the Vienna Convention, can result in a departure from the original intent on the basis of a tacit agreement between the parties'.[182]

While this appears to provide explicit recognition of tacit amendment by subsequent practice as constituting authentic interpretation, it has been noted in the work of the ILC that the Court may have been merely making a point relating to the interpretation of treaties, rather than referring to their amendment, 'since the "original" intent of the parties is not necessarily conclusive for the interpretation of a treaty'.[183] This observation is consistent with the proper use of the Vienna rules and seems more probable than endorsement of tacit amendment.

In terms of dynamics between treaty parties, however, how could a supposed amendment by practice come to be challenged? For practice to meet the requirements of article 31(3)(b) there must be no treaty party dissenting from the practice. Yet for any challenge to arise on the ground that the resultant meaning given to the treaty is inadmissible because it amounts to a procedurally defective amendment, at least one party must express opposition. To support a practice, or to acquiesce in it sufficiently to be shown to have agreed to it, and then challenge it seems an improbable posture to assume.[184]

Thus one difficulty in investigating issues of interpretations encroaching on, or circumventing, amendment provisions in treaties is how it can be shown that there is a properly established interpretation which may have been changed by practice such as to constitute an amendment. The case of the UN Security Council voting practice, for example, was not one where an established interpretation was overturned. Only where an incontrovertible meaning is now changed by practice to a meaning which the term in issue could not bear as its ordinary meaning would a clear conflict between interpretation and amendment truly arise, but this would be a conflict engineered by all the parties collectively. There is little in the case law of international courts and tribunals that really fits this specification, the nearest cases having been presented in the work of the ILC on subsequent agreements and practice and shown to be distinguishable from the clear-cut case.[185]

---

[181] [2009] ICJ Reports 214. at 242, para 64.

[182] [2009] ICJ Reports 214. at 242, para 64.

[183] Nolte (ILC Special Rapporteur), 'Second Report on Subsequent agreements and subsequent practice in relation to interpretation of treaties', A/CN.4/671 (26 March 2014), p 50, para 115.

[184] The position of those with interests under a treaty may, however, be different if the treaty is of a kind which affords individuals reliance on the treaty; but see, for example, *Hassan v UK*, Application no 29750/09, Judgment of 16 September 2014, para 101, where the ECtHR considered that 'a consistent practice on the part of the High Contracting Parties, subsequent to their ratification of the Convention, could be taken as establishing their agreement not only as regards interpretation but even to modify the text of the Convention'; see also L Hill-Cawthorne 'The Grand Chamber Judgment in *Hassan v UK*', 16 September 2014 <http://www.ejiltalk.org>; as to the practice in issue on derogations from the Convention, see also *Smith v Ministry of Defence* [2013] UKSC 41, at para 60.

[185] Nolte, 'Second Report', A/CN.4/671 (26 March 2014), at pp 52–60.

The proposed draft conclusion in the continuing work of the ILC seems, therefore, the best that can be suggested in advising a presumption that the parties through their practice intend to interpret the treaty rather than change it and noting the lack of general recognition of changed meaning being established by the subsequent practice of the parties.[186] Even were some form of tacit amendment by subsequent practice to be recognized as an interpretative possibility it would be less likely to be readily achieved in the case of multilateral treaties than bilateral ones because of the required degree of participation in the practice, the extent of uniformity which would be necessary, and the unanimity of agreement which would have to be demonstrated.

4.8 Subsequent practice in international organizations

The role of international organizations in treaty interpretation has been considered generally in Chapter 4 above. There is little in the output of international organizations that specifically bears on the role of subsequent practice in the Vienna rules, other than the work of the ILC and the judgments, opinions, and decisions of international courts and tribunals.[187] The current work of the ILC includes consideration of subsequent agreements and subsequent practice in relation to treaty interpretation, but the Commission has not yet considered in any detail treaties establishing international organizations.[188] Subsequent practice under such treaties raises particular issues because the principle underlying this element of the Vienna rules is that practice demonstrating the agreement of the parties as to the meaning of a treaty is a strong indicator of that meaning; but the practice of, or within, an organization is in principle attributable to the organization itself and does not necessarily demonstrate the specific concurrence of the individual parties to the treaty setting it up. Nevertheless, practice within international organizations is taken into account, allying the Vienna rules to a further provision of the Vienna Convention considered below

4.8.1 Whose practice in the organization?

The first point to note is that both the 1969 Vienna Convention and that of 1986 (the latter specifically relating to treaties to which international organizations are parties, but not yet in force) refer to subsequent practice in the application of the treaty which 'establishes the agreement of the parties' regarding its interpretation. This does not say whose practice is to be taken into account. There is no specific

---

[186] Nolte, 'Second Report' on Subsequent agreements and subsequent practice in relation to interpretation of treaties', A/CN.4/671 (26 March 2014), at p 69, para 166, draft conclusion 11.

[187] See C F Amerasinghe, *Principles of Institutional Law of International Organizations* (Cambridge: CUP, 2nd edn, 2005), at 49–55.

[188] See Nolte (ILC Special Rapporteur), 'Second Report', p 33, fn 158, flagging up treaties establishing international organizations as a matter to be addressed more specifically at a later stage of the work on the topic.

requirement here that the practice be that of state parties individually, though it has been noted that in relation to the provision in the 1969 Convention the practice contemplated is that of states, not organizations.[189] A reasonable expectation is that relevant practice will usually be that of those on whom the obligation of performance falls, but obviously this depends on the nature of the obligation and treaty provision in issue.[190] Hence where states by treaty entrust performance of activities to an organization, how those activities are conducted can constitute practice under the treaty; but whether such practice establishes agreement of the parties regarding the treaty's interpretation may require account to be taken of further factors. These may include assessment of the powers of the organ acting in the matter, the potential for any other body in the organization to control the organ, the manner in which states parties to the treaty participate in the activities of the organization, etc.

It is appropriate, therefore, to distinguish between consideration of subsequent practice in connection with interpretation of the powers and functions in a treaty establishing an international organization—its constitution, and any contribution of international organizations to the interpretative function of subsequent practice more generally.

4.8.2 Practice in relation to a treaty establishing an organization

Article 5 of the 1969 Vienna Convention provides that the Convention 'applies to any treaty which is the constituent instrument of an international organization and to any treaty adopted within an international organization without prejudice to any relevant rules of the organization'. Article 5 of the 1986 Vienna Convention is to like effect; but there the reference to 'rules of the organization' is amplified by a definition of that phrase as 'the constituent instruments, decisions and resolutions adopted in accordance with them, and established practice of the organization' (article 2(1)(j)). Thus established practice of the organization is specifically envisaged in the latter case as falling within the rules of the organization.[191]

---

[189] H G Schermers and N M Blokker, *International Institutional Law: Unity within Diversity* (Boston: Martinus Nijhoff, 2003), at 841, § 1347.

[190] Cf Amerasinghe, *Principles of Institutional Law of International Organizations*, at 51, pointing out that practice in international organizations would generally not be based on a sense of obligation so much as exercise of a discretion, the interpretative value following from conduct of the organ being pursued in the belief it was acting lawfully under the organization's constitutive instrument.

[191] On practice in international organizations, see E Lauterpacht, 'The Development of the Law of International Organisation by the Decisions of International Tribunals' (1976-IV) 152 *Recueil des Cours* 379, at 448–65, and on whose acts are relevant, see 458–59; C Peters, in a detailed and useful study adducing further material, suggests that, although article (2)(1)(j) of the 1986 Convention may not be strictly germane to interpretation of the 1969 Convention, '[a]ll things considered, the language, history and purpose of Art. 5 [1969 Vienna Convention] lead to the conclusion that established practice is part of the rules of the organization regardless of the difficulties of contextual interpretation': C Peters, 'Subsequent Practice and Established Practice of International Organizations: Two Sides of the Same Coin?' (2011) 3 *Goettingen Journal of International Law* 617, at 629.

These provisions leave no doubt over the applicability of the Vienna rules to a treaty which is the constitution of an international organization, but the modalities of taking into account subsequent practice are less clear. The ICJ has expressly confirmed applicability of the Vienna rules in its advisory opinion in *Legality of the Use by a State of Nuclear Weapons in Armed Conflict*.[192] The central issue was whether asking a question about the legality of use of nuclear weapons came within the scope of the activities of the World Health Organization (WHO). Having referred to its own previous consistent practice of following the principles and rules generally applicable to the interpretation of treaties when interpreting the UN Charter, the Court noted:

But the constituent instruments of international organizations are also treaties of a particular type; their object is to create new subjects of law endowed with a certain autonomy, to which the parties entrust the task of realizing common goals. Such treaties can raise specific problems of interpretation owing, *inter alia*, to their character which is conventional and at the same time institutional; the very nature of the organization created, the objectives which have been assigned to it by its founders, the imperatives associated with the effective performance of its functions, as well as its own practice, are all elements which may deserve special attention when the time comes to interpret these constituent treaties.[193]

The Court's reference to the relevance of an organization's 'own practice' as an interpretative element deserving special attention is to be noted. The Court followed this by singling out the 1969 Vienna Convention's provision on subsequent practice for complete quotation in its brief reference to some elements of the general rule. It listed the occasions on which it had previously applied the rule on subsequent practice and stated that it would apply it in the present case 'for the purpose of determining whether, according to the WHO Constitution, the question to which it has been asked to reply arises "within the scope of [the] activities" of that Organization.'[194]

The Court thus appears to have equated the organization's own practice with subsequent practice in the Vienna rules.[195] When it came to examine the practice of the WHO, the Court used the practice in an essentially confirmatory role, having determined the meaning using a textual approach first, combined with assessment of the legitimate functions of the organization in the light of the treaty's

---

[192] [1996] ICJ Reports 66, Opinion of 8 July 1996. The Court held that the request for an opinion submitted by the WHO did not relate to a question arising within the scope of WHO's activities and that a condition essential to founding its jurisdiction was absent.

[193] [1996] ICJ Reports 66, at 75, para 19.   [194] [1996] ICJ Reports 66, at para 19.

[195] See, however, C M Brölmann, 'Specialized Rules of Treaty Interpretation: International Organizations', Chapter 20 in D B Hollis (ed), *The Oxford Guide to Treaties* (Oxford: OUP, 2012), at 515–16 identifying application of a constitutive treaty as attributable to the organization itself and therefore as practice which 'cannot be put on the same footing as the interpretive tool envisaged by Article 31(3)(b) of the [Vienna Convention]' (at p 515, footnote omitted); see also Schermers and Blokker, *International Institutional Law: Unity within Diversity*, at 841, to the effect that as the 1969 Vienna Convention refers to the practice of states and not of organizations: 'Article 31(3)(b) of the Vienna Convention seems to be incorrect as a foundation on which "practice of the organization" may rest.'

object and purpose, refined by application of the specialty principle (confining a specialized agency to its prescribed area of activity).

Of further interest is what the Court treated as practice. In the preamble to its resolution asking for the Court's opinion on the legality of use of nuclear weapons, the Assembly of the WHO referred to reports and resolutions within the organization prior to the request for the Court's opinion. The Court found that none of these constituted a practice of the WHO such as to show that it treated the legality of use of nuclear weapons as a matter for that organization's attention.[196] The Court reached this conclusion not because it did not view resolutions of an organization as practice, nor because they and secretariat reports were not to be regarded as authoritative expressions of the position of the organization, but because they addressed the *effects* of use of nuclear weapons and therefore did not, in their substance, sustain an argument that the issue sent to the Court was treated by the organization as within the scope of its activities. That the Court engaged with the content of the instruments makes it clear that such output of an international organization has the potential to constitute subsequent practice for the purposes of the Vienna rules.

The only WHO resolution which did raise the issue of legality of use of nuclear weapons was the one seeking the Court's opinion. As the Court observed, however, this resolution was adopted almost immediately the matter had been raised and was itself adopted in the face of opposition. The Court therefore concluded:

… [the resolution] could not be taken to express or to amount on its own to a practice establishing an agreement between the members of the Organization to interpret its Constitution as empowering it to address the question of the legality of the use of nuclear weapons.[197]

Hence the Court's opinion in this case indicates a rationale for treating resolutions of an organization as relevant practice if they establish agreement of the members of an organization, which is in line with the provision on subsequent practice in the Vienna rules. In contrast, however, it has been pointed out that in its Advisory Opinion on the *Wall in Occupied Palestinian Territory*, the Court took account of the evolution of practice of the General Assembly and Security Council of the United Nations without investigating whether the extent of support for the practice showed agreement of all Member States.[198]

In the *Wall* case the Court had to decide whether article 12 of the UN Charter precluded the General Assembly adopting a resolution requesting an advisory opinion because the Security Council was engaged in consideration of matters of international peace and security in the Middle East.[199] The Court noted that,

---

[196] *Legality of the Use by a State of Nuclear Weapons in Armed Conflict* [1996] ICJ Reports 66, at 81, para 27.

[197] [1996] ICJ Reports 66, at 81, para 27.

[198] Peters, 'Subsequent Practice and Established Practice of International Organizations: Two Sides of the Same Coin?' (2011) 3 *Goettingen Journal of International Law* 617, at 623–4.

[199] *Legal Consequences of the Construction of a Wall in the Occupied Palestinian Territory* [2004] ICJ Reports 136.

as regards the practice of the United Nations, both the General Assembly and the Security Council initially interpreted and applied article 12 to the effect that the Assembly could not make a recommendation on a question concerning the maintenance of international peace and security while the matter remained on the Council's agenda, but that this interpretation of article 12 had evolved subsequently. The Court further noted that there has been an increasing tendency over time for the General Assembly and the Security Council to deal in parallel with the same matter concerning the maintenance of international peace and security.[200] Both as regards the original interpretation by the UN organs and as evidence of the evolving practice, the Court gave numerous specific examples of the practice; but without investigating the extent of support for each resolution, recommendation or decision, the Court concluded that 'the *accepted practice* of the General Assembly, as it has evolved, is consistent with Article 12, paragraph 1, of the Charter'.[201]

The Court did not mention the Vienna rules until a much later stage and in connection with a different point; but if it was following the line it had taken in the *Use of Nuclear Weapons* case, Peters notes that something must have influenced the way the provision on subsequent practice in the Vienna rules applied:

This could be the rule of customary law as codified in Art. 5 [of the Vienna Convention]. Further, the established practice of the United Nations could have created a rule of the organization with the content that its subsequent practice does not strictly require the agreement of *all* the Member States.[202]

It has also been argued elsewhere that the practice of international organizations in fulfilment of their constitutional remit may in some sense have an independent basis rather than being purely interpretative of their constitutive treaty as drawn up by the founding states, particularly when membership and functions have grown.[203] This seems implicit in the Court's recognition that interpretation may evolve through the political organs of the UN.[204] However, as noted above, the

---

[200] [2004] ICJ Reports 136, at 149, para 27.

[201] [2004] ICJ Reports 136, at 150, para 28 (emphasis added).

[202] Peters, 'Subsequent Practice and Established Practice of International Organizations: Two Sides of the Same Coin?', at 624.

[203] See Amerasinghe, *Principles of Institutional Law of International Organizations*, at 53 and Lachs [1964] *Yearbook of the ILC*, vol I, Part 1, p 286, para 46; Brölmann, 'Specialized Rules of Treaty Interpretation: International Organizations', Chapter 20 in Hollis (ed), *The Oxford Guide to Treaties* (Oxford: OUP, 2012); and L B de Chazournes, 'Subsequent Practice, Practices and 'Family Resemblance': Towards Embedding Subsequent Practice in its Operative Milieu', Chapter 6 in Nolte, *Treaties and Subsequent Practice*, at 57–9.

[204] See *Legal Consequences of the Construction of a Wall in the Occupied Palestinian Territory (Advisory Opinion)* [2004] ICJ Reports 136, at 149–50, paras 27–28, where the Court noted that the General Assembly had originally refused to recommend measures when a question concerning maintenance of international peace and security remained on the agenda of the Security Council, but had later interpreted article 12 of the Charter as precluding recommendations by the Assembly only when the Council was actually exercising its functions; see also the ICJ's consideration of the procedure followed by the Security Council constituting the 'veto' which the Court found in the *Namibia* case had been generally accepted by members of the United Nations and evidenced a general practice of the UN: see section 4.7, above.

ICJ took account of the opposition to the WHO resolution in assessing whether the resolution reflected practice of the organization, so that clarification of the Court's view of the precise modalities of use of practice in interpretation of constitutive treaties is yet to emerge.[205] The ILC may have the opportunity to suggest approaches to this issue in its work on subsequent agreements and practice.

Interpretative practice in relation to constitutional instruments of international organizations may also link with general rules of international law. For example, work within the United Nations is constrained by article 2(7) preserving a realm of 'domestic jurisdiction' of states. The volumes of practice of the organs of the UN interpreting this term has had a more general effect ascribing meaning to the term in international law and deriving support from international law in ascertaining its meaning.[206]

4.8.3 Practice in relation to treaty provisions other than in constitutions of international organizations

This category is concerned with international organizations, including courts and tribunals forming part of international organizations, which have powers to interpret treaties that are not the constitution of the institution of which they form part. Their work is considered throughout this book and is merely noted here as a source of systematic practice in interpretation of the Vienna rules.

Where international organizations have a role in developing rules on matters within their sphere of activity, furthering interpretation of treaties in a manner that assists their useful application in accordance with the policies which the organization seeks to promote may be seen more as a substantive function in developing the law than one which develops practice of the organization in relation to interpretation. For example, the UN High Commissioner for Refugees acts as a catalyst for interpretation of the UN Convention on Refugees, particularly through the publication of the UNHCR Handbook on Procedures and Criteria for Determining Refugee Status.[207]

4.8.4 Does practice of courts and tribunals constitute precedent?

Many international courts and tribunals are established within the framework of an international organization, although ad hoc arbitrations between states are still a feature of the international scene, often using the facilities of the Permanent Court of Arbitration. It is perhaps inevitable that where judgments, awards, and decisions are made within single systems, and often relating to matters forming

---

[205] See also Amerasinghe, *Principles of Institutional Law of International Organizations*, at 53–4.
[206] See *Repertory of Practice of United Nations Organs,* at <http://www.un.org/law/repertory>.
[207] See introduction to 1992 edition of the Handbook; while the Handbook records the practice of states parties to the Convention, by also taking into account exchanges of views between the UNHCR Office and the authorities of the parties, the Handbook provides coordinated evidence of practice and an institutional input; see also section 4.4 above on the role of the Handbook.

a distinct community of interests, attempts will be made to shape reasoning in a coherent form, drawing inspiration from the efforts of predecessors.

Decisions of international courts and tribunals only bind the parties to a particular dispute unless otherwise established. This is inherent in a system of multifarious treaties each with potentially differing sets of parties to them. However, the governing instruments establishing some of these courts and tribunals may make this explicit. Thus article 59 of the Statute of the ICJ provides: 'The decision of the Court has no binding force except between the parties and in respect of that particular case.'[208] Yet the judgments and opinions of the ICJ are full of references to its previous case law and occasionally to decisions of others. Similarly courts and tribunals having jurisdiction in the growing number of specialist fields, such as human rights, world trade, investments between private parties and states, tax, international criminal law etc, all are building up great bodies of case law which often furnishes reasoning and guidance somewhat akin to precedent used ad hoc to sustain reasoning in later judgments, awards, and decisions.

The approach of the ICJ to propositions of law established in its previous cases (and those heard at the Permanent Court of International Justice) is that of the civil law's *jurisprudence constante* rather than the common law's notion of binding precedent. *Jurisprudence constante* (now commonly just 'jurisprudence' when used in the context of the case law of an international court or tribunal) respects propositions of law more on the basis of weight of repetition than authority of source: 'a precedent becomes a source of law when it has become "settled jurisprudence" (*jurisprudence constante*) through an uninterrupted line of judicial decisions'.[209] An excellent illustration of this is the way in which the ICJ built up its use of the Vienna rules, listing its earlier applications of the rules to demonstrate progressively its established position on their applicability.[210] The ICJ leans towards this approach. It does refer to precedents and, in application of article 38 of its Statute, may refer to 'other judicial decisions…as subsidiary means for the determination of rules of law'.[211]

---

[208] It may be that treaty provisions on dispute settlement tend to be more concerned with issues of compliance and finality than precedent: see eg the Convention on the Settlement of Investment Disputes between States and Nationals of Other States, Washington, 1965, article 53 (1) 'The award shall be binding on the parties and shall not be subject to any appeal or to any other remedy except those provided for in this Convention.'

[209] See B Luppi and F Parisi, 'Judicial Creativity and Judicial Errors: an Organizational Perspective' (2010) 6 *Journal of Institutional Economics* 91, at 93; see also: R L Henry, 'Jurisprudence Constante and Stare Decisis Contrasted' (1929) 15 *American Bar Assoc Journal* 11; M Shahabbuddeen, *Precedent in the World Court* (Cambridge: Grotius, 1996); J Gill, 'Is There a Special Role for Precedent in Investment Arbitration?' (2010) 25 *ICSID Review* 87; I M Ten Cate, 'The Costs of Consistency: Precedent in Investment Treaty Arbitration' (2012–2013) 51 *Colum J Transnat'l L* 418.

[210] See Chapter 1 section 2.2 above; for further examples of the ICJ explicitly referring to its own jurisprudence, see *Ambatielos case (Greece v United Kingdom)* [1953] ICJ Reports 10, at 19: 'The Court is not departing from the principle, which is well-established in international law and accepted by its own jurisprudence as well as that of the Permanent Court of International Justice, to the effect that…'; *Accordance with International Law of the Unilateral Declaration of Independence in Respect of Kosovo* [2010] ICJ Reports 404 at 417, para 31: 'Accordingly, the consistent jurisprudence of the Court has determined that…'.

[211] See, eg, *Nottebohm case (Liechtenstein v Guatemala)* [1953] ICJ Reports 111 at 119: 'Since the Alabama case, it has been generally recognized, following the earlier precedents, that, in the absence

While, however, it is clear that the ICJ does follow its jurisprudence and precedents in the senses described above, the cases of the Court are generally too varied and distinct (except where grouped together to produce effectively the same judgments) for there to be many examples of cases where it has to interpret a second or further time the same treaty terms. In contrast, some of the courts and tribunals concerned with specialist fields are often interpreting a single treaty or treaties of closely similar type and are therefore more likely to encounter the same treaty provisions for interpretation anew. Here, the idea of both precedent and jurisprudence take on a rather different appearance depending on whether there is a strong element of continuity of the court or tribunal or whether it is constituted for each occasion. For example, the ECtHR is a body with some degree of continuity, while arbitral tribunals under the treaty setting up the International Centre for Settlement of Investment Disputes (ICSID) are composed of arbitrators selected for each case. In the latter cases, the ideas of *jurisprudence constante* or precedent sit ill with the absence of any collegial affiliation beyond the community of specialism which the ICSID may foster. While there are studies showing how in these specialisms judges and arbitrators may treat decisions relating to the same or similar treaties and situations, there is little to suggest that there is any coherent approach to case law or jurisprudence in regard to interpretation of treaties.[212] Unfortunately, although increasing reference has been made to the Vienna rules, which might be expected to encourage coherence in their application, actual familiarity with the rules and full and proper use of them have not been uniformly apparent in investment arbitration.[213]

4.9 Possible overlap with relevant rules of international law

The next chapter shows how potentially wide is the requirement in article 31(3)(c) to take into account in treaty interpretation 'any relevant rules of international

of any agreement to the contrary, an international tribunal has the right to decide as to its own jurisdiction ...', and see *Case concerning Delimitation of the Maritime Boundary in the Gulf of Maine Area (Canada/United States of America)* [1984] ICJ Reports 246, at paras 143 and 147, *Maritime Delimitation and Territorial Questions between Qatar and Bahrain (Qatar v Bahrain)* [2001] ICJ Reports 40, at 110, para 227, and *Case concerning the Land and Maritime Boundary between Cameroon and Nigeria (Cameroon v Nigeria: Equatorial Guinea Intervening)* [2002] ICJ Reports 303, at 415, paras 222–3.

[212] For a useful review of the role of prior awards or decisions in interpretation of bilateral investment treaties, with helpful comparisons with similar issues in other areas, see J R Weeramantry, *Treaty Interpretation in Investment Arbitration* (Oxford: OUP, 2012), 116–27; on 'legal certainty and *jurisprudence constante*' in WTO bodies, see I Van Damme, *Treaty Interpretation by the WTO Appellate Body* (Oxford: OUP, 2009), 195–203; see also M Paparinskis 'Sources of Law and Arbitral Interpretations of Pari Materia Investment Protection Rules', Chapter 5 in O K Fauchald, and A Nollkaemper (eds), *The Practice of International and National Courts and the (De-)Fragmentation of International Law* (Oxford: Hart Publishing, 2012).

[213] See Chapter 10, section 6 below; and cf *Canadian Cattlemen for Fair Trade v United States*, UNCITRAL (NAFTA), Award on Jurisdiction, 28 January 2008, paras 49–51, asserting the relevance of other arbitral awards as supplementary means of interpretation; and see A Orakhelashvili, 'Principles of Treaty Interpretation in the NAFTA Arbitral Award on *Canadian Cattlemen*' (2009) 26 *Journal of International Arbitration* 159, 167–69.

law applicable in the relations between the parties'. Subsequent practice of states parties to a treaty may take the form of their entering into further agreements in relation to the same or related subject matter or such further agreements may establish obligations which apply in their relations.[214] In the *Abyei Arbitration* the tribunal hedged its bets as to the basis on which it should take into account some agreements of 2008 when interpreting the Comprehensive Peace Agreement of 2005 (CPA):

> In the Tribunal's view, the 2008 Agreements serve to clarify the meaning of provisions of the CPA as "subsequent practice" pursuant to Article 31(3)(b). The phrase "subsequent practice" has been widely interpreted and is not restricted to specific, interpretative treaties. The 2008 Agreements constitute relevant subsequent practice, since the Agreements make specific reference to sections of the CPA: ... As such, these 2008 Agreements reaffirm the relevant provisions of these elements of the CPA and must be taken into account in interpreting the CPA. The 2008 Agreements are thus admissible and relevant for purposes of assessing the reasonableness of the ABC [Abyei Boundaries Commission] Experts' interpretation of the Formula [the phrase defining the Abyei Area in dispute] as expressed in the Abyei Protocol. ... Even if one were to consider that the 2008 Agreements do not constitute relevant "subsequent practice," the 2008 Agreements would still inform the interpretation of the CPA as "relevant rules ... applicable in the relations between the parties" pursuant to Article 31(3)(c) of the Vienna Convention.'[215]

5. Conclusions

A proven agreement of all parties on interpretation of their treaty is usually the best evidence of its meaning. This is so even though the Vienna rules separate consideration of agreements made at the time of conclusion of a treaty from subsequent agreements (the latter evidenced by being recorded or shown through sufficient practice). Because the general rule is a single rule composed of several elements, and because of the particular significance of the agreement of the parties on a treaty's interpretation, such agreements are not subordinate to the elements in the first paragraph of the general rule. A somewhat different element to be taken into account is any unilateral instrument connected to the conclusion of the treaty and accepted by the other parties as related to it. Instruments of this kind may contain interpretative declarations, the effects of which vary according to the particular circumstances.

---

[214] See Chapter 7, section 3.2.2.
[215] *The Abyei Arbitration (The Government of Sudan/The Sudan People's Liberation Movement/Army)*, Final Award of 22 July 2009, paras 654–5 (footnote omitted), <http://www.pca-cpa.org>; and see R Moloo, 'When Actions Speak Louder Than Words: The Relevance of Subsequent Party Conduct to Treaty Interpretation' (2013) 31 *Berkeley JIL* 39, at 45–46.

7

The General Rule: (3) Relevant Rules of International Law and Special Meanings

Relevant rules of international law applicable between parties—time factors—special meanings

...it is a rule of interpretation that a text emanating from a Government must, in principle, be interpreted as producing and intended to produce effects in accordance with existing law and not in violation of it.[1]

Article 31
General rule of interpretation

...

3. There shall be taken into account, together with the context:

...

(c) any relevant rules of international law applicable in the relations between the parties.

4. A special meaning shall be given to a term if it is established that the parties so intended.

1. Introduction

This chapter takes up the last two elements of the general rule for treaty interpretation. They are rather a juxtaposition of opposites. Article 31(3)(c) concerns the circumstances in which rules from the broad sweep of international law may be brought into play in treaty interpretation. Article 31(4) addresses the situation where the interpretative exercise is narrowed by attribution by the parties of a particular meaning to a term of a treaty. The former identifies the circumstances in which the interpreter may use matter from the body of law outside the treaty. The latter narrows the focus to a particular or peculiar use of a term within the treaty, most readily indicated by a definition provision.

---

[1] *Case concerning the Right of Passage over Indian Territory (Preliminary Objections) (Portugal & India)* [1957] ICJ Reports 125 at 142.

The provision on rules of international law had its genesis in an attempt to deal with an issue which, in the context of general international law, is commonly labelled the 'intertemporal law'. This concept addresses two questions: first, whether the legal significance of facts in a particular situation is to be assessed as at the time of relevant events rather than at the time at which a difference or dispute is being resolved; and, second, what account is to be taken of changes or developments in international law in any intervening period.

The recent flowering of case law referring to article 31(3)(c) has shown that it has a capacity to become applicable in a greater variety of circumstances than its origins would suggest. The provision has been the subject of extensive recent study in the ILC in the context of its work on fragmentation of international law.[2] The formulation and application of article 31(3)(c) provides something of an illustration of the very problem it addresses. Should it be interpreted as at the moment of conclusion of the Vienna Convention, at the moment at which this assessment of it is being read, or at the moment at which some other treaty is being interpreted by reference to it? That the last of these three possibilities is the case is clear from the context and location of the provision in the Vienna rules. It is in a section of the Convention headed 'Interpretation of Treaties'. Even though not hierarchical, or invariably to be applied sequentially, the general rule in article 31 is conceptually clear: progression from terms to context, through any agreements at the time of conclusion of a treaty, to subsequent agreements, subsequent practice, and thence to relevant rules of international law. The framework suggests that had the reference to international law been to that law as at the time of negotiation or conclusion of a treaty, the reference to it would logically have placed it in paragraph (1) or (2) of article 31. If the preparatory work tends towards revealing the origins of article 31(3)(c) in the first limb of the intertemporal law, the words eventually used and practice subsequent to the entry into force of the Vienna Convention show wider actual application of the provision than to resolve intertemporal issues. Nevertheless, the time element is frequently a part of the picture when the provision is being invoked.

Transposing the intertemporal law principle from the context of general international law to that of treaty interpretation, the central questions are: first, whether a treaty provision is to be interpreted as if at the time of the treaty's negotiation, conclusion, ratification (accession, acceptance, or whatever), or some other time; and, second, whether the meaning of a treaty provision can evolve, particularly in the light of changes in international law. In the preceding chapter an example was given in the approach of the European Court of Human Rights accepting that some terms in themselves incorporate the idea that their scope is sufficiently wide to allow an 'evolutive' interpretation. Although it was argued in that chapter that such evolutive interpretation was limited to the extent of adopting meanings coming within a concept already present in the treaty when negotiated, the

---

[2] See ILC Fifty-eighth Session, 'Report of the Study Group on Fragmentation of International Law: Difficulties arising from the Diversification and Expansion of International Law', finalized by M Koskenniemi, 13 April 2006, A/CN.4/L.682 and A/CN.4/L.682/Corr.1, pp 206–44 and ILC Report on its Fifty-eighth Session (2006), UN Gen. Ass., Official Records, Sixty-first Session, Supplement No 10 (A/61/10), pp 400–23.

development of subsequent practice provides a further means by which evolution of the treaty's content can take place at the instance of the parties to a treaty.

Absent such practice, however, is there scope for evolutionary interpretation by reference to developments in the law outside the immediate confines of a particular treaty? Decisions in recent years applying article 31(3)(c) suggest an affirmative answer. This is sustained by the expansion of international law into regulation of new areas, particularly by treaties not only creating specific obligations but also establishing general principles, such as those on environmental matters. Such rules may need to be taken into account when interpreting treaties pre-dating these developments. However, this is to further the process of interpretation, not to displace the treaty.

Article 31(3)(c) is concerned with the role of international obligations of the parties to the treaty undergoing interpretation and, implicitly and through its history, with the effect of changes in legal obligations since a treaty's conclusion. This does not deal specifically with other factors having a bearing on the interpretation of terms that are subject to evolutionary interpretation through changes not of legal obligations but linguistic practice, scientific and technical developments, political and social influences, etc.[3] However, because the ILC's preparatory work for this provision tackled time factors in treaty interpretation, using the intertemporal law as its starting point, this chapter includes an overview of these factors.

Almost the converse of the application of rules of international law in the interpretative process is the rule which provides for terms of a treaty to be given a special meaning if the parties so intended. This introduces the one element of the interpretative process which explicitly looks to an intention of the parties, this being to give their very own sense to a term which they use. A provision which might have been placed at the very start of the general rule because of its potential to short-circuit the carousel of the Vienna rules, comes at the end because of its relatively minor usage and its dependence on evidence from the range of possible sources, including those identified earlier in the general rule.

1.1 The intertemporal rule in general international law

An understanding of the nature of the intertemporal principle, rule, or law (to grace an ill-defined notion with labels suggesting a clarity which it does not warrant) is a necessary precursor to examining this part of the Vienna rules.[4] The first part of the intertemporal principle is usually expressed in the words used by Judge Huber in the *Island of Palmas (Netherlands v USA)* (1928): '...a juridical fact must be appreciated in the light of the law contemporary with it, and not the law in force at the time

---

[3] For evolutionary interpretation, see Chapter 10, section 4 below.

[4] Judge Elias notes that the principle has sometimes been described as 'international intertemporal law', sometimes as the 'theory', 'principle' or 'doctrine' of intertemporal law: T O Elias, 'The doctrine of Intertemporal Law' (1980) 74 AJIL 285, where each usage is ascribed to cited authors. The ILC refers to 'the general principle of intertemporal law' in paragraph (1) of its commentary on draft article 13 of its 'Draft articles on the Responsibility of States for Internationally Wrongful Acts' and provides further analysis and examples of application of the principle in that commentary: see ILC, Report on the work of its Fifty-third Session (2001), General Assembly, Official Records, Fifty-Sixth Session,

when a dispute in regard to it arises or falls to be settled'.[5] However, to treat this as a general rule for determining what law is applicable in any dispute requires excessive extrapolation from the facts of the case. The central issue in the *Island of Palmas* case was whether the 'root of title' to certain territory in Spain's discovery of the island could have provided an effective basis for transfer of sovereignty over it to the USA by treaty in 1898 when weighed against the claim of the Netherlands to sovereignty over the same territory based on intervening centuries of peaceful and effective possession or occupation. Discovery was a mode of acquisition of sovereignty fully recognized in the sixteenth century, the time of discovery of the island in this case. However, possession or occupation as a mode of acquisition of sovereignty had become recognized as increasingly significant in those intervening centuries.

In the event Judge Huber found in favour of the claim of the Netherlands. He had supplemented his statement on applicability of contemporaneous law to a juridical fact (explained by Higgins as 'a fact with juridical significance')[6] with the further explanation that:

The same principle which subjects the act creative of a right to the law in force at the time the right arises, demands that the existence of the right, in other words its continued manifestation, shall follow the conditions required by the evolution of law.[7]

This shows the intertemporal law as really having two limbs, both of which played a part when the ILC attempted to codify its role in the draft articles on the law of treaties. However, transformation of the principle proved impossible in anything resembling Judge Huber's formulation. The principal or first proposition, although a reasonable starting point, is too narrow to allow for the range of possibilities which the text of a treaty, and other elements considered in treaty interpretation, might require to be taken into account. The second limb, if applied in its broadest possible application, could undermine rights properly established when they were acquired and thus negate the first proposition.[8] Appropriate in the context of assessment of particular facts relating to territorial acquisition, the significance of the second limb is simply that international law relating to sovereignty over territory requires that a state effectively maintains any title which it has validly acquired.[9] This does not have an obvious potential for extension to treaty interpretation generally.

1.2 Time factors in treaty interpretation

At any given moment when a treaty is being interpreted several different time factors may be relevant. For example, if a 'legal' term is used in a treaty, the interpreter needs to decide whether the meaning, or starting point for interpretation, is the

---

Supplement No 10 (A/56/10), chapter IV; see also E Bjorge, *The Evolutionary Interpretation of Treaties* (Oxford: OUP, 2014), Chapter 4, 'The Intertemporal Law'.

[5] (1928) 2 RIAA 829 at 845.

[6] R Higgins, 'Some Observations on the Inter-Temporal Rule in International Law' in J Makarczyk (ed), *Theory of International Law at the Threshold of the 21st Century* (The Hague: Kluwer, 1996), at 173.

[7] *Island of Palmas* (1928) 2 RIAA 829.   [8] See Higgins, 'Some Observations', at 174.

[9] Higgins, at 174.

meaning at the time the treaty was negotiated, concluded, entered into force, or some other time. If the interpretation depends on a range of facts, assessment or appreciation of the legal significance of those facts may require application of the considerations which Judge Huber addressed. The treaty, or one of its provisions, may 'speak' to a different time from its conclusion. In other words, the treaty or a provision in it may envisage an obligation or right being predicated on a lapse of time or on a specific occurrence. There may be time factors relevant to reservations and objections to reservations. The terms of a treaty may be open to evolutionary interpretation.[10] Finally, and most pertinently in the context of the provision of article 31(3)(c) as it was finally adopted, international law may have marched on since the conclusion of the treaty and the interpreter needs to know whether, and how, to relate any such developments to the particular task of interpretation.

The main underlying question is to what extent changed circumstances affect interpretation of a treaty. No universal answer is to be found in a general rule such as that of the intertemporal law, but the solution lies rather in the particular treaty itself. If the changed circumstances are factual, the issue is whether the treaty envisaged the possibility of change. If this is not clear after application of the general rule of interpretation, article 32 of the Vienna Convention indicates that the circumstances of conclusion of the treaty are a supplementary means for its interpretation. This supplementary means clearly points to facts weighing with those who negotiated the treaty and at the time of its conclusion. If the facts in issue at the time of interpretation differ from those at the time of conclusion of the treaty, there are three possibilities: (1) that the treaty envisaged such changes; (2) that the situation remains within the scope of effective interpretation of the treaty; or (3) that the change is so fundamental that the treaty cannot be applied.

In the first of these possibilities, the treaty may have envisaged change in a general way or in a more particular sense. An example of allowing for change in a general way is the evolutionary interpretation envisaged in human rights treaties.[11] Somewhat more specific circumstances were covered in the *Danube Dams* case, where growing environmental concerns were seen by one party as a bar to performing the treaty.[12] The ICJ found that the treaty required the parties to maintain the quality of the water of the Danube and to protect nature, thus recognizing that there would be developments in environmental science and law.[13]

The second possibility arises where facts have changed radically but remain within the scope of effective interpretation of the treaty. In the *Iron Rhine* case, nineteenth-century treaties had expected a long life for the railway from Belgium

---

[10] On evolutionary interpretation, see Chapter 10, section 4 below.

[11] See Chapter 6, section 4.6 above and Chapter 10, section 4 below.

[12] *Case concerning the Gabčíkovo-Nagymaros Project (Hungary/Slovakia)* [1997] ICJ Reports 7.

[13] *Case concerning the Gabčíkovo-Nagymaros Project (Hungary/Slovakia)* [1997] ICJ Reports 7, at para 140, and see section 4.7 below; see further C Warbrick, 'Introduction' to *The Iron Rhine ("IJzeren Rijn") Railway (Belgium–Netherlands) Award of 2005* (ed B Macmahon) (The Hague: TMC Asser Press, 2007); see also *Indus Waters Kishenganga Arbitration (Pakistan v India)* Final Award of 20 December 2013, <http://www.pca-cpa.org/> at para 111, where the Court of Arbitration noted in contrast to the *Iron Rhine* case, the treaty in issue expressly limited the extent to which the Court could have recourse to, and apply, sources of law beyond that treaty (considered further in section 5.3.4 below).

to Germany across the Netherlands.[14] Belgium and the Netherlands, the parties to these treaties, had made some provision for maintenance, extension, and upgrading, but could not have foreseen the advances in electrification, track design and specification, freight stock, etc, all developments which needed to be considered when the largely disused line was being considered for a comprehensive revival, restoration, renewal, and redirection. The arbitral tribunal considered that this was not a case of conceptual or generic terms in the treaty being in issue, but rather of new technical developments to be taken into account. The tribunal found that 'an evolutive interpretation, which would ensure an application of the treaty that would be effective in terms of its object and purpose will be preferred to a strict application of the intertemporal rule'.[15]

The third possibility is covered by article 62 of the Vienna Convention. The essence of this is that an unforeseen and fundamental change of circumstances from those existing at the time of conclusion of a treaty may not be invoked as a ground for terminating, suspending, or withdrawing from the treaty unless '(a) the existence of those circumstances constituted an essential basis of the consent of the parties to be bound by the treaty; and (b) the effect of the change is radically to transform the extent of obligations still to be performed under the treaty'. This is not so much an approach to interpreting a treaty in changed circumstances as a circumstance for investigating whether the treaty can apply at all. So fundamental a change in circumstances will be difficult to show.

As for the effect on treaty interpretation of changes in international law, a general statement of the ICJ in the *Namibia* case needs to be examined in the context in which it was made, as it might otherwise be thought to be a panacea for the problems of the intertemporal law:

... an international instrument has to be interpreted and applied within the framework of the entire legal system prevailing at the time of the interpretation.[16]

The case concerned the legal consequences of continued assertion by South Africa of control over what was then South West Africa even though the League of Nations had ceased to exist. In the paragraphs leading up to the statement

---

[14] *Arbitration regarding the Iron Rhine ("IJzeren Rijn") Railway (Belgium/Netherlands)*, (2005) XXVII RIAA 35, p 66 para 58, and see sections 4.1.2, 4.2, and 4.7 above; see also: Declaration of Judge Higgins in *Kasikili/Sedudu Island (Botswana/Namibia)* [1999] ICJ Reports 1113 at 1114, para 3, who in considering the application of a treaty of 1890 to select one from two channels of a river as a boundary, stated: 'The Court is indeed, for this particular task, entitled to look at all the criteria the Parties have suggested as relevant. This is not to discover a mythical "ordinary meaning" within the Treaty, but rather because the general terminology chosen long ago falls to be decided today. To use contemporary knowledge and scientific data to assist in fulfilling that task is not at all inconsistent with the intertemporal rule in the Island of Palmas Award...'; and Warbrick, 'Introduction' to *The Iron Rhine*.

[15] *Arbitration regarding the Iron Rhine ("IJzeren Rijn") Railway (Belgium/Netherlands)*, para 80.

[16] Advisory Opinion on *Legal consequences for States of the continued presence of South Africa in Namibia (South West Africa), notwithstanding Security Council Resolution 276 (1970)* [1971] ICJ Reports 16 at 31, para 53, and on 'evolutionary interpretation' see Chapter 10, section 4 below.

quoted above, the ICJ had referred to the original concept of a 'sacred trust of civilisation' embodied in the system of mandates under the supervision of the League of Nations, and the subsequent development of international law making the principle of self-determination applicable to all non-self-governing territories under the Charter of the United Nations. Self-determination had not developed as a legal principle in the era of the League in the way that it did after the founding of the UN. In the sentences immediately preceding the dictum, the Court stated:

Mindful as it is of the primary necessity of interpreting an instrument in accordance with the intentions of the parties at the time of its conclusion, the Court is bound to take into account the fact that the concepts embodied in Article 22 of the Covenant—'the strenuous conditions of the modern world' and 'the well-being and development' of the peoples concerned—were not static, but were by definition *evolutionary,* as also, therefore, was the concept of the 'sacred trust'. The parties to the Covenant must consequently be deemed to have accepted them as such.[17]

It can be seen that the Court found guidance within the treaty itself on temporal concerns as to how developing international law, and the principle of self-determination, was to apply to the mandates. The Court used the same concept of a provision being 'evolutionary' as found in relation to some other treaties, most notably human rights treaties.[18] This use of guidance from the content of the treaty itself on how to treat temporal issues is not an exception to a generally applicable intertemporal rule but 'an application of a wider principle—intention of the parties, reflected by reference to the objects and purpose—that guides the law of treaties'.[19] Nevertheless, reference is still made to the intertemporal law and the prominent absence from article 31(3)(c) of guidance on the issues which it poses leaves to the interpreter a need to be aware of the background to the laconic nature of that provision.

2. History and Preparatory Work of Article 31(3)(c)

The origins of this element of the Vienna rules are found in the principles disclosed above, but the formulation eventually adopted offers no guidance for its modern application. In the work of the International Law Commission, the first draft of the provision which became article 31(3)(c) was a projected draft article 56 intended to take account of the impact of the intertemporal law as part of draft articles on the application of treaties rather than just their interpretation:

(1) A treaty is to be interpreted in the light of the law in force at the time when the treaty was drawn up.

---

[17] [1971] ICJ Reports 16 at 31, para 53, (emphasis added).
[18] See further Higgins, 'Some Observations', at 173–7.
[19] Higgins, at 181.

(2) Subject to paragraph 1, the application of a treaty shall be governed by the rules of international law in force at the time when the treaty is applied.[20]

The formulation of paragraph (1) was an attempt to transpose into the law of treaties the well-established wording of the first branch of the intertemporal rule from the *Island of Palmas* case quoted above.[21] The second paragraph of the draft was a less nuanced version of Judge Huber's expanded version, or continuation, of the principle. The first of several examples given by the Special Rapporteur of the ILC (Waldock), in explaining the proposal, was from an arbitral award in 1909 in which the tribunal had had to decide how to apply a seventeenth-century treaty determining the frontier between two adjacent states when it became necessary to extend the frontier to the limit of the territorial sea.[22] Because the treaty had as its object the definitive settlement of the frontier, the tribunal found that the seventeenth-century principle of drawing a line out perpendicular from the coast was applicable rather than the 'line of equidistance' which was of more modern usage. The treaty had envisaged a final, once-and-for-all determination of the frontier applicable at its entry into force. This showed clearly that in any later interpretation of the treaty the principles applying at that time governed the matter. In contrast, while the direction of the line was determined by the seventeenth-century principle, the treaty of that era had not specified the breadth of the territorial sea on which there had been no clear rule at the time. Hence, in applying the treaty in the twentieth century, the law of that time was appropriate for ascertaining how far out the line went by reference to the developing law on the breadth of the territorial sea.

While there was a certain attraction in the way the Special Rapporteur drew up and illustrated the provision to reflect the two limbs of the intertemporal law, with the contrast between interpretation in the first and application in the second, it can be seen from the range of time factors indicated above that the 'simple' formulation of the intertemporal principle could not be usefully transposed to the Vienna rules without more—much more. Yet the ILC, in the event, plumped for less.

The ILC considered the initial proposal in a wide-ranging debate, including discussion of the intertemporal law itself, whether there was a clear line between interpretation and application, and, if so (or in any event), whether the two paragraphs of draft article 56 contradicted one another. The upshot of the debate was that the essential concept in the first paragraph (interpretation in the light of international law as at the time of the treaty's conclusion) was transferred to the 'general

---

[20] [1964] *Yearbook of ILC*, vol II, pp 8-9 and see Waldock's commentary there.

[21] See section 1.1 above; the ILC's Commentary on the draft articles indicated that: 'This element, as previously indicated, appeared in paragraph 1 of the text provisionally adopted in 1964, which stated that, *inter alia*, the ordinary meaning to be given to the terms of a treaty is to be determined "in the light of the general rules of international law *in force at the time of its conclusion*." The emphasized words were a reflection of the general principle that a juridical fact must be appreciated in the light of the law contemporary with it.' [1966] *Yearbook of ILC*, vol II, p 222, para 16.

[22] *Grisbardana* (*Sweden v Norway*) (1909) 2 RIAA 159–60, [1916] Scott Hague Crt Rep 130, and Waldock, commentary on draft articles [1964] *Yearbook of ILC*, vol II, p 9, para 2.

rules' in the new draft articles on interpretation.[23] The second paragraph of draft article 56 was converted into a provision requiring interpretation to take into account 'the emergence of any later rule of customary international law affecting the subject-matter of the treaty and binding upon all the parties'.[24] This latter element was briefly hived off into a separate draft provision and was adjusted to deal with the way in which operation of a treaty may be modified, sealing the departure of that clause from the rules of interpretation (though the eventual article 31(3)(c) became wide enough to contain the same thought).[25]

The abridged formulation stating that a treaty's terms were to be interpreted 'in the light of the rules of international law [in force at the time of its conclusion]' continued to be the subject of controversy.[26] While removal of the phrase which had been included in square brackets seemed to destroy the *raison d'être* of the provision, and leave a rather banal and obvious statement, agreement could not be reached for this phrase's retention. The ILC, evidently applying the principle 'less is more', decided to eliminate all detail:

> ...the Commission considered that the formula used in the 1964 text was unsatisfactory, since it covered only partially the question of the so-called inter-temporal law...It further considered that correct application of the temporal element would normally be indicated by interpretation of the term *in good faith*. The Commission therefore concluded that it should omit the temporal element and revise the reference to international law.[27]

However, adoption of the apparently innocuous reference to 'any relevant rules' of international law appears to have provided a classic treaty-makers' compromise—elegant but uninformative, the latter particularly so in consequence of the potential in the word 'relevant' to resurrect precisely the issues laid bare in the original draft article 56. Thus, in the final version sent to the Vienna conference in 1969 (and not significantly changed there), specific reference to the content of the intertemporal principle was lost from the rules on interpretation, although it lurks in disguised form in article 31(3)(c) and in the opening reference to good faith in article 31(1). The issue of intertemporal law is also apparent in other provisions of the Vienna Convention such as articles 53 and 63 on peremptory norms (overriding rules of international law, or *jus cogens*), and the effect of the onward march of time and events can be seen in article 62 (fundamental change of circumstances), article 30 (application of successive treaties relating to the same subject matter), and Part IV (amendment and modification of treaties).

---

[23] Draft Article 70(1)(b) in Waldock, Third Report on the Law of Treaties [1964] *Yearbook of ILC*, vol II, p 52 and commentary at p 56, para 15; see also [1964] *Yearbook of ILC*, vol I, pp. 33–40.

[24] Waldock, Third Report on the Law of Treaties [1964] *Yearbook of ILC*, vol II at p 53, draft article 73(a).

[25] See draft article 69A, [1964] *Yearbook of ILC* vol I, p 325; in the debate on this provision (which became draft article 68 at the 1966 session of the ILC) it was agreed to delete the element dealing with emergent rules of customary international law: [1966] *Yearbook of ILC*, vol I, part II, pp 163–87.

[26] [1966] *Yearbook of ILC*, vol I, part II, at p 309 (square brackets in original); the word 'general' had previously been included in this formulation before 'international law' (at p 183) but had been deleted: see section 3.2.2 below.

[27] [1966] *Yearbook of ILC*, vol II, p 222, para 16 (emphasis added).

Perhaps the position on the temporal relationship between terms of a treaty and international law was best summarized towards the end of the ILC debate by the Special Rapporteur (Waldock):

The question whether the terms used were intended to have a fixed content or to change in meaning with the evolution of the law could be decided only by interpreting the intention of the parties.[28]

There was some discussion in the ILC of other points relating to article 31(3)(c). These are taken up with the specific issues below.

3. Ordinary Meaning of Article 31(3)(c) in Context, etc

3.1 There shall be taken into account, together with the context...

The obligatory character of article 31(3)(c) is the same as that of the provisions which immediately precede it. This means that the provision must be applied where it has a role in any particular instance, not that there will always be a role for its application. However, while the status of the subparagraph is clear in that sense, Professor Greig has noted that article 31 could be read as importing a different relationship between its subparagraph (c) and the opening words of the article from that which subparagraphs (a) and (b) have.[29] He starts from the perception that the phrase 'together with the context' suggests that all the elements of article 31(3) 'should be equally applicable to the interpretative process at the time of that context'.[30] While subparagraphs (a) and (b) (*subsequent* agreement and *subsequent* practice) relate to what were future events at the time of a treaty's conclusion, he notes that subparagraph (c) does not contain any such time indication. However, he accepts that the presence of two subparagraphs dealing with future events gives the third one scope to cover both rules of international law as it was at the time of conclusion of the treaty and at the time the interpretation is being made.[31] Nevertheless, he sees the resultant wide scope of article 31(3)(c) as somewhat anomalous given what he characterizes as the Convention's 'restricted version of context' (that is, one which is limited to textual elements rather than surrounding circumstances), given the limited expansion of this by reference to the treaty's object and purpose, and given the limitations in article 32 on situations in which surrounding circumstances may be taken into account.

Leaving such criticism to one side while examining the remaining text ('any relevant rules of international law applicable in the relations between the parties'), the key questions are: What rules are 'relevant'? Can the 'forward' reach of 'international law' include potentially the whole of that law in force at the time when the interpretation is being made? Does the description 'applicable in the relations

---

[28] [1966] *Yearbook of ILC*, vol I, part II, p 199, para 9.
[29] D W Greig, *Intertemporality and The Law of Treaties* (London: BIICL, 2001), 46.
[30] Greig, 46.   [31] Greig, 46.

between the parties' have some limiting role as regards the extent of international law that is applicable?

3.2 Relevant rules of international law

3.2.1 Relevance

It seems reasonable to take the ordinary meaning of 'relevant' rules of international law as referring to those touching on the same subject matter as the treaty provision or provisions being interpreted or which in any way affect that interpretation. The word 'relevant', however, is equally apt to re-introduce temporal considerations and, particularly when linked with 'applicable in the relations between the parties', to bring into consideration obligations flowing from other treaties where these relate to the same subject matter. In what senses then can rules of international law be 'relevant' to the interpretation of a particular treaty? Professor McLachlan provides a helpful general answer:

> . . . article 31(3)(c) expresses a more general principle of treaty interpretation, namely that of *systemic integration* within the international legal system. The foundation of this principle is that treaties are themselves creatures of international law. However wide their subject matter, they are all nevertheless limited in scope and are predicated for their existence and operation on being part of the international law system.[7] As such, they must be 'applied and interpreted against the background of the general principles of international law',[8] and, as Verzijl put it . . . a treaty must be deemed 'to refer to such principles for all questions which it does not itself resolve expressly and in a different way.'[9]

> [7] See Koskenniemi 'Study on the Function and Scope of the *lex specialis* rule and the question of self-contained regimes' (ILC(LVI)/SG/FIL/CRD.1 and Add. 1) ('Koskenniemi'), para. 160.
> [8] McNair *The Law of Treaties* (Oxford: OUP, 1961), p. 466.
> [9] Supra [per Verzijl P., *Georges Pinson Case* (1927–8) A.D. no. 292].[32]

3.2.2 Rules of international law

A number of considerations may arise in the particular context of 'rules of international law'. 'International law' will be a somewhat imprecise term for those who are wedded to the distinction between public international law and private international law. However, it is not surprising that the ILC, being a UN body, should have used the unqualified term 'international law'.

First, in the context of treaties creating obligations between states, 'international law' can be read as referring to public international law. This is clear from article 2(1)(a) in its definition of 'treaty' referring to a written agreement 'governed by international law'.[33] Second, one of the most widely used starting points for a

[32] C McLachlan, 'The Principle of Systemic Integration and Article 31(3)(c) of the Vienna Convention' (2005) 54 ICLQ 279 at 280 (original emphasis); and see P Merkouris, *Article 31(3)(c) of the VCLT and the Principle of Systemic Integration* (Ph D Thesis, 2010), pp 36–39, <https://qmro.qmul.ac.uk/jspui/handle/123456789/477>.

[33] Other Vienna Convention provisions which refer to 'international law' are the Preamble, article 3 (several mentions, principally excluding from the scope of the Vienna Convention agreements

definition or description of public international law is that in article 38 of the Statute of the ICJ. That provision sets out the sources of the law (broadly, treaties, customary law, general principles, and, as subsidiary sources, judicial decisions and academic writing) to be used by the ICJ whose function (the Statute states) is to decide disputes 'in accordance with international law'. Hence the elements listed in article 38 are equated with international law. More generally, it is also probably the case that nowadays the term 'international law' without adjectival qualification denotes public international law, 'private' international law being so specified or put under the description 'conflict of laws'.

Therefore, while it seems clear enough that the reference to 'any relevant rules of international law' in its context, and in the light of the object and purpose of a treaty on the law of treaties, takes one to public international law, this does not precisely identify the extent of that area of law that is brought into consideration. This is not the place for a doctrinal disquisition on what international law is or whether it is law at all. The assumption that it is law must have been made by anyone who accepts that rules of international law govern treaty interpretation. However, the practical point is the question whether 'rules of international law' in article 31(3)(c) include the provisions of treaties, and if so of all treaties? Can treaties properly be described as international law or are they simply a source of obligation binding pursuant to international law?[34] The latter view imports an obvious analogy with contract, an analogy that is unsatisfactory because of the very different roles treaties can play, but helpful here as illustrating the difference between an obligation in the law and one created in application of the law. Or should a distinction be made between 'law-making' treaties and those that simply create specific obligations for the parties?

Answers to this question are more the province of books on (public) international law. But the various issues (whether 'international law' here means only customary law and general principles, whether regional and local international law are included, whether one treaty is to be interpreted in the light of other treaties, etc) did attract attention in a debate on deletion of the word 'general' which had been included as qualifying 'international law' in the draft of the general rule.[35]

---

between 'States and other subjects of international law'); article 4 (non-retroactivity of Vienna Convention is without prejudice to application of rules to which treaties 'would be subject under international law independently of the Convention'); article 38 (nothing in the Vienna Convention provisions relating to third state is to preclude a rule set out in a treaty from becoming binding on a third state 'as a customary rule of international law'); article 43 (invalidity or other reason for non-applicability of treaty obligations not to impair the duty of a state to fulfil any obligation in the treaty to which it would be subject 'under international law' independently of the treaty); article 52 (a treaty is void if its conclusion has been procured by the threat or use of force in violation of 'the principles of international law' in the UN Charter); article 53 (a treaty is void if, at the time of its conclusion, it conflicts with a peremptory norm of 'general international law'); article 64 (a treaty becomes void and terminates if it conflicts with a new peremptory norm of 'general international law'); and article 71 (consequences of the invalidity of a treaty which conflicts with a peremptory norm of general international law).

[34] G Fitzmaurice, *'Some Problems Regarding the Formal Sources of International Law' Symbolae Verzijl* (The Hague: Nijhoff, 1958), 153.

[35] [1966] *Yearbook of ILC*, vol I, part II, pp 183–200.

There is no authoritative definition of the term 'general international law' but the ILC used the term repeatedly in its debates and included it in some provisions of the Vienna Convention.[36]

'General international law' would exclude treaties only if a narrow meaning were attributed to it. Therefore, the deletion of 'general' must suggest strongly that treaties are included in the unqualified use of 'international law'. The records of the ILC are thin on this issue but support inclusion of treaties in the term. Jiménez de Aréchaga welcomed the emerging text referring to international law:

...[the] new text should be maintained, because it set out the important principle that a treaty constituted a new legal element which was additional to the other legal relationships between the parties and should be interpreted within the framework of other rules of international law in force between them. But it should not be qualified by the insertion of the word 'general', which would exclude specific or regional rules of international law binding on the parties. That was a particularly important matter where one treaty had to be interpreted in the light of other treaties binding on the parties.[37]

More indirect support comes from the fact that the suggestion of including the word 'customary' in place of 'general' was not taken up when Verdross proposed this: 'to express it more clearly, reference should be made to the rules of "customary" international law, because every treaty contained rules of international law.'[38] Yasseen clearly viewed an unqualified reference to international law as including treaties:

The omission of the word 'general' before the words 'international law' was justified, because a treaty concluded between several States should be interpreted in the light of the special international rules applying to those States, whether they were customary rules or rules of written law. It must be emphasized, however, that to be taken into consideration in interpreting the treaty, those rules, although not 'general', must be 'common' to the parties to the treaty.[39]

Thus the ordinary usage of 'international law' to include treaties is supported by the preparatory work. Further support in subsequent practice is considered in section 4 below.[40]

This does not, however, entirely conclude discussion of the matter. In the present context the reference is to 'rules of international law'. The notion of 'rules' differs from obligations, the former importing the idea of something imposed, the latter being undertaken voluntarily. This might suggest a distinction between those treaties which codify rules of customary law and those which simply establish

---

[36] See articles 53, 64, and 71. See also Koskenniemi, 'Report of the Study Group on Fragmentation of International Law: Difficulties arising from the Diversification and Expansion of International Law', at 254, para 3 headed 'The nature and operation of "general international law"?'; and for a study of the term in a particular context, see M Wood, 'The International Tribunal for the Law of the Sea and General International Law' (2007) 22 *International Journal of Marine and Coastal Law* 351.

[37] [1966] *Yearbook of ILC*, vol I, part II, p 190, para 70.

[38] [1966] *Yearbook of ILC*, vol I, part II at p 191, para 74.

[39] [1966] *Yearbook of ILC*, vol I, part II at p 197, para 52.

[40] See sections 4.3 and 4.4 below.

particular commitments which are voluntarily assumed. It seem clear from the preponderant meaning of 'international law', the ILC preparatory work above, the developing practice considered below, and ILC and academic studies, that other relevant treaties between parties in dispute about interpretation of a treaty between them are viewed as admissible in treaty interpretation, whether by being subsumed within international law (as the source from which they draw their force of obligation), or as facts necessarily relevant to the issue under consideration, or, more specifically, in application of the general rule of international law that 'every treaty in force is binding upon the parties to it and must be performed by them in good faith' (the principle *pacta sunt servanda,* as codified in article 26 of the Vienna Convention).

The further specification 'applicable in the relations between the parties' tends to support the conclusion that treaty obligations are covered by article 31(3)(c). International law is axiomatically applicable in relations between states, whereas treaty obligations are distinctly a matter of relations between the parties.

3.3 Which are 'the parties'?

The scope of the limitation in article 31(3)(c) to rules that are applicable in the relations between 'the parties' cannot be determined solely by reference to the ordinary meaning of this term, nor is it clear from the context. The first issue is whether the reference is to the parties to a dispute or difference over the meaning of a treaty, or to parties to the treaty being interpreted. Even if the latter, the question which recurs in the case of a multilateral treaty is whether the meaning is just those of the parties to the treaty who have a dispute or difference over interpretation, or a group of parties who have established some particular international regime among themselves, or whether the reference is to all parties to the treaty which is being invoked to provide applicable rules.

On the face of it, the position should be clear since 'party' has a special meaning in the Vienna Convention by virtue of article 2(1)(g), where the term is defined to mean 'a State which has consented to be bound by the treaty and for which the treaty is in force'. The plural in common usage in treaty parlance is 'states parties', but the Vienna Convention abbreviates this to 'parties'.

However, this does not conclusively resolve the matter. In immediate proximity to article 31(3)(c) are references to 'parties' in articles 31(2)(a) (an agreement relating to the treaty made between 'all the parties' in connection with its conclusion), article 31(2)(b) (an instrument made by 'one or more parties' in connection with the conclusion of the treaty and accepted by 'the other parties' as an instrument related to it), and in article 31(3)(a) (a subsequent agreement between 'the parties' regarding the treaty's interpretation or application). These references are clearly to states which have some relationship to the treaty in question, rather than to those which have some question between them as to the treaty's meaning. Less clear is whether these provisions really are limited to parties as defined in article 2, viz those states which have consented to be bound and for which the treaty is in force.

There is little logical or rational difficulty in applying the strict definition in relation to article 31(3)(a). Only those for whom the treaty is in force have a direct interest and obvious right to reach agreement on how to interpret it, though even here there may be some doubt because of the potential impact of such agreement on those who have signed a treaty subject to ratification and may be proceeding to ratification on a different interpretative basis from that now agreed among the parties. More problematic, however, is the meaning of 'parties' in article 31(2) (a) and (b). Both subparagraphs refer to acts of 'parties' in connection with the conclusion of a treaty. The better view sees conclusion as a process starting at authentication of the text and potentially stretching through to consent of states to be bound, but not including entry into force.[41] Yet at the time of conclusion states would only be 'parties' in the sense defined in the Vienna Convention if it was one of those treaties by which states become bound by signature alone (ie without being subject to ratification) and which come into force at that point without delay. Otherwise both limbs of the definition of 'party' in article 2(1)(g) (a state having consented to be bound and for which the treaty is in force) could not be fulfilled by two or more states in treaty relations with one another. This does not appear to have caused any problems in application of these provisions of the Vienna rules, probably because interpretative issues that are argued out in the public domain usually involve states which are bound by the treaty in question.

In the immediate context of article 31(3)(c), the further qualification of relevant rules of international law requiring that these be 'applicable in the relations between the parties' gives an impression that the phrase must narrow the interpretative quest by excluding some rules of international law that are not applicable in such relations. Setting to one side peremptory norms of general international law (*jus cogens*), as described in article 53 of the Vienna Convention and being rules from which departure is not permitted, states may generally come to their own agreements on the rules that are to apply between themselves, provided they do not violate their obligations to others. Even where rules are set out in a multilateral treaty, permitted reservations modify the rules applicable in relations between parties and permissive rules may be exercised in ways which create a variety of possible obligations.

Thus, article 31(3)(c) has been drawn wide enough to cover rules of international law subject to, or including, any permissible modification or extension by treaty applicable to those states involved in the particular interpretative process. Nevertheless, it is not clear from the text of article 31(3)(c) whether the latter states are the only ones to be considered in applying the rule. The context suggests that 'parties' does not necessarily mean all the parties to the treaty being interpreted. The inclusion of 'all' before 'the parties' in article 31(2)(a) is unambiguous. This might suggest that where 'all parties' is meant, this is stated. However, other references in the Vienna rules to the 'parties' can bear the meaning of 'all' even though the word is not included. In article 31(3)(c) the immediate context is slightly different. The

---

[41] See Chapter 6, section 2.1.1 above for the meaning of 'conclusion' of a treaty.

omission of 'all' is combined with the phrase 'applicable in the relations between the parties', wording which may import the idea of *significant* relations, which makes more sense if referring to relations between the parties having an immediate interest in the issue of interpretation, rather than to all states parties to the treaty that is being interpreted. The phrase 'relations between the parties' (with 'legal' included before 'relations') also occurs in article 72 of the Vienna Convention.[42] That wording is in the context of suspension of a treaty between some parties only; but in view of that clear context, it goes no further than showing that the wording in article 31(3)(c) could refer to only some of the parties.

It seems clear that the point cannot be resolved by analysis alone. It has exercised the ILC study group on fragmentation of international law, academic investigation, and has begun to attract attention in practice. These further sources of guidance are considered below.

4. Issues and Practice

The instruction in article 31(3)(c) to take into account relevant rules of international law applicable in the relations between the parties appeared for a long time to be a dead letter, at least as regards explicit reliance on it.[43] However, this did not mean that courts and tribunals were ignoring international law in interpreting treaties. They were simply following established practice but not linking any particular aspect of their practice to this treaty provision. The need to identify a role, and more positively the opportunity to make the rule 'operational', was identified by Professor Sands when reflecting on issues that had arisen over the developing 'precautionary principle' in environmental law and what account should be taken of its potential impact on interpretation of treaties that had no specific reference to the rule but were of a kind on which environmental law had a bearing.[44] Subsequently, consideration of the role of the rule became part of the ILC's work of 'fragmentation' of international law.[45] The developing practice of relying on the

---

[42] Article 72(1): 'Unless the treaty otherwise provides or the parties otherwise agree, the suspension of the operation of a treaty under its provisions or in accordance with the present Convention: (a) releases the parties between which the operation of the treaty is suspended from the obligation to perform the treaty in their mutual relations during the period of the suspension; (b) does not otherwise affect the legal relations between the parties established by the treaty.'

[43] See H Thirlway, 'The Law and Procedure of the International Court of Justice 1960–1989 Part Three' (1991) LXII BYBIL 1 at 58, pointing out that the rule did not resolve the intertemporal problem, that it was not immediately apparent that it had anything to do with it, and concluding that '[i]t is therefore doubtful whether this sub-paragraph will be of any assistance in the task of treaty interpretation'.

[44] P Sands, 'Treaty, Custom and the Cross-fertilization of International Law' (1998) 1 *Yale Human Rights & Development Law Journal* 85.

[45] See the Koskenniemi 'Report of the Study Group on Fragmentation of International Law: Difficulties arising from the Diversification and Expansion of International Law', further Report of 18 July 2006, A/CN.4/L.702, and ILC Report on its Fifty-eighth Session (2006), UN Gen. Ass., Official Records, Sixty-first Session, Supplement No 10 (A/61/10), pp 400–23.

rule has also been the subject of a thorough study under the more optimistic rubric of 'systemic integration'.[46]

It may also be helpful to consider a detailed analysis of case law from both before and after the conclusion of the Vienna Convention by Merkouris who has suggested that use of the various elements of article 31(3)(c) is actually based on a single criterion, which he names 'the proximity criterion'.[47] He identifies 'four different manifestations of the proximity criterion':

'i) terminological proximity;
ii) subject-matter proximity;
iii) shared signatory parties ('actor') proximity; and
iv) temporal proximity.'[48]

These are self-explanatory and may prove useful to have in mind, particularly when considering the potential interpretative contribution from other treaties, a contribution which ought to be subject to careful justification but whose legitimacy some courts and tribunals appear to assume.

4.1 Terms

4.1.1 Extent of relevant 'international law'

Several questions present themselves for consideration in relation to this issue. First is whether this provision is referring to rules of international law relevant to the interpretation as distinct from any rules relevant to the legal relations of the parties or obligations pertaining to the matter in issue. It seems clear from the context that the provision is concerned only with interpretation. Thus relevant rules must be those which can aid the quest for the meaning of a treaty provision, not those applying to a situation generally. Of course, the latter will not necessarily be excluded from consideration in the case. If a court or tribunal is charged with resolving an international dispute, and is not limited to identifying the correct interpretation of a treaty, international law may be relevant to resolution of the dispute; but that is for reasons other than article 31(3)(c).

However, this distinction is easier to make in principle than in practice. Part of the difficulty lies in the fact that the interpretative exercise identified at the outset of the Vienna rules (and in the function of courts, lawyers, and others) is interpretation of a *treaty,* while detailed elements of the rules necessarily also address interpretation of the *terms* of a treaty. A further factor complicating analysis is that interpretation is often difficult to separate from application of provisions, understandably enough perhaps when a treaty is being considered in the context of a specific issue or dispute.

---

[46] McLachlan, 'The Principle of Systemic Integration and Article 31(3)(c) of the Vienna Convention' (2005) 54 ICLQ 279.

[47] P Merkouris, *Article 31(3)(c) of the VCLT and the Principle of Systemic Integration* (Ph D Thesis, 2010), pp 36–78, <https://qmro.qmul.ac.uk/jspui/handle/123456789/477>.

[48] Merkouris, at 78.

The majority judgment of the ICJ in the *Oil Platforms* case illustrates well some of the issues identified in the preceding paragraphs. That judgment treated at some length the rules of international law on the use of force. Yet some of the judges in separate opinions in that case, as well as commentators, observed that this use of international law was not for the purposes of treaty interpretation but more to ascertain law which might apply to the facts which had arisen.[49]

The term 'international law' has been considered above in the context of its ordinary meaning.[50] This is not limited to customary international law. A broad meaning (and in particular one including treaty obligations) is also suggested by the references to 'any' rule and 'applicable in the relations between the parties'. The question whether 'international law' in North American Free Trade Agreement (NAFTA) meant just 'customary' international law was a core issue in *Pope & Talbot v Canada (Damages Phase)*.[51] There, interpretation was in the context of a NAFTA treaty provision (though the tribunal had included reference to article 31(3)(c) when confirming the applicability of the Vienna rules at an earlier phase of the case[52]). The analogous point, however, which is significant for present purposes is that the tribunal used what it saw as the definition of international law, viz the elements which article 38 of the Statute of the ICJ directs the ICJ to apply as 'international law'. The tribunal noted that this is a broader concept than customary international law.[53]

More recently a panel set up by the Dispute Settlement Body (DSB) in the WTO considered article 31(3)(c) in the *Biotech* case.[54] This arose from complaints over a moratorium by the EU on approval of agricultural products affected by genetic modification and other EU measures regarding such 'biotech products'. One issue was whether the Convention on Biological Diversity and the Protocol on Biosafety were treaties to be taken into account when interpreting rights and obligations under relevant WTO treaties. The Panel stated: 'In our view, there can be no doubt that treaties and customary rules of international law are "rules of international law" within the meaning of Article 31(3)(c)' (though there were more problematic issues as regards the content of those instruments and the fact that some only of the disputants were parties to them).[55]

A specific link between the Vienna Convention provision and article 38 of the ICJ Statute was made as long ago as 1975 by the ECtHR, identifying 'general

---

[49] *Oil Platforms (Islamic Republic of Iran v United States of America) (Merits)* [2003] ICJ Reports 161m and see sections 4.3 and 4.5 below.

[50] See section 3.2.2 above.

[51] *Arbitration under Chapter Eleven of NAFTA, Pope & Talbot v Canada (Award in respect of Damages)* (2002) 41 ILM 1347.

[52] *Arbitration under Chapter Eleven of NAFTA, Pope & Talbot v Canada (Interim Award)* 26 June 2000, paras 65–68.

[53] *Arbitration under Chapter Eleven of NAFTA, Pope & Talbot v Canada (Award in respect of Damages)* at 1356, para 46.

[54] *European Communities—Measures Affecting the Approval and Marketing of Biotech Products*, Reports of the Panel, 29 September 2006, WT/DS291-3/R; see further section 4.1.3 below.

[55] *European Communities—Measures Affecting the Approval and Marketing of Biotech Products*, Reports of the Panel, 29 September 2006, WT/DS291-3/R at p 332, para 7.67.

principles of law recognised by civilised nations' (ICJ Statute, article 38(1)(c)) as relevant to the interpretation of the term 'civil rights' in article 6 of the European Convention on Human Rights:

Article 31 para. 3 (c) of the Vienna Convention indicates that account is to be taken, together with the context, of 'any relevant rules of international law applicable in the relations between the parties'. Among those rules are general principles of law and especially 'general principles of law recognized by civilized nations' (Article 38 para. 1 (c) of the Statute of the International Court of Justice)...

The principle whereby a civil claim must be capable of being submitted to a judge ranks as one of the universally 'recognised' fundamental principles of law; the same is true of the principle of international law which forbids the denial of justice. Article 6 para. 1 (art. 6–1) must be read in the light of these principles.[56]

It might seem reasonable to conclude that the Vienna Convention reference to international law includes all the elements of article 38 of the ICJ Statute on an equal footing. However, while this seems clear as regards treaties, custom, and general principles (that is paragraphs (a) to (c) of article 38), 'judicial decisions and the teachings of the most highly qualified publicists of the various nations' are characterized by paragraph (d) of article 38 as 'subsidiary means for the determination of rules of law'. Nevertheless, since article 31(3)(c) of the Vienna Convention requires attention to be paid to relevant 'rules' of international law, if use of judicial decisions and teachings do lead to identification of such rules, their use must be taken as acceptable in treaty interpretation. Certainly courts and tribunals do make free use of such material without apparently seeing any need to find a specific justification in the Vienna rules.

4.1.2 'Rules'

Case law is insufficiently developed to give a clear indication of the scope of the term 'rules' in the present context.[57] That such rules are those applying in relations between states points to their being legal rules. However, there is some debate whether international law includes a more extensive concept of law and whether instruments which are not binding may legitimately influence interpretation. That this debate extends to the concept of 'rules' was acknowledged in the *Iron Rhine* case:

There is considerable debate as to what, within the field of environmental law, constitutes 'rules' or 'principles'; what is 'soft law'; and which environmental treaty law or principles have contributed to the development of customary international law. Without entering further into those controversies, the Tribunal notes that in all of these categories 'environment' is broadly referred to as including air, water, land, flora and fauna, natural ecosystems and sites, human health and safety, and climate. The emerging principles, whatever their

---

[56] *Golder v the United Kingdom* Series A, vol 18 (Judgment of 21 February 1975), p 17, para 35.
[57] For a brief jurisprudential summary of the concepts of rules, principles, measures, etc see M Leir, 'Canadian Practice in International Law, 1998–99' (1999) 37 *Canadian Yearbook of International Law* 317 at 320; and, more extensively, W L Twining and D Miers, *How to Do Things with Rules: A Primer of Interpretation* (Cambridge: CUP, 5th edn, 2010).

current status, make reference to conservation, management, notions of prevention and of sustainable development, and protection for future generations...[58]

The arbitral tribunal did not find it necessary to go far into the meaning of rules because it found that the duty of states to prevent or mitigate harm to the environment had become a principle of international law.[59]

The ECtHR has made its own particular contribution to the expansion of the range of 'rules' which might be taken into account under article 31(3)(c) of the Vienna Convention.[60] This was recognized by the House of Lords in the context of article 31(3)(c) in *A and Others v Secretary of State for the Home Department (No 2)*, where examples of the range of instruments used by the Human Rights court are conveniently cited.[61] Some of those instruments do not appear to be binding in themselves (though the position is more complex because they may amount to statements of customary international law or have other relevant aspects connecting them with the Vienna rules).

The Court has noted that it has 'never considered the provisions of the Convention [on Human Rights] as the sole framework of reference for the interpretation of the rights and freedoms enshrined therein'.[62] In *Demir and Baykara v Turkey* the Court spelt out the extent to which it takes into account general international law and other international texts and instruments when interpreting the European Convention. Its approach has reflected its view of the Convention as a 'living' instrument which is to be interpreted 'in the light of present-day conditions' and taking account of 'evolving norms of national and international law'.[63] The Court recalled cases in which it had referred to multilateral treaties, such as the UN Convention on the Rights of the Child, 1989 and ILO Conventions on Forced Labour and Abolition of Slavery, [64] but it also identified article 31(3)(c) of the Vienna Convention as including general principles of law. The Court also referred to its classification of the prohibition of torture as a peremptory norm of international law evidenced not only by multilateral conventions but also by a decision of the International Criminal Tribunal for the Former Yugoslavia and the judgment of the House of Lords in *ex parte Pinochet (No 3)*.[65] The Court further noted that in a number of judgments it had made interpretative use of intrinsically non-binding instruments of Council of Europe bodies, such as recommendations and resolutions of the Committee of Ministers and the Parliamentary Assembly.

---

[58] *Arbitration regarding the Iron Rhine ("IJzeren Rijn") Railway (Belgium/Netherlands)*, (2005) XXVII RIAA 35, p 66 para 58, and see sections 4.2 and 4.7 below.

[59] (2005) XXVII RIAA 35 at para 59.

[60] See Chapter 4, section 3.5 above and Chapter 10, section 4.2 below.

[61] Per Lord Bingham, [2005] 3 WLR 1249 at 1268–70, paras 29–31.

[62] *Demir and Baykara v Turkey* (Application no 34503/97), Judgment of 12 November 2008, para 67 and see generally M Fitzmaurice, 'Dynamic (Evolutive) Interpretation of Treaties: Part I' (2008) 21 *Hague Yrbk IL* 101 and Part II (2009) 22 *Hague Yrbk IL* 3.

[63] *Demir and Baykara v Turkey*, at para 68.

[64] See also *National Union of Rail, Maritime and Transport Workers v the United Kingdom* (Application no 31045/10), Judgment of 8 April 2014, para 76.

[65] *Demir and Baykara v Turkey*, at paras 71–73.

More controversially, perhaps, the Court observed that that 'in searching for common ground among the norms of international law it has never distinguished between sources of law according to whether or not they have been signed or ratified by the respondent State'.[66] It listed numerous cases and circumstances in which it had taken account of instruments which had not become binding on respondent states in cases before it.[67] While in some instances the Court had adopted this position in the light of the evolution of domestic laws in parallel with a multilateral treaty or evidence that provisions of a treaty reflected customary international law, in other instances the Court had adopted a generous view of what may be taken into account in identifying common international or domestic law standards of European states when interpreting the European Convention:

The Court, in defining the meaning of terms and notions in the text of the Convention, can and must take into account elements of international law other than the Convention, the interpretation of such elements by competent organs, and the practice of European States reflecting their common values. The consensus emerging from specialised international instruments and from the practice of Contracting States may constitute a relevant consideration for the Court when it interprets the provisions of the Convention in specific cases.

In this context, it is not necessary for the respondent State to have ratified the entire collection of instruments that are applicable in respect of the precise subject matter of the case concerned. It will be sufficient for the Court that the relevant international instruments denote a continuous evolution in the norms and principles applied in international law or in the domestic law of the majority of member States of the Council of Europe and show, in a precise area, that there is common ground in modern societies....[68]

The *Demir and Baykara* case concerned the right of municipal council employees to form trade unions, to engage in collective bargaining, and to enter into collective agreements. The right in article 11 of the European Convention 'to form and to join trade unions' was qualified to allow a state to impose restrictions on the exercise of these rights by 'members...of the administration of the State'. It can be seen from the way in which these rights are so briefly defined, and from the need to give effective application to an evolving regime, that interpretation of the Convention necessarily requires identification of standards from sources outside the treaty itself. Justifying reference to instruments to which a respondent state is not a party, the Court linked the international law background to the issue before it with its consideration of the object and purpose of the Convention:

Being made up of a set of rules and principles that are accepted by the vast majority of States, the common international or domestic law standards of European States reflect a reality that the Court cannot disregard when it is called upon to clarify the scope of a Convention provision that more conventional means of interpretation have not enabled it to establish with a sufficient degree of certainty.[69]

---

[66] Application no. 34503/97, at para 78.
[67] Application no. 34503/97, at paras 76–84.
[68] Application no. 34503/97, at paras 85–86, cross-reference omitted.
[69] Application no. 34503/97, at para 76.

This appears to recognize that the range of materials being taken into account was not typical of treaty interpretation. Nevertheless, *Demir* has been followed, particularly prominently in *RMT v UK* where the ECtHR again took an expansive view of the Convention's provision relating to trade union activities.[70] Such a broad potential attributed by the Court to article 31(3)(c) of the Vienna Convention is not to be taken as something automatically applying to treaties in general but, rather, an approach which takes account of the particular interpretative circumstances of the European Convention on Human Rights.

More generally, principles which constitute emerging rules of international law are sometimes described as 'soft law'. The role of soft law in treaty interpretation is itself still emerging.[71] Some other courts and tribunals take a stricter view of 'rules' than does the ECtHR. Thus, for example, in the *Biotech* case, the WTO panel concluded that the precautionary principle could only be considered a rule of international law if it had become a general principle of international law (which, it found, it had not).[72]

What is clear from these cases is that the notion of a 'rule' cannot usefully be taken in isolation from 'international law', and that the examples in this section must therefore be read in conjunction with the interpretation of the other terms of article 31(3)(c) considered in this chapter.

4.1.3 Applicable in the relations between which 'parties'?

Practice and academic investigation of this phrase sheds little light on the rather uncertain outcome of textual investigation of the term 'parties' (section 3.3 above). The conclusion of the textual and contextual inquiry was that the phrase could refer to parties to the treaty that is being interpreted, rather than to parties to any dispute about its meaning; but whether the focus is on examination of relations between *all* the parties to the treaty, whether the situation is similar to that of subsequent practice (where the practice must be the concordant practice of a sufficient number of parties coupled with acquiescence and imputed concurrence of the rest), or whether there is some other interpretation to be given to the term remains unclear.

---

[70] *National Union of Rail, Maritime and Transport Workers v UK* (Application no 31045/10), Judgment of 8 April 2014; a further example of the ECtHR's use of a treaty to which a state was not a party is *Rantsev v Cyprus and Russia* (Application no 25965/04), Judgment of 7 January 2010, where, in interpreting provisions protecting against slavery etc (article 4 of the Human Rights Convention), the Court found it unnecessary to consider whether the particular treatment constituted 'slavery', 'servitude' or 'forced and compulsory labour', concluding instead that 'trafficking' itself, within the meaning of treaties including the Council of Europe's the Anti-Trafficking Convention to which Russia was not a party, fell within article 4 of the Human Rights Convention (para 282).

[71] See the reference to soft law in the *Arbitration regarding the Iron Rhine ("IJzeren Rijn") Railway (Belgium/Netherlands)* (2005) XXVII UNRIAA 35 at 66, para 58, where the arbitral tribunal, in the context of article 31(3)(c) of the Vienna Convention, noted the controversy over what constituted 'soft law' but did not have to decide whether it had an independent role in treaty interpretation.

[72] *European Communities—Measures Affecting the Approval and Marketing of Biotech Products*, Reports of the Panel, 29 September 2006, WT/DS291-3/R at 333 at para 7.67.

Reasoning and decisions of judicial bodies which have looked at this issue, and academic writing on the topic, help to identify the issues and possibilities without producing any firm outcome. It is in connection with dispute settlement in the WTO and in human rights cases that the most significant attention has been given to the matter. Although the actual decisions of the DSBs have not generally specifically linked to this provision in the Vienna rules their decision to consider particular material, what they have actually done has been revealing in some instances. It needs to be noted that disputes within the WTO are not limited to those between only two states parties to a treaty. Groups of states may be involved on one side or both. The European Union is often involved. Further, members of the WTO may make representations in cases in which they are not the primary disputants. Thus, the proceedings of the DSBs provide an opportunity for the wider constituency of interested members of the WTO to be involved in consideration of the interpretation in issue. It would therefore be less surprising if the outcome reflected a view on the relations between the *disputing parties*, moderated by any account taken of the more extensive web of relations of all participants (that is those submitting views in the dispute procedure), with the presumed acquiescence of non-participants in the background.

As the rules of international law derived from other sources than treaties generally apply axiomatically to all states, the issue of whether the phrase 'applicable in the relations between the parties' refers to all parties to the treaty under interpretation normally only arises in connection with use of one or more other treaties in the process of interpretation. In this context Professor McLachlan has identified four possibilities which provide a useful structure for examination of the issues and practice, also taking into account work of the ILC on fragmentation.[73]

(i) All parties to the treaty being interpreted must be parties to any other treaty being used

The first possibility is that the rule may require that all parties to the treaty under interpretation also be parties to any other treaties or instruments relied upon.[74] The ILC reported that in its study group it had been suggested that this was 'a clear but very narrow standard', but that resulting problems might be alleviated by distinguishing between using the other treaty or treaties in the process of interpretation

---

[73] McLachlan, 'The Principle of Systemic Integration and Article 31(3)(c) of the Vienna Convention' (2005) 54 ICLQ 279, at 314 ff. See also Koskenniemi, 'Report of the Study Group on Fragmentation of International Law: Difficulties arising from the Diversification and Expansion of International Law', at 237ff; M Fitzmaurice, 'Canons of Treaty Interpretation: Selected Case Studies from the World Trade Organization and the North American Free Trade Agreement' (2007) 10 *Austrian Review of International and European Law* 43; J Pauwelyn, *Conflict of Norms in Public International Law: How WTO Law Relates to other Rules of International law* (Cambridge: CUP, 2003), 253–74; J Meltzer, 'Interpreting the WTO Agreements—A Commentary on Professor Pauwelyn's Approach' (2003–2004) 25 *Mich J Int'l L* 917; and J Pauwelyn, 'Reply to Joshua Meltzer' (2003–2004) 25 *Mich J Int'l L* 923.

[74] See McLachlan, 'The Principle of Systemic Integration and Article 31(3)(c) of the Vienna Convention', at 314.

of a treaty and in its application.[75] Some support for the 'narrow standard' appears to have been given by a WTO panel in the *Biotech* case:

...we note that Article 31(3)(c) does not refer to 'one or more parties'. Nor does it refer to 'the parties to a dispute'. We further note that Article 2.1(g) of the *Vienna Convention* defines the meaning of the term 'party' for the purposes of the *Vienna Convention*. Thus, 'party' means 'a State which has consented to be bound by the treaty and for which the treaty is in force'. It may be inferred from these elements that the rules of international law applicable in the relations between 'the parties' are the rules of international law applicable in the relations between the States which have consented to be bound by the treaty which is being interpreted, and for which that treaty is in force. This understanding of the term 'the parties' leads logically to the view that the rules of international law to be taken into account in interpreting the WTO agreements at issue in this dispute are those which are applicable in the relations between the WTO Members.[76]

In consequence of this understanding of article 31(3)(c), the panel found that it could not take account of the Convention on Biological Diversity and the Protocol on Biosafety in interpreting relevant WTO treaties. The USA, one of the parties to the *Biotech* dispute, was not a party to either of the treaties and others involved in the dispute were not parties to the Protocol so that those treaties were not 'applicable' in the relations between these WTO Members and all other WTO Members.[77]

The main perceived problem in the case of interpretation of WTO treaties is that, given the very extensive membership of that organization, the number of other multilateral treaties that could be invoked to aid interpretation of WTO instruments would be severely limited by giving the rule its strictest meaning, and bilateral treaties would all be excluded. However, it may be argued that if the objective of article 31(3)(c) is integration of interpretation of a treaty into the system of international law, the question should not be whether all the members are parties to another treaty to be used in interpretation of a WTO instrument but rather whether the provisions of that other treaty state rules of international law. If the provisions of that other treaty do not state rules of international law, on the face of it they do not come within the scope of article 31(3)(c). That does not necessarily exclude them from consideration in treaty interpretation if they provide guidance on the ordinary meaning of a term or can be invoked on the basis of some other element of the Vienna rules, such as in the form of supplementary means of interpretation.

---

[75] ILC Report on the work of its Fifty-seventh Session (2005), General Assembly, Official Records, Sixtieth Session, Supplement No 10 (A/60/10), p 217, para 472(a).

[76] *European Communities—Measures Affecting the Approval and Marketing of Biotech Products*, Reports of the Panel, 29 September 2006, WT/DS291-3/R at 333, para 7.68 (the footnotes, omitted from the extract, contain substantial support, including a thorough examination of the context and of past practice in the WTO); see also section 4.1.1 above and M Fitzmaurice, 'Canons of Treaty Interpretation: Selected Case Studies from the World Trade Organization and the North American Free Trade Agreement' (2007) 10 *Austrian Review of International and European Law* 43.

[77] Reports of the Panel paras 7.74 and 7.75.

It should be noted that when the ILC was considering fragmentation of international law, the case law applying article 31(3)(c) was still at a fairly early stage of its development. It has been pointed out that the panel in *Biotech* was not confronted with a situation in which all the parties to a dispute were parties to other potentially relevant treaties to which uninvolved members of the WTO were not parties; hence, the panel specifically found that it did not need to take any position on that.[78]

It has also been pointed out that since the panel report in *Biotech*, the WTO Appellate Body has left open the meaning of 'parties' in article 31(3)(c).[79] Noting the need to exercise caution in drawing guidance from an international agreement to which not all WTO Members are party, the Appellate Body acknowledged the ILC's view that the Vienna Convention provision is an expression of the 'principle of systemic integration' and indicated that:

In a multilateral context such as the WTO, when recourse is had to a non-WTO rule for the purposes of interpreting provisions of the WTO agreements, a delicate balance must be struck between, on the one hand, taking due account of an individual WTO Member's international obligations and, on the other hand, ensuring a consistent and harmonious approach to the interpretation of WTO law among all WTO Members.[80]

In the particular case the matter did not have to be decided in those terms because the Appellate Body found that the provision of the other treaty put forward by some parties to the dispute was not 'relevant' and could not, therefore, meet the requirements of article 31(3)(c) in any event. While relevance may prove helpful in resolving the problem in some cases, the ILC's suggestion that the distinction between interpretation and application could be deployed to allow legal obligations to be upheld in the guise of application where participation in the 'other' treaty is not sufficiently extensive to permit its use for interpretation, may need to be approached with caution. If another set of treaty obligations is to be applied to displace those in the treaty under interpretation, the treaty under interpretation must at least be open to being interpreted to allow this. However, if the treaty under interpretation allows another one to prevail, that is not an *interpretative* effect but rather an application of rules regulating application of parallel or successive treaties dealing with the same subject. Thus, as a solution to the problem of apparently competing treaty obligations, it seems doubtful whether the suggested distinction between interpretation and application (which has not been maintained in the ILC's final conclusions on fragmentation) could help.[81]

---

[78] Reports of the Panel at para 7.72 and for analysis of this, see P Merkouris, 'Keep Calm and Call...', <http://www.ejiltalk.org/> 19 June 2014; see also P Merkouris, *Article 31(3)(c) of the VCLT and the Principle of Systemic Integration* (Ph D Thesis, 2010), pp 36–9, <https://qmro.qmul.ac.uk/jspui/handle/123456789/477>.

[79] See P Merkouris, 'Keep Calm and Call...', <http://www.ejiltalk.org/> post published 19 June 2014 discussing the case of *EC—Large Civil Aircraft* WT/DS316/AB/R, 316ABR (2011)

[80] *EC—Large Civil Aircraft* at p 363, para 845.

[81] See also doubts expressed by Judge Higgins over the prospect of article 31(3)(c) providing an overall answer to systemic fragmentation: R Higgins, 'A Babel of Judicial Voices: Ruminations from the Bench' (2006) 55 ICLQ 791 at 803–4.

Nevertheless, it must be noted that in practice reference is sometimes made to obligations under other treaties in the guise of application without differentiating this from interpretation using article 31(3)(c). For example, in *HN v Poland*[82] the ECtHR emphasized that the European Convention on Human Rights:

> ... must be applied in accordance with principles of international law rights (see ... *Al-Adsani v. the United Kingdom* [GC], no. 35763/97, § 55, ECHR 2001-XI). Consequently ... the positive obligations that Article 8 of the Convention lays on the Contracting States in the matter of reuniting a parent with his or her children must be interpreted in the light of the Hague Convention of 25 October 1980 on the Civil Aspects of International Child Abduction, all the more so where the respondent state is also a party to that instrument ...[83]

If the last part of this extract is to be read as basing an interpretation of the European Convention on a principle of international law which is applicable whether or not a particular party to the European Convention is a party to a treaty which states the principle, this seems wholly consistent with article 31(3)(c). The mention of the respondent state actually being a party can be seen as reflecting prudent judicial inclination to focus on obligations of the state party to the proceedings, rather than a clear adoption of an interpretation of article 31(3)(c) that only parties to proceedings need be parties to another treaty for it to be invoked as an aid to interpretation.

(ii) All parties to the dispute over interpretation must be parties to any other treaty being used

The second possibility canvassed by Professor McLachlan is that the problem posed by the phrase in article 31(3)(c) could be met by permitting reference to another treaty if the treaty parties in dispute are also parties to the other treaty.[84] The advantage claimed for this approach is that it would broaden the range of treaties potentially applicable for interpretation purposes, though it would be capricious, in effect being dependent on which particular treaty partners were in dispute.

As an actual interpretation of the Vienna Convention provision, however, the approach finds little support in case law. In a WTO case a panel report, in further proceedings in the *United States—Shrimp* case, noted that the Appellate Body in

---

[82] *HN v Poland*, App no 77710/01 (Judgment of 13 September 2005).

[83] *HN v Poland*, App no 77710/01 (Judgment of 13 September 2005) at para 75. One of the cases mentioned, *Al-Adsani* (citation in quoted extract), did specifically refer to article 31(3)(c) of the Vienna Convention, and reference to that provision as making a link with other treaties has become more common at the ECtHR: see, eg, *X v Latvia* (Application no. 27853/09), Judgment of 26 November 2013, at paras 92–101 making extensive reference to particular provisions and the 'philosophy' of the 1980 Hague Convention. See also *Behrami v France*, ECtHR App no 71412/01 (Judgment of 2 May 2007), para 122, taking into account rules of international law in the UN Charter without assuming the role of authoritative interpreter of the Charter; and Lord Bingham in *R (on the application of Al-Jedda) v Secretary of State for Defence* [2007] UKHL 58 at para 36, citing *Behrami* and other ECtHR cases in the context of the interpretative principle laid down in article 31(3)(c) of the Vienna Convention.

[84] McLachlan, 'The Principle of Systemic Integration and Article 31(3)(c) of the Vienna Convention' at 314.

the earlier phase had referred to a number of international agreements, many of which have been ratified or otherwise accepted 'by the parties to this dispute'.[85] The panel referred in the very next sentence to article 31(3)(c), the juxtaposition making it appear that the test for that provision's application was whether the parties to the dispute (rather than to the treaty under interpretation) were parties to the other instruments. This, however, gives scant support for that proposition. Both principal parties to the later phase of the case had accepted or become committed to apply all but one of the instruments mentioned by the Appellate Body in the relevant part of its report at the earlier stage.[86] True, the Appellate Body had referred to article 31(3)(c) in its earlier decision, but that was in a different context. The Appellate Body had been considering whether the USA had acted in a discriminatory fashion in applying its legislation on shrimping to foreign fishers of shrimps.[87] The evidence had been that one of the requirements of the governing US legislation had been consultation with relevant foreign governments, a requirement which, the Appellate Body noted, was seen in the pattern of those international instruments to which it referred. That was analysis of the facts to determine whether there had been discrimination. It was, in terms of treaty handling, application, not part of interpretation. Further, as observed by Pauwelyn, the panel in that case did not address the issue of whether other members of the WTO were in fact parties to the instruments and in the more recent case of *Chile—Price Band System* that panel specifically left aside the question of whether a rule of international law in the terms of article 31(3)(c) should be applicable between *all* parties to the WTO Agreement to qualify for a role in interpretation.[88]

The absence of support for this interpretation in the case of multilateral treaties must, however, be considered in conjunction with the position as regards bilateral treaties. In general, the point made in response to the ILC's suggested use of a distinction between interpretation and application applies here too. A bilateral treaty could only be invoked as an aid to interpretation of a multilateral treaty if the multilateral treaty is open to the interpretation that such a consideration is possible. Pauwelyn has noted that the WTO Appellate Body referred to principles recognized in double taxation treaties in interpreting the term 'foreign-source income'.[89] Pauwelyn suggests that though the Appellate Body did not give an explicit basis

---

[85] *United States—Import Prohibition of Certain Shrimp and Shrimp Products (Malaysian Recourse to Article 21.5)* WT/DS58/RW, 15 June 2001 at para 5.57; the same matter went to the Appellate Body (WT/DS58/AB/RW, 22 October 2001), but it did not focus on article 31(3)(c) of the Vienna Convention.

[86] *United States—Import Prohibition of Certain Shrimp and Shrimp Products (Malaysian Recourse to Article 21.5)* WT/DS58/RW, 15 June 2001 at para 5.57.

[87] *United States—Import Prohibition of Certain Shrimp and Shrimp Products*, WT/DS58/AB/R, 12 October 1998, paras 161 ff.

[88] Pauwelyn, *Conflict of Norms in Public International Law: How WTO Law Relates to other Rules of International Law*, at 260, and *Chile—Price Band System* WT/DS207/R (2002), para 7.85 (where the panel found that the other agreement that had been invoked did not yield a 'relevant' rule on international law).

[89] Pauwelyn, *Conflict of Norms*, at 260–1, referring to *US Tax Treatment for Foreign Sales Corporations (EU Recourse to Article 21.5)* WT/DS108/AB/RW (2002).

for this approach, it could be interpreted as reflecting the 'common intentions' of all WTO members and, or alternatively, the ordinary meaning, thus applying article 31(3)(c) and 31(1), respectively of the Vienna Convention. This seems a fair assessment, although it is difficult to see why it is necessary to introduce the notion of 'common intentions'. The use in treaty interpretation of provisions based on a common model, or standard form with variants, is a common practice in other matters such as bilateral investment treaties, extradition treaties, air services agreements, etc.[90] This seems within the range of 'rules of international law' as that notion has been (implicitly) interpreted in the practice of arbitral tribunals; but it could also be seen as simply part of the quest to find the ordinary meaning.

(iii) A rule being invoked from any other treaty must be shown to be a customary rule

The third possibility examined by Professor McLachlan is that if a treaty being invoked is one by which not all parties to the one being interpreted are bound, only a rule which can be shown to represent customary law can be given an interpretative role. Professor McLachlan suggests that it could be inappropriately restrictive in two ways.[91] First, he suggests that it could preclude reference to widely accepted treaties, such as the UN Convention on the Law of the Sea, to which not all states are parties and whose content is not all a litany of statements of customary international law.[92] Second, treaties on specialist subjects could be excluded on the basis that not all the parties to the treaty being interpreted are parties to the specialist treaties.[93] It is difficult to evaluate these objections without a concrete situation in which an interpretative issue is posed. Nevertheless, both criticisms seem to assume that a treaty will only state a rule of customary international law if all states are parties to it and if the treaty as a whole is viewed as reflecting customary rules. Yet the Vienna rules themselves are an example of the rather different position that has been authoritatively endorsed. By no means are all states parties to the Vienna Convention and its provisions cannot all be said to state customary international law. Some provisions do, however, do so. The Vienna rules themselves are now generally applied as relevant rules of international law applying in the relations between parties to treaties, including such application by the WTO DSBs.

(iv) A rule being invoked in another treaty must have been implicitly accepted or tolerated by all parties to the treaty under interpretation

The fourth possibility is that propounded by Pauwelyn (and briefly mentioned above).[94] This suggests that not all the parties to the WTO agreement under

---

[90] See section 4.4.1 below.
[91] McLachlan, 'The Principle of Systemic Integration and Article 31(3)(c) of the Vienna Convention' (2005) 54 ICLQ 279, at 314.
[92] McLachlan, at 314.   [93] McLachlan, at 314.
[94] Pauwelyn, *Conflict of Norms*, at 257–63, supports this approach in the case of the WTO Covered Agreements.

interpretation need to have formally become bound by the rule in the other treaty that is to be invoked in the interpretative process:

… the criterion is rather that the rule can be said to be at least *implicitly* accepted or tolerated by all WTO members, in the sense that the rule can reasonably be said to express the common intention or understanding of all members as to what the particular WTO term means.[95]

Once again it can be observed that this seems close to saying that the rule stated in the 'other' treaty is sufficiently established to constitute a rule of customary international law or, if not, sufficiently accepted to constitute an interpretative agreement. It is implicit in that notion that where a treaty states a rule of customary international law, it is not necessary that every state be a party to the treaty for that to be so and, likewise, express agreement of every party is not regarded as indispensable if there has been sufficient acquiescence.

4.1.4 Conclusion as to 'parties'

These four possibilities provide an analytical framework, without resolving the matter. The International Law Commission has also not resolved it. The fourth of the possibilities discussed above offers an approach broadly comparable to the emerging interpretation of paragraph (3)(b) of article 31. This is to the effect that the stronger the evidence provided of a common understanding, the greater the weight to be given to this element of the general rule in a particular case. The ILC has not offered a prescriptive formula to apply uniformly in every situation, but in its 2006 Report offered some guidance of a more subtle nature:

Application of other treaty rules. Article 31(3)(c) also requires the interpreter to consider other treaty-based rules so as to arrive at a consistent meaning. Such other rules are of particular relevance where parties to the treaty under interpretation are also parties to the other treaty, where the treaty rule has passed into or expresses customary international law or where they provide evidence of the common understanding of the parties as to the object and purpose of the treaty under interpretation or as to the meaning of a particular term.[96]

4.2 Intertemporal and temporal issues

Although the remote origins of the rule in article 31(3)(c) are in the work of the ILC considering the intertemporal law, the absence of the intertemporal rule in recognizable form from the final version of the rules may explain why explicit connection in case law between the rule and the intertemporal law is rare. In the 'Iron

---

[95] Pauwelyn, *Conflict of Norms* at 261 (footnote omitted).
[96] ILC Report on the work of its Fifty-eighth Session (2006), General Assembly, Official Records, Sixty-first Session, Supplement No 10 (A/61/10), 414–15, para 21; but note the caution sounded by Judge Higgins: R Higgins, 'A Babel of Judicial Voices: Ruminations from the Bench' (2006) 55 ICLQ 791 at 803–4.

Rhine Railway' arbitration, however, the arbitral tribunal did specifically recognize the intertemporal rule as being one of the 'relevant rules' of international law to which the Vienna Convention refers.[97] The point at issue was allocation of cost of revival, adaptation, and modernization of a railway, costs which would be augmented by the need to respect environmental concerns. At the root of the matter was article XII of a treaty of 1839, which referred to costs and expenses of extension of a 'new road' or 'new canal' (terms later extended to include the railway in issue) from Belgium across the Netherlands.[98]

The tribunal referred to the acceptance in treaty interpretation that some terms, such as conceptual or generic terms, are to be taken as having a meaning necessarily following evolution of the law.[99] As the clearest analysis of the linkage of the Vienna rule to the intertemporal law, the Arbitral Tribunal's statement needs to be seen in full:

Article 31, paragraph 3, subparagraph (c) of the Vienna Convention also requires there to be taken into account 'any relevant rules of international law applicable in the relations between the parties.' The intertemporal rule would seem to be one such 'relevant rule.' By this, regard should be had in interpreting Article XII to juridical facts as they stood in 1839. In particular, it is certainly the case that, in 1839, it was envisaged that the costs for any extension of a new road or canal that Belgium might ask for would be limited and relatively modest. The great advances that were later to be made in electrification, track design and specification, freight stock, and so forth—and the concomitant costs—could not have been foreseen by the Parties. At the same time, this rule does not require the Tribunal to be oblivious either to later facts that bear on the effective application of the treaty, nor indeed to all later legal developments. It has long been established that the understanding of conceptual or generic terms in a treaty may be seen as 'an essentially relative question; it depends upon the development of international relations' *(Nationality Decrees Issued in Tunis and Morocco, P.C.I.J. Series B, No. 4 (1923),* p. 24). Some terms are 'not static, but were by definition evolutionary... The parties to the Covenant must consequently be deemed to have accepted them as such' *(Namibia (SW Africa) Advisory Opinion, I.C.J. Reports 1971,* p.16 at p. 31). Where a term can be classified as generic 'the presumption necessarily arises that its meaning was intended to follow the evolution of the law and to correspond with the meaning attached to the expression by the law in force at any given time' *(Aegean Sea Continental Shelf (Greece/Turkey), Judgment, I.C.J. Reports 1978,* p. 3 at p. 32, para 77). A similar finding was made by the WTO Appellate Body when it had to interpret the term 'natural resources' in Article XX, paragraph (g) of the WTO Agreement *(United States—Import Prohibition of Certain Shrimp and Shrimp Products,* WTIDS58/AB/R, 12 October 1998, para. 130).[100]

In the present case, the tribunal found that although it was not a situation in which conceptual or generic terms were in issue, but rather a matter of new technical railway developments, an 'evolutive interpretation' would be preferred to

---

[97] *Arbitration regarding the Iron Rhine ("IJzeren Rijn ") Railway (Belgium/Netherlands),* (2005) XXVII RIAA 35 at 72, para 79.

[98] (2005) XXVII RIAA 35 at 48, para 17 (the text of the treaty provision is given in French in the award).

[99] (2005) XXVII RIAA 35, and see Chapter 5, para 3.3.5 above, on generic terms.

[100] (2005) XXVII RIAA 35 at 72–3, para 79.

'a strict application of the intertemporal rule' in order to ensure an application of the treaty that would be 'effective in terms of its object and purpose'.[101] Noting further that, 'notwithstanding the intertemporal rule', writers had recognized that the object and purpose of a treaty might lead to evolution and dynamism playing a part in treaty interpretation, the tribunal found that since the treaty of 1839 had no fixed duration and saw the railway between Belgium and Germany as aimed at contributing to the stability needed in the separation of Belgium and the Netherlands, adaptation and modernization of the railway should be taken as within the scope of the original treaty but with certain provisions of international law 'read into' it as they apply today.[102]

Two points particularly attract attention in this award. First, the reference to 'strict application' of the intertemporal rule only takes account of the first element in Judge Huber's formulation in the *Island of Palmas* case.[103] He himself directed how account should be taken of developments in the law.[104] Second, when indicating that modern international law must be read into the 1839 treaty, the tribunal referred back to its analysis of the rules of treaty interpretation and, particularly, the applicability of developing environmental law in the context of the Vienna Convention's article 31(3)(c) (significant in the instant case because of the Netherlands' requirement that measures of noise abatement be taken and tunnelling used where habitat protection was needed).[105]

That the second limb of the intertemporal rule as formulated by Judge Huber is applicable to treaty interpretation is perhaps best evidenced by the Vienna rules themselves. This is both shown by their content and their applicability. As regards content, while the general rule in article 31 takes the interpreter to the original object and purpose (via the text and context), and article 32 brings into consideration the circumstances of the treaties conclusion and preparatory work where appropriate, those elements linked to the time of conclusion are combined with aspects later in time through the references to any subsequent agreement, subsequent practice and (if the treaty is correctly interpreted to include them)any developments falling within article 31(3)(c).[106] As regards applicability of the Vienna rules, their acceptance as a codification of customary international law bears the analysis that they contain both the interpretative rules as they were at the time of the treaty's conclusion, but also the content of those rules as clarified, amplified, or developed since then.

Thus, in *Territorial Dispute (Libyan Arab Jamahiriya/Chad)* the ICJ applied the Vienna rules to a whole series of treaties dating from 1898 that were listed in one

---

[101] (2005) XXVII RIAA 35 at 73, para 80.

[102] (2005) XXVII RIAA 35 at 73–5, paras 81–84 on 'evolutive interpretation'; and see para 84 on 'provisions of international law as they apply today' being 'read into' the 1839 treaty.

[103] See section 1.1 above.   [104] See section 1.1 above.

[105] *Iron Rhine Arbitration*, at 66–7, paras 58–59; see also C Djeffal, 'The Iron Rhine Case – A Treaty's Journey from Peace to Sustainable Development' (2011) 71 *Zaörv* 3.

[106] On the effects of developments in international law on treaty interpretation, see the conclusion of this section and section 4.7 below.

of 1955.[107] Similarly in the 1999 river frontier case *Botswana/Namibia*, having specifically referred to the Vienna rules, the ICJ stated:

In order to illuminate the meaning of words agreed upon in 1890, there is nothing that prevents the Court from taking into account the present-day state of scientific knowledge, as reflected in the documentary material submitted to it by the Parties....[108]

Probably the most useful conclusion that can be found at present on the issue of intertemporality in relation to treaty interpretation is that of the ILC in its 2006 Report:

Inter-temporality. International law is a dynamic legal system. A treaty may convey whether in applying article 31 (3) (c) the interpreter should refer only to rules of international law in force at the time of the conclusion of the treaty or may also take into account subsequent changes in the law. Moreover, the meaning of a treaty provision may also be affected by subsequent developments, especially where there are subsequent developments in customary law and general principles of law.[109]

4.3 Clarifying meaning by reference to international law

Located in its immediate context of treaty interpretation, article 31(3)(c) implicitly invites the interpreter to draw a distinction between using rules of international law as part of the apparatus of treaty interpretation and applying the rules of international law directly to the facts in the context of which the treaty is being considered. The former is within the scope of the Vienna rules, the latter not.

However, there appears to be a prime example of conflation of these two ideas in the judgment of the ICJ in the *Oil Platforms* case.[110] That case concerned the destruction of Iranian oil platforms by the USA when the latter was defending shipping in the Gulf at a time of war between Iran and Iraq. The Court had concluded in the initial phase (1996) that the only dispute within its jurisdiction was over the interpretation and the application of article X(1) ('freedom of commerce') of a Treaty of Amity, Economic Relations, etc of 1955.[111] Iran argued that in destroying its oil platforms in the Gulf, the USA had violated this provision. In 1996 the Court had, however, also taken account of article XX(1)(d) of the same treaty, which stated that the treaty did not 'preclude the application of measures ... necessary to fulfil the obligations of a High Contracting Party for the maintenance or restoration of international peace and security, or necessary to protect its essential security interests'. The Court took the view that article XX(1)(d)

---

[107] [1994] ICJ Reports 6.

[108] *Kasikili/Sedudu Island (Botswana/Namibia)* [1999] ICJ Reports 1045 at 1060, para 20.

[109] ILC Report on the work of its Fifty-eighth Session (2006), General Assembly, Official Records, Sixty-first Session, Supplement No 10 (A/61/10), 415, para (22) (footnotes omitted).

[110] *Oil Platforms (Islamic Republic of Iran v United States of America) (Merits)* [2003] ICJ Reports 161 and see section 4.5 below; for commentary, see F D Berman, 'Treaty "Interpretation" in a Judicial Context' (2004) 29 *Yale Journal of International Law* 315; D French, 'Treaty Interpretation and the Incorporation of Extraneous Legal Rules' (2006) 55 ICLQ 281.

[111] *Oil Platforms (Islamic Republic of Iran v United States of America) (Preliminary Objection)* [1996–II] ICJ Reports 820, para 53.

was 'confined to affording the Parties a possible defence on the merits to be used should the occasion arise'.[112]

At the stage of considering the merits, however, the reasoning in the majority judgment took the general international law of self-defence as the starting point, making reference to article 31(3)(c) of the Vienna Convention in support of this approach.[113] Using general international law, rather than starting with the treaty terms and applying the whole process of the Vienna rules systematically, the ICJ found that the USA could not justify its destruction of the platforms by reliance on article XX(1)(d). The Court nevertheless found that the USA had not violated article X(1). The absence of a finding of a violation prompts the question whether, given the Court's earlier view that article XX(1)(d) could afford a defence 'should the occasion arise', it was necessary to embark on a consideration of that article at all and whether the approach it took was in any way what article 31(3)(c) mandates.

Powerful criticism has been made of the judgment in *Oil Platforms*, including prominently that of two ICJ judges in their separate opinions (though concurring in the result). On the majority's approach to interpretation, Judge Higgins wrote:

The Court has, however, not interpreted Article XX, paragraph 1 *(d)*, by reference to the rules on treaty interpretation. It has rather invoked the concept of treaty interpretation to displace the applicable law. It has replaced the terms of Article XX, paragraph 1 *(d)*, with those of international law on the use of force and all sight of the text of Article XX, paragraph 1 *(d)*, is lost.[114]

Judge Kooijmans similarly took the view that the question was not whether the USA had acted in self-defence under general international law but whether it had violated a treaty. He considered that once the Court had concluded that the USA had not violated article X(1), article XX(1)(d) was not relevant to the decision on the claim made by Iran:

...the approach taken by the Court is putting the cart before the horse. The Court rightly starts by saying that it is its competence to interpret and apply Article XX, paragraph 1 *(d)* (Judgment, para. 33), but it does so by directly applying the criteria of self-defence under Charter law and customary law and continues to do so until it reaches its conclusion in paragraph 78.

The proper approach in my view would have been to scrutinize the meaning of the words 'necessary to protect the essential security interests' in Article XX, paragraph 1 *(d)*....[115]

The role of treaty interpretation is clearest when seen in the context of a particular treaty provision. When it is a matter of considering how a treaty contributes to the law applicable to a particular situation, interpretation of a treaty may become interwoven with issues of its application in the circumstances; but that is still a

---

[112] [1996–II] ICJ Reports 820, at para 20.
[113] [2003] ICJ Reports 161 at 182, para 41.
[114] [2003] ICJ Reports 225 at 238, Separate Opinion at para 49.
[115] [2003] ICJ Reports at 259, Separate Opinion at paras 42–43; and for Judge Kooijmans' explanation of using article 31(3)(c) to lead to supplementary means to provide standards in applying a treaty provision, see section 4.5 below.

different matter from the application of international law directly to the given facts. In the *US—Shrimp* case (whether US restrictions on shrimp imports could be justified as an environmental measure to protect turtles), the Appellate Body of the WTO specifically referred to article 31(3)(c) and identified its function.[116] The structure of the provision in issue was one in which permissible measures for environmental protection and other purposes were listed, the whole list being governed by the requirement in the provision's chapeau (the introductory words) that measures were to be such that they did not constitute 'arbitrary or unjustifiable discrimination between countries where the same conditions prevail, or a disguised restriction on international trade'.

The Appellate Body considered the role of good faith and stated that abuse of treaty rights amounted to a violation of the treaty conferring those rights.[117] However, it distinguished between abuse of rights as an aspect of the general principle requiring good faith in application of a treaty and stated that 'our task here is to interpret the language of the chapeau, seeking additional interpretative guidance, as appropriate, from the general principles of international law'.[118] Nevertheless, it remains difficult to separate out the general deployment of international law, its role as an interpretative guide, and the balancing of rights under the treaty in the part of the Appellate Body's Report which immediately followed its reference to article 31(3)(c):

The task of interpreting and applying the chapeau is, hence, essentially the delicate one of locating and marking out a line of equilibrium between the right of a Member to invoke an exception under Article XX and the rights of the other Members under varying substantive provisions (e.g., Article XI) of the GATT 1994, so that neither of the competing rights will cancel out the other and thereby distort and nullify or impair the balance of rights and obligations constructed by the Members themselves in that Agreement. The location of the line of equilibrium, as expressed in the chapeau, is not fixed and unchanging; the line moves as the kind and the shape of the measures at stake vary and as the facts making up specific cases differ.[119]

It can be seen that the Appellate Body here elides the task of interpreting and that of applying the provision. In this case there seems more justification for this than in some others. The structure of the provision in issue rather dictated this. There was an issue of interpretation over the relationship of the list of excepted measures to the governing conditions in the chapeau, an interpretative issue resulting in a range of possible outcomes when applied to particular facts.

More difficult to explain is the invocation of article 31(3)(c) in the ECtHR judgment in *Loizidou v Turkey.*[120] In that case the applicant's complaints included one that Turkey was responsible for her being denied access to her property in Northern

---

[116] *United States—Import Prohibition of Certain Shrimp and Shrimp Products*, WTO Report of Appellate Board AB-1998-4, WT/DS58/AB/R, 12 October 1998, para 158, footnote 157.
[117] For these aspects of the case see Chapter 5, section 2.4.4 above.
[118] *United States—Import Prohibition of Certain Shrimp and Shrimp Products*, para 158.
[119] *United States—Import Prohibition of Certain Shrimp and Shrimp Products*, para 159.
[120] [1996] ECHR 15318/89.

Cyprus before, during, and after a demonstration in 1989 by Greek Cypriot women when they crossed into Northern Cyprus where they were detained and returned across the buffer zone to Greek Cypriot territory by Turkish soldiers and Turkish Cypriot police. Turkey had limited its acceptance of the compulsory jurisdiction of the Court to matters raised in respect of facts which had occurred after that acceptance. Turkey argued that the applicant had lost title to her property in Northern Cyprus well before that acceptance and at the latest in 1985 by the promulgation of a constitutional provision by the Turkish Republic of Northern Cyprus (TRNC).

Invoking the Vienna Convention's article 31(3)(c), the Court asserted that 'the principles underlying the [Human Rights] Convention cannot be interpreted and applied in a vacuum'.[121] It then rejected the Turkish contention on the basis *(inter alia)* of resolutions of the UN refusing recognition of the TRNC, thus providing a ground for also rejecting the asserted consequence of the TRNC's constitution. The idea that the European Convention is not to be interpreted and applied in a vacuum seems unassailable; but while this means that assessing the Turkish argument in the context of the international legal position of the TRNC was a legitimate exercise, that does not make it an exercise of treaty interpretation. In contrast, had article 31(3)(c) been specifically invoked in the *Loizidou* judgment in the context of the issue whether the deprivation of property had been subject to 'conditions provided for by law' (Protocol 1 to the European Convention), it can be seen that the invalidity of the TRNC constitution under international law would have been relevant to the question whether the Protocol's wording was to be interpreted to cover law derived from the purported constitution.

4.4 Reference to other treaties

Courts and tribunals, national and international, appear to have no hesitation over using provisions in treaties other than the one being applied as aids to interpretation where the same, similar, or different term sheds light on the meaning under consideration. This is such an accepted and established practice that it is hard to find any situation in which justification in terms of the Vienna rules has been presented. The reason for this is not hard to see. In the context of 'the relentless rise in the use of treaties as a means for ordering international civil society'[122] what can be seen, particularly in connection with bilateral treaties but also more generally, is that reference is commonly made in interpretation of one treaty to others in the same subject area:

Each state brings to the negotiating table a lexicon which is derived from prior treaties (bilateral or multilateral) into which it has entered with other states. The resulting text in each case may be different. It is, after all, the product of a specific negotiation. But it will inevitably share common elements with what has gone before.[123]

---

[121] [1996] ECHR 15318/89 at para 43.

[122] McLachlan, 'The Principle of Systemic Integration and Article 31(3)(c) of the Vienna Convention' (2005) 54 ICLQ 279, at 283.

[123] McLachlan, at 283.

Where the common element is simply the ordinary meaning of a word, reference in the interpretative process to its use in other treaties may be a legitimate means of identifying its ordinary meaning, with the added utility derived from finding such use in a similar context if available. At the other end of the spectrum, use of a term in a 'law-making treaty' may constitute an element of what has so evidently become a rule of customary international law that the rule in article 31(3)(c) seems clearly applicable. In other cases, reference to other treaties may simply be part of the history of the law on the subject or part of the facts relating to an issue. As courts and tribunals do not generally particularize the peg on which they hang their use in interpreting one treaty of terms in other treaties, it seems appropriate to mention the practice here in the context of international law and relations between the parties.

4.4.1 *Reference to international law stated in common form treaties*

The term 'common form treaties' is used here to refer to treaties that constitute a group, resembling one another in form and content through their derivation from a common model, or covering the same subject matter in similar provisions. They tend, of course, to have individual variations but use many of the same terms and approaches. Examples are Bilateral Investment Treaties (BITs), Double Taxation Agreements, Air Services Agreements, and Extradition Treaties.[124] In such cases there may be coincidence of terminology, which can assist by guiding the interpreter to the ordinary meaning or by identifying a relevant obligation arising from the treaty relations between the same parties (see below). There may, however, be sufficient identity of provisions in a range of common form treaties as to enable identification of a formulation of a relevant general rule of international law. Thus, for example, in *Pope & Talbot v Canada* at both the merits and damages phases of the case the tribunal took account of the regime established by BITs to inform its interpretation of the NAFTA. At the merits stage, the tribunal noted that the NAFTA provision on a standard of treatment for foreign investors 'in accordance with international law, including fair and equitable treatment and full protection and security' (article 1105) grew out of provisions of BITs which were a principal source of the 'general obligations of states with regard to their treatment of foreign investment'.[125] The tribunal therefore used the BIT regime to interpret article

---

[124] See, for example, the acceptance by an arbitral tribunal that many of the standard bilateral aviation clauses would be based on those in the first 'Bermuda' agreement and should therefore be taken into account in relation to an agreement involving a state not party to it: *Air Transport Agreement (USA v Italy)* (1965) 4 ILM 974 and P Merkouris, *Article 31(3)(c) of the VCLT and the Principle of Systemic Integration* (Ph D Thesis, 2010), pp 46–8, <https://qmro.qmul.ac.uk/jspui/handle/123456789/477>. If the link with other treaties is weak or not sufficient for those treaties to be brought into the interpretative process through this element of the general rule, a more appropriate classification for their being taken into consideration may be as supplementary means: see *Churchill Mining PLC and Planet Mining Pty Ltd v Republic of Indonesia* ICSID Case No ARB/12/14 and 12/40 (Decision on Jurisdiction, 24 February 2014) at paras 195–207.

[125] *Arbitration under Chapter Eleven of NAFTA, Pope & Talbot v Canada (Merits)*, Award of 10 April 2001, paras 110 ff, at <http://www.naftalaw.org/disputes_canada_pope.htm> and see section 4.1.1 above.

1105 as setting a standard in line with that of the BITs. At the damages phase, the tribunal also took account of BITs in assessing Canada's argument over the customary international law standard prescribed by the Free Trade Commission's interpretation of article 1105 of the NAFTA:

> Canada's views on the appropriate standard of customary international law for today were perhaps shaped by its erroneous belief that only some 70 bilateral investment treaties have been negotiated; however, the true number, now acknowledged by Canada, is in excess of 1800. Therefore, applying the ordinary rules for determining the content of custom in international law, one must conclude that the practice of states is now represented by those treaties.[126]

It is to be noted that this example from the *Pope & Talbot* case is truly an example of use of common form treaties to identify customary international law rules as an aid to interpretation of the NAFTA, the reference to 'practice' of states being a reference to the practice element of customary international law rather than practice of states in application of the NAFTA establishing their agreement regarding the interpretation of that treaty.

4.4.2 Reference to the same word as used in other treaties

Courts and tribunals refer to other treaties where the same word is used as in the provision in issue. As noted above, this is commonly explicable as part of the quest for the appropriate ordinary meaning by reference to usage in another treaty context. However, where treaty relations between the same parties are governed by different treaties bearing on the same issue, other rules of international law may be relevant to interpretation, such as the rules on successive treaties on the same subject matter or modification between only some of the parties.[127]

4.4.3 Reference to terms or phrases used in treaties on the same subject

Reference may be made to the same word or term used in another treaty where there is a provision on the same or a related topic even though the treaties may not be part of a group or from a common model. Once again, such a reference may be merely to assist in finding the ordinary meaning. However, even though the other treaty may not be one based on a common model, it could nevertheless be indicative of a position or practice which has become established in international law. In the WTO *US—Shrimp* case, the Appellate Body had to decide whether 'exhaustible natural resources' in the GATT 1994 included living species as well as mineral and other resources.[128] Having noted that the usage of 'natural resources' in the

---

[126] *Arbitration under Chapter Eleven of NAFTA, Pope & Talbot v Canada (Award in respect of Damages)* (2002) 41 ILM 1347 at 1358, para 62 (footnotes omitted).

[127] See, eg, Vienna Convention articles 30 and 41, and reference to the former in *Pope & Talbot v Canada (Merits)*, (2002) 41 ILM 1347, para 115, note 112.

[128] *United States—Import Prohibition of Certain Shrimp and Shrimp Products*, WTIDS58/AB/R, 12 October 1998, paras 127 ff.

treaty was by definition evolutionary, the Appellate Body referred to provisions in the UN Convention on the Law of the Sea that showed a link between use of the term 'natural resources' (article 56) and 'living resources' (articles 61 and 62). Reading this with provisions in another treaty and various associated international legal instruments, the Appellate Body concluded that 'it is too late in the day to suppose that article XX(g) of the GATT 1994 may be read as referring only to the conservation of exhaustible mineral or other non-living natural resources'.[129] Similarly, on the question of whether the turtles which the measures in issue intended to protect were 'exhaustible', the Appellate Body concluded that they were, since all the sea turtles were listed in the Convention on International Trade in Endangered Species of Wild Fauna and Flora which referred to 'species threatened with extinction'.[130]

There is a converse consideration in that it cannot be assumed that provisions on the same or a similar topic have become established as being applicable outside their own treaty or aiding interpretation of another one. Although in principle article 31(3)(c) provides locus for considering another treaty where its provision or provisions state or reflect rules of international law, courts and tribunals need to examine this in conjunction with context, object and purpose, other elements of treaty interpretation, and the jurisdiction which they exercise. Thus, in one of the parallel *MOX Plant* cases, the International Tribunal for the Law of the Sea stated:

> …the application of international law rules on interpretation of treaties to identical or similar provisions of different treaties may not yield the same results, having regard to, *inter alia,* differences in the respective contexts, objects and purposes, subsequent practice of parties and *travaux préparatoires*…[131]

4.4.4 Requirement to take into account another treaty

That provisions of another treaty can fall within the scope of article 31(3)(c) was explicitly stated by the ICJ in *Djibouti v France* (2008).[132] In that case the central issue was whether France had violated obligation under its 1986 Convention on Mutual Assistance in Criminal Matters with Djibouti by not handing over evidence gathered in an investigation into the death of a French national in Djibouti and requested by the latter's judicial authorities. France had been concerned that handing over requested documents would reveal intelligence material.

The 1986 Convention permitted the requested state to refuse to meet the request if to do so was 'likely to prejudice its sovereignty, its security, its *ordre public* or other of its essential interests'. The Court found that the reasons adduced by the French judge for refusal fell within this provision, but that France was in breach of

---

[129] WTIDS58/AB/R, 12 October 1998, at para 127.

[130] WTIDS58/AB/R, 12 October 1998, at para 132.

[131] *The MOX Plant Case (Ireland v United Kingdom)* (ITLOS) Judgment of 3 December 2001, para 51 at <http://www.itlos.org/case_documents/2001/document_en_197.pdf>.

[132] *Certain Questions of Mutual Assistance in Criminal Matters (Djibouti v France)*, [2008] ICJ Reports 177 at 219, para 113.

the treaty to the extent that it had not communicated to Djibouti its reasons for refusal of mutual assistance.

Djibouti also argued that France's failure to produce the requested evidence (as well as other acts of France in pursuance of the judicial investigation in France) was a breach of a 1977 bilateral Treaty of Friendship and Co-operation. Article 1 of that Treaty stated that the parties 'decide to found the relations between their two countries on equality, mutual respect and peace'. This was followed by provisions referring to specific areas, such as culture, science, technology, and education, and setting up a Co-operation Commission 'to oversee the implementation of the principles and the pursuit of the objectives defined in the... Treaty and in the conventions and specific agreements entered into between the two Governments'. The Commission's remit comprised all matters of cooperation, 'as well as the application of the various agreements entered into between the two States' (articles 6 and 7).

The ICJ noted that mutual assistance in criminal matters, which was the subject of the 1986 Convention, was not a matter mentioned in the areas of cooperation listed in the 1977 treaty. It therefore questioned whether the 1977 treaty could have any juridical impact on the 1986 Convention. In the *Nicaragua* and *Oil Platforms* cases the Court had considered the effect of a general provision envisaging bilateral peace and friendship. The Court had concluded that such a provision was to be regarded as fixing an objective, in the light of which the other treaty provisions were to be interpreted and applied; but the provision was not by itself a source of an obligation which could be independently violated.[133]

In the present case, the general provision on friendship and cooperation was being invoked in relation to a separate treaty, which raised the somewhat different question of whether the general principles stated in the 1977 Treaty could also inform the way in which obligations in the 1986 Convention were to be understood and applied. The Court considered that, in line with its previous case law, this could have been the case had the 1986 Convention made specific reference to cooperation in an area designated by the 1977 Treaty; but the provisions of the 1977 Treaty did not include cooperation in the judicial field. Nevertheless, the ICJ concluded:

The provisions of the 1977 Treaty of Friendship and Co-operation are 'relevant rules' within the meaning of Article 31, paragraph (3) *(c)*, of the Vienna Convention. That is so even though they are formulated in a broad and general manner, having an aspirational character. According to the most fundamental of these rules, equality and mutual respect are to govern relations between the two countries; co-operation and friendship are to be preserved and strengthened. While this does not provide specific operational guidance as to the practical application of the Convention of 1986, that Convention must nevertheless be interpreted and applied in a manner which takes into account the friendship and co-operation which France and Djibouti posited as the basis of their mutual relations in the Treaty of 1977.

---

[133] *Military and Paramilitary Activities in and against Nicaragua (Nicaragua v United States of America) (Merits)* [1986] ICJ Reports 14, at 136–37 and *Oil Platforms (Islamic Republic of Iran v United States of America) (Jurisdiction)* [1996–II] ICJ Reports 803, at 813–15.

The Court thus accepts that the Treaty of Friendship and Co-operation of 1977 does have a certain bearing on the interpretation and application of the Convention on Mutual Assistance in Criminal Matters of 1986. But this is as far as the relationship between the two instruments can be explained in legal terms. An interpretation of the 1986 Convention duly taking into account the spirit of friendship and co-operation stipulated in the 1977 Treaty cannot possibly stand in the way of a party to that Convention relying on a clause contained in it which allows for non-performance of a conventional obligation under certain circumstances.[134]

This analysis does not explain all situations where another treaty may be relevant to interpreting particular provisions; but it does confirm that, in addition to rules of international law from other sources, article 31(3)(c) of the Vienna Convention can bring into account other relevant treaty relations between states who are trying to resolve a difference or dispute over interpretation of a treaty.

4.5 Filling gaps by reference to general international law

This heading covers two distinct roles for article 31(3)(c): first, supporting an interpretation by reference to general rules of international law, and, second, using such rules to achieve an interpretation where the issue comes within the general scheme of a treaty but is not covered by its terms, or not fully covered. The distinction may not be that readily drawn. In *Golder v United Kingdom*,[135] the ECtHR had to consider whether article 6 of the European Convention, guaranteeing an individual a fair and public hearing 'in the determination of his civil rights and obligations', entitled a prisoner to consult a lawyer so as to institute civil proceedings or only gave the right to a hearing in existing proceedings. Using the other provisions of the Vienna rules to establish a basis for the former understanding of the text, the Court specifically referred to article 31(3)(c) and stated:

The principle whereby a civil claim must be capable of being submitted to a judge ranks as one of the universally 'recognised' fundamental principles of law; the same is true of the principle of international law which forbids the denial of justice. Article 6 para. 1 (art. 6-1) must be read in the light of these principles.[136]

Thus, although the provision of the European Convention did not in terms guarantee the right of access to a court, application of the Vienna rules produced this conclusion:

Taking all the preceding considerations together, it follows that the right of access constitutes an element which is inherent in the right stated by Article 6... This is not an extensive interpretation forcing new obligations on the Contracting States: it is based on the very terms of the first sentence of Article 6 para. 1 (art. 6-1) read in its context and having regard to the object and purpose of the Convention, a lawmaking treaty (see the Wemhoff judgment of 27 June 1968, Series A no. 7, p. 23, para. 8), and to general principles of law.[137]

---

[134] *Djibouti v France* [2008] ICJ Reports 177 at 37–8, paras 113–114.
[135] ECHR No 4451/70 (Judgment of 21 February 1975), and see Chapter 5, section 3.3.2 above.
[136] ECHR No 4451/70, at para 35.
[137] ECHR No 4451/70, at para 35.

More recently, and using a similar approach, in *Mamatkulov and Askarov v Turkey* the ECtHR invoked article 31(3)(c) of the Vienna Convention when relying on a common interpretative outcome in decisions of other courts, tribunals, and institutions applying a number of other treaties.[138] The applicants were resisting extradition from Turkey to Uzbekistan, fearing torture and injustice there. In the proceedings in Strasbourg, the President of the relevant Chamber of the European Court had indicated as an interim measure that the applicants should not be handed over before the Chamber met. When it did meet, the Chamber extended the interim measure until further notice, but the applicants were handed over a mere four days later.[139]

In deciding whether extradition of the applicants constituted a breach of the obligation in article 34 of the European Convention to refrain from any act or omission that may hinder the effective exercise of an individual applicant's right of application, the Court noted that in a number of recent decisions and orders, international courts and institutions had stressed the importance and purpose of interim measures and had pointed out that compliance with such measures was necessary to ensure the effectiveness of their decisions on the merits. In proceedings concerning international disputes, the purpose of interim measures was to preserve the parties' rights, thus enabling the body hearing the dispute to give effect to the consequences which a finding of responsibility would entail.[140] The Court observed that:

…the International Court of Justice, the Inter-American Court of Human Rights, the Human Rights Committee and the Committee against Torture of the United Nations, although operating under different treaty provisions to those of the Court, have confirmed in their reasoning in recent decisions that the preservation of the asserted rights of the parties in the face of the risk of irreparable damage represents an essential objective of interim measures in international law.[141]

In concluding that extradition in these circumstances was a breach of the obligations in article 34, the Court relied on the principle of effectiveness inherent in article 31(1) of the Vienna Convention and 'the general principles of international law, the law of treaties and international case-law'.[142]

A brief account has been given in section 4.3 above of the *Oil Platforms* case.[143] There the majority used article 31(3)(c) as a peg for a lengthy consideration of the international law on self-defence. It is difficult to see this use of the Vienna Convention provision as a legitimate extension of the treaty in issue or as the necessary means of filling in any omission from it. The Court only had jurisdiction in

---

[138] Application nos 46827/99 and 46951/99 (Judgment of 4 February 2005).
[139] Application nos 46827/99 and 46951/99, paras 24–27.
[140] Application nos 46827/99 and 46951/99, para 113.
[141] Application nos 46827/99 and 46951/99, para 124; the ICJ case on this issue (*LaGrand*) is considered in Chapter 9, section 4.3 below.
[142] Application nos 46827/99 and 46951/99, para 123.
[143] *Oil Platforms (Islamic Republic of Iran v United States of America) (Merits)* [2003] ICJ Reports 161.

the matter under the USA–Iran Treaty of 1955, not jurisdiction to consider generally whether there had been breaches by either side of international law beyond
the treaty. However, international law could have an interpretative role in supplementing provisions of the treaty. The distinction is perhaps best expressed by Judge
Kooijmans who, in conjunction with other criticisms of the approach taken by the
majority (considered below), stated:

> ...the Court...has to decide whether the actions against the platform can be qualified as
> measures necessary to protect the United States security interests in the sense of Article XX,
> paragraph 1 *(d)*, of the 1955 Treaty, not whether they were justified as measures taken
> in self-defence under international law. It can be readily admitted that if these measures
> involve the use of force, the rules of general international law become relevant for the
> question whether these measures can qualify as being 'necessary'. But that is something
> completely different from putting these measures directly to the test of the general rules
> of law on the use of force. The relationship is in my opinion aptly reflected in the deci-
> sion of the Iran-United States Claims Tribunal in the *Amoco International Finance* case
> when it said with regard to the 1955 Treaty that 'the rules of customary law may be use-
> ful...to ascertain the meaning of undefined terms in its text or, more generally, to aid
> interpretation and implementation of its provisions' (15 Iran-U.S. CTR 189, p. 222,
> para. 112).[144]

Readers may conclude that the view of Judge Kooijmans shows the proper
application of article 31(3)(c). The majority's approach seems to display a rather
loose reading of this provision. Judge Kooijmans explained how he envisaged international law being deployed to assist interpretation:

> ...neither Article XX, paragraph 1 *(d)*, itself nor any other provision of the Treaty contains
> elements which enable the Court to apply the legality test with regard to the question
> whether measures, taken to protect the essential security interests, are necessary indeed.
> The Court, therefore, has no choice but to rely for this purpose on the body of general
> international law.
>   General international law is therefore indispensable as a standard of interpretation of the
> provisions of the 1955 Treaty. If the measures taken involve the use of force, it is therefore
> the rules on the use of force which have to be called in in order to enable the Court to
> appreciate the lawfulness of these measures.[145]

This approach determines which rules of international law are relevant by lock-
ing on to the term 'necessary' in the treaty. Though it may appear that the effect
is to bring in a broad sweep of international law, the difference of approach from
that of the majority judgment is very considerable. The extent of the international
law inquiry is confined to the context of the treaty provision, aiding its interpretation and, ultimately, its application. Such application continues to represent
application of the treaty to the situation, not direct application of international
law to it.

---

[144] *Oil Platforms (Islamic Republic of Iran v United States of America) (Merits)* [2003] ICJ Reports
246 at 253–54, Separate Opinion at para 23.
[145] [2003] ICJ Reports at 261, paras 48–49.

It seems reasonable to summarize the position by adopting an academic assessment made in connection with human rights treaties that:

…the purpose of interpreting by reference to 'relevant rules' is, normally, not to defer the provisions being interpreted to the scope and effect of those 'relevant rules,' but to clarify the content of the former by referring to the latter. 'Relevant rules' may not, generally speaking, override or limit the scope or effect of a provision…[146]

4.6 Parallel and conflicting obligations

The possibility of parallel or conflicting obligations arising under different treaties, or as between a treaty and other sources of international law, has begun to be encountered by courts and tribunals. That article 31(3)(c) may have a useful role in handling such potential conflicts has been considered in academic study, in the work of the ILC, and in some instances when the provision has been invoked in judgments and rulings of courts and tribunals.[147] Foremost examples of the latter are three judgments of the ECtHR on whether state immunity can stand as a bar to civil claims in the light of the entitlement to a fair and public hearing in the determination of civil rights and obligations, as guaranteed by article 6 of European Convention on Human Rights. Having decided in *Golder v the United Kingdom*[148] that article 6 was to be interpreted as securing a right of access to courts to institute proceedings, could such a right of access be defeated by the procedural bar of state immunity? That immunity is well established in customary international law. It is also sustained in another Council of Europe Convention, the 1972 Basle Convention.[149] That Convention reflects the restrictive doctrine of state immunity, codifying customary law's limitations on the scope of state immunity, but specifically preserving it for personal injury claims unless the injury was caused in the territory of the forum state and the author of the damage was present in that territory at the time when the injury occurred.

The ECtHR found that there had been no breach of the Human Rights Convention by the operation of state immunity to defeat the applicants' domestic claims in the cases *Al-Adsani v UK* (originating in a damages claim against Kuwait alleging that injuries were caused by torture in Kuwait), *Fogarty v United Kingdom* (originating in a claim against USA alleging sex discrimination by its Embassy in London), and

---

[146] A Orakhelashvili, 'Restrictive Interpretation of Human Rights Treaties in the Recent Jurisprudence of the European Court of Human Rights' (2003) 14 EJIL 529 at 537; and see *Jones v Ministry of the Interior of the Kingdom of Saudi Arabia et al* (CA) [2005] QB 699 at 719–20, para 25 (appeal to House of Lords dismissed [2006] UKHL 26).

[147] See Sands, 'Treaty, Custom…' (1998) 1 *Yale Human Rights & Development Law Journal* 85, at 102 ff; McLachlan, 'The Principle of Systemic Integration and Article 31(3)(c)' (2005) 54 ICLQ 279; Pauwelyn, *Conflict of Norms in Public International Law: How WTO Law Relates to Other Rules of International Law;* and Koskenniemi 'Report of the Study Group on Fragmentation of International Law: Difficulties arising from the Diversification and Expansion of International Law', at p 207, para 412.

[148] See section 4.5 above.

[149] European Convention on State Immunity, Basle [1972] ETS No 74.

McElhinney v Ireland & UK (originating in a claim for personal injuries alleged to have been caused by a British soldier).[150] In reasoning common to the three judgments, the Court referred to Vienna Convention, article 31(3)(c) and, recalling its previous dictum that the European Convention, including article 6, was not to be interpreted in a vacuum, stated:

... The Court must be mindful of the Convention's special character as a human rights treaty, and it must also take the relevant rules of international law into account. ... The Convention should so far as possible be interpreted in harmony with other rules of international law of which it forms part, including those relating to the grant of State immunity.

It follows that measures taken by a High Contracting Party which reflect generally recognised rules of public international law on State immunity cannot in principle be regarded as imposing a disproportionate restriction on the right of access to a court as embodied in Article 6 § 1. Just as the right of access to a court is an inherent part of the fair trial guarantee in that Article, so some restrictions on access must likewise be regarded as inherent, an example being those limitations generally accepted by the community of nations as part of the doctrine of State immunity.[151]

It has been noted that the Court was engaged in evaluating international law on state immunity in relation to the protection guaranteed by the European Convention, rather than solely resolving a matter of interpretation of the latter.[152] While this may be the underlying position, there is at the very least an aspect of the matter that directly concerns interpretation of the European Convention. The provisions of the Convention are drawn in terms of broad principle, needing particularization when applied to specific cases. Hence an interpretative apparatus has had to be developed, not to the exclusion of the Vienna rules, but applying and complementing them. Hence notions such as proportionality and margin of appreciation inform the judgments of the Court. In using such concepts when taking account of the relevant rules of international law on state immunity, the Court has been applying article 31(3)(c) to the task of interpreting article 6 of the European Convention.

4.7 Taking account of international law developments

There is a clear link between the idea of taking account of developments of international law when interpreting a treaty and the intertemporal law, a link which initiated the sequence of drafts which led to article 31(3)(c).[153] A particular issue

---

[150] *Al-Adsani v United Kingdom*, App no 35763/97, 123 ILR 24; *Fogarty v United Kingdom*, App no 37112/97, 123 ILR 54; and *McElhinney v Ireland*, App no 31253/96, 123 ILR 73 (all three judgments in 2001).

[151] *Al-Adsani*, paras 55–56; *McElhinney*, paras 36–37; and, *Fogarty*, paras 35–36.

[152] See McLachlan, 'The Principle of Systemic Integration and Article 31(3)(c)' (2005) 54 ICLQ 279, at 305–6; cf *Bankovic & Others v Belgium & Others (Admissibility)*, App no 52207/99, where the ECtHR cited article 31(3)(c) as relevant to interpretation of the concept of 'jurisdiction' in the European Convention on Human Rights, but did not derive assistance from other treaties or find occasion to investigate general international law in detail: see esp paras 58 and 78.

[153] See section 1.1 above.

in the realm of treaty interpretation is what account is to be taken of developments in international law, particularly the striking emergence of new specialist fields such as environmental law and human rights law.

In the *Iron Rhine* case the arbitral tribunal explained that developing environmental law was to be taken into account in treaty interpretation:

…Provisions of general international law are also applicable to the relations between the Parties, and thus should be taken into account in interpreting Article XII of the 1839 Treaty of Separation and Article IV of the Iron Rhine Treaty. Further, international environmental law has relevance to the relations between the Parties…

…Environmental law and the law on development stand not as alternatives but as mutually reinforcing, integral concepts, which require that where development may cause significant harm to the environment there is a duty to prevent, or at least mitigate, such harm… This duty, in the opinion of the Tribunal, has now become a principle of general international law. This principle applies not only in autonomous activities but also in activities undertaken in implementation of specific treaties between the Parties.[154]

In adopting this approach, the tribunal found support in the *Gabčíkovo-Nagymaros* case, where the ICJ was confronted with arguments that emerging environmental concerns over a project to develop the hydro-electric potential of the Danube (as well as improving navigability, flood control, regulation of ice discharge, and the protection of the natural environment), justified abandonment or renegotiation of a bilateral treaty between Hungary and Slovakia (originally Czechoslovakia).[155] Most of the argument and reasoning in the judgment was couched in terms of breach, suspension, and termination of the treaty. However, the Court did consider some argument explicitly relying on an approach to treaty interpretation. Slovakia (or its predecessor) had taken unilateral measures in response to Hungarian termination of the treaty. The Court noted that:

With a view to justifying those actions, Slovakia invoked what it described as 'the principle of approximate application', expressed by Judge Sir Hersch Lauterpacht in the following terms:

'It is a sound principle of law that whenever a legal instrument of continuing validity cannot be applied literally owing to the conduct of one of the parties, it must, without allowing that party to take advantage of its own conduct, be applied in a way approximating most closely to its primary object. To do that is to interpret and to give effect to the instrument—not to change it.'(Admissibility of Hearings of Petitioners by the Committee on South West Africa, separate opinion of Sir Hersch Lauterpacht, I.C.J. Reports 1956, p. 46.)

It claimed that this is a principle of international law and a general principle of law.[156]

The Court did not find it necessary to determine whether there was such a general principle because, even if there were, it could only be employed within the limits of the treaty in question which, it found, the Slovak measures exceeded.

---

[154] *Arbitration regarding the Iron Rhine ("IJzeren Rijn") Railway (Belgium/Netherlands)*, (2005) XXVII RIAA 35, pp 66–67, paras 58–59, and see sections 4.1.2 and 4.2 above.
[155] *Case concerning the Gabčíkovo-Nagymaros Project (Hungary/ Slovakia)* [1997] ICJ Reports 7.
[156] [1997] ICJ Reports 7 at 53, para 75.

Nevertheless, the Court did give a clear indication that developments in environmental law were to be taken into account, and did so quite clearly in a context of treaty interpretation:

In order to evaluate the environmental risks, current standards must be taken into consideration. This is not only allowed by the wording of Articles 15 and 19 [of the bilateral treaty between Hungary and Czechoslovakia], but even prescribed, to the extent that these articles impose a continuing—and thus necessarily evolving—obligation on the parties to maintain the quality of the water of the Danube and to protect nature...

Throughout the ages, mankind has, for economic and other reasons, constantly interfered with nature. In the past, this was often done without consideration of the effects upon the environment. Owing to new scientific insights and to a growing awareness of the risks for mankind—for present and future generations—of pursuit of such interventions at an unconsidered and unabated pace, new norms and standards have been developed, set forth in a great number of instruments during the last two decades. Such new norms have to be taken into consideration, and such new standards given proper weight, not only when States contemplate new activities but also when continuing with activities begun in the past. This need to reconcile economic development with protection of the environment is aptly expressed in the concept of sustainable development...[157]

5. Special Meanings

5.1 Introduction

The notion of a special meaning includes two distinct categories. One is the meaning which a term has in a particular area of human endeavour; the other is a particular meaning given by someone using a term that differs from the more common meaning or meanings. The former is essentially an ordinary meaning in the particular context. It may be a term of art, but the context leaves no room for doubt once the term is recognized as such. Terms in the second category require some indication from the user that their meaning differs from the expected one.

The Vienna rules cover both situations; but courts and tribunals do not always make it clear whether they are considering a meaning that is 'ordinary' in the particular context or 'special' because the intention of the user to give the term a particular meaning is apparent. Article 31(4) of the Vienna Convention is most apt to cover the second category, referring to what the parties intended, though it is broad enough to cover the first if it has not already been taken into account under paragraph (1) of the article.

Article 31(4) presents two main issues: first, in what circumstances is reliance to be placed on this provision if investigating a particular meaning of a term in a treaty, and, second, how is the intention of the parties to be identified?

---

[157] [1997] ICJ Reports 7 at para 140; see also the *Biotech* case, section 4.1.1 above, at para 7.86, where the Panel indicated that it was prepared to consider whether the precautionary principle fitted within the category of rules of customary law or the recognized general principles of law, though ultimately finding that it had not established itself sufficiently firmly as either.

5.2 History and preparatory work

The first formulation of the Vienna rules, in the Third Report of the Special Rapporteur (Waldock), envisaged giving a meaning to a term of a treaty other than its natural and ordinary meaning 'if it is established conclusively that the parties employed the term in the treaty with that special meaning'.[158] Further provision was made for reference to 'other evidence or indications of the intentions of the parties and, in particular, to the preparatory work of the treaty, the circumstances surrounding its conclusion and the subsequent practice of parties' in order to establish such special meaning.[159]

There was little debate in the ILC on these drafts. When the provision on special meanings was consolidated into a separate draft article, the commentary recorded that some members of the ILC doubted the need to include provision on this point, noting that 'technical or special use of the term normally appears from the context and the technical or special meaning becomes, as it were, the ordinary meaning in the particular context' (the first category of special meaning suggested above).[160] The main reason given in favour of including a specific provision on the point was to emphasize that the burden of proof lies on the party invoking the special meaning of the term, and the strictness of the proof required.[161] This concern reflected the stress laid on this point in the two cases mentioned in the commentary.[162]

On separation into a distinct draft article, the provision on special meanings lost its link with preparatory work as a source of evidence. The Special Rapporteur (Waldock), responding to a comment by a state, explained the proposed transfer of the provision to the first draft article on interpretation in a way which introduced some uncertainty into what had been an explicit reference to use of preparatory work as a possible source of evidence of a special meaning:

The establishment of a 'special meaning' is not one of the purposes for which article 70 admits recourse to *travaux préparatoires,* and unless the 'special meaning' rule is made part of article 69, means of interpretation necessary to establish a special meaning may appear to be excluded.[163]

While this indicates that the primary means of establishing a special meaning was now to be application of the general rule of interpretation, the reference to

---

[158] [1964] *Yearbook of ILC*, vol II, p 52, draft article 70(3).
[159] [1964] *Yearbook of ILC*, vol II, p 52, draft article 71(2)(c).
[160] [1964] *Yearbook of ILC*, vol II, p 205, para 18.
[161] [1964] *Yearbook of ILC*, vol II, p 205, para 18. These points were retained in the final version of the ILC's commentary on the draft articles: [1966] *Yearbook of ILC*, vol II, p 222.
[162] *Legal Status of Eastern Greenland* PCIJ (1933), Series A/B, No 53, p 22 at 49 and Advisory Opinion on *Conditions of Admission of a State to Membership in the United Nations* [1948] ICJ 57 at 63. Discussion of the term 'Greenland' in the first of these cases did not focus on a particular provision in a treaty but rather on its usage in legislative and administrative acts in the territory; but the ILC seems to have been concerned more with the burden of proof in showing a special meaning than how the context could guide the interpreter to an ordinary meaning to be ascribed to a term in a treaty.
[163] [1966] *Yearbook of ILC*, vol II, p 100, para 22.

establishment of a special meaning not being a purpose of the provision on recourse to preparatory work may reasonably be taken as meaning that such establishment was not a purpose separate from those of confirming or determining the meaning in the specified circumstances.

There was not very much debate about how a special meaning would be established. One view was that, given the requirements that the proponent of a special meaning had the burden of proving it, 'there should be no need to resort to auxiliary means of interpretation in order to establish that special meaning'.[164] The Special Rapporteur (Waldock) gave his own opinion that 'where a special meaning could be established by special evidence, it was very probable that that meaning would appear in the context of the treaty'.[165] To the suggestion that a provision on special meanings was unnecessary because any special meaning given by the parties to a term would be an ordinary meaning in the context of the treaty, he responded that 'that proposition was too subtle to be understood by many of those who would be likely to interpret treaties' and that the proposed provision was therefore necessary.[166]

In a manner that is rather more typical of treaty negotiations than deliberations of a group of experts, the question how it could be established, without recourse to the further means of interpretation, that the parties intended a term to have a special meaning was left to the drafting committee.[167] When the draft emerged, the debate was about where the provision should be placed, without objection to the assumption of the initiator of the discussion who had suggested:

...it might be better if paragraph 4 were placed immediately after paragraph 1; that would show the process of interpretation more clearly. Paragraph 4 provided that a special meaning should be given to a term if it was established that the parties so intended. How was that intention to be established? Presumably by the rules of interpretation set out in paragraphs 2 and 3, and in article 70 [ultimately incorporated into article 32]. The purpose of interpretation was to ascertain which of several ordinary meanings was the one intended or whether a special meaning was given to a term.[168]

The hesitant inclusion of a place for the provision on special meanings at the end of the general rule was effectively endorsed by the vote to accept the drafting committee's proposal on this after the observation that:

Paragraph 4, on the other hand, dealt with a minor point which was of limited application; in fact, the Drafting Committee had even considered dropping that provision altogether. It would therefore detract from the importance of paragraph 1 if the contents of paragraph 4 were incorporated in it or placed immediately after it as a new paragraph 2. Such a change would also have the disadvantage of breaking the continuity of the [general rule]...[169]

---

[164] Mr Ruda, [1964] *Yearbook of ILC*, vol I, p 283, para 10.
[165] Mr Ruda, [1964] *Yearbook of ILC*, vol I, at p 309.
[166] [1966] *Yearbook of ILC* vol I, part II, p 198, para 3.
[167] See observation of R Ago, [1966] *Yearbook of the ILC*, vol I, part II at p 205, para 24.
[168] [1966] *Yearbook of the ILC*, vol I, part II at p 267, para 97.
[169] Mr Jimenez de Arechaga, [1966] *Yearbook of ILC*, vol I, part II, p 269, para 9.

Thus the outcome of the work of the ILC was to change the original idea of a special meaning derived principally from evidence of the intention of the parties, in particular by reference to the preparatory work, to one which was centred on the primary means of interpretation. This would leave as the most obvious cases of special meanings those in a treaty's definition provision, elsewhere in the context, or in any of the instruments identified by application of the rest of the general rule.[170] But it also leaves an uncertain impression over the extent to which supplementary means can be invoked as support for a special meaning. Applying the Vienna rules, this would only be permissible within an interpretative exercise justifying reliance on supplementary means by reference to article 32. However, such an exercise would envisage recourse to preparatory work 'to confirm' any meaning that emerged in the course of interpretation without any prerequisite of finding ambiguity. Hence if good evidence of an intended special meaning were produced from preparatory work, this could trigger reassessment of the meaning reached by application of the general rule.[171]

As a footnote to the preparatory work of article 31(4), one member of the ILC gave his view that the reference to 'the parties' whose intention was to establish a special meaning should be understood as meaning the parties which had participated in the authentication of the treaty, not in its conclusion.[172] However, article 2(1)(g) of the Vienna Convention defines a party as a state 'which has consented to be bound by the treaty and for which the treaty is in force'. There seems no ground to displace such a clear definition by reference to a single view expressed in the preparatory work, particularly as any consensus on a special meaning recorded in the preparatory work would be admissible if the circumstances envisaged in article 32 arose.[173]

5.3 Issues and practice

5.3.1 Special meaning and ordinary meaning distinguished

Selection of a particular meaning from a range of possible meanings by reference to the context may lead to a particular sense being mandated by the subject matter—for example, where a word is a term of art.[174] This is the thought expressed by some members of the ILC (considered in section 5.1 above). There appears, however, to be a reluctance on the part of courts and tribunals to class a meaning

---

[170] The Special Rapporteur (Waldock) also suggested that an interpretative declaration could be evidence of a special meaning [1965] *Yearbook of ILC*, vol II, p 49, para 2.

[171] On the role of preparatory work to confirm a meaning, see Chapter 8 below. For a full analysis of the history of the provision on special meanings and use of preparatory work in their ascertainment, see J D Mortenson, 'Is the Vienna Convention Hostile to Drafting History?' (2013) 107 AJIL 780.

[172] Mr Bartos, [1966] *Yearbook of ILC*, vol I, part II, p 192, para 90.

[173] The Convention's definition of 'party' was mentioned by one delegation at the Vienna conference as an example of a term being given a special meaning (United Nations Conference on the Law of Treaties, Second Session (9 April–22 May 1969), Official Records: Summary Records, p 47, para 32.

[174] See, eg, the discussion of 'Thalweg' in relation to boundaries at rivers in Chapter 5, section 3.3.4 above.

as 'special' if there is any way it can be justified as 'ordinary'. The ILC Special Rapporteur (Waldock) noted that 'in most cases in which a special meaning of a term had been pleaded, the tribunals appeared to have rejected the special meaning'.[175] In *Witold Litwa v Poland* the ECHR preferred to use an extended meaning of 'alcoholics' to include drinkers who are not addicted, rather than accept Poland's argument that the parties had intended a special meaning.[176] In *Georgia v Russian Federation* Russia had argued that the term 'dispute' should be given a special meaning derived from the context of provisions distinguishing a 'matter', 'complaints', and 'disputes', the latter being alleged to mean only matters or complaints which had proceeded through the stages stipulated by the treaty for a dispute to crystallize.[177] However, the ICJ declined to ascribe a narrower interpretation than usually given to the word as generally understood and as used in comparable compromissory clauses in treaties drawn up around the same time as the one in issue.[178]

It is probably of no great consequence whether an interpreter finds the route to the appropriate meaning through an understanding of what is an 'ordinary' meaning or whether such a meaning is viewed as 'special'. Provided the interpreter uses all appropriate evidence to evaluate the probable meanings the correct result should be ascertainable.

5.3.2 Burden of establishing a special meaning

That the burden falls on the party urging a special meaning is clear; but which party this is in given circumstances may not always be incontestable. In the frontier dispute between El Salvador and Honduras (with Nicaragua intervening), one of the several provisions in the special agreement listing issues for the ICJ to decide invited the Court 'to determine the legal situation of the…maritime spaces'.[179] There was disagreement between the parties whether or not this empowered the Court (which heard the case as a Chamber rather than the full court) to delimit a maritime boundary. 'Delimitation' of areas is a well-recognized term for entrusting to international courts and tribunals jurisdiction to mark out boundaries or frontiers. It was the term that had been used in the present case in relation to land frontiers. In contrast, 'determining the legal situation' could have meant something different. El Salvador claimed that the relevant waters were subject to a condominium in favour of the three coastal states of the Gulf of Fonseca. Legal status of an area is different from its extent. One of the arguments put by Honduras was that the constitution of El Salvador did not permit delimitation of the waters of

---

[175] [1964] *Yearbook of ILC*, vol I, p 309, para 6.

[176] ECHR App no 26629/95 (Judgment of 4 April 2000), considered in Chapter 1, section 5.1 above.

[177] *Application of the International Convention on the Elimination of All Forms of Racial Discrimination (Georgia v Russian Federation), (Preliminary Objections)* [2011] ICJ Reports 70 at 82–3, paras 26–7.

[178] [2011] ICJ Reports 70 at 84, para 29.

[179] *Case Concerning the Land, Island and Maritime Frontier Dispute (El Salvador/Honduras: Nicaragua intervening)* [1992] ICJ Reports 351.

the Gulf, that the different wording was to accommodate these sensibilities, and that it was for the Court to decide whether the status of the waters left it open to it to make a delimitation. The majority of the chamber of the ICJ construed the issue as putting an evidential burden on Honduras:

In essence, it is arguing that a special meaning—one comprising the concept of delimitation—was intended by the Parties to attach to the phrase 'determine the legal situation of the... maritime spaces'. The onus is therefore on Honduras to establish that such was the case.[180]

The Chamber found that to accept the contention of Honduras would be to accept that the parties were not in complete agreement over jurisdiction, which it must therefore lack on this issue.[181] Judge Torres Bernárdez, dissenting on this point, started with analysis of the Spanish term *determinar* for 'determine' in the phrase 'determine the legal situation. He found that this word could convey the idea of setting limits, hence delimitation.[182] The majority had also regarded this as a possible meaning if the word was taken in isolation, but the context and construction of the sentence had made it clear that what was being determined was the legal situation, not the limits, of the waters.[183] In contrast, Judge Torres Bernárdez considered that once it was admitted that delimit could be an ordinary meaning of *determinar,* the onus fell on El Salvador to establish, as a special meaning, that it excluded delimitation.[184]

This example may be unusual in that neither party appears to have advanced a particular special meaning which it could be required to establish. It suggests that there may remain an unresolved issue whether article 31(4) offers a further way, within the general rule, of selecting from a range of ordinary meanings or whether it is really to be viewed as a particular rule to be brought into play when a meaning at odds with the normal processes for selection of an ordinary meaning is being advanced.

5.3.3 *Evidence required to establish a special meaning*

In recommending inclusion of a provision on special meanings, Waldock noted that the PCIJ 'had decided that evidence of the special meaning to be attached to a term was admissible but that the burden of proof was upon the party desiring to establish that special meaning'.[185] He said that 'he personally thought that where a special meaning could be established by special evidence, it was very probable that that meaning would appear in the context of the treaty'.[186] The most common way in which a special meaning is indicated is by including a definition article in a treaty. Beyond that there is little practice showing clearly what would amount to the necessary 'special evidence'. If no definition is provided it is a matter of assessing the intent of the parties in the light of the available evidence.

---

[180] [1992] ICJ Reports 351 at 585, para 377.
[182] [1992] ICJ Reports 351 at 720, para 192.
[184] [1992] ICJ Reports 351 at 721, para 193.
[185] [1964] *Yearbook of ILC*, vol I, p 309, para 6.
[186] [1964] *Yearbook of ILC*, vol I, p 309, para 6.

[181] [1992] ICJ Reports 351 at 585, para 378.
[183] [1992] ICJ Reports 351 at 583, para 373.

A good example of the contrasting situations is given in the *Roma Rights* case (UK House of Lords) concerning the Convention Relating to the Status of Refugees, Geneva, 1951 and its 1967 Protocol:

> It is also noteworthy that article 31(4) of the Vienna Convention requires a special meaning to be given to a term if it is established that the parties so intended. That rule is pertinent, first, because the [Geneva] Convention gives a special, defined, meaning to 'refugee' and, secondly, because the parties have made plain that '*refouler*', whatever its wider dictionary definition, is in this context to be understood as meaning 'return'.[187]

With regard to the second of these special meanings, it would not normally be the case that a special meaning is to be linked with the treaty in one language only unless the meaning is in doubt and the treaty specifies that that language is to prevail.[188] In the present case, however, the Convention itself provided evidence of how the English and French understanding of the special meaning were to be aligned by including the French term in the English title and text of article 33: 'Prohibition of expulsion or return ("refoulement")...No contracting state shall expel or return ("refouler") a refugee...'. Lord Bingham put it this way:

> ...the French verb refouler and the French noun refoulement are, in article 33, the subject of a stipulative definition: they must be understood as having the meaning of the English verb and noun 'return'.[189]

Where material is generally regarded as providing an authoritative interpretation of a treaty, it seems plausible to accept from it a special meaning.[190] Where a special meaning is recorded in the preparatory work, its effect on interpretation is probably no different from that of other statements or declarations in preparatory work, but confirmation of this is not readily found.

---

[187] *R v Immigration Officer at Prague Airport ex parte European Roma Rights Centre* [2004] UKHL 55, [2005] 2 AC 1 at 31, para 18, per Lord Bingham.

[188] See *Case Concerning Military and Paramilitary Activities in and Against Nicaragua (Nicaragua v United States of America) (Jurisdiction and Admissibility)* [1984] ICJ Reports 392 at 537.

[189] *R v Immigration Officer at Prague Airport ex parte European Roma Rights Centre* at 29, para 15; but the usage may also seem apt to import into the word 'return' the content signified by the French word; for it seems to have been the intention of including the French term that its meaning should prevail: see D Shelton, 'Reconcilable Differences? The Interpretation of Multilingual Treaties' (1997) 20 *Hastings International and Comparative Law Review* 611 at 623; see also the extensive consideration of *refoulement* by the US Supreme Court in *Sale v Haitian Centers Council* 509 US 155 (1993) at 179 ff, particularly at 180, indicating that the legal meaning of 'return' in the Convention is narrower than its common meaning, a conclusion which the Court considered was 'reinforced by the parenthetical reference to "*refouler*," a French word that is *not* an exact synonym for the English word "return" '; but cf: H H Koh, 'The "Haiti Paradigm" in United States Human Rights Policy' (1993–1994) 103 *Yale LJ* 2391 at 2416: '*Haitian Centers Council* takes its place atop a line of recent Supreme Court precedent misconstruing international treaties'; UNHCR, Advisory Opinion on the Extraterritorial Application of Non-refoulement Obligations under the 1951 Convention relating to the Status of Refugees and its 1967 Protocol [2007] European Human Rights LR 484; and G S Goodwin-Gill and J McAdam, *The Refugee in International Law* (Oxford: OUP, 3rd edn, 2007), Chapter 5.

[190] See the suggestion in *UBS AG v Revenue and Customs Commissioners* [2005] STC (SCD) 589 at 598, para 10, in relation to the use of the Commentary on the OECD model for double taxation treaties, though courts which heard appeals in the case preferred a rather more limited approach to the Vienna Convention: see (2006) 8 ITLR 595 at 608–9, and (2007) 9 ITLR 767.

5.3.4 *Special meanings and special regimes*

It does not follow that because a rule or regime may be correctly characterized as a *lex specialis* terms in a treaty establishing the rule or regime are to be viewed as having a special meaning. This is apparent from the opinion of Lord Steyn in *Mullen*.[191] Where a conviction was set aside because the accused had been brought before the court by unjust means rather than because his guilt was in doubt, was he entitled to compensation under legislation giving effect to article 14(6) on 'miscarriage of justice' in the International Covenant on Civil and Political Rights 1966? Lord Steyn considered that the Court of Appeal had erred in relying on what had been described there as 'the ordinary use of English' and in concluding that because the phrase 'miscarriage of justice' was wide enough to cover the circumstances of the case (ie where the guilt of the claimant was not in doubt but he should not have been unlawfully deported to stand trial in England), the Covenant required compensation to be paid. Lord Steyn stressed that what was relevant was 'the autonomous meaning of the concept in article 14(6)' of the Covenant.[192] He considered that 'the obvious and sensible construction is that article 14(6) is a lex specialis' to be read in the context of the treaty (which did not require that a particular meaning be imputed to it in the light of the presumption of innocence in article 14(2)).[193] It can be seen that this is not to attribute a special meaning to 'miscarriage of justice', but simply acknowledges that the term is to be interpreted in the sense of the Covenant, rather than as it might be in English law.

In line with the freedom inherent in the right of states to draw up their treaties as they wish, states (and international organizations) may include their own rules of interpretation. It is also possible to see the principle underlying recognition that parties may attribute a special meaning to a term that they use as supporting the possibility that parties to a treaty may include special interpretative principles which differ from those in the Vienna rules, or which place a different weight on one or more of the elements of interpretation, a possibility which is also consistent with choosing the arbiters of interpretation. This freedom is confirmed by the practice of states in their treaty making. There do not, however, appear to be examples of wholesale displacement of the Vienna rules.

A prominent example of a particular rule of interpretation in a treaty is article 22(2) of the Rome Statute of the International Criminal Court (2002):

The definition of a crime shall be strictly construed and shall not be extended by analogy. In case of ambiguity, the definition shall be interpreted in favour of the person being investigated, prosecuted or convicted.[194]

---

[191] *R v Secretary of State for the Home Department ex parte Mullen* [2004] UKHL 18, [2005] 1 AC 1.

[192] [2004] UKHL 18, [2005] 1 AC 1 at 39, para 36; see also Chapter 1, section 4.1 above.

[193] [2004] UKHL 18, [2005] 1 AC 1 at 39, para 36.

[194] See also article 9 of the Rome Statute on 'elements of crimes' which are to assist the Court in the interpretation and application of the provisions defining crimes.

It can readily be seen that inclusion of such a provision in a treaty dealing with international criminal law properly provides a special rule appropriate to the subject matter, rather than a wholesale replacement of the Vienna rules which are of a general character and, in the interpretation of the Rome Statute, would apply to article 22 taking account of the context as an element of the general rule.[195] This is consistent with the principle that general provisions do not derogate from special ones.[196]

A more general interpretative provision may be included in a treaty circumscribing the interpretative role of an arbitral tribunal. For example, in the Indus Waters arbitration the treaty included in an annexure providing for a Court of Arbitration:

Except as the Parties may otherwise agree, the law to be applied by the Court shall be this Treaty and, whenever necessary for its interpretation or application, but only to the extent necessary for that purpose, the following in the order in which they are listed:

  (a) International conventions establishing rules which are expressly recognized by the Parties.
  (b) Customary international law.[197]

Such a provision clearly attempts to limit recourse to extraneous application of international rules, perhaps to counter wide-ranging approaches such as those criticized above in the ICJ's *Oil Platforms* case.[198] In the *Indus Waters* case, the Court followed the Vienna rules applicable as customary law but took care in following its mandate on applicable law as quoted above.[199]

6. Conclusions

The origins of article 31(3)(c) in attempts to incorporate the intertemporal rule into the rules of interpretation became obscured as the provision was pared down to its somewhat opaque final version. To the extent that the provision can bring

---

[195] See also Chapter 10, section 5.2 below.

[196] See also Chapter 8, section 4.5.4 below on maxims and presumptions; and on general and special provisions, cf discussion of *Hosaka v United Airlines* in Chapter 8, section 4.3.1 below.

[197] *Indus Waters Kishenganga Arbitration (Pakistan v India)* Partial Award of 18 February 2013, Addendum Annexure G, p A-38, para 29, <http://www.pca-cpa.org/>.

[198] See section 4.1.1 above; cf *Indus Waters Kishenganga Arbitration (Pakistan v India)* Final Award of 20 December 2013, where the Court, being more concerned at this stage with application than interpretation, while acknowledging that the principles of international environmental law were to be taken into account even when interpreting treaties concluded before the development of that body of law, nevertheless took careful account of the limits imposed by the treaty in issue on the application of any customary principles of environmental law: 'The Court's authority is more limited and extends only to mitigating significant harm. Beyond that point, prescription by the Court is not only unnecessary, it is prohibited by the Treaty. If customary international law were applied not to circumscribe, but to negate rights expressly granted in the Treaty, this would no longer be "*interpretation or application*" of the Treaty but the substitution of customary law *in place of* the Treaty' (Final Award, paras 111–112, original emphasis <http://www.pca-cpa.org/>).

[199] This included consideration of an argument that a special meaning of a term had been established, an argument which the Court rejected on the basis that the term was not specifically defined and was used in several senses in the treaty: Partial Award, 18 February 2013, paras 385–86, and see Decision of 20 December 2013 on India's Request for Clarification or Interpretation, para 29.

into play obligations of international law which have arisen after conclusion of the treaty, the time element is still present; but use of this calls for fine judgement in assessing whether the proper interpretation is that the treaty is one which envisaged interpretation in the light of the circumstances at the time of its conclusion or, having been drawn up to endure and adapt, requires account to be taken of later developments.

More specifically, roles for the rule in article 31(3)(c) may include:

(a) resolving time issues (including application of the intertemporal law);
(b) completing the legal picture, or filling gaps, in a treaty by reference to general international law;
(c) deriving guidance from other treaty provisions;
(d) resolving conflicting obligations arising under different treaties;
(e) taking account of international law developments.

Special meanings will sometimes be established by a provision defining the terms used in a particular treaty, or in parts of a treaty; but such meanings otherwise require proof by the proponent that a special meaning was intended by the parties.

B. Supplementary Means of Interpretation

8

Supplementary Means of Interpretation

Supplementary means of interpretation—preparatory work and circumstances of conclusion—confirming meaning—determining meaning if general rule leaves ambiguity or obscurity, or results in absurdity or unreasonable meaning

This formulation [the precursor to article 32] seemed to the Commission about as near as it is possible to get to reconciling the principle of the primacy of the text with frequent and quite normal recourse to *travaux préparatoires* without any too nice regard for the question whether the text itself is clear. Moreover, the rule...is inherently flexible, since the question whether the text can be said to be 'clear' is in some degree subjective.[1]

It would hardly be an exaggeration to say that in almost every case involving the interpretation of a treaty one or both of the parties seeks to invoke the preparatory work.[2]

Article 32
Supplementary means of interpretation

Recourse may be had to supplementary means of interpretation, including the preparatory work of the treaty and the circumstances of its conclusion, in order to confirm the meaning resulting from the application of article 31, or to determine the meaning when the interpretation according to article 31:

(a) leaves the meaning ambiguous or obscure; or
(b) leads to a result which is manifestly absurd or unreasonable.

1. Introduction

This chapter covers use of all supplementary means of interpretation. These are supplementary to those in the general rule in article 31. However, their function is not dictated by the label 'supplementary' but by the terms of article 32. In fact their function is not dictated or dictatorial. In contrast to the mandatory formulation of the general rule, supplementary means are ones to which recourse 'may' be had. Conditions are stated in article 32 governing their use, but these are not so

---

[1] Sir Humphrey Waldock, 'Sixth Report on the Law of Treaties' [1966] *Yearbook of ILC*, vol II, pp 99–100, para 20.
[2] A D McNair, *The Law of Treaties* (Oxford: OUP, 2nd edn, 1961), 412.

restrictive as they may appear. Supplementary means are not listed exhaustively in the Vienna Convention, though those most commonly used are mentioned. The most controversial issues arise over use of preparatory work. The meaning and scope of the term 'preparatory work' have been considered in Chapters 1 and 3 above.[3] The principal remaining issues are when preparatory work may be invoked in treaty interpretation, how it relates to the other Vienna rules, and what weight is to be given to its very varied content.

The Vienna Convention's provision on preparatory work exposed the most significant difference in approach to treaty interpretation among members of the ILC. It was the only part of the Vienna rules on which there was a substantial debate at the Vienna Conference in the first session (1968). These differences in approach can be marked out as a divide between those who asserted the primacy of the text of a treaty as revealing the commitments of the parties and those (principally the US delegation) who saw the interpretative quest as a direct investigation of the intentions of the parties and of their shared expectations, with aid in that task being sought from wherever it could be found. This is to put the opposing camps in the most extreme light. Attaching the labels 'textual' and 'intention seeking' to the different approaches serves mainly to hide the realities and practicalities of treaty interpretation. Once these realities and practicalities are examined, it can be seen that the differences between the two approaches are not as great as they may appear. The core issue is what information and material outside the text of a treaty can be brought into the task of interpreting it and how this is done.

The second key to understanding the provision lies in the distinction between examining or surveying information and material, on the one hand, and using it for a particular purpose, on the other. It is one thing to read the history of a provision, quite another to say that that history is the one element which identifies the correct meaning. The provision of the Vienna Convention appears to draw a firm distinction between using the supplementary means to 'confirm' and to 'determine' the meaning of a treaty provision. The gateway to the former use of supplementary means is that the correct interpretation appears ascertainable by application of the general rule. The prerequisites for using supplementary means to 'determine' the meaning are ambiguity, obscurity, absurdity, or unreasonableness (which must be 'manifest', in the case of the last two possibilities). It will, however, be seen that these clear lines of approach (particularly confirmation) were not intended to be applied too rigidly, nor are they in practice. 'Frequent and quite normal recourse to *travaux préparatoires*' was the thought underlying the ILC's approach, as indicated in the first quotation at the head of this chapter.

There is thus both something of a paradox and an illustration in the interpretation and application of article 32 to preparatory work. Only by giving the provision the most narrow of literal meanings that it could bear does the provision look as limiting as its critics suggest. Yet by taking account of its own preparatory work in the manner that that preparatory work indicates, is it clear that such a

---

[3] See Chapter 1, section 3.4 and Chapter 3, section 4 above.

limited role is not correctly attributed to it. An expansive meaning of 'confirm' is confirmed by the preparatory work. There is also plenty of evidence that a literal approach to treaty interpretation has not been applied to this element of the Vienna rules, which is a good indicator that an excessively literal approach does not hold sway in treaty interpretation generally.

2. History and Preparatory Work

2.1 Separating supplementary means from the general rule

Although the first draft of the Vienna rules was somewhat different in its layout and detail from the final text, the way in which the provisions were separated revealed the thought that certain evidence of meaning should only be used to confirm the meaning found by applying the general rule or to establish the meaning in circumstances of ambiguity, uncertainty, etc.[4] However, the separation of the 'general rule' from 'supplementary means' was not so clearly drawn as in the final version of the rules. It was this separation which was the source of controversy at the Vienna Conference and the cause of an unsuccessful attempt by the US delegation to integrate the content of articles 31 and 32 into a single provision. The core of the criticisms made by Professor McDougal (USA) of the draft rules lay in the relationship between these two provisions. Professor McDougal saw the designation 'supplementary' for article 32 as confirming primacy of a purely literal approach. To him this meant that the focus of treaty interpretation was directed to an impossible quest for an ordinary textual meaning. It meant (to him) dismissal of context in the broad sense which he gave the word, with relegation of preparatory work to a limited role, and then only after crossing excessively high hurdles. He foresaw the likely result as a general failure to consider important indicators of the 'shared expectations' of the parties and 'community values'.

Somewhat paradoxically, Professor McDougal's criticisms would only have proved cogent if interpreters had adopted an extremely literal (and rather distorted) reading of the Vienna rules, if they ignored much of the ordinary meaning of their terms, abandoned the content of article 31 beyond its first paragraph, and dismissed the abundant guidance in the ILC's preparatory work as to how the Vienna rules were to provide the launch pad for reaching proper interpretations.[5] Showing that this has not been the result is the role of the section on practice (section 4) of this chapter. However, even at the introductory phase of studying this topic, a reader of the Vienna rules and of the records of the ILC's work (including the contribution of Professor Waldock as Special Rapporteur) can see that the approach is not purely textual, and that *looking at* preparatory work and the circumstances of

---

[4] See Waldock, 'Third Report' [1964] *Yearbook of ILC*, vol II, p 52, draft articles 70 and 71.
[5] See H W Briggs, 'The *Travaux Préparatoires* of the Vienna Convention on the Law of Treaties' (1971) 65 AJIL 705, at 709–10.

a treaty's conclusion is not excluded. Thus, it is difficult to see the 'rigidities and restrictions' which Professor McDougal asserted were common knowledge.[6]

Professor McDougal sought to underline the importance of preparatory work and surrounding circumstances by citing the role of Professor Waldock at the Vienna Conference, describing his presence as 'the best testimony, not always mute' of the impossibility of applying the textuality approach. He noted that reference to Professor Waldock had often been necessary at the Vienna Conference in tribute 'not to his skill in flipping the pages of a dictionary or as a logician, but rather to his very special knowledge of all the circumstances attending the framing of our draft Convention'.[7] Although oratorically engaging, this is not persuasive. The Vienna Conference was not simply engaged in interpretation of a concluded treaty but was continuing the preparatory work of the Vienna Convention begun by the ILC. This demanded a somewhat different perception and approach. It also seems more reasonable to regard reference to Professor Waldock at the Conference for an account of the work of the ILC as something of a proxy for consulting the extensive preparatory work, a short cut to acquiring a fuller version of the thinking behind drafts that had been presented to the ILC. Courts, tribunals, writers, and other interpreters of treaties have, in practice, very much treated the records of the ILC as an aid to looking into that thinking.

At all events, Professor McDougal did not convince the Vienna Conference that reference to preparatory work and surrounding circumstances was an approach to interpretation that should be put on exactly the same footing as the elements of the general rule: for the proposal to combine the articles on interpretation was rejected.[8] Yet the separation of the two articles into general rule and supplementary means has not proved a bar to reference to preparatory work, circumstances of conclusion or other supplementary means. The Vienna rules have generally been taken as allowing liberal reference to preparatory work, even if a decisive role in determining an interpretation is more limited. In addition, where the explanations of a preparatory body are likely to be useful to an interpreter, these are now commonly readily available, if not always in their raw form, then in published commentaries, explanatory reports, and such like.

This is not to say that there are no difficulties with the rules and how they have been applied in some cases.[9] But it is suggested here that the principal difficulty has

---

[6] Statement of Professor McDougal, US Delegation, to Committee of the Whole, Vienna Conference, 19 April 1968, as reproduced at (1968) 62 AJIL 1021; the summary records set out a somewhat abridged and less colourful version of the statement: UN Conference on the Law of Treaties, Summary Records of First Session (26 March–24 May 1968), 167–8.

[7] McDougal Statement, US Delegation, to Committee of the Whole, Vienna Conference, 19 April 1968, as reproduced at (1968) 62 AJIL 1021, at 1025.

[8] The US proposal for an amendment combining the first two articles of the Vienna rules and placing all the elements on the same footing was rejected by 66 votes to 8, with 10 abstentions, UN Conference on the Law of Treaties, First and Second Sessions (1968 & 1969), Documents of the Vienna Conference (UN, New York, 1971), p 150, para 271(a). For an example of the ICJ treating explanations to a Diplomatic Conference by an ILC Special Rapporteur as an admissible part of the preparatory work, see the *Avena* case considered in section 4.1.2 below.

[9] See, eg, J Klabbers, 'International Legal Histories: The Declining Importance of *Travaux Préparatoires* in Treaty Interpretation?' (2003) L NILR 267 and M Ris, 'Treaty Interpretation and

not proved to be the catalogue of limitations suggested by Professor McDougal. Nor is it easy to find evidence that quantities of other useful material revealing the shared expectations of the parties have been excluded from consideration because of application of the Vienna rules. The main difficulty has been over the indication in the Vienna rules that one permissible use of preparatory work is to 'confirm' a meaning achieved by application of the general rule. If the preparatory work, so far from confirming that meaning, suggests that that interpretation is wrong, does the interpretation stand (but unconfirmed), or may it be displaced? It will be submitted here that that is not the insuperable problem that it may appear to be on a literal reading of article 32, and that in practice means can be found, compatible with the Vienna rules, for using preparatory work in the way such work was meant to be used. Non-confirming preparatory work could, for example, lead to exploration of a hitherto unnoticed ambiguity in the text and reopen evaluation of the meaning. Such a possibility is considered further below, but in understanding the role of preparatory work it is helpful first to look more closely at Professor McDougal's criticisms.

Professor McDougal linked the stigma which he saw as being attached to preparatory work by classifying it as 'supplementary means' with his perception of undue literalism being required by the general rule. He saw 'context' as being defined by reference not to 'factual circumstances attending the conclusion of the treaty, but to mere verbal texts'.[10] His understanding was that 'object and purpose' referred 'not to the actual common intent of the parties, explicitly rejected as the goal of interpretation, but rather to mere words about "object and purpose" intrinsic to the text'.[11] This view seems to have led him to underestimate the role envisaged by the Vienna rules for circumstances of conclusion of a treaty. The first basis given for his strictures about these perceived rigidities and restrictions was that principles of interpretation had seldom been considered as mandatory rules of law, 'precluding examination of relevant circumstances'.[12] 'Precluding examination' of 'relevant circumstances' seems as much to overstate the purport of the scheme of the rules as the suggestion that the combination of the reference to ordinary meaning and the rules on admissibility of preparatory work were being employed in a way 'to foreclose inquiry'.[13]

ICJ Recourse to Travaux Préparatoires: Towards a Proposed Amendment of Articles 31 and 32 of the Vienna Convention on the Law of Treaties' (1991) 14 *B C Int'l & Comp L Rev* 111; but note that the former does not purport to take stock of the current position in an empirical fashion (at 269) and notes that 'interpretation consistently takes place with the help of the *travaux préparatoires*, but is rarely based on the *travaux préparatoires* alone' (at 288), while the latter reviews the case law of the ICJ mainly before it specifically endorsed use of the Vienna rules, suggesting that reference to supplementary means should be as part of the context of a treaty if requested by a party and that the ICJ and UN should have a role in identifying a collecting preparatory work (at 135); and see A I Aust, *Modern Treaty Law and Practice* (Cambridge: CUP, 3rd edn, 2012), 217–20.

[10] McDougal Statement (1968) 62 AJIL 1021.   [11] (1968) 62 AJIL 1012, at 1021–22.

[12] 62 AJIL 1012, at 1022.

[13] 62 AJIL 1012, at 1022; and cf J D Mortenson, 'The Travaux of Travaux: Is the Vienna Convention Hostile to Drafting History?' (2013) 107 AJIL 780, at 810: 'McDougal's speech probably caused more confusion about treaty interpretation than any intervention on the subject before or since. He so badly mischaracterized the ILC draft—and did so with such flair . . .—that his description

An initial reply to these criticisms is to note that by suggesting that 'context' should properly mean the 'factual circumstances attending the conclusion of the treaty', Professor McDougal was giving 'context' a wider meaning than what might be viewed as its primary or ordinary meaning, or at least than its principal dictionary definition.[14] Much more significant, however, is that his criticism does not appear to take account of the reference to 'the circumstances of its [a treaty's] conclusion' receiving explicit mention, along with preparatory work, in article 32. It would be a distinctly odd reading of the term 'context' in article 31 that included in it 'the circumstances of conclusion', when precisely the same concept is given a specific role as a 'supplementary means' elsewhere in the rules.

2.2 Ready reference to preparatory work distinguished from basing interpretations on it alone

Underlying Professor McDougal's criticisms seems to be the notion that a great array of interpretative aids, only admitted in a limited way in article 32, was being excluded by the approach taken in separating the two articles. This was compounded, in the view of Professor McDougal, by the 'high preclusionary hurdles—designed to foreclose automatic, habitual recourse to such "supplementary means"'[15] This is wholly at odds with the balance envisaged by the ILC between primacy of the text and the ILC's expectation of 'frequent and quite normal recourse' to preparatory work noted at the head of this chapter. The Vienna rules do not impose any hurdle to *looking* at the preparatory work. This is confirmed by looking at the preparatory work in the records of the work of the ILC. In his comments on the first draft of what became the Vienna rules, the Special Rapporteur (Waldock) explained the proposed provision on preparatory work (which did not then bear the epithet 'supplementary means', but which did categorize the conditions for use of preparatory work) as being 'permissive in character'. The aim was to recognize

---

has taken on a totemic power that it does not deserve. In essence, he claimed that the ILC draft created a "preclusionary hierarchy" of sources that was "rigid and restrictive" in its celebration of the bare dictionary meaning of text that would take precedence over every conceivable countervailing factor, and that it "relegated" preparatory work to a "subordinate position" vis-à-vis every other source of meaning.' (footnotes omitted).

[14] The *Oxford English Dictionary* gives as the fourth meaning (after three obsolete ones): 'The whole structure of a connected passage regarded in its bearing upon any of the parts which constitute it; the parts which immediately precede or follow any particular passage or "text" and determine its meaning.' But cf the example given in the OED of 'context theory': 'According to this theory, what a word means depends upon its connection in past experience with some other thing.' It would be in line with the approach of the Vienna rules, but not that of Professor McDougal, to point out that the first of these two definitions is given as the concrete usage originating some 400 years ago (and in continuing general use), while the latter is last in the list, after transferred and figurative senses, is an 'attributive and combination' usage, and was only a little more than 30 years old at the time of the Vienna Conference. Nevertheless, selection of the former as the ordinary use when interpreting the Vienna rules would not fulfil the requirements of those rules without also taking account of the context in the Convention (including the fact of reference to 'circumstances of conclusion' being a separate element), subsequent practice, and the preparatory work.

[15] McDougal Statement (1968) 62 AJIL 1021, at 1022.

'the propriety of recourse to extraneous evidence or indications of the intentions of the parties'.[16] Preparatory work was therefore regarded as evidence to be used for specified purposes. He saw no difficulty in using such evidence to determine the meaning of an ambiguous or obscure term, or of a term whose ordinary meaning gave an absurd or unreasonable result. Most revealing were his observations on the distinction between reference to the preparatory work and the actual use made of such work:

> There is, however, a difference between examining and basing a finding upon *travaux préparatoires*, and the Court itself has more than once referred to them as confirming an interpretation otherwise arrived at from a study of the text. Moreover, it is the constant practice of States and tribunals to examine any relevant *travaux préparatoires* for such light as they may throw upon the treaty. It would therefore be unrealistic to suggest, even by implication, that there is any actual bar upon mere reference to *travaux préparatoires* whenever the meaning of the terms is clear.[17]

What is clear from this is that the invariable practice was (and still is) to look at the preparatory work when there is a question of treaty interpretation; but actually basing a finding on such material needs to take place in more controlled conditions if the agreement of the parties is not to be replaced by the content of unconsummated exchanges of proposals and arguments that preceded finalization of the treaty. It is difficult to find fault with the Special Rapporteur's further comment:

> Recourse to *travaux préparatoires* as a subsidiary means of interpreting the text, as already indicated, is frequent both in State practice and in cases before international tribunals. Today, it is generally recognized that some caution is needed in the use of *travaux préparatoires* as a means of interpretation. They are not, except in the case mentioned [reference to agreements, instruments, and documents annexed to a treaty or drawn up in connection with its conclusion], an authentic means of interpretation. They are simply evidence to be weighed against any other relevant evidence of the intentions of the parties, and their cogency depends on the extent to which they furnish proof of the *common* understanding of the parties as to the meaning attached to the terms of the treaty. Statements of individual parties during the negotiations are therefore of small value in the absence of evidence that they were assented to by the other parties.[18]

2.3 Distinction between use of supplementary means 'to confirm' and 'to determine' the meaning

These observations of the Special Rapporteur related to the first draft of the rules which differed from what was ultimately agreed, but this does not affect their relevance as indicating the analysis of the established role of preparatory works in treaty interpretation. The role of supplementary means of interpretation, and in

---

[16] Waldock, 'Third Report on the Law of Treaties' [1964] *Yearbook of the ILC*, vol II, p 58, para 20.
[17] [1964] *Yearbook of the ILC*, vol II, p 58, para 20 (footnotes omitted).
[18] [1964] *Yearbook of the ILC*, vol II, p 58, para 21 (footnotes omitted, emphasis in original).

particular preparatory work, was eventually put into two categories differentiated by the functions of 'confirming' and 'determining' meaning. In its commentary on its final version of the draft articles, the ILC noted that the first of these had a further significance in its scheme of rules of interpretation:

The fact that article 28 [now 32] admits recourse to the supplementary means for the purpose of 'confirming' the meaning resulting from the application of article 27 [now 31] establishes a general link between the two articles and maintains the unity of the process of interpretation.[19]

Thus the preparatory work of the Vienna Convention effectively confirms the propriety of examining the preparatory work, without precondition, of any treaty whose interpretation is in issue and sets this in the context of 'the unity of the process of interpretation'.

Recourse to preparatory work is always permissible under the Vienna rules to 'confirm' the meaning reached by application of the general rule in article 31. Where the qualifying conditions (ambiguity or obscurity of meaning, or manifest absurdity or unreasonableness of result) are met for use of preparatory work to 'determine' the meaning, the Vienna rules appear to envisage what is in effect replacement of an unsatisfactory interpretation produced by the general rule with one yielded up by the preparatory work. The two roles for preparatory work appear very different in their significance for interpretation. Although both are presented under the title 'supplementary means of interpretation', 'to determine' the meaning is very much to fulfil a primary role in treaty interpretation, while confirmation is only secondary and supportive.

However, the difference in roles may not be so great in practice as it appears to be. A literal reading of article 32 would result in a very limited role for preparatory work if the qualifying conditions for a determining role are not met. Preparatory work could be invoked to show that a meaning that is already plain, unambiguous, and neither absurd nor unreasonable is indeed the correct one. Other than as a congratulatory acknowledgement of the drafting and inherent clarity of a treaty, that would produce no real result from invoking the preparatory work. Investigating preparatory work to see whether it does in fact 'confirm' a particular meaning carries with it the implicit possibility that it does not do this. What then? The options are either to stick with the meaning achieved by the general rule or investigate the other meaning or meanings which the preparatory work suggests.

The ILC's approach to this provision suggests that the reality is that if the interpreter finds that the preparatory work suggests a meaning which was not the one which would be first choice after applying the general rule, and which would not have immediately struck the interpreter as within the obvious range of interpretative options, the interpreter will have to reconsider the position. It would be absurd to think otherwise. This reality is further exemplified by the present investigation

---

[19] [1966] *Yearbook of ILC*, vol II, p 220, para 10.

of what is meant by 'confirm' a meaning. In the first epigraph to this chapter, the ILC Special Rapporteur's view is given that the formulation of the provision that is now article 32 was to give effect to the Commission's aim of 'reconciling the principle of the primacy of the text...with frequent and quite normal recourse to *travaux préparatoires* without any too nice regard for the question whether the text itself is clear'.[20] An interpreter with that prime piece of preparatory work already in mind would need to interpret 'confirm' in the context of all the Vienna rules and the whole exercise of treaty interpretation.

Despite the apparent clear meaning of 'confirm', the Special Rapporteur's explanation goes on to suggest that the subjectivity in deciding whether a term is 'clear' imports flexibility into the rule. Hence 'confirm' offers the option of not confirming and the possibility of transforming the exercise into one where the preparatory work leads to revisiting the application of the general rule to find a permissible interpretation which is then confirmed. Another possibility is that the investigation may lead to a conclusion that there is a hitherto unperceived ambiguity (or one or more of the other qualifying conditions) such that the exploration of the preparatory work is transformed from a potential confirming role to one of determining the meaning. Treaty interpretation is not working out a simple equation. This is best illustrated by the examples in the section on practice below.

Two further pieces of preparatory work of the Vienna Convention support the case for giving 'confirm' a broad meaning. First, early versions of the text had proposed recourse to further means of interpretation 'to verify or confirm' the meaning ascertained by application of the general rule. In response to suggestions that confirmation was unnecessary if the meaning of a term was clear, the Special Rapporteur (Waldock) noted that it was 'unrealistic to imagine that the preparatory work was not really consulted by States, organizations and tribunals whenever they saw fit, before or at any stage of the proceedings, even though they might afterwards pretend that they had not given it much attention'.[21] However, he recognized that 'the reference to confirmation and, *a fortiori*, verification tended to undermine the text of a treaty in the sense that there was an express authorization to interpret it in the light of something else; nevertheless that was what happened in practice'.[22] This was acknowledgement that consulting the preparatory work had to be accepted as having the potential to modify an attitude formed towards the treaty text. Second, the Special Rapporteur later explained that 'verify' had been deleted because the idea of 'verification' was contained in 'confirmation'.[23] Hence 'confirm' was viewed as having a wider meaning than 'verify', one which could possibly embrace adjustment of an assumption that the meaning was clear.

---

[20] Sir Humphrey Waldock, 'Sixth Report on the Law of Treaties' [1966] *Yearbook of ILC*, vol II, p 99, para 20.
[21] [1964] *Yearbook of ILC*, vol I, p 314, para 65.
[22] [1964] *Yearbook of ILC*, vol I, p 314, para 65.
[23] [1966] *Yearbook of ILC*, vol I, pt II, p 270, para 34.

3. Meaning of 'Recourse' and 'Supplementary'

The opening words of article 32 ('Recourse may be had to supplementary means of interpretation') invite particular attention to two terms: the meaning of 'recourse' and the scope of 'supplementary means'.

3.1 'Recourse'

Descriptions commonly used for considering the preparatory work are 'consulting' or 'examining' it. That the Vienna Convention provision uses the term 'recourse' has attracted little attention, probably because the circumstances of use of supplementary means of interpretation are addressed as part of the substance of the article. Controversy therefore has surrounded the interpretation of the descriptions of the circumstances, rather than the introductory word. In the light of the differentiation made by the ILC between looking at preparatory work and actually basing an interpretation on it, the term 'recourse' is apt to cover making use of the preparatory work (or other supplementary means) for the ends described in the provision, without implying that looking at preparatory work to see if it may assist is proscribed.

Were the Vienna Convention's interpretative apparatus to be deployed in making an interpretation of 'recourse', it would provide a good illustration of some of the elements of the rules. First, dictionary definitions would show that no single ordinary meaning can be isolated but that some meanings fit the context and practice better than others.[24] These meanings must, of course, be read in the context of the more specific directions in the article on how supplementary means are to be used; thus, the division is between use for confirmation and determination of meaning. However, the meanings do not exclude (and may even chime in with) the distinction recorded in the ILC's work between examining the preparatory work and basing a determination upon it.[25]

3.2 'Supplementary'

Any need for interpretation of the term 'supplementary' is largely subsumed by the substantive content of article 32, indicating the circumstances in which additional means of interpretation come into play for specified purposes; by practice,

---

[24] *Oxford English Dictionary* (1989) definitions 3.a and 4.a include the notion of resorting to someone or something for assistance or help, while the obsolete definition 5.a 'usual or habitual going or resorting to a place' captures the thought that preparatory work is something to which resort may be usual or habitual. It is also to be noted that the ICJ, in its Advisory Opinion on *Legality of the Threat or Use of Nuclear Weapons*, faced with possible divergences between the English and French texts of the question that was posed, used 'recourse to nuclear weapons' to refer to the threat or use of nuclear weapons, thus suggesting that 'recourse' does not necessarily only mean actual use: [1996–I] ICJ Reports 226, at 238, para 20.

[25] See section 2 above.

which includes liberal reference to both means specifically mentioned and others whose use is warranted by particular circumstances; and by the practical dynamics of interpretation which are assisted by awareness of the underlying thinking of the ILC and the clarificatory effect of the debate at the Vienna Conference on the amendment proposed by the USA.[26] As with 'recourse', an interpretative exercise, starting with an ordinary meaning for 'supplementary', would reveal some definitional notions at the root 'supplement' which are germane to its use here. That a supplement is something added as 'an enhancement' (in some senses, 'to complete' a work or provide reinforcement), and also 'something added 'to make good a deficiency', embraces (if rather obliquely) the two potential functions of recourse to preparatory work (confirmation and determination of meaning).[27] It may be useful to note that the dictionary definitions do not include any suggestion of 'subordinate'.

The equivalent French phrase in the Vienna Convention may suggest more ready access to further means of interpretation, using the term *des moyens complémentaires*. An English dictionary invites comparison of 'French *supplémentaire* (1790)' with 'supplementary' and 'modern French *compl[é]mentaire*' with 'complementary' as a matter of etymology, which may raise the question of whether there is correct alignment of meaning between the languages. However, the notions of 'completing' or 'perfecting' in the English term 'complementary' do not exclude dealing with 'deficiencies' according to further parts of the definition, while 'supplement' is defined to include 'enhancement' as well as 'make good a deficiency'.[28] The content of article 32 is capable of bearing both the notions of completing and making good. Examination of practice may, therefore, prove the most useful way of ascertaining the meaning and effect of the term 'supplementary'.[29]

3.3 Further supplementary means

More difficult is establishing the identity of other supplementary means of interpretation, given that the only immediate contextual clue is the word 'including' which introduces preparatory work and circumstances of conclusion of the treaty.[30] What lies beyond? 'Means of interpretation', when used in the context of the Vienna rules, appears to refer to material or substantive matters to be taken under consideration, rather than general interpretative principles of an analytical kind such as lawyers are accustomed to apply.[31] An example of the latter is the *eiusdem generis* principle. This assists in deciding whether an item is to be regarded

---

[26] See section 2 above.   [27] *OED* online 2012, definitions 1 and 2.
[28] *OED* online entries.   [29] See section 4 below.
[30] The French text (*notamment aux travaux préparatoires et aux circonstances dans lesquelles le traité a été conclu*) may carry the slightly different, or additional, connotation that the preparatory work and the circumstances of conclusion are the most significant supplementary means.
[31] Cf McNair, *The Law of Treaties*, Chapter XXII, and Aust, *Modern Treaty Law and Practice*, 220–1, listing further maxims and techniques commonly used by lawyers in interpretation.

as included in a list by applying a test of its similarity to items specifically mentioned in the list. Preparatory work and circumstances of conclusion are material elements linked to the particular treaty undergoing interpretation: the *eiusdem generis* principle is not a material element linked in a similar way, but rather a general interpretative principle which may be applicable in approaching particular material.

This distinction between material and general interpretative principles could be of importance, particularly given the somewhat optional character of recourse to supplementary means. Lawyer's techniques, often encapsulated in well-known maxims, could be particularly useful in applying the general rule rather than depending on the accessibility being governed by whether recourse is had to the supplementary means of interpretation. However, the Vienna rules are not exclusionary and article 32 is not so restrictively applied. Thus, even though well-known interpretative devices, such as the *eiusdem generis* principle, *expressio unius exclusio alterius*, or *a contrario* could fall within the ordinary meaning of 'supplementary means', these devices are not rigidly viewed as exclusively within the province of that rule.[32]

3.4 Relationship between supplementary means and the general rule

For an interpreter, the initial difference between the general rule and supplementary means is that the elements of the general rule have mandatory application (a treaty 'shall be interpreted in good faith...', 'There shall be taken into account', etc), the word 'shall' being used in treaties to denote obligation. In contrast, the supplementary means of interpretation are available to an interpreter ('Recourse may be had'), but their use is not expressed to be mandatory. This does not mean that supplementary means can be characterized as always *subordinate* to the general rule. Indeed, in the circumstances where the provisions of article 32 of the Vienna Convention envisage use of supplementary means 'to determine' the meaning, they are potentially dominant, albeit only after application of the general rule has left ambiguity, obscurity, etc in the result.

In finding a distinction between the general rule and supplementary means of interpretation to be both justified and desirable, the ILC looked mainly at the role of preparatory work and how it differed in character from the elements of the general rule:

The elements of interpretation in article [now 31] all relate to the agreement between the parties *at the time when or after it received authentic expression in the text*. *Ex hypothesi* this is not the case with preparatory work which does not, in consequence, have the same authentic character as an element of interpretation.[33]

---

[32] See further section 4.5.4 below.
[33] Commentary on draft articles [1966] *Yearbook of the ILC*, vol. II, p. 220, para (10), emphasis in original.

Noting that records of treaty negotiations can be incomplete or misleading and require particular discretion to determine their interpretative value, the Commission nevertheless pointed out that:

... the provisions of article [now 32] by no means have the effect of drawing a rigid line between the 'supplementary' means of interpretation and the means included in article [31]. The fact that article [32] admits recourse to the supplementary means for the purpose of 'confirming' the meaning resulting from the application of article [31] establishes a general link between the two articles and maintains the unity of the process of interpretation.[34]

The most common understanding of 'confirming' something does inherently link article 32 to article 31, quite apart from the explicit references to article 31 in article 32. Yet the ILC's notion of 'the unity of the process of interpretation', and the general link with the provisions in article 31 which it saw as established by the term 'confirm', are sometimes overlooked or misunderstood.[35] This may in part be due to the way in which article 32 gives such apparent prominence to the determining role of supplementary means by singling out, in separately denoted subparagraphs, the situation where an interpretation according to the general rule leaves the meaning ambiguous or obscure or produces a result which is manifestly absurd or unreasonable.[36] However, as has already been emphasized, the more precisely defined circumstances in which preparatory work may 'determine' meaning must not be taken to eclipse the general acceptability of reading the preparatory work for purposes covered by the term 'confirm' ranging from providing help in understanding provisions of a treaty to working with the general rule to give them meaning. Practice provides many examples of the integration of preparatory work in the process of interpretation thus preserving the unity of the latter which the ILC sought.

4. Issues and Practice

This section tracks the two gateways which are established by article 32 and illustrates modalities of use of supplementary means. The first gateway is where application of the general rule has produced what appears to be the correct meaning which may lead to recourse to supplementary means to confirm the meaning. The main issues here are identifying the circumstances in which confirmation is to be sought and the nature of such confirmation. The second gateway is where, after application of the general rule, there remains one or more of ambiguity, obscurity, manifest absurdity, or unreasonableness. This gateway leads to use of supplementary means to determine the meaning.[37] Here the main issues are the nature of

---

[34] [1966] *Yearbook of the ILC*, vol II, p 220, para 10.

[35] See also sections 2.1 and 2.3 above.

[36] See J D Mortenson, 'The Travaux of Travaux: Is the Vienna Convention Hostile to Drafting History?' (2013) 107 AJIL 780, at 786.

[37] It is wide of the mark to treat these gateways as simply factors affecting the meaning of the terms in question; see, for example, in assessing whether an attempt to secure local remedies was a

the four entry points for this gateway and how, once reached, the supplementary means lead to a determination of the meaning. As a preliminary matter, however, it must be noted that only sometimes do courts and tribunals identify which of these gateways they are using. In other instances their use is not explicit or there is no sign of them being used at all.

4.1 Systematic use of gateways, unsystematic use, and by-passing them

4.1.1 Explicit reference to the qualifying gateway

If circumstances arise where supplementary means have to be used to determine the meaning of provisions in a treaty, the qualifying conditions for their use are more likely to be clearly identified than where the rather loose notion of confirming a meaning is being applied. However, as courts and tribunals pay increasing attention to the Vienna rules, they do quite often state that they are using supplementary means (most commonly preparatory work) to confirm a meaning reached by applying the general rule.

For example, explicit reference to the route being followed to consideration of the preparatory work was made in the dispute between Indonesia and Malaysia concerning sovereignty over certain islands.[38] The ICJ had to decide whether a reference in an 1891 Convention to a boundary following a line of latitude continuing eastward across the island of Sebatik should be taken as extending beyond that island to separate out further islands then under Dutch sovereignty from those under British sovereignty.

The Court found that the object and purpose of the 1891 treaty was delimitation of boundaries between Dutch and British possessions within the island of Borneo itself and to resolve the status of the island of Sebatik. It found nothing in the treaty to suggest that the parties had intended to delimit the boundary between their possessions to the east of the islands of Borneo and Sebatik or to attribute sovereignty over any other islands.[39] Having concluded that the treaty provision read in context and in the light of the Convention's object and purpose could not be interpreted as establishing an allocation line determining sovereignty over the islands out to sea to the east of the island of Sebatik, the Court explained that it was not necessary to resort to supplementary means of interpretation to determine

---

prerequisite to arbitration of an investment dispute, the assertion that: 'As a matter of treaty interpretation, however, [the disputed provision] cannot be construed as an absolute impediment to arbitration. Where recourse to the domestic judiciary is unilaterally prevented or hindered by the host State, any such interpretation would lead to the kind of absurd or unreasonable result proscribed by Article 32 of the Vienna Convention ...': *BG Group Plc v Argentina* (UNCITRAL) Final Award of 24 December 2007, at para 147. The Vienna rules make no such proscription but enable a court or tribunal carrying out a proper interpretative exercise to have recourse to supplementary means to determine the meaning in such a situation.

[38] *Sovereignty over Pulau Litigan and Pulau Sipadan (Indonesia/Malaysia)* [2002] ICJ Reports 625.
[39] [2002] ICJ Reports 625, at para 51.

the meaning of the treaty but that it would have recourse to such supplementary means in order 'to seek a possible confirmation of its interpretation of the text of the Convention.'[40] In doing this, the Court examined not only the documents which preceded the treaty but also the history of assertions of rights by the British North Borneo Company and others, and the setting up of a joint commission by Great Britain and the Netherlands.

In this case the circumstances leading to the conclusion of the Convention were considered along with the accompanying documents forming the actual preparatory work. Since the only hint of possible extension of the line of latitude eastwards of Sebatik was in a document which had not been passed to the other side, and on a map which did not include the disputed islands, the Court found nothing in the preparatory work or circumstances of conclusion to support the Indonesian case for such an extension.[41] Explicit use of the gateway of confirmation not only led to further substantiation of the meaning derived by application of the general rule, but also enabled the Court to evaluate the submissions of one party as to the intention of the parties to the treaty.

4.1.2 Reaching the preparatory work informally

Courts do not always indicate that the application of the general rule has led to a 'clear' meaning which is to be confirmed by reference to the preparatory work or that one of the circumstances is present which could make the preparatory work determinative of the meaning of a term or provision. This may reflect the way litigation works, with the arguments of the parties influencing the elements and shape of a court's judgment, or it may be that use of preparatory work is so much part of lawyers' interpretative apparatus that resort to consideration of it is instinctive rather than formalistic.

Thus, for example, in the *Avena* case[42] the ICJ rehearsed the arguments of the disputing parties over the preparatory work before deciding the meaning of the requirement in article 36 of the Vienna Convention on Consular Relations 1963 (here 'the Consular Convention') that the authorities of a state must inform arrested nationals of other parties 'without delay' of their right to ask for their consul to be informed of their arrest. One issue was whether 'without delay' was a synonym for 'immediately', ie immediately upon arrest. The Court found an accumulation of factors negating acceptance of 'immediately' as the correct meaning. It started its own analysis by noting that the Consular Convention offered no precise meaning through any definition provision, thus implicitly eliminating the possibility of any special meaning being established in application of article 31(4) of the Vienna Convention; but the Court did explicitly state that the terms would therefore have

---

[40] [2002] ICJ Reports 625, at para 53.
[41] [2002] ICJ Reports 625, paras 56–58. The Court then considered subsequent practice of relevant parties, including publication of maps.
[42] *Case concerning Avena and other Mexican Nationals (Mexico v USA)* [2004] ICJ Reports 12.

to be interpreted applying the customary law rules set out in articles 31 and 32 of the Vienna Convention.[43] The Court observed that such was the variety of terms used in the different language versions of the Consular Convention for 'without delay' and 'immediately' (in that Convention's article 14) that recourse to dictionary definitions gave no assistance.[44] This analysis effectively reflected articles 31(1) and 33 of the Vienna Convention.

Since it was clear that neither article 36 of the Consular Convention nor any of its other provisions envisage a consular officer acting in person as the legal representative of the accused or being directly involved in the criminal justice process, the Court found no indication that the object and purpose of the treaty meant that 'without delay' was to be understood as 'immediately upon arrest and before interrogation'.[45] Having thus, in effect, made its initial approach via articles 31(4), 33, and 31(1) of the Vienna Convention, the Court proceeded directly to its own assessment of the preparatory work of the Consular Convention. This revealed various strands. The ILC Special Rapporteur had explained that the Commission had proposed 'without undue delay' to allow for special circumstances which might permit information about consular notification not being given at once. There had been no consensus for including a specific time requirement for notification, no proposal to use 'immediately', and no suggestion that the time factor was linked in any way to the start of interrogation.[46] There was convergence on deletion of 'undue' from the phrase 'no undue delay', a deletion which had been proposed to avoid the implication that some delay was permissible. The Court thus concluded that 'without delay' was not necessarily to be interpreted as 'immediately' upon arrest, although there was nonetheless a duty upon the arresting authorities to give that information to an arrested person as soon as it was realized that the person was, or probably was, a foreign national.[47]

The most significant points to note in this judgment are: first, the ease with which the Court swept into its consideration of the preparatory work having worked through some of the components of the general rule; second, the Court's admission to a prominent place in the argument of the recorded use by the diplomatic conference of the Special Rapporteur's explanations of the ILC's work; third, the Court's reference to individual contributions by delegations at the diplomatic conference to give a fair account of the development of the treaty text; and, finally, the Court did not make a clear distinction between use of the preparatory work to confirm a meaning and to establish a meaning (though it had noted irreconcilable variations of dictionary meanings of the terms used in the different languages), but rather used the preparatory work in a cumulative analysis to negate a meaning of 'immediately'. This seems quite a vivid reassurance that the fears of Professor McDougal over 'preclusionary hurdles' preventing use of preparatory work and circumstances of conclusion need not be obstructive in practice.

---

[43] [2004] ICJ Reports 12, at 48, para 83.
[44] [2004] ICJ Reports 12, at 48, para 84.   [45] [2004] ICJ Reports 12, at 48, para 85.
[46] [2004] ICJ Reports 12, at 48–49, para 86.
[47] [2004] ICJ Reports 12, at 47, para 80, and at 48–49, paras 86–88.

4.1.3 Incidental use of supplementary means

Reference to preparatory work and circumstances of conclusion of treaties is quite often included in a judgment or award's narrative account of the background. For example, in the *Arrest Warrant* case, three of the ICJ judges who considered the extent of universal jurisdiction of states, gave an account of the development of the concept of universal jurisdiction.[48] They found that states had jurisdiction under certain treaties (such as those concerning torture, hostages, hijacking, etc), jurisdiction which could be described as 'treaty-based broad extraterritorial jurisdiction'. In addition under those treaties the parties had jurisdiction to prosecute an offender found in their territory, jurisdiction which was only 'universal' by loose use of language, being really 'obligatory territorial jurisdiction over persons, albeit in relation to acts committed elsewhere'.[49] In examining the treaties relevant to this conclusion, the Joint Separate Opinion referred to preparatory work of the Conventions to explain their history, interpretation, and intended operation.[50] It can readily be recognized that such reference to supplementary means does not need justifying by use of one of the Vienna rules' gateways. It was simply part of the exposition of the historical development of the law and its analysis.

Incidental reference to preparatory work also occurs from time to time when courts and tribunals refer to accounts, analysis, and conclusions in works by authors having a focus on a particular treaty.[51]

4.1.4 Admitting preparatory work introduced by parties

There is an understandable tendency on the part of courts and tribunals to admit into consideration preparatory work which is proffered as such by both, or all, parties to a dispute.[52] Indeed, it is quite difficult to exclude mention of material which is unilaterally submitted even if it does not clearly form part of the preparatory work. Typically, the main presentation of material and argument to international

---

[48] *Case concerning the Arrest Warrant of 11 April 2000 (Congo v Belgium)*, Joint Separate Opinion of Judges Higgins, Kooijmans and Buergenthal [2002] ICJ Reports 63, at 68–72, paras 19–31; the majority judgment did not address this matter; for another example of incidental reference to preparatory work, see *Re Norway's Application (Nos 1 and 2)* [1990] 1 AC 723, at 799, where the House of Lords recounts preparatory work of a Hague Convention showing that no difficulty had arisen in practical application of bilateral agreements on the same subject despite differences among states in their national law over meaning of 'civil and commercial matters'.

[49] *Arrest Warrant* case, Joint Separate Opinion, [2002] ICJ Reports 63, at para 41.

[50] See, eg, [2002] ICJ Reports 63, at paras 27 and 35.

[51] See, eg, references to UNHCR *Handbook* section 4.5.3 below; C H Schreuer, *The ICSID Convention: A Commentary on the Convention on the Settlement of Investment Disputes between States and Nationals of Other States* (Cambridge: CUP, 2001); and *Polyukhovich v Commonwealth of Australia* (1991) 172 CLR 501 FC 91/026, at para 105.

[52] See, eg, the WTO Appellate Body: 'We observe, as a preliminary matter, that this appeal does *not* raise the question whether... [two Secretariat documents] constitute "supplementary means of interpretation...". Both participants agree that they do, and we see no reason to disagree.' *United States—Measures Affecting the Cross-Border Supply of Gambling and Betting Services*, Report of 7 April 2005, WT/DS285/AB/R, para 196, and for further on this case, see sections 4.3.1 and 4.4.1 below.

courts and tribunals is in writing. Judges or arbitrators may reject material from consideration, or exclude it from their reasoning, but cannot readily prevent it being brought to their notice.

However, even where there is a firm determination by a court or tribunal that recourse to preparatory work is not necessary to reach a proper interpretation, the wide scope offered by article 32 for use of preparatory material to confirm a meaning may combine with a court's inclination to acknowledge the introduction of material by the parties. Thus, for example, in *Georgia v Russia*, the ICJ determined that a provision of the treaty referring to a dispute 'which is not settled by negotiation' set preconditions to bringing a case before the Court. The Court nevertheless considered that, given the extensive arguments of the parties and the Court's previous practice of resorting to the preparatory work to confirm its reading of a provision, a presentation of the parties' positions and an examination of the preparatory work was warranted.[53] In the event, the Court noted that, while no firm inferences could be drawn from the drafting history of the Convention as to whether negotiations or the procedures expressly provided for in the Convention were meant as preconditions for recourse to the Court, it was possible nevertheless to conclude that the materials constituting the preparatory work 'do not suggest a different conclusion from that at which the Court has already arrived through the main method of ordinary meaning interpretation'.[54] This invites consideration of the role of confirming a meaning and, implicitly, raises the question of how to proceed if the preparatory work does suggest a different conclusion from that achieved by application of the general rule.

4.2 Confirming meaning

4.2.1 Confirming a clear meaning

In using the Vienna rules, the ICJ is sometimes quite explicit that it is using the preparatory work simply to confirm a meaning that is already clear from applying the general rule. For example, in *Territorial Dispute (Libya/Chad)* the ICJ used the general rule to establish that it was clear that in a 1955 treaty, when the parties stated that they recognized frontiers that resulted from instruments listed in an annex to the treaty, they acknowledged that these instruments defined all the frontiers even if demarcation on the ground had been left over to later work in some instances.[55] Accordingly, the Court stated:

The Court considers that it is not necessary to refer to the *travaux préparatoires* to elucidate the content of the 1955 Treaty; but, as in previous cases, it finds it possible by reference to

---

[53] *Application of the International Convention on the Elimination of All Forms of Racial Discrimination (Georgia v Russian Federation), (Preliminary Objections)*, [2011] ICJ Reports 70, at 128–9, paras 142–6, at para 142 listing previous cases in which the practice of examination to confirm a meaning had been followed.

[54] *Application of the International Convention on the Elimination of All Forms of Racial Discrimination (Georgia v Russian Federation), (Preliminary Objections)*, at 130, para 147.

[55] [1994] ICJ Reports 6.

the *travaux* to confirm its reading of the text, namely that the Treaty constitutes an agreement between the parties which, inter alia, defines the frontiers.[56]

It may legitimately be asked why, if the meaning was so clear from application of the general rule, was it necessary to consider the preparatory work at all? The general answer is that, as acknowledged by the ILC's Special Rapporteur (Waldock) and many others, in virtually all cases where there is an issue of treaty interpretation, it is the practice to look at the preparatory work even if nothing comes of it. In the particular case, there are some deductions that can be made from reading the Court's account of the preparatory work; but it probably boils down to doing justice to the parties and their arguments, and completing the interpretative exercise. The records showed that in negotiating the 1955 treaty, the Libyan negotiators had wished to leave aside the issues of frontiers but had been persuaded that these should be determined, even in the case of one frontier in a treaty of 1919 which was difficult to apply because of events subsequent to that date. The Libyan leader had nevertheless stated in the 1955 negotiations that the 1919 Agreement was 'acceptable' and that 'implementation' of it was to be left to the 'near future'. The Court found that 'implementation' could only mean 'operations to demarcate the frontier on the ground'.[57] Thus this exploration of the negotiating history showed respect for the fact that there were, possibly, grounds for arguing that something had been left aside at one stage in the negotiation of the treaty, that this warranted examination, but that the intended outcome was clear enough.

The evident influence that preparatory work can exert, even when a court is vigorously asserting that its role is only confirmatory, is well shown in the judgment of the ECtHR in *Bankovic & Others v Belgium & Others*.[58] The Court had to decide whether the parties' commitment to 'secure to everyone within their jurisdiction' respect for rights under the European Convention on Human Rights had extraterritorial reach when NATO forces caused death, injury, and damage in Serbia, which was not a party to the Convention:

Finally, the Court finds clear confirmation of this essentially territorial notion of jurisdiction in the *travaux préparatoires* which demonstrate that the Expert Intergovernmental Committee replaced the words 'all persons residing within their territories' with a reference to persons 'within their jurisdiction' with a view to expanding the Convention's application to others who may not reside, in a legal sense, but who are, nevertheless, on the territory of the Contracting States...

However, the scope of Article 1, at issue in the present case, is determinative of the very scope of the Contracting Parties' positive obligations and, as such, of the scope and reach of the entire Convention system of human rights' protection... In any event, the extracts from the *travaux préparatoires* detailed above constitute a clear indication of the intended meaning of Article 1 of the Convention which cannot be ignored. The Court would emphasise

---

[56] [1994] ICJ Reports 6, at 27–28, para 55.
[57] [1994] ICJ Reports 6, at 27–28, para 55.
[58] Application no 52207/99, Decision on Admissibility (2001).

that it is not interpreting Article 1 'solely' in accordance with the *travaux préparatoires* or finding those *travaux* 'decisive'; rather this preparatory material constitutes clear confirmatory evidence of the ordinary meaning of Article 1 of the Convention as already identified by the Court (Article 32 of the Vienna Convention 1969).[59]

The ICJ and other courts and tribunals do not always express in direct or simple terms that they are using preparatory work to confirm a meaning even when using preparatory work in that role. For example, the ICJ has several times phrased its conclusions in terms indicating that it does not view the preparatory work as contradicting an interpretation at which the Court has arrived by other means:

... none of the sources of interpretation referred to in the relevant Articles of the Vienna Convention on the Law of Treaties, including the preparatory work, contradict the conclusions drawn from the terms of Article 41 read in their context and in the light of the object and purpose of the Statute.[60]

The Court concludes from this that ... the text of Article 11 of UNCLOS and the *travaux préparatoires* do not preclude the possibility of interpreting restrictively the concept of harbour works ... so as to avoid or mitigate the problem of excessive length identified by the ILC.[61]

Finding that preparatory work does not 'contradict' a conclusion, 'preclude' the possibility of interpreting a term in a particular way, and does not 'suggest a different conclusion', all indicate a form of confirmation, but give it a formulation which leaves hanging the implicit questions: what would have happened if there had been a contradiction? Could preparatory work preclude an otherwise proper interpretation? This has not been resolved in the practice of courts and tribunals. There are few cases that even come near to producing an interpretation that is entirely clear yet directly contradicted by preparatory work which is itself crystal clear.

4.2.2 Role of 'confirming' when preparatory work contradicts meaning afforded by application of general rule

One of the most prominent of recent ICJ cases in which preparatory work was in issue was *Qatar v Bahrain* in 1995.[62] The case shows that whatever the correct evaluation of the relationship between application of the general rule and recourse to preparatory work, any relevant and accessible preparatory work will normally be considered, but its confirmatory role may depend on how the material is to be read. The case inspired consideration of the problem of what the interpreter is to

---

[59] Application no 52207/99, Decision on Admissibility (2001), at paras 63 and 65.

[60] *LaGrand (Germany v USA)* [2001] ICJ Reports 466, at 506, para 109, and see the ICJ case *Application of the International Convention etc (Georgia v Russian Federation)* (2011), quoted at the end of section 4.1.4 above to the effect that the *travaux* in that case 'do not suggest a different conclusion'.

[61] *Maritime Delimitation in the Black Sea (Romania v Ukraine)* [2009] ICJ Reports 62, at 106, para 134.

[62] *Maritime Delimitation and Territorial Questions between Qatar and Bahrain (Qatar v Bahrain), (Jurisdiction and Admissibility)* [1995] ICJ Reports 6; and see Chapter 5, section 2.4.1 above, for the role of 'good faith' in interpretation in this case.

do if the preparatory work fails to confirm a meaning which emerges from application of the general rule, or if it can be read as tending to contradict that meaning. However, although the difference in approach between the majority and the principal dissent (Judge Schwebel) looks to be over how article 32 of the Vienna Convention applies, it is suggested here that the real difference was over how the preparatory work was to be read and understood. Nevertheless, the case warrants detailed attention as providing occasion for consideration of a difficult issue relating to preparatory work.

The dispute concerned maritime delimitation and territorial claims. A preliminary issue was whether Bahrain had agreed to the ICJ being seised of the case by Qatar individually rather than by joint submission by the two states. Arcane though this matter might appear, it was not merely a point for procedural obstruction. The substantial concern was how to define the extent of the dispute to be considered by the Court, in addition to the important point of legal principle that the Court's jurisdiction is wholly dependent on the consent of the parties in dispute.

For many years the two states had been in dispute over their maritime and territorial claims. Since independence, attempts had been made to resolve these disputes through the good offices of the ruler of Saudi Arabia. In the background was the possibility of reference to the ICJ. What aspects of the differences were to be included, and how the issues were to be formulated, in any agreement to submit the dispute to the Court were the core of the persistent disagreement, rather than the principle of judicial settlement itself. One suggestion in the course of negotiations was that the agreement to submit the case to the Court should have two annexes, one Qatari and the other Bahraini, each state defining in its annex the subjects of dispute it wanted to refer to the Court. This idea was not taken up. That it was suggested, however, shows that great importance was attached to how the dispute was formulated.

The ICJ had previously held that exchanges of letters in 1987 and minutes of discussions in 1990 ('the Doha minutes') amounted to treaties.[63] The issue in the 1995 stage of the case was interpretation of provisions on submission to the ICJ, with a focus on the Arabic word transliterated as 'al-tarafan', a dual usage which Qatar translated as 'the parties' and Bahrain as 'the two parties'.[64] This was in the context of a period ending in May 1991 being reserved to try to reach a settlement through the good offices of the Saudi King. The Doha minutes (in translation) recorded agreement that: 'Once that period has elapsed, the {two} parties may submit the matter to the International Court of Justice in accordance with the Bahraini formula [a definition of the subject and scope of the commitment to jurisdiction], which has been accepted by Qatar, and with the procedures consequent on it.'[65]

---

[63] *Maritime Delimitation and Territorial Questions between Qatar and Bahrain (Qatar v Bahrain) (Jurisdiction and Admissibility)* [1994] ICJ Reports 112.
[64] [1994] ICJ Reports 112, para 34.
[65] [1994] ICJ Reports 112, para 30, in the translation used by the Court from the Arabic.

Did the controversial term 'al-tarafan' mean each state could individually start proceedings at the ICJ or did they have to be instituted by both together (the common process of submitting a case by special agreement[66])? Qatar had made a unilateral application to the ICJ. If the agreements actually required Bahrain's concurrence, Qatar's application would have been insufficient to establish the Court's jurisdiction. The point had been closely examined in the negotiations leading to the words used. An early draft had been unambiguous, reading in translation: 'either of the two parties may submit the matter to the International Court of Justice'. This had been changed at the proposal of Bahrain to the potentially ambiguous expression 'al-tarafan'. Qatar had accepted that.

The majority of judges (supporting the Court's finding in favour of the permissibility of unilateral submission) started with the word 'may' in the complete phrase. This they found to indicate an option rather than an obligation, and hence suggested that the ordinary meaning of the words in that context was that either could submit the case. This was supported, in the view of the majority, by further contextual analysis. That the possibility of submitting the case was to be suspended until expiry of the stated period of Saudi mediation militated in favour of the possibility of unilateral submission to the Court, as did the reference to the Bahraini formula which in the circumstances left open the only procedural possibility that each party might submit distinct claims in the absence of agreement defining their scope.

The majority of the Court found this meaning so clear from application of the general rule of interpretation that the judges did not consider it necessary to resort to supplementary means of interpretation in order to *determine* the meaning of the Doha Minutes. The Court nevertheless did have recourse to these supplementary means 'in order to seek a possible confirmation of its interpretation of the text'.[67] It prefaced its consideration of the preparatory work by stating the need for caution on account of its perception that the preparatory work was fragmentary. On what might be thought the crucial change from 'either of the two parties' to 'the {two} parties' (al-tarafan), the majority said:

The Court is unable to see why the abandonment of a form of words corresponding to the interpretation given by Qatar to the Doha Minutes should imply that they must be interpreted in accordance with Bahrain's thesis. As a result, it does not consider that the *travaux préparatoires*, in the form in which they have been submitted to it—i.e., limited to the various drafts mentioned above—can provide it with conclusive supplementary elements for the interpretation of the text adopted; whatever may have been the motives of each of the Parties, the Court can only confine itself to the actual terms of the Minutes as the expression of their common intention, and to the interpretation of them which it has already given.[68]

---

[66] Such joint applications following the special agreement of the parties ('compromis') are denoted in the practice of the Court by the names of the parties being separated by '/' rather than the 'v' used where a party has unilaterally brought the case without there being a compromis.

[67] [1994] ICJ Reports 112, para 40.   [68] [1994] ICJ Reports 112, para 41.

Nevertheless, it seems difficult when working with English translations of the phrase 'either of the two parties' to resist the apparently obvious implication of the deletion of 'either of' as removing the possibility of submission by either of them alone. And that was the gist of the dissent of Judge Schwebel.[69] Emphasizing that the central objective of treaty interpretation was finding the intention of the parties, and noting the controversial nature of the Vienna rules in the time leading up to their adoption, Judge Schwebel found that what the text and context of the Doha minutes left so unclear was crystal clear when the minutes were analysed with the assistance of the preparatory work.[70] Thus, he concluded, particularly in the light of the change in wording, that the correct interpretation was that an application to the Court required *joint* submission of the case.

Judge Schwebel noted that in 1987, in a draft for a letter submitting the case to the Court, Qatar provided for 'preparing the *necessary* Special Agreement in this respect...'.[71] This suggested that Qatar, no less than Bahrain, saw conclusion of a special agreement, that is joint submission, as 'necessary'. Further:

If the object of the Parties—if their common intention—was to make clear that 'both Qatar *and* Bahrain had the right to make a unilateral application to the Court', the provision that 'either of the two parties may submit the matter' would have been left unchanged. That wording achieved that object clearly, simply, and precisely. As it was, that unchanged phraseology authorized either of the two Parties to make unilateral application to the Court. To suggest that the change of that phraseology to 'the two parties' rather imports that each of the Parties—because of that change—is entitled to make a unilateral application to the Court is unintelligible.[72]

For present purposes, however, Judge Schwebel's dissenting opinion is as interesting for his approach as for his conclusion. While he was at pains to reiterate the American objections to the Vienna Convention's formulation as if it labelled preparatory work a 'subsidiary' means, and (in effect) to support McDougal and the New Haven school's approach to treaty interpretation as being a matter of finding (in paraphrase) the shared intentions of the parties modified by any community values, in fact in his handling of the preparatory work in this case, Judge Schwebel's approach seems very much in line with what the Vienna rules mandate. He found the term in issue to be ambiguous: 'The expression in the Doha Minutes of "al-tarafan", however translated, is quintessentially unclear; as the Court itself acknowledges, it is capable of being construed as meaning jointly or separately.'[73] He therefore reached the proper interpretation by looking at the preparatory work—all precisely as mandated by article 32.

In contrast, the majority had expressly found it unnecessary to resort to the preparatory work to make a *determination* of the correct meaning, but rather sought *confirmation* of the ordinary meaning as they found it to be. This resulted in the rather elliptical conclusion to the effect that the preparatory work could not

---

[69] [1995] ICJ Reports 27. [70] [1995] ICJ Reports 27, at 38.
[71] [1995] ICJ Reports 27, at 33. [72] [1995] ICJ Reports 27, at 34–35.
[73] [1995] ICJ Reports 27, at 37.

provide the Court with conclusive evidence in support of the interpretation which it had reached, but that there was no clear contradiction. This approach seems equally in line with the Vienna rules, perhaps reflecting more faithfully the differentiation between the general rule and supplementary means, even if the Court's assessment of the inconclusive nature of the preparatory work, particularly as regards the change of wording at the crucial point, may be thought to be less in tune with seemingly obvious inferences.[74]

While, therefore, different conclusions were reached, it is not clear that their divergence is attributable to the Vienna rules or to a fault line in them. If the difference in result had to be characterized in terms of approach, it might reasonably be summarized as the majority view giving preference to what those judges saw as a meaning which was clear in its context over unclear preparatory work, while Judge Schwebel gave precedence to what he saw as clear conclusions to be drawn from the preparatory work rather than to a term which was ambiguous and not clarified by its context. However, neither approach fell outside article 32. The majority and Judge Schwebel only really differed as to how to interpret the preparatory work.

Nevertheless, the discussion offered by the two judgments does reveal an apparent difficulty in the Vienna rules. The majority judgment (understandably, given that the issues did not arise for those judges) does not disclose what the position would have been had they found their interpretation to be clearly contradicted by the preparatory work. Perhaps finding this frustrating, Judge Schwebel explored the possibility that the Court in reality discounted the preparatory work because it did not confirm the meaning to which its analysis had led.[75] If that were the position, he found it would be hard to reconcile with interpretation of a treaty in good faith 'which is the cardinal injunction of the Vienna Convention's rule of interpretation. The *travaux préparatoires* are no less evidence of the intention of the Parties when they contradict as when they confirm the allegedly clear meaning of the text or context of treaty provisions.'[76]

Judge Schwebel homed in on this in a contribution to a book, his chapter being titled 'May Preparatory Work be Used to Correct rather than Confirm the "Clear" Meaning of a Treaty Provision?'.[77] This helpfully sets out relevant extracts from

---

[74] See para 41 of judgment, *ad fin.*

[75] Schwebel, dissenting, [1995] ICJ Reports 27, at 39.   [76] [1995] ICJ Reports 27, at 39.

[77] S Schwebel, 'May Preparatory Work be Used to Correct rather than Confirm the "Clear" Meaning of a Treaty Provision?' in J Makarczyk (ed), *Theory of International Law at the Threshold of the 21st Century* (The Hague: Kluwer, 1996) 541, republished electronically at <http://www.transnational-dispute-management.com>, *Transnational Dispute Management*, vol 2, no 5 (Nov 2005); and for a response, see M H Mendelson, 'Comment on "May Preparatory Work be Used to Correct Rather than Confirm the 'Clear' Meaning of a Treaty Provision?"', *Transnational Dispute Management*, vol 2, no 5 (Nov 2005). The problem appears to have been tackled head on (but not with specific reference to the Vienna rules) by the Swiss Federal Supreme Court in *Bosshard Partners Intertrading AG v Sunlight AG* [1980] 3 CMLR 664, at 674–75, para 21: 'If the wording is clear and its meaning, as it appears from the ordinary use of language and the subject and purpose of the treaty, is not patently contrary to sense, a differing interpretation only comes into question if it must be inferred with certainty, from the context or the legislative history of the treaty, that the contracting States had an agreed intention which differs from the wording' (footnote omitted). Since no authority

the preparatory work of the ILC and notes that more extensive use is made of pre-paratory work in practice, even where it contradicts an apparently plain meaning. Paradoxically perhaps, the problem presents itself in its most acute form only if one adopts a very literal meaning of 'to confirm' in article 32 of the Vienna Convention. If the whole of articles 31 and 32 are deployed in relation to that term, the picture is rather different. Even the ordinary meaning of 'confirm' is not monolithic. In a transitive mood, I may contact someone to confirm a provisional booking which I have made. I am actually going a little further than I had when originally booking because I am making firm something which previously was not. In an interroga-tive mood, I may telephone an airline or hotel asking them to confirm that they have received my internet booking and payment, and are keeping my reservation. I expect an affirmative response, but lurking is the fear that something may have gone wrong, in which case I will have to think again. Both situations show the comparable potential in the Vienna Convention's usage of 'confirm'.

Judge Schwebel considered that the Vienna Convention could hardly be said to be reflective of customary international law if it did not in fact fairly reflect state practice and judicial precedent:

That practice and precedent demonstrate that preparatory work is often brought to bear on the interpretation of treaties, by the parties to those treaties and by their interpreters, and this whether the *travaux préparatoires* confirm or correct an interpretation otherwise arrived at.[78]

That this reflects the meaning of the Vienna Convention provision is 'confirmed' in the preparatory work in the ILC.[79] However, it does not show exactly what should happen if preparatory work reveals an intended divergence from the ordi-nary meaning; nor has exploration of the issue thrown up a clear example. *Qatar v Bahrain* did not precisely pose the issue because it could reasonably be argued that there was uncertainty as to meaning in both text and preparatory work.

Perhaps the Vienna Convention's use in article 32 of 'confirm' comes closest to an example of the preparatory work, in combination with practice, contradicting an ordinary meaning, if a very narrow meaning is ascribed to 'confirm'. As well as the ILC's own view at the head of this chapter and the statements of the Special Rapporteur (Waldock) set out above,[80] there were also further observations in the preparatory work which may be taken as providing guidance on this issue. First, Yasseen in the ILC made clear the role he saw for preparatory work in relation to the 'clarity' of a text, stating that:

...the clearness or ambiguity of a provision was a relative matter; sometimes one had to refer [to] the preparatory work or look at the circumstances surrounding the conclusion

---

or example is given in support of this assertion, it would be difficult to sustain in the face of the Vienna rules.

[78] Schwebel, 'May Preparatory Work be Used to Correct rather than Confirm the "Clear" Meaning of a Treaty Provision?' 547.

[79] See references to records of ILC in sections 2.2 and 2.3 above.

[80] See sections 1 and 2.3 above.

of the treaty in order to determine whether the text was really clear and whether the seeming clarity was not simply a deceptive appearance. He could not accept an article which would impose a chronological order and which would permit reference to preparatory work only after it had been decided that the text was not clear, that decision itself, being often influenced by the consultation of the same sources.[81]

The Special Rapporteur (Waldock) acknowledged this, noting that it was sometimes impossible to understand clearly even the object and purpose of the treaty without such reference.[82] At the Vienna Conference, the issue was addressed head on by the delegate of Portugal:

What would happen if, though the text was apparently clear, in seeking confirmation in the preparatory work and other surrounding circumstances a divergent meaning came to light? It was impossible to be sure in advance that those circumstances would confirm the textual meaning of the treaty. If the emphasis were placed on good faith, it would appear that in such a case those circumstances should be taken into consideration. . . .[83]

The outcome at Vienna was inconclusive save in the sense that the conference endorsed the distinction between the general rule and supplementary means. Analysis without examples is difficult to evaluate; but it is also difficult to find examples of situations in which an unquestionable interpretation ascertained by proper application of the general rule is directly contradicted by a clear indication in preparatory work of the common understanding as to the meaning held by all negotiators. Close, perhaps, are two examples given in Chapter 1, above. The most firmly established meaning of an 'alcoholic' (as one who is addicted to alcohol rather than temporarily drunk) would not in fact have been confirmed by the preparatory work, whereas a broader connotation of drunkenness, which the Court found established from the context, was strongly supported by the preparatory work.[84] Similarly, the place where an arbitral award was 'made' was not necessarily where it was signed but, as shown by the preparatory work, was a reference to the place of arbitration.[85] In both these situations reference to the preparatory work shows that a primary meaning which was, or might have been thought to be, clear was contradicted by the preparatory work. In both cases the correct meaning was not so far removed from ordinary meanings and usage of the words in issue as to preclude the proper meaning being deduced by application of the general rule, the preparatory work giving strong confirmation of this.[86]

---

[81] [1964] *Yearbook of ILC*, vol I, p 313, para 56.

[82] [1964] *Yearbook of ILC*, vol I, p 313, para 57.

[83] United Nations Conference on the Law of Treaties, Official Records: First Session, p 183, para 56; and see Schwebel, 'May Preparatory Work be Used to Correct rather than Confirm the "Clear" Meaning of a Treaty Provision?', at 544–47.

[84] See *Litwa v Poland* in Chapter 1, section 5.1 above.

[85] See *Hiscox v Outhwaite* considered in Chapter 1, section 5.4 above; and see below. It is to be noted that in *Hiscox v Outhwaite* the higher courts in the UK reached their conclusion without the benefit of the Vienna rules; but the facts are helpful as illustrating how proper use of the Vienna rules in academic analysis of the problem had assisted the court of first instance to a conclusion in line with the eventual legislation that was required to reverse the interpretation given by the higher courts.

[86] Further examples of preparatory work in apparent conflict with an interpretation reached by application of the general rule of interpretation are *Young, James and Webster v UK* (ECtHR)

In any event, a divergent meaning disclosed by the preparatory work would be present in the interpreter's mind throughout any competently conducted interpretative exercise.[87] In such circumstances the unity of the Vienna rules is perhaps of greater significance than the *supplementary* character of the means identified in article 32, the rather elastic concepts of ambiguity, etc allowing for recourse to the preparatory work to determine the meaning in appropriate cases. Hence the real question would be what weight is to be given to the preparatory work. Here courts and tribunals may draw inspiration from Waldock's introductory reflection on the topic to the effect that preparatory work does not provide authentic interpretation but 'simply evidence to be weighed against any other relevant evidence of the intentions of the parties' whose ' cogency depends on the extent to which they furnish proof of the *common* understanding of the parties as to the meaning attached to the terms of the treaty.'[88]

4.2.3 *Using supplementary means to confirm 'intention'*

Although the Vienna rules do not make the search for the intention of the parties a specific aim of treaty interpretation, reference to preparatory work almost inevitably points the thoughts of the interpreter in the direction of seeking the intention of the parties as much as towards the meaning of a term in a text. This was indeed explicitly stated in the explanation given by Waldock in the ILC.[89] Hence it is not surprising to find references to the intentions of the drafters of treaty provisions when preparatory work is being assessed. A good example of this is in the ICJ's Advisory Opinion on the *Wall in Occupied Palestinian Territory*.[90] One issue was whether the Fourth Geneva Convention, 1949, applied in the occupied territory of Palestine. That Convention stated that it applied (inter alia) to 'all cases of declared war or of any other armed conflict which may arise between two or more of the High Contracting Parties' (article 2(1)) and to 'all cases of partial or total occupation of the territory of a High Contracting Party, even if the said occupation meets with no armed resistance' (article 2(2)). Where the wall was in occupied Palestine, an entity whose statehood had not fully crystallized, was application of this provision excluded by the reference to 'territory of a High Contracting Party'? The Court had noted that Switzerland had concluded that, as a depositary of the Geneva Conventions, it was not in a position to decide whether the request in 1989 from the 'Palestine Liberation Movement' [*sic*] in

---

Application nos 7601/76 and 7806/77, Judgment of 13 August 1981 (considered further in chapter 10, section 5.1 below) and investment arbitrations following *Salini Costruttori SpA v Kingdom of Morocco* ICSID Case No. ARB/00/4 (Decision on Jurisdiction, 16 July 2001) (see further Chapter 10, section 6.2.1 below).

[87] For a realistic approach to the situation where material providing supplementary means of interpretation may itself have been the trigger for finding ambiguity, see *HICEE B.V. v Slovak Republic*, PCA Case No. 2009-11, Partial Award, 23 May 2011, relevant extract in section 4.3.1 below.

[88] Section 2.2 above.   [89] See section 2.2 above.

[90] *Legal Consequences of the Construction of a Wall in the Occupied Palestinian Territory* [2004] ICJ Reports 136.

the name of the 'State of Palestine' to accede inter alia to the Fourth Geneva Convention could be considered as an instrument of accession.[91] Hence there remained an issue whether the occupied territory was territory in respect of which the Conventions applied.

Making explicit reference to the Vienna rules, the Court identified two conditions of applicability in article 2(1) of the Fourth Geneva Convention: existence of an armed conflict, and that such conflict was between two contracting parties. It deduced from this that if those two conditions were satisfied, the Convention applied in any territory occupied in the course of the conflict by one of the contracting parties. This was not limited by article 2(2) because the object of that paragraph was not to restrict the scope of application of the Convention, as defined by article 2(1), by excluding territories not falling under the sovereignty of one of the contracting parties. It was directed 'simply to making it clear that, even if occupation effected during the conflict met no armed resistance, the Convention is still applicable'.[92]

The Court supported this interpretation by stating that it reflected 'the *intention* of the drafters of the Fourth Geneva Convention to protect civilians who find themselves, in whatever way, in the hands of the occupying Power'.[93] This was shown by contrasting the provision with that of the Hague Regulations of 1907 whose drafters 'were as much concerned with protecting the rights of a State whose territory is occupied, as with protecting the inhabitants of that territory', while 'the drafters of the Fourth Geneva Convention sought to guarantee the protection of civilians in time of war, regardless of the status of the occupied territories'.[94] In support of the latter proposition the Court referred to article 47 of the Geneva Convention. Although it is correct that article 47 provides rules for protection of persons in occupied territory without reference to such territory being that of a party to the Convention, the main support for assertions about the intentions of the drafters was to be found in the preparatory work. From examination of this, and having recited extracts from the material, the Court concluded that: 'The drafters of the second paragraph of article 2 thus had no intention, when they inserted that paragraph into the Convention, of restricting the latter's scope of application. They were merely seeking to provide for cases of occupation without combat, such as the occupation of Bohemia and Moravia by Germany in 1939.'[95]

This illustration of the use of preparatory work to ascertain the intention of the drafters shows a prominent role for the preparatory work in clarifying the meaning of a text whose literal sense could appear limitative of the application of the Geneva Convention. It should be emphasized, however, that this was only part of a fuller interpretative exercise, making use of other elements of the Vienna rules, including

---

[91] [2004] ICJ Reports 136, at 173, para 91.
[92] [2004] ICJ Reports 136, at 174, para 95.
[93] [2004] ICJ Reports 136, at 174, para 95 (emphasis added).
[94] [2004] ICJ Reports 136, at 174, para 95.
[95] [2004] ICJ Reports 136, at 174, para 95.

subsequent agreement by states parties to the Fourth Geneva Convention in their approval at a 1999 conference of the interpretation that the Convention applied to the occupied territory under consideration.[96]

4.2.4 Using supplementary means to 'reinforce' an interpretation

The term 'confirm' in article 32 is very loosely interpreted in practice, reference to preparatory work and circumstances of conclusion being made to substantiate an interpretation that is emerging as much as confirming one which is already pretty much clear. An example of this is in the *Legality of Use of Force* cases (2004),[97] where the ICJ interpreted provisions of its Statute in the context of the regime for access to the Court by states not parties to the Statute, including the reference in article 35(2) of the Statute to 'the special provisions contained in treaties in force'. The Court used the general rule to identify possible interpretations of 'treaties in force' and continued:

The first interpretation, according to which Article 35, paragraph 2, refers to treaties in force at the time that the Statute came into force, is in fact reinforced by an examination of the *travaux préparatoires* of the text. Since the Statute of the Permanent Court of International Justice contained substantially the same provision, which was used as a model when the Statute of the present Court was drafted, it will be necessary to examine the drafting history of both Statutes....[98]

It seems fair to observe that how the Court chooses to introduce its consideration of preparatory work is less significant than whether it makes use of such work in some sort of confirmatory role or to determine the meaning where other means leave this unclear. Thus, in introducing the former role, it is difficult to see any distinction between the description above of the preparatory work as 'reinforcing' a possible interpretation and that in another case where the ICJ stated that 'further confirmation' of the Court's reading of a particular provision was to be found in the preparatory work.[99]

---

[96] See especially [2004] ICJ Reports 136, at 175, para 96. See also the comparable interpretative exercise referring to the intention of the drafters of the International Covenant on Civil and Political Rights, in paras 108–9 of the same advisory opinion. For other explicit references to seeking intention via preparatory work, see: *Pope & Talbot v Canada (Award in respect of Damages)* (NAFTA) (2002) 41 ILM 1347, at 1357, para 26: '...it is common and proper to turn to the negotiating history of an agreement to see if that might shed some light on the intention of the signatories', and *Klöckner v Cameroon* (ICSID Ad Hoc Committee on Annulment, 3 May 1985) 114 ILR 152, at 286, paras 118–19: 'The preparatory works of the Convention seem to indicate that the intention was to limit the institution of annulment proceedings.'

[97] *Case concerning Legality of Use of Force (Serbia and Montenegro v Belgium) (Preliminary Objections)* [2004] ICJ Reports 279, and see also other cases by the same Applicant on *Legality of Use of Force (Serbia and Montenegro v Canada, France, Germany, Italy, Netherlands, Portugal, United Kingdom) (Preliminary Objections)* [2004] ICJ Reports where the same wording recurs.

[98] *Case concerning Legality of Use of Force (Serbia and Montenegro v Belgium) (Preliminary Objections)* at para 103.

[99] *Border and Transborder Armed Actions (Nicaragua v Honduras) (Jurisdiction and Admissibility)* [1988] ICJ Reports 69, at 85, para 37.

4.2.5 Using preparatory work as general support

Allusion to preparatory work on an apparently incidental basis to support an interpretative argument is quite common. This can be justified as a use of supplementary means to confirm a meaning in a very general sense, or as less respectful of the more structured approach which the separation of the general rule and the supplementary means indicates, if read literally. So for example, in a lengthy note on interpretation of the 1965 Washington Convention's requirements as to nationality, when considering whether these had to be met by a company at the date of entering into a concession agreement or also at the date of making a request for arbitration, an International Centre for Settlement of Investment Disputes (ICSID) arbitral tribunal set out arguments including those based on analysis of the text, views of commentators, and interpretations by previous arbitral tribunals.[100] Following the latter, the tribunal simply noted that 'the *travaux préparatoires* of the Convention support the single requirement, *see* Documents... Vol. II, 287 etc'.[101]

4.2.6 Reciting and using preparatory work contrasted

The practice of the European Court of Human Rights (ECtHR) in recounting the development of relevant provisions has already been shown.[102] However, that Court makes a definite distinction between stating the record from the preparatory work and deploying that material in an interpretative exercise. This distinction is not always so clearly made. For example, in *US v Kostadinov* the Court of Appeals (Second Circuit) considered the meaning of 'mission' in the Vienna Convention on Diplomatic Relations.[103] Although the Convention defined 'members of the mission' and 'premises of the mission', the term 'mission' was not defined separately. Did the fact that someone had an office in the Bulgarian trade mission in New York entitle them to immunities? The Court set out relevant provisions of the Convention and indicated that those provisions were better understood after examining the groundwork performed by the ILC and the discussions by the delegates to the Vienna Conference which prepared the Convention.[104] The Court used this background to show that the lower court had placed emphasis on the physical aspect of the mission, whereas it could be shown from the preparatory material that a mission in the diplomatic sense consists of a group of people sent by one state to another, not the premises which they occupy in the receiving state. This Court's further use of the preparatory work in its detailed support of this and its analysis of the provisions on immunity together formed the basis for

---

[100] *Vacuum Salt v Ghana* ICSID Case No ARB/92/1, (1994) 4 ICSID Rep 329, at 337–38, para 29, fn 9.

[101] (1994) 4 ICSID Rep 329, at 337–38, para 29, fn 9.

[102] See, eg, *Litwa v Poland* in Chapter 1, section 5.1 above.

[103] 99 ILR 103, 734 F 2d 905 (1984) (Sup Crt, certiorari denied).

[104] 99 ILR 103, 734 F 2d 905 (1984), at 106 and 907, respectively.

the interpretation denying immunity. While this approach may appear to give a greater role to the preparatory work than the Vienna rules would now warrant, unless a particular effort is made to separate systematically the elements identified by the rules, a narrative with provisions interwoven with preparatory work may make the most coherent presentation of a reasoned interpretation.

4.3 Determining meaning

4.3.1 Qualifying conditions: 'ambiguous or obscure' or 'manifestly absurd or unreasonable'

Ambiguity or obscurity in the meaning produced by application of the general rule are notions which leave generous scope for resort to supplementary means such as preparatory work. The range of ordinary meanings of a term will often be extensive and the issue giving rise to the investigation of possible interpretations may itself point to the possibility of different meanings. That a word has various dictionary definitions, while raising the ordinary notion of ambiguity, does not necessarily mean that there is ambiguity in the sense of article 32 of the Vienna Convention.[105] The Vienna rules look here to ambiguity that remains after the application of the general rule—that is, after deploying all relevant elements of the whole of article 31, not merely the ambiguity of multiple senses in a dictionary. The context, subsequent agreement, subsequent practice, etc may resolve any such ambiguity without the need for determination by supplementary means.

However, the approach of the ILC was based on the suggestion of Waldock as Special Rapporteur reproduced at the head of this chapter and indicating reconciliation of the principle of the primacy of the text 'with frequent and quite normal recourse to *travaux préparatoires* without any too nice regard for the question whether the text itself is clear'. Waldock suggested that the proposed rule was 'inherently flexible, since the question whether the text can be said to be 'clear' is in some degree subjective'. Nevertheless, it can be dictionary definitions that initially point strongly to ambiguity, and courts and tribunals have not generally analysed too closely what is meant by ambiguity in article 32. Of course dictionaries give many words more than one meaning. 'Ambiguous' itself bears seven meanings of which the one indicated as most common offers multiple choice of somewhat different senses: 'Admitting more than one interpretation, or explanation; of double meaning, or of several possible meanings; equivocal'.[106] The dictionary stage, if it occurs in interpretation, is likely to be at the outset of the interpretative exercise, but that sets the ground for ultimate consideration of preparatory work if the

---

[105] Cf G G Fitzmaurice, 'The Law and Procedure of the International Court of Justice 1951–4: Treaty Interpretation and Other Points' (1957) 33 BYBIL 203, at 216 suggesting a threshold in relation to ambiguity: 'It is . . . not sufficient in itself that a text is *capable* of bearing more than one meaning. These meanings must be equally valid meanings, or at any rate, even if one may appear more possible and likely than the other, both must attain a reasonable degree of possibility and probability, not only grammatically but as a matter of substance and sense' (original emphasis).

[106] *Oxford English Dictionary*.

general rule provides no clear resolution. Thus, in considering the meaning of 'without delay' in the *Avena* case, the ICJ observed that 'dictionary definitions, in the various languages of the Vienna Convention [on Consular Relations], offer diverse meanings of the term "without delay" (and also of "immediately"). It is therefore necessary to look elsewhere for an understanding of this term'.[107] Taking the view that neither the treaty as normally understood, nor its object and purpose, suggested that 'without delay' was to be understood as 'immediately upon arrest and before interrogation', the Court wove a number of points from the preparatory work into its argument leading to the conclusion that 'by application of the usual rules of interpretation' there was a duty on the arresting authorities to give the required information to an arrested person as soon as it was realized that the person was a foreign national.[108]

In that case the ICJ gave little to indicate the precise role it was affording the preparatory work. Although following a brief account of ordinary meaning and context, the preponderant analysis of the preparatory work suggested that the use of this supplementary means of interpretation went beyond mere confirmation. In contrast, the Appellate Body of the WTO made the process much clearer in *US—Measures Affecting Gambling*. It noted that of the 13 dictionaries consulted by the Panel on the meaning of 'sporting', some included gambling in the definition while others did not.[109] Nevertheless, it was not this that led the Appellate Body to conclude that there was ambiguity. It was only after investigating the context and possible subsequent agreement that the conclusion of ambiguity was affirmed, which opened the door to determining the meaning by using supplementary means. Thus the Appellate Body stated specifically: 'application of the general rule of interpretation set out in Article 31 of the *Vienna Convention* leaves the meaning of "other recreational services (except sporting)" ambiguous...Accordingly, we are required, in this case, to turn to the supplementary means of interpretation provided for in Article 32 of the *Vienna Convention*.'[110]

These cases show what may be described as at least the presence of dictionary-derived ambiguity, leading the way to reasoning drawn from preparatory work. A different situation is where material introduced as supplementary means of interpretation is what suggests that there is ambiguity. In *HICEE v Slovak Republic* an arbitral tribunal considered that Dutch explanatory notes drawn up by one

---

[107] *Case concerning Avena and other Mexican Nationals (Mexico v USA)* [2004] ICJ Reports 12, at 48, para 84, considered further in section 4.1.2 above.

[108] [2004] ICJ Reports 12, at 48–9, paras 84–88.

[109] *United States—Measures Affecting the Cross-Border Supply of Gambling and Betting Services* WTO Appellate Body Report of 7 April 2005, WT/DS285/AB/R, para 165 and fn 193, also noting that: 'Some of the definitions appear to contradict one another. For instance, the *Shorter Oxford English Dictionary* definition quoted by the Panel defines "sporting" as both "characterized by sportsmanlike conduct"; and "[d]esignating an inferior sportsman or a person interested in sport from purely mercenary motives" ', and see further on this case section 4.4.1 below.

[110] *United States—Measures Affecting the Cross-Border Supply of Gambling and Betting Services* WTO Appellate Body Report of 7 April 2005, WT/DS285/AB/R, at para 195.

party to a bilateral investment treaty resolved uncertainty as to whether the term 'directly' referred to an investment made only in a company incorporated in the host state but not in a subsidiary of such a company, or whether it meant any company in the host state that was not a subsidiary of a company incorporated in a third state.[111] As to how the ambiguity had been identified, the Tribunal stated:

It may be objected...that the whole Treaty Interpretation Issue might never have entered anyone's mind in the first place had it not been for the Dutch Explanatory Notes, in other words that it is not admissible to introduce the Notes in order to give rise to an ambiguity. But the Tribunal is unable to follow so counterfactual a line of argument. The plain fact is that the Explanatory Notes were put in argument before it, with a provenance and a relevance that cannot be gainsaid. Whether the ambiguity in the text would otherwise have occurred to either side in this dispute, or to the Counsel representing it, is a hypothetical issue on which it would not be proper for a tribunal to speculate. Suffice it to say that the Tribunal, having been confronted with the treaty text and by the highly professional argument put before it on both sides, has registered the ambiguity in its 'ordinary meaning' and is bound to note that ambiguities exist *a fortiori*; their existence does not depend on the skill of counsel in arguing how they should be resolved.[112]

Ambiguity is not, of course, confined to one word having two or more meanings. A text may be ambiguous where provisions read together leave open different possible interpretations. In *Hosaka v United Airlines*, a US Court of Appeals endorsed the proposition that: 'It is axiomatic that an agreement subject to two or more reasonable interpretations...is ambiguous.'[113] This case (which is considered in more detail below) concerned the 1929 Warsaw Convention which provided a set of uniform rules to be applied in national systems of law in claims against carriers asserting liability for death, injury, loss, or damage during international carriage by air. Article 28 of the Convention provided that:

(1) [any such claim was to be brought in one of four specified places] 'at the option of the plaintiff'; and

(2) 'questions of procedure shall be governed by the law of the court seised of the case'.

In issue was whether a court in a place selected by the plaintiff from one of the four specified options could decline jurisdiction on the basis that it was not the appropriate court (ie applying the doctrine of *'forum non conveniens'*)? If a national system of law characterized application of the doctrine as a procedural matter, did that doctrine or the option exercised by the plaintiff prevail? This might seem an obvious situation in which to apply the principle that general provisions (such as the one on questions of procedure) do not derogate from specific ones. However,

---

[111] *HICEE B.V. v Slovak Republic*, PCA Case No. 2009-11, Partial Award, 23 May 2011; for further consideration of this case, see section 4.5.4 below.
[112] *HICEE B.V. v Slovak Republic*, para 138.
[113] 305 F.3d 989 (9th Cir. 2002), at 995, certiorari denied 537 U.S. 1227.

the Court found the text to be ambiguous, affording two possible interpretations, both of which it considered reasonable.[114]

Obscurity is less commonly instanced than ambiguity as the specific gateway to determination from the preparatory work. In practice, courts and tribunals tend to contrast provisions that are 'clear' with those that are 'uncertain'. Thus, for example, the tribunal in *Prosecutor v Dusko Tadić* stated:

> ...since at least with regard to the issue of discriminatory intent those statements may not be taken to be part of the 'context' of the Statute, it may be argued that they comprise a part of the *travaux préparatoires*...Under customary international law, as codified in Article 32 of the Vienna Convention referred to above, the *travaux* constitute a supplementary means of interpretation and may only be resorted to when the text of a treaty or any other international norm-creating instrument is *ambiguous or obscure*. As the wording of Article 5 is clear and does not give rise to uncertainty...there is no need to rely upon those statements.[115]

It is harder to find specific reference to a result of application of the general rule being expressly found to be 'manifestly absurd or unreasonable' (article 32(b)).[116] 'Monstrous', 'absurd', 'a nonsense or at least a tautology', and 'not reasonable' are some of the terms used to indicate the grounds on which arbitrators have rejected interpretations in case law pre-dating the Vienna Convention.[117] These suggest that these requirements for supplementary means to be determinative are considerably more demanding than an interpretation according to the general rule being merely unpalatable.

Article 32(b) has, however, occasionally been mentioned in a rather different context from being a gateway to use of supplementary means. This is to support rejection of a suggested meaning of a treaty provision on the basis that it would produce a result that is manifestly absurd or unreasonable.[118] Such invocation of

---

[114] 305 F.3d 989, at 994–6; for the use made of the preparatory work, circumstances of conclusion, and the further approach of the Court in finding that the option of the plaintiff prevailed, see section 4.4.2 below.

[115] [1999] ICTY2 (15 July 1999), 124 ILR61, at 183–84, para 303; note that the statement that supplementary means of interpretation may *only* be resorted to when the text of a treaty is ambiguous or obscure is incomplete: ambiguity is only a precondition for recourse to preparatory work *to determine* meaning, not when *confirming* meaning; and see, similarly risking conveying an incomplete impression, Report of the ILC Sixty-eighth Session, (2013) Supplement No. 10 A/68/1, p 14, Conclusion 1, Commentary, para (3).

[116] Absurdity was explicitly cited as a ground for using supplementary means in *United States—Measures Affecting the Cross-Border Supply of Gambling and Betting Services* WTO Appellate Body, Report of 7 April 2005, WT/DS285/AB/R, at para 236, but ambiguity had been found as well: see further section 4.4.1 below; see also *Indonesia—Certain Measures affecting the Automobile Industry*, WTO Panel, Report of 2 July 1998, at paras 5.332 ff, where a WTO Panel used the absurdity of the consequences of one party's argument as a ground for examining the preparatory work.

[117] See citations and analysis in the *Rhine Chlorides case (Netherlands v France)*, Arbitral Award of 12 March 2004, 144 ILR 259, at 297–99, paras 73–76, considered further in Chapter 1, section 5.2 above.

[118] See, eg, *Pope & Talbot v Canada (Merits Phase 2)* (2000) (NAFTA), 122 ILR 352, at 384, para 118, fn. 115 and *(Award in respect of Damages)* (2002) 41 ILM 1347 at 1350, where the tribunal relied on the argument against an interpretation that it would produce a result which was absurd in the sense of article 32 of the Vienna Convention because another provision in the treaty would apply to produce exactly the result of the interpretation in issue; and in similar vein: *Ethyl Corp v Canada (Jurisdiction)* (NAFTA) (1999) 38 ILM 708, at 728–29, para 85, and 734, fn 34.

this test is not four-square within article 32(b), since there it is a lead-in to using supplementary means of interpretation to *determine* the meaning when application of the general rule produces an unsatisfactory result. However, absurdity of result is sometimes argued as an aid to excluding meanings when identifying the ordinary meaning of a term.

An example of use of the concept of absurdity which could trigger reference to the preparatory work was offered in *Champion Trading Co, J T Wahba & Others v Egypt*.[119] An ICSID tribunal upheld the ordinary meaning of the provision in the 1965 Washington Convention, which excluded dual nationals from invoking protection under the Convention against a host country of the investment when also a national of that country. In doing so the tribunal noted reference made by the respondent to the preparatory work which showed that early drafts allowing protection for dual nationals had been changed by unanimous decision to exclude such protection explicitly. However, while upholding that clear meaning for application in the instant case, the tribunal speculated that:

This Tribunal does not rule out that situations might arise where the exclusion of dual nationals could lead to a result which was manifestly absurd or unreasonable (Vienna Convention, article (32)(b)). One could envisage a situation where a country continues to apply the *jus sanguinis* over many generations. It might for instance be questionable if the third or fourth foreign born generation, which has no ties whatsoever with the country of its forefathers, could still be considered to have, for the purpose of the Convention, the nationality of this state.[120]

It is, however, difficult to see how reliance on article 32 could produce a different interpretation that would avail such potential claimants of remote generations. The preparatory work would still confirm the clear exclusion. It seems more likely that the concept of 'effective nationality' would prove the focus of interpretative development through the application of article 31(3)(c) of the Vienna Convention, a concept which was considered in the present case but which did not avail when the link of nationality was not tenuous and artificially imposed.

4.3.2 *Ambiguous by reference to availability of another word having one of the claimed meanings*

In the example given in Chapter 1 above, in the case of *Hiscox v Outhwaite*[121] one of the central issues was where an arbitral award is 'made' within the meaning of the New York Convention on Recognition and Enforcement of Foreign Arbitral Awards. When the arbitrator signed an award in Paris, was the award 'made' in France despite all other connections in the arbitration being with England? In the context of execution of legal documents, judgments, and so on, the point at which the award became concluded would commonly be taken as the moment at which it

---

[119] ICSID Case No ARB/02/9, Decision on Jurisdiction, 21 October 2003.
[120] ICSID Case No ARB/02/9, Decision on Jurisdiction, 21 October 2003, at 288.
[121] [1992] 1 AC 562 and see Chapter 1, section 5.4 above.

was signed. Nevertheless, delivery could fit the bill if that was identifiable as completion of the process. However, even given that possible uncertainty (one which was canvassed in the case), the strong inclination of the judiciary in England was towards viewing signature as the concluding act. Only the judge at first instance pointed out that had the New York Convention used the term 'signed', that would have been unambiguous. 'Made' was a different word from 'signed'. Hence he found ambiguity where the other judges did not.[122]

4.4 Modalities of use of supplementary means

4.4.1 Using and construing preparatory work

Consistent with the ILC's aim of stating only those rules of interpretation which have general application, its authorization of 'recourse' to supplementary means does not prescribe how that recourse is to be made or how the supplementary means are to be read, other than by reference to the purpose of such recourse as being either to confirm or determine a meaning. Because of the diversity of preparatory work and relevant circumstances it would, in any event, have been a hopeless task to try to include guidance in the Vienna rules. Courts and tribunals, and other interpreters, have to work out for themselves what to make of these supplementary means.

Using supplementary means for confirmation of a meaning may involve no more than recounting the stages of development of a provision. For example, in *Witold Litwa v Poland*[123] the issue was whether the word 'alcoholics' necessarily imported the notion of someone suffering addiction or could include those who are merely under the influence of too much alcohol. Having determined by application of the general rule that the latter was the correct meaning, the ECtHR found confirmation in the preparatory work, whose relevant features the Court had set out in the 'Facts' section of its judgment. This showed how the concern to allow for domestic measures on drunkenness had become transformed in drafting. The history spoke for itself, but formally its role was only confirmatory.

Rather different was the situation in the WTO Appeal Body's Report on *US—Measures Affecting Gambling*.[124] The issue was whether gambling came within the US schedule of commitments annexed to the General Agreement on Trade in Services (GATS), which included an entry 'OTHER RECREATIONAL SERVICES (except sporting)'. This entry remained ambiguous after applying the general rule of interpretation, it being unclear whether 'sporting' included gambling. Hence it was necessary to rely on supplementary means to determine the meaning of 'sporting'. In preparation for adoption of the GATS, the GATT

---

[122] See Chapter 1, section 5.4.
[123] ECHR App no 26629/95 (judgment of 4 April 2000); see fuller account in Chapter 1, section 5.1 above.
[124] *United States—Measures Affecting the Cross-Border Supply of Gambling and Betting Services* WTO Appellate Body Report of 7 April 2005, WT/DS285/AB/R.

Secretariat had circulated 'document W/120' to assist in defining services by providing a 'services sectoral classification list'. The list incorporated references to the 'United Nations' Provisional Central Product Classification' (CPC), which is a very detailed and multi-level classification of goods and services. The Secretariat had also circulated a document known as the '1993 Scheduling Guidelines', designed to assist in determining what should be put in a WTO Member State's annex to the GATS and how entries should be expressed. Classification was to be based on the document W/120 list, with any necessary further refinements of sectoral classifications being achieved by reference to the more detailed taxonomy in the CPC. Although W/120 and the 1993 Guidelines were not agreements on interpretation in the sense of the Vienna general rule, there was no dispute that they were preparatory work and that the USA had indicated that it had used W/120 in preparing its Annex and had sought to follow the 1993 Guidelines.[125] The CPC did not include gambling in its detailed entries for 'sporting services', but did include it in as a separate sub-class of 'other recreational services'. It was clear from this, and reinforced by the scheme of the CPC, that inclusion in one class meant exclusion from any other class, and that the reference in the US Annex to 'sporting' did not include gambling.

This simplified account of the reasoning of the WTO's Appellate Body cannot do full justice to the way in which the analysis of the preparatory work was interwoven with the relevant circumstances, and how account was taken of the context in achieving an interpretation by full application of the Vienna rules. The case does, however, illustrate how interpretation and application of preparatory work may require more than a historical tracing of the development of a provision.

While it is a consistent theme in international and national treaty interpretation that preparatory work is to be used with caution, the consequences for how such work is to be read is less clear. The contrast between an internationalist approach and a nationalist one was given in relation to the New York Convention on Recognition and Enforcement of Foreign Arbitral Awards in Chapter 1 above.[126] In courts in the United Kingdom there has been a line of cases referring to the 'bull's eye' approach. This gives the impression that preparatory work is only relevant where it directly addresses and resolves the precise point in issue. The approach was formulated in *Effort Shipping Company Limited v Linden Management*:

Although the text of a convention must be accorded primacy in matters of interpretation, it is well settled that the travaux préparatoires of an international convention may be used as supplementary means of interpretation: compare article 31 of the Vienna Convention on the Law of Treaties, Vienna, 23 May 1969. Following *Fothergill v. Monarch Airlines Ltd.* [1981] A.C. 251, I would be quite prepared, in an appropriate case involving truly feasible alternative interpretations of a convention, to allow the evidence contained in the travaux préparatoires to be determinative of the question of construction. But that is only possible where the court is satisfied that the travaux préparatoires clearly and indisputably point to

---

[125] WT/DS285/AB/R, at paras 196 and 207.   [126] Chapter 1, section 5.4 above.

a definite legal intention: see *Fothergill v. Monarch Airlines Ltd.*, per Lord Wilberforce, at p. 278C. *Only a bull's-eye counts. Nothing less will do.*[127]

It is puzzling that, while mentioning article 31, this statement does not focus on article 32 of the Vienna Convention and the specific roles of preparatory work in either confirming or determining the meaning of a treaty provision. The risk of the bull's eye test is twofold: it subverts the grounds for use of preparatory work and it may lead to a much narrower view of the role of preparatory work than that in the Vienna rules. Although its use in relation to acts of the European Community and EU may not represent a central role in treaty interpretation, repeated reference to it suggests that it may gain a purchase there.[128]

It is certainly the case that caution has always been the touchstone for use of preparatory work in treaty interpretation. It bears repeating in this context that its role is probably best summarised by the ILC's Special Rapporteur (Waldock) as 'simply evidence to be weighed against any other relevant evidence of the intentions of the parties', and pointing out that its cogency depends on the extent to which it furnishes 'proof of the *common* understanding of the parties as to the meaning attached to the terms of the treaty'.[129] Were the bull's eye approach to emphasize the particular importance of caution where the preparatory work is fulfilling the 'determinative' role envisaged in the Vienna rules, this could be seen as broadly in line with the idea that the cogency of the preparatory work as evidence of a particular meaning depends on how clearly it shows a common understanding. If the preparatory work is not being used to add weight to other evidence of meaning, it needs to be very strong to stand on its own.

Unfortunately, however, the effect of the bull's eye approach seems more narrowing than that. In the formulation offered above, the bull's eye approach refers to 'determination' of meaning; but because this is not set on the context of article 32 of the Vienna Convention, it remains unclear whether the approach is limited to 'determining' meaning in the sense and circumstances of article 32, or whether it applies to exclude use of preparatory work as confirming an interpretation already indicated by application of the general rule. This could constitute a severe

---

[127] [1998] AC 605, at 623, per Lord Steyn, emphasis added; the comments which follow are based on a fuller account in R Gardiner, 'The Role of Preparatory Work in Treaty Interpretation', Chapter 5 in A Orakhelashvili and S Williams (eds), *40 Years of the Vienna Convention on the Law of Treaties* (London: BIICL, 2010), 97–104.

[128] See *Re Council Regulation (EEC) 1768/92 and Council Regulation (EC) 1901/2006, re Application No. SPC/GB/95/010 by E I du Pont Nemours & Co for an extension of an SPC* [2009] EWHC 1112, at para 17 where the test, in its application to European Community legislation, was based on it elaboration in *Higgs v R* [2008] EWCA Crim 1324. There the wording in issue was traced back to two treaties; the decision was reversed on appeal but without reference to the account to be taken of preparatory work: [2009] EWCA Civ 966. Other references to the bull's eye test include: *Bayerische Motoren Werke AG v Round & Metal Ltd* [2012] EWHC 2099 (Pat), at paras 61–3; *Fortis Bank S.A./ N.V. v Indian Overseas Bank* [2011] EWCA Civ 58, para 51; *Green Lane Products v PMS International Group* [2008] EWCA Civ 358, at para 74 (CA); *Nova Productions v Mazooma Games* [2007] RPC 589, at 603, para 42 (CA); *R (Mullen) v Secretary of State for the Home Department* [2005] 1 AC 1, at 45; *Serena Navigation Ltd and Another v Dera Commercial Establishment and Another (The "Limnos")* [2008] 2 Lloyd's Rep. 166, at 168 and 171.

[129] See sections 2.2 and 2.3 above.

limitation. Preparatory work is often too diffuse to be helpful at all. Very rarely does it provide a bull's eye. However, it is quite often somewhere in between these extremes, and it can occasionally be quite revealing even where the precise issue was not in the negotiators' minds, as is shown by the example of *Hiscox v Outhwaite*.[130] It therefore seems unfortunate that courts in the UK are tending to follow *Fothergill* and the bull's eye approach rather than using article 32 of the Vienna Convention itself as the starting point for an approach to the use of preparatory work in treaty interpretation.

Even if the preparatory work can be read as dealing only with part of the issue in dispute, it may have a role. For example, where the European Patent Convention (EPC) described exclusions from patentability, in considering the extent of the exceptions, the Court of Appeal in England asked 'What help can be had from the *travaux preparatoires* to the EPC?', continuing: 'The answer is not a lot.'[131] But, the judgment added, 'one can at least find confirmation that no overarching principle was intended', and '... one other thing emerges—by its absence. There is no indication of any intention as to how the categories should be construed—either restrictively or widely'; and, referring to the categories of exceptions from patentability: 'the categories are disparate with differing policies behind each. There is no reason to suppose there is some common factor (particularly abstractness) linking them. The *travaux preparatoires* at least confirm this.'[132]

4.4.2 Reading preparatory work to show agreement to exclude

The notion of using preparatory work to confirm a meaning established by applying the general rule can lead an interpreter to find the meaning of a term by showing that the course of the negotiations excluded an interpretation that is being put forward. For example, in the WTO *Lamb Meat* case[133] one of the issues which the panel had to decide was what enterprises constituted relevant 'domestic industries' for the purposes of taking into account producers of like products. Were farmers who had reared live lambs in the same industry as importers of fresh, chilled, and frozen lamb meat, or did those who processed and traded in lamb meat constitute the comparable domestic industry? The definition of domestic industries in the relevant treaty included assessment of whether the domestic enterprises were producers of like or directly competitive products or those whose collective output of the like or directly competitive products constituted a major proportion of the total domestic production of those products.[134]

The panel applied the general rule, starting with the proposition that '[t]o us, the ordinary meaning of this phrase is straightforward: the producers *of an article*

---

[130] [1992] 1 AC 562, and see the study of this case in Chapter 1, section 5.4 above.
[131] *Aerotel Ltd v Telco Holdings Ltd and others* [2007] 1 All ER 225 at 232, para 11.
[132] [2007] 1 All ER 225 at 232, at paras 11, 12 and at 238, para 38.
[133] *United States—Safeguard Measures on Imports of Fresh, Chilled or Frozen Lamb Meat from New Zealand and Australia* WT/DS177/R (2000).
[134] Safeguards Agreement, article 4.1(c).

are those who make *that* article',[135] and proceeded through consideration of context and other relevant interpretative matters. The Panel included consideration of the reasoning of other Panel reports in cases concerning the same wording in comparable agreements. All this led to the conclusion that 'domestic industries' had a narrow interpretation, that is, referring to 'the producers as a whole of the like end-product, i.e., lamb meat in this case'.[136] In approaching the preparatory work for confirmation, the Panel noted that in a Panel Report pre-dating the negotiation of the current Safeguards Agreement, the Panel had found that the only way a wide interpretation of 'domestic industry' could be adopted would be by amending the treaty through negotiation. Hence, when at the Uruguay Round the negotiators came to consider the industry definition, they did so against this background. Since proposals for, and objections to, changing the 'domestic industry' definition were extensively discussed in the Uruguay Round negotiations without any agreement to broaden the industry definition, the exclusion of any wider meaning was effectively confirmed.[137]

However, even where a provision which would have covered precisely the case in point is shown by the preparatory work to have been rejected or deleted in the course of negotiations, that may not demonstrate conclusively that the issue is not covered in some way in the final text.[138] One example of this, already examined above, is *Qatar v Bahrain* (1995) where deletion of a clear provision was considered by the ICJ not to preclude its interpretation of words in the agreement in the very sense whose clearer expression had been rejected.[139]

Extensive consideration of the role in interpretation of rejection of a proposed provision was given by a US Court of Appeals in *Hosaka v United Airlines*, where the Court used the preparatory work in support of an interpretation which it based on the text of the provision read in the light of the object and purpose of the treaty, also finding support in a judicial decision in another state.[140] Only when it had looked at these other elements did the Court pursue consideration of the preparatory work. Thus although the Court was not specifically applying the Vienna Convention, it followed much the same line of approach found there.

In this case the Court had to decide whether the plaintiff's choice from four defined national jurisdictions identified in the 1929 Warsaw Convention on international carriage by air could be set aside on the ground that the chosen one was not appropriate (using the doctrine known as *'forum non conveniens'*). The

---

[135] *United States—Safeguard Measures on Imports of Fresh, Chilled or Frozen Lamb Meat from New Zealand and Australia* WT/DS177/R (2000) at para 7.67 (original emphasis).

[136] WT/DS177/R (2000) at para 7.109.   [137] WT/DS177/R (2000) at para 7.110–14.

[138] A good example of a record in preparatory work of an apparently clear exclusion of a proposed right which nevertheless was not determinative of an interpretation issue is in the case of *Young, James and Webster v UK* at the ECtHR, cited and considered below in Chapter 10, section 5.1 below. See also the academic discussion of the interpretative consequences of exclusion of a provision of chemical weapons from the Statute of the International Criminal Court, Rome, 1998 considered below in Chapter 10, section 5.2 below.

[139] See section 4.2.2 above.

[140] 305 F.3d 989 (9th Cir. 2002), certiorari denied 537 U.S. 1227; for details of the treaty provisions in issue and the Court's finding of ambiguity see section 4.3.1 above.

Convention described the selection as 'at the option of the plaintiff', but also indicated that 'questions of procedure shall be governed by the law of the court seized of the case'. The doctrine of *forum non conveniens* was viewed as procedural under the relevant law in the instant case.

The Court looked first to the objectives of the Convention. It noted that the main purpose of the Convention was to achieve uniformity of rules governing claims relating to international carriage by air.[141] It found that the Convention created 'a self-contained code on jurisdiction' and harmonized different national views on jurisdiction. Application of the doctrine of *forum non conveniens* would undermine the goal of uniformity. A plaintiff could be denied the right in some countries to sue in one of the four specified forums, but not denied that right in others. It also would subject actions brought under the Convention to a doctrine which had been described in earlier case law as 'vague and discretionary.'[142] The Court therefore concluded from its analysis of the text: 'The doctrine of forum non conveniens is inconsistent with the Convention's dual purposes of uniformity and balance.'[143]

The Court found support in the preparatory work for its view that the Convention did not allow invocation of *forum non conveniens*. At the 1929 conference, the British delegation had proposed adding a provision substantially equivalent to the doctrine. The delegation considered this would give the courts 'more latitude to repress vexatious litigation, as in the case where the 'forum' of another country would be naturally indicated as being that where the debates should take place'.[144] Unfortunately, how this proposal was viewed at the conference is not known as the records simply state: 'The British Delegation did not insist.'[145] The Court in *Hosaka* noted that this left it unclear whether the proposal had been considered and rejected by the delegates or was merely abandoned by the British when other proposals for amending the draft article were accepted; but the Court observed:

That said, the failed British amendment is not irrelevant. That the British delegation proposed an explicit incorporation of the doctrine of forum non conveniens strongly suggests that the contracting parties were cognizant of the doctrine and did not understand Article 28(2) as silently incorporating, or acquiescing in, its application. It is even more difficult to construe Article 28(2) as silently incorporating or acquiescing in the application of forum non conveniens when one considers the historical context in which the British amendment was offered and, more generally, in which the treaty was drafted and negotiated.[146]

This reading of the preparatory work led the Court of Appeals to consider what is described in article 32 of the Vienna Convention as 'the circumstances of conclusion' of a treaty. Having examined the approaches of different legal systems and

---

[141] 305 F.3d 989 (9th Cir. 2002) at 996.   [142] 305 F.3d 989 (9th Cir. 2002) at 997.
[143] 305 F.3d 989 (9th Cir. 2002) at 997.
[144] Second International Conference on Private Aeronautical Law, 4–12 October 1929, Minutes translated by R. Horner and D Legrez (1975) at 299.
[145] Second International Conference on Private Aeronautical Law, 4–12 October 1929, 169.
[146] 305 F.3d 989 at 998.

traditions at the time of the negotiation of the 1929 Convention, the Court declined to 'infer from the treaty's incorporation of local procedural law that the drafters acquiesced in the application of *forum non conveniens*, a concept that was (and is) both alien to and unwelcome by the majority of the contracting parties. *Forum non conveniens*, which permits a Court having jurisdiction to decline it, is a feature of the common law.'[147] The Court saw the Warsaw Convention as drafted by 'civil law jurists, to whom *forum non conveniens* was an alien concept' and 'generally is unknown in legal systems following the continental civil law model'.[148] The Court therefore considered that: 'In this historical light, it is unreasonable to infer that the "continental jurists,"...would have succumbed to the British, common law point of view.'[149] Thus it concluded that:

The more reasonable inference is that the delegates, if they had intended to permit the application of forum non conveniens, would have done so explicitly.[150]

It can be seen that this approach allows something of a supporting role for preparatory work which the 'bull's eye' approach of some British courts tends to exclude without apparent regard to the Vienna provisions.[151] The approach of the US Court of Appeals seems more closely in line with the description in article 32 of the Vienna Convention of preparatory work and circumstances of conclusion of the treaty as being generally available to 'confirm' the meaning that has been ascertained by application of the general rule in article 31, as contrasted with the more prescriptive circumstances for use of supplementary means to 'determine' the meaning.

As a footnote to this case it should be noted that although the decision in *Hosaka* is generally well attuned to the principles of treaty interpretation, it was at odds with an earlier US judicial indication by the Fifth Circuit on the issue of *forum non conveniens* under the same treaty. However, the *Hosaka* court found that the earlier decision had not considered the purposes, drafting history, and post-ratification understanding of the parties, means of construction which had been indicated by the Supreme Court as applicable to treaty interpretation in decisions after the Fifth Circuit's analysis. As well as studying the preparatory work of the 1929 Warsaw Convention, the Court in *Hosaka* did examine the preparatory work of the 1999 Montreal Convention (designed to replace the 1929 treaty) to see whether there was an indication of subsequent agreement on the interpretation of the Warsaw Convention. It found that: 'In sum, although *forum non conveniens* was discussed at length in Montreal, the drafting history does not paint a coherent picture of the parties' understanding of the Warsaw Convention'. However, the Court specifically indicated that its conclusion on the provisions of the Warsaw Convention was not an expression of opinion as to interpretation of the Montreal Convention's provisions on the same point.[152]

---

[147] 305 F.3d 989 at 999.   [148] 305 F.3d 989 at 999.   [149] 305 F.3d 989 at 999.
[150] 305 F.3d 989 at 999.   [151] See section 4.4.1 above.
[152] On use of preparatory work to produce a different result in relation to the Convention for the Unification of Certain Rules for International Carriage by Air, Montreal, 1999, see *Pierre-Louis v Newvac* 584 F.3d 1052 (US Court of Appeals 11th Cir, 2009), where the Court upheld rejection of

4.4.3 Deduction from absence from preparatory work

The mere absence from the preparatory work of reference to an issue, or even discussion of an issue and rejection of inclusion of any provision on the matter, is unlikely to prove dispositive if a difference emerges over interpretation.[153] However, absence of mention of the point may be part of the picture that leads to an interpretation.[154] In this sense practice in use of preparatory work goes beyond the narrow confines of either confirming or determining the meaning. If closer to the former than the latter, consideration of the preparatory work is in some instances treated as more supportive of argument than confirmatory of meaning.

An example arose in the course of the ICSID arbitration *Compañía de Aguas del Aconquija SA & Vivendi Universal v Argentine Republic*.[155] The ICSID Convention includes provisions ensuring that arbitrators and conciliators have the necessary qualities (independence, impartiality, etc). These requirements are implemented by rules of procedure adopted by the ICSID Administrative Council.[156] The Convention also specifies grounds on which parties to arbitration proceedings may seek annulment of an arbitral award (including improper constitution of the tribunal, exceeding powers, corruption, and failure to state reasons). An application for annulment is determined by an ad hoc committee appointed by the Chairman of the Administrative Council. The Convention specifies that various of its articles and chapters apply to such a committee, but this list does not include chapter V on replacement and disqualification of arbitrators and conciliators. However, the rules of procedure make good this omission by applying their implementing rules on these matters to members of an ad hoc committee just as to arbitrators and conciliators.

In the *Compañía de Aguas* case, one party sought to challenge the President of the Committee on the basis that a partner in his law firm had previously acted for

---

jurisdiction on the ground that a French court in Martinique was the appropriate forum; the French then court rejected jurisdiction on the basis that the plaintiff had opted for the US court and that precluded their jurisdiction under the Montreal Convention, but the US Court of Appeals nevertheless refused to allow the Florida court's decision on *forum non conveniens* to be set aside: *Galbert v West Caribbean Airways* 715 F.3d 1290 (US Court of Appeals, 11th Cir, 2013).

[153] See, eg, *Re Attorney-General and Ward* 104 ILR 222 at 237, where the Canadian Supreme Court, when considering whether state complicity in persecution is a prerequisite to a valid refugee claim under the Refugee Convention, found no evidence in the drafting history suggesting that persecution was linked to state action: 'The omission of a reference to state action does not tell us much, however. The question was apparently never discussed, and the text does not reveal that any link to state action is required.'

[154] See, eg, *European Molecular Biology Laboratory Arbitration (EMBL v Germany)*, Award of 29 June 1990, 105 ILR 1 at 55–56, where the tribunal stated that had there been 'a common intention to grant the Director-General the unrestricted legal status of the "diplomatic agent" [this] would have clearly surfaced during the negotiations. As the parties were not able to present minutes on the framing of the HQA, the question would have had to remain open.' For further consideration of this case, see Chapter 6, section 3.2.

[155] ICSID Case No ARB/97/3, Decision on the Challenge to the President of the Committee in Annulment Proceedings, 3 October 2001.

[156] Convention on the Settlement of Investment Disputes between States and Nationals of Other States, Washington, 1965, article 6.

one of the disputing parties in an unrelated matter. Could the rules implementing the Convention's chapter on replacement and disqualification of arbitrators and conciliators validly extend to the situation of members of ad hoc committees when the Convention had omitted the chapter from its list of provisions applicable to such committees?

This list was comprehensive and seemed a considered one. Therefore a literal reading produced a clear result that the Convention's rules on disqualification did not apply. Yet, given the importance of the matter, it was difficult not to wonder whether disqualification of committee members must simply have been overlooked. The committee noted that the omitted chapter's provisions were plainly apt for application to ad hoc committees. Such application would also be consistent with the object and purpose of the Convention in producing awards from bodies whose members were independent and impartial. Ad hoc committees had an important function in this regard. The committee noted that 'the *travaux préparatoires* of the Convention do not suggest that there was any particular reason for excluding the application of Chapter V'.[157] No party to the Convention had at the time of the adoption of the arbitration rules suggested any such reason. The rule in question had been adopted unanimously and had been treated by the Administrative Council (on which all states parties were represented) as uncontroversial, nor had there been any objection when revised rules were adopted. Unanimous adoption of the rules, if not an actual agreement on interpretation of the Convention, at least amounted to subsequent practice relevant to its interpretation, a fact which (in combination with the other interpretative points) led the committee to conclude that the rule applying chapter V to disqualification of members of an *ad hoc* committee was consistent with a proper interpretation of the Convention.[158] Thus it can be seen that the silence of the preparatory work was a significant element in showing that a conclusion at odds with a literal reading of a provision was within a permissible range of interpretations when taken with other interpretative elements.

In the *Oil Platforms* case at the ICJ, an interpretative issue arose over article I of the Treaty of Amity, Economic Relations and Consular Rights, 1955, which provided: 'There shall be firm and enduring peace and sincere friendship between the United States...and Iran.[159] Iran asserted that this did not merely state a recommendation or desire, but imposed actual obligations on the Contracting Parties, requiring them to maintain long-lasting peaceful and friendly relations.[160] Finding, to the contrary, that the provision only fixed 'an objective, in the light of which the other Treaty provisions are to be interpreted and applied', the ICJ stated:

...it may be thought that, if that Article had the scope that Iran gives it, the Parties would have been led to point out its importance during the negotiations or the process of ratification. However, the Court does not have before it any Iranian document in support of this

---

[157] ICSID Case No ARB/97/3 (2001), para 12.
[158] ICSID Case No ARB/97/3 (2001), paras 9–13.
[159] *Oil Platforms (Iran v USA) (Preliminary Objections)* [1996] ICJ Reports 803.
[160] [1996] ICJ Reports 803 at 812, para 25.

argument. As for the United States documents introduced by the two Parties, they show that at no time did the United States regard Article I as having the meaning now given to it by the Applicant.[161]

4.4.4 *Change of word or words during negotiation of treaty*

Tribunals approach with caution assertions as to the conclusions to be drawn from a change in wording during the drafting process of a treaty, particularly if there is no record at all of why the change was made. Such changes are, of course, commonly recounted where a judgment or award gives the history of the development of a provision.[162] Where the records are a sparse succession of drafts, courts and tribunals may be reluctant to conclude that a change from the wording proposed by, or favouring, one party to a dispute to the wording espoused by the other party necessarily means that the latter's preferred meaning is correct. This was the position taken by the majority in *Qatar v Bahrain*.[163] Equally, rejection of a change of wording without explanation or consensus on the meaning of retained words may yield no assistance on interpretation.[164]

4.4.5 *Exclusion of preparatory work from consideration*

One of the concerns over describing the means of interpretation in article 32 as 'supplementary', and over the inclusion of prerequisites for their use to determine (rather than just confirm) the meaning of a treaty provision, was that interpreters would be barred from access to relevant material in preparatory work. The grounds for this fear were open to question. In the *Lotus* case, the PCIJ, having recounted the preparatory work as presented by the French government, had stated that 'there is no occasion to have regard to preparatory work if the text of a convention is

---

[161] [1996] ICJ Reports 803 at 814, paras 28–29; see also *In The Matter of an Arbitration before a Tribunal constituted in accordance with Article 26 of the Energy Charter Treaty and the 1976 UNCITRAL Arbitration Rules, Hulley Enterprises Limited (Cyprus) v The Russian Federation*, Final Award of 18 July 2014, para 1415 where an arbitral tribunal, having found that the interpretation of the relevant treaty provision according to the general rule of interpretation resulted in a meaning which was not ambiguous, obscure etc, and did not therefore need any other rule of interpretation, nevertheless also found that the preparatory work did not support the limited reading asserted by the Respondent because if a change of wording had been motivated by an intention to limit the scope of the provision, the Tribunal would have expected such a motivation to have been expressed in the record..

[162] See, eg, *LaGrand (Germany v USA)* [2001] ICJ Reports 466, where the ICJ traced the parallel changes in the development of the French and English texts of part of its statute with explanations where these were recorded (see further Chapter 9, sections 4.4, 4.5, and 4.9 below; see also, in like vein, *Litwa v Poland* (ECtHR), considered in Chapter 1, section 5.1 above; and *Casado v Chile* ICSID Case No ARB/98/2, Award of 25 September 2001, where an arbitral tribunal considered the indication in preparatory work of how the term 'prescribe' had ended up as 'recommend', describing such recourse as debatable ('*la methode, discutable, d 'interprétation*'), at para 18.

[163] See section 4.2.2 above; see also *Tariffs Applied by Canada to Certain US-origin Agricultural Products* NAFTA Arbitral Panel (Secretariat File No CDA-95–2008-01) Final Report of the Panel 2 December 1996 at para 153.

[164] See, eg, *R v Secretary of State for the Home Department ex parte Mullen* [2004] UKHL 18, [2005] 1 AC 1 at 46, para 52.

sufficiently clear in itself', but then proceeded to examine the preparatory work in some detail.[165] As regards case law of the ICJ, the notion of complete exclusion of the preparatory work in the case of clear meaning had receded by the time of the Vienna Conference in 1968–69. Rosenne had powerfully made the point in the deliberations of the ILC:

> It was true that there existed a number of apparently consistent pronouncements by the International Court of Justice and arbitral tribunals to the effect that *travaux préparatoires* had only been used to confirm what had been found to be the clear meaning of the text of a treaty. However, that case law would be much more convincing if from the outset the Court or tribunal had refused to admit consideration of *travaux préparatoires* until it had first established whether or not the text was clear, but in fact, what had happened was that on all those occasions the *travaux préparatoires* had been fully and extensively placed before the Court or arbitral tribunal by one or other of the parties, if not by both. In the circumstances, to state that the *travaux préparatoires* had been used only to confirm an opinion already arrived at on the basis of the text of the treaty was coming close to a legal fiction.[166]

Thus it is difficult to detect substance for the fears that Vienna rules would confirm, or introduce, real limitations on the role of the preparatory work.[167] In practice, preparatory work is admitted in evidence or is within the material proffered by the litigants. Inevitably it comes to the attention of the judges, even if the use they actually make of it should be controlled by the Vienna rules.

A good example of this is the ICJ's *La Grand* case.[168] In interpreting the requirement in the Vienna Convention on Consular Relations that an arrested alien be informed without delay of 'his rights' under the treaty provision 'if he so requests' to have the consul of his nationality informed of the arrest, one question was whether there was a violation of an individual's own rights. For the claimant state (Germany), this could have provided a ground of complaint additional to its allegation that the USA directly violated its rights to have its national informed of their rights. If an individual had the right to be informed that he could ask for the consul to be informed, Germany would have a claim in right of diplomatic protection of one of its nationals if breach of that right went unremedied.

Germany argued that every national of a party to the Consular Convention who entered territory of another party had the right to be appropriately informed if arrested. Germany saw this as the ordinary meaning of the terms of the Consular Convention, which included a reference to informing 'the person concerned' of 'his rights'. The context supported this by indicating that it was for the arrested person to decide whether consular notification was to take place, thus showing that such notification was an individual right of the national concerned. Germany

---

[165] *Case of the SS 'Lotus' (France v Turkey)* PCIJ (1927), Series A, No 10, pp 16–17.

[166] [1964] *Yearbook of the ILC*, vol I, p 283, para 17.

[167] Cf J Klabbers, 'International Legal Histories: The Declining Importance of *Travaux Préparatoires* in Treaty Interpretation?' (2003) L NILR 267, discussing the ambivalence of lawyers towards preparatory work, and indicating that 'recourse to historical origins is so pervasive that the qualification of *travaux préparatoires* as mere supplementary means of interpretation seems rather inadequate' (at 284).

[168] *LaGrand (Germany v United States of America)* [2001] ICJ Reports 466.

argued that the preparatory work of the Consular Convention supported this interpretation.[169]

The USA based its case against this reading principally on the conceptual argument that the Consular Convention concerned the rights of states to offer consular assistance and that, even if expressed in terms of individuals' rights, treatment due to individuals under the Consular Convention was 'inextricably linked to and derived from the right of the State, acting through its consular officer'. The USA pointed out that the relevant provision started out with an indication that it was included with a view 'to facilitating the exercise of consular functions relating to nationals of the sending State', wording which did not support the notion that the provision gave individual nationals particular rights or treatment in the context of a criminal prosecution.[170] According to the USA, the preparatory work did not reflect a consensus that article 36 was addressing immutable individual rights, as opposed to individual rights derived from those of states.[171]

The Court found that the provision did create individual rights which could be invoked by the state of nationality of the detained person. The Court placed emphasis on the words 'his rights' and on the further provision that the state of nationality was not permitted to exercise its right to provide consular assistance to the detained 'if he expressly opposes such action'.[172] The judgment stated:

The clarity of these provisions, viewed in their context, admits of no doubt. It follows, as has been held on a number of occasions, that the Court must apply these as they stand (see Acquisition of Polish Nationality, Advisory Opinion, 1923, P.C.I.J., Series B, No. 7, p. 20; Competence of the General Assembly for the Admission of a State to the United Nations, Advisory Opinion, I.C.J. Reports 1950, p. 8; Arbitral Award of 31 July 1989, Judgment, I.C.J. Reports 1991, pp. 69–70, para. 48; Territorial Dispute (Libyan Arab Jamahiriya/ Chad), Judgment, I.C.J. Reports 1994, p. 25, para. 51).[173]

It can be seen that the Court was fully regaled with the relevant preparatory work, and with the differing interpretations of it, but did not find it necessary or helpful to bring it into its judgment.

4.4.6 May preparatory work be deployed as context?

The short answer is that preparatory work clearly does *not* itself fall within the meaning of 'context' given by the Vienna Convention's article 31(2). But this does not entirely exclude the possibility that the preparatory work might contain an element of context so defined, such as the record of an agreement made by all the prospective parties as to the meaning of a term. However, the requirement in article 31(2) that such an agreement be 'made between all the parties in connection

---

[169] [2001] ICJ Reports 466 at 492–3, para 75.
[170] [2001] ICJ Reports 466 at 493, para 76.
[171] [2001] ICJ Reports 466 at 494, para 76.
[172] [2001] ICJ Reports 466 at 494, paras 77–78.
[173] [2001] ICJ Reports 466 at 494, para 77.

with the conclusion of the treaty' could usually be expected to be met by some connecting factor close to the time of signature, such as a record of the point in the final act of a conference or a reference there to its presence in some particular document within the collective preparatory work.

Any confusion over this may, at least in part, owe its origin to the broader sense of 'context' used by Professor McDougal in his campaign, as part of the USA delegation at the Vienna Conference, against the proposed formulation of the set of articles which became the Vienna rules. To him, 'context' seems to have meant everything pertinent to the negotiation of a treaty. In terms of the Vienna rules that is closer to the idea of 'circumstances of its [the treaty's] conclusion' in article 32. However, it was in fact the USA which, in the *US—Measures Affecting Gambling* case, successfully persuaded the WTO's Appellate Body that a Panel had been wrong in treating two documents which were part of the preparatory work as 'context'.[174] Although generally accepted then and subsequently as useful guidance on classification of services in Annexes to the GATS, those documents did not fit the definition of context in the Vienna rules, in contrast to the Annexes themselves, which did.

The formal significance of this distinction lies in the use to be made of preparatory work as a 'supplementary' means of interpretation. In the *US—Measures Affecting Gambling* the Appellate Body corrected the Panel's classification of the two guidance documents as context. This led the Appellate Body to follow the correct approach in applying the Vienna rules, so that it reached the conclusion by the proper route that there was ambiguity (and absurdity) such as to warrant determining the meaning by recourse to the preparatory work. Although use of the correct route to the interpretation did not in this case ultimately produce a different conclusion on the particular point, proper use of the preparatory work is important for the integrity of the interpretative process, given the regular stress now laid on the applicability of the Vienna rules by courts and tribunals. Nevertheless, it is also important to note that use to confirm or determine meaning does not preclude other reference to the preparatory work, for example where this reveals part of the helpful background, as in *Litwa v Poland* (meaning of 'alcoholics').[175] In the Vienna Convention's terms this may involve combination of use of preparatory work and circumstances of the treaty's conclusion, but this is not a reference to context in the sense in which that term is used in the Vienna rules.

4.4.7 Using preparatory work to identify or confirm object and purpose

Resort may be made to the preparatory work to identify or confirm the object and purpose of a treaty. For example, at the Jurisdiction and Admissibility phase

---

[174] *United States—Measures Affecting the Cross-Border Supply of Gambling and Betting Services* WTO Appellate Body Report of 7 April 2005, WT/DS285/AB/R, paras 169–78 and see further on this case in section 4.4.1 above.
[175] See Chapter 1, section 5.1 above.

of *Nicaragua v Honduras*[176] the ICJ had to determine whether two articles of the Pact of Bogotá provided one combined route to bring a case before the Court (as Honduras argued), or two separate avenues. Finding that it was clear from the text of the treaty that there were two distinct lines of recourse, the Court supported this by reference to the object and purpose as confirmed by the preparatory work:

It is, moreover, quite clear from the Pact that the purpose of the American States in drafting it was to reinforce their mutual commitments with regard to judicial settlement. This is also confirmed by the *travaux préparatoires:* the discussion at the meeting of Committee... the delegate of Colombia explained... 'that the principal procedure for the peaceful settlement of disputes of conflicts between the American States had to be judicial procedure before the International Court of Justice'... Honduras's argument would however imply that the commitment... would, in fact, be emptied of all content, if for any reason, the dispute were not subjected to prior conciliation. Such a solution would be clearly contrary to both the object and purpose of the Pact.[177]

Another example is the ICSID arbitration in *Banro American Resources v Congo*.[178] The tribunal considered whether pursuit of diplomatic action in parallel with initiation of arbitration proceeding by, or in respect of, companies of different nationality within a group, where the state of nationality of one company was not a party to the 1965 Washington (ICSID) Convention, vitiated the tribunal's jurisdiction. Against the backdrop of the relationships of the various companies and states, the tribunal considered the objectives of the Washington Convention. Having recounted these objectives in describing features and consequences of the ICSID system, the tribunal stated that:

This objective of taking disputes between host States and foreign private investors out of the political and diplomatic realm in order to submit them to legal settlement mechanisms was emphasized several times during the course of the travaux préparatoires of the Washington Convention.[179]

The tribunal supported this statement with quotations from the preparatory work.

4.4.8 *Effect of interpretation recorded in preparatory work*

Article 31(2) of the Vienna Convention incorporates into the context of a treaty any interpretative agreement made between all its parties and any instrument made by one or more of them if accepted by the other parties. However, in both these situations the rule only applies if the agreement or instrument was made 'in connection with the conclusion of the treaty'. There are, however, instances where negotiating states agree an interpretation while drawing up a provision, or where

---

[176] *Border and Transborder Armed Actions (Nicaragua v Honduras) (Jurisdiction and Admissibility)* [1988] ICJ Reports 69.

[177] [1988] ICJ Reports 69 at 89, para 46.

[178] *Banro American Resources, Inc. and Société Aurifère du Kivu et du Maniema SARL v Democratic Republic of the Congo* ICSID Case No ARB/98/7, Award of 1 September 2000.

[179] ICSID Case No ARB/98/7, Award of 1 September 2000 at para 16.

one state's interpretation is endorsed at that time by the other negotiating states. If this is only recorded in the preparatory work, without being endorsed in a final act or some other instrument connected with the conclusion of the treaty, is such an interpretation dispositive?

Although the preparatory work is one of the supplementary means of interpretation rather than part of the general rule (which includes article 31(2)), interpretations recorded in the preparatory work are likely to have force proportionate to their clarity of meaning and the comprehensiveness of their endorsement. For example, the meaning of 'return' in the Convention and Protocol on Refugees offers scope for interpretative difficulties given that the Convention defines refugee status in relation to persons outside their country of nationality, does not accord rights of entry into other countries, but does impose obligations on parties not to expel or return refugees to face persecution. In examining the preparatory work to determine whether the USA had an obligation not to turn back boats carrying people who had left Haiti in the hope of entering the USA to seek protection as refugees there, the US Supreme Court found that the negotiating history of what became article 33 included endorsement of a Swiss interpretation of the first draft to the effect that:

… the word 'expulsion' related to a refugee already admitted into a country, whereas the word 'return' ('*refoulement*') related to a refugee *already within the territory but not yet resident there*.[180]

The Dutch delegation had referred to this at a later stage in the diplomatic conference. He noted that the Swiss interpretation had received support from several delegations at the time it was given and, detecting a possible consensus in its favour, he stated:

In order to dispel any possible ambiguity and to reassure his Government, he wished to have it placed on record that the Conference was in agreement with the interpretation that the possibility of mass migrations across frontiers or of attempted mass migrations was not covered by article 33.

'There being no objection, the PRESIDENT *ruled* that the interpretation given by the Netherlands representative should be placed on record.'[181]

While the US Supreme Court felt able to draw appropriate conclusions as to the support this gave to the interpretation it derived from the text and context, it noted that the significance of the conference President's comment that the remarks should be placed on record was not entirely clear.[182] However, little value can be derived from the Court's approach. The Court did not apply the Vienna rules. Its use of context was sketchy and it did not consider subsequent practice and

---

[180] *Sale v Haitian Centers Council* 509 US 155 at 185 (1993) (emphasis in original).

[181] 509 US 155 at 185 (1993) at 186 (inverted commas and emphasis in original); for different views on the extent of the obligation of non-refoulment, see decision of The Inter-American Commission for Human Rights in *The Haitian Centre for Human Rights v United States*, case no 10.675, report no 51/96 (1997) and, on 'non-refoulment' in connection with a range of international legal materials, the ECtHR in *Hirsi Jamaa and Others v Italy* Application no 27765/09, Judgment of 23 February 2012.

[182] See further G S Goodwin-Gill and J McAdam, *The Refugee in International Law* (Oxford: OUP, 3rd edn, 2007), Chapter 5 and UNHCR, Advisory Opinion on the Extraterritorial Application of

international law obligations which might have been relevant to interpretation, such as the general prohibition on sending individuals to states where they may be tortured or suffer abuse of their human rights.[183]

The structure of the Vienna rules emphasizes the caution with which preparatory work is to be approached. Even if there were ambiguity over the meaning of 'return', it would require a strong indication of complete agreement for the preparatory work to determine the meaning. Given that the Vienna Convention gives no firm status even to an interpretative declaration made on conclusion of a treaty, it is difficult to see statements in minutes as records of interpretative agreement unless the complete record is quite clear or the interpretation is in some way directly incorporated into the process of conclusion of the treaty such as by repetition in a Final Act.

4.4.9 Reading preparatory work in combination with other supplementary means

It may not always be clear whether material forms part of the preparatory work or whether it is being considered on the basis of being other supplementary means, such as circumstances of conclusion. If, for example, a provision is based on, but not identical to, terms in another treaty or instrument the explanation of the extent and effect of such 'borrowing' may play a clarificatory role. Thus, in *Johnston v Ireland*, a central issue for the ECtHR to determine was whether the right to marry in article 12 of the European Convention included a guarantee of availability of a legal process for dissolution.[184] The preparatory work showed that that article was based on article 16 of the 1948 Universal Declaration of Human Rights, which included for men and women 'equal rights as to marriage, during marriage and at its dissolution'. In explaining why the draft of what became article 12 was not as extensive as article 16 of the 1948 Declaration, the Rapporteur of the Council of Europe's Committee on Legal and Administrative Questions, had said:

In mentioning the particular Article [of the Universal Declaration], we have used only that part of the paragraph of the Article which affirms the right to marry and to found a family, but not the subsequent provisions of the Article concerning equal rights after marriage, since we only guarantee the right to marry.[30]

---

[30] *Travaux Préparatoires*, vol. 1, p. 268.[185]

Non-refoulement Obligations under the 1951 Convention relating to the Status of Refugees and its 1967 Protocol [2007] *European Human Rights LR* 484.

[183] The dissenting view of Blackmun J relied (in part) on the proposition that oral statements of treaty negotiators are only conditionally admissible: '…even the general rule of treaty construction allowing limited resort to *travaux preparatoires* "has no application to oral statements made by those engaged in negotiating the treaty which were not embodied in any writing and were not communicated to the government of the negotiator or to its ratifying body."…' (509 US at 195, citation omitted). In the light of the conference president's direction that the interpretation be recorded, it seems difficult to view it as 'not embodied in any writing', even though there may be considerable doubts whether the process amounted to endorsement by the conference.

[184] (1987) 9 EHRR 203.

[185] (1987) 9 EHRR 203 at 219, para 52 (square brackets in original).

Accordingly, the Court, having started with the proposition that the words used in article 12 did not on their face include a right to divorce, supplemented that with its view that 'the travaux préparatoires disclose no intention to include in article 12... any guarantee of a right to have the ties of marriage dissolved by divorce'.[186] Obviously where the preparatory work includes a history explaining how a particular provision developed from an earlier one, this can provide a useful confirmation of a textual interpretation, even if the earlier provision was not an actual draft but a separate legal instrument.

4.5 Circumstances of conclusion and other supplementary means

Given that the supplementary means envisaged by article 32 of the Vienna Convention are not indicated, other than that they include preparatory work and circumstances of conclusion of a treaty, it seems reasonable to take it that they are only limited by the requirement that any such means must be consistent with the Vienna rules unless otherwise agreed in the particular treaty. The host of canons of interpretation formulated over the centuries and the prevalent general maxims of construction commonly used by lawyers are too numerous to attempt to list. However, because the circumstances of conclusion of a treaty are specifically mentioned, this element of treaty interpretation warrants specific consideration, as do certain other means which have assumed prominence or may be encountered in the earlier case law but whose place in the scheme of the Vienna rules is uncertain.

4.5.1 *Meaning of 'circumstances of conclusion'*

What is meant by the circumstances of conclusion is not indicated in the Vienna Convention. The circumstances which cause a treaty to be drawn up, affect its content, and attach to its conclusion, are all factors which are in practice taken into account. They overlap or interact with other elements in the Vienna rules, such as the object and purpose of a treaty, instruments which may be made in connection with conclusion of a treaty, and the preparatory work. It is particularly likely that the circumstances of conclusion and the preparatory work will both be considered in the situations envisaged by article 32 of the Vienna Convention. As noted in Chapter 3 above, it is not always clear how far back in the history of a treaty its preparatory work extends. Consequently, it may not always be clear when an interpretative argument moves from considering the circumstances of conclusion of a treaty to its preparatory work. Commonly the two factors are interwoven, circumstances of conclusion receiving incidental references.

An example is in the ICJ's judgment in the *Case Concerning Legality of Use of Force (Serbia and Montenegro v Belgium) (Jurisdiction)*, where the Court found

---

[186] (1987) 9 EHRR 203 at 219, para 52.

that Serbia and Montenegro was not a member of the UN and therefore did not have access to the Court under article 35(1) of the Court's Statute.[187] Turning to whether there could be access as a non-member under article 35(2) of the Statute, the Court invoked the Vienna Convention's reference to both preparatory work and circumstances of conclusion when examining the history of article 35(2). One issue was whether the reference there to jurisdiction based on 'treaties in force' meant those in force at the time of entry into force of the Statute or when a particular matter was being referred to the Court. Having found that these words could produce differing meanings, the Court looked at their origins in the predecessor treaty, the Statute of the PCIJ, at its preparatory work, and at practice of the PCIJ.

The Court found that the provision had been included to cover cases contemplated in agreements made in the aftermath of the First World War before the Statute entered into force, but it found the preparatory work for its own Statute less helpful. What little discussion there was of the article was 'provisional and somewhat cursory' and 'took place at a stage in the planning of the future international organization when it was not yet settled whether the Permanent Court would be preserved or replaced by a new court'.[188] The former of these two observations can be seen as a comment on the nature or quality of the evidence provided by the preparatory work, the latter as a relevant circumstance. Among other factors, in reaching its conclusion that the present Statute must be interpreted in the same way as the equivalent in the predecessor instrument, the Court noted that it was possible that no treaties from that time existed with such a provision, none having been brought to its attention, but that that 'circumstance' did not support the alternative interpretation allowing access on the basis of any treaty (being one providing for reference of a dispute to the Court), if in force subsequent to the Statute.[189] Thus the Court alluded to the circumstances of conclusion in conjunction with its analysis of the preparatory work and in relation to the potential effect of the provision in issue, but all in conjunction with analysis of the preparatory work.[190]

Another example is the *Canadian Agricultural Tariffs* arbitration.[191] The USA and Canada entered into a Free Trade Agreement (FTA) in 1988 which allowed some quantitative restrictions on imports of agricultural products. They replaced this with the North American Free Trade Agreement (NAFTA), which preserved several provisions of the FTA and entered into force in January 1994. Both became

---

[187] [2004] ICJ Reports 279 at 314–15, para 91 and other cases by the same applicant on the same matter.

[188] [2004] ICJ Reports 279 at 323, para 113.

[189] [2004] ICJ Reports 279 at 323, para 113.

[190] See also *Oil Platforms (Preliminary Objection)* [1996] ICJ Reports 803 at paras 24 ff where the parties referred to the circumstances in which the Treaty of Amity, Economic Relations and Consular Rights had been negotiated, though the Court did not single these circumstances out from other factors when examining the history of the treaty and making comparisons with others of a similar kind; see further section 4.4.3 above.

[191] *Tariffs Applied by Canada to Certain US-origin Agricultural Products* NAFTA Arbitral Panel (Secretariat File No CDA-95–2008-01), Final Report of the Panel, 2 December 1996.

parties to the WTO Agreement on Agriculture, which came into force a year later. The central issue in the arbitration was whether tariffs applied by Canada to US agricultural products which exceeded their allotted quota after the NAFTA and WTO agreements came into force breached the NAFTA prohibition on new tariffs. The WTO arrangements envisaged quantitative restrictions being replaced by tariffs. In deciding that the preserved FTA provisions had the effect of bringing into the NAFTA the replacement regime for agricultural non-tariff barriers established under the WTO, the arbitral panel examined the sequence of negotiations of the three treaties and considered statements and documents which did not strictly form part of the preparatory work of the NAFTA. While the panel's conclusion was essentially based on the text of the three treaties, the circumstances of conclusion were taken into account. The panel joined together its examination of the preparatory work and the circumstances of conclusion to justify use of some material whose admissibility might otherwise have been uncertain.[192]

Circumstances of conclusion may also be allied to preparatory work when being used in a purely confirmatory role.[193]

4.5.2 Comparison with provisions in other treaties or associated material as a circumstance of conclusion

As has been noted above, courts and tribunals often make comparisons between wording of a treaty in issue and that in other treaties without indicating any basis in the Vienna rules for this. If, however, the comparable treaty provisions were part of a line of treaties in some sense linked such as by subject matter, and even more so if reference was made to them in the preparatory work, they may be treated as part of the history and warrant consideration as part of the circumstances of conclusion.

Even where reference is made to the Vienna rules, attribution to a particular rule may not be conclusive. For example, in the *Chilean Price Band* case, a WTO Panel referred to article 32 of the Vienna Convention in explaining its use of documents pre-dating the treaty which it was interpreting.[194] These documents were not, in its view, strictly part of the preparatory work, but they did shed light on what the negotiators intended to express in using certain terms of art. The Panel justified this on the basis that article 32 refers to the 'circumstances of conclusion of the treaty'. It quoted the observation of Yasseen in the ILC that:

...the very nature of a convention as an act of will made it essential to take into account all the work which had led to the formation of that will—*all material which the parties had had before them when drafting the final text.*[195]

---

[192] *Tariffs Applied by Canada...*, Final Report of the Panel, 2 December 1996 at paras 154 and 179.

[193] See, eg, *Sovereignty over Pulau Litigan and Pulau Sipadan (Indonesia/Malaysia)* [2002] ICJ Reports 625 at 653–56, paras 53–58.

[194] *Chile—Price Band System and Safeguard Measures Relating to Certain Agricultural Products* WT/DS207/R, 3 May 2002, para 7.35, fn 596.

[195] WT/DS207/R at para 7.35 and fn 536, citing [1966] *Yearbook of the ILC*, vol I, pt II, p 204, para 25, emphasis added by Panel.

The Appellate Body considered that the panel had not correctly applied article 32, though as regards the scope of 'circumstances of conclusion', it noted that the parties had accepted that the material constituted information admissible under the rules of the WTO's Dispute Settlement Mechanism, even though one of them had not accepted that it was admissible as a supplementary means of interpretation.[196]

This left the position unclear but it is perhaps indicative of the rather free-ranging interpretation given to the Vienna rules in that courts and tribunals do make use of interpretative arguments involving comparison of characteristics of different treaties and associated material which may loosely be regarded as part of the circumstances of conclusion of the treaty in issue or which may simply be valuable illustrations when seeking the meaning of a particular provision. Thus, for example, in the *Oil Platforms* case, the ICJ contrasted the types of treaties in which a general proposition affirming enduring peace and friendship is accompanied by procedural measures (explicit reference to certain provisions of the UN Charter, consultation between parties in certain circumstances such as an armed conflict with a third state, etc), and treaties such as the one in issue envisaging quite different matters (trade, consular relations, etc). Such comparison was for the purpose of identification of the object and purpose of the treaty, but seems to base itself on consideration of a wider range of materials which may be thought more aptly the province of supplementary means of interpretation.

4.5.3 Commentaries, explanatory reports, academic writing, etc

Commentaries, explanatory reports, and similar documents may be written at the same time as a treaty is being drawn up. Such material may be acknowledged in some way when a treaty is adopted or concluded, or it may be prepared after that stage. The descriptive terms for such materials are not uniformly applied, but the broad distinction is between those which are in some way linked with the preparation, conclusion, or implementation of a treaty and those which are prepared quite separately. The former may come within article 31(2)(a) or they may constitute part of the preparatory work. The latter category (quite separate material) may be admissible under article 31(3)(c) to the extent that it states international law as recognized in article 38 of the Statute of the ICJ. However, the subsidiary status given to such material in the Statute makes for a somewhat uneasy fit within the idea of 'rules of international law applicable in the relations between the parties'. This suggests that this material may be best viewed as within the category of supplementary means of interpretation, depending somewhat on its content.[197]

There are many sets of commentaries by the ILC and other bodies involved in preparatory work of treaties but these remain part of the preparatory work unless

---

[196] *Chile—Price Band System and Safeguard Measures Relating to Certain Agricultural Products*, AB-2002–2, (2002) WT/DS207/AB/R at para 230 and fn 206.
[197] See Chapter 7, section 3.2.2 above.

given some enhanced status at conclusion of a treaty. Of those specifically endorsed at the time of conclusion of treaties, prominent examples are the explanatory reports which accompany many of the conventions drawn up within the Council of Europe and those relating to Conventions drawn up by the Hague Conference on Private International Law.[198] An example of explanatory material developed in successive editions after the adoption of a treaty is the 'Handbook' promulgated by the UN High Commissioner for Refugees (UNHCR) in connection with the UN Convention on Refugees.[199] The precise basis for use of such materials is not always made clear.[200] While this may lead to failure to respect the distinction between the general rule and supplementary means of treaty interpretation, guides and commentaries are likely to contain a mixture of analysis of text, references to preparatory work, compilations of practice, etc. Their interpretative role is thus more likely to depend on which of these elements is being used than on their general character as a source of learning. The assumption seems to be that where an issue is covered in a commentary or explanatory report in a way which shows clearly the collective

---

[198] See Council of Europe Treaty Series (formerly European Treaty Series) at <http://conventions.coe.int/>.

[199] UNHCR Handbook on Procedures and Criteria for Determining Refugee Status under the 1951 Convention and the 1967 Protocol relating to the Status of Refugees, 1992. The Handbook has been used in interpretation of the UN Convention on Refugees on several occasions in English and other courts, Lord Bingham noting that it 'is recognised as an important source of guidance on matters to which it relates', *Sepet and Another v Secretary of State for the Home Department* [2003] UKHL 15, [2003] 1 WLR 856 at 864; and see *R v Secretary of State for the Home Department, ex parte Adan* [2001] 2 AC 477 at 490 (House of Lords), citing and quoting the preambular reference to the Handbook in 'Joint Position of the European Union' adopted on 4 March 1996 (OJ 1996 L 63, p 2). However, the Handbook takes account of practice of states and their communications with the UNHCR and may therefore be seen as reflecting subsequent practice or agreed implementation, rather than supplementary means of interpretation; but cf *Chan Yee Kin v Minister for Immigration* 90 ILR 138 (Australia HC, 1989), per Mason CJ at 145: 'I regard the Handbook more as a practical guide for the use of those who are required to determine whether or not a person is a refugee than as a document purporting to interpret the meaning of the relevant parts of the Convention'; *Ward v Attorney General of Canada* [1993] 2 SCR 689 (Supreme Court of Canada) 103 DLR (4th) 1, para 34: 'While not formally binding on signatory states, the Handbook has been endorsed by the states which are members of the Executive Committee of the UNHCR, including Canada, and has been relied upon by the courts of signatory states'; and *Sale v Haitian Centers Council* 509 US 155 (1993) (US Supreme Court) at 182 and 197.

[200] See, eg, *R v Secretary of State for the Home Department, Ex parte Read* [1989] AC 1014 at 1052 where the UK House of Lords referred to the Explanatory Report on the Convention on the Transfer of Sentenced Persons: 'Although it does not purport to be an authoritative interpretation of the Convention, it is available as an aid to construction as part of the "travaux preparatoires" and under article 31 of the Vienna Convention...'; cf *R v Secretary of State for the Home Department ex parte Mullen* [2004] UKHL 18, [2005] 1 AC 1 at 44–45, para 48, per Lord Steyn: 'But the explanatory report has great persuasive value in the process of interpretation. For example, it is a basis on which states sign and ratify the Protocol. Inevitably, state practice will be based on the explanatory report, and in this way it becomes directly relevant to the interpretation of article 14(6): article 31(3)(b) of the Vienna Convention on the Law of Treaties'; Advocate-General Jacobs in *In re Eurofood IFSC Ltd* [2006] Ch 508 at 511 on interpretation of the Regulation successor to the European Union Convention on Insolvency Proceedings stated: 'I consider that the explanatory report on the Convention written by Professor Miguel Virgos and Mr Etienne Schmit ("the Virgos-Schmit report") may provide useful guidance when interpreting the Regulation (...the Virgos-Schmit report "was discussed extensively and agreed to by the expert delegates but, unlike the Convention, was not formally approved by the Council of Ministers. Nevertheless, it will have considerable authority for courts in member states"). (Similarly the Court of Justice has on countless occasions referred to the explanatory reports on the

intention of those who drew up the treaty, this will be recognized as an aid to the correct interpretation.[201] This is also a possible source of guidance where treaties are based on model provisions, such as treaties for the avoidance of double taxation.[202] Where a treaty concerns a subject that is developing, arrangements may be made for continued production of explanatory and interpretative material.[203]

Commentaries written by independent experts may assume a role of almost equal value to those endorsed by the parties.[204] This may result in uncertainties of status as in the case of the 'Explanatory Report on the 1980 Hague Child Abduction Convention', prepared by Elisa Pérez-Vera and published by The Hague Conference on Private International Law (HCCH) in 1982.[205] Professor Pérez-Vera had been Rapporteur of the Commission which prepared the Convention, but her report was drawn up after the Convention's conclusion and frankly acknowledges that 'it is possible that, despite the [Rapporteur's] efforts to remain objective, certain passages reflect a viewpoint which is in part subjective'.[206] It has nevertheless been influential in proceedings concerning child abduction.[207]

Brussels Convention of 27 September 1968 on Jurisdiction and the Enforcement of Judgments in Civil and Commercial Matters (principally the Jenard report (OJ 1979 C 59, p 1) and the Schlosser report on the Convention on the Accession of Denmark, Ireland and the United Kingdom to the Brussels Convention (OJ 1979 C 59, p 71))'; and *Malachtou v Armefti* 88 ILR 199 at 215 (Cyprus Supreme Court), referring to the European Convention on the Legal Status of Children Born out of Wedlock: 'The Explanatory Report is a supplementary means of interpretation.'

[201] See Lord Steyn, *ex parte Mullen* [2004] UKHL 18, [2005] 1 AC 1 .

[202] These may be based on the OECD model to which reference is made in numerous cases, together with commentary; see, eg, *Staatssecretaris van Financiën v X* (Netherlands, Hoge Raad) 5 ITLR 818, paras 3.6 and 3.7 referring to explanatory notes and commentary to tax treaties, and *National Westminster Bank plc v USA* (US Court of Federal Claims) 6 ITLR 292 at 304: 'Both this court and others have recognised that the Organisation for Economic Co-Operation and Development's (OECD's) 1977 Model Double Taxation Convention on Income and on Capital (the model treaty) and the accompanying Explanatory Commentary on Article 7 Concerning the Taxation of Business Profits (the Commentary) serve as a meaningful guide in interpreting treaties that are based on its provisions…'; but cf *Russell v Commissioner of Taxation* (Federal Court of Australia) 13 ITLR 538, *Commissioner of Taxation v SNF (Australia) Pty Ltd* (Federal Court of Australia) [2011] FCAFC 74, and see further F Engelen, *Interpretation of Tax Treaties under International Law* (Amsterdam: IBFD Publications BV, 2004) at 439 ff.

[203] See, eg, International Convention on the Harmonized Commodity Description and Coding System, Brussels, 14 June 1983 [1988] ATS 30, articles 6–7 setting up a committee whose functions include preparing 'Explanatory Notes, Classification Opinions or other advice as guides to the interpretation of the Harmonized System', considered in *Turbon International GmbH v Oberfinanzdirektion Koblenz* (ECJ Case C-250/05) [2006] All ER (D) 384.

[204] See, eg, the 'Commentary on the Refugee Convention, Articles 2–11, 13–37' by Professor Grahl-Madsen (republished by the UNHCR Department of International Protection, October 1997) and references to that work in *A and Others v Secretary of State for the Home Department* [2004] UKHL 56, [2005] 2 AC 68 at para 69, *R v Immigration Officer at Prague Airport ex parte European Roma Rights Centre* [2004] UKHL 55, [2005] 2 AC 1 at paras 13, 14, 17, and 70 and *In re B (FC) (2002), R v Special Adjudicator ex parte Hoxha* [2005] UKHL 19, [2005] 4 All ER 580 at paras 15 and 68.

[205] *Actes et documents de la Quatorzième session* (1980), HCCH Publications (1982), <http://www.hcch.net/upload/expl28.pdf>.

[206] *Actes et documents de la Quatorzième session*, p. 428.

[207] See the many cases logged on the HCCH database (INCADAT) as referring to the Report, and cf *Abbott v Abbott* 130 S.Ct. 1983 at 1995, where the US Supreme Court noted that the Federal Register identified the Pérez-Vera Report as the 'official history' of the Convention and 'a source of

The growing role of explanatory reports received recognition in the context of the Convention on International Interests in Mobile Equipment and its Protocol specific to Aircraft Equipment (2001) where a resolution in the Final Act mandated preparation of an 'official commentary' by the Chairman of the Drafting Committee, being 'CONSCIOUS of the need for an official commentary on these texts as an aid for those called upon to work with these documents and RECOGNISING the increasing use of commentaries of this type in the context of modern, technical commercial law instruments'.[208]

Likewise, academic guides and studies are often used by courts and tribunals to assist them in analysis of text, preparatory work, comparative case law, and argument on controversial issues.[209]

4.5.4 Other supplementary means

There are few references in case law linking material considered in judgments, decisions, and awards to supplementary means other than preparatory work and circumstances of conclusion; but it is clear that these are not the only supplementary means that are admissible, even if it is sometimes difficult to determine whether this or some other category in the Vienna rules is the most appropriate classification.

For example, some have seen maxims as supplementary means of interpretation. The history of treaty interpretation before the Vienna Convention is full of attempts to identify and list rules or 'canons' of interpretation, presumptions and 'maxims' (often graced with Latin, or in some cases French, expression). Chapter 2 above contains many pointers to the main literature on the subject and thence to much further material. Whether these items are now appropriately considered as other 'supplementary means' of interpretation is not clear. Some are better seen as useful adjuncts to the apparatus for identifying which ordinary meaning is to be given a term rather than supplementary means, but it is convenient to consider the present role of canons, presumptions, and maxims here in one place.[210] There is

---

background on the meaning of the provisions of the Convention', but found that it, the Court, 'need not decide whether this Report should be given greater weight than a scholarly commentary', though it nevertheless pointed out that the Report supported the interpretation which the Court adopted; see Chapter 4, section 4.2.3 above for further consideration of this case.

[208] See R Goode, *Cape Town Convention and Aircraft Protocol Official Commentary* (UNIDROIT, 3rd edn, 2013).

[209] See, eg, *K v Secretary of State for the Home Department* [2007] 1 All ER 671 at 684, where Lord Bingham noted that the consensus in the case law (that for the purposes the UN Convention on Refugees a family group could be a particular social group) was clearly reflected in academic literature which he cited; and see *Attorney General v Zaoui* [2006] 2 LRC 206 (NZ Supreme Court) at 220 ff, where the judgment tracks the Vienna rules, taking in academic and other materials at appropriate stages; see also the endorsement by Lord Steyn of Bossuyt's 'Guide to the "travaux préparatoires" of the International Covenant on Civil and Political Rights' in *R v Secretary of State for the Home Department ex parte Mullen* [2004] UKHL 18, [2005] 1 AC 1; and see *Churchill Mining PLC and Planet Mining Pty Ltd v Republic of Indonesia* ICSID Case No. ARB/12/14 and 12/40 (Decision on Jurisdiction, 24 February 2014) at paras 182–88 on use of 'doctrinal writings'.

[210] See Aust, *Modern Treaty Law and Practice*, 220–1 where the maxims are considered as supplementary means of interpretation.

no authoritative definition of 'canons' of interpretation or construction, 'presumptions', or of 'maxims' in the specific context of treaty interpretation. Their usage sometimes makes them overlap, and their content and value is indeterminate.

The ILC in its preparatory work on the Vienna rules mostly avoided use of these terms. In its Commentary on the then draft articles to form the Vienna rules the Commission noted that some jurists 'express reservations as to the obligatory character of certain of the so-called canons of interpretation', and indicated that it had 'confined itself to trying to isolate and codify the comparatively few general principles which appear to constitute general rules for the interpretation of treaties'.[211] This endorsed the analysis by the ILC's Special Rapporteur, Sir Humphrey Waldock, who treated the principles and maxims of interpretation then in common use warily. Taking as examples ones frequently referred to in their Latin forms ('*ut res magis valeat quam pereat, contra proferentem, eiusdem generis, expressio unius est exclusio alterius, generalia specialibus non derogant*'), he characterized these as 'for the most part, principles of logic and good sense valuable only as guides to assist in appreciating the meaning', principles whose use was thus 'discretionary rather than obligatory'.[212] It is clear that the ILC's approach was to focus its own efforts on stating principles which could stand as rules.

Two categories of canons and maxims may be identified. The first consists of the type instanced by Waldock. These are certainly not excluded by the Vienna rules from use in the interpretative exercise; but, given that the rules are only a framework for treaty interpretation, leaving modalities of their application very much to the interpreter, these common principles of construction may be as useful in application of the general rule as they could be as supplementary means. A second, rather different, category comprises presumptions based on requirements of justice rather than techniques of construction. Examples of the latter category are presumptions of criminal law, such as the principles that a person should not be charged unless the alleged acts constituted a crime identified by law (*nullum crimen sine lege*) and the injunction that where there is doubt to favour the accused (*in dubio pro reo*), which could be relevant to interpreting definitions of international criminal offences.[213]

One interpretative means of particular application in treaty interpretation, and still used by some interpreters, is the 'restrictive principle' (*in dubio mitius*).[214] It has been retained in Oppenheim, where examples and analysis are cited:

The principle of *in dubio mitius* applies in interpreting treaties, in deference to the sovereignty of states. If the meaning of a term is ambiguous, that meaning is to be preferred

---

[211] [1966] *Yearbook of the ILC*, vol II, p 218–9, paras 1 and 4–5. An early draft considered by the ILC did single out a specific canon or maxim for inclusion as a separate article headed 'Effective interpretation of the terms: *ut res magis valeat quam pereat*'. This was rejected on several grounds, the chairman stating as a summary: 'In so far as it stated a logical rule, it was in any case implicit in the earlier provisions ... of the draft and there was perhaps no need to state it explicitly'. [1964] *Yearbook of the ILC*, vol I, p 288–91, and conclusion at p 291 para 119.

[212] Waldock, 'Third Report on the Law of Treaties' [1964] *Yearbook of the ILC*, vol II, p 54, paras 5–6.

[213] See Chapter 10, section 4.2 below.

[214] On restrictive interpretation see Chapter 2, section 6 above.

which is less onerous to the party assuming an obligation, or which interferes less with the territorial and personal supremacy of a party, or involves less general restrictions upon the parties.[215]

There have, nevertheless, long been grounds for questioning whether the restrictive principle should be applied to treaties which are primarily for the protection of individuals, such as human rights instruments.[216] More generally, however, the whole idea of a restrictive approach as a principle of interpretation has now become open to question in the light of observations by the ICJ in the *Navigational and Related Rights Case (Costa Rica v Nicaragua)*.[217] The Court indicated that it would make its interpretation in terms of customary international law as reflected in the 1969 Vienna Convention.[218] The court preceded its interpretation of a key disputed phrase with an indication that restrictive interpretation is not part of the general rule.

The case concerned the extent of Costa Rica's rights on the section of the San Juan river where the right bank, ie the Costa Rican side, marks the border between Costa Rica and Nicaragua pursuant to an 1858 'Treaty of Limits'. Nicaragua had argued that Costa Rica's right of free navigation for commercial purposes (*con objetos de comercio*) should be interpreted narrowly because it represented a limitation of the 'exclusive *dominium* and *imperium* over the waters of the San Juan river' (ie sovereignty) which was conferred on Nicaragua by article VI of the treaty. The Court was not convinced:

While it is certainly true that limitations of the sovereignty of a State over its territory are not to be presumed, this does not mean that treaty provisions establishing such limitations, such as those that are in issue in the present case, should for this reason be interpreted *a priori* in a restrictive way. A treaty provision which has the purpose of limiting the sovereign powers of a State must be interpreted like any other provision of a treaty, i.e. in accordance with the intentions of its authors as reflected by the text of the treaty and the other relevant factors in terms of interpretation.

A simple reading of Article VI shows that the Parties did not intend to establish any hierarchy as between Nicaragua's sovereignty over the river and Costa Rica's right of free navigation, characterized as 'perpetual', with each of these affirmations counter-balancing the other. Nicaragua's sovereignty is affirmed only to the extent that it does not prejudice the substance of Costa Rica's right of free navigation in its domain, the establishment of which is precisely the point at issue; the right of free navigation, albeit 'perpetual', is granted only on condition that it does not prejudice the key prerogatives of territorial sovereignty.

---

[215] R Jennings and A Watts (eds), *Oppenheim's International Law*, vol I (London: Longman, 9th edn, 1992), 1278 (footnote omitted); and see, eg, WTO Appellate Body *Report on EC Measures Concerning Meat and Meat Products (Hormones)* WT/DS26/AB/R, WT/DS48/AB/R (1998), 64–65, para 70.

[216] See A Orakhelashvili, 'Restrictive Interpretation of Human Rights Treaties in the Recent Jurisprudence of the European Court of Human Rights' (2003) 14 EJIL 529, where an analysis is made in the light of the Vienna rules.

[217] *Dispute regarding Navigational and Related Rights (Costa Rica v Nicaragua)* [2009] ICJ Reports 214.

[218] [2009] ICJ Reports 214 at 237, para 47.

There are thus no grounds for supposing, *a priori*, that the words 'libre navegación ... con objetos de comercio' should be given a specially restrictive interpretation, any more than an extensive one.[219]

This firmly negates any idea that a restrictive approach should generally be taken to treaty provisions, even ones which concern matters near to the core of sovereignty such as those affecting territory. However, the indication in the judgment that restrictive interpretation has no '*a priori*' application seems not to rule out the possibility that if the normal process of treaty interpretation in accordance with the Vienna rules leads to a finely balanced outcome, the restrictive approach might still offer an element weighing in favour of the result which least impinges on the sovereignty of a protagonist which is being required to yield some right to another party.

A further approach which is now even more anomalous is the idea that an appeal can be made to the 'spirit' of a treaty. This notion has probably lost any role it once had in treaty interpretation, at least in that form.[220] However, it can be seen that the definition of 'context' in the general rule as including the whole text of a treaty allows account to be taken of the scheme and economy of a treaty; the reference to object and purpose there brings into consideration the aim of the treaty as a whole; and where the circumstances of conclusion come to be considered, these may indicate the motivation and ethos that generated the treaty's terms. Thus, the spirit may be revealed, but rather as inherent in the outcome of a more systematic approach to treaty interpretation.

One case in which 'other' supplementary means were specifically considered concerned reliance on a document which did not fall within any category in the general rule, and was not preparatory work. This was the investment arbitration *HICEE v Slovak Republic*.[221] The case concerned interpretation of a bilateral investment treaty (BIT) between the Netherlands and Czechoslovakia, the Slovak Republic being a party as successor to the latter state. At the preliminary phase the central issue was whether the phrase 'invested either directly or through an investor of a third State' applied to a company incorporated in the respondent state, that company being a subsidiary of another company incorporated there and owned by the foreign claimant (the ultimate holding thus being a 'sub-subsidiary').

---

[219] *Dispute regarding Navigational and Related Rights (Costa Rica v Nicaragua)* [2009] ICJ Reports 214 at 237–8, para 48; and cf *Whaling in the Antarctic (Australia v Japan: New Zealand intervening)*, Judgment of 31 March 2014, para 58, where the ICJ, considering in particular the context and the treaty's object and purpose, stated: 'Taking into account the preamble and other relevant provisions of the Convention referred to above, the Court observes that neither a restrictive nor an expansive interpretation of Article VIII [the provision in issue] is justified'.

[220] See references to the spirit of a treaty in *Case of the SS "Wimbledon"* (PCIJ) (1923) Series A, no 1, 23; Advisory Opinion on *Conditions of Admission of a State to Membership in the United Nations* [1948] ICJ Reports 57 at 63; *Interpretation of Peace Treaties* [1950] ICJ Reports 221 at 228–29; *South West Africa (Preliminary Objections)* [1962] ICJ Reports 319 at 336; *AAPL v Sri Lanka* (ICSID) 106 ILR 417 at 445, paras 51–52, *New Zealand Maori Council v AG* (NZ Court of Appeal) 120 ILR 462 at 544; and see J Klabbers, 'On Rationalism in Politics: Interpretation of Treaties and the World Trade Organization' (2005) 74 *Nordic JIL* 405 at 421 ff.

[221] *HICEE B.V. v Slovak Republic*, PCA Case No. 2009-11, Partial Award, 23 May 2011.

Did 'directly' mean any investment was covered which an investor itself held in a state party to the BIT as contrasted with an investment there made through a holding company in a third state; or did 'directly' mean that the BIT covered an investor's subsidiary in the host state but not an investment held more remotely there, that is, as a sub-subsidiary? A contextual argument was derived from the contrast between holding 'directly' and through an investor of a third state. In other words 'directly' referred to an investment that was not made via a third state, but otherwise imposed no restriction on a chain of subsidiaries. For the majority, the general rule of interpretation did not resolve possible uncertainty. Such uncertainty was supported, or instigated, by a statement in Dutch Explanatory Notes produced from the archives of the respondent state (Slovakia):

Normally, investment protection agreements also cover investments in the host country made by a Dutch company's subsidiary which is already established in the host country ('subsidiary'–'sub-subsidiary' structure). Czechoslovakia wishes to exclude the 'sub-subsidiary' from the scope of this Agreement, because this is in fact a company created by a Czechoslovakian legal entity, and Czechoslovakia does not want to grant, in particular, transfer rights to such company. This restriction can be dealt with by incorporating a new company directly from the Netherlands.[222]

The document containing this statement was not part of the preparatory work as it had been drawn up as part of the Dutch process for approval of the treaty. It could not be viewed as an agreement between the parties at the time of, or subsequent to, the conclusion of the treaty, there being no evidence of agreement by Czechoslovakia. Nor was there any evidence to suggest that the explanatory notes could amount to an instrument made by one party in connection with the conclusion of the treaty and accepted by the other party as related to the treaty since there was no evidence of such acceptance.

The majority view of the tribunal was that the material should nevertheless be taken into account. It considered that the government of the Netherlands had, in the process of giving consent to the treaty, 'expressed itself formally, publicly, and in writing (with reasons) as to what had been intended by the key phrase', and the government of Slovakia in the arbitration espoused the same meaning.[223] The Tribunal noted that the material did not fall within categories enumerated in the Vienna rules but that did not mean it should be left out of consideration:

To do so...would not...be reconcilable with the requirement that a treaty is to be interpreted 'in good faith', which the Vienna Convention consciously placed at the very head of the provisions dealing with interpretation. And the Tribunal recalls once more (as set out above) that the category of supplementary materials that a tribunal is authorized to have recourse to, in order to confirm the meaning resulting from the application of article 31, or to determine the meaning when the interpretation according to article 31 leaves the meaning ambiguous or obscure, is, on the terms of the Convention, not closed. The Tribunal is therefore in no doubt that the Dutch Explanatory Notes, given their terms and content, taken together with the viewpoint adopted in these proceedings by Slovakia, constitute

---

[222] PCA Case No. 2009-11 (2011) at para 126.   [223] Award para 126.

valid supplementary material which the Tribunal may, and in the circumstances must, take into account in dealing with the question before it.[224]

5. Conclusions

The supplementary means of interpretation indicated in the Vienna rules are not an exclusive list. They are 'supplementary' rather than subordinate. There is, however, a differentiation in their roles. When used 'to confirm' meaning they are of a lesser role that the general rule, but when used 'to determine' meaning they are dominant. They may always be considered to help in understanding a treaty and with a view to assessing their availability for one of the roles identified in article 32. Their admissibility in the operative reasoning of an interpretation is differentiated by function—that is, according to whether they are to *confirm* a meaning reached by applying the general rule or to *determine* the meaning of a treaty provision.

In the latter case supplementary means (most commonly preparatory work) may only be used if the result of deploying the general rule leaves the meaning ambiguous or obscure or produces a result which is manifestly absurd or unreasonable. These preconditions do *not* apply to use of preparatory work to confirm the meaning reached by application of the general rule, nor to its use for general understanding of the treaty.

The relationship between the general rule and the supplementary means of interpretation suggests that if preparatory work does not confirm the clear meaning given to a treaty provision by applying the general rule, the preparatory work is not to be taken into account. When applied in practice, however, the small amount of case law touching on this issue suggests that this is not what generally happens and some evaluation of the preparatory work takes place.

Application of the general rule tends in such cases not to produce so clear an outcome that strong evidence in preparatory work, and in the circumstances of conclusion, of a possible different meaning will be ignored. In practice, awareness of the preparatory work may reveal at an early stage the possibility of ambiguity.

Hence the general rule and supplementary means may in extreme cases operate like a see-saw, with the relatively much stronger element carrying preponderant weight. This may usually be justifiable on the basis of the application of the general rule either producing a clearer outcome than that suggested in the preparatory work or producing a result that meets the preconditions set in article 32 for the preparatory work to be determinative. It should not be forgotten, however, that the general rule includes elements in its third paragraph which may lead away from meanings suggested by the preparatory work. The records of preparatory work are commonly inconclusive and are to be approached with considerable caution.

---

[224] Award para 126, footnote omitted.

C. Languages

9

Languages

Treaties authenticated in two or more languages

The conclusion which I have reached is that in French, as in English, it is possible to write with a precision which permits of only one possible construction, but....[1]

Article 33
Interpretation of treaties authenticated in two or more languages

1. When a treaty has been authenticated in two or more languages, the text is equally authoritative in each language, unless the treaty provides or the parties agree that, in case of divergence, a particular text shall prevail.
2. A version of the treaty in a language other than one of those in which the text was authenticated shall be considered an authentic text only if the treaty so provides or the parties so agree.
3. The terms of the treaty are presumed to have the same meaning in each authentic text.
4. Except where a particular text prevails in accordance with paragraph 1, when a comparison of the authentic texts discloses a difference of meaning which the application of articles 31 and 32 does not remove, the meaning which best reconciles the texts, having regard to the object and purpose of the treaty, shall be adopted.

1. Introduction

From the fact that many judgments and awards of international courts and tribunals only mention articles 31 and 32 of the Vienna Convention, as if these constituted the whole law of treaty interpretation, it might be concluded that article 33 is the poor relation in the set. This rather conceals the fact that these courts and tribunals have an international composition and may themselves be working in more than one language, from the outset using different languages when approaching terms in the text. However, while such international capabilities can inject an often valuable element into the thinking and understanding of judges and arbitrators in relation to any legal document, the use of different languages in recording the same agreement can have disadvantages as well as advantages.

---

[1] Donaldson J in *Corocraft v Pan American Airways* [1969] 1 QB 616. For the continuation of the quotation see section 4.8 below.

Language is a medium which can be coloured by differences related to culture, society, philosophy, and perhaps even thought processes.[2] Comparison of authoritative different language texts of a treaty can play a helpful role in removing uncertainties residing in one or more of them. It can also throw up ambiguities or alternative possibilities which may not arise, or be so readily apparent, if a single language has been used.[3]

This chapter considers the roles languages can play in treaty interpretation. Case law specifically referring to the Vienna rules is relatively sparse on this topic even though comparison of terms in different languages has long been routine and has become even more necessary with the increasing number of treaties authenticated in multiple languages. Routine comparisons, though important in their particular contexts, yield up few points of general guidance in application of the Vienna rules. Hence the preparatory work assumes a greater role in explaining the text of article 33.

2. History and Preparatory Work

The Vienna Convention's single article on interpretation of 'treaties authenticated in two or more languages' was developed by the ILC from two draft articles.[4] The provisions on languages were always viewed as within the section of the draft convention concerning interpretation of treaties; but in the report of the Special Rapporteur (Waldock) in which he first presented this section, and in the debates in the ILC, the various draft provisions which became the two articles constituting the

---

[2] On factors affecting choice of language in treaty making, see J K Gamble and C Ku, 'Choice of Language in Bilateral Treaties: Fifty Years of Changing State Practice' (1992–93) 3 *Indiana International and Comparative Law Review* 233 and on trends in languages for treaties, see J K Gamble, L Kolb, and C Graml, 'Choice of Official Text in Multilateral Treaties: The Interplay of Law, Politics, Language, Pragmatism and (Multi)-Nationalism' (2014) 12 *Santa Clara J Int'l L* 29.

[3] On practice in use of language in treaties, including use of a 'neutral' language (a language which is not the primary one of any of the parties), see A I Aust, *Modern Treaty Law and Practice* (Cambridge: CUP, 3rd edn, 2012), 222–5.

[4] Draft article 74 'Treaties drawn up in two or more languages' and draft article 75 'Interpretation of treaties having two or more texts or versions', in Waldock (Special Rapporteur), 'Third Report on the Law of Treaties' [1964] *Yearbook of the ILC*, vol II, p 62. In that report Professor Waldock used the adjective 'plurilingual' to describe such treaties, a usage which carried over into the ILC's commentary on the draft articles in [1966] *Yearbook of the ILC*, vol II, pp 219 and 224 ff. However, Professor Waldock elsewhere used 'multilingual' (see, eg, [1966] *Yearbook of the ILC*, vol II, p 103, para 11), and the report of the UN Secretariat, commissioned by the ILC in the present context, used 'multilingual' in its title (but both adjectives in the text): *Preparation of multilingual treaties*, Doc A/CN.4/187 [1966] *Yearbook of the ILC*, vol II, p 104. Members of the ILC, and comments of states, use the two terms without making any obvious distinction between them. A distinction is sometimes made between 'multilateral' treaties and 'plurilateral' ones, the latter involving a limited number of states having some common interest or object affecting only a restricted number or group of states (see G G Fitzmaurice (Special Rapporteur), 'Report on the Law of Treaties' [1956] *Yearbook of the ILC*, vol II, p 122, para 55, fn 26 and Aust, *Modern Treaty Law and Practice* at 125). There does not, however, seem to be a useful analogy to be drawn in the present context from that attribution of meaning to words having a construction similar to 'multilingual' and 'plurilingual'.

general rule and the supplementary means of interpretation were set out together, with commentary or debate immediately following them. Then, separately, followed the provisions on languages with their commentary or debate. The significance of this is that a residual impression has persisted that there is some faint divide, putting the provisions on languages at a slight remove from the other two articles on interpretation.

Nevertheless, although they handled the draft language articles separately from the rest of the section on interpretation, the ILC and its Special Rapporteur were at pains to explain:

The existence of more than one authentic text clearly introduces a new element—comparison of the texts—into the interpretation of the treaty. But it does not involve a different system of interpretation. Plurilingual in expression, the treaty remains a single treaty with a single set of terms the interpretation of which is governed by the rules set out in articles 27 and 28 [now 31 and 32].[5]

The main issues in the development of article 33 were, first, the proper characterization of the status of the different languages used and, second, how much detail the rules on this topic should contain. The first of these was essentially a matter of identification of an authentic text or texts, definition of terms, and attribution of effects. Given that there is one treaty, albeit in different languages, are these to be described as different language 'texts', different language 'versions', or in some other way? Is a text 'authentic' or 'authoritative', or both, if it is 'established' or 'expressed' in different languages? What is the meaning and effect of describing a translation as 'official'? The second set of issues was whether there existed practice and principles of interpretation on the use to be made of different languages sufficiently detailed to be converted into rules.[6]

These two sets of issues—that is, the status of instruments written in different languages and the methods of reconciling divergent meanings in those languages—have such obvious points of contact that they were in due course amalgamated. It also needs to be borne in mind that the ILC was working up the rest of a set of articles on the law of treaties. Of these other provisions, the draft which became article 10 of the Vienna Convention is particularly relevant in the present context. The concept there of 'authentication'—that is, establishing a text as definitive—associates the term 'authentic' with the process of finalizing the text, leaving 'authoritative' available to describe the subsequent status and effect of a text which has been authenticated. The parties may have agreed in the treaty to give one authoritative text priority if a divergence of meaning can be attributed to the

---

[5] [1966] *Yearbook of the ILC*, vol II, p 225, para 7, commentary on draft article 29 (now 33); and see Waldock (Special Rapporteur), 'Third Report on the Law of Treaties' [1964] *Yearbook of the ILC*, vol II, p 63, para 5: 'But it needs to be stressed that in law there is only one treaty—one set of terms accepted by the parties and one common intention with respect to those terms—even when two authentic texts appear to diverge.'

[6] For a detailed analysis of the work of the ILC on this article see P Germer, 'Interpretation of Plurilingual Treaties: A Study of Article 33 of the Vienna Convention on the Law of Treaties' (1970) 11 *Harvard International Law Journal* 400.

same provision in the different languages, or they may have deliberately rejected this possibility by giving several languages equally authoritative status.

While, however, establishing the status of texts or versions is clearly important, it is the second set of issues—whether rules or principles can be identified for reconciling differences among the languages—which concern the substantive role of languages in interpretation. In this second area the ILC was able to draw on a very thorough, and then recent, study by Dr Hardy of how language issues had previously been approached in treaty interpretation.[7] This study was so comprehensive, and enriched by so many examples of past practice, that it was cited extensively by the Special Rapporteur (Waldock) in his initial report on the topic.[8] But while the study and report revealed many useful techniques for extracting the correct meaning from divergent language texts, the ILC found these practices insufficiently established and uniform to provide a comprehensive code. The Commission, therefore, whittled away the original attempt by its Rapporteur to codify the practice. This reduced it to such an extent that it contained no real guidance on how to resolve interpretative uncertainties resulting from use of different languages. It was at the Vienna Conference that an amendment was made to the ILC draft introducing the object and purpose of a treaty as the guideline for reconciliation of texts in different languages where there are divergences which cannot be removed by application of the other Vienna rules.

The first of the two draft articles on languages, as originally proposed by the Special Rapporteur (Waldock), specified which texts were authoritative. It set out a rule which provided, first, that when 'the text' of a treaty is authenticated in two or more languages, 'the texts of the treaty are authoritative in each language unless otherwise specified'; and, second, that 'a version' drawn up in a language other than one in which the text of the treaty was authenticated would be considered authentic and authoritative if the treaty so provided, if the parties so agreed, or if an international organization so prescribed in respect of a treaty drawn up within that organization.[9]

This proposal resulted in quite a flurry of concern about the nature of a treaty whose terms were stated in two or more languages and whether it was necessary to avoid using the plural 'texts' to reduce the risk of creating an impression that there could be more than one 'text' of a treaty.[10] The difficulty was capturing the

---

[7] J Hardy, 'The Interpretation of Plurilingual Treaties by International Courts and Tribunals' (1961) 37 BYBIL 72–155.

[8] 'Third Report on the Law of Treaties' [1964] *Yearbook of the ILC*, vol II, pp 62–65.

[9] Draft article 74 [1964] *Yearbook of the ILC*, vol II, p 62. The proposed provision relating to versions in different languages drawn up within an international organization led to a memorandum prepared by the UN Secretariat: *Preparation of multilingual treaties*, Doc A/CN.4/187 [1966] *Yearbook of the ILC*, vol II, p 104; the Special Rapporteur (Waldock) felt that the memorandum shed an interesting light on the practice of international organizations in the preparation of multilingual instruments, but in view of the inclusion of a particular provision on international organizations (article 5 of the Vienna Convention), reference to them was dropped from the draft article on interpretation of treaties drawn up in two or more languages: see Waldock, Sixth Report on the Law of Treaties [1966] *Yearbook of the ILC*, vol II, p 102, para 1 and p 103, para 8.

[10] Waldock, 'Sixth Report' [1966] *Yearbook of the ILC*, vol II, pp 101–3.

idea of there being only a *single* agreement but expressed in different languages. Treaties tend to be published with the different languages presented as complete units, either successively or in separate documents. In any event, whether a complete set of a treaty's articles in each language is printed successively or separately, or whether the articles are printed individually in each language side by side, readers are likely to think of each set of provisions in each language as a text, although parallel presentation may reduce this propensity. Usage in multilateral treaties has been virtually uniform in referring to 'texts' in the relevant article or testimonium in which the languages that have been used are identified. The Charter of the United Nations provides a typical formulation: 'The present Charter, of which the Chinese, French, Russian, English, and Spanish *texts* are equally authentic...'.[11]

The possible alternative, that the terms set out in different languages were different 'versions', faced the objection that this word suggested an even greater departure from the concept of unity of a treaty. The matter was only partly resolved by devising a provision which includes several texts in one, viz 'the text' is equally authoritative in each language, unless it is provided or agreed that, in case of divergence, 'a particular text' is to prevail. In reality, the provision acknowledges the customary usage of referring to authentic texts in different languages as 'texts' in the plural. However, it reserves the term 'version' to describe a complete set of the provisions in a language in which the treaty was not originally authenticated but which is stated in the treaty to be authentic, or has been so agreed by the parties.[12] The significance of this part of the history of the provision is that the ILC came to recognize that the important point for treaty interpretation was being clear about which text or texts were authoritative and could be used in interpretation either on an equal footing or, in specified circumstances, with one prevailing.

It was this perceived priority of the need to identify authoritative texts, and the inherent link between such texts and the proposed substantive rules on the use of different languages in interpretation, which led to combining the two original draft articles on languages into a single one more precisely targeted on interpretation.[13] Thus the original simple recognition, as it had appeared in the first draft, of the equal authority of the text in each language in which it has been authenticated was given an interpretative slant by particularizing the exception so that it is 'in the case of divergence' that a particular text is to prevail where this is agreed in the treaty or otherwise agreed by the parties. The second paragraph of the original first article on languages was reduced to an ancillary definition, indicating that a 'version' in a language which was not one in which the treaty was originally authenticated is to be considered authentic if so agreed in the treaty or by the parties. Thus the term

---

[11] Article 111 (emphasis added).

[12] See, eg, the testimonium of the 'Chicago Convention' 1944 in section 4.5 below.

[13] This was the first reason given by the Special Rapporteur (Waldock) for combining the draft provisions in a single article. His second reason was 'that the presentation of the rules in a single article may help to avoid any appearance of over-emphasizing the significance of the multilingual character of a treaty as an element in treaty interpretation': [1966] *Yearbook of the ILC*, vol II, p 103, para 11.

'version' came to include the new entrant in the collectivity of languages of a particular treaty. The result has been described thus:

...a *text* of a treaty denotes any rendition in a language in which it was authenticated, while *version* refers also to languages other than those in which the text was authenticated.[14]

Evidently if a version comes to be considered an authentic text in accordance with article 33(2) it is then to be regarded as a 'text' for the purposes of paragraphs (3) and (4) of that article.

It appears from the records of the discussions that some members of the ILC thought that a proper approach would be for an interpreter to investigate the treaty in all its languages before deciding on its meaning. However, this was seen as too demanding and a proposal to make comparison of languages compulsory in every case was rejected. Instead a scheme was adopted under which only where a divergence came to light would it be necessary to embark on comparison of the languages. This all seems to have been predicated on there being a dispute or difference over interpretation and circumstances in which one or other party would bring any divergence or relevant issue arising from differences in language to the attention of the interpreter. Particular recognition was given by the Special Rapporteur (Waldock) to the difficulty many would have in investigating all parallel languages whenever interpreting a treaty:

While it was true that the interpreter normally undertook such a comparison, it would be going too far to give that process the status of a criterion for the determination of an interpretation according to law. To erect comparison into one of the means of legal interpretation set out in article 69 [ultimately 31] would imply that it was no longer possible to rely on a single text as an expression of the will of the parties until a difficulty arose and that it was necessary to consult all the authentic texts for that purpose; such a procedure would have a number of drawbacks and would, in particular, involve practical difficulties for the legal advisers of the newly independent States, who did not always have staff familiar with the many languages used in drafting international treaties.[15]

In considering how an interpreter is to treat different languages, the ILC was animated by a clear principle:

...The unity of the treaty and of each of its terms is of fundamental importance in the interpretation of plurilingual treaties and it is safeguarded by combining with the principle of the equal authority of authentic texts the presumption that the terms are intended to have the same meaning in each text. This presumption requires that every effort should be made to find a common meaning for the texts before preferring one to another....[16]

In the first draft of this article, the Special Rapporteur (Waldock) had suggested two rules for coping with variations of meaning among different languages. First, if a term was capable of being given more than one meaning compatible with the

[14] M Tabory, *Multilingualism in International Law and Institutions* (Alphen aan den Rijn: Sijthoff, 1980), 171.
[15] [1966] *Yearbook of the ILC*, vol I, pt II, p 211, para 35.
[16] [1966] *Yearbook of the ILC*, vol II, p 225, para 7, commentary on draft article 29.

objects and purposes of the treaty, a meaning common to both or all the texts was to be adopted. Second, if the ordinary meaning in one authentic text was clear and compatible with the objects and purposes of the treaty, while in another it was uncertain owing to the obscurity of the term, the former was to be adopted.[17] These detailed proposals were swiftly dropped and the provisions became progressively pared down until the final proposal of the Commission simply required that if comparison of texts revealed any difference which was not resolved by being directed to one which was to have priority or by application of the other rules of interpretation, 'a meaning which as far as possible reconciles the texts shall be adopted'.[18]

The drawback with this was that it offered no means of achieving such a reconciliation. At the Vienna Conference, the USA proposed substituting for the words quoted immediately above: 'a meaning shall be adopted which is most consonant with the object and purpose of the treaty'.[19] There was little debate and the matter was referred to the drafting committee which combined the ILC's proposal with the idea of taking account of the object and purpose of a treaty wherever reconciliation cannot be achieved by applying the other rules of treaty interpretation.[20]

3. Ordinary Meaning of Terms in Article 33

The history of the development of article 33 in the preceding section has covered most of the issues relating to the ordinary meaning of the provisions eventually adopted. 'Authentic' and 'authoritative' present no particular issues when read in the context of the Vienna Convention's scheme of treaty-making. 'Text' and 'version' may have particular or special meanings as disclosed by the preparatory work, though these are more a matter of usage in the light of how authenticity is established rather than any departure from meanings falling within the range of what is ordinary for those words.

More controversial is the notion of 'reconciling' provisions which have different meanings in different languages. The context suggests a contrast between the case where one language is specified as prevailing and the situation where two or more equally authentic but differing statements of the same proposition have to be brought into harmony or made compatible. As article 33(4) requires that regard be had to the object and purpose of the treaty when achieving this reconciliation, the process seems more one of selecting a meaning by application of that criterion than trying to find commonality between elements of provisions whose differences have

---

[17] Draft article 75(2) and (3) [1964] *Yearbook of the ILC*, vol II, p 62.
[18] Draft article 29 [1966] *Yearbook of the ILC*, vol II, p 224.
[19] See Reports of Committee of the Whole, United Nations Conference on the Law of Treaties: Official Records: Documents of the Conference, A/CONF.39/14, p 151, parallel proposals and sub-amendments mentioned there, and debate in United Nations Conference on the Law of Treaties: First Session (March–May 1968), Summary Records, A/CONF.39/11/Add.2., pp 188–90.
[20] See Documents of the Conference, A/CONF.39/14, p 152.

already become so apparent as to raise the need for reconciliation. In the leading ICJ case the Court viewed interpretation by reference to the object and purpose of the particular treaty as the principal content of the notion of 'reconciliation'.[21]

4. Issues and Practice

4.1 Interpretation by reference
first to only one of several languages

In many instances an interpreter will use just one language, even where several are authoritative. The decision of the ILC not to include a requirement to consider all languages as part of the general rule of interpretation was linked to its inclusion in article 33(3) of the presumption that the terms of a treaty have the same meaning in each authentic text.[22]

Strictly speaking, according to the letter of the Vienna Convention, the presumption of the equality of the texts and the absence of an express directive to compare the texts sanction the reliance on any single authentic version for routine interpretation.[23]

However, the thinking underlying this aspect of the Vienna rules only fits the case of 'routine' interpretation, this presumably being where there is no reason to believe that there is any issue affected by the choice of language of the text which is being interpreted. If a difference or dispute over interpretation is being presented to a court or tribunal, comparison of texts is likely to be essential. Nor does the 'single text for routine interpretation' approach wholly absolve the individual adviser who is called on to make an interpretation of a term which is thought to need investigation, even in the absence of any dispute, from being aware of the possible need to check other languages or finding another person competent to do so.[24]

Even the ICJ, however, does not feel the need to show its working in all languages in which a treaty is authentic when setting out the linguistic elements of its reasoning. In its judgment in the *LaGrand* case, once the issue had arisen whether the English text differed from the French, the Court discussed only those two texts.[25]

---

[21] See consideration of *LaGrand Case (Germany v USA)* [2001] ICJ Reports 466 in section 4.9 below and further consideration of the same case in sections 4.1, 4.4, and 4.5 below.

[22] For the history of the presumption, see C B Kuner, 'The Interpretation of Multilateral Treaties: Comparison of Texts Versus the Presumption of Similar Meaning' (1991) 40 ICLQ 953, at 954.

[23] Tabory, *Multilingualism in International Law*, at 198, and see also at 199–200 where the difficulties which this approach can cause are noted and the desirability of making comparisons between the languages is recognized; see also *Restatement (Third) Foreign Relations Law of the United States* (St Paul, Minn: American Law Institute, 1987), para 325, reporters' note 2, referring to recognition of equality of authentic texts and the presumption: 'An international tribunal, therefore, may consider any convenient text unless an argument is addressed to some other text.'

[24] See ILC debate [1966] *Yearbook of the ILC*, vol I, pt II, pp 208–11.

[25] *LaGrand Case (Germany v USA)* [2001] ICJ Reports 466, and see section 4.1 below.

However, this should not be taken as indicating that one or more languages may be selected at will. The German memorial submitted to the Court in *LaGrand* had set out and compared the Chinese, Spanish, and Russian texts of the relevant provisions.[26] Thus those languages were before the Court even if it did not see it as necessary to refer to them to support its conclusion.

The endorsement by the ILC of the presumption of identity of meaning, when linked with the practice of reliance on the text of a treaty in one language, has been criticized for being likely to contribute to failure to identify significant differences between the languages of particular provisions.[27] This likelihood was recognized in the ILC commentary on its draft articles:

Few plurilingual treaties containing more than one or two articles are without some discrepancy between the texts. The different genius of the languages, the absence of a complete *consensus ad idem*, or lack of sufficient time to co-ordinate the texts may result in minor or even major discrepancies in the meaning of the texts.[28]

Practical examples of unrevealed discrepancies between languages are *ipso facto* not easy to find, though there is some evidence of them.[29] There may be a greater risk when using languages that are not authentic—that is to say 'official' translations—where differences may have been undetected, ignored, or swept under the carpet.

The conclusion must be that the interpreter may legitimately use a single language for 'routine' interpretation or in circumstances which otherwise mandate this (such as a requirement in domestic legislation, though in this case the legislation is being interpreted rather than the treaty), but a prudent interpreter needs to be very aware of the possibility that language differences may be relevant. These need not necessarily complicate the process, and can assist in elucidating the meaning.

4.2 Use of 'versions', 'official', and other texts

Obviously the more a treaty is invoked and applied within a national legal system, the more likely it is that the language of that state will be the point of first resort, even if that text is not an authentic one but some form of official translation, whether promulgated in legislation or published by the authorities of the state. Provided such an official version is complete, an alert interpreter will see from

---

[26] See Memorial of 16 September 1999, paras 4.149–4.150.

[27] See C B Kuner, 'The Interpretation of Multilateral Treaties: Comparison of Texts Versus the Presumption of Similar Meaning' (1991) 40 ICLQ 953, at 958 and 960–61; and on the Nuremberg Charter and judgments, see G Acquaviva, 'At the Origins of Crimes against Humanity: Clues to a Proper Understanding of the "Nullum Crimen" Principle in the Nuremberg Judgment' (2011) 9 *J of Int Crim Justice* 881.

[28] [1966] *Yearbook of the ILC*, vol II, p 225, para 6; and see the many examples of difficulties and confusions in multilingual treaties in D Shelton, 'Reconcilable Differences? The Interpretation of Multilingual Treaties' (1997) 20 *Hastings International and Comparative Law Review* 611.

[29] See, eg, Kuner (1991) 40 ICLQ 953, at 958 and the Anglo–Russian and Russo–American treaties considered in section 4.2.

the final clauses or testimonium which languages are authentic and which, if any, prevails.

However, even where a treaty is being considered in a dispute between states, rather than within a national legal order, reliance is sometimes placed on one language only, most probably on grounds of accessibility. For example, in the *Taba Award*[30] the main treaty was that of 1906 concerning the boundary between the former Turkish Sultanate and the Khedivate of Egypt (at the time occupied by Great Britain). The award records how the Turkish negotiators insisted on the text being in Turkish, which was endorsed as the language of the authentic text. However, the treaty was translated into Arabic and thence into English, with inconsistencies. The scope of these translation issues was revealed by differences which appeared in fresh translations made in preparation for the arbitration.[31] However, in the period from the agreement to the arbitration, reliance had apparently been placed on English translations which had been published in various official sources. Hence the Tribunal decided that, unless it specified otherwise, it would 'follow the general practice of the Parties and refer to the contemporaneous English translation…'.[32] A key feature in this case was identifying the boundary from the location of pillars set up as markers in implementation of the agreement. Thus the decision not to look too far back into the different language versions of the agreement which governed the location of the pillars, and any linguistic divergences relating to the agreement, must be seen as coloured by the greater significance to be attached to how the treaty had been implemented in practice.

An example of a significant discrepancy between an authentic language and official translations is in two agreements, the Anglo–Russian Convention on the Pacific Northwest of 1825 and the Russo–American Convention of 18/30 March 1867 (the 'Alaska Purchase' agreement).[33] Professor Butler has explored a marked difference between the texts of 1825 and 1867, which were authentic solely in French, and their English and Russian translations.[34] A key provision referred to a coastal strip of North America which was to be Russian territory under the 1825 Convention, a provision which was repeated in the 1867 treaty. The French text identified this as '*dix lieues marines de l'océan*' which was 'ten marine leagues' in the English translation presented to the US Senate. However, all official Russian texts referred to the Russian equivalent of '10 nautical miles'.[35] Professor Butler noted that as ten marine leagues would equate to at least 30 nautical miles, this discrepancy would have produced an enormous difference in result. Professor Butler notes that the history of the 1825 and 1867 conventions was investigated in the 1893 Bering Sea Fur-Seal Arbitration and the 1903 Alaska Boundary Arbitration

---

[30] *Arbitral Award in the Dispute Concerning Certain Boundary Pillars between the Arab Republic of Egypt and the State of Israel* (Egypt–Israel Arbitration Tribunal, the 'Taba' Award, 1988) 80 ILR 226.

[31] 80 ILR 226, at 253–4, paras 45 and 47–48.

[32] *Arbitral Award in the Dispute Concerning Certain Boundary Pillars between the Arab Republic of Egypt and the State of Israel*, at 253, para 45.

[33] See W E Butler, 'The 1867 Russo–American Convention: Some Textual Issues' (1991) 40 ICLQ 457.

[34] (1991) 40 ICLQ 457.   [35] (1991) 40 ICLQ 457, at 458.

without this difference between the authentic text and the Russian version emerging, ten marine leagues having been accepted by all as 'appropriate'.[36] In such circumstances, however, it is easy to envisage that a divergent official translation put into public circulation could give rise to issues of possible estoppel or, if given practical effect, establishment of an interpretation or amendment by practice.

4.3 Presumption of the same meaning in all authentic texts

Comparison of the text in different authentic languages is routine in international litigation but the resources necessary to carry this out may make such comparison impracticable in everyday interpretation, or at least until a sufficiently critical issue emerges.[37] The presumption in article 33(3) may assist in identifying the ordinary meaning or confirm a meaning that seems clear from initial interpretation in only one language. If, however, comparison reveals a divergence in meaning, the first attempt at resolving the matter should use all applicable interpretative elements in articles 31 and 32. As the ILC put it: 'This presumption requires that every effort should be made to find a common meaning for the texts before preferring one to another...'.[38] Only if these fail does the need arise to adopt the meaning which best reconciles the texts, having regard to the object and purpose of the treaty.

Attention is sometimes drawn to the judgment of a Chamber of the ICJ in the *Elettronica Sicula* case, where it had been argued that there was a difference between 'immovable property or interests therein' and *'diritti reali'* in the equally authoritative texts of the 1948 Treaty of Friendship, Commerce and Navigation between the USA and Italy.[39] At issue was whether the American owners of shares in an Italian company had the necessary interest to receive protection when the relevant immovable property belonged to the Italian company. The Chamber noted that the English term had a wide scope (including, for example, future interests) and that, though there was a potential divergence, it was possible to interpret the English and Italian texts 'as meaning much the same thing'.[40]

While this is in line with the objective of finding a common meaning, too much should not be read into the particular case as the ICJ did not have to pursue this point to its conclusion, finding that the facts did not show any violation of the treaty. Rather greater precision would usually be required than finding a loosely similar meaning. The Appellate Body of the WTO, in *US—Softwood*

---

[36] (1991) 40 ICLQ 457, at 462–63.

[37] For a specific approach in the case of tax treaties, arguing that a comparison of authentic texts is particularly necessary in the case of tax treaties and giving background to some of the issues raised here, see R X Resch, 'Not in Good Faith—A Critique of the Vienna Convention Rule of Interpretation Concerning its Application to Plurilingual (Tax) Treaties' [2014] *British Tax Review* 307.

[38] [1966] *Yearbook of the ILC*, vol II, p 225, para 7, commentary on draft article 29, and see section 2 above.

[39] *Case Concerning Elettronica Sicula SpA (ELSI) (USA v Italy)* [1989] ICJ Reports 15; see also *Kasikili/Sedudu Island (Botswana/Namibia)* [1999] ICJ Reports 1045, at para 25 where, referring to article 33(3), the ICJ treated 'centre of the channel' and the German *'Thalweg'* as synonyms.

[40] [1989] ICJ Reports 15, at 79, para 132.

Lumber, concluded from the presumption that: 'It follows that the treaty interpreter should seek the meaning that gives effect, simultaneously, to all the terms of the treaty, as they are used in each authentic language.'[41] In that case, the general issue was whether conferring a right to harvest timber from stumps remaining in the ground amounted to provision of 'goods'. The Panel had used law dictionary definitions which suggested that an attribute of 'goods' was that they be movable. The Appeal Body noted, however, that the more general dictionary definition did not view goods as property and possessions that are necessarily movable. Further, the French term '*biens*' and the Spanish '*bienes*', which were in texts in equally authoritative languages, bore ordinary meanings which included a wide range of property, including immovable property. The Appellate Body observed that these corresponded more closely to a broad definition of 'goods', which they adopted.[42]

4.4 How many languages must be considered if there is a need to reconcile texts?

Once the presumption of conformity of meaning in different authentic languages has been rebutted by showing a potential difference of meaning between equivalent portions of the text in any two languages, how many languages need to be used to reach the correct interpretation? The obviously prudent course is to check all authoritative languages. However, in the *LaGrand* case the ICJ did not use all the available languages when setting out its analysis.[43] The Court had indicated by way of provisional measures under article 41 of its Statute that the USA should not execute a German national pending the final decision of the Court on issues relating to consular access. One of the German submissions at the later merits phase of the case was that the USA, by executing *LaGrand* contrary to the requirement of those provisional measures, was in breach of its international legal obligation to comply with the Court's order. The USA denied that an order indicating provisional measures created such an obligation.

In determining that its orders of provisional measures are mandatory for parties in a case before it, the Court only referred in its reasoning to the French and English texts of its Statute. It began by applying article 31(1) of the Vienna Convention. It noted that the relevant part of article 41 of its Statute provided that '*La Cour a le pouvoir d'indiquer . . . quelles mesures conservatoires . . . doivent être prises*' and that '*En attendant l'arrêt définitif, l'indication de ces mesures est immédiatement*

---

[41] *United States—Final Countervailing Duty Determination with Respect to Certain Softwood Lumber from Canada*, WT/DS257/AB/R (2004) p 22, para 59 (footnote omitted).

[42] WT/DS257/AB/R (2004), at paras 59–60; see also *European Communities—Conditions for the Granting of Tariff Preferences to Developing Countries*, WT/DS246/AB/R (2004), p 59, para 147, and *United States—Subsidies on Upland Cotton*, WT/DS267/AB/R (2005), p 159, para 424, (both decisions using French and Spanish for support in interpretation).

[43] *LaGrand Case (Germany v USA)* [2001] ICJ Reports 466, and see sections 4.1 above and 4.5 and 4.9 below.

notifiée…'. While *'indiquer'* and *'l'indication'* could be seen as neutral as to any mandatory character of the measures, *'doivent'* gave an imperative character to what was to be done. The comparable English words were: 'The Court shall have the power to *indicate…* any provisional measures which *ought* to be taken…' and that 'Pending the final decision, notice of the measures *suggested* shall forthwith be given…'.[44]

The Court referred to the assertions of the USA that use in the English version of 'indicate' instead of 'order', of 'ought' instead of 'must' or 'shall', and of 'suggested' instead of 'ordered', implied that decisions under article 41 lacked mandatory effect. However, while still at the stage of addressing the ordinary meaning of the terms used, the Court considered it might be argued 'having regard to the fact that in 1920 the French text was the original version, that such terms as "indicate" and "ought" have a meaning equivalent to "order" and "must" or "shall"'.[45] One may note in parenthesis that this observation depends for its factual basis on the preparatory work of the original version of the Statute and would thus come more appropriately under article 32 of the Vienna Convention (which the Court considered later in its judgment). In any event, the Court concluded that it was 'faced with two texts which are not in total harmony' and proceeded to apply article 33(4) of the Vienna Convention to reconcile the texts by reference to the object and purpose of the Statute.[46]

It may be wondered why the ICJ considered the provisions of its Statute only in French and English. As noted above, in its Memorial to the Court, Germany had set out the relevant provisions in Chinese, Russian, and Spanish as well, and had analysed the relevant words in all languages.[47] These reinforced the fact of divergence, showing further differences, at the very least of nuance. However, it may reasonably be concluded that any divergence between meaning in any two authentic languages displaces the presumption of uniformity and opens the door to finding the meaning by reconciliation of differences applying article 33(4) of the Vienna Convention. Here the Court simply kept to its own working languages, perhaps on the basis that these were sufficient to disclose 'incongruity' and were particularly appropriate for consideration in that the original Statute (that of the PCIJ) was in French and English.

Slightly different from a need to reconcile terms that could lead to differing interpretations when comparing authentic texts is the situation where one language is more strongly supportive of a particular interpretation than is another. This was the situation found by the ICJ in *Georgia v Russia* where an issue was whether an attempt to settle a dispute was a prerequisite to the Court's jurisdiction.[48]

---

[44] [2001] ICJ Reports 466, at 501–2, paras 99–100 (emphasis in original).
[45] [2001] ICJ Reports 466, at para 100.   [46] [2001] ICJ Reports 466, at para 101.
[47] See section 4.1 above.
[48] *Application of the International Convention on the Elimination of All Forms of Racial Discrimination (Georgia v Russian Federation) (Preliminary Objections)*, [2011] ICJ Reports 70, at 122, paras 123 ff; the reasoning found by looking at the variation of tenses in the different languages was supportive of the argument based on effectiveness, as to which see Chapter 5, sections 2.4.5 and 5.3.6 above.

The English phrase used the present tense to refer to a dispute 'which is not settled', while the French used the future perfect tense *'qui n'aura pas été réglé'*. The Court noted that use of the future perfect tense further reinforced the idea (which was contextually present in any event) that some previous action (an attempt to settle the dispute) must have taken place before another action (referral to the Court) could be pursued. The other three authentic of the treaty (Chinese, Russian, and Spanish) did not, the Court found, contradict this interpretation.[49]

4.5 Is the 'original' language of a treaty particularly significant for interpretation?

It has been suggested that:

The original language may of course prevail on account of its greater clarity, either because the other text represents a faulty translation or because particular phraseology is more meaningful in the language of the legal system in which it originated.[50]

However, the term 'original' when used in conjunction with the language of a treaty is not authoritatively defined in international law. It does, however, commonly appear in the final clauses or testimonium of a treaty to identify the authenticated text.[51] Treaties have sometimes specified a particular language as the one in which they were drawn up even if other languages are also authentic, though in recent times this is more likely to be in the context of how one or more additional languages are to be established so that they can be added as equally authentic.[52]

In a study of the interpretation of plurilingual treaties, Dr Hardy took the original language to be the one in which the text was actually first drafted, and then examined the possible significance of the original language for treaty interpretation.[53] However, while the ILC acknowledged the great value of Dr Hardy's study in this area, on this point it did not follow it.[54] This seems to have been because the ILC was keen to work from the principle of equal authority of each language when a treaty has been authenticated in two or more languages, joined with the presumption that terms of a treaty have the same meaning in each authentic text. In the scheme of article 33 of

---

[49] [2011] ICJ Reports 70, at 126, para 135.

[50] *Restatement (Third) Foreign Relations Law of the United States* (St Paul, Minn.: American Law Institute, 1987), para 325, reporters' note 2.

[51] See, eg, the Vienna Convention, article 85: 'The original of the present Convention, of which the Chinese, English, French, Russian and Spanish texts are equally authentic, shall be deposited with the Secretary-General of the United Nations.'

[52] See Hardy, 'The Interpretation of Plurilingual Treaties by International Courts and Tribunals' (1961) 37 BYBIL 72, at 98–99, and below.

[53] (1961) 37 BYBIL 72, at 98; in the ILC debates, Verdross suggested that if authentic texts proved irreconcilable, the language to be considered should be that in which the treaty had been drawn up [1966] *Yearbook of the ILC*, vol I, pt II, p 208, para 5; this solution, while having some attractions, would only work where it could be shown that a complete text was negotiated and drafted entirely from thoughts and proposals in a single language, which would not be the typical process for drawing up modern multilateral treaties.

[54] See debate in 874th Meeting, 21 June 1966 (1966) *Yearbook of the ILC*, vol I, pt II, pp 208–11, paras 5–34.

the Vienna Convention, in the case of divergence of meaning where a particular language is not specified as prevailing, paragraph (4) takes the interpreter to the preceding two articles. If the situation reaches the supplementary means of interpretation, and the conditions prescribed in article 32 are met, the interpreter is taken to the preparatory work and the circumstances of conclusion of the treaty. If these show that a particular language captured a manifestly intended meaning which one or more of the other languages failed to replicate, then that language assumes a significance by that route rather than by an assumption that the language of negotiation, or that in which the text was first drawn up, has some inherent priority.

It should be noted that the eventual absence from the Vienna rules of a provision referring to the original language of a treaty did not lead the ICJ to feel it should exclude mention of the original language of its Statute in *LaGrand:*

It might however be argued, having regard to the fact that in 1920 the French text was the original version, that such terms as 'indicate' and 'ought' have a meaning equivalent to 'order' and 'must' or 'shall'.[55]

There is, however, no certainty that the root of the divergence does not lie in the language originally used rather than the other authentic texts in which the treaty has been concluded.[56] Nor is it necessarily the case that a single language will have been the original for all parts of the treaty, and the source of a difficulty may be the switch from one language to another as appears to have been the case in *Litwa v Poland* (measures relating to 'drunkenness' subsequently formulated by reference to '*l'alcoolisme*').[57]

Although in the *LaGrand* case, the ICJ alluded to the original text being drafted in French, that was part of the argument for concluding that the two texts were not in harmony. The Court based its reconciliation of them on the object and purpose of its Statute. In *R (on the application of the Federation of Tour Operators and Others) v HM Treasury* the process was broadly in line with the rule in article 33(4) of the Vienna Convention, even if the route to the conclusion on that point was not very well mapped out.[58] In challenging the imposition of an air passenger duty, the claimants argued that the duty fell within the prohibition of 'fees, dues or other charges' in respect solely of the right of entry into or exit from a party's territory, a prohibition imposed by article 15 of the Convention on International Civil Aviation, Chicago, 1944.

The claimants asserted that the provision prohibited taxes as well as charges.[59] They relied, inter alia, on the equivalent texts in French ('*droits, taxes ou autres*

---

[55] *LaGrand Case (Germany v USA)* [2001] ICJ Reports 466, at 501–2, para 100.

[56] See observation of the Special Rapporteur (Waldock) 874th Meeting, 21 June 1966 [1966] *Yearbook of the ILC*, vol I, pt II, pp 210–11, para 33.

[57] See Chapter 1, section 5.1.

[58] [2007] EWHC 2062 (Admin), [2007] All ER (D) 18.

[59] The distinction was explained by reference to a resolution of the Council of the International Civil Aviation Organization stating that 'charges are levies to defray the costs of providing facilities and services for civil aviation while taxes are levies to raise general national and local government revenues that are applied for non-aviation purposes': [2007] EWHC 2062 (Admin), [2007] All ER (D) 18, at para 45.

redevances') and Spanish ('*derechos, impuestos u otros gravemenes*'). The court quoted and used the Vienna rules, hearing expert evidence that '*taxe*' in the French text was used in the strict sense of 'a compulsory levy of the same nature as a tax but intended to finance a particular public service and payable only by the users of the service', that had it been intended to denote a tax in the English sense, '*impôt*' would have been used (though it was accepted that '*taxe*' does often means 'tax'), and that in both the Spanish and the Russian texts words were used which unequivocally translated as 'taxes'.[60] Despite these indications of the ordinary meaning, charges of a similar kind to the air passenger duty had been levied around the world without breach of the Convention being established. In reaching an interpretation, therefore, the judge attached weight to this subsequent practice (as well as other interpretative factors). In relation to the issue of whether one language had priority, the testimonium of the Chicago Convention showed that its original language had been English, but not that English was to prevail:

DONE at Chicago the seventh day of December 1944, in the English language. A text drawn up in the English, French and Spanish languages, each of which shall be of equal authenticity, shall be open for signature at Washington, D.C. Both texts shall be deposited in the archives of the Government of the United States of America. . . .[61]

Authentic versions in French, Spanish, and Russian were added by Protocols of 1968 and 1977. With regard to the value to be attached to these languages, the judge stated that:

[Counsel for the defendants] was right to give some primacy to the English text, not because it is more authentic than the other texts, but because the travaux were in English, and reference to them necessarily involves reference to the English texts. Furthermore, the texts in the other languages are translations from the English, and could not have been intended to change the meaning of the English.[62]

It may be suggested that it should be the substance of the preparatory work, and the development and meaning of terms disclosed there, which attracts interpretative weight rather than the language of the records and the one to which they necessarily referred, but if (as seems quite clear in this instance) the texts in other languages were later translations, the conclusion that these were intended to reflect the same concept as the English original seems cogent. Nevertheless, a more general formulation of the approach of the Vienna rules on this issue is given in the Award in the *Young Loan* arbitration concerning the London Debt Agreement (LDA) 1953, whose final clauses stated that the agreement was in three original texts, in English, French, and German, all three texts being equally authoritative:

It may be directly inferred from the final clause of the LDA in conjunction with Article 33(1) of the [Vienna Convention] that the English text of the Agreement and the Annexes thereto carry no special interpretative weight merely because the Agreement was largely—and

---

[60] [2007] EWHC 2062 (Admin), [2007] All ER (D) 18, at para 52.
[61] Convention on International Civil Aviation, Chicago, 1944.
[62] [2007] EWHC 2062 (Admin), [2007] All ER (D) 18, at para 80.

undisputedly, as far as the disputed claim is concerned— drafted in that language and discussed in English by the committees concerned with it on the basis of English texts. The Tribunal takes the view that the habit occasionally found in earlier international practice of referring to the basic or original text as an aid to interpretation is now, as a general rule, incompatible with the principle, incorporated in Article 33(1) of the [Vienna Convention], of the equal status of all authentic texts in plurilingual treaties. The interpretational maxim of the special importance or precedence—whatever form it may take—of the original text would relegate the other authentic texts again to the status of subordinated translations.[63]

4.6 Translation of terms and legal concepts in different languages

Where a term in a treaty is of a kind which can be said to have a 'legal' or 'technical' meaning, a problem for an interpreter who is using a different language from one or more authoritative languages is whether the interpretative process reaches progressively beyond the ordinary meaning of the translated term to its conceptual meaning—that is, the meaning given to it within the relevant skill or field of activity—and then further still into the background of that skill or activity in the society in which the particular language is prevalent. The problem is in principle the same whether or not the interpreter is using, as a first resort, an authoritative text, a version of the treaty, or an official translation. Put more simply, if, for example, the issue is the meaning of a legal term, is the term to be investigated as a matter of the legal meaning in each language, or is an interpreter to consider how legal systems using the language would handle the problem in issue? Clearly if the context is specialist or technical, words in issue are to be interpreted in that context. But this does not make it clear whether a whole scheme, approach, or ethos of a legal system is to be enlisted to make good deficiencies in drafting or uncertainties of wording.

The best illustration of this is provided by cases applying the 'Warsaw Convention', a 1929 treaty which aimed to establish a uniform regime in relation to carriage by air, covering (among other things) liability for death or injury. The Warsaw Convention was concluded solely in French.[64] Courts in different jurisdictions have had to consider whether the Convention envisages compensation for 'mental injury' (used here to describe psychological harm, mental anguish, nervous shock, stress disorders, etc). Article 17 of the Convention provides:

Le transporteur est responsable du dommage survenu en cas de mort, de blessure ou de toute autre lésion corporelle subie par un voyageur lorsque l'accident qui a causé le dommage s'est produit à bord de l'aéronef...

---

[63] *Arbitral Tribunal for the Agreement on German External Debt ('Young Loan' case), (Belgium, France, Switzerland, UK and USA v Federal Republic of Germany)* 59 ILR 495, at para 17 (footnote omitted).

[64] Later amending Protocols used English and other languages as well as French, but provided that French was to prevail in the case of divergence. A revised Convention, concluded at Montreal in 1999, uses a whole panoply of languages. The various changes do not affect the issue considered here.

This was translated in the British Carriage by Air Act 1932 as:

The carrier is liable for damage sustained in the event of the death or wounding of a passenger or any bodily injury suffered by a passenger, if the accident which caused the damage so sustained took place on board the aircraft....

Two of the issues which arise are whether 'bodily injury' ('*lésion corporelle*') could include mental injury and, if so, whether there must be a causal link between the bodily injury and the mental injury. Among the many situations which have been considered are the cases where a passenger suffers nothing but mental anguish as a result of a near disaster, and the case of a passenger who suffers some physical injury but the contemporaneous mental injury is not directly related to the physical one. The former is the case where the aircraft is pulled out of a dive just at the last moment and the passenger suffers no physical harm but has suffered mentally from the expectation of an imminent crash; the latter is where in an emergency evacuation the passenger pinches or cuts a finger closing the seat table, suffers nothing else physically, but is subject to shock and consequent stress disorder from having to evacuate an aircraft which is about to explode. As French was the sole language of the Convention in its original form, the interpretative issue considered here is whether uncertainties over the meaning of 'damage sustained in the event of...any bodily injury' are to be resolved by looking at the ordinary meaning of the French words or investigating what meaning the whole apparatus of French law, or a French court, would give, or have given, to the terms.

Cases considering these issues have not generally invoked article 33 of the Vienna Convention, though there has been peripheral mention of the Vienna rules in some. This is not surprising as only in amended versions of the Warsaw Convention were other languages introduced, while French continued to prevail in the case of divergence. In principle, article 33(4) guides the interpreter towards application of articles 31 and 32 of the Vienna Convention. This would suggest that the ordinary meaning is the starting point, with practice, preparatory work, and other elements being considered as appropriate. Most courts considering bodily injury and issues of causation in Warsaw Convention cases have loosely followed this approach, or some elements of it, but US courts have taken the view in some cases that they should look to French legal concepts.[65] The latter approach is not necessarily ruled out by article 33(4) because recourse to the ordinary meaning can include a search among meanings appropriate to a particular subject.[66]

In *Eastern Airlines v Floyd*, where passengers had brought claims for mental distress when an aircraft's engines were restarted only moments before the aircraft

---

[65] The Warsaw Convention was proclaimed in French in the USA with an unofficial translation appended to the proclamation: see P S Bechky, 'Mismanagement and Misinterpretation: U.S. Judicial Implementation of the Warsaw Convention in Air Disaster Litigation' [1994–95] 60 *Journal of Air Law & Commerce* 455, at 477.

[66] See Chapter 5, section 3.3.2 above.

would have ditched in the ocean, the US Supreme Court undertook quite a detailed examination of French law:

We must consider the 'French legal meaning' of 'lésion corporelle' for guidance as to the shared expectations of the parties to the Convention because the Convention was drafted in French by continental jurists.[67]

While the underlying premise that the Convention was *solely* the product of continental jurists is open to question and qualification, the significant point here is that the use of French as the sole language for the treaty led the Court to investigate not just dictionary translations but the whole approach of the French legal system:

...In 1929, as in the present day, lawyers trained in French civil law would rely on the following principal sources of French law: (1) legislation, (2) judicial decisions, and (3) scholarly writing...Our review of these materials indicates neither that 'lésion corporelle' was a widely used legal term in French law nor that the term specifically encompassed psychic injuries...[68]

Noting that in 1929 France, unlike many other countries, permitted tort or delict recovery for mental distress, the Supreme Court nevertheless found that that *general* proposition of French law did not demonstrate that the *specific* phrase chosen by the negotiators covered purely psychic injury.[69] The Court also considered other interpretative factors very thoroughly and concluded that an air carrier could not be held liable under article 17 when an accident had not caused a passenger to suffer death, physical injury, or physical manifestation of injury. The Court expressed no view as to whether passengers could recover for mental injuries that are accompanied by physical injuries.

More recently in *Ehrlich v Eastern Airlines*, a US Court of Appeal had to consider whether there could be liability for mental injuries unrelated to physical injuries which the plaintiffs claimed to have suffered when an aircraft, having overshot the end of a runway, was abruptly halted by an arrestor bed shortly before it would have run into the sea.[70] Although physical injuries were alleged to have occurred during this incident and the subsequent emergency evacuation of the aircraft, the mental harm was not alleged to flow from those injuries but from the accident itself.

The Court investigated the French legal meaning of '*dommage survenu en cas de...lésion corporelle*'. Following *Floyd* it did not look to French law to discover when a party could *generally* recover compensation for a mental injury, but rather it sought guidance from French law on the narrow issue in the particular appeal. While the Court found French law in 1929 envisaged recovery for non-physical injury in certain circumstances causing grief, sentimental loss, etc ('*dommage moral*'), this was not an analogous case. No French case prior to 1929 had been produced to the Court in which a party was allowed to recover for their own mental injuries caused by fright or shock suffered during an accident where they did not flow from

---

[67] 499 US 530, at 536 (1991); see also see also *Air France v Saks* 470 US 392 (1985) and *El Al v Tseng* 525 US 155 (1999).
[68] 499 US 530, at 538.   [69] 499 US 530, at 539.
[70] 360 F. 3d. 366 (2004) (2nd Cir.).

physical injuries sustained by that same party.[71] Although some commentators had nevertheless suggested that French law did then permit such recovery, the Court was 'not persuaded that French jurists in 1929 would have read the phrase "dommage survenu en cas de... *lésion* corporelle" in a manner which would have held a carrier liable for a passenger's mental injury in the absence of a *causal relationship* between such pain and suffering and a physical injury'.[72]

Can these examples of very thorough investigation of French law as it was in 1929 be taken as indicators of how article 33 of the Vienna Convention is to be applied? The USA is not a party to the Vienna Convention and the principle applied by its courts of seeking the shared expectations of the parties may allow admission of a slightly wider-ranging investigation than envisaged by the Vienna rules and have different implications for the intertemporal law. Unfortunately, there is insufficient practice explicitly using the Vienna rules in similar circumstances to yield up firm guidance.

It seems reasonable to suggest, however, that the approach taken by some judges in the UK may prove more likely to be the one followed if closer application of the Vienna rules becomes established practice. Although a highly eclectic approach to the Vienna rules is still a feature of many English cases, a few useful pointers to their possible application can be found. In *King v Bristow Helicopters*[73] a helicopter came down onto a floating platform in the North Sea following engine failure. It was engulfed in smoke and seemed at risk of toppling into the sea. A passenger claimed he had suffered post-traumatic stress disorder which resulted in peptic ulcer disease. The House of Lords allowed the case to proceed on the basis that a peptic ulcer was a bodily consequence which could be brought on by mental effects of the accident. It regarded this as a sufficient causal link under the Convention. In another appeal heard at the same time, the House of Lords ruled that a victim of an assault on an aircraft, which had produced no bodily injury but resulted in a psychiatric illness, could not recover compensation under the Convention. Although one of the judges mentioned some of the elements of the Vienna rules *en passant*, they were not systematically applied.[74] However, Lord Steyn observed:

It follows from the scheme of the [Warsaw] Convention, and indeed from its very nature as an international trade law convention, that the basic concepts it employs to achieve its purpose are autonomous concepts. It is irrelevant what bodily injury means in other contexts in national legal systems. The correct inquiry is to determine the autonomous or independent meaning of 'bodily injury' in the Convention....[75]

---

[71] 360 F. 3d. 366 (2004) (2nd Cir.), at 380.

[72] 360 F. 3d. 366 (2004) (2nd Cir.), at 381 (original emphasis); many other points of analysis and strands of case law, including decisions of courts in other states parties to the Warsaw Convention, are set out in *Ehrlich* but do not relate to the point of treaty interpretation considered here.

[73] *King v Bristow Helicopters Ltd, Morris v KLM Royal Dutch Airlines* [2002] Lloyd's Rep 745.

[74] [2002] Lloyd's Rep 745, at 763, para 80, per Lord Hope.

[75] [2002] Lloyd's Rep 745, at 750, para 16; other judges used differing mixes of elements of treaty interpretation.

This approach, which seems in line with that of the Vienna rules, did not exclude investigation of the meaning of the relevant words in French or their relationship to the circumstances in which the Warsaw Convention was concluded.[76] Lord Steyn also took account of the practice in application of the Convention and comparison of its development through amendments with another transport convention also having a French text. In the Convention on International Carriage by Rail, the phrase '*toute autre atteinte a l'integrité corporelle*' was successively modified to read '*...l'integrité corporelle ou mentale*' and '*...l'integrité physique or [ou] psychique du voyageur*', showing that '*corporelle*' may not have been regarded by French draftsmen as sufficient to include mental harm.[77] The main difference between this and the approach of the US courts in their attitude to the Convention's French connections is that the House of Lords did not place so much stress on the French legal system's understanding of the terms as used in 1929. That could be one element of the interpretative process, but the approach of Lord Steyn brings a different perspective to the significance of the French language, viewing the matter as combining translation of words with understanding terms of a treaty which are subjected to interpretation in different jurisdictions, as well as to intermittent development through formal means of amendment or revision.

It is not so common for modern treaties to have such strong links with a single language, though it still occurs that a particular language may be specified as prevailing in the case of divergence.[78] However, the point made here is that an interpreter will need to decide how far it is necessary to pursue terms into the legal systems in which a particular language leads them (though this in itself may raise difficulties where a language is associated with different legal systems). There is no

---

[76] [2002] Lloyd's Rep 745, at 750–51.

[77] [2002] Lloyd's Rep 745, at 751–52; in contrast, the Montreal Conference 1999, accompanied its rather anaemic revision of the Warsaw Convention with a statement in the conference records, in keeping with that ethos: 'The expression "bodily injury" is included on the basis of the fact that in some States damages for mental injuries are recoverable under certain circumstances, that jurisprudence in this area is developing and that it is not intended to interfere with this development, having regard to jurisprudence in areas other than international carriage by air'; see M Mercer, 'Liability of Air Carriers for Mental Injury under the Warsaw Convention' (2003) XXVIII *Air & Space Law* 147, at 175.

[78] There is no inherent reason why parties should not formulate their own solutions. In some cases treaties have met the problem of divergent meanings in different languages by other means than giving a specified language prevalence: see examples of an extradition treaty requiring the interpretation most favourable to extradition and one commonly found in tax treaties, in D Shelton, 'Reconcilable Differences? The Interpretation of Multilingual Treaties' (1997) 20 *Hastings International and Comparative Law Review* 611, at 623; the provision in the OECD model double taxation agreement (that undefined terms are to be interpreted according to each party's own laws unless otherwise required by the context) has been the subject of extensive studies, some with particular emphasis on the Vienna rules: see, eg, J Avery Jones, 'The Interpretation of Tax Treaties with Particular Reference to Article 3(2) of the OECD Model' [1984] *British Tax Review* 14–54 and 90–108, and F Engelen, *Interpretation of Tax Treaties under International Law* (Amsterdam: IBFD Publications BV, 2004), chapter 10, section 10.10.

hard and fast rule which can be offered, but the best guide will probably be the context, supported if appropriate by the preparatory work.[79]

Courts may also have to consider whether they are being asked to give a 'special meaning' to a term when applying the first stage of reconciliation under article 33(4) of the Vienna Convention. As that stage involves applying the general rule in article 31, the investigation should look to whether there was manifestly an intent to give a term a special meaning. Although of the judges in *Fothergill v Monarch Airlines* only Lord Diplock looked closely at the Vienna rules, on this point Lord Wilberforce considered the difficulty of selecting between the ordinary and special meanings of a French term.[80] The issue was whether loss of contents of a traveller's suitcase came within the meaning of 'damage' which was a translation from the French text's '*avarie*', the latter prevailing if there was divergence. Lord Wilberforce said:

> ...the word 'avarie' would not I think convey a clear meaning to an English mind without assistance...for 'avarie' is, or may be, a term of art. There were five dictionaries involved, of evidently different standards: some of English publication, others of French. I regard the latter, which provide an analysis, as of greater value than the former, which provide a translation—since then we have to interpret the translation...They seem to me to show that 'avarie' has both an ordinary meaning and a special meaning as a term of maritime law. In the ordinary meaning, the word signifies physical damage to a movable; in its special meaning, it is capable of meaning physical damage, or loss, including partial loss. In my opinion this does not carry the matter much beyond the English text: both use words of some ambiguity; perhaps the French text points somewhat more in the direction of partial loss than does the English...An attempt was made to carry the argument from the French text further by suggesting that 'avarie' means 'average' and 'average' means partial loss. But I cannot accept that it is sound, in effect, to retranslate 'avarie' by 'average' when in fact it is translated by 'damage.' Clearly 'average' could not be sensibly inserted in the English text in replacement for 'damage.' Nor am I persuaded that 'average,' though it may have to do with partial loss, means partial loss.[81]

Looking at this in the light of the requirement in article 31(4) of the Vienna Convention that if any special meaning is to be adopted it must be shown that the parties intended it, it seems clear that any reconciliation of differences of meaning in different languages must respect that requirement too. Hence a technical meaning should not be adopted from one language, even if it appears to have been the 'source' language, unless there is cogent other evidence that that was what was intended.[82] Essentially, however, the underlying difference is between seeing the aim of interpretation as being to find an autonomous meaning of terms in a treaty and a more specific quest for original intent. The Vienna rules tend strongly towards the former, the latter being accorded only appropriate weight when identified in the ways envisaged by the rules.

---

[79] See also the *Öztürk* case before the ECtHR, Chapter 5, section 3.3.8 above and further examples given there.
[80] [1981] AC 251.   [81] [1981] AC 251, at 274.
[82] See sections 4.5 above and 4.10 below.

4.7 Reconciliation where one or more texts are clear but another is ambiguous

The ILC did not retain from its first draft articles the principle that where two or more authentic languages could produce different meanings, a meaning common to both or all should prevail. Nor did it retain the specific provision that the ordinary meaning of a term in one authentic text if clear and compatible with the objects and purposes of the treaty should be preferred over that in another language if uncertain there owing to the ambiguity or obscurity of the term.[83] However, the requirement in article 33(4) to achieve a meaning which best reconciles the texts, having regard to the object and purpose of the treaty, does not exclude the possibility of concluding that the meaning which is clear in one of the texts is the correct one.[84]

Thus in *Nicaragua v Honduras* the ICJ dismissed argument based on a possible ambiguity in the French text of article XXXII of the Pact of Bogotá in favour of an interpretation which was more in line with the ordinary meaning and construction of the provision and consistent with it in Spanish, English, and Portuguese.[85] That article provided for compulsory jurisdiction of the ICJ but only if conciliation under the Pact had failed. One issue in this case was whether article XXXII was linked with the article preceding it. That was a provision formulated as a general acceptance by the parties to the Pact of the compulsory jurisdiction of the ICJ over disputes between them very much in terms following article 36(2) of the Statute of the ICJ (the 'optional clause'). Honduras contended that the two provisions were linked together so that the Court lacked jurisdiction over its dispute with Nicaragua because there had been no attempt at conciliation.

The Court rejected this, finding that each provision set out an autonomous basis for its jurisdiction. Article XXXII made no reference to article XXXI. Its terms did not suggest a link, but there was one qualification regarding the French text of article XXXII, which stated that in the prescribed circumstances, the party had '*le droit de porter la question devant la Cour*'. This could have been read as referring back to a question which was the subject of a dispute referred to the Court under article XXXI. The Court observed, however, that the word 'question' left room for uncertainty, in contrast with '*differend* (dispute)', which was used in article XXXI and would have been perfectly clear. Nevertheless, the ordinary meaning of the text of article XXXII was clear and the provisions in other languages referring to

---

[83] See section 2 above.
[84] Cf *Elettronica Sicula SpA (ELSI) (USA v Italy)* [1989] ICJ Reports 15, at 70–71, para 118, where the ICJ was invited by Italy to apply article 33(4) of the Vienna Convention as embodying the restrictive approach to interpretation so that the reference in the Italian text of the relevant treaty to '*diritti*' (rights) should be preferred to the reference to 'interests' in the English text, the former being narrower than the latter; the Court found that the facts made it unnecessary to decide this issue; and see section 4.3 above.
[85] *Border and Transborder Armed Actions (Nicaragua v Honduras)* [1988] ICJ Reports 69.

the entitlement to have recourse to the Court indicated that the conclusion that the two articles were linked would not be justified.[86]

Another example, though pre-dating the Vienna Convention, is in the judgment of the ECtHR in *Wemhoff v Germany*.[87] The applicant had alleged that the length of his detention on remand violated his right to 'trial within a reasonable time or to release pending trial' (article 5(3) of the European Convention on Human Rights). One issue was whether the reasonable time ran until the start of trial or until judgment. The Court rejected the interpretation maintained by the German government that it was the time of appearance before the trial court that marked the end of the period with which article 5(3) was concerned. The Court accepted that the English text of the Convention allowed such an interpretation, but considered that the word 'trial' could equally refer to the whole of the proceedings before the court, not just their beginning. But while the English text admitted two interpretations, the French text (of equal authority) allowed only one. According to it, the obligation to release an accused person within a reasonable time continued until that person has been '*jugée*'—that is, until the day of the judgment that terminates the trial. Confronted with two versions of a treaty which are equally authoritative but not exactly the same, the Court followed what it saw as established international law precedents, interpreting them in a way that would reconcile them as far as possible. The Court explicitly recognized that it was necessary to seek the interpretation that was most appropriate in order to realize the aim and achieve the object of the treaty. The Court found it impossible to see why the protection against unduly long detention on remand which article 5 seeks to ensure for persons suspected of offences should not continue up to delivery of judgment rather than cease at the moment the trial opens.

In the US case *Busby v State of Alaska*[88] article 33 of the Vienna Convention was explored and applied as customary law, the USA not being a party to the Vienna Convention. Busby, a former resident of Alaska had his driving licence revoked there. He acquired an international driving permit in Nicaragua. He was later prosecuted in Alaska for driving there while his licence was revoked. The law of Alaska defined a driver's licence to include the privilege to drive whether or not the person concerned held a valid licence there or issued in another jurisdiction.[89] Busby argued that he could nevertheless rely on his international permit in conjunction with the UN Convention on Road Traffic,[90] one argument being that his Alaskan permit had not been physically confiscated before he drove on the occasion when he was apprehended.

The English text of article 24(5) of the UN Convention recognized the right of a subdivision of a party to withdraw the right to use an international permit on the basis of non-discriminatory application of local law to such effect, indicating that the authority 'withdrawing the use of the permit may withdraw and retain the

---

[86] [1988] ICJ Reports 69, at 89, para 45.

[87] Judgment of 27 June 1968, Series A no 7, p 23.

[88] 40 P 3d 807 (Alaska Ct App, 2002).   [89] 40 P 3d 807, at 812.

[90] Convention on Road Traffic, Geneva, 1949 [1955] ATS 2.

permit until the period of the withdrawal of use expires or until the holder leaves the territory of that Contracting State'. That the English text used 'withdraw' in connection with both use of the international permit and its physical possession could have suggested that the two withdrawals had to run together. In contrast, the equally authoritative French text used '*retirer*' for withdrawing the right to drive and '*pourra se faire remettre le permis*' for requiring surrender of the international permit. Relying on the presumption in article 33(3) of the Vienna Convention that the two languages are to produce the same meaning, the court accepted the guidance given by the structure and language of the provision in French. The court also saw this reconciliation as mandated by the objective and purpose of the Convention which (in allowing parties to maintain domestic withdrawal of the right to drive) could not have encompassed the possibility of drivers obtaining new international permits 'and then play a game of "cat and mouse" with countries that had previously suspended their license'.[91]

More complex is the case where there are inconsistencies in the terminology used in equally authentic languages. A good example of this in the *Rhine Chlorides* case.[92] The Protocol in issue was authentic in French, German, and Dutch. The Tribunal noted a succession of inconsistencies and discrepancies among the terms used in the different languages.[93] While the Tribunal considered these carefully, it did not identify one particular language as revealing the proper interpretation. Instead, it built up an interpretation reflecting the position that the terms in the different languages had not been sufficiently precisely used to enable it to depart from the meaning which the text conveyed through application of all the relevant rules.[94]

There were somewhat similar difficulties arising from the way questions were framed for an Advisory Opinion of The Seabed Disputes Chamber of the International Tribunal for the Law of the Sea.[95] This perhaps required not so much a reconciliation of the differing languages but analysis of their use of terms to describe quite different concepts. The distinction was between 'responsibility' meaning to have an obligation ('responsibility to ensure') and 'responsibility' meaning liability ('responsibility and liability for damage'). The former sense emerged from the context relating to a particular provision as stated in English, as well as from the expressions in other languages, which were not direct verbal equivalents. Thus, for example, 'States are responsible for the fulfilment...' has a sense of stating an obligation rather than a liability when contrasted with other provisions in the treaty referring specifically to liability. That meaning was confirmed by the other languages used for the treaty, such as the French '*il incombe de*', which denoted an obligation incumbent on a party. Hence the Chamber was

---

[91] 40 P 3d 807, at 815.

[92] *Case Concerning the Auditing of Accounts (Netherlands v France)*, Arbitral Award of 12 March 2004, 144 ILR 259; for an account of this case, see Chapter 1, section 5.2 above.

[93] 144 ILR 259, at 304, para 89 ff,

[94] Some of the terms in issue are in the account given in Chapter 1, section 5.2 above.

[95] *Responsibilities and Obligations of States Sponsoring Persons and Entities with respect to Activities in the Area* (Advisory Opinion) (2011) ITLOS Case No 17, paras 64–71.

able by such comparisons to identify those questions which went to identifying obligations and the one which went to the measure of liability.[96]

Perhaps the sternest test of the Vienna provision on reconciling differing languages arose in *Kiliç v Turkmenistan*.[97] As is so often the case, there were complicating factors in that there was a preliminary issue of identifying which texts were authentic and there were particular problems of working with different translations of crucial wording. Effectively, the issue was whether the bilateral treaty in issue required a claimant to have taken steps towards achieving a domestic remedy. The tribunal was faced with a discrepancy over authentic languages in that in Russian there was a reference (as translated) to two authentic copies in the Turkish, Turkmen, English, and Russian languages, while in English there were stated to be two authentic copies in only English and Russian. No texts signed by the parties were produced in Turkish and Turkmen, although there was an 'official' Turkish language text, that is a Turkish version of the bilateral investment treaty (BIT) published in Turkey's Official Gazette.

The authentic text in English was, in the polite terms of the tribunal, 'grammatically incorrect' and 'inelegant'.[98] It could equally be said to deficient in its syntax. It stated that a dispute 'can be submitted, as the investor may choose' to one of three specified tribunals:

provided that, if the investor concerned has brought the dispute before the courts of justice of the Party that is a party to the dispute and a final award has not been rendered within one year.[99]

The equally authentic text in Russian, as at first translated into English for the case, worded the proviso as:

on the condition that, if the concerned investor submitted the conflict to the court of the Party, that is a Party to the conflict, and a final arbitral award on compensation of damages has not been rendered within one year.[100]

A later translation from the Russian 'made sense' of the provision by eliminating the word 'if' so that the proviso clearly contained a requirement to submit the case to the domestic court first:

… on the condition that the concerned investor submitted the conflict to the court of the Party, that is a Party to the conflict, and a final arbitral award on compensation of damages has not been rendered within one year.[101]

The explanation for this changed translation was that the first translation was:

… a literal translation of the words in Russian in the order in which they appear in the Russian text. However, it does not accurately reflect the meaning of the Russian version of

---

[96] (2011) ITLOS Case No 17, paras 69–71.

[97] ICSID Case No. ARB/10/1, Decision of 7 May 2012 on Article VII.2 of the Turkey–Turkmenistan Bilateral Investment Treaty, 1997; the Award of 2 July 2013 did not affect the language issues discussed here; cf contrary interpretation in *Muhammet Çap v Turkmenistan* ICSID Case No. ARB/12/6, 13 February 2015.

[98] Decision of May 2012, para 9.14.   [99] Decision of May 2012, para 2.10.

[100] Decision of May 2012, para 2.11.   [101] Decision of May 2012, para 4.19 *ad fin.*

this segment of Article VII.2 of the BIT ... This is because the phrase '... [Russian text] ...', which literally reads word-by-word in Russian '... on the condition that, if' is used in order to make the sentence conditional but should correctly be translated as '... on the condition that' to properly convey the meaning. The 'if' in the Russian text is part of the correct syntax needed in Russian to create the conditional, but it does not create a second or separate conditional. In fact, the complete phrase '... [Russian text] ...' is used in Russian as a single expression to mean 'on the condition that' or 'if'.'[102]

It seems, therefore, that the Russian usage goes one step further than the unnecessarily portentous 'in the event that' which is so commonly used as a substitute for 'if'. The Russian usage, however, combines the two (if correctly explained). The Turkish official text (translated into English) essentially matched the second Russian translation (making reference to a domestic court a precondition).

The evidence at the hearing of the issues over the authentic text and the meaning and effect of the jurisdiction provision can, at its most favourable, best be described as unsatisfactory. Put simply, and not in terms used in the award, it seems that the Russian text could be made clear by 'proper' translation, while the English text was syntactically hopeless. A core issue was whether proper translation involves interpretation. The tribunal stated that it considered 'it to be necessary and proper for a translation to convey accurately the complete sense of the Russian text when it is translated into English.'[103]

The Tribunal concluded that attempting to interpret the relevant English text in accordance with article 31 of the Vienna Convention left its meaning ambiguous or obscure. Looking to the circumstances of conclusion as a supplementary means of interpretation, the tribunal found an authentic Turkish text of a Turkey–Kazakhstan BIT negotiated at about the same time, which followed the second Russian sense of the Turkey–Turkmenistan BIT. Thus in all languages except the English text of the latter treaty, first recourse to the local courts was mandatory.

The Tribunal found these circumstances sufficient to adopt the interpretation that such prior recourse to local courts was mandatory. Had it been necessary to follow article 31(4) of the Vienna Convention, the Tribunal concluded, the ambiguity of the English text could only be reconciled with the clearly mandatory outcome in the explained Russian text by a determination that the English formula also required a mandatory recourse to the local courts on the basis that 'what is plainly mandatory cannot be optional, but what may either be mandatory or optional, can be seen as mandatory'.[104] In other words, because the best that could be extracted from the English wording was that domestic recourse was either optional or mandatory, since the Russian could only mean the latter, the Tribunal should endorse that meaning as the only one compatible with both languages.

---

[102] Decision of May 2012, para 4.20.   [103] Decision of May 2012, para 8.8.
[104] Decision of May 2012, para 9.23 (original punctuation).

4.8 Different punctuation in different languages

Where equally authentic texts in different languages have different punctuation, or a different syntax in the interaction between punctuation and words, can this guide the interpreter? What is ambiguous in one language may be made clear in another by reference to punctuation. Unfortunately, this is usually a remote hope. Quite apart from the variability of punctuation practices in different languages, even in relation to a single language punctuation rules may not be sufficiently recognized as having a particular effect.

An example of such differences is provided by the facts in *Corocraft v Pan American Airways*, although the case pre-dated the Vienna rules and would not, in the event, have been readily resolved by application of article 33.[105] That case was yet another which concerned provisions in the Warsaw Convention relating to uniform rules for international carriage by air, in this case carriage of cargo. The Convention included rules relating to documents of carriage, to some extent comparable to documents used in carriage by sea, and a regime of liability with limitations on compensation depending on weight of the cargo. The Convention made mandatory inclusion of certain information in an 'air consignment note'. Failure to include the required particulars would result in the airline losing its right to limit its liability. The Convention was solely authentic in French. Article 8(i) required the document of carriage to state: '*le poids, la quantité, le volume ou les dimensions de la marchandise*'. This was translated in the implementing UK statute as: 'the weight, the quantity and the volume or dimensions of the goods'.[106] The question was whether the authoritative French text produced what was described as a 'choice' as opposed to an 'accumulation'.[107] In other words, was it 'one out of four' or 'three out of four'? Experts in the French language disagreed, which led the judge at first instance to remark in continuation of the quotation at the head of this chapter:

The conclusion which I have reached is that in French, as in English, it is possible to write with a precision which permits of only one possible construction, but that, in the absence of such precision, subject-matter and context carry great weight and, in particular, permit a comma to be construed conjunctively when the strict application of grammatical rules might dictate a disjunctive construction. Similar considerations apply to the word 'ou.' The interesting problem of the true nature of an invitation by an airline operator to fly to 'London, Brussels, Rome or Paris' and to partake *en route* of a meal consisting of 'corn flakes, egg, tea or coffee'—to take an example explored in evidence—is not difficult of solution, even if it may involve some criticism both of the airline's use of English and of its catering.[108]

The conclusion of the judge at first instance depended in part on his appreciation of another part of the treaty where there was a similar list of requirements set

---

[105] [1969] 1 QB 616; and on punctuation generally, see Chapter 5, section 4.2.6 above.
[106] Schedule to Carriage by Air Act 1932.   [107] [1969] 1 QB 616, at 632.
[108] [1969] 1 QB 616, at 633.

out in the French version in the same manner. This had been interpreted in almost all jurisdictions as meaning three out of four elements were required. This aspect of the context and practice were elements which carried considerable weight with the judge in his decision that the English statutory version reflected the correct interpretation. However, the Court of Appeal reversed this on the basis that, the French text of the provision being ambiguous, it should be interpreted so as to make good commercial sense. It considered that the weight was usually the key factor (in most cases determining the freight charges as well as the limitation of compensation), and the volume or dimensions did not need to be stated except when one or other might be necessary or useful.

Had this been a case decided by applying the Vienna rules, it seems that the approach of the judge at first instance, which gave more weight to the contextual arguments as well as practice in implementation of the Convention to the extent that it was concordant, would be more in line with the Vienna rules. The Court of Appeal did consider practice in a more restricted way but introduced the test of commercial good sense without showing that this was mandated by text, context, concordant practice, or preparatory work. Although the case shows how problems of punctuation could reveal differences of understanding between languages, in the instant case it would not have been a matter for application of article 33(4) of the Vienna rules because the English language was only used in an official translation, not an authoritative version of the text. Hence, while the English Statute's clarification of the punctuation and syntax shows the legislature's imprimatur for the understanding of one party to the treaty, that would not resolve the ambiguity of the authoritative text, unless the clarification had come to reflect the general practice of the parties to be taken into account under article 31(3)(b) of the Vienna Convention.

A reluctance to attach significance to a difference in punctuation of the text of a treaty in different authoritative languages was shown in the WTO Appellate Body's Report on *US—Measures Affecting Gambling*.[109] One issue was whether a limitation imposed in US law, a limitation which could be construed as resulting in a zero quota, fell within the undertaking of parties to the General Agreement on Trade in Services not to adopt or maintain certain measures unless otherwise specified in a schedule submitted by the particular party. The prohibited measures were described as:

…limitations on the total number of service operations or on the total quantity of service output expressed in terms of designated numerical units in the form of quotas or the requirement of an economic needs test.[110]

The French and Spanish texts had a comma between the phrases equivalent to 'terms of designated numerical units' and 'in the form of quotas'. The USA asserted

---

[109] *United States—Measures Affecting the Cross-Border Supply of Gambling and Betting Services* WTO Appellate Body Report of 7 April 2005, WT/DS285/AB/R.
[110] Article XVI (2) (c).

that the WTO Panel (against whose Report it was appealing) had read over into the English text the commas present in the French and Spanish, resulting in identification of three types of limitations in subparagraph (c) when, properly interpreted, there were only two, neither of which covered the US measures.

The Appellate Body did not think it useful to make 'a careful dissection of the use of commas' within the grammatical structure of each language. It found all three languages grammatically ambiguous. All three could be read as identifying either two or three limitations on the total number of service operations or on the total quantity of service output. The Appellate Body preferred to look to the language of the provision which showed, in its first part, that the target of the limitations covered by the provision was twofold—that is limitations on the number of service operations and on the quantity of service output, both being quantitative in nature. The second part of the provision, in providing detail of the type of limitations covered, modified the first part. This applied differently to the two elements of the first part in that, for example, the term 'numerical units' would be more naturally used to refer to 'output' than to 'operations'. The Appellate Body saw scope for overlap among the elements of the provision—that is between limitations on the number of service operations and limitations on the quantity of service output, or between limitations in the form of quotas and limitations in the form of an economic needs test. It concluded that the limitations which were covered could not be viewed as taking a single form; nor were they to be constrained in a formulaic manner. Hence even if subparagraph (c) were to be read as referring to only two types of limitations, it did not follow that it would not catch a measure equivalent to a zero quota.[111]

Clearly such analysis of the substance of provisions in their context (and, as in this case coupled with further consideration of the rest of the treaty and its preparatory work) is likely to provide a better basis for treaty interpretation than differences in punctuation.[112]

4.9 Reconciliation of language differences by reference to object and purpose

Where a difference of meaning falls to be resolved under article 33(4) of the Vienna Convention, the presupposition is that no language has been identified as the one to prevail in such circumstances and the differences in meaning among the languages cannot be removed by the application of articles 31 and 32. Inherent in the idea of reconciliation, coupled with the premise that no single language prevails in the face of equally authentic texts, is the implication that this is not a matter of selecting one or several languages that are to be taken as expressing the meaning correctly, but rather,

---

[111] WTO Appellate Body Report of 7 April 2005, WT/DS285/AB/R, at paras 242–52.

[112] See, however, the significance of a comma in the Nuremberg Charter, considered in Chapter 5, section 4.2.6 above.

that an interpretative outcome is to be found which respects the different languages but extracts from the treaty the best reconciliation of the differences. This is easier said than done, and the case law suggests that selection of the meaning from one of the different languages may be what happens in practice if there is no *via media*. Further, the ILC appears to have recognized that once every effort had been made to find a common meaning, the next step might be to prefer one text to another.[113]

In the *Chile—Price Band System* case, the Appellate Body at the WTO emphasized the significance of the term 'reconcile' in article 33(4) of the Vienna Convention.[114] In interpreting the phrase 'ordinary customs duties' in the two relevant treaties, the Panel had detected a difference between these words and those in the French and Spanish authentic texts.[115] The Panel had characterized the English phrase as having an empirical character, the French and Spanish as normative. Disagreeing with the Panel's conclusions that a normative connotation required exclusion of what the Panel described as 'exogenous' factors (such as world market prices) from the basis for a WTO member's levy of customs duties, the Appellate Body stated:

…the Panel came to this conclusion by interpreting the French and Spanish versions of the term 'ordinary customs duty' to mean something *different* from the ordinary meaning of the English version of that term. It is difficult to see how, in doing so, the Panel took into account the rule of interpretation codified in Article 33(4) of the Vienna Convention whereby 'when a comparison of the authentic texts discloses a difference of meaning…, the meaning which best *reconciles* the texts…shall be adopted.'[116]

Unfortunately, the Appellate Body did not have to explore further what reconciliation actually demands. The applicability of the phrase 'ordinary customs duties' was only in issue in a supporting argument. Having found the Panel wrong in requiring exclusion of exogenous factors, the Appellate Body was able simply to reverse the Panel on this point, while noting that this did not affect its view on the main issue.[117]

A contrasting explanation of reconciliation is suggested in the *Young Loan* arbitration.[118] The Agreement on German External Debts, London, 1953 (LDA) established a scheme for repayment of certain debts. Protection for creditors against changes in currency values was given by requiring payments to be made in 'the least

---

[113] See section 4.3 above.

[114] *Chile—Price Band System and Safeguard Measures Relating to Certain Agricultural Products*, AB-2002-2 (2002) WT/DS207/AB/R, at para 271.

[115] These phrases were '*droits de douane proprement dits*' and '*derechos de aduana propiamente dichos*'. The Panel had reasoned that: 'The dictionary meaning of "ordinary" is "occurring in regular custom or practice", "of common or everyday occurrence, frequent, abundant", "of the usual kind, not singular or exceptional, commonplace, mundane". "*Propiamente dicho*" has been translated as "true (something)" or "(something)" "in the strict sense". "*Proprement dit*" has been explained as "*au sens exact et restreint, au sens propre*" and "*stricto sensu*".' AB-2002-2 (2002) WT/DS207/AB/R, at para 265, note 243.

[116] AB-2002-2 (2002) WT/DS207/AB/R, at para 271 (emphasis added).

[117] AB-2002-2 (2002) WT/DS207/AB/R, at paras 278–80.

[118] *Arbitral Tribunal for the Agreement on German External Debt* ('*Young Loan*' case) (*Belgium, France, Switzerland, UK and USA v Federal Republic of Germany*) 59 ILR 495.

depreciated currency' of those specified. Equally authoritative texts expressed this
as '*Währung mit der geringsten Abwertung*' and '*devise la moins dépréciée*'.[119] When
the German mark was revalued to a higher level in the international monetary
system, the issue was whether this phrase covered that situation, or only applied
in selecting among currencies when one or more had been lowered in value (this
being in a time of formal fixed parities).

The Tribunal found that '*Abwertung*' was relatively clear in technical language,
meaning reduction in the external value of a currency by an act of government,
although in everyday usage '*formelle Abwertung*' would tend to be used to describe
devaluation by governmental act in contrast to the economic phenomenon of
depreciation of a currency.[120] The English and French phrases would normally
describe the economic phenomenon of depreciation, 'devaluation' or '*dévaluation*'
being the term for formal or governmental lowering of value.[121] If one currency
was adjusted upwards in value, others could be seen to have 'depreciated' in value
against it. But if the treaty only contemplated the case of a formal devaluation of a
currency in relation to gold or the dollar in the Bretton Woods system, it did not
mean that selection of the currency was to take into account a revaluation of a currency that had appreciated. Faced with these terms, the Tribunal carefully applied
the rules in the articles 31 and 32 of the Vienna Convention, including in particular the context and the object and purpose of the treaty, finding that the provision
was limited to devaluation and did not contemplate revaluation.

Having resolved the interpretation by application of the general rule, and confirmed this by reference to the preparatory work, the Tribunal found that any possible discrepancy between the texts would be resolved by reference to the object
and purpose of the treaty:

The repeated reference by Article 33(4) of the VCT [Vienna Convention] to the 'object and
purpose' of the treaty means in effect nothing else that that any person having to interpret a
plurilingual international treaty has the opportunity of resolving any divergence in the texts
which persists, after the principles of Articles 31 and 32 of the VCT have been applied,
by opting, for a final interpretation, for one or the other text which in his opinion most
closely approaches the 'object and purpose' of the treaty. Application of Article 33(4) of the
VCT to the case under decision means that the Arbitral Tribunal has the right—and the
duty—to adopt that interpretation of the clause in dispute which most closely approaches
the object and purpose of the LDA.

In deciding which text is to be granted priority, certain of the traditional principles
of treaty interpretation, which apply when the texts of plurilingual international treaties
diverge irreconcilably, offer no help having regard to the unambiguous wording of Article
33(4) of the VCT in this respect....[122]

The indication here that this phase of the interpretative exercise involves granting one text priority seems at first at odds with the requirement of article 33(4) to
reconcile the texts and, in doing so, to have regard to the object and purpose of the

---

[119] 59 ILR 495, at 529–30, para 15.   [120] 59 ILR 495, at 530–31, para 18.
[121] 59 ILR 495, at 530–31, para 18.   [122] 59 ILR 495, at 548–49, paras 39–40.

treaty. However, the award does state that it is considering the case of texts which diverge 'irreconcilably', so that no reconciliation is possible. In practice, the likelihood is that if interpretation is the subject of litigation, the divergence will be significant and the interpretation urged by one or other party based on their favoured text will have to be selected. Hence in the reference in article 33(4) to a meaning which best 'reconciles' the texts, reconciliation may well result in more weight being attached to a particular language or in that one appearing to be selected in the final outcome. It can be seen, however, in the *Young Loan* case that the English and French words were wide enough to include the meaning attributed to the German text. So there was in fact a reconciliation in the sense of a meaning being found which was within the range of possibilities in all three languages, even if the Tribunal seems to have viewed this as in some sense selecting the meaning of the German text as that most closely approaching the object and purpose of the treaty.

The Vienna Convention only requires the interpreter, when adopting a meaning which best reconciles the texts, to have regard to the object and purpose of the treaty. It may reasonably be understood that the 'best' reconciliation could involve taking account of other factors provided that regard is had to the object and purpose. However, the explicit reference to object and purpose, and the silence as to any other means of achieving reconciliation, puts the object and purpose in pole position. This was recognized by the Tribunal in the *Young Loan* case. The Tribunal rejected traditional principles as ruled out by the express reference in article 33(4) to the object and purpose, thus eliminating selection of the clearest text, the 'lowest common denominator', and the *contra proferentem* rule.[123]

In the *LaGrand* case, the ICJ took the object and purpose of the Statute as the central means of reconciliation of the apparent divergences between the French and English texts.[124] However, in reaching its consideration of that element of interpretation, the Court noted that in line with article 111 of the Charter of the UN, the French and English texts of the Statute were equally authentic. Neither Charter nor Statute indicated how to proceed in cases of divergence, nor had the parties made any agreement on this. This observation satisfied the Court that the proviso of article 33(1) of the Vienna Convention ('unless the treaty provides or the parties agree that…a particular text shall prevail') did not come into play. However, the Court does not appear to have quite followed the sequence which leads through to using the object and purpose to achieve reconciliation. Article 33(4) envisages such use of object and purpose 'when a comparison of the authentic texts discloses a difference of meaning which the application of Articles 31 and 32 does not remove'. The Court did first approach the languages issue by applying article 31; but it only applied article 32, by looking at the preparatory work, *after* applying article 33(4).[125]

---

[123] 59 ILR 495, at 549–50, paras 40–42.

[124] For the relevant issues and citation of this case, see sections 4.1, 4.4, and 4.5 above.

[125] In an earlier case, one ICJ judge noted that article 33(4) could not be used to produce 'any solution which seeks to give a special meaning to the French text, which meaning cannot be collected from the Chinese, the English, the Russian and the Spanish': see Separate Opinion of Judge Jennings

In applying article 33(4), the Court linked object and purpose with context—more in the manner suggested by article 31(1). The Court saw the object and purpose of the Statute as being to enable the Court to fulfil the functions in the Statute and the basic function of judicial settlement of international disputes by binding decisions. The context in which the powers in the Statute to order provisional measures was conferred was ensuring that the Court was not hampered in the exercise of its functions by the respective rights of the parties, a dispute not being preserved. These elements combined to produce the conclusion that provisional measures had to be binding.[126]

4.10 Using preparatory work in reconciling differences between languages

May preparatory work (and other supplementary means of interpretation) be used in the process of reconciliation of differences of meaning in different languages? The short answer is that such use is virtually inevitable and is also sensible. The *LaGrand* case, which has had the leading role in this chapter as the one in which the ICJ expressly applied article 33 of the Vienna Convention, attests to this. Although the Vienna rules were not mentioned in the ICJ's earlier judgment in the jurisdiction phase of *Nicaragua v USA*, the preparatory work of its Statute also featured there.[127]

Nicaragua had deposited a declaration accepting the jurisdiction of the PCIJ at the same time as signing the Statute of the PCIJ and related Protocol, both subject to ratification. Ratification of the Statute and Protocol had not been completed before the PCIJ was replaced by the ICJ. A provision in the latter's Statute provided for declarations made under the PCIJ Statute to continue in effect as if under the equivalent provision in the successor ICJ's Statute. The only condition which such declarations had to fulfil was that they should be 'still in force' or '*faites pour une durée qui n'est pas encore expirée*'.[128]

The English version appeared to require that the declaration had entered into force and remained in force, while the French version was apt to cover any declaration which had not exceeded any time limit to which it was subject or had not otherwise expired. The USA argued that both languages should be read as meaning that in order to continue to take effect, a declaration must continue to be 'binding'. The Court, however, considered that it should interpret the provision on the basis of the text actually used. Neither English nor French used 'binding' and the preparatory work showed no hint that this had ever been suggested. Further, the preparatory work showed that the French negotiators had deliberately

---

in *Case concerning Military and Paramilitary Activities in and against Nicaragua (Nicaragua v USA) (Jurisdiction and Admissibility)* [1984] ICJ Reports 392, at 538, considered further in section 4.10.

[126] *LaGrand Case (Germany v USA)* [2001] ICJ Reports 466, at 502–3, para 102.

[127] *Case concerning Military and Paramilitary Activities in and against Nicaragua (Nicaragua v USA) (Jurisdiction and Admissibility)* [1984] ICJ Reports 392.

[128] [1984] ICJ Reports 392, at 405, para 28.

departed from the obvious equivalent of the English text which would have been '*encore en vigueur*'. Since the provision for continuation of declarations did not include a requirement that a declarant state had been a party to the PCIJ Statute and Protocol, the Nicaraguan declaration had a certain validity that could be preserved or destroyed, an appreciation of the position which was not excluded by the English text. The Court also examined the circumstances of conclusion which it found supported its interpretation in the sense of the French text.[129]

Some judges, in separate opinions specifically referring to article 33 of the Vienna Convention, were critical of the Court's approach on this point. But the significant point for present purposes is that this was on the basis of their analyses which included consideration of the preparatory work, not because they considered that reference to preparatory work or circumstances of conclusion was inadmissible when seeking to reconcile points of difference between languages.[130] Rosenne has noted that the ILC envisaged reference to preparatory work to evaluate different languages:

A close study of the rules for the interpretation of a multi-lingual treaty embodied in articles 31 to 33 of the Vienna Convention...suggests that what the International Law Commission wanted to stress, when it put forward the draft of these rules, was, in case of doubt, the importance of determining the history of the multi-lingual texts concerned in order to establish their interrelationship as a matter of fact, as the point of departure for an operation designed to establish the intention of the parties to the treaty in question.[131]

5. Conclusions

Although the provisions for interpretation of treaties authenticated in more than one language are sometimes omitted from mention as part of the Vienna rules, they are treaty provisions equal to the other rules. Where they are applicable they can play a significant part in treaty interpretation. The first principle is that a treaty authenticated in more than one language is a single treaty and has one and the same proper interpretation in whichever language it is read. Unless one language is specified as having priority, if there is divergent meaning, and if it is not possible to achieve a harmonious interpretation by applying the rules of interpretation to all the languages, the meaning to be adopted in the one which best reconciles the texts, having regard to the object and purpose of the treaty.

---

[129] [1984] ICJ Reports 392, at 405–11.

[130] See, eg, the opinion of Judge Jennings, *Case concerning Military and Paramilitary Activities in and against Nicaragua (Nicaragua v USA) (Jurisdiction and Admissibility)* [1984] ICJ Reports 392, at 537–9.

[131] S Rosenne, 'On Multi-lingual interpretation' (1971) 6 *Israel Law Review* 360, at 362–3 (footnotes omitted).

PART III

CONCLUSION

10

Criticism, Themes, Issues, and Conclusions

Criticisms of the Vienna rules — inadequacy of traditional analyses — originalist, constructivist, and evolutionary approaches — inconsistent and incomplete application of the rules — examples from particular regimes — conclusions

[T]he structure of Articles 31 to 33 of the Vienna Convention has become the virtually indispensable scaffolding for the reasoning on questions of treaty interpretation, and this despite the intention of the authors of the Convention that it should not establish anything like a hierarchy of rules.[1]

International law's canon for interpreting international agreements is codified in the Vienna Convention on the Law of Treaties. Its provisions have become something of a *clause de style* in international judgments and arbitral awards: whether routinely and briefly referred to or solemnly reproduced verbatim, they are not always systematically applied. But a failure to apply the rules of interpretation properly may distort the resulting elucidation of the agreement made by the parties and do them an injustice by retroactively changing the legal regime under which they had arranged and managed their affairs.'[2]

No claim can be made that the Vienna rules provide a comprehensive set of rules for treaty interpretation that will achieve uniform application and a single possible outcome in every case. At the very least, however, they offer a list of ingredients, a coherent structure, and some guidance on method. Yet increasingly abundant references to the Vienna rules are frequently not matched by use of them to engage with all the items mandated by the rules or are marked by failure to deploy them in the proper manner. The result is that the case law displays such a disparate picture as to make criticism vulnerable to the very defects which so many of the judgments, awards, and decisions present – that is, the criticisms are based on an incomplete picture of how the rules should work. Criticism of the rules based on interpretations reached by inadequate application of them is directed at the wrong

---

[1] H Thirlway, 'The Law and Procedure of the International Court of Justice 1960–1989, Supplement 2006: Part Three' (2006) 77 BYBIL 1, at 19; see also this and further studies reproduced in H Thirlway, *The Law and Procedure of the International Court of Justice: Fifty Years of Jurisprudence* (Oxford: OUP, 2013).

[2] M H Arsanjani and W M Reisman, 'Interpreting Treaties for the Benefit of Third Parties: The "Salvors' Doctrine" and the Use of Legislative History in Investment Treaties' (2010) 104 AJIL 597, at 598–9.

target. It is not the rules that are at fault but incomplete knowledge of their content and application. This chapter, nevertheless, picks up some of the criticisms and looks at the development of application of the Vienna rules, supplementing the study in Part II above with brief reference to theory, themes, and issues.

The idea of looking beyond the Vienna Convention for the law of treaties has several distinct aspects.[3] First, the law is not static. Several decades have passed since the time at which the Convention's provisions were thought out. The rules of interpretation therefore now need to take into account more recent developments and difficulties, in particular those revealed by practice and case law. Second, the Convention did not provide a complete code covering all details of the law of treaties. Some parts of the law have proved to require more detailed consideration such as the rules on reservations and the distinction between reservations, interpretative declarations, and conditional declarations. Third, since the Vienna rules only provide basic guidance on interpretation, and principally what is to be taken into account rather than great detail of how interpretative elements are to be used, there is a whole further level of the interpretative exercise.

It seems important to stress at the outset that the ILC in conceiving the Vienna rules on treaty interpretation never saw them as complete formulae in the sense of lists of ingredients to be used every time, still less as algorithms in the sense of sets of sequential instructions. Rather, the Commission saw them as key principles to be applied following their own inherent logic and on the basis of which interpreters would exercise their own skills of judgement, insight, and their experience of legal processes.

In the light of these aims it is understandable that the Vienna rules were not made more extensive or more ambitious. While analysis of treaty interpretation, elaboration of theories, and identification of traits may prove helpful and revealing, that should not replace an understanding of the rules as a starting point and framework. General descriptions of approaches, such as 'textual', 'teleological', 'purposive', or 'evolutionary' are *not*, individually or collectively, a substitute for actual familiarity with all the elements of the rules and full use of them. However, these general descriptions of approaches to treaty interpretation may help analysis and provide useful indicators of further topics for consideration, with emphasis on the proviso just noted.

A further aspect of the development of study of treaty interpretation is the emergence of special fields, such as treaty interpretation in world trade law, human rights, international investment, tax, etc. Such is the extent of case law in these areas that there is sufficient to warrant complete books on treaty interpretation for each one.[4] These provide excellent accounts of the subject with copious examples far beyond the scope of the present work. No attempt is made here to outline the issues specific to each subject area which this mass of case law raises. Some of it has

---

[3] Cf E Cannizzaro (ed), *The Law of Treaties Beyond the Vienna Convention* (Oxford: OUP, 2011).

[4] See eg I Van Damme, *Treaty Interpretation by the WTO Appellate Body* (Oxford: OUP, 2009); G Letsas, *A Theory of Interpretation of the European Convention on Human Rights* (Oxford:

been used to illustrate points in the preceding chapters. What is attempted here is to pick out some of the developments in these areas that illustrate aspects of the Vienna rules pertinent to criticism or explanation of them.

The main themes of this concluding chapter are that: the Vienna rules provide a framework for interpretative reasoning for all treaties, even if they only take the interpreter part of the way; the more vague the wording of a treaty, the greater scope which the interpreter has to exercise discretion; such exercise of discretion needs to be based on a full understanding of all the rules and must be carried out in good faith.

1. The notion of 'rules' of interpretation

1.1 Reviewing 'interpretation'

The process of interpretation is described above in Chapter 1 as 'giving' meaning to the treaty. This followed the firm rejection by Waldock of any notion that the process of interpretation is 'a mere mechanical one of drawing inevitable meanings from the words in a text, or of searching for and discovering some pre-existing specific intention of the parties with respect to every situation arising under a treaty.' 'In most instances', he wrote, 'interpretation involves *giving* a meaning to a text'.[5]

The significance of 'giving' meaning rather than 'finding' meaning is twofold. 'Finding' meaning steers an interpreter towards scrutinising the text to discern a meaning within it. It also implies looking for the 'original' meaning. While both these elements play a part in the process envisaged by the Vienna rules, *finding* the meaning embodies a much narrower approach than that of *giving* a meaning to the text and does not accurately reflect the Vienna rules. This is, first, because the principles in the Vienna rules are *not* exclusively 'textual' in the sense of drawing meaning solely from the text, despite the epithet 'textual' being applied to them as adverse criticism.[6] Second, interpretation is not a quest aiming to find the 'original' meaning, though in cases where such a concept is appropriate the Vienna rules include that possibility. Third, 'giving' meaning better reflects the process of interpretation because the skill of the interpreter lies in identifying the appropriate meaning through a range of elements which simply delving into the wording of the treaty may not yield up. Skills of assessment and judgement are required to weigh up the interpretative elements and to produce the proper outcome.

OUP, 2007); J R Weeramantry, *Treaty Interpretation in Investment Arbitration* (Oxford: OUP, 2012); N Shelton, *Interpretation and Application of Tax Treaties* (London: LexisNexis, 2004); F Engelen, *Interpretation of Tax Treaties Under International Law* (Amsterdam: IBFD Publications BV, 2004).

[5] [1964] *Yearbook of the ILC*, vol.II, p 53, para (1): see Chapter 1, section 3.6 above.
[6] The ILC used 'textual' to differentiate the approach in the draft articles from an unregulated search for intention, indicating an approach using the text as the starting point: see Chapter 1 above.

1.2 What can 'rules' achieve?

Of the many criticisms which can be made of the Vienna rules some may be the result of false expectations raised by dubbing them 'rules'. The nature and role of rules has been investigated both in the context of the WTO and more generally by Jan Klabbers.[7] In part of the latter analysis he examines an assessment by H Jefferson Powell of the virtues required by judges and, in his summation, attractively concludes that '[w]hat matters is not virtuoso technique, but virtuous reading'.[8] Recognizing a 'morality of disagreement', he approves an approach which engages in debate as part of 'the art and politics of interpretation':

This calls for rules on how to conduct the debate, of course, but rules of interpretation cannot play that role, for their main function is to stifle today's debate in the name of yesterday's (seeming) agreement. [9]

In his conclusions Klabbers emphasizes the significance of *who* constitutes the readership of texts and the importance of good faith in their approach to interpretation of them. In relation to the proliferation of third party determination of legal issues he states:

Yet, curiously enough, with the creation of all those courts and tribunals, it would seem that the call for rules on interpretation has not diminished: quite the contrary, it has increased. . . .

Any rule, any treaty, can be misread . . . this is also why the notion of good faith is included in the general rule on interpretation as laid down in article 31. It is perhaps time to re-discover this particular element of the rule: the reference to the virtues—the good faith—of the interpreter. This suggests that individuals should approach the interpretation of texts with humility, acquiescence, integrity and candour, as Powell proposes, rather than with the mechanistic sense of applying a rule as if it were mathematics.[10]

There is every reason to concur in the importance of debate to resolve disagreement, to doubt whether more rules would solve problems of how texts are read, to avoid mechanistic approaches, and above all to sustain the importance of good

---

[7] J Klabbers, 'On Rationalism in Politics: Interpretation of Treaties and the World Trade Organization' (2005) 74 *Nordic JIL* 405, and J Klabbers, 'Virtuous Interpretation' in M Fitzmaurice, O Elias, and P Merkouris (eds), *Treaty Interpretation and the Vienna Convention on the Law of Treaties: 30 Years on* (Leiden: Brill, 2010); see also J Klabbers, writing that 'The main function served by the Vienna Convention's rules, then, is as something of a battlefield: the continuation of politics by other means', and '. . . rules on interpretation can do little more than set the outward parameters: certain things are not acceptable to begin with . . .' <http://opiniojuris.org/2009/03/>.

[8] Klabbers, 'Virtuous Interpretation' in M Fitzmaurice and others (eds), *Treaty Interpretation and the Vienna Convention on the Law of Treaties: 30 Years* on, at pp 34–6, citing, at p 36, H Jefferson Powell, *Constitutional Conscience: The Moral Dimension of Judicial Decision* (Chicago: University of Chicago Press, 2008); on the moral dimension in interpretation of the European Convention on Human Rights, see G Letsas, *A Theory of Interpretation of the European Convention on Human Rights* (Oxford: OUP, 2007).

[9] Klabbers, 'Virtuous Interpretation', at p 35.

[10] Klabbers, 'Virtuous Interpretation' in Fitzmaurice and others (eds), *Treaty Interpretation and the Vienna Convention on the Law of Treaties: 30 Years on*, at p 37 referring to H Jefferson Powell, *Constitutional Conscience: The Moral Dimension of Judicial Decision*.

faith in leading towards virtuous interpretation. It is less clear that the 'main' function of rules of interpretation is to stifle debate, that there is actually a demand for more rules, or that a mechanistic approach (firmly rejected by the ILC) would, or could in any practical sense, prevail over, or act as a counterpoint to, good faith. Klabbers also points out 'appeals to rules never settle a debate, but only begin the interpretative process that constitutes the international system'.[11] This nicely captures the role of the Vienna rules in providing a starting point and framework for interpretation though at present, far from there being a demand for more rules, even the existing rules ones are sometimes briefly mentioned only to be incompletely used.[12]

As regards the role of 'debate' in interpretation, this is difficult to isolate from the individual circumstances in which a need for interpretation arises. Where there is an emerging difference of view between parties to a treaty, the most common treaty provision for initial resolution of differences actually favours debate, usually termed 'negotiation' in typical treaty language. However, this is far from the only circumstance in which a need for interpretation arises, unilateral interpretation being probably the most common (and most commonly uncontroversial). An interpreter may therefore need to gauge whether their perception of the meaning is likely to prove uncontroversial or, if not, whether an interpretation is likely to require negotiation, third party determination, or amendment of the terms of the treaty.

In a general sense the role of debate in treaty interpretation may be more or less prominent depending on the view taken as to what a treaty is, or what the subject and content is of a particular treaty. McDougal's concept of a treaty as 'a continuing process of communication and collaboration between the parties in the shaping and sharing of demanded values' greatly favours the 'debate' approach to interpretation.[13] Philip Allott's definition of a treaty as 'a disagreement reduced to writing' effectively emphasizes the potential need to resolve differences over interpretation.[14]

These descriptions may convey something of the reality of treaties; but a further reality is that states do regulate their conduct by application of established agreements, do generally seek to abide by their commitments in treaties, and often do make provision in advance for resolving differences in current understanding of a treaty, or over their inclinations in implementing it, on the basis of what has been agreed in the past. There is a discernible difference between debate to ascertain

---

[11] J Klabbers, 'The Meaning of Rules' (2006) 20(3) *International Relations* 295, see also J Tobin, 'Seeking to Persuade: A Constructive Approach to Human Rights Treaty Interpretation' (2010) 23 *Harv Hum Rts J* 1.

[12] See, for example, section 5.2 below; and see further M Waibel, 'Uniformity versus specialization (2): A uniform regime of treaty interpretation?' Chapter 13 in C J Tams, A Tzanakopoulos and others (eds), *Research Handbook On The Law Of Treaties* (Cheltenham: Edward Elgar, 2014), 386–88.

[13] See Chapter 2, section 6 above; cf H G Cohen, 'International Law's Erie Moment' (2013) 34 *Mich J Int'l L* 249, at 257; on this and the development of the Vienna rules, see further Klabbers, 'Virtuous Interpretation', at pp 23–31.

[14] P Allott, 'The Concept of International Law' (1999) 10 EJIL 31, at 43.

what obligations are acceptable to both or all parties and interpretation to establish what is understood to have been agreed. Reducing the notion of international agreement to a continuing process of communication or just an ongoing debate would be to deny the idea of commitment and of a treaty itself. If the parties wish to develop new obligations, then they may decide to amend or terminate a treaty. If, however, they differ over the extent of obligations in an established agreement, or as to whether they wish to maintain it in existence, a realistic assessment of the interpretation to be placed on the treaty is necessary.

The Vienna rules seek to provide some guidance on how to achieve this. Far from having a main function of stifling debate, the Vienna rules import the product of any such debate into the general rule of interpretation itself. A significant set of elements of the general rule, which is lost on many interpreters who go no further than the first paragraph of article 31, is the requirement to take into account agreements on interpretation and evidence of uniform practice amounting to agreement. Interpretative agreements between the parties are necessarily the result of negotiation or debate, while practice in relation to a problematic treaty provision may be the outcome of discussions leading to understandings on what practices to adopt in application of the treaty. Of course, where such agreements and practice take hold, third party dispute settlement is not engaged, which may explain why instances pointing up these elements of the general rule do not feature so greatly in studies of treaty interpretation. The current work of the ILC on subsequent agreements and subsequent practice in relation to interpretation of treaties may encourage greater familiarity with these parts of the general rule.

As further evidence that the Vienna provisions on interpretation were not conceived as in any sense to be applied mechanistically or as if mathematical formulae, the views of the ILC itself bear repeating. Waldock, the principal architect of the rules, had himself emphasized earlier warnings against viewing treaty interpretation as a mechanical operation, concluding that:

This is obviously a task which calls for investigation, weighing of evidence, judgment, foresight, and a nice appreciation of a number of factors varying from case to case. No canons of interpretation can be of absolute and universal utility in performing such a task, and it seems desirable that any idea that they can be should be dispelled.[15]

More specifically in relation to 'rules' he indicated that:

.... any 'principles' found by the Commission to be 'rules' should, so far as seems advisable, be formulated as such. In a sense all 'rules' of interpretation have the character of 'guidelines' since their application in a particular case depends so much on the appreciation of the context and the circumstances of the point to be interpreted.[16]

---

[15] [1964] *Yearbook of the ILC*, vol.II, p. 53, para (1), quoting from and citing Part III of the Harvard draft codification of international law in (1935) 29 AJIL Supp. 653, at 946, and see Chapter 1 section 3.6 above.

[16] Extract from Sixth Report of Special Rapporteur (Waldock), [1966] *Yearbook of the ILC*, vol. II, page 94, para 1.

Finally, provided the Vienna rules are understood and used in the manner in which they were designed to be, the result is not a mechanical approach to interpretation. It was the primacy of good faith which was one of the motivating factors in persuading the ILC to draw up the rules:

[T]he Commission confined itself to trying to isolate and codify the comparatively few general principles which appear to constitute general rules for the interpretation of treaties. Admittedly, the task of formulating even these rules is not easy, but the Commission considered that there were cogent reasons why it should be attempted. First, the interpretation of treaties in good faith and according to law is essential if the *pacta sunt servanda* rule is to have any real meaning. ... [17]

2. Ambiguity and vagueness distinguished

... texts can be either vague or ambiguous.... The two terms are sometimes used interchangeably, and, when this is the case, they both mark a general lack of what we might call 'determinacy' (or 'clarity' or 'certainty') of meaning. But the terms 'vague' and 'ambiguous' also have technical (or more precise) meanings, such that there is a real difference in their meaning. [18]

Good faith and fidelity to what the parties to a treaty have agreed must motivate the interpreter in using the available interpretative elements. However, treaty provisions vary in their formulation from the very general to the extremely particular. While the latter may contain more of their own interpretative solutions, the former may benefit from analysis somewhat analogous to that applied to national constitutions. For example, as a prelude to investigating 'originalist' and 'constructivist' approaches to interpretation of constitutions, Professor Solum defines certain terms. [19] The first distinction which he makes is between 'ambiguity' and 'vagueness'. [20] This may be useful in the context of treaty interpretation, though perhaps in a different way from that of its application to constitutional interpretation. In Professor Solum's usage 'ambiguity refers to the multiplicity of sense' or, as expressed in one of the dictionary meanings, 'capability of being understood in two or more ways'. [21] He explains vagueness as 'the existence of borderline cases: a

---

[17] Commentary on draft articles [1966] *Yearbook of the ILC*, vol. II, pp 218–19, para (5).

[18] L B Solum, 'The Interpretation-Construction Distinction' (2010–2011) 27 *Const Comment* 95, at 97 (footnote omitted); see also L B Solum, 'Originalism and Constitutional Construction' (2013–2014) 82 *Fordham L Rev* 453, and S T Helmersen, 'Evolutive Treaty Interpretation: Legality, Semantics and Distinctions' (2013) 6 *European Journal of Legal Studies* 127, at 142–44.

[19] L B Solum, 'The Interpretation-Construction Distinction' (2010–2011) 27 *Const. Comment* 95; see also L B Solum, 'Originalism and Constitutional Construction' (2013–2014) 82 *Fordham L Rev* 453; for general material on the originalist and constructivist debate, see Solum, 'The Interpretation-Construction Distinction', at 95, note 1 and G Letsas, 'Intentionalism and the Interpretation of the ECHR' in Fitzmaurice and others (eds), *Treaty Interpretation and the Vienna Convention on the Law of Treaties: 30 Years on*, at 258.

[20] At 97–98.   [21] *Oxford English Dictionary*, meaning 3.a.

term is vague if there are cases where the term might or might not apply'.[22] The example which he uses of the former (ambiguity) is 'cool', with two substantial uses denoting temperature or a certain relaxed style. 'Vagueness' is exemplified by 'tall', for which the starting point is indeterminate (though the context may provide a rough indication). Professor Solum notes that a word or phrase can be both vague and ambiguous, 'cool' being ambiguous as described above, but when used of temperature it is also vague.[23]

The other pair of preliminary definitions given in the same study contrasts 'semantic content' and 'legal content'. Semantic content is described as 'the linguistic meaning of the text' whereas the legal content is the effect or doctrines which the words or provisions produce.[24] An example is the US constitutional provision that Congress shall make no law abridging the freedom of speech. 'Freedom' has a readily identified semantic meaning, but its legal content is what has led to a number of doctrines such as that forbidding prior restraint of utterance or publication. 'Prior restraint' is not present in the words of the text but principles precluding prior restraint in most circumstances have been found to be the legal content of the regime envisaged by the constitutional provision.[25] Put another way:

Legal interpretation turns a semantic 'text' into a legal norm... The semantic meaning of a text is the totality of all meanings that may be attached to the language in question (the public language) or in the private lexicon of the text's author (the private code). To interpret a text is to choose its legal meaning from among a number of semantic possibilities—to decide which of a text's semantic meanings constitutes its proper legal meaning. The semantic meaning of the text determines its semantic potential... The legal meaning carries this potential into practice.[26]

The definitions given above lead to development of the argument that interpretation is what yields semantic content and recognizes or discovers the linguistic meaning, while it is construction which determines legal content or legal effect. The further idea is that ambiguity 'characteristically can be resolved by interpretation', although evidence from the context may not always achieve this resolution.[27] Construction, however, goes further by (in paraphrase) elaborating or extrapolating from the semantic meaning the rules or regime which can actually be applied.[28]

---

[22] L B Solum, 'The Interpretation-Construction Distinction' (2010–2011) 27 *Const. Comment* 95, at 98, footnote omitted.

[23] Solum at 98; it can also be noted that 'tall' could likewise be described as ambiguous as well as vague, though there is little risk that a 'tall story' will be taken as having anything much to do with height.

[24] Solum at 98–99.

[25] Solum at 99–100.

[26] A Barak, *Purposive Interpretation in Law* (Princeton: Princeton University Press, 2007), 6–7 (footnote omitted).

[27] Solum, 'The Interpretation-Construction Distinction', at 102.

[28] Solum at 102 *et seq* where the theory and analysis is applied particularly to constitutional construction.

The immediate significance for treaty interpretation of this careful labelling of features of interpretative circumstances lies in its implication that the *modus operandi* may have to vary according to the particular treaty. A human rights treaty formulating rights in very broad terms is quite different from an agreement specifying in minute detail how taxation is to fall upon those engaged in international activities. This is not a matter of categorizing types of treaties so much as looking at how their provisions are formulated. In somewhat different terms, the ICJ has shown signs of an approach based on the way a treaty is drafted by adopting the concept that some terms in treaties are to be taken as 'generic'.[29]

Discussion of approaches to US constitutional interpretation offers a further parallel. This is the contrast between the approach of 'originalists', who look for the original intention of the constitution's framers, and that of 'living constitutionalists' who consider that the constitution should be interpreted in the light of developments up to the moment of interpretation.[30] This suggests comparison with the issues of time in treaty interpretation, the intertemporal law, and evolutionary interpretation.[31]

The general point here is that as regards the life of a treaty, the Vienna rules envisage taking into account a range of elements, potentially extending from before its birth to the moment of interpretation, though with some differentiation in the value to be attributed to the various elements. In treaty interpretation it is not a firm dichotomy between original intention and living instrument strategies. The rules allow for a more bespoke approach. The treaty itself may steer the interpreter in one direction or another. The use of preparatory work, though supplementary rather than part of the general rule, extends from assisting a general understanding, through a very wide notion of 'confirming' meaning, to a much more closely conditioned role of 'determining' meaning. The reality, however, is that the interplay between the elements of the general rule and supplementary means may depend on the strength and clarity of the one or the other, as may the interplay between the elements of the general rules itself.

A good example of this is the rule that abstentions by permanent members of the Security Council on non-procedural matters, matters which require their 'concurring' votes, are not treated as non-concurring. The records show that in the negotiation of the Charter of the UN the question was raised whether the abstention of any one of the permanent members would have the same effect as a negative vote by that member in preventing the Security Council from reaching a decision on such a matter.[32] The answer took the somewhat oblique angle along

---

[29] See section 4.1 below, and P Merkouris, *Article 31(3)(c) of the VCLT and the Principle of Systemic Integration* (Ph D Thesis, 2010) pp 97–8 and 114–21; <https://qmro.qmul.ac.uk/jspui/handle/123456789/477>.

[30] L B Solum, 'The Interpretation-Construction Distinction' (2010–2011) 27 *Const. Comment* 95, at 130.

[31] See Chapter 1, section 3.5, and Chapter 7, sections 1.1 and 1.2 above and, on evolutionary interpretation, section 4 below.

[32] S A Tiewul, 'Namibia and the Unanimity Principle in the Security Council: Is Abstention a Concurring Vote?' (1974) 11 *U Ghana LJ* 20, at 24–5.

the lines that permanent members could not be expected to assume obligations to act in serious matters of international peace and security in consequence of a decision in which they had not concurred, but a proposed amendment that might have clarified the matter was not adopted.[33] How the practice developed a clear interpretation from qualified reception initially to unchallengeable acceptance, and the relevant dynamics in both Security Council and among the general membership of the UN, has been well described.[34] Evaluating a clear practice as set against an unclear intention in the preparatory work is by no means uncommon in treaty interpretation.

3. 'Textual', 'teleological', 'seeking intention', and other approaches

The dominant analysis of treaty interpretation when the Vienna rules were being drawn up still holds sway in several writings although with some reformulation and additions. Analysis tends to identify underlying theories, bases or trends such as 'textual', 'purposive', 'evolutionary', etc. Sometimes these are brought to the forefront in the practice of certain courts and tribunals, the Vienna rules being merely mentioned as a waypoint to freer pastureland. The three most common approaches are described in terms such as 'textual', 'teleological', and 'seeking intention', though the latter two are perhaps better indicated by Pauwelyn and Elsig in terms of 'underlying objective' and 'party intent'.[35] These descriptions are apt because they indicate more closely the approaches sometimes taken in substitution for the Vienna rules or where application of the rules is limited to the first paragraph (or parts of the first paragraph) of the general rule.

In their analysis of what international tribunals actually do when interpreting treaties and how their behaviour can be explained, Pauwelyn and Elsig provide useful insights into what can look like interpretative choices as presented by courts and tribunals. They offer 'a taxonomy of the most important and most commonly discussed choices of interpretation techniques that tribunals must select from', well described in question form in the largely self-explanatory headings of Part II of their study:

A. The Dominant Hermeneutic: Text, Party Intent, or Underlying Objective?
B. Timing: Original or Evolutionary Interpretation?
C. Activism: Work-to-Rule or Gap-Filling Approach?

---

[33] Tiewul, 'Namibia and the Unanimity Principle in the Security Council' (1974) 11 *U Ghana LJ* 20, at 25–26.

[34] Tiewul, at 26–35 and 40, fn 71.

[35] J Pauwelyn and M Elsig, 'The Politics of Treaty Interpretation: Variations and Explanations across International Tribunals', Chapter 18 in J L Dunoff and M A Pollack (eds), *Interdisciplinary Perspectives on International Law and International Relations: The State of the Art* (Cambridge: CUP, 2012), 450.

D. Case-by-Case Analysis or Rule of Precedent?
E. Linkage: Self-Contained or Systemic Interpretation?[36]

The authors' identification of these 'interpretative choices' is to set the frame for seeking explanations of how and why international tribunals opt for one approach rather than another. This is a challenging exercise in which the dynamics at work are explained and shown in schematic forms. This exercise is not further explored here, but the classifications of choice and the examples which the authors give do usefully prompt some questions as to whether courts and tribunals have grasped how the Vienna rules were designed to work. The general rule is emphatically not *à la carte* as is suggested by the idea of these questions as encapsulating 'interpretative choices' among techniques. The scheme of the Vienna rules envisages that *all* the elements of the general rule present in any particular case are to be weighed up together and against one another. Even if one looks at the first paragraph of article 31 separately, as does heading A, in the Vienna rules the ordinary meaning of a treaty term is to be identified in the context and in the light of the treaty's object and purpose, rather than programming any one of these elements as the dominant force.

Similarly, 'timing' in the sense of selecting original or evolutionary interpretation in heading B, although it receded behind the veil when article 31(3)(c) was winnowed down to its present form, was left in the Vienna rules to be identified by full interpretation of the treaty. A complete application of the Vienna rules is a process which could take into account considerations such as whether it involved a one-off transaction, long-term expectation of continuing application and development, drafting in terms which are generic and would inevitably need elaboration, etc. However, these factors should not be evaluated as if a choice between two strategies. They are contained in the general rule. There are increasing indications from the ICJ that no *a priori* restrictive or expansive approach is appropriate, contrary to what is implied by heading C. The individual treaty itself postulates the proper course to adopt through the assessment of factors (including ones such as those just mentioned).[37]

In terms of the Vienna rules, heading D's choice between a case-by-case approach and one of precedent resolves itself in different senses. A treaty governing the work of a court or tribunal may direct that a case has binding effect only on the parties in the particular case; but this leaves open whether judgments, decisions, and awards may constitute practice amounting to agreed interpretation as envisaged by article 31(3)(b) of the Vienna Convention if there is sufficient unopposed repetition in a system of independent adjudication accepted in advance by the parties to a treaty.

---

[36] Pauwelyn and Elsig 'The Politics of Treaty Interpretation', 449–59.

[37] See *Dispute regarding Navigational and Related Rights (Costa Rica v Nicaragua)* [2009] ICJ Reports 214, considered in Chapter 8 section 4.5.4 above, and, with a more specific link to context and object and purpose, *Whaling in the Antarctic (Australia v Japan: New Zealand intervening)*, Judgment of 31 March 2014, para 58, where the ICJ stated: 'Taking into account the preamble and other relevant provisions of the Convention referred to above, the Court observes that neither a restrictive nor an expansive interpretation of Article VIII [the provision in issue] is justified'.

Similarly, the response to heading E is that this is the element addressed in article 31(3)(c), and thus to be taken into account in combination with the other elements of the general rule.

A particular aspect of the question in this last heading is the extent to which the Vienna rules mandate reference to other international obligations (that is those under other treaties).[38] While article 31(3)(c) is the only direct indication of a link to be made to other treaty obligations in the interpretative process, further possible avenues of approach may be open. The simplest is where the treaty itself makes a direct reference to another one. A second possibility is that one or more terms in issue are such as to have an ordinary meaning which it is appropriate to select because of its established use (particularly if frequent) in other treaties. In some circumstances the object and purpose may also point to a link.[39] The significance of these possibilities is that they show how it is the full range of elements present in relation to each particular treaty which guide the interpreter, not a general choice of some predominant means.

Although not aiming at analysis of the Vienna rules, Pauwelyn and Elsig do actually show how tribunals have often misunderstood the rules. They describe the Vienna Convention as offering two main principles:

> The first is that treaties must be interpreted in 'good faith,' in accordance with the 'ordinary meaning' of the 'terms' or text of the treaty, in their 'context,' and in light of the treaty's 'object and purpose.' [fn citing Vienna Convention] This summing up of text, context, and purpose is described as a holistic, non-hierarchical exercise, albeit one that starts with the text of the treaty (Abi-Saab 2010). The VCLT's second main principle is that the 'preparatory work of the treaty and the circumstances of its conclusion' are only secondary sources of interpretation to confirm meaning established under the first principle or in case the meaning of the treaty remains unclear or leads to an absurd result. [fn citing Vienna Convention, article 32][40]

This analysis suggests undue limits to the material to be taken into account in treaty interpretation and unbalances the elements of the process encapsulated in the rules. Describing article 31(1) as the first of two 'main' principles, and as the second that preparatory work and circumstances of conclusion are only 'secondary sources' of interpretation, omits from the set of rules subsequent agreement and practice constituting agreement (both 'authentic' means of interpretation in the ILC's view), leaves out the role of rules of international law applicable in the relations between the parties, ignores special meanings, and omits the role of

---

[38] Cf A van Aaken, 'Defragmentation of International Law through Constitutional Interpretation: A Methodological Proposal' (2009) 16 *Indiana Journal of Global Legal Studies* 483, at 495–98; and see Chapter 7, section 3.2.2 above.

[39] For examples of the various possibilities, see van Aaken, at 495–96.

[40] Pauwelyn and Elsig, 'The Politics of Treaty Interpretation', at 448; the work cited in the quotation is G Abi-Saab, "The Appellate Body and Treaty Interpretation," in Fitzmaurice and others (eds), *Treaty Interpretation and the Vienna Convention on the Law of Treaties: 30 Years on*, 99–109.

supplementary means specifically 'to determine' the meaning when the itemised preconditions are met. In the latter instance, where supplementary means 'determine' the meaning, preparatory work and circumstances of conclusion are clearly not 'secondary' but predominant.

Taken collectively, the interpretative choices which Pauwelyn and Elsig identify are essentially in harmony with, and substantially contained within, the Vienna rules, but only if rolled up into evaluation of all the elements in the rules. Where courts and tribunals adopt just one of the choices—that is, selecting one element of the Vienna rules to the exclusion or automatic relegation of others—they have effectively abandoned the rules or fallen prey to the temptation of 'excessive molecularization'.[41] It is the case, however, that the rules only gently hint at the proper method of their deployment, necessitating an act of interpretation to that end. There is, therefore, the resultant requirement of judgement to take the interpretative exercise to its conclusion in each case; but without proper consideration of all the elements in the rules, the foundation for the exercise of discretion and judgement is not laid.

3.1 'Textual' does not mean 'literal' and is an unhelpful label

A major criticism of the Vienna rules, most prominently advanced by Professor McDougal at the Vienna Conference and in his other writing, was that the proposed rules were highly restrictive, with what he described as an 'insistent emphasis upon an impossible, conformity-imposing textuality'.[42] Some have seen the rules as including a 'literal' approach to interpretation, even if combined with other techniques.[43]

Such views are ill-founded. The ILC, in its work on the draft rules, used the term 'textual' to indicate that the text was to be taken as an authentic expression of the intention of the parties and that, consequently, the text was to be 'the *starting point* of interpretation' rather than 'an investigation *ab initio* into the intention of the parties'.[44] As Letsas notes: 'There are no general theories of textual interpretation.'[45] He rightly indicates that 'textualism is an unfortunate label to the extent that it advocates strict interpretation in order to avoid recourse to extra-textual arguments.'[46] The Vienna rules themselves clearly include a range of elements going beyond the text of the treaty itself. 'Context' is defined to include material outside the treaty text proper; subsequent agreements and practice are both outside the

---

[41] See warning in introduction to Chapter 5 above.

[42] M S McDougal, 'The International Law Commission's Draft Articles upon Interpretation: Textuality *Redivivus*' (1967) 61 AJIL 992.

[43] See eg G G Lawrie, 'The Application and Interpretation of the Vienna Convention on the Law of Treaties' [1972] HKLJ 261, at 274.

[44] See Chapter 1 above, text to fn 8, emphasis added.

[45] G Letsas, 'Intentionalism and the Interpretation of the ECHR' in Fitzmaurice and others (eds), *Treaty Interpretation and the Vienna Convention on the Law of Treaties: 30 Years on*, at 266.

[46] Letsas, at 266.

treaty text itself, while the latter does not necessitate any text at all; relevant rules of international law applicable in the relations between the parties are not within the treaty text; preparatory work, the circumstances of the treaty's conclusion, and material for use as other supplementary means, are likewise not part of the treaty text. Thus the term 'textual' is a misleading label to place on the approach of the Vienna rules.

The misunderstandings about the Vienna rules and the supposition of their insistence on textuality are helpfully analysed by Villiger, who notes as one of the reasons for this:

… somewhat unfortunately—and here indeed lies a misunderstanding—the forceful United States campaign in Vienna most likely led to this conclusion: because its delegation criticized the alleged textuality of Articles 31 and 32, a *rejection* of the US amendment appeared to imply that the articles were textual.[47]

3.2 'Teleological' is not warranted as a description of the general approach

Just as it is misleading to characterize the Vienna rules as 'textual', so it can be inaccurate to derive from them a 'teleological' approach. This is not inaccuracy in the sense that the rules exclude purpose from the relevant elements, but inaccuracy in two ways. First, the proper approach requires that all the elements present in any given interpretative exercise are considered and evaluated. This includes the object and purpose of the treaty which has a particular role in relation to the identification of the ordinary meaning, while the 'context' requires consideration of the whole treaty and other defined matter. Second, there is no warrant for using a teleological approach as a compendious substitute for the rules.

Thus, for example, caution is needed in evaluating the following explanation of the work of the Inter-American Court of Human Rights:

Although the Court usually begins its reasoning by looking at the text, it has, in general, not relied on a primarily textual approach but rather resorted to other means of interpretation. The Court's reluctance to assign a more prominent role to a provision's ordinary meaning is ultimately the consequence of the Court's emphasis on object and purpose. Thus, the Court stressed that

… the 'ordinary meaning' of terms cannot of itself become the sole rule, for it must always be considered within its context and, in particular, in the light of the object and purpose of the treaty.[52]

In the Inter-American Court's jurisprudence the 'object and purpose' appears to play the most important role among the different means of interpretation. A characteristic feature of this Court's object and purpose-based approach is its emphasis on the overriding aim of the Convention as a whole to effectively protect human rights…

---

[47] M E Villiger, 'The Rules on Interpretation—Misgivings, Misunderstandings, Miscarriage? The 'Crucible' Intended by the International Law Commission', Chapter 6 in Cannizzaro (ed), *The Law of Treaties Beyond the Vienna Convention*, at 117 (original emphasis).

⁵² *Proposed Amendments of the Naturalization Provisions of the Constitution of Costa Rica*, Advisory Opinion OC-4/84, Inter-American Court of Human Rights, Series A, No. 4 (19 January 1984), para. 23; *Article 55 of the American Convention on Human Rights*, Advisory Opinion OC-20/09, Inter-American Court of Human Rights, Series A, No. 20 (29 September 2009), para. 26.[48]

This analysis seems to suggest that a textual approach and one which has regard to the treaty's object and purpose are different 'means of interpretation' rather than elements of a single general rule. Yet in this quotation above from the Inter-American Court's own judgment, the Court indicates an approach to identifying the ordinary meaning of a term using context and object and purpose in just the way envisaged by the ILC for use of these elements, rather than choosing between a textual and a teleological approach. If the product of the Court's application of rules of interpretation has been to place weight on object and purpose and on effectiveness, this may be a legitimate evaluation of treaty provisions drafted in a manner which is both ambiguous and vague in the senses described above.[49] Only if the Court omitted consideration of the elements required by the general rule, substituting a purely general teleological interpretation for application of the rules of interpretation, would the approach be at odds with the Vienna Convention.

Substitution of a general teleological interpretation for application of the Vienna rules is what has occurred in some judgments of *ad hoc* international criminal tribunals.[50] This is plainly at odds with the approach mandated by the Vienna rules and highlights the danger of analysis which views differentiation between textual and teleological as admissible in contrast to the synthesis envisaged by the Vienna provisions.

3.3 Seeking intention

If the ILC used the term 'textual' primarily to identify the process of interpretation as one which does not involve launching into a separate quest to find the intention of the parties, the Commission may also have had in mind some of the difficulties which Hersch Lauterpacht identified in the rules of interpretation used before the adoption of the Vienna rules:

It may be added that in so far as 'revealing the intention of the parties' has in itself assumed the complexion of a somewhat stereotyped formula, it may, on occasions, conceal the true difficulties of interpretation. For the question frequently arises whether the intention of the parties can be the decisive factor in cases where, as often happens in international

⁴⁸ G Nolte (ILC Special Rapporteur), 'First Report on subsequent agreements and subsequent practice in relation to treaty interpretation', A/CN.4/660 (19 March 2013), paras 19–20 (further footnotes omitted).

⁴⁹ Cf L Lixinski, 'Treaty Interpretation by the Inter-American Court of Human Rights: Expansionism at the Service of the Unity of International Law' (2010) 21 EJIL 585, examining case law of the Inter-American Court and its particular approach to treaty interpretation in the light of article 29 of the American Convention; see also section 5.1 below.

⁵⁰ See section 5.2 below.

instruments, the treaty—far from giving expression to any common intention of the parties—actually registers the absence of any common intention (either in general or in relation to the subject-matter of the dispute) or contains provisions which are mutually inconsistent and which the creative work of interpretation must reduce to some coherent meaning.[51]

Lauterpacht followed this statement with an analogy to the use of 'presumed intention' of the parties to a contract and noted: 'In the international sphere the occasions for such necessity of acting on implied intention are more frequent'.[52] The need to avoid the danger which the ILC saw in using the term 'intent'—that the interpreter would head off in an entirely unconstrained quest for the putative content of the minds of the negotiating states—suggests the need for an even greater caution in *implying* such content. If the terms 'intent' or 'presumed intent' are to be used, it is in the sense that what is being described is the product of application of the Vienna rules. As the ICJ has put it, a treaty provision is to be interpreted 'in accordance with the intentions of its authors *as reflected by the text of the treaty and the other relevant factors in terms of interpretation*'.[53]

The ILC has more recently explained the position in its commentary on one of its draft conclusions on interpretation of treaty terms capable of evolving over time. There it refers to the possible role of subsequent agreements and subsequent practice in providing assistance in determining whether or not 'the presumed intention of the parties upon the conclusion of the treaty was to give a term used a meaning which is capable of evolving over time'.[54] The ILC commented that:

[The draft conclusion] by using the phrase 'presumed intention', refers to the intention of the parties as determined through the application of the various means of interpretation which are recognized in articles 31 and 32 [of the Vienna Convention]. The 'presumed intention' is thus not a separately identifiable original will, and the *travaux préparatoires* are not the primary basis for determining the presumed intention of the parties, but they are only, as article 32 indicates, a supplementary means of interpretation.[55]

This makes it clear that what is envisaged by the reference to 'presumed intention' is not any imputed intention independent of a complete and proper application of the Vienna rules, but simply the result of their use. This has been helpfully

---

[51] H Lauterpacht, 'Restrictive Interpretation and the Principle of Effectiveness in the Interpretation of Treaties' (1949) XXVI BYBIL 48, at 52 (footnotes omitted).

[52] Lauterpacht, at 52; cf G Letsas, *A Theory of Interpretation of the European Convention on Human Rights* (Oxford: OUP, 2007), at 71–72 usefully analysing intention in terms of 'intentions of principle', 'intentions of detail' and 'meta-intentions', but concluding that 'any theory of interpretation for the ECHR (or any international treaty) must at some stage stand outside the drafters' intentions and provide a normative justification based on values of political morality' (at 71–72).

[53] *Dispute regarding Navigational and Related Rights (Costa Rica v Nicaragua)* [2009] ICJ Reports 214, at 237, para 48 (emphasis added).

[54] Draft conclusion 3 in ILC Report on the Work of its Sixty-fifth Session (2013), General Assembly Official Records, Sixty-eighth Session, Supplement No. 10 (A/68/10), Chapter IV, p 12.

[55] ILC Report on the Work of its Sixty-fifth Session (2013), General Assembly Official Records, Sixty-eighth Session, Supplement No. 10 (A/68/10), p 27 para (9).

described as the 'objectivized, or objective, nature of "the intention of the parties"'.[56] There remains, of course, the same danger that has arisen with the terms 'textual' and 'teleological' that some interpreters will seize on the term 'intention' as offering a short cut or the means to avoid the sometimes laborious task of applying the rules fully.

4. Evolutionary Interpretation

...the evolutionary interpretation of treaties is not a separate method of interpretation; it is rather the result of a proper application of the usual means of interpretation, as means by which to establish the intention of the parties.... The 'intention of the parties' is a construct to be derived from the articulation of the 'means of interpretation admissible' in the process of interpretation...'.[57]

This extract from a comprehensive study of evolutionary interpretation answers the main question relevant here, namely whether evolutionary interpretation is a distinct method or means of interpretation. Following the same approach as the extract and the emerging view of the ILC, the answer is that where evolution in the meaning of the terms of a treaty occurs, identification of the interpretation as 'evolutionary' is the result of the proper application of the Vienna rules.[58] The topic is nevertheless of considerable importance in treaty interpretation because it addresses problems of time factors, one of the most difficult issues in treaty interpretation.

'Evolutionary interpretation' and its cognate 'evolutive interpretation' are terms which have been put into circulation mainly through case law and, in particular, through analysis of pronouncements of courts and tribunals, most notably of the ICJ and the ECtHR.[59] There is no standard definition of either term in relation to usage in legal contexts, but the gist is that the meaning of treaty terms may change over time. In the sense considered here, this evolution is without the

---

[56] E Bjorge, *The Evolutionary Interpretation of Treaties* (Oxford: OUP, 2014), 2–3 (footnote omitted).

[57] Bjorge, 2 (footnote omitted).

[58] Commentary on draft Conclusion 3 in Chapter IV of the ILC Report on the Work of its Sixty-fifth Session (2013), p 27, para (8) (footnote omitted): 'In the final analysis, most international courts and tribunals have not recognized evolutive interpretation as a separate form of interpretation, but instead have arrived at such an evolutive interpretation in application of the various means of interpretation which are mentioned in articles 31 and 32 of the Vienna Convention...Any evolutive interpretation of the meaning of a term over time must therefore result from the ordinary process of treaty interpretation'; and M Fitzmaurice, 'Interpretation of Human Rights Treaties', chapter 31 in D Shelton (ed), *The Oxford Handbook of International Human Rights Law* (Oxford: OUP, 2013), at 745. The terms 'evolutionary interpretation' and 'evolutive interpretation' are treated here as indistinguishable, but the former is preferred as closer to common usage.

[59] For examples from other international judicial bodies, such as WTO, International Tribunal on the Law of the Sea, and the Inter-American Court of Human Rights, see ILC Report on the Work of its Sixty-fifth Session (2013), General Assembly Official Records, Sixty-eighth Session, Supplement No. 10 (A/68/10), Chapter IV, p 26, para (7).

specific intervention of the parties to amend or modify the terms and distinct from attribution of meaning by showing practice evidencing agreement.[60] There are three main areas of focus:

1. Terms of a treaty may be such as to embrace change of meaning, perhaps most commonly to expand their coverage so as to include new activities, scientific advances, technological developments etc where these would not have been specifically conceived at the time the treaty was drawn up.

2. The treaty may constitute a regime of a nature inherently adapted to development, perhaps where the treaty's provisions could be viewed as having 'constitutional' characteristics, such as treaties giving powers to an international organization or stating broad propositions of principle which necessarily involve elaboration to have precise effect.

3. Developments elsewhere in the legal system may impact on the particular treaty, where there are, for example, emerging fields of law such as environmental law, or later treaties on the same subject or ones in some way related.

These categories, which are not mutually exclusive, may help in analysis of evolutionary interpretation but, as the observation at the head of this section notes, the labels 'evolutionary interpretation' and 'evolutive interpretation' do not provide distinct means of interpreting treaties. The situation which they depict is better viewed as harnessing the results of proper interpretation in accordance with the Vienna rules.[61]

4.1 The International Court of Justice

The ICJ used the term 'evolutionary' in its *Namibia* advisory opinion in the context of the system of mandates set up under the League of Nations. The Court considered that the guiding concepts in the Covenant of the League 'were not static, but were by definition *evolutionary*…The parties to the Covenant must

---

[60] Draft conclusion 3 in the work of the ILC on subsequent agreements and subsequent practice in relation to the interpretation of treaties states: 'Subsequent agreements and subsequent practice under articles 31 and 32 may assist in determining whether or not the presumed intention of the parties upon the conclusion of the treaty was to give a term used a meaning which is capable of evolving over time.' ILC Report on the Work of its Sixty-fifth Session (2013), p 24; this suggests that subsequent agreements and subsequent practice in the Vienna rules may be prominent elements leading towards a conclusion that an evolutionary interpretation is appropriate.

[61] Cf J Arato, 'Subsequent Practice and Evolutive Interpretation: Techniques of Treaty Interpretation over Time and Their Diverse Consequences' (2010) 9 *The Law and Practice of International Courts and Tribunals* 443 where evolutive interpretation is analysed as a 'technique' compared with subsequent practice as a technique; this approach may be broadly in line with the current work of the ILC on subsequent agreements and subsequent practice in relation to treaty interpretation, but the emphasis in the present work is directed to how the elements of the general rule, the supplementary means and the provisions on languages work together to give meaning to a treaty rather than viewing any elements (particularly those of the general rule) as distinct means of interpretation.

consequently be deemed to have accepted them as such.'[62] The ICJ has not subsequently made great use of the description 'evolutionary', though it has implicitly done so, for example in a number of cases where it has assessed use of a term as 'generic'. More specifically, in the *Navigational and Related Rights case (Costa Rica v Nicaragua)* the Court reviewed the circumstances in which it had previously had to consider how to interpret a term whose meaning had evolved since the conclusion of the treaty at issue.[63] In that case the ICJ transposed to interpretation of treaty provisions the approach which it had adopted in the *Aegean Sea* case interpreting a Greek reservation to exclude disputes relating to 'territorial status'; it interpreted this term as extending to the continental shelf even though that area was not a known legal concept at the time of the relevant 1928 treaty.[64] In the *Navigational and Related Rights case (Costa Rica v Nicaragua)* the Court identified the underlying idea as being that:

...where the parties have used generic terms in a treaty, the parties necessarily having been aware that the meaning of the terms was likely to evolve over time, and where the treaty has been entered into for a very long period or is 'of continuing duration', the parties must be presumed, as a general rule, to have intended those terms to have an evolving meaning.[65]

This suggests three elements as indicators that evolutionary interpretation is appropriate:

- use of language adapted to evolve, such as 'generic' terms;
- long or indefinite duration of the treaty;
- consequent general presumption of awareness and intention of the parties that those terms would evolve.[66]

A significant point to note from the development of the ICJ's approach to evolutionary interpretation is that it seems in line with the Vienna rules, although its opinion in the *Namibia* case was given very soon after the conclusion of the Vienna Convention and many years before the ICJ's specific endorsement of the Vienna rules. As shown in the quotation from that case above, the Court looked to see that the terms and concepts used in the treaty were 'by definition evolutionary' and 'deemed' that the parties must therefore have accepted them as such. In other words the Court did not set off on an inquiry into the intentions of the parties outside the treaty but, as the Court put it in *Navigational and Related Rights (Costa*

---

[62] *Legal consequences for States of the continued presence of South Africa in Namibia (South West Africa), notwithstanding Security Council resolution 276 (1970)* [1971] *ICJ Reports* 16, at 31, para 53 (emphasis added); and see fuller extract and consideration of this case in Chapter 7, section 1.2 above.

[63] *Dispute regarding Navigational and Related Rights (Costa Rica v Nicaragua)* [2009] ICJ Reports 214, at 242–4, paras 63–71, and see further consideration of this case in Chapter 6, section 4.7 above.

[64] *Aegean Sea Continental Shelf (Greece v. Turkey)* [1978] ICJ Reports 3; see Chapter 5, section 3.3.5 above.

[65] *Dispute regarding Navigational etc (Costa Rica v Nicaragua)* [2009] ICJ Reports 214, at 243, para 66.

[66] See also S T Helmersen, 'Evolutive Treaty Interpretation: Legality, Semantics and Distinctions' (2013) 6 *European Journal of Legal Studies* 127.

Rica v Nicaragua), based its assessment on 'the intentions of its authors as reflected by the text of the treaty', that is, through interpretation of the treaty.[67] Criticism that such an approach does not look to the actual intentions of the parties may misunderstand the objective effect of application of the Vienna rules to give a meaning to the text of a treaty. The emerging reliance by the ILC on the 'presumed intention' of the parties, in the context of the role of subsequent agreements and subsequent practice in interpretation, indirectly supports the idea of deeming parties to have accepted evolutionary interpretation by suggesting one type of relevant evidence, but this is always with the understanding that 'presumed intention' is the product of proper application of the Vienna rules.

Individual judges of the ICJ have explored evolutionary interpretation more extensively. A particularly useful account of the relevant case law was given by Judge Guillaume in the *Navigational and Related Rights case (Costa Rica v Nicaragua)* where he identified contrasting approaches:

The question of the effect of the passage of time on treaty interpretation has been the subject of spirited debate in the literature between proponents of 'contemporaneous' (also called 'fixed reference') interpretation and advocates of 'evolutionary' (also called 'mobile reference') interpretation. Thus, within the International Law Commission 'there was support for the principle of contemporaneity as well as the evolutive approach', but a consensus seems to have emerged to the effect that the problem should be resolved through the application of ordinary methods of treaty interpretation.[68]

This confirms that problems presented by time considerations should be resolved by 'ordinary methods' of treaty interpretation. Nevertheless, analysis, such as that of Judge Guillaume, does offer broader help in tackling those problems. Expansion of the meaning resulting from development of new activities or technologies potentially coming within a generic or vague term is a different situation from one where new rules of law have to be considered. The latter directs attention to article 31(3)(c) of the Vienna Convention's general rule, while the former requires appropriate resolution of terms that may be 'vague' but in appropriate circumstances are properly subjected to evolutionary interpretation.[69]

---

[67] *Dispute regarding Navigational and Related Rights (Costa Rica v Nicaragua)* [2009] ICJ Reports 214, at 237, para 48. See further Bjorge, *The Evolutionary Interpretation of Treaties* and cf M Dawidowicz, 'The Effect of the Passage of Time on the Interpretation of Treaties: Some Reflections on *Costa Rica v. Nicaragua*' (2011) 24 *Leiden Journal of International Law* 201.

[68] *Dispute regarding Navigational and Related Rights (Costa Rica v Nicaragua)*, Declaration of Judge ad hoc Guillaume, [2009] ICJ Reports 214, at 296–6, para 9 (footnotes omitted) and paras 10–15 listing and analysing examples of interpretations falling into either category ('fixed' or 'mobile' reference) or showing features from both.

[69] The *'Iron Rhine'* arbitral award offers a very good example of account being taken of developments coming within article 31(3)(c): see Chapter 7, sections 4.1.2, 4.2, and 4.7 above; cf the ICJ judgment in the *Danube Dams* case, *Case concerning the Gabčíkovo-Nagymaros Project (Hungary/Slovakia)* [1997] ICJ Reports 7, at 67–68, para 112: 'By inserting these evolving provisions [previously enumerated articles] in the Treaty, the parties recognized the potential necessity to adapt the Project. Consequently, the Treaty is not static, and is open to adapt to emerging norms of international law.' It has been noted, however, that the Court was here suggesting the parties reach further agreement

A further aspect of the approach taken by the ICJ to evolutionary interpretation is the significance which the Court attaches to institutional arrangements. In the *Whaling* case the Court described the role of the Commission set up under the International Whaling Convention. That Convention incorporated a Schedule setting out provisions regulating the conservation of whale stocks or the management of the whaling industry.[70] These provisions can be amended by the Commission, and have been amended to such an extent that the ICJ observed: 'The functions conferred on the Commission have made the Convention an evolving instrument'.[71]

The significance of institutional arrangements in relation to evolutionary interpretation and for interpretation of 'vague' provisions is particularly apparent in the case of treaties establishing courts to consider issues of human rights. The contribution of the ECtHR to developing the idea of evolutionary interpretation is briefly considered here, and the role of institutional arrangements in interpretation of human rights treaties in the following section.

4.2 The European Court of Human Rights

'Vague', in the sense discussed above, is the description which best characterizes many of the formulations in human rights treaties. Hence it is no surprise that decisions of the ECtHR have established a number of doctrines based on the principles in the European Convention on Human Rights and the Court has provided the cradle for development of 'evolutive' interpretation in line with the concept of the Convention as a 'living instrument'. This points to 'dynamic' rather than 'static' interpretation.[72]

It has been noted that there are two main ways in which evolutive interpretation may occur.[73] First, there may be a change to an interpretation that at a particular point reflected a settled meaning, whether settled by absence of different understanding at the time of drafting, by practice, or by decision of a competent institution. Second, there may be an interpretation 'applying a provision to a novel set of circumstances which were not anticipated during drafting, ratification, or previous

---

on this and it is therefore questionable whether this should be regarded as evolutive interpretation: Helmersen, 'Evolutive Treaty Interpretation: Legality, Semantics and Distinctions', at 132.

[70] *Whaling in the Antarctic (Australia v Japan: New Zealand intervening)*, Judgment of 31 March 2014, para 45; and for full analysis of issues of interpretation raised in this case, see M Fitzmaurice, 'The Whaling Convention and Thorny Issues of Interpretation', in D Tamada and M Fitzmaurice (eds), *Whaling in the Antarctic: The Judgment and its Implications* (Nijhoff/Brill, forthcoming).

[71] *Whaling in the Antarctic (Australia v Japan: New Zealand intervening)*, Judgment of 31 March 2014, para 45; and see Bjorge, *The Evolutionary Interpretation of Treaties*, 80–2.

[72] See M Fitzmaurice, 'Dynamic (Evolutive) Interpretation of Treaties: Part I' (2008) 21 *Hague Yearbook of International Law* 101 and 'Part II' (2009) 22 *Hague Yearbook of International Law* 3; P-M Dupuy 'Evolutionary Interpretation of Treaties: Between Memory and Prophecy', Chapter 7 in E Cannizzaro (ed), *The Law of Treaties Beyond the Vienna Convention* (Oxford: OUP, 2011); K Dzehtsiarou and C O'Mahony, 'Evolutive Interpretation of Rights Provisions: A Comparison of the European Court of Human Rights and the U.S. Supreme Court' (2013) 44 *Columbia Human Rights Law Review* 309.

[73] Dzehtsiarou and O'Mahony, at 319.

case law and thus on which no settled understanding actually exists'.[74] The former type of change is akin to amendment.[75] The latter may most readily attract the epithet 'dynamic', particularly if viewed as in some way drawing a wider inspiration than an immediate literal impression would afford if taken without regard to context and other factors.

The ECtHR's jurisprudence is mainly in this second category, although there are examples of judgments which are at odds with earlier ones or seem substantially so (and thus within the first category).[76] 'Evolutive' is generally directly equated with the 'living instrument' approach as stated by the ECtHR in the *Tyrer* (corporal punishment) case:

[T]he Convention is a living instrument which, as the Commission rightly stressed, must be interpreted in the light of present-day conditions. In the case now before it the Court cannot but be influenced by the developments and commonly accepted standards in the penal policy of the Member States of the Council of Europe in this field.[77]

Though in different language, this can be seen to be based on a somewhat similar idea to that of the ICJ in the *Namibia* case above. The ECtHR explicitly makes this link, referring to:

the Court's well-established approach to the Convention as a living instrument which must be interpreted in the light of present-day conditions... a principle which reflects the general rule that the interpretation of international treaties requires consideration of the evolution of the relevant legal norms and concepts (see *Demir and Baykara v. Turkey* [GC], no. 34503/97, § 153, ECHR 2008; and *Advisory Opinion on Legal Consequences for States of the Continued Presence of South Africa in Namibia (South West Africa) Notwithstanding Security Council Resolution 276 (1970)*, [1971] International Court of Justice Reports 16, pp. 31-32, § 53).[78]

The notion of the European Convention as a 'living instrument' in the 1978 *Tyrer* case has become a 'given' in the jurisprudence of the ECtHR.[79] However, the actual description 'evolutive' is perhaps more commonly found in the separate and dissenting judgments. The general idea is that an approximation of a current consensus is to be taken into account in interpreting the vague terms of the Convention, such consensus not being confined to too precise an analysis of domestic laws and international instruments.[80] The case law of the ECtHR

---

[74] Dzehtsiarou and O'Mahony, at 319.   [75] Dzehtsiarou and O'Mahony, at 319.

[76] See for example *Goodwin v UK* (Application no 28957/95), Judgment of 11 July 2002, at paras 73–5 explaining the basis for the Court not following its earlier judgments.

[77] *Tyrer v United Kingdom*, Series A, No 26, (1979–80) 2 EHRR 1, at 10, para 31.

[78] *Ternovskis v Latvia* (Application no 33637/02), Judgment of 29 April 2014, para 49 (further citations of ECtHR jurisprudence omitted).

[79] See, for example, *X v Austria* (Application no 19010/07), Judgment of 19 February 2013, para 139: '...given that the Convention is a living instrument...'.

[80] Cf K Dzehtsiarou, 'European Consensus and the Evolutive Interpretation of the European Convention on Human Rights' (2011) 12 *German LJ* 1730; see also A Mowbray, ' The Creativity of the European Court of Human Rights' (2005) 5 *Human Rights Law Review* 57, contrasting the 'living instrument' doctrine and the 'practical and effective' doctrine.

on evolutive interpretation is too extensive for detailed analysis such as has been thoroughly undertaken elsewhere.[81] In the present context, however, it may be helpful to note that Letsas suggests that the Court introduced the notion of a living instrument 'with a view to understand better the principles that underpin the Convention, regardless of how states themselves apply these principles'.[82] Letsas also observes that the jurisprudence of the ECtHR shows a 'shift from commonly accepted standards in domestic legislation to signs of evolution of attitudes among modern societies', leading to a conclusion that the Court has been 'primarily interested in evolution towards the moral truth of the ECHR rights, not in evolution towards some commonly accepted standard, regardless of its content'.[83]

While it can be seen that article 31(3)(c) of the Vienna Convention is a mandate for taking into account relevant obligations from other international sources, and is a provision to which the ECtHR has been making increasing reference, as the Court does not confine itself strictly to obligations binding on all relevant parties, the central question here is whether the Court's approach applies, or is consistent with, the Vienna rules.[84] Does the Court's view of the European Convention and its own function warrant what looks like a rather sweeping reliance on the object and purpose of the Convention?

In the 1975 *Golder* case, where the Court found that a right to have access to a court was necessarily inherent in a provision which may appear to safeguard rights to due process in the course of proceedings, the Court was attentive to formulating reasons fitting the Vienna rules.[85] While this may be viewed as a dynamic approach, it is less appropriately labelled evolutive since the decision did not rely on any approximation of consensus or on a range of external sources of growing applicability.

The difficulty with the approach in *Tyrer* is that the analysis of the growing consensus is sparse and not based on materials constituting obligations which would fit within article 31(3)(c). It can be suggested, however, that there are elements of underpinning for this type of evolutive interpretation in the Vienna rules: the principles of good faith, effectiveness, taking into account context, object and purpose, considering general rules of international law and obligations in other instruments, and so forth; but these only provide a limited platform in the case of a treaty whose provisions are vague and are combined with establishment of institutions which, even if not originally designed for evolutive initiatives, have been revamped to give

---

[81] See, for example, G Letsas, *A Theory of Interpretation of the European Convention on Human Rights* (Oxford: OUP, 2007), M Fitzmaurice, 'Dynamic (Evolutive) Interpretation of Treaties: Part I' (2008) 21 *Hague Yearbook of International Law* 101 and 'Part II' (2009) 22 *Hague Yearbook of International Law* 3.

[82] Letsas, *A Theory of Interpretation*, at 75.   [83] Letsas, at 77 and 79.

[84] On the Court's use of article 31(3)(c), see J Arato, 'Constitutional Transformation in the ECtHR: Strasbourg's Expansive Recourse to External Rules of International Law' (2011–2012) 37 *Brook J Int'l L* 349; and V P Tzevelekos, 'The Use of Article 31(3)(C) of the VCLT in the Case Law of the ECtHR: An Effective Anti-Fragmentation Tool or a Selective Loophole for the Reinforcement of Human Rights Teleology—Between Evolution and Systemic Integration' (2009–2010) 31 *Mich J Int'l L* 621.

[85] See further Chapter 7, section 4.5 above.

sharper focus to that end. A possible conclusion is that human rights treaties warrant distinct consideration, not because interpretative rules different from those in the Vienna Convention apply but because the treaty provisions are drawn up in a way which takes the interpreter beyond the rules. The case law which human rights treaties have generated illustrates particularly well the way in which the Vienna rules lead to interpretation embracing development of doctrines necessary to give meaning to 'vague' provisions when accompanied by institutions to this end.

5. Particular Regimes

That the growing case law in particular areas has been so extensive as to warrant complete individual studies of interpretation of treaties on human rights, the WTO, tax, investment, etc has been noted at the start of this chapter. Does this indicate that particular regimes demand or establish special rules of interpretation? Apart from occasional suggestions in commentary, there is little to suggest from practice that the Vienna rules are not the proper rules for interpretation of all treaties, at least as a starting point.[86] Taking up an earlier theme of this chapter, however, it is suggested that where treaties are drawn up in 'vague' terms—that is, where the substantive rules are vague and combined with provisions setting up institutions for their interpretation—the Vienna rules can only constitute the foundation for more developed approaches to interpretation. This is illustrated here by a brief study of human rights treaties.[87] In contrast, where there have been stronger suggestions that the Vienna rules are inappropriate in the case of international criminal law treaties, examination of case law suggests that it is inadequate appreciation or incomplete application of the Vienna rules which is the foundation for the claim that international criminal law is a special case for which the rules are not suitable.

5.1 International Human Rights Law

There may be some good reasons for identifying the treaties establishing international human rights law as a category showing special features. Perhaps the most

---

[86] See B Çali, 'Specialized Rules of Treaty Interpretation: Human Rights' Chapter 21 in Hollis (ed), *The Oxford Guide to Treaties* where arguments on both sides are given leading to the conclusion that human rights treaty law does not constitute an exceptional regime such as to exclude the Vienna rules but that 'special rules of interpretation called for by human rights treaties have been crystallized under the overarching umbrella of effectiveness' (at p 547); see also Weiler noting 'the emergence of different hermeneutics across the landscape of judicial treaty interpretation', J H H Weiler, 'The Interpretation of Treaties—A Re-examination' (2010) 21 EJIL 507; cf the different sense in which treaties setting the constitutions of international organizations may form a special class of treaty, as considered in Chapter 4, section 2.2 above.

[87] For a somewhat analogous view that in WTO dispute resolution interpretation goes beyond the Vienna rules embracing the WTO's unique 'inherited intellectual culture', see F Smith, 'Power, Rules, and the WTO' (2013) 54 *Boston College L R* 1063.

significant one from the standpoint of the law of treaties is that, in a loose sense, human rights treaties (starting with those guaranteeing rights of minorities and refugees as forerunners of more modern ones), are more concerned with individuals than the relations of treaty parties with one another, although the latter is the basis of all treaties and plays some part in the guarantee of the rights.

This, however, does not seem to be so significant a factor in their interpretation as contrasted with the way in which they are drafted. Typically, in treaties in this area broad descriptions of rights are coupled with mechanisms to ensure (or encourage) respect for them. Thus, for example, the European Convention on Human Rights in its original form used only some 11 articles to define the rights, out of a total of 61 articles. The great majority of the Convention's provisions concerned the various bodies for 'collective enforcement' (in the words of the preamble) of the rights through petitions and cases taken to the relevant institutions. At that time these were the Commission, Court, Committee of Ministers, and Secretariat.[88] In other words, most of the Convention was concerned with setting up the bodies and mechanisms to guarantee the rights and freedoms stated in the opening provisions.

Formulating rights in broad and brief terms in a treaty which sets up elaborate institutions gives the appearance of a recipe for those institutions to undertake extensive interpretation. The provisions defining rights are, in terms which this chapter has explored, 'vague' rather than 'ambiguous'; that is, they are likely to result in cases where the provisions might or might not apply, as contrasted with using terms having two or more quite distinct senses.[89] Although institutionally quite different from a national or supreme constitutional court, the ECtHR is interpreting provisions drafted in terms which invite comparison in their manner of formulation with, for example, the US Bill of Rights. Seeking once more the assistance of the definitions and analysis summarized above, it might be thought that 'ambiguities in legal texts can (usually) be resolved by interpretation, but constitutional vagueness always requires construction'.[90] However, recollecting that such a distinction between ambiguity and vagueness is not always clear cut, and that a distinction between interpretation and construction is not clearly identifiable in treaty interpretation, can transposition of these ideas help with a human rights treaty? It may be that they help explain the combination of use of the Vienna rules and development of themes or approaches by the ECtHR.

Although the case law of the ECtHR dates back to well before the 1969 Vienna Convention entered into force in 1980, the ECtHR referred to its rules for treaty interpretation a few times before the latter date on the basis that the provisions on interpretation 'enunciate in essence generally accepted principles of international

---

[88] Convention for the Protection of Human Rights and Fundamental Freedoms, Rome, 1950; the institutions were reformed to replace the existing European Commission and Court of Human Rights with a new permanent Court from the entry into force of Protocol 11 in 1998.

[89] See section 2 above.

[90] L B Solum, 'The Interpretation-Construction Distinction' (2010–2011) *27 Const. Comment* 95, at 98.

law'.[91] However, while there are cases where the Court has given a careful account of how it is applying the rules of interpretation, for the most part explicit reference to the Vienna rules is rare.[92] This does not necessarily indicate that they are not being used by the Court since it is common for courts and tribunals not to allude to rules which they use every day.[93] What it does suggest is that, where the main provisions of a treaty that are likely to need interpretation are in such broad and economical terms, the rules will only help the interpreter a smaller part of the way than in the case of more detailed treaty provisions.

The two areas briefly examined here are the way in which the Court has used the Vienna rules and the extent to which its development of principles guiding its interpretation and application of the European Convention in particular aspects align with the Vienna rules. The former of these has already been partly considered in relation to specific issues as they occur throughout the present study. One aspect of particular interest here, however, is the way in which the ECtHR has used preparatory work.

In *Litwa v Poland* the Court used preparatory work in its role of confirming a meaning ascribed to the term 'alcoholics' reached by application of the general rule. This was despite their particular application of the general rule appearing to produce a reading which went against a strict meaning of the term 'alcoholics', and even though the arguments which it deployed could readily have justified using the preparatory work to determine the meaning without stretching the general rule.[94] Less easy to accommodate to the Vienna rules is the judgment of the ECtHR in *Young, James and Webster v UK*.[95] In issue was whether the right to form and to join trade unions (article 11) included, by inference, a right not to be compelled to join an association or trade union. In summary, as a result of agreement between trade unions and employers 'a closed shop' was formed, the nature of which was to require the applicants, if they were to remain employees, to become members of one of the specified trade unions. The preparatory work of the European Convention included an explanation that:

On account of the difficulties raised by the 'closed-shop system' in certain countries, the Conference [of Officials preparing the draft articles] in this connection considered that it was undesirable to introduce into the Convention a rule under which 'no one may be

---

[91] *Golder v United Kingdom* ECHR No. 4451/70, Judgment of 21 February 1975, para 29, where the ECtHR also noted that, in accordance with article 5 of the Vienna Convention, its use of the Vienna rules in interpreting the European Convention is subject, where appropriate, to 'any relevant rules' of the Council of Europe, the organization within which the Court is established; see further Bjorge, *The Evolutionary Interpretation of Treaties*, 30–31.

[92] On the sparsity of references in the Court's jurisprudence to the rules, see G Letsas, 'Strasbourg's Interpretive Ethic: Lessons for the International Lawyer' (2010) 21 EJIL 509, at 512 ff; for an example of an explicit application of the rules, see *Litwa v Poland* considered in Chapter 1, section 5.1 above.

[93] The Court's acceptance of the role of the Vienna rules is, for example, indicated by its reference to its 'constant practice of interpreting the Convention in the light of the rules set out in the Vienna Convention on the Law of Treaties': *Hassan v UK* Application no 29750/09, Judgment of 16 September 2014, para 100.

[94] See Chapter 1, section 5.1 above.

[95] Application nos 7601/76 and 7806/77, Judgment of 13 August 1981.

compelled to belong to an association' which features in [Article 20 par. 2 of] the United Nations Universal Declaration.[96]

This appeared to indicate that a right to opt out of a closed shop was deliberately not included in the Convention. Did this mean that the right to join a trade union could *not* be interpreted as including a right not to be compelled to join? The Court stated that it did not 'consider it necessary to answer this question on this occasion', apparently meaning it was unnecessary to address the general question whether the positive right to join was not matched by a negative right, ie not to join.[97] The Court did add, however, that 'the notion of a freedom implies some measure of freedom of choice as to its exercise', and that assuming from the preparatory work that a general rule of the kind in the Universal Declaration of Human Rights was deliberately omitted 'it does not follow that the negative aspect of a person's freedom of association falls completely outside the ambit of [article 11] and that each and every compulsion to join a particular trade union is compatible with the intention of that provision'.[98]

The Court considered that 'to construe [article 11] as permitting every kind of compulsion in the field of trade union membership would strike at the very substance of the freedom it is designed to guarantee' and, emphasizing that it was dealing with individual cases rather than the principle of the closed shop, the Court found that:

a threat of dismissal involving loss of livelihood is a most serious form of compulsion...directed against persons engaged...before the introduction of any obligation to join a particular trade union....[S]uch a form of compulsion, in the circumstances of the case, strikes at the very substance of the freedom guaranteed by [article 11]....[99]

It may seem near the limit of reasonable argument for the Court to have viewed the rejection of a general right not to be forced into a closed shop as meaning merely that 'compulsion to join a particular trade union may not always be contrary to the Convention'; but it seems that the Court was ultimately seeking to attribute a fair meaning to the right to 'freedom of association with others' in circumstances where the closed shop was to be imposed on applicants who were already in employment, a circumstance which was not the specific basis for the rejection of the proposed general right not to be obliged to join a particular union. Hence a loosely drafted provision stating the Convention right was matched by a rejection of a general rule having a loosely indicated basis, viz 'difficulties raised by the "closed-shop system"'.

The ECtHR has developed a number of interpretative strategies enabling it to attempt a consistent approach to some of the Human Rights Convention's broadly drawn provisions. Particularly well known among these are that the Convention is to be taken as 'a living instrument' (*Tyrer*, 1978) with scope for 'evolutive'

---

[96] Judgment of 13 August 1981, para 51. [97] Judgment of 13 August 1981, para 52.
[98] Judgment of 13 August 1981, para 52.
[99] Judgment of 13 August 1981, paras 52 and 55.

interpretation (*Soering v UK*, 1989), the principle of 'proportionality' ('*Belgian Linguistics*', 1968), and the doctrine of 'margin of appreciation' (*Engel v Netherlands*, 1976).[100] These interpretative approaches of the Court, noted above with indications of early cases in which they were mentioned, have become consistent elements in the jurisprudence of the Court. It can be seen that they date from long before the new Court came into being in 1998. The question considered here is how they relate, if at all, to the Vienna rules.

One way of answering this is to suggest that the Vienna rules only furnish a first step in giving meaning to the terms defining the rights in the European Convention. The Convention is only a little less laconic in its exposition of freedom of expression than the statement in the US Constitution's first amendment that 'Congress shall make no law...abridging the freedom of speech'. As noted above, that statement contains no overt reference to freedom from 'prior restraint', but the courts charged with its interpretation had to develop the legal content of the concept of freedom of speech. While in the broadly comparable situation the ECtHR has been given some indication by the Vienna rules of the materials to be taken into account and how to go about giving meaning to the terms of a treaty, a major component of the Court's approach is its mandate from the European Convention 'to ensure the observance of the engagements undertaken by the High Contracting Parties in the Convention and the Protocols thereto'.[101] This requires giving effective meaning to the rights.

A broadly similar position obtains in the case law under the American Convention on Human Rights, 1969. Although article 29 of that Convention ('Restrictions Regarding Interpretation') contains provisions on its interpretation, these are not exactly special rules of interpretation but are expressed as exclusionary principles mainly relating the stated rights to those of others or protected under other instruments. They do, however, guide the Inter-American Court of Human Rights in its approach to interpretation. The Court nevertheless shows signs that it values compatibility of its approach with that of the Vienna rules, stating:

This evolutive interpretation is consistent with the general rules of interpretation set forth in Article 29 of the American Convention, as well those set forth in the Vienna Convention....[102]

---

[100] *Tyrer v UK* (Application no 5856/72) Judgment of 15 March 1978, *Soering v UK* (Application no 14038/88) Judgment of 7 July 1989, *Case Relating to Certain Aspects of the Laws on the Use of Languages in Education in Belgium (Merits)* (Application no 2126/64 and others) Judgment of 23 July 1968, *Engel v Netherlands* (Application no 5370/72 and others) Judgment of 8 June 1976.

[101] Preamble to European Convention on Human Rights as amended by Protocols No. 11 and No. 14 (CETS No. 194), article 19. The interpretative significance of the moral dimension of this work of the Court beyond the Vienna rules has been convincingly shown by G Letsas in *A Theory of Interpretation of the European Convention on Human Rights* (Oxford: OUP, 2007) and Letsas, 'Strasbourg's Interpretive Ethic: Lessons for the International Lawyer' (2010) 21 EJIL 509. For further study of interpretation of the Convention see M Fitzmaurice, 'Dynamic (Evolutive) Interpretation of Treaties: Part I' (2008) 21 *Hague Yearbook of International Law* 101, 'Part II' (2009) 22 *Hague Yearbook of International Law* 3, and M Fitzmaurice, 'Interpretation of Human Rights Treaties', Chapter 31 in Shelton (ed), *The Oxford Handbook of International Human Rights Law*; and Bjorge, *The Evolutionary Interpretation of Treaties*.

[102] *Case of the "Mapiripán Massacre" v Colombia (Merits, Reparations, and Costs)*, Judgment of 15 September 2005, para 106 (citations from earlier jurisprudence omitted); cf Lixinski: 'the

5.2 International Criminal Law

International criminal law is sometimes said to require special rules of interpretation because of presumptions which are particularly applicable to defend the position of the accused. Thus, for example, in interpreting the definition of a crime, any ambiguity or uncertainty must be resolved in favour of the accused. Unfortunately discussion of this has been ill served by judgments of tribunals having jurisdiction over criminal matters which purport to apply the Vienna rules but whose use of them is rather far removed from their proper application. The consequence is that criticism is sometimes levelled against the rules when it should be directed to their misuse.

This is well illustrated by a judgment of the Appeals Chamber of the International Criminal Tribunal for the former Yugoslavia (ICTY) in the *Tadić* case.[103] In one part of this judgment the Tribunal shifts the test for inclusion within the status of 'protected person' from whether the persons concerned are 'nationals' (in the relevant treaty's terms) to one of their ethnicity.[104] The supporting argument is based on general intent deduced from reference in the preparatory work to the different matter of retention of status by those who become refugees, and from a very general assessment of object and purpose.[105] This generalized teleological approach is not one which the Vienna rules envisage. The primary reference to object and purpose in the first part of the general rule is to their use as a means of identifying the ordinary meaning of the terms that are to be interpreted. The tribunal in the *Tadić* case made no attempt to find the ordinary meaning of 'protected person' in the proper way. Further, the use it made of preparatory work was not by way of supplementing the general rule. The tribunal did not attempt to confirm a meaning derived by use of the general rule, did not identify the prerequisites for resort to preparatory work (if purporting to use it to *determine* the meaning), and did not limit itself to using the preparatory work to illuminate the common understanding of the parties.

Thus this part of the judgment paid scant regard to proper application of the Vienna rules. Yet later in the same judgment the Vienna rules were specifically invoked (albeit somewhat inaccurately describing the content of article 32) to reject any use of the preparatory work because the meaning of the terms in question was said to be clear.[106] The latter part of the judgment does, however, come

Inter-American Court applies general cannons of interpretation, but it derives them from the specific rules of interpretation of Article 29, instead of the VCLT', L Lixinski, 'Treaty Interpretation by the Inter-American Court of Human Rights: Expansionism at the Service of the Unity of International Law' (2010) 21 EJIL 585, at 602; and see Fitzmaurice, 'Interpretation of Human Rights Treaties', Chapter 31 in Shelton (ed), *The Oxford Handbook of International Human Rights Law*, at 757–9.

[103] *The Prosecutor v Duško Tadić* (Appeals Chamber), Judgment of 15 July 1999, IT-94-1-A.
[104] Judgment of 15 July 1999, IT-94-1-A, paras 163–169.
[105] Judgment of 15 July 1999, IT-94-1-A, para 164.
[106] Judgment of 15 July 1999, IT-94-1-A, paras 298–304, esp at 303.

nearer to the approach which the Vienna rules mandate than the earlier part, but both show that inadequate application of the Vienna rules provides a poor start.

Attention to the use of the Vienna rules by special criminal tribunals has been somewhat obscured by the origins of those tribunals created by the UN Security Council through resolutions rather than having their foundations in treaty form. Whether the Vienna rules are appropriate for such application is not the issue here.[107] If rules are applied, they should be applied properly. Unfortunately, it looks as if the uncertainty about whether the rules correctly apply may have contributed to the idea that modifications of them or bowdlerisation is permissible, so that a halfway house is entered, somewhere between a broad-brush teleological approach and proper application of the rules. One result which has been noticed is that contradictory results have been achieved where issues of jurisdiction have arisen in contrast with issues of substance.[108] For the former (jurisdiction), the extreme teleological scheme produces broad jurisdiction, while for the latter, closer adherence to the Vienna rules produces a result more nearly matching the requirements of criminal law for strict interpretation, favouring of the accused where there is doubt.

How is the extreme teleological approach different from the dynamic or evolutive approach of the ECtHR and other human rights tribunals? Put generally, a human rights treaty enumerating rights in 'vague' terms, with institutions designed to resolve the vagueness in a manner consonant with an object and purpose stated in general terms, is to be contrasted with bodies whose raison d'être is to achieve justice by respecting precise definitions of crimes and jurisdiction consonant with respect for international justice.[109] As indicated above, the status of the constitutive instruments of the ICTY is not such as to unquestionably attract the application of the Vienna rules but, if applying them, it is not acceptable to misapply them.

Another example of inadequate application of the Vienna rules is provided by a Chamber of the Special Tribunal for Lebanon in *Ayyash et al*.[110] The Chamber took the view that paragraph (1) of article 31 of the Vienna Convention gave it carte blanche to apply a general teleological approach, stating after its caveat about the questionable applicability of the Vienna rules to UNSC resolutions:

rules must be interpreted 'in good faith in accordance with the ordinary meaning to be given to the terms of the treaty in their context and in the light of its object and purpose'.

---

[107] For a review of some issues over approaches to interpretation in international criminal law, see L Grover, 'A Call to Arms: Fundamental Dilemmas Confronting the Interpretation of Crimes in the Rome Statute of the International Criminal Court' (2010) 21 EJIL 543; D Jacobs, 'International Criminal Law', Chapter 17 in J d'Aspremont and J Kammerhofer (eds), *International Legal Positivism in a Post-Modern World* (Cambridge: CUP, 2014).

[108] W A Schabas, 'Interpreting the Statutes of the *ad hoc* tribunals' in L C Vorah et al (eds), *Man's Inhumanity to Man: Essays on International Law in Honour of Antonio Cassese* (The Hague: Kluwer Law International, 2003), 847 at 887.

[109] See, for example, final recital of Preamble to Rome Statute of the International Criminal Court, 1999.

[110] *The Prosecutor v Ayyash et al*, 16 February 2011, Interlocutory STL-11-01/1, STL Casebook 2011, 29.

The latter portion of this clause embodies the principle of teleological interpretation, which emphasises the need to construe the provisions of a treaty in such a manner as to render them effective and operational with a view to attaining the purpose for which they were agreed upon.[111]

This is unfortunate. It misrepresents article 31(1), substituting 'rules' for the actual opening reference to a 'treaty' (ie the text) and its terms, ignoring the grammar and syntax (which associates the object and purpose with the ascertaining of the ordinary meaning) and then, in that and the subsequent paragraph, treats the ill-described provision as a basis for concluding that the Vienna rules are simply a direction to produce a generally teleological outcome. Given that the same judgment manages to quote from the ILC's commentary on the draft articles emerging as the VCLT on the principle of effectiveness, one might have hoped that it would have paid closer attention to the actual Vienna rules on interpretation, and at least as regards object and purpose should have found in the commentary the explanation:

the ordinary meaning of a term is not to be determined in the abstract but in the context of the treaty and in the light of its object and purpose.[112]

That these are but two examples of poor use of the Vienna rules by *ad hoc* tribunals having international criminal jurisdiction is confirmed by the observation that in those tribunals the rules 'appear to have been available by analogy' and that 'although for the most part justified, their application was frequently chaotic and unsystematic'.[113] This assessment, though clearly correct, probably understates the considerable harm done by misleading and incomplete application of the Vienna rules. Such practice violates the principle of unity of application of the rules, as well as diverging on numerous occasions from the proper use of their elements.

The start of the work of the International Criminal Court (ICC) might be expected to lead to systematic interpretation of treaty provisions. The governing instruments were drafted in preparatory bodies and sessions of a diplomatic conference, a process which allowed for more deliberative negotiation than was possible in the UN Security Council in its work on the *ad hoc* tribunals. Hence it could be hoped that the Court might interpret treaty terms with more comprehensive and confident use of the Vienna rules. Academic discussion of some of the issues which may arise does not, unfortunately, lead to confidence that this will be the case.

A good illustration is debate over whether chemical and biological weapons are included in the term 'poison', 'poisoned', and 'poisonous' etc in the definition of war crimes in the ICC's constitution (the Rome Statute).[114] A full interpretation of these terms would require extensive evaluation of a range of material, but two pertinent pieces of information in that process would be: first, that a proposed

---

[111] *The Prosecutor v Ayyash et al*, at 55–6, para 28.
[112] ILC Commentary on draft articles, [1966] Yearbook of the ILC, vol II, p 221, para 12.
[113] S Darcy and J Powderly (eds), *Judicial Creativity at the International Criminal Tribunals* (Oxford: OUP, 2010), at 5.
[114] Article 8(2)(b)(xvii) and (xviii).

provision expressly referring to chemical or biological weapons was deleted at the last moment from the list of crimes in the Rome Statute and, second, a provision which did make it into the final text restated the principle of criminal law favouring the accused: 'The definition of a crime shall be strictly construed and shall not be extended by analogy. In case of ambiguity, the definition shall be interpreted in favour of the person being investigated, prosecuted or convicted.'[115]

Discussion of the interpretation of 'poison', 'poisoned', and 'poisonous' has, unfortunately, at times proceeded on the polarized basis of whether a dictionary definition of ordinary meaning of the terms above would trump the intention of the parties supposedly revealed by the last minute excision recorded in the preparatory work, or vice versa.[116] This has been accompanied by expression of views that the Vienna rules should not apply at all to the ICC Statute or even to international criminal law generally.[117] Such disapplication is suggested as being necessary to respect the presumptions in favour of the accused, or that application of the rules needs to be modified to take account of the presumptions.

None of these approaches seems based upon complete application of the Vienna rules. The rules may certainly be open to criticism, but in any particular case criticism needs to be based on a full assessment of their application. There is no mechanistic rule that one element trumps another. It was well recognized in the work of the ILC, ultimately reflected in the rules, that dictionary meanings are likely to be multiple and would therefore need to be selected (as just one part of the whole process of interpretation) by reference to the context and by taking account of the object and purpose. It was also recognized by the ILC, and in the resultant rules, that preparatory work was to be widely consulted, particularly in the category of 'confirming' a meaning; but such work was to be used more cautiously 'to determine' the meaning when this could not readily be ascertained by application of the general rule. Hence *in the latter case only* (that is, 'to determine' the meaning), use of supplementary means is to be subject to the prerequisite of finding ambiguity, obscurity etc.

In the case of 'poison', one of many meanings in the *Oxford English Dictionary* may well appear to extend to chemical and biological weapons. This would be accommodated in the first, very general, sense ('material that causes illness or death when introduced into or absorbed by a living organism'), but the same dictionary includes a specialist meaning in chemistry and biochemistry ('substance which reduces or blocks the activity of a catalyst...'). Thus at the very least, and as a

---

[115] Article 22 Rome Statute, embodying the fundamental principles requiring crimes to be established by law and doubts resolved in favour of the accused (*nullum crimen*, or *nulla poena, sine lege*, and *in dubio pro rei*); see also R Cryer, 'Royalism and The King: Article 21 of the Rome Statute and the Politics of Sources' (2009) 12 *New Criminal Law Review* 390.

[116] See discussions at <http://opiniojuris.org/2013/08/23/syria-chemical-weapons-incoherence-vclt/>, <http://www.ejiltalk.org/can-the-icc-prosecute-for-use-of-chemical-weapons-in-syria/> and <http://www.ejiltalk.org/treaty-interpretation-the-vclt-and-the-icc-statute-a-response-to-kevin-jon-heller-dov-jacobs/#more-9136>.

[117] See discussions at <http://opiniojuris.org/2013/08/23/syria-chemical-weapons-incoherence-vclt/>, etc.

starting point, there are grounds to question whether the term in the Statute is used in the general sense or with the meaning allied to chemicals. Given the context, which includes in article 22 the embodiment of the presumption in favour of the accused, these differing uses in the dictionary might alone be enough to intimate to an interpreter the existence of ambiguity (whose own definition is multiple and includes: 'indistinct, not clearly defined, admitting more than one interpretation, or of several possible meanings').

The existence of such ambiguity through there being several possible meanings is 'confirmed' by uncertainty surrounding the reason for deletion of specific reference to chemical weapons from the proposed crime at the final stage of negotiation. The context—that is, the whole treaty—makes it clear that the existence of *any* uncertainty is what is significant. In this case that is all that the preparatory work need confirm, without having to be clear on what was the actual intention of the negotiators in their selection of terms. Once uncertainty is shown, the provision of article 22 relating to ambiguity is plainly applicable.

Obviously a proper interpretative exercise would also require a full application of the general rule, including examination of rules of international law applicable in relations between the parties (particularly in the sense of in the other relevant treaty obligations) and consideration of the circumstances of conclusion. However, even from this short introduction to the issues, it can be seen that the proper application of the Vienna rules offers a more detailed process rather than deciding whether a meaning plucked from the dictionary trumps any intention that may be deduced from preparatory work or vice versa.

6. Inconsistent Interpretations

6.1 Is there always a single interpretation that is correct?

If the Vienna rules provide a single set of principles of treaty interpretation, does it follow that the rules are defective if their application leaves open the possibility that different courts and tribunals may interpret the same treaty provisions in a different sense or if their interpretation differs from an intention clearly expressed in preparatory work? The answer lies in the role and purpose of the Vienna rules. It was always a given that there was no mechanical method of ascertaining meaning but that there could be rules giving general guidance on the paths to be followed. However, while the rules constitute a uniform set of principles which should maximize the possibility of reaching a proper interpretation, because of the need for 'investigation, weighing of evidence, judgment, foresight, and a nice appreciation of a number of factors varying from case to case' (in Waldock's phrase above), the outcome of essentially the same exercise may not invariably be uniform. Examining the few instances of divergent interpretations may show how uniform rules nevertheless could provide a better starting point, though no guarantee of uniform outcomes.

In its general approach the WTO Appellate Body continues to stress that the principles of interpretation in the Vienna rules are to be followed in a holistic fashion. In *United States—Continued Zeroing* the Appellate Body stated:

...the enterprise of interpretation is intended to ascertain the proper meaning of a provision; one that fits harmoniously with the terms, context, and object and purpose of the treaty.... The purpose of such an exercise is therefore to narrow the range of interpretations, not to generate conflicting, competing interpretations. Interpretative tools cannot be applied selectively or in isolation from one another. It would be a subversion of the interpretative disciplines of the Vienna Convention if application of those disciplines yielded contradiction instead of coherence and harmony among, and effect to, all relevant treaty provisions.[118]

However, the case law of the Appellate Body reveals a difficult question concerning the Vienna rules arising from a provision in the 'Anti-Dumping Agreement' which directs the approach of a WTO panel to reviewing measures adopted by national authorities in application of the Agreement. As regards facts established by the national authorities, the panel is to

determine whether the authorities' establishment of the facts was proper and whether their evaluation of those facts was unbiased and objective. If the establishment of the facts was proper and the evaluation was unbiased and objective, even though the panel might have reached a different conclusion, the evaluation shall not be overturned.[119]

As regards interpretation of the Anti-Dumping Agreement:

the panel shall interpret the relevant provisions of the Agreement in accordance with customary rules of interpretation of public international law. Where the panel finds that a relevant provision of the Agreement admits of *more than one permissible interpretation*, the panel shall find the authorities' measure to be in conformity with the Agreement if it rests upon one of those permissible interpretations.[120]

It can be seen that as regards both fact and interpretation, these provisions are designed to define the extent to which the WTO panel is to pay respect to the decisions of the national authorities. However, as regards interpretation of the international agreement, there is something of an apparent contradiction. The panel is to follow customary rules of interpretation, which aim to result in a single meaning, while the second sentence of the provision in question suggests multiple meanings. The provision might therefore be thought to suggest that the Vienna rules, as a statement of customary law, envisage different 'permissible' interpretations of the same provision. Yet although the Vienna rules do not provide a mechanical route to a 'correct' result, their proper application should lead to a single autonomous meaning of a treaty or at least the meaning that is legally relevant to the matter in issue.

---

[118] *United States—Continued Existence and Application of Zeroing Methodology*, Report of Appellate Body, WT/DS350/AB/R. 4 February 2009, para 273, footnote omitted.

[119] Agreement on Implementation of Article VI of the General Agreement on Tariffs and Trade 1994 ('the Anti-Dumping Agreement'), article 17.6(i).

[120] Article 17.6(ii), emphasis added.

In application of the Anti-Dumping Agreement, the Appellate Body has adopted an approach which views the reference to 'permissible interpretations' as requiring the interpretative process to be interrupted at a point where differing 'permissible' interpretations have been revealed:

> ... the proper interpretation of the second sentence of Article 17.6(ii) must itself be consistent with the rules and principles set out in the *Vienna Convention*. This means that it cannot be interpreted in a way that would render it redundant, or that derogates from the customary rules of interpretation of public international law. However, the second sentence allows for the possibility that the application of the rules of the *Vienna Convention* may give rise to an interpretative range and, if it does, an interpretation falling within that range is permissible and must be given effect by holding the measure to be in conformity with the covered agreement. The function of the second sentence is thus to give effect to the interpretative range rather than to require the interpreter to pursue further the interpretative exercise to the point where only one interpretation within that range may prevail.[121]

This approach accepts that the interpretative exercise *could* be pursued to result in a single interpretation but that the Anti-Dumping Agreement mandates acceptance of any one which a party has adopted within a range of permissible interpretations. The Appellate Body excludes from such a range the mere existence of multiple possible meanings.[122] It also excludes contradictory interpretations from forming part of a range.[123] Hence, if applying the Vienna rules is seen as a process of 'progressive encirclement' (in the description used by an arbitral tribunal), the Appellate Body views the process as stopping before entering the innermost circle.[124]

Unfortunately, application of the metaphor cannot be illustrated from the Report in *United States—Continued Zeroing* because the Appellate Body found that the interpretations offered as alternatives to the one which it espoused would be 'flatly contradictory' and 'repugnant to the customary rules of treaty interpretation'.[125] The possibility of parallel permissible interpretations should, in any event, be seen as peculiar to any treaty which, like the Anti-Dumping Agreement, envisages this.[126] Normally a treaty provision has only one correct interpretation,

---

[121] *United States—Continued Existence and Application of Zeroing Methodology*, Report, at para 272.

[122] *United States—Continued Existence and Application of Zeroing Methodology*, Report, at para 268.

[123] *United States—Continued Existence and Application of Zeroing Methodology*, Report, at para 273.

[124] On 'progressive encirclement' see *Aguas del Tunari v Bolivia* (ICSID ARB/02/03), Award of 21 October 2005, para 91, and Chapter 5, epigraph and introduction, above; and see further D McRae, 'Treaty Interpretation by the WTO Appellate Body: The Conundrum of Article 17(6) of the WTO Antidumping Agreement', Chapter 10 in E Cannizzaro (ed), *The Law of Treaties Beyond the Vienna Convention* (Oxford: OUP, 2011).

[125] *United States—Continued Existence and Application of Zeroing Methodology*, Report, at para 317.

[126] In a more extended study of this case, McRae helpfully provides an analysis of the Anti-Dumping Agreement problem with a suggested approach for a solution having a focus on the need for rigorous analysis of the term 'permissible' by the Appellate Body to provide the threshold for determining what is permissible: McRae, 'Treaty Interpretation by the WTO Appellate Body: The Conundrum of Article 17(6) of the WTO Antidumping Agreement', Chapter 10 in Cannizzaro

even though there may be scope for great divergence of opinion as to what that interpretation is.

6.2   Divergence over the same terms or from preparatory work: investment disputes

A most fertile area for finding differing interpretations of the same provision, or of ones that are the same or closely similar in different treaties, is in judgments, awards, and decisions of international tribunals relating to bilateral investment treaties (BITs).[127] The number of these treaties is considerable, while the literature analysing the work of tribunal is voluminous. However, the Vienna rules have hitherto only been sketchily applied in many cases, despite frequent reference to them.[128] A specific criticism made by Roberts of the arbitral tribunals is that 'their jurisprudence frequently resembles a house of cards built largely by reference to other tribunal awards and academic opinions, with little consideration of the views and practices of states in general or the treaty parties in particular'.[129] What is suggested here is that a more coherent body of case law could have been achieved had judgments or awards been faithfully based on the common scheme of interpretation in the Vienna rules, even if this would not necessarily ensure complete uniformity of outcomes for controversial issues.

Reinisch has identified and analysed groups of cases where he notes dangers that have arisen, including 'the threat of divergent or even conflicting outcomes' of investment disputes. In summary, these are, first, where different tribunals have reached different interpretations of the same provision or same type of provision, such as interpretations of (a) 'umbrella' clauses (general provisions on scope); (b) most favoured nation (MFN) clauses; (c) provisions for a 'state of necessity';

(ed), *The Law of Treaties Beyond the Vienna Convention*, at 180–3; McRae suggests that in analysing the competing arguments of the disputing parties, 'the greater the balance between the different approaches, the more likelihood that it can be said that there are two permissible interpretations, even though if the process went further one would be chosen'. This seems fairly close to the analysis in the text above.

[127] For a specific account of treaty interpretation in this context, see J R Weeramantry, *Treaty Interpretation in Investment Arbitration* (Oxford: OUP, 2012) whose bibliography helpfully lists numerous relevant books and articles.

[128] See O K Fauchald, 'The Legal Reasoning of ICSID Tribunals—An Empirical Analysis' (2008) 19 EJIL 301, at 314 stating that out of the 98 decisions examined '[a] clear majority of the references were limited to Article 31(1)' of the Vienna Convention; A Saldarriaga, 'Investment Awards and the Rules of Interpretation of the Vienna Convention: Making Room for Improvement' (2013) 28 *ICSID Review* 197, esp at 204–10 showing inadequate use or misuse of the Vienna rules; M Waibel, 'International Investment Law and Treaty Interpretation' in R Hofmann and C Tams (eds), *From Clinical Isolation To Systemic Integration*, (Baden-Baden: Nomos Verlagsgesellschaft, 2011) <http://ssrn.com/abstract=1930725> at p 29: 'My hypothesis is that many investment awards demonstrate a cavalier attitude to treaty interpretation. The contrast with the interpretative practice of a highly developed and institutionalized adjudicatory body like the WTO dispute settlement body is particularly striking' (footnote omitted).

[129] A Roberts, 'Power and Persuasion in Investment Treaty Interpretation: The Dual Role of States' (2010) 104 AJIL 179.

second, cases where the same dispute was arbitrated under two different bilateral investment agreements.[130]

To these may be added the numerous awards and decisions on the meaning and role of the term 'investment' in the Washington Convention which set up the International Centre for Settlement of Investment Disputes (the ICSID Convention), the institution under whose auspices many of the investment arbitrations take place.[131] Some of the contrasting cases on the meaning of 'investment', on 'umbrella clauses', and on MFN clauses are briefly considered here to show how poor use of the Vienna rules has contributed to the confusing picture on these topics and how systematic use of the rules could have produced more consistent results.

6.2.1 *Meaning of 'investment'*

The first group of cases concern the term 'investment' which occurs without definition in article 25 of the ICSID Convention. This provides for the jurisdiction of the ICSID to extend to 'any legal disputes arising directly out of an investment'. BITs typically include a definition of 'investment', many with considerable specificity; and they contain other provisions relevant to jurisdiction, commonly including each state's advance consent to arbitration being established by the treaty itself.

ICSID tribunals investigating the meaning of 'investment' have broadly speaking split into two groups, one comprising those which consider that the bare term 'investment' in article 25 has a primary role in prescribing jurisdiction, and the other consisting of those which view article 25 as leaving it to the particular BIT to provide a definition of 'investment' identifying thereby the extent of acceptance of an ICSID tribunal's jurisdiction. A modified approach in this second camp views the ICSID Convention as providing some outer boundary of what falls within the jurisdiction of the Centre while the relevant BIT provides the detailed definition subject only to its elements falling within the outer boundary. The awards and decisions giving article 25 a primary role have led to development of expandable menus of criteria of what constitutes an investment, broadly reflecting a 'constructivist' approach of the kind discussed above but failing to take into account all the Vienna rules.

A convenient starting point for considering cases on the role and meaning of 'investment' in article 25 is *Salini v Morocco* (the 'first *Salini*' case).[132] Here the Tribunal initiated the transformation of some elements, such as contribution to economic development, duration, participation in risk, etc which were said to

---

[130] A Reinisch, 'The Proliferation of International Dispute Settlement Mechanisms: The Threat of Fragmentation vs. the Promise of a More Effective System? Some Reflections From the Perspective of Investment Arbitration', Chapter 7 in I Buffard, J Crawford, A Pellet, and S Wittich (eds), *International Law between Universalism and Fragmentation: Festschrift in Honour of Gerhard Hafner* (Leiden: Nijhoff, 2008), at 114 ff where the contrasting cases are cited and analysed.

[131] Convention on the Settlement of Investment Disputes between States and Nationals of Other States, Washington, 1965; see further Chapter 4, section 3.4 above.

[132] *Salini Costruttori SpA v Kingdom of Morocco* ICSID Case No. ARB/00/4 (Decision on Jurisdiction, 16 July 2001); see generally: P-E Dupont, 'The Notion of ICSID Investment: Ongoing "Confusion" or "Emerging Synthesis"?' (2011)12 *J World Investment & Trade* 245; J Fellenbaum,

be characteristic of an investment, into the basis of a list of prerequisites for an investment to come within the scope of article 25.[133] The brief reasoning given in the *Salini* decision did not cite the Vienna rules, made no proper analysis in terms of treaty interpretation, but relied (at least in part) on writings which included descriptions of characteristics of investments without any clear indication of what was the catalyst converting these characteristics into obligatory elements. Although the tribunal found that there was an investment in these terms in the particular case, its decision has led to successive tribunals using, and in some cases expanding, the catalogue of characteristics imputed to the term 'investment' as if such components were obligatory.

For the most part tribunals contributing to this approach have shown little real awareness of the contents and proper use of the Vienna rules, though several have mentioned them. One of the key issues is the relationship between 'investment' as used in the ICSID Convention and the detailed definitions commonly found in BITs. Although a few tribunals considering investment disputes have mentioned article 31(3) of the Vienna Convention, they do not appear to have considered whether regular inclusion of definitions of 'investment' in BITs amounts to practice by parties to the ICSID Convention such as to constitute agreement among them as to the *method* of giving meaning to the term 'investment' as distinct from establishing a uniform content for that term.[134]

Similarly, although several tribunals have mentioned article 31(3)(c) of the Vienna Convention, their approach to it does not reveal awareness that its reference to rules of international law covers obligations established by treaty as well as international law generally, such that BIT provisions must be taken into account when interpreting the ICSID Convention. Surprisingly, given the tendency to draw from general ideas about interpretation, the tribunals seem not to have considered, as a possible supplementary element, the legal principle that a general provision does not detract from a specific one (*generalia specialibus non derogant*). The view that the general provision supplies an outer boundary to the meaning of investment may well be sound, but it would be more firmly established if there were examples of actual provisions in BITs falling outside any possible meaning

---

'*GEA v. Ukraine* and the Battle of Treaty Interpretation Principles Over the *Salini* Test' (2011) 27 *Arbitration International* 249.

[133] ICSID Case No. ARB/00/4 (Decision on Jurisdiction, 16 July 2001) paras 50–58.

[134] In *Mihaly International Corporation v Democratic Socialist Republic of Sri Lanka*, ICSID Case No. ARB/00/2, at para 33, the Tribunal noted that the ICSID Convention left the definition of investment to be worked out in the subsequent practice of states; but that is slightly different from showing as part of an interpretation that subsequent practice has now provided sufficient evidence to constitute an agreement to the effect, evidence of which the Tribunal noted had not been presented by the parties (ICSID Case No. ARB/00/2, at para 34): see G Nolte (ed), *Treaties and Subsequent Practice* (Oxford: OUP, 2013), at 233–4, and on use of subsequent practice generally by ICSID tribunals as an interpretative element, Nolte, at 232–37; See also A Roberts, 'Power and Persuasion in Investment Treaty Interpretation: The Dual Role of States' (2010) 104 AJIL 179, at 179–80 and 198–202; C Schreuer, 'Diversity and Harmonization of Treaty Interpretation in Investment Arbitration' in M Fitzmaurice, O Elias, and P Merkouris (eds), *Treaty Interpretation and the Vienna Convention on the Law of Treaties: 30 Years On* (Leiden: Nijhoff, 2010), 129, at 139–47;

of 'investment' rather than positing hypothetical extreme cases and using these to justify imposition of invented entry hurdles for matters well within any ordinary meaning of 'investment'.

Further, the Tribunal in the first *Salini* case did not fully consider the context, the circumstances of conclusion, or the preparatory work. In its decision the Tribunal quoted from the 'Report of the Executive Directors on the ICSID Convention' that accompanied the draft of the ICSID Convention at its adoption and which stated: 'No attempt was made to define the term 'investment' given the essential requirement of consent by the parties, and the mechanism through which Contracting States can make known in advance, if they so desire, the classes of disputes which they would or would not consider submitting to the Centre (art. 25(4))'.[135]

The reference to paragraph (4) of article 25 alone should put an interpreter on notice that the immediate context requires further investigation, quite apart from the standard requirement to engage this element of interpretation when seeking the ordinary meaning of a term. There is also a fair argument that the Report accompanying the Convention could itself be viewed as context in the senses indicated in article 31(2) of the Vienna Convention.[136] Yet no detailed analysis was made of the import of paragraph (4) of article 25 of the ICSID Convention or of the significance and consequences of the passage from the Report quoted by the Tribunal.

Even if the Report is to be regarded as preparatory work rather than context, having quoted from it the *Salini* Tribunal looked no further at the preparatory work. Failure to employ the supplementary means in article 32 of the Vienna Convention properly, or at all, has been the hallmark of the branch of the case law rejecting jurisdiction on the basis of the term 'investment' in the ICSID Convention, as has been well demonstrated by J D Mortenson.[137]

Some other tribunals have taken into account the preparatory work of the ICSID Convention so as to recognize the BITs as the primary source for the meaning of 'investment', although even these tribunals have not regularly undertaken comprehensive application of the Vienna rules in the sense indicated above.[138] It has been noted that in the case of bilateral treaties such as the BITs which confer rights on

and O K Fauchald, 'The Legal Reasoning of ICSID Tribunals—An Empirical Analysis' (2008) 19 EJIL 301, at 343–49.

[135] *Salini Costruttori SpA v Kingdom of Morocco,* ICSID Case No. ARB/00/4 (Decision on Jurisdiction, 16 July 2001) para 51; and see B Legum and W Kirtley, 'The Status of the Report of the Executive Directors on the ICSID Convention' (2012) 27 *ICSID Review* 159.

[136] Legum and Kirtley, 'The Status of the Report of the Executive Directors on the ICSID Convention'; see also Fauchald, 'The Legal Reasoning of ICSID Tribunals—An Empirical Analysis', at 329–30 on whether the Report constitutes an interpretative agreement or preparatory work.

[137] J D Mortenson, 'The Meaning of "Investment": ICSID's Travaux and the Domain of International Investment Law' (2010) 51 *Harvard ILJ* 257; see also A R Parra, *The History of ICSID* (Oxford: OUP, 2012), 276–85.

[138] In contrast, an approach which carefully deploys the Vienna rules is provided by the decision in *Ambiente Ufficio S.p.A. and others v Argentine Republic,* ICSID Case No. ARB/08/9 (Decision on Jurisdiction and Admissibility, 8 February 2013).

individuals they, as third parties, will not have as ready access as states to preparatory work (though it is doubtful whether proper records of such treaties are generally kept, let alone made public). [139] However, this is not so likely to be a difficulty in the case of preparatory work of a modern multilateral treaty such as the ICSID Convention. In any event, the investor reading an applicable BIT could legitimately expect that that treaty's definition of 'investment' would apply rather than an imputed expansion of the term in another treaty.

This is not the place for a detailed analysis of the case law, but it has been well analysed by Fellenbaum as divisible into teleological and textual approaches.[140] The outcomes show clearly that there is no substitute for taking account of the full content and proper application of the Vienna rules. Retaining general approaches such as 'textual', 'teleological', or 'originalist intention' only achieves an ineffective approximation to application of the Vienna rules with, typically, excessive focus on the first element of the general rule or a misunderstanding of the potential uses of preparatory work. The mere nod so often given to the Vienna rules has been nicely described as 'something of a *clause de style* in international judgments and arbitral awards: whether routinely and briefly referred to or solemnly reproduced verbatim, they are not always systematically applied'.[141]

The continuation of this last assessment is equally telling: 'But a failure to apply the rules of interpretation properly may distort the resulting elucidation of the agreement made by the parties and do them an injustice by retroactively changing the legal regime under which they had arranged and managed their affairs.'[142] To this may be added the potential injustice to the third party, the investor, where jurisdiction is denied on an inadequately reasoned basis.

On a happier note, in contrast to the insouciance of many tribunals, a cogent example of how comprehensive use of the Vienna rules can lead to well grounded reasoning is provided in the decision in *Ambiente Ufficio v Argentina*.[143] This decision

---

[139] Cf M H Arsanjani and W M Reisman, 'Interpreting Treaties for the Benefit of Third Parties: The "Salvors' Doctrine" and the Use of Legislative History in Investment Treaties' (2010) 104 AJIL 597, at 603–4, where difficulties of access to preparatory work are described in relation to both multilateral and bilateral treaties.

[140] Fellenbaum, '*GEA v. Ukraine* and the Battle of Treaty Interpretation Principles Over the *Salini* Test' (2011) 27 *Arbitration International* 249.

[141] Arsanjani and Reisman, 'Interpreting Treaties for the Benefit of Third Parties: The "Salvors' Doctrine" and the Use of Legislative History in Investment Treaties', at 598–9, quoted more extensively at the head of this chapter. On fragmentation in application of the rules of interpretation see M Waibel, 'Uniformity versus specialization (2): A uniform regime of treaty interpretation?', Chapter 13 in C J Tams, A Tzanakopoulos, and others (eds), *Research Handbook On The Law Of Treaties* (Cheltenham: Edward Elgar, 2014).

[142] Arsanjani and Reisman, 'Interpreting Treaties for the Benefit of Third Parties', at 599.

[143] *Ambiente Ufficio S.p.A. and others v Argentine Republic*, ICSID Case No. ARB/08/9, Decision on Jurisdiction and Admissibility, 8 February 2013, paras 441–474. The dissenting arbitrator (S Torres Bernárdez) also referred to the Vienna rules but not in the same structured form as the majority. He criticized their decision, among other things, for a 'rather heterodox application of the treaty interpretation system' in opening the interpretive reasoning with the background to adoption of article 25 of the ICSID Convention. It may be helpful to recall, however, Waldock's account of the ILC's approach: 'There had certainly been no intention of discouraging automatic recourse to

gives a clear indication of how it uses the pertinent elements of the general rule and carefully indicates how the circumstances of conclusion confirm its interpretation, along with the preparatory work.

As can be seen, in evaluating the various elements set by the Vienna rules there is scope for differing assessments. Thus while proper use of the Vienna rules does not guarantee a uniform outcome in interpreting 'investment' in the ICSID Convention, at least more of the tribunals exploring this matter could have been expected to find the right track if they had employed the rules systematically and produced arguments fully reflective of all the elements in the rules.[144]

6.2.2 'Umbrella' clauses

The treaty dynamics underlying differing interpretations of 'umbrella' clauses—general provisions in BITs requiring states to observe commitments made to, or obligations undertaken towards, investors—are different from the issues over 'investment'. In establishing the meaning of 'investment' there is a common multilateral treaty (the ICSID Convention) linked to a large number of BITs, that is to say associated with the Convention by the BITs' common provision for reference to ICSID arbitration and frequently by their inclusion of a detailed definition of 'investment'. In contrast, in the 'umbrella' clause cases the divergent outcomes are over interpretation of differing BITs whose exact wording of the clause may vary but which give rise to a common issue of interpretation. The issue is whether the jurisdiction of an international tribunal can be invoked under these umbrella provisions in disputes arising from contracts between a state party to a BIT and a national of the other party.[145]

In *SGS v Pakistan*, in rejecting a broad meaning of the clause, the Tribunal's approach to treaty interpretation was sketched out in its statement:

A treaty interpreter must of course seek to give effect to the object and purpose projected by that Article [the umbrella clause] and by the BIT as a whole. That object and purpose must be ascertained, in the first instance, from the text itself of Article 11 and the rest of the BIT.[174] Applying these familiar norms of customary international law on treaty interpretation, we do not find a convincing basis for accepting the Claimant's contention....

---

preparatory work for the general understanding of a treaty', UN Conference on the Law of Treaties: Official Records, First Session, Vienna, 1968: Summary Records, p 184, para 69; starting an interpretation by reciting the background to a provision, including its history from the preparatory work, is in line with this and can be found elsewhere (for example in the practice of the ECtHR) provided care is taken over actual use of the preparatory work in the interpretative process, as shown in the majority decision in *Ambiente Ufficio*, para 455 (emphasizing the role of the Vienna Convention's general rule), and paras 473–474 (noting that the preparatory work *confirmed* the meaning derived by application of the general rule and, if there were ambiguity, clearly resolving the ambiguity in the same sense). See also C Lévesque, '*Abaclat and Others v Argentine Republic*: The Definition of Investment' (2012) 27 *ICSID Review* 247.

[144] See A Saldarriaga, 'Investment Awards and the Rules of Interpretation of the Vienna Convention: Making Room for Improvement' (2013) 28 *ICSID Review* 197.

[145] For an overview and analysis of case law on umbrella clauses see Weeramantry, *Treaty Interpretation in Investment Arbitration*, 168–77.

Unfortunately, neither this allusion to object and purpose, nor the interpretative analysis which followed, showed a close adherence to the 'familiar norms of customary international law on treaty interpretation' in the sense of the Vienna rules. The rules were not mentioned in *SGS v Pakistan*. The closest the Tribunal reached to them was the citation of the NAFTA '*ADF*' case which included a bare reference to articles 31 and 32 in a footnote in support of a rather general assertion that specific provisions needed to be read 'not just in relation to each other, but also in the context of the entire structure of NAFTA if a treaty interpreter is to ascertain and understand the real shape and content of the bargain actually struck by the three sovereign Parties'.[147] Thus any real application of the Vienna rules was absent.

In the contrasting case *SGS v Philippines* the Tribunal held that it had jurisdiction under an umbrella clause of broadly similar wording, though the substantive obligation of payment under the relevant contract was dependent on the amounts owing being definitively acknowledged or determined in accordance with that contract.[148] In reciting the arguments of the parties and in its own assessment, the Tribunal made brief references to the Vienna rules, but more significantly the Tribunal did at least undertake an interpretative exercise more closely focused on text and context, while in *SGS v Pakistan* the Tribunal showed more concern with what it saw as the difficult consequences of a broad interpretation.[149] After these two cases arbitral tribunals have followed one line or other, with variants. Real use of the Vienna rules has been sparse and it can be suggested that had they been fully deployed, the argument and reasoning over umbrella clauses could have had a better structure and focus.[150]

6.2.3 'Most Favoured Nation' clauses

A third area in which investment arbitration awards show outright divergence is over MFN provisions in BITs. These divergences seem egregious in that in some cases different arbitral tribunals have reached different conclusions over whether investors invoking the very same BIT can take advantage of dispute settlement provisions in other agreements of the same state party under an MFN provision. Few, if any, of the arbitral tribunals concerned have done much more than simplistically

---

[146] *SGS Société Générale de Surveillance S.A. v Islamic Republic of Pakistan*, ICSID Case No. ARB/01/13, Decision of 6 Aug 2003, para 165.

[147] *ADF Group Inc. v United States of America*, ICSID Case No. ARB (AF)/00/1, Final Award, para 149 and fn 153.

[148] *SGS Société Générale de Surveillance S.A. v Republic of the Philippines* ICSID Case No. ARB/02/6, Decision of 29 January 2004 (Objections to Jurisdiction).

[149] See Weeramantry, *Treaty Interpretation in Investment Arbitration*, 174–75.

[150] For detailed analysis of the case law hitherto, see J Antony, 'Umbrella Clauses Since *SGS v. Pakistan* and *SGS v. Philippines*—A Developing Consensus' (2013) 29 *Arbitration International* 607.

pick out parts of the first paragraph of article 31 of the Vienna Convention, to which some have added the odd mention of another element from the general rule. Although systematic application of the Vienna rules has been noticeably lacking, on one point many of the tribunals agree, namely that they must interpret the words of the particular treaty which they are applying.

Because of the considerable variation in wording of MFN provisions leading to numerous cases and analyses of them, detailed exposition of the interpretative arguments is not given here.[151] Just one observation seems worth adding to mention of the absence of substantial application of the Vienna rules. It is surprising, given that several tribunals have managed to invoke article 31(1) of the Vienna rules, how little reference is made to the context in the sense of the full text of the BITs, and proportionately less surprising, given how little attention is paid in the case law to supplementary means of interpretation, that virtually no mention is made of the circumstances of conclusion of the BITs,

Thus it might have been expected that in the context of MFN provisions as formulated in many BITs, there would have been more exploration of the significance of the words 'in its territory' qualifying the treatment of an investment by the state party. Investigation of this is surprisingly sparse. However, in *Impregilo v Argentina,* Argentina argued 'that the MFN clause refers to treatment by the Contracting Party "within its own territory", whereas arbitration takes place outside Argentina and beyond its sovereign powers'.[152] Rejecting this, the Arbitral Tribunal responded by accepting that the words 'within its own territory' limited the scope of the MFN clause but considered that in the instant case 'the question as to what legal protection Argentina shall give to foreign investors is in no way an issue over which Argentina has no power to decide, nor is it tied to any particular territory.'[153]

Leaving to one side any obscurity in this formulation by the Tribunal, where is the full analysis of the context or of the object and purpose of the treaty? Where is recourse to the circumstances of conclusion for confirmation of the interpretation supposedly reached in application of the general rule? For example, analysis of the relevant BIT might reveal an immediate contextual contrast between article 8(2) (submission to the competent judicial or administrative courts of the Party 'in whose territory the investment is made') and article 8(3) (if unresolved after eighteen months the dispute 'may be referred to international arbitration'). Failure to examine context may be the explanation for the neglect of a useful clue to be

---

[151] See Weeramantry, *Treaty Interpretation in Investment Arbitration,* 177–82; Z Douglas, 'The MFN Clause in Investment Arbitration: Treaty Interpretation Off the Rails' (2011) 2 *J Int'l Dispute Settlement* 97; S W Schill, 'Allocating Adjudicatory Authority: Most-Favoured-Nation Clauses as a Basis of Jurisdiction—A Reply to Zachary Douglas' (2011) 2 *J Int'l Dispute Settlement* 353 for overview and analysis, and M J Valasek and E-A Ménard, '*Impregilo SpA v Argentine Republic* and *Hochtief AG v The Argentine Republic*—Making Sense of Dissents: The Jurisprudence Inconstante of the MFN Clause' (2012) 27 *ICSID Review* 21.

[152] *Impregilo S.p.A. v Argentine Republic*, ICSID Case No. ARB/07/17, Award 21 June 2011, at para 97(b).

[153] ICSID Case No. ARB/07/17, Award 21 June 2011, at para 100.

found in the contrast between resolution in courts in the territory of the state party and international arbitration.

Likewise, reference to the circumstances of conclusion, far from confirming a scheme which views international arbitration as part of treatment within a territory, could show provision for external resolution of disputes as being precisely the remedy sought for the problems encountered by investors in their treatment within a territory before BITs were conceived. A key reason for making BITs was to protect against the mistreatment within a territory. Such mistreatment had given rise to the attempts to 'internationalize' investment contracts and provide secure international arbitration. In this sense international arbitration is not a matter of geographical treatment but a reference to treatment outside a territorial legal system.[154]

Of course, interpretation of words such as 'in the territory of' is only part of the complete exercise, but this is an illustration of how full application of the Vienna rules could help tribunals engage with the whole range of relevant material. Again, there is a bright spot. In *ICS Inspection v Argentina* the Arbitral Tribunal, in reasoning leading to its conclusion that the MFN clause did not extend to international dispute resolution, quoted the full text of articles 31 and 32 of the Vienna Convention and embarked on a comprehensive exercise of treaty interpretation, including a focus on the point discussed above in relation to territory.[155] This was in marked contrast, both in process and outcome, to *National Grid v Argentina* and *AWG Group Ltd v Argentina*, where the same MFN provision had been interpreted as extending arbitral jurisdiction by reference to treaties making provision for claimants of nationalities other than that of these claimants.[156] In the award in *ICS Inspection v Argentina* can be seen an example of thorough application of the Vienna rules, though there is the slightly strange invocation of the 'principle of contemporaneity' to describe analysis of what is plainly the type of supplementary means described in the Vienna rules as 'circumstances of conclusion', recourse to which in the particular case would have been amply justified whether to confirm or to determine the meaning.[157]

A sensible conclusion is that cogency and consistency would be likely to be enhanced were the Vienna rules to be used fully, rather than piecemeal and with only lip service as is customarily paid to the first paragraph of the general rule, and with occasional selective use of other provisions. This is not entirely in the hands of arbitrators since the way in which cases are pleaded and evidence is produced inevitably affects the decisions and awards. Nevertheless, it has been suggested that improvement in use of the Vienna rules could be advanced by three steps: 'capacity

---

[154] Cf the proper interpretation of the place of arbitration contrasted with the decision in *Hiscox v Outhwaite* in Chapter 1, section 5.4 above.

[155] *ICS Inspection and Control Services Limited (United Kingdom) v The Republic of Argentina*, UNCITRAL, PCA Case No. 2010-9, Award on Jurisdiction, 10 February 2012.

[156] *National Grid plc v The Argentine Republic*, UNCITRAL arbitration, Decision on Jurisdiction, 20 June 2006; *AWG Group Ltd. v The Argentine Republic*, UNCITRAL arbitration, Decision on Jurisdiction, 3 August 2006.

[157] *ICS Inspection v Argentina*, at paras 290–95.

building', meaning improving awareness among counsel and arbitrators; 'explicit rationality', that is inducing expectation that clear explanations are given of the interpretative process being employed; and 'scrutiny', meaning wide ranging review input from those observing the work of investment arbitral tribunals, such as academic commentators.[158]

7. Conclusion

Metaphors may have a role, if limited, in helping to understand how the Vienna rules should guide an interpreter. The ILC's 'crucible' metaphor remains one of the most useful explanations of the much misunderstood general rule. Ask whether the rules are more in the nature of formulae than algorithms and one is taken to loose analogies with lists of ingredients and step-by-step instructions on how to bake a cake. Neither fits the bill, but both correctly suggest some features of the rules.

The suggestion quoted at the head of this chapter, that the structure provided by the Vienna rules 'has become the virtually indispensable scaffolding for the reasoning on questions of treaty interpretation', particularly nicely sums up the role of the rules, even if 'indispensable' may be conceal an unhealthily large number of cases where passing reference to the rules has substituted for thorough application.

The key points remain unchanging. The rules apply as a starting point for *all* treaty interpretation. The general rule is the *whole* of article 31 of the Vienna Convention, not just its first paragraph. The further paragraphs of article 31 are not secondary or subordinate. They provide elements such as subsequent agreement and practice which, if present in any given case, may have very great interpretative weight in the crucible. Consideration of supplementary means is not confined to situations of ambiguity, obscurity, etc. Such means have a wider role in assisting understanding and in confirming meaning when the preconditions for their role to 'determine' meaning are not met. Good faith, which is the first element mentioned in the rules, should control the whole process of interpretation.

---

[158] See A Saldarriaga, 'Investment Awards and the Rules of Interpretation of the Vienna Convention: Making Room for Improvement' (2013) 28 *ICSID Review* 197, at 213–15.

Bibliography

Note: This bibliography refers to material primarily of use in relation to the rules of interpretation in the Vienna Convention on the Law of Treaties, 1969. Other helpful bibliographies relating to earlier material on treaty interpretation include those in:

Harvard Law School, Faculty of, 'The Law of Treaties', Part III of Harvard Draft Codification of International Law (1935) 29 *AJIL Supp.* 653, at 671–85; and

Treaties and other International Agreements: The Role of the United States Senate, Senate Committee on Foreign Relations, 106th Congress, *2d Session,* S. PRT.106–71 (2001), Appendix 1, p 295, part B.4 'Interpretation', at pp 303–7.

See also online: I Van Damme, *Oxford Bibliography on Treaty Interpretation* <http://www.oxfordbibliographies.com/view/document/obo-9780199796953/obo-9780199796953-0053.xml>

BOOKS AND CHAPTERS IN BOOKS

Aldrich, G H, *The Jurisprudence of the Iran–United States Claims Tribunal* (Oxford: Clarendon Press, 1996)

Amerasinghe, C F, *Principles of Institutional Law of International Organizations* (Cambridge: CUP, 2nd edn, 2005)

Aryal, R S, *Interpretation of Treaties: Law and Practice* (New Delhi: Deep & Deep, 2003)

Aust, A, *'Law of Treaties'*, Chapter 11 in J P Grant and J C Barker (eds), *The Harvard Research in International Law: Contemporary Analysis and Appraisal* (New York: W S Hein, 2007)

Aust, A, *Modern Treaty Law and Practice* (Cambridge: CUP, 3rd edn, 2013)

Bederman, D J, *Classical Canons: Rhetoric, Classicism and Treaty Interpretation* (Aldershot: Ashgate, 2001)

Bjorge, E, *The Evolutionary Interpretation of Treaties* (Oxford: OUP, 2014)

Boyle, A E, and Chinkin, C, *The Making of International Law* (Oxford: OUP, 2007)

Brower, C N, and Brueschke, J D, *The Iran–United States Claims Tribunal* (The Hague: Martinus Nijhoff, 1998)

Butler, W E, *The Russian Law of Treaties* (London: Simmonds & Hill, 1997)

Cannizzaro, E (ed), *The Law of Treaties Beyond the Vienna Convention* (Oxford: OUP, 2011)

Chang, Y-T, *The Interpretation of Treaties by Judicial Tribunals* (New York: Columbia University Press, 1933)

Cheng, Bin, *General Principles of Law as Applied by International Courts and Tribunals* (London: Stevens and Sons, 1953, and Cambridge: Grotius Publications, 1987 reprint)

Clapham, A, *Brierly's Law of Nations* (Oxford: OUP, 2012)

Corten, O, and Klein, P (eds), *The Vienna Conventions on the Law of Treaties: A Commentary* (Oxford: OUP, 2011)

Crawford, J, *Brownlie's Principles of Public International Law* (Oxford: OUP, 8th edn, 2012)

Dalton, R E, 'National Treaty Law and Policy: United States' in M Leigh, M R Blakeslee, and L B Ederington (eds), *National Treaty Law and Practice* (Washington DC: ASIL, 1999)

Degan, V D, *L'interprétation des Accords en Droit International* (The Hague: M Nijhoff, 1963)

Dhokalia, R P, *The Codification of International Law* (Manchester: Manchester University Press, 1970)

Dörr, O, and Schmalenbach, K (eds), *The Vienna Convention on the Law of Treaties: A Commentary* (Berlin: Springer, 2012)

Elias, T O, *The Modern Law of Treaties* (Dobbs Ferry, NY: Oceana Publications, 1974)

Engelen, F, *Interpretation of Tax Treaties Under International Law* (Amsterdam: IBFD Publications BV, 2004)

Fitzmaurice, G, 'Some Problems Regarding the Formal Sources of International Law' *Symbolae Verzijl* (The Hague: Nijhoff, 1958)

Fitzmaurice, M, 'The Practical Working of the Law of Treaties' in M Evans (ed), *International Law* (Oxford: OUP, 3rd edn, 2010)

Fitzmaurice, M, 'Interpretation of Human Rights Treaties', Chapter 31 in D Shelton (ed), *The Oxford Handbook of International Human Rights Law* (Oxford: OUP, 2013)

Fitzmaurice, M, 'The Whaling Convention and Thorny Issues of Interpretation', in D Tamada, and M Fitzmaurice (eds), *Whaling in the Antarctic: The Judgment and its Implications* (Nijhoff/Brill, forthcoming)

Fitzmaurice, M, Elias O, and Merkouris P (eds), *Treaty Interpretation and the Vienna Convention on the Law of Treaties: 30 Years on* (Leiden: Brill, 2010)

Gardiner, R K, *International Law* (Harlow: Pearson/Longman, 2003)

Gardiner, R K, 'Interpreting Treaties in the United Kingdom', Chapter 7 in M Freeman (ed), *Legislation and the Courts* (Dartmouth: Aldershot, 1997)

Greig, D W, *Intertemporality and The Law of Treaties* (London: BIICL, 2001)

Grotius, H, *De Jure Belli ac Pacis*, Bk II, chapter 16 (translation by F W Kelsey, 1925) (New York: Oceana, reprint 1964)

Haraszti, G, *Some Fundamental Problems of the Law of Treaties* (Budapest: Akadémiai Kiado, 1973)

Hoffmeister, F, 'The Contribution of EU Practice to International Law', in M Cremona (ed), *Developments in EU External Relations Law* (Oxford: OUP, 2008)

Hollis, D B (ed), *The Oxford Guide to Treaties* (Oxford: OUP, 2012)

Hollis, D B, Blakeslee, M R, and Ederington, L B (eds), *National Treaty Law and Practice* (Leiden: Martinus Nijhoff, 2005)

Horn, F, *Reservations and Interpretative Declarations to Multilateral Treaties* (Amsterdam: North-Holland, 1988)

Hudson, M O, *The Permanent Court of International Justice 1920–1942* (New York, NY: Macmillan, 1943)

Jacobs, D, 'Positivism and International Criminal Law: The Principle of Legality as a Rule of Conflict of Theories' in J d'Aspremont, and J Kammerhofer (eds), *International Legal Positivism World* (Cambridge: CUP, 2014)

Jacobs, F, and Roberts, S (eds), *The Effect of Treaties in Domestic Law* (London: Sweet & Maxwell, 1987)

Jennings, R, and Watts, A (eds), *Oppenheim's International Law*, vol I (London: Longman, 9th edn, 1992)

Joyner, D H, *Interpreting the Nuclear Non-Proliferation Treaty* (Oxford: OUP, 2011)

Kaufmann-Kohler, G, 'Interpretation of Treaties: How Do Arbitral Tribunals Interpret Dispute Settlement Provisions Embodied in Investment Treaties?', Chapter 13 in L Mistelis, and J Lew (eds), *Pervasive Problems in International Arbitration* (The Netherlands: Kluwer, 2006)

Klabbers, J, and Lefeber, R (eds), *Essays on the Law of Treaties: A Collection of Essays in Honour of Bert Vierdag* (The Hague: Martinus Nijhoff, 1998)

Kolb, R, *La bonne foi en droit international public* (Paris: Presses universitaires de France, 2000)

Lauterpacht, E (ed), *International Law, the Collected Papers of Hersch Lauterpacht* (Cambridge: CUP, 1978), vol 4, part VIII

Letsas, G, *A Theory of Interpretation of the European Convention on Human Rights* (Oxford: OUP, 2007)

Linderfalk, U, *On the Interpretation of Treaties: The Modern International Law as Expressed in the 1969 Vienna Convention on the Law of Treaties* (Dordrecht: Springer, 2007)

McDougal, M S, Lasswell, H D, and Miller, J C, *The Interpretation of Agreements and World Public Order: Principles of Content and Procedure* (New Haven, CT: Yale University Press, 1967, re-issued as *The Interpretation of International Agreements* etc with a new introduction and appendices, 1994)

McNair, A D, *The Law of Treaties* (Oxford: OUP, 2nd edn, 1961)

Makarczyk, J (ed), *Theory of International Law at the Threshold of the 21st Century* (The Hague: Kluwer, 1996)

Mann, F A, *Foreign Affairs in English Courts* (Oxford: OUP, 1986)

Merkouris, P, *Article 31(3)(c) of the VCLT and the Principle of Systemic Integration* (Ph D Thesis, 2010) <https://qmro.qmul.ac.uk/jspui/handle/123456789/47>)

Nolte, G (ed), *Treaties and Subsequent Practice* (Oxford: OUP, 2013)

O'Connor, J F, *Good Faith in International Law* (Dartmouth: Aldershot, 1991)

Orakhelashvili, A, *The Interpretation of Acts and Rules in Public International Law* (Oxford: OUP, 2008)

Orakhelashvili, A, and Williams, S (eds), *40 Years of the Vienna Convention on the Law of Treaties* (London: BIICL, 2010)

Paparinskis, M, 'Sources of Law and Arbitral Interpretations of Pari Materia Investment Protection Rules', Chapter 5 in O K Fauchald, and A Nollkaemper (eds), *The Practice of International and National Courts and the (De-)Fragmentation of International Law* (Oxford: Hart Publishing, 2012)

Pauwelyn, J, *Conflict of Norms in Public International Law: How WTO Law Relates to Other Rules of International Law* (Cambridge: CUP, 2003)

Pauwelyn, J and Elsig, M, 'The Politics of Treaty Interpretation: Variations and Explanations across International Tribunals ', Chapter 18 in J L Dunoff and M A Pollack (eds), *Interdisciplinary Perspectives on International Law and International Relations: The State of the Art* (Cambridge: CUP, 2012)

Qureshi, A H, *Interpreting WTO Agreements: Problems and Perspectives* (Cambridge: CUP, 2006)

Reinisch A, 'The Proliferation of International Dispute Settlement Mechanisms: The Threat of Fragmentation vs. the Promise of a More Effective System? Some Reflections From the Perspective of Investment Arbitration', Chapter 7 in I Buffard, J Crawford, A Pellet, and S Wittich (eds), *International Law between Universalism and Fragmentation: Festschrift in Honour of Gerhard Hafner* (Leiden: Nijhoff, 2008)

Rauschning, D, and Wetzel, R, *The Vienna Convention on the Law of Treaties: Travaux Préparatoires* (Frankfurt am Main: Metzner, 1978)

Reuter, P, *Introduction to the Law of Treaties* (trans J Mico and P Haggenmacher) (London: Kegan Paul, 2nd edn, 1995)

Rosenne, S, *The Law of Treaties: A Guide to the Legislative History of the Vienna Convention* (Leyden: A W Sijthoff, 1970)

Rosenne, S, *An International Law Miscellany* (Dordrecht: Nijhoff, 1993)

Schabas, W A, 'Interpreting the Statutes of the *ad hoc* tribunals' in L C Vorah et al. (eds), *Man's Inhumanity to Man: Essays on International Law in Honour of Antonio Cassese* (The Hague: Kluwer Law International, 2003)

Schermers, H G, and Blokker, N M, *International Institutional Law: Unity Within Diversity* (Boston, MA: Martinus Nijhoff, 2003).

Schreuer, C, *The ICSID Convention: A Commentary* (Cambridge: CUP, 2nd edn, 2009)

Schreuer, C, 'Diversity and Harmonization of Treaty Interpretation in Investment Arbitration' in M Fitzmaurice, O Elias and P Merkouris (eds), *Treaty Interpretation and the Vienna Convention on the Law of Treaties: 30 Years On* (Leiden: Nijhoff, 2010) 129

Schwebel, S, 'May Preparatory Work be Used to Correct rather than Confirm the "Clear" Meaning of a Treaty Provision?' in J Makarczyk (ed), *Theory of International Law at the Threshold of the 21st Century* (The Hague: Kluwer, 1996), 541–7

Scobbie, I, 'Wicked Heresies or Legitimate Perspectives? Theory and International Law', Chapter 3 in M Evans (ed), *International Law* (Oxford: OUP, 2nd edn, 2006)

Shaheed, F, *Using International Law in Domestic Courts* (Oxford: Hart Publishing, 2005)

Shelton, N, *Interpretation and Application of Tax Treaties* (London: LexisNexis, 2004)

Sinclair, I, *The Vienna Convention on the Law of Treaties* (Manchester: Manchester University Press, 2nd edn, 1984)

Sinclair, I, *The International Law Commission* (Cambridge: Grotius, 1987)

Slotboom, M, *A Comparison of WTO and EC Law: Do Different Objects and Purposes Matter for Treaty Interpretation?* (London: Cameron May, 2006)

Spiermann, O, *International Legal Argument in the Permanent Court of International Justice: The Rise of the International Judiciary* (Cambridge: CUP, 2005)

Thirlway, H, *The Law and Procedure of the International Court of Justice: Fifty Years of Jurisprudence* (Oxford: OUP, 2013)

Torres Bernárdez, S, 'Interpretation of Treaties by the International Court of Justice following the Adoption of the 1969 Vienna Convention on the Law of Treaties' in G Hafner et al. (eds), *Liber Amicorum: Professor Ignaz Seidl-Hohenveldern in Honour of his 80th Birthday* (The Hague: Kluwer Law International, 1998)

Twining, W L, and Miers, D, *How to Do Things with Rules: A Primer of Interpretation* (London: Butterworths, 1999)

Van Damme, I, *Treaty Interpretation by the WTO Appellate Body* (Oxford: OUP, 2009)

Vattel, E de *The Law of Nations*, Book II, Chap XVII, of *The Interpretation on Treaties* (1758 edition, trans by C G Fenwick) (Washington DC: Carnegie Institution, 1916)

Venzke, I, *How Interpretation Makes International Law* (Oxford: OUP, 2012)

Verwey, D R, *The European Community, the European Union and the International Law of Treaties: A Comparative Legal Analysis of the Community and Union's External Treaty-making Practice* (The Hague: T M C Asser Press, 2004)

Villiger, M E, *Commentary on the 1969 Vienna Convention on the Law of Treaties* (The Hague: Martinus Nijhoff, 2009)

Villiger, M E, 'Articles 31 and 32 of the Vienna Convention on the Law of Treaties in the Case-Law of the European Court of Human Rights' in *Internationale Gemeinschaft und Menschenrechte: Festschrift für Georg Ress zum 70 Geburtstag am 21 Januar 2005* (Cologne: Carl Heymanns Verlag, 2005)

Waibel, M, 'Uniformity versus specialization (2): A uniform regime of treaty interpretation?' Chapter 13 in C J Tams, A Tzanakopoulos, and others (eds), *Research Handbook On The Law Of Treaties* (Cheltenham: Edward Elgar, 2014)

Wälde, T W, 'Interpreting Investment Treaties: Experiences And Examples', Chapter 38 in *International Investment Law for the 21st Century: Essays in Honour of Christoph Schreuer* (C Binder et al., eds) (Oxford: OUP, 2009)

Warbrick, C, 'Introduction' to *The Iron Rhine ("IJzeren Rijn") Railway (Belgium- Netherlands) Award of 2005* (B Macmahon (ed)) (The Hague: TMC Asser Press, 2007)

Watts, A, *The International Law Commission, 1949–1998* (New York: OUP, 1999)

Weeramantry, J R, *Treaty Interpretation in Investment Arbitration* (Oxford: OUP, 2012)

Weiniger, M, 'Jurisdiction Challenges in BIT Arbitrations—Do you read a BIT by Reading a BIT or by Reading into a BIT?', Chapter 12 in L Mistelis and J Lew (eds), *Pervasive Problems in International Arbitration* (The Netherlands: Kluwer, 2006)

Yambrusic, E S, *Treaty Interpretation: Theory and Reality* (Lanham, MD: University Press of America, 1987)

Yü, T-C, *The Interpretation of Treaties* (New York: Columbia University Press, 1927)

Zemanek, K (ed), (assisted by Behrmann, L-R), *Agreements of International Organizations and the Vienna Convention on the Law of Treaties* (New York: Springer-Verlag, 1971)

ARTICLES

Acquaviva, G, 'At the Origins of Crimes against Humanity: Clues to a Proper Understanding of the "Nullum Crimen" Principle in the Nuremberg Judgment' (2011) 9 *J of Int Crim Justice* 881

Allott, P, 'The Concept of International Law' (1999) 10 EJIL 31

Amerasinghe, C F, 'Interpretation Of Texts In Open International Organizations' (1994) 45 BYBIL 175

Arato, J, 'Subsequent Practice and Evolutive Interpretation: Techniques of Treaty Interpretation over Time and Their Diverse Consequences' (2010) 9 *The Law and Practice of International Courts and Tribunals* 443

Arato, J, 'Constitutional Transformation in the ECtHR: Strasbourg's Expansive Recourse to External Rules of International Law' (2011–2012) 37 *Brook J Int'l L* 349

Arato, J, 'Treaty Interpretation and Constitutional Transformation: Informal Change in International Organizations' (2013) 38 *Yale J Int'l L* 289

Arsanjani, M H, and Reisman, W M, 'Interpreting Treaties for the Benefit of Third Parties: The "Salvors' Doctrine" and the Use of Legislative History in Investment Treaties' (2010) 104 AJIL 597

Attal, M, 'The Interpretation of a Treaty by a National Jurisdiction' (2006–07) 28 *Whittier Law Review* 817

Aust, H P, Rodiles, A, and Staubach, P, 'Unity or Uniformity?: Domestic Courts and Treaty Interpretation' (2014) 27 *Leiden Journal of International Law* 75

Baetens, F, 'Muddling the Waters of Treaty Interpretation? Relevant Rules of International Law in the *MOX Plant* OSPAR Arbitration and *EC Biotech* Case' (2008) 77 *Nordic Journal of International Law* 197

Benatar, M, 'From Probative Value to Authentic Interpretation: The Legal Effect of Interpretative Declarations' (2011) 44 *Revue Belge de Droit International* 170

Bechky, P S, 'Mismanagement and Misinterpretation: US Judicial Implementation of the Warsaw Convention in Air Disaster Litigation' (1994–1995) 60 *Journal of Air Law and Commerce* 455

Bederman, D J, 'Revivalist Canons and Treaty Interpretation' (1993–1994) 41 *UCLA Law Review* 953

Berglin, R H, 'Treaty Interpretation and the Impact of Contractual Choice of Forum Clauses on the Jurisdiction of International Tribunals: the Iranian Forum Clause Decisions of the Iran–United States Claims Tribunal' (Winter 1986) 21 *Texas International Law Journal* 39–65

Berman, F D, 'Treaty "Interpretation" in a Judicial Context' (2004) 29 *Yale Journal of International Law* 315

Bernhardt, R, 'Interpretation in International Law' in R Bernhardt (ed), *Encylopedia of Public International Law*, Vol II, 1416 (1995) 11

Bernhardt, R, 'Evolutive Treaty Interpretation, Especially of the European Convention on Human Rights' (1999) 42 *German Yearbook of International Law* 11

Berrisch, G M, 'The Establishment of New Law through Subsequent Practice in GATT' (1991) 16 *North Carolina Journal of International Law and Commercial Regulation* 497

Bilder, R B, and Edwards, R W Jr, 'Review of *Interpretation: The IMF and International Law* by J Gold' (1997) 91 AJIL 405

Bishop, W W, 'Editorial Comment' (1967) 61 AJIL 990

Blackett, A, 'Whither Social Clause? Human Rights, Trade Theory and Treaty Interpretation' (1999–2000) 31 *Columbia Human Rights Law Review* 1

Bos, M, 'Theory and Practice of Treaty Interpretation' (1980) 27 NILR 3

Briggs, H W, 'The *Travaux Préparatoires* of the Vienna Convention on the Law of Treaties' (1971) 65 AJIL 705

Brown, P M, 'The Interpretation of the General Pact for the Renunciation of War' (1929) 23 AJIL 374

Buffard, I, and Zemanek, K, 'The "Object and Purpose" of a Treaty: An Enigma?' (1998) 3 *Austrian Review of International and European Law* 311

Butler, W E, 'The 1867 Russo-American Convention: Some Textual Issues' (1991) 40 ICLQ 457

Cameron, J, and Gray, K R, 'Principles of International Law in the WTO Dispute Settlement Body' (2001) 50 ICLQ 248

Caron, D, 'The United Nations Compensation Commission for Claims Arising out of the 1991 Gulf War: the "Arising Prior To" Decision' (2004–2005) 14 *Journal of Transnational Law and Policy* 309

Chang-Fa Lo, 'Good Faith Use of Dictionary in the Search of Ordinary Meaning under the WTO Dispute Settlement Understanding' (2010) 1 *J Int'l Dispute Settlement* 431

Chang-Fa Lo, 'A Clearer Rule for Dictionary Use Will Not Affect Holistic Approach and Flexibility of Treaty Interpretation—A Rejoinder to Dr Isabelle Van Damme' (2012) 3 *J Int'l Dispute Settlement* 89

Ciorciari, J D, 'The Lawful Scope of Human Rights Criteria in World Bank Credit Decisions: An Interpretive Analysis of the IBRD and IDA Articles of Agreement' (2000) 33 *Cornell International Law Journal* 331

Cohen, H G, 'International Law's Erie Moment' (2013) 34 *Mich J Int'l L* 249

Corten, O, 'The Notion of "Reasonable" in International Law: Legal Discourse, Reason and Contradictions' (1999) 48 ICLQ 613

Coyle, J, 'Incorporative Statutes and the Borrowed Treaty Rule' (2010) 50 *Virginia Journal of International Law* 655

Criddle, E, 'The Vienna Convention on the Law of Treaties in US Treaty Interpretation' (2003–2004) 44 *Virginia Journal of International Law* 431

Crnić-Grotić, V, 'Object and Purpose of Treaties in the Vienna Convention on the Law of Treaties' (1997) 7 *Asian Yearbook of International Law* 141

Cryer, R, 'Royalism and The King: Article 21 of the Rome Statute and the Politics of Sources' (2009) 12 *New Criminal Law Review* 390

Damrosch, L F, 'Interpreting US Treaties in Light of Human Rights Values' (2002–2003) 46 *New York Law School Law Review* 43

Dawidowicz, M, 'The Effect of the Passage of Time on the Interpretation of Treaties: Some Reflections on *Costa Rica v Nicaragua*' (2011) 24 *Leiden Journal of International Law* 201

de Vries, H P, 'Choice of Language' (1963) 3 *Virginia Journal of International Law* 26

Denza, E, 'Bilateral Investment Treaties and EU Rules on Free Transfer: Comment on *Commission v Austria, Commission v Sweden* and *Commission v Finland*' (2010) 35 *European Law Review* 263

Desierto, D A, 'Necessity and Supplementary Means of Interpretation for Non-Precluded Measures in Bilateral Investment Treaties' (2014) 31 *University of Pennsylvania J Int'l L* 827

Djeffal, C, 'The Iron Rhine Case – A Treaty's Journey from Peace to Sustainable Development' (2011) 71 *Zaörv* 3

Douglas, Z, 'The MFN Clause in Investment Arbitration: Treaty Interpretation Off the Rails' (2011) 2 *J Int'l Dispute Settlement* 97

Dupont, P-E, 'The Notion of ICSID Investment: Ongoing "Confusion" or "Emerging Synthesis"?' (2011)12 *J World Investment & Trade* 245

Dzehtsiarou, K, and O'Mahony, C, 'Evolutive Interpretation of Rights Provisions: A Comparison of the European Court of Human Rights and the U.S. Supreme Court' (2013) 44 *Columbia Human Rights Law Review* 309

Elias, T O, 'The Doctrine of Intertemporal Law' (1980) 74 AJIL 285

Engel, S, ' "Living" International Constitutions and the World Court (The Subsequent Practice of International Organs under their Constituent Instruments)' (1967) 16 ICLQ 865

Falk, R A, 'On Treaty Interpretation and the New Haven Approach: Achievements and Prospects' (1967–1968) 8 *Virginia Journal of International Law* 323

Falk, R A, 'Charybdis Responds: A Note on Treaty Interpretation' (1969) 63 AJIL 510

Fastenrath, U, 'Relative Normativity in International Law' (1993) 4 EJIL 305

Fauchald, O K, 'The Legal Reasoning of ICSID Tribunals—An Empirical Analysis' (2008) 19 EJIL 301

Feldman, A M, 'Evolving Treaty Obligations: A Proposal for Analyzing Subsequent Practice Derived From WTO Dispute Settlement' (2009) 41 *NYU J Int'l L & Politics* 655

Fish, S, 'Fish v Fiss' (1984) 36 *Stanford Law Review* 1325

Fitzmaurice, G G, 'The Law and Procedure of the International Court of Justice 1951–4: Treaty Interpretation and Certain Other Points' (1951) 28 BYBIL 1

Fitzmaurice, G G, 'The Law and Procedure of the International Court of Justice 1951–4: Treaty Interpretation and Other Points' (1957) 33 BYBIL 203

Fitzmaurice, G G, '*Vae Victis* or Woe to the Negotiators! Your Treaty or Our "Interpretation" of it?' (1971) 65 AJIL 359

Fitzmaurice, M, 'Canons of Treaty Interpretation: Selected Case Studies from the World Trade Organization and the North American Free Trade Agreement' (2007) 10 *Austrian Review of International and European Law* 41

Fitzmaurice, M, 'The Tale Of Two Judges: Sir Hersch Lauterpacht And Sir Gerald Fitzmaurice—Human Rights and the Interpretation of Treaties' (2008) 61 *Revue Hellénique de Droit International* 126

Fitzmaurice, M, 'Dynamic (Evolutive) Interpretation of Treaties: Part I' (2008) 21 *Hague Yearbook of International Law* 101 and 'Part II' (2009) 22 *Hague Yearbook of International Law* 3

Frankel, S, 'The WTO's Application of "the Customary Rules of Interpretation of Public International Law" to Intellectual Property' (2005) 46 *Virginia Journal of International Law* 365

Frankowska, M, 'The Vienna Convention on the Law of Treaties before United States Courts' (1987–1988) 28 *Virginia Journal of International Law* 281

French, D, 'Treaty Interpretation and the Incorporation of Extraneous Legal Rules' (2006) 55 ICLQ 281

Gamble, J K, 'Multilateral Treaties: The Significance of the Name of the Instrument' (1980) 10 *California Western International Law Journal* 1

Gamble, J K, and Ku, C, 'Choice of Language in Bilateral Treaties: Fifty Years of Changing State Practice' (1992–93) 3 *Indiana International and Comparative Law Review* 233

Gamble, J K, Kolb, L, and Graml, C, 'Choice of Official Text in Multilateral Treaties: The Interplay of Law, Politics, Language, Pragmatism and (Multi)-Nationalism' (2014) 12 *Santa Clara J Int'l L* 29

Gardiner, R, 'Treaty Interpretation in the English Courts since *Fothergill v Monarch Airlines* (1980)' (1995) 44 ICLQ 620

Germer, P, 'Interpretation of Plurilingual Treaties: A Study of Article 33 of the Vienna Convention on the Law of Treaties' (1970) 11 *Harvard International Law Journal* 400

Gill, J, 'Is There a Special Role for Precedent in Investment Arbitration?' (2010) 25 *ICSID Review* 87

Glashausser, A, 'What We Must Never Forget When It Is A Treaty We Are Expounding' (2004–2005) 73 *University of Cincinnati Law Review* 1243

Glashausser, A, 'Difference and Deference in Treaty Interpretation' (2005) 50 *Villanova Law Review* 25

Gottlieb, G, 'The Conceptual World of the Yale School of International Law' (1968) 21 *World Politics* 108

Gourgourinis, A, 'The Distinction Between Interpretation and Application of Norms in International Adjudication' (2011) 2 *J Int'l Dispute Settlement* 31

Grover, L, 'A Call to Arms: Fundamental Dilemmas Confronting the Interpretation of Crimes in the Rome Statute of the International Criminal Court' (2010) 21 EJIL 543

Hafner, G, 'Pros and Cons Ensuing from Fragmentation of International Law' (2003–2004) 25 *Michigan Journal of International Law* 849

Halberstam, M, 'The Use of Legislative History in Treaty Interpretation: The Dual Treaty Approach' (1990–91) 12 *Cardozo Law Review* 1645

Hardy, J, 'The Interpretation of Plurilingual Treaties by International Courts and Tribunals' (1961) 37 BYBIL 72

Harvard Law School, Faculty of, 'The Law of Treaties', Part III of *Harvard Draft Codification of International Law* (1935) 29 AJIL Supp 653

Hassan, T, 'Good Faith in Treaty Formation' (1980–1981) 21 *Virginia Journal of International Law* 443

Heller, K, 'The Uncertain Legal Status of the Aggression Understandings' (2012) 10 *Journal of International Criminal Justice* 229

Helmersen, S T, 'Evolutive Treaty Interpretation: Legality, Semantics and Distinctions' (2013) 6 *European Journal of Legal Studies* 127

Higgins, R, 'Time and the Law: International Perspectives on an Old Problem' (1997) 46 ICLQ 501

Higgins, R, 'A Babel of Judicial Voices: Ruminations from the Bench' (2006) 55 ICLQ 791

Hollis, D, 'A New Supreme Court Case on Treaty Interpretation', 29 June 2009, <http://opiniojuris.org/>, accessed 8 June 2010

Hollis, D, 'The Supreme Court takes Treaty Interpretation Seriously: Abbott v. Abbott', 17 May 2010, <http://opiniojuris.org/>, accessed 8 June 2010

Jackson, J H, 'International Law Status of WTO Dispute Settlement Reports: Obligation to Comply or Option to "Buy Out"?' (2004) 98 AJIL 109

Jackson, J H, 'Process and Procedure in WTO Dispute Settlement' (2009) 42 *Cornell International Law Journal* 233

Jacobs, F G, 'Varieties of Approach to Treaty Interpretation: With Special Reference to the Draft Convention on the Law of Treaties before the Vienna Diplomatic Conference' (1969) 18 ICLQ 318

Jarreau, J S, 'Interpreting the General Agreement on Trade in Services and the WTO Instruments Relevant to the International Trade of Financial Services: The Lawyer's Perspective' (1999–2000) 25 *North Carolina Journal of International Law and Commercial Regulation* 1

Johnstone, I, 'Treaty Interpretation: the Authority of Interpretive Communities' (1990–91) 12 *Michigan Journal of International Law* 371

Jonas, D S, and Saunders, T N, 'The Object and Purpose of a Treaty: Three Interpretive Methods' (2009) <http://works.bepress.com/david_jonas/!>, accessed 18 June 2010

Kearney, R D, and Dalton, R E, 'The Treaty on Treaties' (1970) 64 AJIL 495

Keith, K J, *Interpreting Treaties, Statutes and Contracts* (Occasional Paper No 19, New Zealand Centre for Public Law, Wellington, 2009)

Kozlowski, A, 'Interpretation of Treaties in the Light of the Relationship Between International Law and the Law of the European Communities (European Union)' (2002–2003) 26 *Polish Yearbook of International Law* 115

Klabbers, J, 'How to Defeat a Treaty's Object and Purpose Pending Entry into Force: Toward Manifest Intent' (2001) 34 *Vanderbilt Journal of Transnational Law* 283

Klabbers, J, 'International Legal Histories: The Declining Importance of *Travaux Préparatoires* in Treaty Interpretation?' (2003) L NILR 267

Klabbers, J, 'On Rationalism in Politics: Interpretation of Treaties and the World Trade Organization' (2005) 74 *Nordic Journal of International Law* 405

Klabbers, J, 'The Meaning of Rules' (2006) 20 *International Relations* 295

Kuner, C B, 'The Interpretation of Multilateral Treaties: Comparison of Texts Versus the Presumption of Similar Meaning' (1991) 40 ICLQ 953

Labuschagne, J M T, 'Interpretation of Multilingual Treaties' (1999) 24 *South African Yearbook of International Law* 323

Larsen, P B, 'Between Scylla and Charybdis in Treaty Interpretation' (1969) 63 AJIL 108

Lauterpacht, E, 'The Development of the Law of International Organisation by the Decisions of International Tribunals' (1976-IV) 152 *Recueil des Cours* 379

Lauterpacht, H, 'Restrictive Interpretation and the Principle of Effectiveness in the Interpretation of Treaties' (1949) XXVI BYBIL 48

Legum, B, and Kirtley W, 'The Status of the Report of the Executive Directors on the ICSID Convention' (2012) 27 *ICSID Review* 159

Leir, M, 'Canadian Practice in International Law, 1998–99' (1999) 37 *Canadian Yearbook of International Law* 317

Letsas, G, 'The Truth in Autonomous Concepts: How to Interpret the ECHR' (2004) 15 EJIL 279

Letsas, G, 'Strasbourg's Interpretive Ethic: Lessons for the International Lawyer' (2010) 21 EJIL 509

Linderfalk, U, 'Is the Hierarchical Structure of Articles 31 and 32 of the Vienna Convention Real or Not? Interpreting the Rules of Interpretation' (2007) 54 NILR 133

Linderfalk, U, 'Who Are "the Parties"? Article 31, Paragraph 3(c) of the 1969 Vienna Convention and the "Principle of Systemic Integration" Revisited' (2008) 55 *Netherlands International Law Review* 343

Lindsley, L, 'The Beagle Channel Settlement: Vatican Mediation Resolves a Century-Old Dispute' (1987) 29 *Journal of Church and State* 435

Lipstein, K, 'Some Practical Comparative Law: The Interpretation of Multi-Lingual Treaties with Special Regard to the EEC Treaties' (1973–1974) 48 *Tulane Law Review* 907

Madden, M K, '*Abbott v. Abbott*: Reviving Good Faith and Rejecting Ambiguity in Treaty Jurisprudence' (2012) 71 *Maryland LR* 575

Mahoney, C J, 'Treaties as Contracts: Textualism, Contract Theory, and the Interpretation of Treaties' (2006–07) 116 *Yale Law Journal* 824

Marceau, G, 'WTO Dispute Settlement and Human Rights' (2002) 13 EJIL 753

Marks, S, 'Reservations Unhinged: The *Belilos* Case before the European Court of Human Rights' (1990) 39 ICLQ 300

Marouf, F E, 'The Role of Foreign Authorities in U.S. Asylum Adjudication' (2013) 45 *NYU J Int'l L & Pol* 391

McDorman, T L, 'Access to Information under Article 9 of the OSPAR Convention (Ireland v United Kingdom)' (2004) 98 AJIL 330

McDougal, M S, 'Statement of Professor Myres S McDougal, United States Delegation, to Committee of the Whole, April 19, 1968' (1968) 62 AJIL 1021

McDougal, M S, 'The International Law Commission's Draft Articles upon Interpretation: Textuality *Redivivus*' (1967) 61 AJIL 992

McLachlan, C, 'The Principle of Systemic Integration and Article 31(3)(c) of the Vienna Convention' (2005) 54 ICLQ 279

McLachlan, C, 'Investment Treaties and General International Law' (2008) 57 ICLQ 361

McNeill, J H, 'International Agreements: Recent US–UK Practice Concerning the Memorandum of Understanding' (1994) 88 AJIL 821

McRae, D M, 'The Legal Effect of Interpretative Declarations' (1978) 49 BYBIL 155

Mechlem, K, 'Treaty Bodies and the Interpretation of Human Rights' (2009) 42 *Vanderbilt Journal of Transnational Law* 905

Meltzer, J, 'Interpreting the WTO Agreements—A Commentary on Professor Pauwelyn's Approach' (2003–2004) 25 *Michigan Journal of International Law* 917

Milanovic, M, 'The ICJ and Evolutionary Treaty Interpretation' 14 July 2009 <http://www.ejiltalk.org/the-icj-and-evolutionary-treaty-interpretation/>, accessed 17 June 2010

Moloo, R, 'When Actions Speak Louder Than Words: The Relevance of Subsequent Party Conduct to Treaty Interpretation' (2013) 31 *Berkeley JIL* 39

Moore, J N, 'Treaty Interpretation, the Constitution and the Rule of Law' (2001–2002) 42 *Virginia Journal of International Law* 163

Mortenson, J D, 'The Meaning of 'Investment': ICSID's Travaux and the Domain of International Investment Law' (2010) 51 *Harvard ILJ* 257

Mortenson, J D, 'Is the Vienna Convention Hostile to Drafting History?' (2013) 107 AJIL 780

Mowbray, A, 'The Creativity of the European Court of Human Rights' (2005) 5 *Human Rights Law Review* 57

Mundorff, K, 'Other Peoples' Children: A Textual and Contextual Interpretation of the Genocide Convention, Article 2(e)' (2009) 50 *Harvard International Law Journal* 61

Myers, D P, 'The Names and Scope of Treaties' (1957) 51 AJIL 575

Nelson, L D M, 'Declarations, Statements and "Disguised Reservations" with respect to the Convention on the Law of the Sea' (2001) 50 ICLQ 767

Orakhelashvili, A, 'Restrictive Interpretation of Human Rights Treaties in the Recent Jurisprudence of the European Court of Human Rights' (2003) 14 EJIL 529

Orakhelashvilli, A, 'Principles of Treaty Interpretation in the NAFTA Arbitral Award on *Canadian Cattlemen*' (2009) 26 *Journal of International Arbitration* 159

Ortino, F, 'Treaty Interpretation and the WTO Appellate Body Report in US—Gambling: A Critique' 9 (2006) *Journal of International Economic Law* 117

Pan, E J, 'Authoritative Interpretation of Agreements: Developing More Responsive International Administrative Regimes' (1997) 38 *Harvard International Law Journal* 503

Pauwelyn, J, 'Reply to Joshua Meltzer' (2003–2004) 25 *Michigan Journal of International Law* 923

Resch, R X, 'Not in Good Faith—A Critique of the Vienna Convention Rule of Interpretation Concerning its Application to Plurilingual (Tax) Treaties' [2014] *British Tax Review* 307.

Ris, M, 'Treaty Interpretation and ICJ Recourse to Travaux Préparatoires: Towards a Proposed Amendment of Articles 31 and 32 of the Vienna Convention on the Law of Treaties' (1991) 14 *Boston College International and Comparative Law Review* 111

Roberts, A, 'Power and Persuasion in Investment Treaty Interpretation: The Dual Role of States' (2010) 104 AJIL 179

Rosenne, S, 'Interpretation of Treaties in the Restatement and the International Law Commission's Draft Articles: A Comparison' (1966) 5 *Columbia Journal of Transnational Law* 205

Rosenne, S, 'On Multi-lingual Interpretation' (1971) 6 *Israel Law Review* 360

Rosenne, S, 'The Election of Five Members of the International Court of Justice in 1981' (1982) 76 AJIL 364

Rothwell, D R, 'Australian Cases Involving Questions of Public International Law 1997 and 1998' (1998) 19 *Australian Yearbook of International Law* 119

Sands, P, 'Treaty, Custom and the Cross-fertilization of International Law' (1998) 1 *Yale Human Rights and Development Law Journal* 85

Sapienza, R, 'Les Déclarations Interprétatives Unilatérales et l'Interprétation des Traités' (1999) 103 *Revue Generale de Droit International Public* 601

Schill, S W, 'Allocating Adjudicatory Authority: Most-Favoured-Nation Clauses as a Basis of Jurisdiction—A Reply to Zachary Douglas' (2011) 2 *J Int'l Dispute Settlement* 353

Schönberg, S and Fric, K, 'Finishing, Refining, Polishing: on the Use of Travaux Préparatoires as an Aid to the Interpretation of Community Legislation' (2003) 28(2) *European Law Review* 149

Schreuer, C H, 'The Interpretation of Treaties by Domestic Courts' (1971) 45 BYBIL 255

Schwarzenberger, G, 'Myths and Realities of Treaty Interpretation: Articles 27–29 of the Vienna Draft Convention on the Law of Treaties' (1968) 9 *Virginia Journal of International Law* 1, also in (1969) 22 *Criminal Law Review* 205

Schwelb, E, 'Crimes Against Humanity' (1946) 23 BYBIL 178

Shelton, D, 'Reconcilable Differences? The Interpretation of Multilingual Treaties' (1997) 20 *Hastings International and Comparative Law Review* 611

Sinclair, I, 'The Principles of Treaty Interpretation and their application by the English Courts' (1963) 12 ICLQ 508

Shanker, D, 'The Vienna Convention on the Law of Treaties, the Dispute Settlement System of the WTO and the Doha Declaration on the TRIPs Agreement' (2002) 36 *Journal of World Trade* 721

Slade, A, 'Good Faith and the Trips Agreement: Putting Flesh on the Trips 'Objectives' (2014) 63 ICLQ 353

Slotboom, M M, 'Do Different Treaty Purposes Matter for Treaty Interpretation?: The Elimination of Discriminatory Internal Taxes in EC and WTO Law' (2001) 4 *Journal of International Economic Law* 557

Smith, F, 'Power, Rules, and the WTO' (2013) 54 *Boston College L R* 1063

Smith, R T, 'Tax Treaty Interpretation by the Judiciary' (1995–1996) 49 *Tax Law* 845

Sofaer, A D, 'Treaty Interpretation: A Comment' (1989) 137 *University of Pennsylvania Law Review* 1437

Spadi, F, 'Pulau Ligitan and Pulau Sipadan: New Parameters for the Concept of Dependency in the Maritime Environment? The ICJ Judgment of 17 December 2002' (2003) 18 *International Journal of Marine and Coastal Law* 295

Ten Cate, I M, 'The Costs of Consistency: Precedent in Investment Treaty Arbitration' (2012–2013) 51 *Colum. J Transnat'l L* 418

Thirlway, H, 'The Law and Procedure of the International Court of Justice 1960–1989 Part Three' (1991) LXII BYBIL 1

Thirlway, H, 'The Law and Procedure of the International Court of Justice 1960–1989, Supplement 2006: Part Three' (2006) 77 BYBIL 1

Tobin, J, 'Seeking to Persuade: A Constructive Approach to Human Rights Treaty Interpretation' (2010) 23 *Harv Hum Rts J* 1

Tuzmukhamedov, B, 'Interpretation of Discrepancies in Russian and English Texts of International Treaties and Possible Impact on Implementation: A Case Study of the ABM Treaty' (1994) 21 *Polish Yearbook of International Law* 213

Tzevelekos, V P, 'The Use of Article 31(3)(C) of the VCLT in the Case Law of the ECtHR: An Effective Anti-Fragmentation Tool or a Selective Loophole for the Reinforcement of Human Rights Teleology—Between Evolution and Systemic Integration' (2009–2010) 31 *Mich J Int'l L* 621

Vagts, D F, 'Treaty Interpretation and the New American Ways of Law Reading' (1993) 4 EJIL 472

Van Aaken, A, 'Defragmentation of International Law through Constitutional Interpretat ion: A Methodological Proposal' (2009) 16 *Indiana Journal of Global Legal Studies* 483

Van Alstine, M P, 'Dynamic Treaty Interpretation' (1998) 146 *University of Pennsylvania Law Review* 687

Van Alstine, M P, 'The Death of Good Faith in Treaty Jurisprudence and a Call for Resurrection' (2004–05) 93 *Georgetown Law Journal* 1885

Van Damme, I, 'On 'Good Faith Use of Dictionary in the Search of Ordinary Meaning under the WTO Dispute Settlement Understanding'—A Reply to Professor Chang-Fa Lo' (2011) 2 *J Int'l Dispute Settlement* 231

Vandevelde, K J, 'Treaty Interpretation from a Negotiator's Perspective' (1988) 21 *Vanderbilt Journal of Transnational Law* 281

Vazquez, C M, 'Laughing at Treaties' (1999) 99 *Columbia Law Review* 2154

Vierdag, E W, 'The Time of the "Conclusion" of a Multilateral Treaty: Article 30 of the Vienna Convention and Related Provisions' (1988) LIX BYBIL 75

Walker, G K, and Noyes, J E, 'Definitions for the 1982 Law of the Sea Convention' (2001–2002) 32 *California Western International Law Journal* 343

Weisstub, D N, 'Conceptual Foundations of the Interpretation of Agreements' (1970) 22 *World Politics* 255

Wessel, J, 'Relational Contract Theory and Treaty Interpretation: End-Game Treaties v Dynamic Obligations' (2004) 60 *NYU Annual Survey of American Law* 149

White, G, 'Treaty Interpretation: The Vienna Convention "Code" as Applied by the World Trade Organization Judiciary' (1999) 20 *Australian Yearbook of International Law* 319

Wildhaber, L, 'The European Convention on Human Rights and International Law' (2007) 56 ICLQ 217

Wood, M, 'Security Council Working Methods and Procedures' (1996) 45 *International and Comparative Law Quarterly* 150

Wood, M, 'The Interpretation of Security Council resolutions' (1998) 2 *Max Planck Yearbook of United Nations Law* 73

Wood, M, 'The International Tribunal for the Law of the Sea and General International Law' (2007) 22(3) *International Journal of Marine and Coastal Law* 351

Yasseen, M K, 'L'Interprétation des Traités d'après la Convention de Vienne sur le Droit des Traités' (1976-III) 151 *Hague Recueil* 1

Zang, D, 'Textualism in GATT/WTO Jurisprudence: Lessons for the Constitutionalization Debate' (2005–2006) 33 *Syracuse Journal of International Law and Commerce* 393

Zemanek, K, 'The "Object and Purpose" of a Treaty: An Enigma?' (1999) 3 *Austrian Review of International and European Law* 311

Index

Printed and bound by CPI Group (UK) Ltd, Croydon, CR0 4YY